C. Hart Merriam, Leonhard Stejneger, Charles Henry Gilbert, Charles V. Riley

The Death Valley Expedition

A Biological Survey of Parts of California, Nevada, Arizona, and Utah

C. Hart Merriam, Leonhard Stejneger, Charles Henry Gilbert, Charles V. Riley

The Death Valley Expedition

A Biological Survey of Parts of California, Nevada, Arizona, and Utah

ISBN/EAN: 9783744670791

Printed in Europe, USA, Canada, Australia, Japan

Cover: Foto ©Andreas Hilbeck / pixelio.de

More available books at **www.hansebooks.com**

U. S. DEPARTMENT OF AGRICULTURE
DIVISION OF ORNITHOLOGY AND MAMMALOGY

NORTH AMERICAN FAUNA

No. 7

PUBLISHED BY AUTHORITY OF THE SECRETARY OF AGRICULTURE

[Actual date of publication, May 31, 1893]

THE DEATH VALLEY EXPEDITION

A BIOLOGICAL SURVEY OF PARTS OF CALIFORNIA, NEVADA, ARIZONA, AND UTAH

PART II

1. Report on Birds. By A. K. FISHER, M. D.
2. Report on Reptiles and Batrachians. By LEONHARD STEJNEGER
3. Report on Fishes. By CHARLES H. GILBERT, Ph. D.
4. Report on Insects. By C. V. RILEY, Ph. D.
5. Report on Mollusks. By R. E. C. STEARNS, Ph. D.
6. Report on Desert Trees and Shrubs. By C. HART MERRIAM, M. D.
7. Report on Desert Cactuses and Yuccas. By C. HART MERRIAM, M. D.
8. List of Localities. By T. S. PALMER

WASHINGTON
GOVERNMENT PRINTING OFFICE
1893

LETTER OF TRANSMITTAL.

U. S. DEPARTMENT OF AGRICULTURE,
Washington, D. C., December 28, 1892.

SIR: I have the honor to transmit herewith the manuscript of North American Fauna, No. 7, consisting of Part II of the report on the results of the Death Valley Expedition, a biological survey of southern California, southern Nevada, and parts of Utah and Arizona, carried on by your authority in 1891. It consists of the special reports on birds, reptiles, batrachians, fishes, molluscs, insects, and the desert shrubs, cactuses, and yuccas, and is accompanied by a list of localities.

Part I, comprising the general report (itinerary, description of the region, and discussion of life zones) and the report on mammals, is not yet ready for the press.

Respectfully,
C. HART MERRIAM,
Chief of Division of
Ornithology and Mammalogy.

Hon. J. M. RUSK,
Secretary of Agriculture.

CONTENTS.

	PAGE.
Report on Birds. By A. K. Fisher, M. D	7-158
Report on Reptiles and Batrachians. By Leonhard Stejneger	159-228
Report on Fishes. By Charles H. Gilbert, Ph. D	229-234
Report on Insects. By C. V. Riley, Ph. D., S. W. Williston, P. R. Uhler, and Lawrence Bruner	235-268
Report on Mollusks. By R. E. C. Stearns, Ph. D	269-283
Report on Desert Trees and Shrubs. By C. Hart Merriam, M. D	285-343
Report on Desert Cactuses and Yuccas. By C. Hart Merriam, M. D	345-359
List of Localities. By T. S. Palmer	361-384

ILLUSTRATIONS.

PLATES.

Frontispiece: Mohave Desert, California, showing tree yuccas.

Plate I. 1, *Sceloporus clarkii*; 2, *S. magister*; 3, *S. zosteromus*; 4, *S. orcutti*; 5, *S. boulengeri*; 6, *S. floridanus*.
II. 1, *Phrynosoma cornutum*; 2, *P. blainvillii*; 3, *P. goodei*; 4, *P. platyrhinos*.
III. 1, *Xantusia vigilis*; 2, *Salvadora hexalepis*; 3, *Bufo halophilus*; 4, *B. boreas nelsoni*, subsp. nov.; 5, *Rana fisheri*, sp. nov.
IV. *Sauromalus ater*.
V. *Empetrichthys merriami* gen. et. sp. nov.
VI. 1, *Rhinichthys nevadensis* sp. nov.; 2, *R. velifer* sp. nov.
VII. *Opuntia acanthocarpa*.
VIII. *Opuntia acanthocarpa*.
IX. *Opuntia whipplei*.
X. *Opuntia parryi*.
XI. *Opuntia rutila*.
XII. *Yucca baccata*.
XIII. *Yucca arborescens*.
XIV. *Yucca macrocarpa*.

FIGURES IN TEXT.

Fig. 1. *Amnicola micrococcus*, page 277.
 2. *Fluminicola merriami*, page 282.

MAPS.

Map 1. General route map of the expedition.
 2. Lower division of the Lower Sonoran zone.
 3. Distribution of LeConte's thrasher (*Harporhynchus lecontei*).
 4. Distribution of the creosote bush (*Larrea tridentata*).
 5. Distribution of the tree yucca (*Yucca arborescens*).

REPORT ON THE ORNITHOLOGY OF THE DEATH VALLEY EXPEDITION OF 1891, COMPRISING NOTES ON THE BIRDS OBSERVED IN SOUTHERN CALIFORNIA, SOUTHERN NEVADA, AND PARTS OF ARIZONA AND UTAH.

By A. K. Fisher, M. D.

The present report includes an enumeration of all the birds observed throughout the region traversed by the different members of the expedition. It was considered advisable to unite all the observations in one general report rather than attempt to treat of the avifauna of special localities in a number of separate papers. At the same time a few local lists may be found under particular areas in Part I.

A number of side trips were made to special localities by small parties, which not only materially increased the observations on the birds already met with, but also added a number of species to the list. Among these trips may be mentioned one made by Dr. Merriam and Mr. Bailey, who extended their observations as far east as St. George, Utah. They were thereby enabled to add valuable notes on several of the birds of the Great Basin not seen elsewhere. After the main party had disbanded in the fall, a trip was made by Mr. Nelson along the coast from San Simeon to Carpenteria, and one to Monterey by Mr. Bailey, which resulted in partially filling up a wide gap among the water birds.

Owing to the unusual interest shown in matters relating to Death Valley, and to the entire absence of reliable information concerning the species inhabiting this area, it seemed best to append a special list of the birds observed there, with brief annotations. This list is believed to be reasonably complete, since the valley was visited by one or more members of the expedition every month except May, from January to June inclusive. A list of the species found in Owens Valley is added for comparison. (See pp. 150-158.)

The known ranges of a number of species were much extended by the expedition, notably in the cases of *Oreortyx pictus plumiferus*, *Dryobates scalaris bairdi*, *Chordeiles texensis*, *Pyrocephalus rubineus mexicanus*, *Calypte costæ*, *Icterus parisorum*, *Leucosticte tephrocotis*, *Junco hyemalis thurberi*, *Spizella atrigularis*, *Peucæa cassini*, *Harporhynchus lecontei*, and a few others; and the distribution of many better-known species was more definitely determined.

The known range of the plumed quail (*Oreortyx pictus plumiferus*) was carried eastward from the eastern slope of the Sierra Nevada to Mount Magruder, Nevada, and to all the desert ranges of southern California west of Death Valley. This valley apparently limits the distribution of this bird on the east, as the species was nowhere seen in the Grapevine or Charleston mountains, although both ranges are well timbered and bear brush which might afford suitable food and shelter.

Baird's woodpecker (*Dryobates scalaris bairdi*) was quite common among the tree yuccas on the Mohave Desert at Hesperia, and its range was extended northward to Vegas Valley, Nevada, and the valley of the Santa Clara, in southwestern Utah, by Dr. Merriam. The vermilion flycatcher also was secured in the same valley, though previously unknown north of Fort Mohave, Ariz. The Texas nighthawk (*Chordeiles texensis*) was found to be a common summer resident in all the valleys east of the Sierra Nevada from Owens Valley, California, to St. George, Utah, where Dr. Merriam secured the eggs. It was taken also in the San Joaquin Valley, California, near Bakersfield. Scott's oriole (*Icterus parisorum*) is another species whose range was carried northward from a short distance above our southern border in California to about latitude 38°, where it was common in places among the tree yuccas, and also on the slopes of some of the desert ranges as high as the junipers and piñons. Along the northern line of distribution it was found in Nevada at the Queen mine in the White Mountains, at Mount Magruder, and in the Juniper Mountains, and in Utah in the Beaverdam Mountains. Costa's humming bird (*Calypte costæ*) was very common wherever water occurred throughout the desert region, ranging northward nearly to latitude 38°, and eastward to the Beaverdam Mountains, Utah. Its nest was frequently found in the low bushes and cactuses on the hillsides near springs and streams.

The discovery that the gray-crowned finch (*Leucosticte tephrocotis*) breeds in the southern Sierra and in the White Mountains is especially interesting both because its breeding range was previously unknown, and because no species of the genus had been recorded from the Sierra Nevada south of about latitude 40°, while the present species was common nearly to the 36th parallel.

Most satisfactory results were accomplished in working out the distribution of Thurber's junco (*Junco hyemalis thurberi*), a recently described race whose range was not definitely known. In the Sierra Nevada it was common from the Yosemite Valley, the most northern point visited by any member of the expedition, to the southern end of the range, and in the desert ranges eastward to the Grapevine and Charleston mountains, where its place was occupied, in winter at least, by its more eastern representative, Shufeldt's junco. The little black-chinned sparrow (*Spizella atrigularis*) was found to be not an uncommon summer resident on the slopes of several of the desert ranges and also on the east slope of the Sierra Nevada as far north as Independence Creek in Kearsarge Pass. This was a great surprise, as heretofore the species has been recorded within our limits only along the southern border, and its presence was not suspected until a specimen was taken in the Panamint Mountains in April.

LeConte's thrasher (*Harporhynchus lecontei*), contrary to our expectations, was a common resident throughout the principal desert valleys from Owens Valley at the east foot of the Sierra Nevada across southern California and Nevada to southwestern Utah, where it was found nearly to the summit of the Beaverdam Mountains. Northward it was observed in Owens Valley almost to Benton, a short distance south of the 38th parallel. It was also taken by Mr. Nelson in the southern part of the San Joaquin Valley, California, about Buena Vista Lake.

The bird life of a region is materially affected by various agencies, such as changes in the character of the country brought about by the destruction of forests, the drying up of springs and water courses, and other causes. But in the High Sierra the sheep industry is doing more than anything else to make that region uninhabitable for certain species of birds and also for other forms of life, as long since pointed out by Mr. Henshaw (Appendix JJ, Annual Report of the Chief of Engineers for 1876, p. 225). During the summer the sheep almost totally destroy all the smaller plants and shrubs which, except in the wet meadows, do not grow again until the following spring. The writer has walked for miles along the hillsides where these animals had recently grazed without seeing a plant of any description save the larger woody shrubs. That the destruction of vegetation by sheep in this region is a potent cause of the scarcity of ground-inhabiting birds is evident by contrast to anyone visiting the national parks where no sheep are allowed to graze and where the vegetation is consequently uninjured and many species of birds abundant.

One member of the expedition, Mr. Vernon Bailey, traversed the Virgin Valley in southwestern Utah and eastern Nevada and the Detrital and Sacramento valleys, Arizona, during the winter of 1888-'89. His notes on several of the birds observed are incorporated in the present report.

With few exceptions it was thought better not to include matter from published reports partially covering the same region, since most of this material has been republished already in Mr. Belding's Land Birds of the Pacific Coast District.

In the following report 290 species and subspecies of birds are dwelt upon at greater or less length. The nomenclature adopted is that of the American Ornithologists' Union.

The writer wishes to extend his sincere thanks to all members of the expedition who assisted in collecting specimens or information for the present report. He wishes also to acknowledge the kindness of Mr. L. Belding, who furnished data on certain birds observed by him during a short trip to the Yosemite National Park in June, 1891. In all important instances credit is given to the observer under the head of each species.

Without this substantial help, so freely given, little more than a fragmentary report would have been possible.

LIST OF BIRDS.

1. Æchmophorus occidentalis.
2. Colymbus nigricollis californicus.
3. Podilymbus podiceps.
4. Urinator imber.
5. Urinator pacificus.
6. Urinator lumme.
7. Uria troile californica.
8. Larus glaucescens.
9. Larus californicus.
10. Larus delawarensis.
11. Larus heermanni.
12. Larus philadelphia.
13. Sterna maxima.
14. Phalacrocorax dilophus albociliatus.
15. Phalacrocorax penicillatus.
16. Phalacrocorax pelagicus resplendens.
17. Pelecanus erythrorhynchos.
18. Pelecanus californicus.
19. Merganser americanus.
20. Merganser serrator.
21. Anas boschas.
22. Anas strepera.
23. Anas americana.
24. Anas carolinensis.
25. Anas discors.
26. Anas cyanoptera.
27. Spatula clypeata.
28. Dafila acuta.
29. Aythya americana.
30. Aythya vallisneria.
31. Aythya collaris.
32. Glaucionetta clangula americana.
33. Charitonetta albeola.
34. Histrionicus histrionicus.
35. Oidemia americana.
36. Oidemia perspicillata.
37. Erismatura rubida.
38. Chen hyperborea.
39. Anser albifrons gambeli.
40. Branta canadensis hutchinsii.
41. Branta canadensis occidentalis.
42. Dendrocygna fulva.
43. Plegadis guarauna.
44. Botaurus lentiginosus.
45. Ardea herodias.
46. Ardea egretta.
47. Ardea virescens.
48. Nycticorax nycticorax nævius.
49. Grus canadensis.
50. Rallus virginianus.
51. Porzana carolina.
52. Fulica americana.
53. Phalaropus tricolor.
54. Recurvirostra americana.
55. Himantopus mexicanus.
56. Gallinago delicata.
57. Tringa minutilla.
58. Ereunetes occidentalis.
59. Calidris arenaria.
60. Limosa fedoa.
61. Totanus melanoleucus.
62. Symphemia semipalmata inornata.
63. Heteractitis incanus.
64. Actitis macularia.
65. Numenius longirostris.
66. Numenius hudsonicus.
67. Charadrius squatarola.
68. Ægialitis vocifera.
69. Ægialitis nivosa.
70. Ægialitis montana.
71. Oreortyx pictus plumiferus.
72. Callipepla californica.
73. Callipepla californica vallicola.
74. Callipepla gambeli.
75. Dendragapus obscurus fuliginosus.
76. Centrocercus urophasianus.
77. Columba fasciata.
78. Zenaidura macroura.
79. Pseudogryphus californianus.
80. Cathartes aura.
81. Elanus leucurus.
82. Circus hudsonius.
83. Accipiter velox.
84. Accipiter cooperi.
85. Accipiter atricapillus striatulus.
86. Buteo borealis calurus.
87. Buteo lineatus elegans.
88. Buteo swainsoni.
89. Archibuteo ferrugineus.
90. Aquila chrysaëtos.
91. Haliaëtus leucocephalus.
92. Falco mexicanus.
93. Falco peregrinus anatum.
94. Falco columbarius.
95. Falco sparverius deserticolus.
96. Pandion haliaëtus caroliuensis.
97. Strix pratincola.
98. Asio wilsonianus.
99. Asio accipitrinus.
100. Syrnium occidentale.

LIST OF BIRDS—Continued.

101. *Megascops asio bendirei.*
102. *Bubo virginianus subarcticus.*
103. *Speotyto cunicularia hypogæa.*
104. *Geococcyx californianus.*
105. *Coccyzus americanus occidentalis.*
106. *Ceryle alcyon.*
107. *Dryobates villosus hyloscopus.*
108. *Dryobates pubescens gairdnerii.*
109. *Dryobates scalaris bairdi.*
110. *Dryobates nuttallii.*
111. *Xenopicus albolarvatus.*
112. *Sphyrapicus varius nuchalis.*
113. *Sphyrapicus ruber.*
114. *Sphyrapicus thyroideus.*
115. *Ceophlœus pileatus.*
116. *Melanerpes formicivorous bairdi.*
117. *Melanerpes torquatus.*
118. *Melanerpes uropygialis.*
119. *Colaptes cafer.*
120. *Phalænoptilus nuttalli.*
121. *Phalænoptilus nuttalli californicus.*
122. *Chordeiles virginianus henryi.*
123. *Chordeiles texensis.*
124. *Cypseloides niger.*
125. *Chætura vauxi.*
126. *Aëronautes melanoleucus.*
127. *Trochilus alexandri.*
128. *Calypte costæ.*
129. *Calypte anna.*
130. *Selasphorus platycercus.*
131. *Selasphorus rufus.*
132. *Stellula calliope.*
133. *Tyrannus tyrannus.*
134. *Tyrannus verticalis.*
135. *Tyrannus vociferans.*
136. *Myiarchus cinerascens.*
137. *Sayornis saya.*
138. *Sayornis nigricans.*
139. *Contopus borealis.*
140. *Contopus richardsonii.*
141. *Empidonax difficilis.*
142. *Empidonax pusillus.*
143. *Empidonax hammondi.*
144. *Empidonax wrightii.*
145. *Pyrocephalus rubineus mexicanus.*
146. *Otocoris alpestris arenicola.*
147. *Otocoris alpestris chrysolæma.*
148. *Pica pica hudsonica.*
149. *Pica nuttalli.*
150. *Cyanocitta stelleri.*
151. *Cyanocitta stelleri frontalis.*
152. *Aphelocoma woodhousei.*
153. *Aphelocoma californica.*
154. *Corvus corax sinuatus.*
155. *Corvus americanus.*
156. *Picicorvus columbianus.*
157. *Cyanocephalus cyanocephalus.*
158. *Molothrus ater.*
159. *Xanthocephalus xanthocephalus.*
160. *Agelaius phœniceus.*
161. *Agelaius gubernator.*
162. *Sturnella magna neglecta.*
163. *Icterus parisorum.*
164. *Icterus bullocki.*
165. *Scolecophagus cyanocephalus.*
166. *Coccothraustes vespertinus.*
167. *Pinicola enucleator.*
168. *Carpodacus purpureus californicus.*
169. *Carpodacus cassini.*
170. *Carpodacus mexicanus frontalis.*
171. *Loxia curvirostra stricklandi.*
172. *Leucosticte tephrocotis.*
173. *Leucosticte atrata.*
174. *Spinus tristis.*
175. *Spinus psaltria.*
176. *Spinus psaltria arizonæ.*
177. *Spinus lawrencei.*
178. *Spinus pinus.*
179. *Poocætes gramineus confinis.*
180. *Ammodramus sandwichensis alaudinus.*
181. *Ammodramus sandwichensis bryanti.*
182. *Choudestes grammacus strigatus.*
183. *Zonotrichia leucophrys.*
184. *Zonotrichia leucophrys intermedia.*
185. *Zonotrichia leucophrys gambeli.*
186. *Zonotrichia coronata.*
187. *Zonotrichia albicollis.*
188. *Spizella monticola ochracea.*
189. *Spizella socialis arizonæ.*
190. *Spizella breweri.*
191. *Spizella atrigularis.*
192. *Junco hyemalis.*
193. *Junco hyemalis shufeldti.*
194. *Junco hyemalis thurberi.*
195. *Junco pinosus.*
196. *Amphispiza bilineata.*
197. *Amphispiza belli.*
198. *Amphispiza belli nevadensis.*
199. *Peucæa cassini.*
200. *Peucæa ruficeps.*
201. *Melospiza fasciata fallax.*
202. *Melospiza fasciata montana.*
203. *Melospiza fasciata heermanni.*
204. *Melospiza fasciata guttata.*
205. *Melospiza fasciata rufina.*
206. *Melospiza fasciata graminea.*
207. *Melospiza lincolni.*
208. *Passerella iliaca unalaschcensis.*

LIST OF BIRDS—Continued.

209. *Passerella iliaca megarhyncha.*
210. *Passerella iliaca schistacea.*
211. *Pipilo maculatus megalonyx.*
212. *Pipilo maculatus oregonus.*
213. *Pipilo chlorurus.*
214. *Pipilo fuscus mesoleucus.*
215. *Pipilo fuscus crissalis.*
216. *Pipilo aberti.*
217. *Habia melanocephala.*
218. *Guiraca cœrulea eurhyncha.*
219. *Passerina amœna.*
220. *Calamospiza melanocorys.*
221. *Piranga ludoviciana.*
222. *Piranga hepatica.*
223. *Progne subis hesperia.*
224. *Petrochelidon lunifrons.*
225. *Chelidon erythrogaster.*
226. *Tachycineta bicolor.*
227. *Tachycineta thalassina.*
228. *Clivicola riparia.*
229. *Stelgidopteryx serripennis.*
230. *Ampelis cedrorum.*
231. *Phainopepla nitens.*
232. *Lanius ludovicianus excubitorides.*
233. *Vireo gilvus swainsoni.*
234. *Vireo solitarius cassinii.*
235. *Vireo solitarius plumbeus.*
236. *Vireo bellii pusillus.*
237. *Vireo vicinior.*
238. *Helminthophila luciæ.*
239. *Helminthophila ruficapilla gutturalis.*
240. *Helminthophila celata lutescens.*
241. *Dendroica æstiva.*
242. *Dendroica auduboni.*
243. *Dendroica nigrescens.*
244. *Dendroica townsendi.*
245. *Dendroica occidentalis.*
246. *Siurus noveboracensis notabilis.*
247. *Geothlypis macgillivrayi.*
248. *Geothlypis trichas occidentalis.*
249. *Icteria virens longicauda.*
250. *Sylvania pusilla pileolata.*
251. *Anthus pennsylvanicus.*
252. *Cinclus mexicanus.*
253. *Oroscoptes montanus.*
254. *Mimus polyglottos.*
255. *Harporhynchus redivivus.*
256. *Harporhynchus lecontei.*
257. *Harporhynchus crissalis.*
258. *Heleodytes brunneicapillus.*
259. *Salpinctes obsoletus.*
260. *Catherpes mexicanus conspersus.*
261. *Thryothorus bewickii spilurus.*
262. *Thryothorus bewickii bairdi.*
263. *Troglodytes aëdon aztecus.*
264. *Cistothorus palustris paludicola.*
265. *Certhia familiaris occidentalis.*
266. *Sitta carolinensis aculeata.*
267. *Sitta canadensis.*
268. *Sitta pygmæa.*
269. *Parus inornatus.*
270. *Parus inornatus griseus.*
271. *Parus gambeli.*
272. *Parus rufescens neglectus.*
273. *Chamæa fasciata henshawi.*
274. *Psaltriparus minimus californicus.*
275. *Psaltriparus plumbeus.*
276. *Auriparus flaviceps.*
277. *Regulus satrapa olivaceus.*
278. *Regulus calendula.*
279. *Polioptila cærulea obscura.*
280. *Polioptila plumbea.*
281. *Polioptila californica.*
282. *Myadestes townsendii.*
283. *Turdus ustulatus.*
284. *Turdus ustulatus swainsonii.*
285. *Turdus aonalaschkæ.*
286. *Turdus aonalaschkæ auduboni.*
287. *Merula migratoria propinqua.*
288. *Hesperocichla nævia.*
289. *Sialia mexicana.*
290. *Sialia arctica.*

Æchmophorus occidentalis. Western Grebe.

The western grebe was seen only in the San Joaquin Valley, where Mr. Nelson observed a few at Buena Vista Lake, in October.

Colymbus nigricollis californicus. Eared Grebe.

The eared grebe was found in most of the larger ponds or lakes throughout the region visited by the expedition. At Owens Lake, Calif., large flocks were seen as late as the middle of June. Hundreds of dead ones were observed along the shore, where they were drifted by the wind. The writer counted the bodies found within the limits of a given distance, and estimated the total for the entire lake shore as 35,000. One of two causes, or both combined, must account for the death of so many. Either the water, which is saturated with salt and soda, is in some way injurious to them, or remaining to search for proper food, which does not exist in the lake, they become so weak from innutrition as to be unable to fly and die of starvation.

The mortality observed is not unusual, but seems to be of regular occurrence. Mr. Nelson, while camped at Keeler, in December, 1890, reported large numbers of dead grebes along the shore, and further stated that a light wind, blowing in shore, brought in half a dozen or more recently dead and excessively emaciated birds.

A specimen was secured on the reservoir at Furnace Creek, Death Valley, by Mr. Bailey April 11, and another on Pahranagat Lake, where many others were seen, May 24. Mr. Nelson saw a single individual in a glacier lake at the head of San Joaquin River, which was more likely the horned grebe; Mr. Stephens found several at Little Owens Lake, May 6–11; and Mr. Palmer observed eight or ten pairs, in full breeding plumage, on Elizabeth Lake July 2, and several on Crane Lake, near Gorman Station, Calif., June 28. Mr. Nelson saw the species at Buena Vista Lake, in the San Joaquin Valley, in October, and found it common along the coast south of San Simeon in November.

The horned grebe (*Colymbus auritus*) may have been associated with the present species in some localities, but it was not identified.

Record of specimens collected of Colymbus nigricollis californicus.

Collector's No.	Sex.	Locality.	Date.	Collector.	Remarks.
....	♂	Death Valley, California	Apr. 11, 1891	V. Bailey	Furnace Creek.
....	♂	Keeler, Inyo Co., Calif.	June 2, 1891	T. S. Palmer	

Podilymbus podiceps. Pied-billed Grebe.

A few dabchicks were seen by Mr. Nelson along the coast between San Simeon and Carpenteria, in November.

Urinator sp.——?

Mr. Nelson reported loons as common along the coast south of San Simeon in November. No adults were observed, all the birds being in immature plumage and remarkably unsuspicious. It is probable that the above note includes two and possibly three species, namely, the Pacific, red-throated, and common loons.

Uria troile californica. California Murre.

The California murre was found by Mr. Bailey to be common along the shore at Monterey, Calif., where a female was secured October 5.

Larus glaucescens. Glaucous-winged Gull.

Mr. Nelson found this species common along the coast of California south of San Simeon in November.

Larus californicus. California Gull.

Mr. Nelson saw three gulls of this species flying up Owens River, California, opposite Lone Pine, in December, 1890. Along the shores of Owens Lake from one to half a dozen were seen almost every day through December. A specimen shot on December 28 had its craw full of duck meat and feathers, and from the actions of its associates when a duck was shot it was evident that they prey upon such game, since the lake affords little other food.

The same observer saw a number of gulls of this species at Buena Vista Lake, in the San Joaquin Valley, in October, and found it common along the coast from San Simeon to Carpenteria, November 4 to December 18, 1891.

Larus delawarensis. Ring-billed Gull.

Mr. Nelson observed the ring-billed gull a few times at Owens Lake, and secured two specimens at a pond abounding in small fish near Lone Pine, in December, 1890. He found it rather common along the coast from San Simeon to Carpenteria, November 4 to December 18, 1891.

Larus heermanni. Heermann's Gull.

Common along the coast from San Simeon to Carpenteria, November 4 to December 18, 1891.

Larus philadelphia. Bonaparte's Gull.

Mr. Nelson saw one immature bird on a small lake near Lone Pine the last of December, 1890, and found a few along the coast from San Simeon to Carpenteria, November 4 to December 18, 1891.

Sterna maxima. Royal Tern.

A large tern, which Mr. Nelson reported as this species, was very common about the bays and inlets along the coast south of San Simeon.

Phalacrocorax dilophus albociliatus. Farallone Cormorant.

Mr. Nelson reported this cormorant as common along the coast from San Simeon to Carpenteria, November 4 to December 18.

Phalacrocorax penicillatus. Brandt's Cormorant.

Common in the same place.

Phalacrocorax pelagicus resplendens. Baird's Cormorant.

Noted by Mr. Nelson at Santa Barbara.

Pelecanus erythrorhynchos. White Pelican.

Mr. Stephens saw a flock of white pelicans sailing high in the air, midway between Haway Meadows and Olancha, at the southern end of Owens Lake, May 15. Mr. Palmer found the wings and shoulder girdle of one of these birds at Crane Lake, near Old Fort Tejon, July 2, and saw an individual on a small lake at Lone Pine, August 23.

Mr. Nelson saw the species at Buena Vista Lake, in the San Joaquin Valley, in October, and observed a large flock on Morro Bay in November.

Pelecanus californicus. California Brown Pelican.

Brown pelicans were common about San Francisco Bay and outside of the Golden Gate during the latter part of September. Mr. Bailey found them numerous at Monterey, September 28 to October 9, and Mr.

Nelson found them abundant all along the coast from San Simeon to Carpenteria, November 4 to December 18.

Merganser americanus. Merganser.

A flock of a dozen or more sheldrakes was seen at Soda Springs (locally known as Kern River Lakes), in the Sierra Nevada the first week in September, and a specimen shot there by Mr. Bailey August 15, belongs to this species.

Merganser serrator. Red-breasted Merganser.

A few red-breasted mergansers, according to Mr. Nelson, were living in the lakes near Lone Pine in December, 1890, and the remains of one were found on the shore of Owens Lake in June. Dr. Merriam shot an adult male in a small pond in Vegas Wash, Nevada, May 2, saw a pair at the Bend of the Colorado, May 3, and noted three females at the mouth of Beaverdam Creek, Arizona, May 9 and 10.

Anas boschas. Mallard.

The first mallard seen was a fine adult male, which was secured as it arose from one of the irrigating ditches in the alfalfa field at Furnace Creek, in Death Valley, January 23. Mr. Nelson noted several small flocks at Saratoga Springs, at the south end of the valley, early in February, and a few in Vegas Wash, Nevada, March 3-6. At Ash Meadows, Nevada, this duck was not uncommon, and a number were secured for the mess during the first three weeks in March. Dr. Merriam saw a pair of mallards and several single birds in Pahranagat Valley, Nevada, May 22-26, and Mr. Stephens noted a few in Oasis Valley, Nevada, March 15-19. In Owens Valley, California, Mr. Nelson found it sparingly about the lakes at Lone Pine in December, 1890; Mr. Stephens saw males and females at Little Owens Lake, May 6-11, and was confident that it bred in the meadows about Olancha, at the foot of Owens Lake, May 16-23. Dr. Merriam shot two and saw others in a small tule pond in Kern Valley, California, June 22, and the writer saw several at the same place July 13. At Walker Basin, California, several females were seen with their broods of young. A specimen of the latter in the down, secured July 13, had its stomach distended with grasshoppers, which insects were abundant everywhere in the neighborhood of the sloughs.

At Bakersfield, in the San Joaquin Valley, a flock of nearly fullgrown birds was flushed from one of the old water ditches on July 19. At a small pond near Trout Meadows, in the Sierra Nevada, Mr. Bailey saw a flock of ten individuals about the middle of August, and on September 7 he and the writer saw a flock containing six birds at the same place. Mr. Nelson saw the species at Buena Vista Lake in October, and along the route from San Simeon to Carpenteria, in November and December.

Anas strepera. Gadwall.

The gadwall did not begin to arrive at Ash Meadows, Nevada, until about March 8, from which time until March 21, when the party left the vicinity, it increased gradually in numbers and furnished, together with many of the other ducks, an agreeable change in the fare. Mr. Nelson found the species in small numbers in the bays and creeks between San Simeon and Carpenteria, Calif., in November and December.

Anas americana. Baldpate; Widgeon.

The spring flight of widgeons began at Ash Meadows, Nevada, about March 8, where they soon became common in the small ponds and sloughs. This was the only locality where the species was at all common.

Mr. Nelson reported two or three seen and one killed at Saratoga Springs, Death Valley, California, early in February; a single bird killed in Pahrump Valley, Nevada, the middle of the same month, and one seen in Vegas Wash, Nevada, about the middle of March. Dr. Merriam mentioned one shot at Furnace Creek in Death Valley, April 8. Mr. Nelson noted a few widgeons in the bays and creeks between San Simeon and Carpenteria, Calif., in November and December.

Anas carolinensis. Green-winged Teal.

Small flocks of green-winged teal were seen at Furnace Creek, Death Valley, January 23 to February 4. They were found either at the reservoir or in the irrigating ditches which flow through the alfalfa field. At Ash Meadows, Nevada, the species was very common, occurring in flocks which varied in size from a few individuals to several hundred birds.

Mr. Nelson found it common at Saratoga Springs, in the southern end of Death Valley, early in February, at Pahrump Ranch, Nevada, February 12–28; and saw small flocks about the large springs in Pahrump and Vegas valleys, March 3–16.

At Hot Springs, Panamint Valley, the writer saw a wing of this species April 20, and Mr. Nelson saw a specimen at the same place in January. The latter observer found it common at Buena Vista Lake in the San Joaquin Valley, California, in October, and between San Simeon and Carpenteria in November and December.

Anas discors. Blue-winged Teal.

The blue-winged teal was met with in two localities only. Mr. Stephens recorded seeing a small flock at Little Owens Lake, May 6–11; and the writer shot an individual out of a mixed flock of cinnamon and green-winged teal at Ash Meadows, Nevada, March 20.

Anas cyanoptera. Cinnamon Teal.

The cinnamon teal is a common species in suitable localities throughout the desert regions of the southern part of the Great Basin. It was first observed at Ash Meadows, Nevada, March 18, at which date a few were found in mixed flocks, and a little later considerable numbers came in, both in flocks by themselves and associated with other ducks. Mr. Nelson observed a female near Jackass Spring, in Cottonwood

Cañon, Panamint Range, June 1. Mr. Stephens saw several about the ponds at Grapevine Spring, California, April 1-4, and one was secured at Hot Spring, Panamint Valley, April 17. On the last trip to Death Valley Mr. Bailey secured a female in the reservoir at Furnace Creek, June 19. It was undoubtedly a pensioner, as its ovaries were undeveloped. During the spring and early summer Dr. Merriam found this duck breeding at numerous warm springs and alkali ponds throughout the districts visited in the Lower Sonoran zone in southern Nevada and southwestern Utah, and at Little Owens Lake, California. A female was killed in a patch of fine watercress in Upper Cottonwood Spring at the east base of the Charleston Mountains, Nevada, April 30; a flock of twenty-two was seen at Vegas Spring, Nevada, May 1, and many were noted in Vegas Wash, May 2. It was seen also in the lower Santa Clara Valley, Utah, May 11-15, and was common throughout Pahranagat Valley, Nevada, May 22-26, where it was breeding in the marshes.

Record of specimens collected of Anas cyanoptera.

Collector's No.	Sex.	Locality.	Date.	Collector.	Remarks.
134	♂ ad ♀	Ash Meadows, Nevada........ Death Valley, California.......	Mar. 20, 1891 June 19, 1891	A. K. Fisher...... V. Bailey.........	Furnace Creek.

Spatula clypeata. Shoveller.

At Lone Pine and Owens Lake, California, Mr. Nelson reported the shoveller as a common species, and at the latter place found it feeding extensively on the larvæ and pupæ of a small fly (*Ephydra hians*) which abounds in the lake. The remains of a large number of these birds were seen about the lake in June. A flock of four was seen on the reservoir at Furnace Creek, in Death Valley, the latter part of January, and the species was common at Ash Meadows, Nevada, where a number were killed early in March. Mr. Palmer found a pair breeding in a pond near Gorman Station, the last of June.

Dafila acuta. Pintail.

The sprigtail was common at Ash Meadows, Nevada, during the first two weeks in March, and many were killed for the mess. Mr. Nelson reported a number seen and some killed at Saratoga Springs, at the south end of Death Valley, February 1, and several seen in Vegas Wash, Nevada, March 3-10.

Aythya americana. Redhead.

The redhead was common at Ash Meadows, Nevada, during the first half of March, and together with the mallard, pintail, widgeon, and gadwall furnished considerable food for the party.

Mr. Nelson saw one in Vegas Valley, Nevada, in March, and Mr. Stephens another at Little Owens Lake, California, early in May.

Aythya vallisneria. Canvasback.

Ash Meadows, Nevada, was the only place where canvasback ducks were met with; a few were killed there early in March.

Aythya collaris. Ring-necked Duck.

The ring-necked duck was found only at Ash Meadows, Nevada, in March, where several in fine adult plumage were shot.

Glaucionetta clangula americana. Golden-eye.

Mr. Nelson saw a few whistlers on the lakes at Lone Pine in December, 1890, the only individuals of this species seen.

Charitonetta albeola. Bufflehead.

Mr. Nelson reported a few buffle headed ducks about the ponds at Lone Pine, California, in December, 1890.

Histrionicus histrionicus. Harlequin Duck.

None of our party saw this species. Mr. Belding, who has been so fortunate as to see a few each year, saw a pair in May, near Crockers, which is about 20 miles northwest of the Yosemite Valley.

Oidemia americana. Scoter.

Mr. Nelson found this scoter not very common at Morro Bay, California, in November.

Oidemia perspicillata. Surf Scoter.

The surf scoter was very common at Morro Bay, California, where Mr. Nelson found mainly immature birds.

Erismatura rubida. Ruddy Duck.

The ruddy duck was first met with at Ash Meadows, Nevada, where a few were killed about the middle of March. Three were seen and secured in the reservoir at Furnace Creek, Death Valley, March 22. Mr. Stephens saw it about the ponds at the ranch at Grapevine Spring, California, April 1-4; and Dr. Merriam observed it in Pahranagat Valley, Nevada, May 22-26. Near the western border of the Mohave Desert in California Mr. Palmer found several in bright plumage on Elizabeth Lake, July 2; one on a pond near Gorman Station on the same day; and several on Castac Lake, July 10. It was probably breeding at all three of these places.

Chen hyperborea. Lesser Snow Goose.

A flock of snow geese was seen by Mr. Nelson about Morro Bay in November, 1891. Mr. Bailey found this species common in flocks in Virgin Valley, where it was first observed near Bunkerville, Nev., January 23, 1889. They frequented the shores of Virgin River, where they fed on the bleached stems and tender roots of a small club-rush. The gullets of two individuals secured contained nothing except the remains of this plant.

Anser albifrons gambeli. White-fronted Goose.

A white-fronted goose remained several days in company with four Canada geese during the latter part of March in the alfalfa field at Furnace Creek, Death Valley, California.

Branta canadensis hutchinsii. Hutchin's Goose.

Very few geese were heard or seen during the time the expedition was in the field. Mr. Nelson reported hearing a flock which passed over the camp at Lone Pine, in Owens Valley, late one evening in December, 1890, and another on the east slope of the Charleston Mountains, Nevada, March 3-16, 1891. At Furnace Creek ranch, Death Valley, four Canada geese and one white-fronted goose remained in the alfalfa field for several days during the latter part of March. The above records may apply to the white-cheeked goose (*Branta c. occidentalis*). Mr. Nelson saw a few Hutchin's geese at Buena Vista Lake, in the San Joaquin Valley, California, in October, and shot a pair near San Simeon. Others were seen at different points along the coast, although nowhere common.

Dendrocygna fulva. Fulvous Tree Duck.

Owens Valley, California, was the only locality where this species was observed. Mr. Stephens found it quite common and unsuspicious at Little Owens Lake, where he secured a pair, May 8. He also saw a flock of a dozen or more at Ash Creek, near the southern end of Owens Lake, June 1.

Record of specimens collected of Dendrocygna fulva.

Collector's No.	Sex.	Locality.	Date.	Collector.	Remarks.
54	♀	Little Owens Lake, California.	May 8, 1891	F. Stephens	
55	♂	......do......	...do...	...do...	

Plegadis guarauna. White-faced Glossy Ibis.

Mr. Stephens saw a small flock of the glossy ibis at Little Owens Lake, May 6-11, and observed one at a springy place at Haway Meadows May 12-14. At Furnace Creek, Death Valley, the wings and tail of a specimen which had been killed near a ditch in the alfalfa field were seen at the ranch.

Botaurus lentiginosus. Bittern.

The bittern was not uncommon at Ash Meadows, Nevada, during the first three weeks in March, where it was seen in the marshes along the irrigating ditches or by the larger springs, in which places small fish were abundant. Dr. Merriam saw several in Pahranagat Valley, Nevada, May 22-26, where it undoubtedly bred. In Owens Valley Mr. Stephens found it at Alvord June 26-28; at Bishop, June 30, and Mr. Nelson shot one near Lone Pine in December, 1890. The latter observer saw the species at the head of Morro Bay, California, and at a small lake near San Luis Obispo in November of the following year.

Ardea herodias. Great Blue Heron.

In California, great blue herons were not uncommon at Bakersfield, in the San Joaquin Valley, where they were seen flying back and forth from the river to their resting grounds, July 17-20. At the following places single individuals were seen: At a small lake near Lone Pine, December, 1890; at Tejon ranch, near the mouth of the Pass, July 13; at Little Owens Lake, June 20; at Kernville, July 12, and at Soda Springs, September 7. Mr. Nelson found the species common in the San Joaquin Valley wherever the streams or lakes furnish it proper surroundings. He reported it common on the coast between San Simeon and Carpenteria, and saw a few near San Luis Obispo and between Carpenteria and Santa Paula in November and December.

Ardea egretta. Egret.

A white egret was seen by Dr. Merriam at a little pool of muddy water between the south end of Panamint Valley and Lone Willow Spring, California, April 24; and another at the Great Bend of the Colorado, May 4. The latter was on the Arizona or east side of the river, opposite the mouth of Vegas Wash. Mr. Nelson saw several about Morro Bay, California, in November.

Ardea virescens. Green Heron.

The green heron was not uncommon along the river, sloughs, and old ditches near Bakersfield, in the San Joaquin Valley, California, July 17–20; one was seen at Elk Bayou, near Tulare, in the same valley, July 22; and Mr. Stephens saw one at Little Owens Lake, California, May 6–11.

Nycticorax nycticorax nævius. Black-crowned Night Heron.

As a matter of course, night herons were rare in a region where streams and lakes containing fish were almost absent. Dr. Merriam saw an adult April 7, resting on a rock near the road in Windy Gap, between Panamint and Death valleys. Several were seen by him on a small alkaline pond at the west end of the Mohave Desert (Antelope Valley), June 28, and one in northwestern Arizona (where Beaverdam Creek joins the Virgin), May 9. Mr. Stephens saw several at Little Owens Lake May 6–11, and Mr. Palmer saw one at Crane Lake, at the west end of the Mohave Desert, June 28, and again July 2. Mr. Bailey shot an immature specimen near the reservoir at Furnace Creek, Death Valley, June 19. Its stomach contained two carp about 5 inches long. At Keeler, in Owens Valley, one was observed near a small fresh-water pond not far from the lake, June 26. At Walker Basin several were seen flying over toward their feeding grounds, and one was observed at the edge of a slough July 13–16.

At Bakersfield, in the San Joaquin Valley, the species was common July 17–20, and at Morro Bay, on the coast, in November.

Grus canadensis. Little Brown Crane.

A little brown crane was seen for several days around the fields and marshes at Ash Meadows, Nevada, and finally was secured March 10. It was a female, and proved to be very good eating. The stomach contained small bulbous rootlets, foliage of young plants, and a quantity of barley, which it had picked up from the place where the horses had been fed.

NOTE.—Mr. Nelson saw four birds at Lone Pine, in Owens Valley, December, 1890, which he thought were whooping cranes, and saw a flock of seventeen sand-hill cranes at the Bend of the Colorado in March. In both cases the birds were too far off for positive identification, and as the region is out of the known range of the former species, it is probable that some other large bird was mistaken for it.

Rallus virginianus. Virginia Rail.

Mr. Nelson reported the species as common at Saratoga Springs in Death Valley, where Mr. Bailey caught a specimen in a trap February 3. One was seen at Ash Meadows, Nevada, about the middle of March, and the species was not uncommon at Lone Pine in Owens Valley, where two were secured June 7-10. Mr. Nelson saw one at the head of Morro Bay, Calif., in November. Dr. Merriam frequently heard a rail among the tules and reeds in Pahranagat Valley, Nevada, May 26, but was unable to say whether it was this species or the sora.

Record of specimens collected of Rallus virginianus.

Collector's No.	Sex.	Locality.	Date.	Collector.	Remarks.
	♀	Death Valley, Calif.	Feb. 3, 1891	V. Bailey	Saratoga Springs.
310	♂ juv.	Owens Valley, Calif.	June 7, 1891	A. K. Fisher	Lone Pine.
326	♂ juv.	......do......	June 10, 1891	....do....	Do.

Porzana carolina. Sora.

A sora rail was seen at Ash Meadows, Nevada, March 10; one at Grapevine Spring, California, the first part of April; and another at Little Owens Lake, early in May. No others were seen.

Fulica americana. Coot.

Coots were common at a number of places where tule marshes occurred. A number were seen in the Mohave Desert, along the edge of the Mohave River at Victor, early in January. In Death Valley it was found common at Saratoga Springs about February 1, and again in the latter part of April. At Ash Meadows, Nevada, it was common during the first three weeks in March, and a few were seen in Vegas Wash, early in the month. In Owens Valley, Mr. Stephens found it common at Little Owens Lake, May 6-11, and at Ash Creek, on the southwestern side of Owens Lake, the first of June. At Lone Pine it was common on the lakes in December, 1890, and at a lake south of the same place, August 23, 1891. A pair with their young was seen in a small pond, June 5. In Nevada, Dr. Merriam observed the species in the marshes in Vegas Wash, May 2; in the valley of the Muddy, May 6; and in Pahranagat Valley, May 24. At the west end of the Mohave Desert, in California, Mr. Palmer found coots common on Elizabeth Lake, July 2, and saw several on Crane Lake and on ponds near Gorman Station,

June 29. Mr. Bailey found it numerous in fresh-water ponds at Monterey.

Several were seen at Soda Springs or Kern River Lakes, in the Sierra Nevada, September 7. Mr. Nelson found it abundant in the lakes and along the streams in the San Joaquin Valley, October 5-27, and along the coast. At San Simeon, he saw a group sunning themselves on a strip of sandy beach just above the reach of the incoming rollers.

Phalaropus tricolor. Wilson's Phalarope.

Mr. Bailey shot an adult male near the overflow of a ditch in the alfalfa field at Furnace Creek ranch, Death Valley, June 19, and Mr. Stephens secured two at Alvord, in Owens Valley, June 27.

Record of specimens collected of Phalaropus tricolor.

Collector's No.	Sex.	Locality.	Date.	Collector.	Remarks.
122	♂	Death Valley, Calif.	June 19, 1891	V. Bailey	Furnace Creek.
	♂	Owens Valley, Calif.	June 27, 1891	F. Stephens	Alvord.
123	♂	....do....	....do....	....do....	Do.

Recurvirostra americana. Avocet.

Avocets were found in a few places both east and west of the Sierra Nevada. A flock of eighteen was seen at Ash Meadows, Nevada, March 15, and most of them secured. Mr. Stephens saw a small flock at Little Owens Lake, California, May 6-11, and the writer saw seven standing at the edge of a bar in Kern River, below Kernville, Calif., July 13. Mr. Nelson found it sparingly about the lakes at Lone Pine, in December, 1890; at Buena Vista Lake, in the San Joaquin Valley, in October; saw one individual at the head of Owens Valley in July; and a few at Morro Bay in November. Dr. Merriam saw a dozen or more at the northwestern end of Owens Lake, June 19.

Himantopus mexicanus. Black-necked Stilt.

Near the west end of the Mohave Desert, in California, Mr. Palmer saw sixteen black-necked stilts at Elizabeth Lake, July 2, and three at Castac Lake, July 10. No others were seen during the entire season.

Gallinago delicata. Wilson's Snipe.

Wilson's snipe were seen in a few localities, both in California and Nevada.

Mr. Nelson saw several in marshy spots near Owens River at Lone Pine, Calif., until the latter part of December, 1890, when a fall in temperature drove them away. Mr. Stephens saw one at Grapevine Spring, California, April 1; a number at Little Owens Lake, May 6-11; and one at Furnace Creek, Death Valley, April 11.

Mr. Bailey flushed one at Resting Springs, California, February 16, and Mr. Nelson saw several near Cottonwood Spring at the east foot of the Charleston Mountains early in March. At Ash Meadows, Nevada, a number were seen and one killed March 16. Mr. Nelson saw one at the head of the Cañada de las Uvas and another at Buena Vista Lake, California, in October, and found the species not common, but generally distributed along the coast marshes between San Simeon and Carpenteria in November and December.

Tringa minutilla. Least Sandpiper.

Least sandpipers were seen in a few places only. Mr. Nelson reported the species as common on the shores of Owens Lake in December, 1890, and along the coast from San Simeon to Carpenteria the following autumn. Two small flocks were seen about an alkaline pond at Hot Springs in Panamint Valley, and a specimen was secured April 22. Near Bakersfield one was flushed from an old irrigating ditch July 19, and Mr. Nelson saw several near a small pond on the east side of Mount Piños, in the latter part of October.

Ereunetes occidentalis. Western Sandpiper.

The western sandpiper was seen in a few localities only. Dr. Merriam shot a specimen out of a flock of four in the Virgin Valley, Nevada, just below the mouth of the Muddy, May 6, and Mr. Stephens found the species rather common along the shore of Little Owens Lake, California, May 6-11. The writer found several in company with snowy plovers, at Keeler, on the shore of Owens Lake the 1st of June. Mr. Nelson reported it as common along the shores of Morro Bay in November.

Calidris arenaria. Sanderling.

Mr. Bailey secured a specimen of this wader at Monterey, Calif., October 3.

Limosa fedoa. Marbled Godwit.

Mr. Nelson reported this godwit as common at Morro Bay, on the coast of California, in November.

Totanus melanoleucus. Greater Yellow-legs.

Mr. Nelson reported several small parties of greater yellow-legs about the ponds at Lone Pine, Calif., in December, 1890, and found the species common at Morro Bay the following November.

Symphemia semipalmata inornata. Western Willet.

Mr. Nelson found the willet common at Morro Bay, Calif., in November.

Heteractitis incanus. Wandering Tattler.

The wandering tattler was common at Monterey, where Mr. Bailey secured a specimen October 3.

Actitis macularia. Spotted Sandpiper.

This species was not rare near the permanent streams. Dr. Merriam found it along several of the water courses in the southern part of the Great Basin, where two were found at the Great Bend of the Colorado

River in Nevada, May 4; several along Beaverdam Creek, northwestern Arizona, May 10; many in Pahranagat Valley, Nevada (where the species was breeding), May 24; and one in Oasis Valley, Nevada, June 1.

Mr. Nelson saw a single individual on Willow Creek Cañon, in the Panamint Mountains, May 22; and observed the species at the head of Owens River and on the western slope of the Sierra Nevada, but found it nowhere common. Mr. Belding saw it at Mirror Lake, in the Yosemite Valley. The writer saw it along Kern River, near Kernville, July 11-12, and at Soda Springs or Kern River Lakes September 5. Mr. Bailey found it common around the fresh-water pools at Monterey early in October.

Numenius longirostris. Long-billed Curlew.

Mr. Nelson saw four sickle-billed curlews on the shore of Owens Lake December 27, and subsequently Mr. Bailey saw a flock of about a dozen. Mr. Stephens observed one near Ash Creek, on the same lake, the last of May.

Numenius hudsonicus. Hudsonian Curlew.

In California Mr. Nelson found the hudsonian curlew at Buena Vista Lake in the San Joaquin Valley in October, and found it common at Morro Bay in November.

Charadrius squatarola. Black-bellied Plover.

The only record of the black-bellied plover was a male secured by Mr. Bailey at Monterey, Calif., October 3.

Ægialitis vocifera. Killdeer Plover.

The killdeer plover is the commonest wader in the desert regions and occurs wherever there is water enough to form marshy places in the vicinity of streams or springs. Dr. Merriam found it particularly abundant at Hot Springs, in Panamint Valley, Calif., April 20-25; at the junction of Beaverdam Creek with the Virgin River, Arizona, May 9; along the Santa Clara River near its junction with the same river, in southwestern Utah, May 11-15; at Willow Spring, in the western part of the Mohave Desert, June 26; at Owens Lake, June 19, and in Kern Valley, California, June 22. In Nevada he found it also, though in less abundance, at Vegas Spring, May 1; at the Bend of the Colorado River, May 4; at Bunkerville, in the Virgin Valley, May 8; in Pahranagat Valley and at Pahranagat Lake, May 22-26;

The writer first observed it at Furnace Creek ranch, Death Valley, in the latter part of January, where it was noisy on moonlight nights; Dr. Merriam observed it at the same place about the middle of April; and Mr. Bailey and the writer found it not uncommon on their last trip to the Valley, June 19-22. One was seen by the latter observer at Resting Springs, California, February 16, and a number at Ash Meadows, Nevada, during the first three weeks of March. Mr. Nelson saw a few solitary individuals about the ranch in Pahrump Valley,

February 12-28; also at the ranch in Vegas Valley, and thence down the Vegas Wash as far as water occurred, March 3-16. In Owens Valley the same observer found it sparingly distributed along Owens River and on the shore of Owens Lake in December, 1890, and the writer found it not uncommon in the same valley, both at Keeler and Lone Pine, June 3-15. In other parts of the valley Mr. Stephens found it at Little Owens Lake, May 6-11; Haway Meadows, May 12-14; Olancha, May 16-23; Ash Creek, May 30 to June 3; Alvord, June 26-28; Bishop, June 30 to July 1; Morans, July 4-7; and at Benton, July 9-10. He also found it rather common in Oasis Valley, Nevada, March 15-19; and at Grapevine Spring, California, April 1-4. In the Sierra Nevada Mr. Nelson found the killdeer at the head of Owens River up to an altitude of 2,440 meters (8,000 feet), and on the western slope from the San Joaquin Valley up into the Yosemite as high as 1,220 meters (4,000 feet); Mr. Stephens found it common at Menache Meadows, May 24-26; and Mr. Dutcher saw one on Big Cottonwood Creek about half a mile below his meteorological camp, September 11. Near the west end of the Mohave Desert Mr. Palmer saw the species at Elizabeth Lake, July 2, and near Crane Lake, June 29. The writer saw killdeers on the eastern slope of Walker Pass, July 1, and Mr. Bailey on the western slope the following day. Several were seen at the South Fork of Kern River, July 3-10; at Kernville, July 11-13; at Walker Basin, July 13-16; and at Bakersfield, in the San Joaquin Valley, July 17-20. At Three Rivers, California, in the western foothills of the Sierra, the killdeer plover was common July 25-30, and on the return trip September 14-17.

Mr. Bailey found it common at Monterey, Calif., September 28 to October 9; and Mr. Nelson reported it as common and generally distributed in the San Joaquin Valley, about San Luis Obispo, and along the coast from San Simeon to Carpenteria and Santa Paula, in November and December.

Record of specimens collected of Ægialitis vocifera.

Collector's No.	Sex.	Locality.	Date.	Collector.	Remarks.
122	♀ ♂	Ash Meadows, Nev .... Death Valley, Calif.............	Mar. 10, 1890 June 19, 1891	A. K. Fisher ...... V. Bailey	Furnace Creek.

Ægialitis nivosa. Snowy Plover.

This handsome little plover was observed by the writer on the shores of Owens Lake, near Keeler, May 30 to June 4, where it was common in small flocks of five or ten on the alkaline flats which border the lake. Like most other birds in the vicinity, it fed extensively, if not exclusively, on a species of small fly (*Ephydra hians* Say), which was found in immense masses near the edge of the lake. Many of these swarms of flies were four or five layers deep and covered an area of 15 or 20 square feet. Some idea can be formed of the inexhaustible supply of food which this insect furnishes for birds when it is known that colonies of equal size occurred at close intervals in suitable localities all around the lake, which has a shore line of between 40 and 50 miles.

The species was evidently breeding at the time, but no eggs or young were found. The birds were tame and unsuspicious, and allowed a person to approach within a few yards before taking wing, and if not too closely pressed would run along ahead of the observer. As Mr. Nelson found the species at this same place December 27, 1890, it is undoubtedly a resident in Owens Valley.

Mr. Bailey found this plover numerous on the beach at Monterey, Calif., September 28 to October 9.

Record of specimens collected of Ægialitis nivosa.

Collector's No.	Sex.	Locality.	Date.	Collector.	Remarks.
276	♂	Keeler, Inyo County, Calif.	June 1, 1891	A. K. Fisher	
277	♂	......do	....do	....do	
278	♂	......do	....do	....do	

Ægialitis montana. Mountain Plover.

According to Mr. Nelson, mountain plovers were common in flocks in October at several places on the open grassy plains in the San Joaquin Valley, Calif.

Oreortyx pictus plumiferus. Plumed Quail.

The known range of the mountain quail was considerably extended by the fieldwork of the expedition. In Cajon Pass, in the San Bernardino Mountains, a small band was seen and an individual secured January 2. In the Panamint Mountains a feather was found in Johnson Cañon, and a pair or so of the birds seen April 6. The Indians, as well as some of the inhabitants of Panamint, knew the bird well, and stated that it was common in many parts of the mountains. Dr. Merriam and Mr. Bailey saw it among the junipers on the north slope of Telescope Peak, April 17–19, and Mr. Nelson found it a common breeding species among the piñons on Willow Creek, Mill Creek, and in Cottonwood Cañon, in the more northern part of the range. Death Valley, with the barren, treeless range immediately to the east, prevents the extension of the species in that direction as effectually as it does the valley quail. In the Argus Range the plumed quail was common. Mr. W. C. Burnett saw a pair at the summit of Shepherd Cañon, and above Maturango Spring the males were heard throughout the day uttering their not unpleasant call notes. At Searl's garden, which is near the southern end of this range, Mr. Stephens heard that they came down into the garden in summer. In the Coso Mountains the species was still more common among the piñons, where several specimens were secured during the latter half of May. In the Inyo Range it was reported as not uncommon at Cerro Gordo, and Mr. Nelson found it common among the nut pines along Waucoba Creek the last of June. On Mount Magruder, Nevada, Dr. Merriam found it common and breeding June 4–9. On this mountain the plumed quails were distributed in pairs, a pair occupying the chaparral on each hillside among the piñons.

In the Sierra Nevada Mr. Stephens heard them west of Little Owens Lake, May 6–11; at Menache Meadows at an altitude of 3,050 meters (10,000 feet), May 24–26; at Independence Creek, where young were seen near the mouth of the cañon, June 18–23; and at Bishop Creek August 4–10. Mr. Nelson found the mountain quail common at the head of Owens River and on the headwaters of the San Joaquin River on the opposite slope. On the western slope of Walker Pass we found it common among the chaparral in the cañons, where it was associated more or less with the valley quail, which was abundant there. At Walker Basin a flock was seen on the hillside above the valley on July 14. In the Sierra Liebre Dr. Merriam saw one near Alamo ranch June 30, and Mr. Palmer found it common on Frazier Mountain, where half-grown young were found July 9. In the southern Sierra Nevada it was common in the Sequoia National Park, and especially near the openings, and coveys of half-grown young were seen every day during the first week in August. It was common also at Horse Corral Meadows August 9–13. A flock was seen at Big Cottonwood Meadows August 26, and another at Round Valley, 12 miles south of Mount Whitney, August 28. At the latter place birds were running about among the bare rocks above timber line. At Soda Springs, or Kern River Lakes, small flocks were seen and several individuals taken September 3. A number were observed around Mineral King the first part of August, and again in September. In the coast ranges Mr. Nelson found the plumed quail common near La Panza the last of October, and in the mountains back of San Simeon in November.

Record of specimens collected of Oreortyx pictus plumiferus.

Collector's No.	Sex.	Locality.	Date.	Collector.	Remarks.
17	♂ ad.	Cajon Pass, Calif.	Jan. 2, 1891	A. K. Fisher.	
	♀	Panamint Mountains, Calif.	May 13, 1891	E. W. Nelson.	
	♂	...... do	...... do	Do.	
	♂	...... do	May 17, 1891	Do.	
	♂	...... do	May 21, 1891	Do.	
234	♂	Argus Range, Calif	May 13, 1891	A. K. Fisher.	
247	♂	Coso Mountains, Calif.	May 23, 1891	Do.	
265	♀	...... do	May 27, 1891	Do.	
266	♀	...... do	...... do	Do.	
361	♂ juv.	Walker Pass, Calif.	July 3, 1891	Do.	
362	♂ juv.	...... do	...... do	Do.	
	♂	Soda Springs, Kern River, Calif.	Aug. 12, 1891	V. Bailey.	

Callipepla californica. California Quail.

The only places from which the typical California quail was recorded are Monterey and Boulder Creek on the coast of California, where Mr. Bailey found it common during the first part of October.

Callipepla californica vallicola. Valley Quail.

The valley quail was found abundantly in many places, and its eastern range in southern California was carefully and definitely mapped. As might be expected, it was found at every point west of the Sierra Nevada visited by members of the expedition. To the east of this range, and the ranges forming its southern continuation, the species was common out to the edge of the Mohave Desert and Salt Wells Valley, and all through Owens Valley as far north at least as Benton, where both Mr. Nelson and Mr. Stephens found it. It was common along the western base of the White Mountains and in the Inyo, Coso, Argus, and Panamint mountains. In the latter range its eastern distribution ends— Death Valley, with the barren, treeless mountains beyond forming a complete barrier to its further extension. The valley quail was not found in the Grapevine Mountains, in Panamint or Saline valleys, or in the Mohave Desert proper, though around the edges of this desert it was seen on the south at the summit of Cajon Pass, on the north at Lone Willow and Leach Point springs, and on the west at Willow Spring and Antelope Valley. The easternmost limits of its range are the San Bernardino Mountains on the south side of the Mohave Desert, and Leach Point Spring on the north side. The latter locality is only a short distance west of the extreme south end of Death Valley. Here Dr. Merriam shot specimens April 25.

In the Panamint range it was common in Johnson and Surprise Cañons, and Mr. Nelson found it in Cottonwood, Mill Creek, and Willow Creek cañons.

In the Argus Range this quail was common in Shepherd Cañon, at Maturango Spring and at other places visited. In the Coso Mountains it was found to range from the lowest part of the valley up through the cañons to the tops of the high peaks, where it was quite closely associated with the mountain quail (*Oreortyx*) during the breeding season. In the Inyo Mountains, Mr. Nelson found it on the east slope at Hunter's arastra and Waucoba Creek, and along the west slope up to the piñons. At Lone Pine, in Owens Valley, young, just able to fly, were seen June 4-15, and at Walker Pass, flocks containing a hundred or more on July 1-2. These flocks were composed of several families, as they contained from ten to fifteen adults and young that varied in size from those just hatched up to half-grown birds. At the west slope of Walker Pass, the valley quail was again found ranging above the lower limit of the mountain quail. At Three Rivers, in the western foothills of the Sierra Nevada, these quails, both adult and young, were found in the oaks feeding on the young acorns July 25-30.

Throughout the San Joaquin Valley, Mr. Nelson found it common about ranches, along water courses or near springs. It was excessively abundant at some of the springs in the hills about the Temploa Mountains and Carrizo Plain. In the week following the expiration of the close season, two men, pot-hunting for the market, were reported to have killed 8,400 quail at a solitary spring in the Temploa Mountains. The men built a brush blind near the spring, which was the only water within a distance of 20 miles, and as evening approached the quails came to it by thousands. One of Mr. Nelson's informants who saw the birds at this place stated that the ground all about the water was covered by a compact body of quails, so that the hunters mowed them down by the score at every discharge. The species was common along the coast from San Simeon to Carpenteria and Santa Paula, in November and December.

Record of specimens collected of Callipepla californica vallicola.

Collector's No.	Sex.	Locality.	Date.	Collector.	Remarks.
10	♂ ad.	Cajon Pass, Calif	Jan. 1, 1891	A. K. Fisher	
65	♀	Lone Willow Spring, Calif	Jan. 16, 1891	....do	
		....do	Jan. 17, 1891	E. W. Nelson	
140	♀	Panamint Mountains, Calif	Mar. 26, 1891	A. K. Fisher	Johnson Cañon.
	♂	....do	Apr. 19, 1891	E. W. Nelson	Surprise Cañon.
	♂	....do	....do	....do	Do.
	♀ juv.	....do	June 13, 1891	....do	
	♂	Argus Range, Calif	Jan. 2, 1891	V. Bailey	Shepherd Cañon.
	♂	....do	....do	....do	Do.
185	♂	....do	Apr. 27, 1891	A. K. Fisher	Do.
244	♂	Coso Mountains, Calif	May 21, 1891	....do	
245	♀	....do	....do	....do	
	juv.	Inyo Mountains, Calif	July 1, 1891	E. W. Nelson	
72	♂ juv.	Owens Lake, Calif	June 3, 1891	F. Stephens	
357	♂ juv.	Walker Pass, Calif	July 1, 1891	A. K. Fisher	
358	♂ juv.	....do	....do	....do	
359	♀ juv.	....do	....do	....do	
376	♀ juv.	Kern River, Calif	July 5, 1891	....do	South Fork.
377	♂ juv.	....do	....do	....do	
404	♂ im.	Three Rivers, Calif	July 28, 1891	....do	

Callipepla gambeli. Gambel's Quail.

Gambel's quail is essentially a desert bird, though rarely found at any great distance from water. It was first observed in winter by our party at Furnace Creek, in Death Valley, where it was reported to have been introduced by the Borax Company from Resting Springs. A few young were seen here June 19-21 by Mr. Bailey and the writer, and a female shot for a specimen had an egg in the lower part of the oviduct. At Resting Springs, California, which is in the Amargosa Valley, it was excessively abundant in February and furnished considerable food for the party. It was so common among the mesquite and other brush that steel traps set for diurnal mammals were often sprung by it, and in a few instances quail were found in traps set in pouched gopher holes. A few were seen at Ash Meadows, Nevada, in March. At the ranch in Pahrump Valley, Nevada, it was fully as abundant as at Resting Springs and was considered a great nuisance by the proprietor of the place, owing to the damage it does to the crops. Mr. Nelson, who was alone in camp for several days in this locality, gives the following notes on its habits: "I noticed that when a flock of quail came to feed on grain left by the horses, an old male usually mounted the top of a tall bush close by and remained on guard for ten or fifteen minutes, then, if everything was quiet, he would fly down among his companions. At the first alarm the flock would take to the bushes, running swiftly, or flying when hard pressed. They roosted in the dense bunches of willows and cottonwoods growing along the ditches. As a rule the birds walked under the roosting place and flew up one or two at a time into the tree or bush, though sometimes they flew into the tree from a distance. When feeding they have a series of low clucking and cooing notes which are kept up almost continually."

Dr. Merriam found Gambel's quail abundant below Mountain Spring, in the southern part of the Charleston Mountains, Nevada, April 29-30, and shot several at Upper Cottonwood Springs, at the east base of the same mountains, April 30. He contributes the following notes concerning its presence in eastern Nevada, northwestern Arizona, and southwestern Utah: In Nevada it was common at the Great Bend of the Colorado, May 4, where several sprung traps set for small mammals; in the Valley of the Virgin and Lower Muddy it was not only abundant but so unwary that it ran along in front of the horses in considerable numbers, early in May; it was tolerably common in the southern part of Pahranagat Valley, May 22-26, but shy and difficult of approach. At the mouth of Beaverdam Creek, northwestern Arizona, and thence up over the Beaverdam Mountains, Utah, it was exceedingly abundant as it was also in the Santa Clara Valley, Utah, May 11-15, and a few were found as far north as the Upper Santa Clara Crossing. The species is said to reach Shoal Creek at the south end of the Escalante Desert occasionally, but is rare there.

Record of specimens collected of Callipepla gambeli.

Collector's No.	Sex.	Locality.	Date.	Collector.	Remarks.
72	♂	Death Valley, Calif.	Jan. 24, 1891	A. K. Fisher	Furnace Creek.
73	♂	......do......	...do......	...do......	Do.
74	♀	......do......	...do......	...do......	Do.
75	♀	......do......	...do......	...do......	Do.
	♂	......do......	June 10, 1891	V. Bailey	Do.
	♀	......do......	...do......	...do......	Do.
102	♂ ad.	Resting Springs, Calif.	Feb. 8, 1891	A. K. Fisher	
104	♂ ad.	......do......	...do......	...do......	
	♂	Pahrump Valley, Nev	Feb. 15, 1891	T. S. Palmer	
28	♂	Ash Meadows, Nev	Mar. 4, 1891	F. Stephens	

Dendragapus obscurus fuliginosus. Sooty Grouse.

The Sooty Grouse was nowhere common, and the only ones seen outside of the Sierra Nevada were one by Mr. Nelson in the upper part of the White Mountains, in July, and a pair by Mr. Stephens at the Queen mill, Nevada, in the same mountains, July 11-16.

On the eastern slope of the Sierra, one was seen by Mr. Stephens at Monache Meadows, the latter part of May; another on Independence Creek about the same time; one adult and two broods, at Bishop Creek, August 4-10; and it was found sparingly at the head of

Owens River, in the latter part of July. In the Sequoia National Park a few were seen both at the saw mill and at Halsted Meadows. At Horse Corral Meadows a flock of ten or fifteen was seen and two secured, August 11. Several were seen in Kings River Cañon about the meadows, August 13-16; at Big Cottonwood Meadows throughout the summer; and grouse were not uncommon near timber line, at Mineral King and vicinity, during August and first half of September. Mr. Nelson found a few about the summit of Mount Piños in October.

Record of specimens collected of Dendragapus obscurus fuliginosus.

Collector's No.	Sex.	Locality.	Date.	Collector.	Remarks.
146	♀ juv.	Sierra Nevada Calif	Aug. 7, 1891	F. Stephens	Bishop Creek.
147	♀ juv.	do	do	do	Do.
150	♀ im.	do	Aug. 9, 1891	do	Do.
151	♀ ad.	do	do	do	Do.
160	♂ ad.	do	Aug. 23, 1891	do	Olancha Peak.
10	♂ ad.	do	July 6, 1891	B. H. Dutcher	Big Cottonwood [Meadows.

Centrocercus urophasianus. Sage Grouse.

On Mount Magruder, on the Nevada side of the boundary line between California and Nevada, many piles of sage hens' excrement were found among sage brush on the main peak, by Dr. Merriam and Mr. Bailey. They were told by a prospector that sage hens used to be common on the mountain, but are very scarce now, having been killed off a few winters ago by unusually deep snow. At the head of Owens River, on the eastern slope of the Sierra Nevada, Mr. Nelson found this bird ranging in among the lower border of the pines (*Pinus jeffreyi*,) where he saw numerous tracks. Near Mammoth Pass also he found it common among the sage brush at about 2,450 meters (8,000 feet) altitude. The same observer stated that the sage hen was a common species in the northern half of the White Mountains up to 3,050 meters (10,000 feet) altitude, where he killed a half-grown bird from a large covey. Mr. Stephens learned from the miners at the Queen mine, Nevada, that this grouse occurred in the gulches around the mines.

Columba fasciata. Band-tailed Pigeon.

At Three Rivers, in the western foothills of the Sierra Nevada, California, Mr. Palmer saw three band-tailed pigeons among the oaks the last of July, and the species was reported to be quite common in the barley stubble of a neighboring ranch. Mr. Nelson found it common among the oaks in the Tehachapi and Temploa mountains, and saw a few about San Luis Obispo during the last of October. Along the route from San Simeon to Carpenteria it was abundant among the oaks in November. Flocks of from 10 to a 100 were feeding on the berries of *Arbutus menziesii* as well as upon acorns. He saw a few flocks between Carpenteria and Santa Paula during the last part of December.

Zenaidura macroura. Mourning Dove.

After the spring migration set in, the mourning dove was a common species all through the desert region wherever water occurred. There was no bird that indicated the close proximity of water with more certainty than the dove, and wherever it was found congregated in any numbers water was confidently looked for. The three following records are the only ones which indicate its presence in the region during the winter: Two were seen drinking from a stream at San Bernardino, Calif., December 28, 1890; one was seen near the roadside at Lone Pine in the same month, and a single individual was found at Furnace Creek in Death Valley, the latter part of January. Migrants were first observed at the last-mentioned place April 9-12, and at Hot Springs, in Panamint Valley, April 21. At Lone Willow Spring Dr. Merriam saw several April 24, and at Leach Point Spring he observed large numbers as they came to the water to drink, and fifteen were secured for food the evening of April 25. In Amargosa Cañon and at Resting Springs they were seen April 27. Mr. Nelson found it exceedingly abundant in the vicinity of springs and streams in the Panamint and Grapevine mountains, where it ranged well up among the piñons. He found them more sparingly at the head of Owens River, in the Sierra Nevada, on both slopes of the Inyo Mountains, and up to the piñons in the White Mountains. They were nesting in various situations, some on the ground sheltered by a bush, others on horizontal branches of cottonwoods, willows, or piñons, and one he found in a small cup-shaped depression on the top of a tall granite boulder 6 feet from the ground. Doves were very common in the Argus Range in Shepherd Cañon and at Maturango Spring, where they filled in very nicely the shortcomings of the mess. In the Coso Mountains the species was just as abundant and occurred up through the cañons to the summit of the range.

Dr. Merriam contributes the following records for eastern Nevada, northwest Arizona, and southwest Utah: In the Charleston Mountains, Nevada, it was seen both at Mountain Spring, and at the Upper Cottonwood Springs at the east foot of the mountains, April 30; at Vegas ranch, May 1; abundant in Vegas Wash and at the Bend of the Colorado, May 2-4; in the valley of the Muddy and Virgin it was common May 7-8; in the Juniper Mountains dozens came to Sheep Spring to drink, the evening of May 18; at Pahroc Spring it was very abundant May 20-22; in Pahranagat Valley it was common and unusually tame May 22-26; at Quartz Spring, on the western slope of the Desert Mountains, it fairly swarmed on the evening of May 22, there being no other water for many miles in any direction; in Oasis Valley it was abundant June 1, feeding on seeds of the bunch grass (*Oryzopsis cuspidata*), and was common on Mount Magruder June 4-9. At the mouth of Beaverdam Creek in northwestern Arizona doves were excessively abundant May 9-10, and were common throughout the juniper belt of the Beaverdam Mountains, Utah, May 10-11. In the Santa Clara Valley, Utah, they were likewise abundant May 11-15.

In Owens Valley, California, the species was abundant from one end to the other. At Lone Pine, during the first part of June, quantities of nests, one of which contained three young, were found in the willow and cottonwood groves. During the last trip to Death Valley, Mr. Bailey and the writer found it common in the Panamint Mountains, and saw four at Furnace Creek June 19-21.

In the Sierra Nevada doves were common in Walker Pass July 1-3; along the valley of Kern River, July 3-13; at Walker Basin, July 13-16; at Bakersfield, in the San Joaquin Valley, July 17-20; at Three Rivers in the western foothills, and along the Kaweah below the pines, the last of July. In the High Sierra Mr. Palmer saw a pair in Kings River Cañon, August 14; Mr. Dutcher shot one and saw others at Big Cottonwood Meadows early in September; and it was seen at Soda Springs and Trout Meadows about the same time. In the Cañada de las Uvas, California, it was abundant at Old Fort Tejon in June and July, and Mr. Stephens found it rather common at Reche Cañon, near San Bernardino, September 22-26. Mr. Nelson reported it as common in the San Joaquin Valley in October, and saw a few along the coast from San Simeon to Carpenteria, and at Santa Paula, in November and December.

Mourning doves furnish a large amount of food to the Indians during the spring and summer. Before migration commences the Indians build rude huts of brush, grass, and weeds, in which to secrete themselves, near the springs and streams. Loopholes are made on the sides toward the water, through which arrows are shot at the birds as they alight to drink.

Record of specimens collected of Zenaidura macroura.

Collector's No.	Sex.	Locality.	Date.	Collector.	Remarks.
299	♀ juv.	Owens Valley, Calif.	June 6, 1891.	A. K. Fisher	Lone Pine.
300	♀ juv.	......do..............	....do......	....do........	Do.

Pseudogryphus californianus. California Vulture.

It was with considerable surprise and pleasure that we found the California vulture still tolerably common in certain localities west of the Sierra Nevada, in California. Mr. Palmer reported seeing one flying above Frazier Mountain July 9, and while on his way to Tejon ranch, July 11, saw three others soaring overhead in company with turkey buzzards, and stated that it was an easy matter to distinguish the two species.

On July 16, about 3 miles from Walker Basin, on the road leading to Bakersfield, in the San Joaquin Valley, Mr. Bailey and the writer saw one of these vultures in company with the turkey buzzards flying about the carcass of a cow. The white on the underside of its wings was plainly visible.

At San Emigdio and the adjacent foothills Mr. Nelson found it quite common in October, and was told that it became very numerous there in winter. He also found it common along the coast near San Simeon, and in the Santa Ynez Mountains. In all these places it was shy and difficult of approach. On the pass at the head of Owens River, July 24, and on the trail above Lone Pine, August 27, Mr. Nelson saw solitary birds which he thought belonged to this species.

Cathartes aura. Turkey Vulture.

The turkey buzzard was seen in various localities, both in the desert and in the mountain regions, but was nowhere common. It was first met with in Death Valley, where a few were seen during the latter part of March. Dr. Merriam saw a number sailing over the Mohave Desert March 29 and 30, and saw several congregated about a dead horse at Furnace Creek, Death Valley, April 11. He saw one in Emigrant Cañon in the Panamint Mountains about the middle of April, and another at Hot Springs, in Panamint Valley, April 20. Mr. Nelson saw a few over Mesquite Valley, and in the Grapevine Mountains in May; found it sparingly in the Inyo Mountains, from the valley to the summit, in the latter part of June, and in the White Mountains in July.

In the Argus Range the writer saw it in Shepherd Cañon and at Maturango Spring, in the latter part of April and first part of May; a few were found at Coso the latter part of May, and around Owens Lake and Lone Pine in June. The species was noted all through Owens Valley, from the southern part to the upper end, and at the base of the White Mountains. On the last trip to Death Valley some were seen at Furnace Creek, June 19–21.

In the Sierra Nevada it was seen at Kernville, along the valley of the Kern River, and in Walker Basin in July; and in the High Sierra at Horse Corral, Big Cottonwood, and Whitney meadows, in August.

It was seen at Old Fort Tejon, and in Tehachapi Valley, California, in June, by Dr. Merriam and Mr. Palmer. In the San Joaquin Valley it was seen at various places from Bakersfield to Visalia and Three Rivers. Mr. Bailey saw it at Monterey the last of September; and Mr. Stephens at Reche Cañon, near San Bernardino, about the same date. In Nevada Dr. Merriam saw it in Vegas Wash, May 3; in the Virgin Valley, May 8; Pahranagat Valley, May 22–26; Ash Meadows, May 30; and a few on Mount Magruder, June 4–8. In the Santa Clara Valley, Utah, it was rather common, May 11–15.

Mr. Nelson found it common in the San Joaquin Valley, in the Tehachapi Mountains, and along the route from San Simeon to Carpenteria about the end of the year.

Elanus leucurus. White-tailed Kite.

Mr. Nelson found the white-tailed kite rather uncommon about San Luis Obispo, where he shot a specimen and saw others in November. The species was not seen elsewhere.

Circus hudsonius. Marsh Hawk.

Wherever there was sufficient water to form considerable areas of marsh land, the marsh hawk was pretty certain to be observed. An adult male was secured at Furnace Creek in Death Valley, January 29; several were seen at Resting Springs in February; and the species was not uncommon at Ash Meadows, Nevada, in March.

In Nevada Mr. Nelson found it common in Pahrump and Vegas valleys in February and March, especially about the ranch in the former place, and Mr. Stephens reported an unusual preponderance of birds in the blue plumage in Oasis Valley about the middle of March. Dr. Merriam saw one in Oasis Valley, June 1; both blue and red birds at Ash Meadows, May 30, and in Pahranagat Valley May 22–26; he shot a male in Meadow Creek Valley May 19, and saw several in the Lower Muddy and Virgin valleys May 6–8.

In California marsh hawks were common in a number of places throughout Owens Valley in winter as well as during the breeding season, and were doubtless attracted by the vast number of meadow mice (*Arvicolæ*) which swarm through the wet meadows and marshes.

Marsh hawks were common along the South Fork of Kern River, where they were seen often through the day skimming over the alfalfa fields and marshes, and in the High Sierra a few were seen at Whitney and Big Cottonwood meadows. At the west end of the Mohave Desert Dr. Merriam saw one near Gorman ranch, June 28; Mr. Bailey found it at Monterey in September, and Mr. Nelson reported it as common in the San Joaquin Valley and around Carpenteria later in the fall.

Accipiter velox. Sharp-shinned Hawk.

We found this species nowhere as common as it is in most of the Eastern States; the total number seen by members of the party, both during migration and in the breeding season, being less than could be seen in southern New York on any day in early September.

The writer saw two at the ranch at Furnace Creek, Death Valley, in the latter part of January; Mr. Nelson observed one at Bennett Wells in the same valley about the same time; and Dr. Merriam saw two at the former place, April 11. The species was seen at Resting Springs, California, the first week in February. In Nevada it was observed at Ash Meadows early in March; Mr. Nelson saw several and killed one at the ranch in Pahrump Valley February 12–28; and saw it among the mesquite thickets on his route from Ash Meadows to the Bend of the Colorado, March 3–16. Dr. Merriam saw one at Vegas Wash May 2; one at the Bend of the Colorado River, Nevada, May 4; one at the west side of the Beaverdam Mountains, Utah, May 10.

In California he saw one in Owens Valley about the middle of June, and one in Kern Valley, June 22. At Hot Springs, in Panamint Valley, Mr. Nelson shot a specimen early in January, and Dr. Merriam saw two during his stay, April 19–24; one in Emigrant Cañon, in the

Panamint Mountains, April 14; and another on the north side of Telescope Peak, April 18; and the writer saw one in Surprise Cañon, April 20.

Mr. Nelson saw the species once or twice in the piñon belt along Waucoba Creek, in the Inyo Mountains, in the latter part of June; and a few in the foothills on the west slope of the Sierra Nevada, in August. Mr. Bailey and the writer observed two or three on the western slope of Walker Pass in the same range July 2–3; one was observed in Kings River Cañon, August 15; and another at Three Rivers in the western foothills, September 13. Mr. Koch secured a pair near their camp in Cottonwood Meadows July 30; Mr. Palmer reported seeing two at Old Fort Tejon; and Mr. Bailey found it not uncommon at Whitney Meadows and at Soda Springs, in August.

Mr. Stephens saw one at Grapevine Spring, California, the first week in April; one at Olancha, at the southern end of Owens Lake, the third week in May, and one at Bishop Creek, early in August. Mr. Bailey saw several at Monterey, during the first week of October. Mr. Nelson found it common in the San Joaquin Valley between Bakersfield and San Emigdio in October, and saw a few along the coast from San Simeon to Carpenteria and Santa Paula in November and December.

Record of specimens collected of Accipiter velox.

Collector's No.	Sex.	Locality.	Date.	Collector.	Remarks.
22	♂ ad.	Sierra Nevada, Calif	July 30, 1891	B. H. Dutcher	Big Cottonwood Meadows.
23	♀ ad.	......do................	...do......	...do......	Do.

Accipiter cooperi. Cooper's Hawk.

This hawk was even more rare than the sharp-shinned, as scarcely two dozen were seen during the time the expedition was in the field. In Cajon Pass in the San Bernardino Mountains, on January 2, the writer decoyed one by imitating the squealing of a mouse; one was seen at Hesperia on the Mohave Desert, January 4; one or two at the ranch at Furnace Creek, Death Valley, the latter part of the same month, and a few were seen at Ash Meadows, Nevada, during the first half of March. Mr. Stephens saw one which had been killed at Searl's garden, on Borax Flat, April 23–26, and one at Bishop Creek, in Owens Valley, the first week in August.

In the Sierra Nevada Mr. Nelson noted the species on the divide between the Merced and San Joaquin rivers; Mr. Bailey saw one on the Kaweah River; two at Whitney Meadows; the writer saw one at the latter place September 2, and secured a specimen at Three Rivers, in the western foothills, July 28. Its stomach contained the remains of a Beechey's spermophile.

Mr. Nelson found a few among the oaks in the lower part of the Tehachapi and Temploa mountains in October, and along the route between San Simeon and Carpenteria in November.

Accipiter atricapillus striatulus. Goshawk.

No specimens of this handsome and daring hawk were taken by any member of the expedition. Mr. Nelson stated that a hawk flew over his camp at Lone Pine, Owens Valley, in December, 1890, which he thought belonged to this species, and Mr. Bailey is quite certain he saw an individual among the sequoias on Kaweah River, and another at Soda Springs, or Kern River Lakes.

Buteo borealis calurus. Western Red-tail.

The western red-tail was observed at most localities visited by members of the expedition in California, Nevada, and Utah. It was seen on the Mohave Desert near Victor, early in January, several were observed in Death Valley between Bennett Wells and Saratoga Springs about the 1st of February, and one at the former place in Death Valley, on June 21.

At Resting Springs, California, a fine specimen was secured, and others seen early in February. In Nevada it was noted at Ash Meadows, in Pahrump Valley, in Vegas Wash, at the Bend of the Colorado, at Pahroc Spring, in Pahranagat Valley, in Oasis Valley, at Mount Magruder, and on the Charleston and Grapevine mountains. On Mount Magruder one was shot by Dr. Merriam as it swooped to pick up a wounded dove, June 7, and another at the mouth of Beaverdam Creek, Arizona, May 9. The stomach of the latter contained a ground squirrel (*Spermophilus tereticaudus*). Several were seen in the Santa Clara Valley, Utah, about the middle of May.

In the Panamint Mountains, California, Dr. Merriam observed it in Emigrant Cañon about the middle of April, and Mr. Bailey and the writer saw one soaring over the summit of Telescope Peak on June 23 and later in the day the former observer killed one near the 'charcoal kilns.' Its stomach contained one pocket gopher (*Thomomys*), two large lizards (*Cnemidophorus tigris* and *Sauromalus ater*), five grasshoppers, and one sand cricket (*Stenopalmatus*). In the northern part of the same mountains Mr. Nelson noted a few, and also in the White and Inyo mountains from the upper limit of the pines down to the valleys. In the Argus Range individuals were seen at Shepherd Cañon and Maturango Spring; and near the road to Lookout Mountain an adult was seen on June 25, beating back and forth over the rocky hillside, evidently hunting for the large lizards known as 'chuck-wallas' (*Sauromalus ater*), which were common in the locality.

It was observed in the Coso Mountains, and in Owens Valley it was found at a number of places, both in winter and summer. It was seen at Old Fort Tejon, Walker Pass, Walker Basin, South Fork of Kern River, and in the High Sierra at Sequoia National Park, Horse Corral, Cottonwood, and Whitney meadows, and Round Valley.

In the San Joaquin Valley it was observed at Bakersfield and Visalia. Mr. Bailey saw it at Monterey, and Mr. Stephens at Reche Cañon near San Bernardino. Mr. Nelson saw it everywhere about the Tehachapi and Temploa mountains and found it common all along the coast from San Simeon to Santa Paula in November and December.

Buteo lineatus elegans. Red-bellied Hawk.

This species was observed mainly in the San Joaquin Valley, where one was seen near an irrigating ditch at Bakersfield, July 18, evidently watching for frogs. At Visalia a fine adult was seen among the oaks, July 22, and at the same place on September 17 and 18 the species was not uncommon. Mr. Nelson reported it as abundant among the oaks on Kings River at the base of the foothills in August, and saw it near the Mission of Santa Ynez and in Gaviota Pass, in November.

Buteo swainsoni. Swainson's Hawk.

Swainson's hawk is apparently a rare species in the region traversed by the expedition. Mr. Nelson saw a number on the western foothills of the Sierra Nevada, and Dr. Merriam shot an adult male on Kern River near Kernville, June 23. Its stomach contained one grasshopper. Several were seen catching grasshoppers in the Cañada de las Uvas, California, June 28–29. At Walker Basin, California, Mr. Bailey and the writer saw a number, and on July 15 the latter observer killed an adult female whose stomach contained about fifty grasshoppers. In Walker Basin a species of grasshopper, which Prof. C. V. Riley kindly identified for the writer as *Camnula pellucida*, was very abundant. In many places a large part of the vegetation ordinarily available as food for these insects was dried up and had lost much of its original nutritive properties, so they had to seek elsewhere for subsistence. This they found in the form of fresh horse droppings which were strewn along the roads and in the corrals. Wherever this substance occurred vast numbers of grasshoppers congregated in a struggling mass, each individual striving to reach the interior of the throng so as to partake of the food. Not only the hawks, but most other birds in the valley, including ducks, ravens, woodpeckers, and sparrows, fed almost exclusively on the grasshoppers.

Archibuteo ferrugineus. Ferruginous Rough-leg.

Very few squirrel hawks were seen by the expedition. Mr. Nelson secured a specimen at Pahrump ranch, and saw others in Vegas and Pahrump valleys and Vegas Wash, March 3–16. A few were seen at Ash Meadows, Nevada, about the same time, but none were secured. Dr. Merriam saw a pair circling over the summit of the highest peak of Mount Magruder, Nevada, June 8, and several times afterward saw them hunting in company in the nut pine groves of the same mountains.

Aquila chrysaëtos. Golden Eagle.

The golden eagle was observed sparingly in a number of widely separated localities by different members of the expedition. One was seen at Ash Meadows, Nevada, March 18, circling over a shallow pond in which a large number of ducks were feeding. Mr. Nelson saw several in Vegas Valley and about the Charleston Mountains, Nevada, March 3-16, and Dr. Merriam saw three among the tree yuccas on the east side of Pahrump Valley, April 29, and one on the Charleston Mountains the following day. One was seen in the Juniper Mountains May 19, and another at Oasis Valley the 1st of June. In California Dr. Merriam observed a pair in Owens Valley, June 10-19, and he and Mr. Palmer saw one near Alamo ranch, in the Sierra Liebre, June 30. According to the Indians, this eagle breeds rarely in the higher portions of the Grapevine, Panamint, Inyo, and White mountains.

In the main Sierra Nevada one was seen on the east slope of Walker Pass, July 2; a pair on the South Fork of the Kern River, July 3-11; one near Little Cottonwood Creek, August 23; a number in Whitney Meadows; and several at and above timber line near Mineral King, September 8-11. At the latter place they probably fed on woodchucks (*Arctomys*) and grouse (*Dendragapus*).

Haliæetus leucocephalus. Bald Eagle.

Two adult bald eagles were seen sitting on a dead mesquite at Ash Meadows, Nevada, about the middle of March. They were the only ones noted during the season.

Falco mexicanus. Prairie Falcon.

Prairie falcons were seen in a number of localities throughout the desert regions as well as among the mountain ranges of southern California and Nevada. In Death Valley, between Bennett Wells and Furnace Creek, one was seen January 22, and at the latter place one was shot from its perch on a haystack where it sat watching a flock of Gambel's quail, January 27, and another was seen in summer on June 20. One was secured at Resting Springs in the Amargosa Desert, February 12, and another at Ash Meadows, Nevada, March 16. At the latter place, where ducks were abundant, this falcon was seen on several occasions to chase single birds, which escaped by dropping in the water among the tules. Mr. Nelson saw a number in Pahrump and Vegas valleys, Nevada, and at the Bend of the Colorado, and one was seen on a cliff in Vegas Wash eating a duck. In the Panamint Mountains one was shot from the top of a cut bank at the mouth of Johnson Cañon, March 26; others were seen in Emigrant Cañon, April 14-15, and in the higher mountains near Telescope Peak, April 17-19. Mr. Nelson found it sparingly about the bases of both the Panamint and Grapevine ranges, where old nests were found on the cliffs. In Nevada Dr. Merriam saw it on Mount Magruder, June 8; in Pahranagat Valley, May 22-26 (breeding in both the Pahranagat and Hyko mountains), and in the Virgin Valley near Bunkerville, May 8. In the Lower Santa Clara Valley, Utah, he saw a pair several times about the cliffs a short distance from the village of St. George, May 11-15.

In Panamint Valley it was seen at Hot Springs April 20, and in the lower end of the valley, January 12. A female was seen in the Coso

Mountains chasing doves, May 19. In Owens Valley the species was seen at a number of localities, and undoubtedly breeds in both the Inyo range and the Sierra Nevada. On the eastern slope of Walker Pass a pair of these falcons were seen flying along the hillsides where quail were abundant.

In the High Sierra a specimen was shot at Big Cottonwood Meadows, August 26; one was seen at Whitney Meadows in the same month, and another at the summit of the pass at the head of Kings River. Mr. Palmer noted the species at Old Fort Tejon, June 28; Mr. Nelson saw it occasionally in the San Joaquin Valley, October 5–27; and saw several along the route from San Simeon to Santa Maria in November, and a few at Cañada de las Uvas and up to the summit of the Temploa Mountains.

Record of specimens collected of Falco mexicanus.

Collector's No.	Sex.	Locality.	Date.	Collector.	Remarks.
83	♂	Panamint Valley, Calif	Jan. 12, 1891.	E. W. Nelson	
	♂	Death Valley, Calif	Jan. 27, 1891.	A. K. Fisher	Furnace Creek.
110	♂	Resting Springs, Calif	Feb. 12, 1891.	....do	
131	♀	Ash Meadows, Calif	Mar. 16, 1891.	....do	
141	♂	Panamint Mountains, Calif	Mar. 25, 1891.	....do	Johnson Cañon.

Falco peregrinus anatum. Duck Hawk.

The only true duck hawk seen by the expedition was observed by Mr. Nelson near the coast west of San Luis Obispo, in November.

Falco columbarius. Pigeon Hawk.

The only records of the pigeon hawk made by the expedition are the following, all in California: Two seen by Mr. Stephens at Little Owens Lake early in May; the remains of one found by the writer near the reservoir at Furnace Creek, Death Valley, June 21; a few seen on the coast by Mr. Nelson between San Simeon and Carpenteria in November, and one in the Ojai Valley, Ventura County, in December.

Falco sparverius deserticolus. Desert Sparrow Hawk.

The sparrow hawk was common in but few places and was nowhere numerous as a summer resident. In Nevada it was not observed except at Ash Meadows, and in Pahrump and Vegas valleys, where it was found in March.

In California one was seen in Cajon Pass in the San Bernardino Mountains, January 1, and another, March 30. In Death Valley it was seen at Mesquite Well, January 21, Bennett Wells at the same date, and again about the middle of April; a pair among the cottonwoods at Furnace Creek, March 22, and one in Mesquite Valley, April 12.

In the Panamint Mountains, Dr. Merriam saw one in Emigrant Cañon, April 14, another on the north side of Telescope Peak, April 17–19, and Mr. Nelson found it rare in this range as well as in the Grapevine range in May. He found a pair nesting at the summit of the divide at the head of Cottonwood Creek in the former range, and a few in the Inyo

Mountains from the upper edge of the piñon belt up to the summit. In the latter range a pair occupied a cavity in a dead *Pinus flexilis* on the divide east of Lone Pine. Dr. Merriam saw a male on the summit of the White Mountains between Deep Spring Valley and Owens Valley, June 9, and Mr. Nelson saw the species in the same mountains and on the plateau at head of Owens Valley the following month.

In the Argus range, above Maturango Spring, a male was seen with a snake in its talons, which was carried to a height of several hundred yards and dropped, for what reason was not evident.

In Owens Valley the sparrow hawk was common at Lone Pine in December, 1890, and was found sparingly in the summer from Little Owens Lake to the head of the valley in the White Mountains. It was seen along the South Fork of Kern River, July 3–10; at Kernville, July 11–12, and was common in Walker Basin, where it was feeding on grasshoppers, July 13–16.

Mr. Palmer found it common on Peru Creek and in Castac Cañon, near Newhall, June 30, and in San Francisquito Pass, July 1. In the High Sierra it was seen at Menache Meadows, May 24–26; was common at Big Cottonwood Meadows during the summer; common at Whitney Meadows from below timberline to some distance above it during the last of August; at Round Valley, 12 miles south of Mount Whitney August 28; at Soda Springs or Kern River Lakes, early in September; and along the Kaweah River in August. Mr. Bailey found it common at Monterey, September 28 to October 9, and Mr. Stephens at Reche Cañon, September 22–24.

Mr. Nelson found it common in the San Joaquin Valley October 5–27 and abundant along the route from San Simeon to Carpenteria and Santa Paula in November and December.

It was common near San Luis Obispo, where one was seen with a small snake in its talons. It was sitting on a fence post eating the snake, and when startled flew off, carrying the reptile.

Record of specimens collected of Falco sparverius deserticolus.

Collector's No.	Sex.	Locality.	Date.	Collector.	Remarks.
33	♂	Sierra Nevada, Calif.	Aug. 12, 1891	B. H. Dutcher	Big Cottonwood Meadows.
428	♂	......do............	Aug. 28, 1891	A. K. Fisher	Round Valley.

Pandion haliaëtus carolinensis. Osprey.

The fish hawk was observed by Dr. Merriam in two localties, Death Valley, California, and Pahranagat Valley, Nevada. In the former place a single individual was seen at Furnace Creek just before dark on April 10. In Pahranagat Valley he saw several at the lake May 24, and in the evening of the same day shot one by mistake for an owl, as it hovered over the camp fire after dark.

At Furnace Creek a specimen was nailed upon the side of the house at the ranch, where it was killed a year or so before our arrival.

Strix pratincola. Barn Owl.

The only barn owl found east of the Sierra Nevada was a dead one seen by Mr. Stephens at Alvord, the last of June. Dr. Merriam and Mr. Palmer found the species abundant at Old Fort Tejon the latter part of June, where a family of young, in one of the large oaks near camp, proved a great nuisance on account of the hissing and shrieking which was kept up all night. The old birds were seen flying in and out among the large oaks on several occasions, as if in pursuit of bats. It is altogether likely that they were thus occupied, as the remains of this mammal have been found repeatedly among their stomach contents, both in Europe and this country. A pouched gopher and a chipmunk, left on the table, disappeared one night, probably through the agency of these birds.

On the South Fork of the Kern River Mr. Bailey secured two specimens July 4, and the species was common at Bakersfield and Visalia, in the San Joaquin Valley, in the latter part of July. Dr. Merriam found it common in the old mission of San Luis Rey, in San Diego County, and Mr. Stephens saw one in Reche Cañon, near San Bernardino. Mr. Nelson found it very common about San Emigdio, Morro Bay, and San Luis Obispo in October and November.

Record of specimens collected of Strix pratincola.

Collector's No.	Sex.	Locality.	Date.	Collector.	Remarks.
	♂	Kern River, Calif	July 4, 1891	V. Bailey	South Fork.
	♀	....do....	....do....	....do....	Do.
402	♀	Visalia, Calif	July 23, 1891	A. K. Fisher	

Asio wilsonianus. Long-eared Owl.

The long-eared owl was seen at a few places only. Mr. Nelson found a flock of eight living in a willow patch at Pahrump ranch, Nevada, February 12-28. All were flushed in an area less than 50 yards in diameter, and each bird had evidently occupied the same place for a considerable time, as the little groups of several dozen pellets plainly showed. Mr. Bailey secured a specimen at Bakersfield, in the San Joaquin Valley, July 18, and another near timber line north of Mineral King in the Sierra Nevada, September 9.

Asio accipitrinus. Short-eared Owl.

Several short-eared owls were seen at Ash Meadows, Nevada, during the early part of March, and Mr. Stephens shot a specimen in Temecula Cañon, San Diego County, California, January 30.

Syrnium occidentale. Spotted Owl.

This species was not met with by any member of our expedition, though the type came from Old Fort Tejon, California, where it was obtained March 6, 1858, by John Xantus.

Megascops asio bendirei. California Screech Owl.

No screech owls were seen or heard east of the Sierra Nevada in California. On the ridge above Walker Basin one was flushed from among the oaks July 14, but was not secured. At Bakersfield, in the San Joaquin Valley, the species was common and was heard at short intervals from dark to daylight, and Mr. Bailey secured a specimen about midnight of July 19, as it sat in the moonlight on a low limb over his bed. At Visalia, in the same valley, it was heard commonly among the big oaks July 22–24, and again September 17 and 18.

Mr. Nelson heard screech owls in different parts of the San Joaquin Valley in October, and along the route from San Simeon to Carpenteria and Santa Paula in November and December.

Record of specimens collected of Megascops asio bendirei.

Collector's No.	Sex.	Locality.	Date.	Collector.	Remarks.
390	♂	Bakersfield, Calif	July 20, 1891.	A. K. Fisher	
403	♀	Visalia, Calif	July 24, 1891.	...do...	

Bubo virginianus subarcticus. Western Horned Owl.

Great horned owls were often heard and occasionally seen at different localities in California and Nevada—in the latter State at Ash Meadows and in the Grapevine and Charleston mountains.

In California, in the Panamint Mountains, it was heard almost nightly in Johnson and Surprise cañons during the first half of April, and by Dr. Merriam in Emigrant Cañon about the same time. In the Argus Range at Shepherd Cañon an individual on several occasions was seen to fly from a certain ledge, where it probably had young; and at Maturango Spring one was flushed from among some boulders on May 7. It was heard all along the South Fork of the Kern River, July 3–11, and at Walker Basin, where two started from a rocky ledge among the hills, and one secured, July 14. Its stomach contained the remains of a wood rat (*Neotoma*) and a scorpion. In the San Joaquin Valley the species was heard at Bakersfield and Visalia in the latter part of July, and in the High Sierra at Sequoia National Park, Horse Corral and Whitney meadows, Soda Springs, and along the Kaweah River, in August and September.

Mr. Bailey heard it at Monterey, September 28 to October 9, and Mr. Stephens at Reche Cañon, September 22–24. Mr. Nelson heard great horned owls in the Tehachapi and Temploa mountains, in the San Joaquin Valley, and secured a specimen near San Luis Obispo.

Record of specimens obtained of Bubo virginianus subarcticus.

Collector's No.	Sex.	Locality.	Date.	Collector.	Remarks.
	im.	Soda Springs, Kern River, Calif.	Aug. 13, 1891	V. Bailey	Fragments.
	♀	San Luis Obispo, Calif	Nov. 29, 1891	E. W. Nelson	

Speotyto cunicularia hypogæa. Burrowing Owl.

The burrowing owl was not met with in any great numbers east of the Sierra Nevada in California or in Nevada. In the latter State several were seen in Ash Meadows, and one was caught at the mouth of the hole of a kangaroo rat (*Dipodomys deserti*) in Oasis Valley in March. In California several were seen about badger holes at Daggett, on the Mohave Desert, January 8–10; a few at Granite Wells January 15 and April 5, and a pair at Lone Willow Spring April 25. Mr. Bailey saw a pair at Bennett Wells, in Death Valley, June 21. A pair was seen in Coso Valley, below Maturango Spring, May 11. In Owens Valley one was seen at Lone Pine June 11; a pair with young at Alvord June 26–29; one at Morans July 4–7, and a few at the head of the valley, near the White Mountains, in July. Mr. Stephens saw it at various places in Salt Wells Valley, where it probably was breeding, May 1–5, and Mr. Bailey and the writer found it common at Indian Wells, in the same valley, July 1. A pair was seen on the eastern slope of Walker Pass July 1, where one was caught in a trap the following morning. A number of times burrowing owls were caught in steel traps set at the holes of badgers, foxes, spermophiles, and kangaroo rats.

Dr. Merriam and Mr. Palmer saw several pairs with full-grown young in the upper part of the Cañada de las Uvas and near Gorman Station, at the west end of Antelope Valley, during the latter part of June and the first week of July. They were living in the burrows of Beechey's spermophile and were catching grasshoppers in the daytime. They saw the species also at Caliente June 24, and in Tehachapi Valley June 25. At Bakersfield, in the San Joaquin Valley, and on the dry plains between Bakersfield and Visalia it was abundant, and as many as a dozen or fifteen were often in sight at once, perched on the mounds in front of the burrows, or on the tops of the telegraph poles.

Mr. Nelson found it generally distributed in the lowlands bordering the coast, between San Simeon and Carpenteria.

Record of specimens collected of Speotyto cunicularia hypogæa.

Collectors' No.	Sex.	Locality.	Date.	Collector.	Remarks.
48	♀	Daggett, Calif.	Jan. 10, 1891	A. K. Fisher	Mohave Desert.
49	♂	do	do	do	Do.
7	♀	do	Feb. 7, 1891	F. Stephens	Do.
62	♂	Granite Wells, Calif.	Jan. 15, 1891	A. K. Fisher	Do.
163	♀	Mojave, Calif.	Sept. 9, 1891	F. Stephens	35 miles northeast.
120	♂	Owens Valley, Calif.	June 26, 1891	do	
	♀ im	Walker Pass, Calif.	July 2, 1891	V. Bailey	
31	♂	Oasis Valley, Nev.	Mar. 15, 1891	F. Stephens	

Geococcyx californianus. Road-runner.

The road-runner or chaparral cock is tolerably common in many of the desert and foothill regions visited by members of the expedition, but on account of its more or less retiring habits comparatively few were seen, though their tracks were common. In Nevada it was very common among the sand dunes and mesquite patches at Ash Meadows, as well as in Vegas Valley and at the Bend of the Colorado, in March, and Mr. Stephens heard it in Oasis Valley.

In California the species is resident in Death Valley, as its numerous tracks seen around the mesquite and other thick growths at Furnace Creek during January and in June conclusively demonstrate.

At Resting Springs in the Amargosa Desert, where it was tolerably common, Mr. Bailey caught one in a steel trap, February 12, and Mr. Nelson found indications of its presence in Mesquite and Saline valleys. In Owens Valley it was very common, judging from the tracks; Mr. Nelson found it common and secured a specimen at Lone Pine in December, 1890; and Dr. Merriam saw one three miles south of that town, June 18, and others at the lower end of the valley on the following day. He saw one in Walker Pass June 22, and Mr. Bailey secured a specimen in the same place July 3. Several were seen along the South Fork of Kern River and at Kernville, June 22-23 and July 3-13, and near Alamo ranch in the Sierra Liebre, June 30. Dr. Merriam saw two near the north end of Cajon Pass in the San Bernardino Mountains, March 29, and found it common in the southern part of San Diego county in Escondido and San Marcos valleys, where it was breeding in patches of branching cactus.

In the Cañada de las Uvas, Mr. Palmer saw one near Castac Lake July 9, and shot one the following day at Old Fort Tejon. In the San Joaquin Valley tracks were seen frequently in the river bottoms and along the borders of thickets near Bakersfield in July, and Mr. Nelson found it common about the foothills at the south and west sides of the valley, October 5-27. The same observer found it along the coast from Morro to Carpenteria in November, and Mr. Bailey at Monterey, September 28 to October 9.

Record of specimens collected of Geococcyx californianus.

Collector's No.	Sex.	Locality.	Date.	Collector.	Remarks.
	♀	Resting Springs, Calif.	Feb. 12, 1891	V. Bailey	
	♂	Walker Pass, Calif.	July 3, 1891	....do....	

Coccyzus americanus occidentalis. California Cuckoo.

At Furnace Creek ranch in Death Valley, a cuckoo was seen among the willows at the edge of the reservoir about sunrise on June 20, and later in the day Mr. Bailey succeeded in securing it (an adult female). In the San Joaquin Valley the species was common at Bakersfield July 17-20, and was heard several times at Visalia among the live oaks July 22-25. In Owens Valley, Mr. Stephens saw one August 11, two miles west of Bishop. No others were recorded.

Ceryle alcyon. Belted Kingfisher.

A kingfisher was seen at San Bernardino, Calif., December 29, 1890. The species was not again met with until the party reached Ash Meadows, Nevada, where a few were seen along the streams during the early part of March. One was seen by Mr. Burnett at Furnace Creek, Death Valley, flying about the reservoir, April 15. Dr. Merriam saw one at Hot Springs, Panamint Valley, April 20, and another in Vegas Wash, Nevada, near the Colorado, May 2.

At Lone Pine, in Owens Valley, it was not uncommon along the river, and Mr. Stephens noted it at Alvord, in the same valley, the last of June. In the Sierra Nevada it was not uncommon at Soda Springs or Kern River lakes, the first of September, and was noted at Three Rivers, in the western foothills, about the middle of the month. Mr. Nelson observed it at the head of the Merced and San Joaquin rivers, and later saw a few individuals along the Kern River, in San Joaquin Valley, in October, and along the streams flowing into the sea between San Simeon, Carpenteria, and Santa Paula, in November and December. Mr. Bailey found it common at Monterey September 28 to October 9.

Dryobates villosus hyloscopus. Cabanis's Woodpecker.

Cabanis's woodpecker was found nowhere common in California, and was not observed at all in Nevada. One was seen above Johnson Cañon in the Panamint Mountains, April 18; Dr. Merriam observed several on the north side of Telescope Peak in the same range, April 17-19, and Mr. Nelson found the species very rare in the northern part of the Panamint and Grapevine Mountains during May and the first part of June. In the Coso Mountains it was seen on several occasions during the last half of May; in the upper part of the Inyo Range a few were seen the last of June; and others on the summit of the White Mountains June 9.

In the Sierra Nevada a few were seen on the east slope, at the head of Owens River, in July; several at Bishop Creek August 4-11; and the species was rather common at Menache Meadows May 24-26. Several were seen on the western slope of Walker Pass July 2; a number along the valley of Kern River July 3-10; and they were not uncommon in Walker Basin, from the bottom of the valley to summit of the ridge, July 13-16. Several were seen in the Sequoia National Park during the first week in August; a few at Horse Corral Meadows August 9-13; one was observed in Kings River Cañon August 15; the species was common at Big Cottonwood Meadows through the summer, at Whitney Meadows September 1, and several were noted from timber line down to below Mineral King September 10-13.

In the Cañada de las Uvas Mr. Palmer saw one or two back of Old Fort Tejon July 6, and a number near the summit of Frazier Mountain July 9.

At Monterey Mr. Bailey found a race of the hairy woodpecker, probably the present subspecies, common from September 28 to October 9; and Mr. Nelson found it sparingly at Mount Piños in October, and in the mountains between San Simeon and Carpenteria November 4 to December 18.

Record of specimens collected of Dryobates villosus hyloscopus.

Collector's No.	Sex.	Locality.	Date.	Collector.	Remarks.
365	♂ ad.	White Mountains, Calif	June 9, 1891	V. Bailey	
375	♀ im.	Walker Pass, Calif	July 2, 1891	A. K. Fisher	
143	♂ im.	Kern River, Calif	July 5, 1891	....do	South Fork.
30	♀ im.	Sierra Nevada, Calif	July 27, 1891	F. Stephens	
31	♂ im.	......do	Aug. 11, 1891	B. H. Dutcher	Big Cottonwood Meadows.
	im.	......do	....do	....do	Do.

Dryobates pubescens gairdnerii. Gairdner's Woodpecker.

Dr. Merriam shot a specimen of this species on the north side of Tehachapi Pass, California, a few miles below the summit, June 25. Mr. Nelson found it rare in the piñon belt of the Panamint and Grapevine mountains May 4 to June 15, and reported a few seen near San Luis Obispo the last of October. These are the only records we have for the species.

Dryobates scalaris bairdi. Baird's Woodpecker.

The known range of this woodpecker was extended considerably by the observations of the expedition. In the Mohave Desert it was not uncommon among the giant yuccas at Hesperia, east of Cajon Pass, where a pair was secured January 4 and 5. Dr. Merriam saw one at the Upper Cottonwood Springs at the east base of the Charleston Mountains, Nevada, April 30, one in Vegas Wash May 2, another near the mouth of the Santa Clara, Utah, May 14, and shot an adult male and saw others in the cottonwoods where Beaverdam Creek joins the Virgin in northwestern Arizona, May 9.

In 1889 Mr. Bailey found it common in the timber along the Santa Clara in January, among the yuccas at Dolan and Mud springs in Detrital Valley, Arizona, in February, and in the river bottom at Fort Mohave in March.

Record of specimens collected of Dryobates scalaris bairdi.

Collector's No.	Sex.	Locality.	Date.	Collector.	Remarks.
	♂	Beaverdam, Ariz	May 9, 1891	C. Hart Merriam	
31	♂	Hesperia, Calif	Jan. 4, 1891	A. K. Fisher	
41	♀	......do	Jan. 5, 1891	....do	

Dryobates nuttallii. Nuttall's Woodpecker.

This species was first observed in Cajon Pass in the San Bernardino Mountains, Calif., where a fine adult male was secured January 2. Mr. Palmer saw several at Old Fort Tejon, July 1, and Dr. Merriam secured a specimen between Walker Basin and Caliente, June 24. In the Sierra Nevada several were seen on the western slope of Walker Pass, July 2—13; it was not uncommon along the valley of Kern River

July 3-13; was common at Walker Basin, July 13-16; and at Three Rivers it was not uncommon, and was found along the East Fork of the Kaweah River as high as the lower edge of the conifers. It was seen on several occasions at Bakersfield, in the San Joaquin Valley, July 17-20; and Mr. Nelson saw several around San Emigdio, and a few along the coast from San Simeon to Carpenteria in November and December, 1891.

Record of specimens collected of Dryobates nuttallii.

Collector's No.	Sex.	Locality.	Date.	Collector.	Remarks.
20	♂	Cajon Pass, Calif.	Jan. 2, 1891	A. K. Fisher	
366	♂ im	Walker Pass, Calif.	July 2, 1891	....do	

Xenopicus albolarvatus. White-headed Woodpecker.

The white-headed woodpecker was rather common in the higher parts of the Sierra Nevada, in California. Mr. Nelson noted a few at the head of Owens River, and found it common on the divide between the Merced and San Joaquin rivers, on the western slope. In the Sequoia National Park it was common, going in pairs and frequenting the more open pine woods. Several were seen at Horse Corral Meadows, August 9-13, and in Kings River Cañon, August 15.

It was seen also at Big Cottonwood Meadows, August 26; at Whitney Meadows the last of August; at Soda Springs or Kern River Lakes, September 3; and along the East Fork of the Kaweah River, from the lower edge of the pines to and above Mineral King, the last of July and September 13-14. Mr. Palmer saw one in Tejon Pass, July 12, and Mr. Nelson observed several near the summit of Mount Piños, in October.

Record of specimens collected of Xenopicus albolarvatus.

Collector's No.	Sex.	Locality.	Date.	Collector.	Remarks.
408	♀	Sierra Nevada, Calif.	July 30, 1891	V. Bailey	East Fork of Kaweah River.
	♂	......do	Aug. 6, 1891	A. K. Fisher	Sequoia National Park.

Sphyrapicus varius nuchalis. Red-naped Sapsucker.

The single record of this woodpecker is a male, killed by Mr. Nelson among the piñons on the west slope of the mountains northwest of Charleston Peak, Nevada, February 12, 1891.

Sphyrapicus ruber. Red-breasted Sapsucker.

The red-breasted woodpecker was not met with east of the Sierra Nevada. Mr. Palmer secured a specimen at Halsted Meadows, in the Sequoia National Park, where it was not uncommon, August 3. It was common at Horse Corral Meadows, around the edges of clearings and in the willow clumps, August 9-13; was seen at Soda Springs or Kern

River Lakes by Mr. Bailey and the writer in August and September; and on the Kaweah River, below the pines, September 12. Mr. Nelson noted it at the head of Owens River and on the western slope, where it was rather more common. He also saw a few at Mount Piños about the middle of October, and Mr. Palmer saw a few in Tejon Pass, July 12.

Record of specimens collected of Sphyrapicus ruber.

Collector's No.	Sex.	Locality.	Date.	Collector.	Remarks.
140	♂	Sierra Nevada, Calif	July 24, 1891	F. Stephens	Horse Corral Meadows.
412	♂ ad.	......do......	Aug. 12, 1891	A. K. Fisher	Do.
413	♂ im.	......do......	...do...	...do...	Kern River Lakes.
	♂ im.	......do......	...do...	V. Bailey	

Sphyrapicus thyroideus. Williamson's Sapsucker.

Williamson's woodpecker is not uncommon in a number of places in the Sierra Nevada, in California. Mr. Nelson saw one at the head of Owens River, and a few on the western slope opposite that place. Several were seen at Horse Corral Meadows, August 11–13; at Whitney Meadows about September 1; and the species was common at Big Cottonwood Meadows, August 25–27, where Mr. Dutcher killed several earlier in the season. It was noted at Soda Springs or Kern River Lakes, early in September; at Mineral King, the last of July and the second week in September, and was seen once on Mount Piños about the middle of October.

Record of specimens collected of Sphyrapicus thyroideus.

Collector's No.	Sex.	Locality.	Date.	Collector.	Remarks.
410	♂	Sierra Nevada, Calif	Aug. 11, 1891	A. K. Fisher	Horse Corral Meadows.
	im.	......do......	Aug. 2, 1891	V. Bailey	Mineral King.
27	♂ im.	......do......	Aug. 4, 1891	B. H. Dutcher	Big Cottonwood Meadows.
28	♂ im.	......do......	...do...	...do...	Do.
29	im.	......do......	...do...	...do...	Do.
423	♂	......do......	Aug. 26, 1891	A. K. Fisher	Do..
156	♂ im.	......do......	Aug. 21, 1891	F. Stephens	Olancha Peak.

Ceophlœus pileatus. Pileated Woodpecker.

This handsome woodpecker was not observed except in the Sierra Nevada, in California, where Mr. Nelson found it common at an altitude of about 1980 meters (6,500 feet) in the Mariposa grove of big trees near Wawona and along the Merced River. The writer heard it a number of times in the Sequoia National Park early in August, and Mr. Palmer saw a pair in Kings River Cañon, August 14.

Melanerpes formicivorus bairdi. California Woodpecker.

The California woodpecker was not seen east of the western slope of the Sierra Nevada. Dr. Merriam found it in Walker Basin June 24; in

Tehachapi Pass, June 25; and in the Cañada de las Uvas, where it was breeding abundantly, June 28-29. At Three Rivers, in the foot hills, the species was common July 25-30, and September 14-17, at which time it was feeding on acorns.

In Walker Basin the writer saw several families along a fence row where they were feeding on grasshoppers, July 13-16, and on the 14th the species was common among the pines on the ridge above the valley.

All along the road between Tulare and Visalia in the San Joaquin Valley, this woodpecker was common among the oaks, July 22-24. As many as ten individuals were seen in one tree.

Mr. Nelson found it common and generally distributed among the oaks in the San Joaquin Valley, and along the route from San Simeon to Santa Paula, during the last three months of the year.

Record of specimens collected of Melanerpes formicivorus bairdi.

Collector's No.	Sex.	Locality.	Date.	Collector.	Remarks.
389	♂	Walker Basin, Calif.	June 14, 1891	A. K. Fisher	
401	♂	Visalia, Calif.	July 23, 1891	do	

Melanerpes torquatus. Lewis's Woodpecker.

This woodpecker was quite common in Walker Basin, where it was seen June 24 and July 13-16. The birds were stationed along the fence rows and on trees, from which they made frequent excursions to the ground to capture grasshoppers. The stomachs of a number examined contained nothing but the remains of this insect.

It was seen by Dr. Merriam and Mr. Palmer near Old Fort Tejon, in the Cañada de las Uvas, the latter part of June. Mr. Nelson saw one on the plateau at the head of Owens Valley in July and on the east slope of the Sierra at the head of Owens River in the latter part of July. At Three Rivers, in the western foothills, it was common among the oaks September 12-17.

Record of specimens collected of Melanerpes torquatus.

Collector's No.	Sex.	Locality.	Date.	Collector.	Remarks.
888	im	Walker Basin, California	July 13, 1891	A. K. Fisher	
	im	do	do	V. Bailey	
	♂ im	do	do	do	
	♀ ad	do	do	do	

Melanerpes uropygialis. Gila Woodpecker.

A specimen of this woodpecker was taken by Mr. Bailey near Fort Mohave, Ariz., in March, 1889.

Colaptes cafer. Red-shafted Flicker.

The red-shafted flicker was seen in many places, though it was comparatively rare over the greater part of the country traversed.

In Nevada, Mr. Nelson saw this woodpecker in Pahrump and Vegas valleys during the latter part of February and first of March. Mr. Stephens observed it in the Grapevine Mountains March 20-26 and found it common at the Queen mine July 11-16. Dr. Merriam saw two in the nut pine zone on Mount Magruder June 6, and the writer shot an individual, the only one seen, at Ash Meadows, March 2. At Pahrump ranch, Mr. Nelson saw where one had drilled four holes through the boards in the gable end of a building used as a granary, and each time a piece of tin had been placed over the hole. When he was there, the bird had just completed a fifth hole, close to the others.

In California, it was common just outside of the town of San Bernardino the last of December, 1890, and was observed in Cajon Pass January 1-2. At Hesperia, in the Mohave Desert, a number were seen among the tree yuccas January 3-4.

Mr. Nelson found the species in the Inyo Mountains the latter part of June, and stated that it occurred wherever there was moisture enough to support a growth of the higher pines in the mountains or of cottonwoods in the valleys. He also found it common from the head of Owens Valley up to timber line in the White Mountains in July. Dr. Merriam saw a red-shafted flicker at Furnace Creek, in Death Valley, April 10, among the willows and mesquite; one at Hot Springs, Panamint Valley, about April 20, and another in the Panamint Mountains a few days earlier. In the Argus Range, the writer saw one at Maturango Spring May 14, several in the Coso Mountains during the latter part of the same month, and a number in the higher portions of the Panamint Mountains the last week in June. In Owens Valley, it was seen by Mr. Nelson at Lone Pine, in December, 1890, and by Mr. Stephens at Independence Creek, Bishop Creek, and Benton during the summer.

This woodpecker was not uncommon in Walker Pass, along the valley of the Kern River, at Kernville, and in Walker Basin during the first half of July. On the High Sierra it was seen in the Sequoia National Park the first week in August; at Horse Corral Meadows August 9-13; in Kings River Cañon August 13-16; at Menache Meadows May 24-26; at Big Cottonwood Meadows June 15 to September; at Whitney Meadows the last of August; Soda Springs or Kern River Lakes, August and first part of September; and at Mineral King and down the west slope to Three Rivers in the foothills during the first two weeks in September.

Dr. Merriam saw it in the Cañada de las Uvas June 28-29, and the writer observed it at Bakersfield July 17-20. Mr. Bailey recorded the species from Monterey September 20 to October 9, and Mr. Nelson reported it common in the Tejon Mountains, in the San Joaquin Valley, at San Luis Obispo, and along the route between San Simeon and Carpenteria during the fall and early winter.

Phalænoptilus nuttalli. Poor-will.

The poor-will was common in a number of localities visited by the expedition. In Death Valley a specimen was obtained at Bennett Wells January 28, another at Saratoga Springs February 4; and the species was seen and heard by Dr. Merriam at Furnace Creek April 10, and in Mesquite Valley April 13. One was seen in the Funeral Mountains March 21. At Ash Meadows, Nevada, one or two were seen and others heard during the first part of March. In Nevada Dr. Merriam found it common on Mount Magruder June 4–9, where he saw and heard one or more every evening and obtained a specimen. On Gold Mountain he heard it at the deserted mining camp June 3, in Pahranagat Valley May 22–26, at Sheep Spring in the Juniper Mountains, May 18, and at Vegas ranch May 1. In Utah he heard it along Shoal Creek, near the Escalante Desert, May 17.

Mr. Nelson found the species in the Panamint and Grapevine mountains, where it was a rare breeder in the sage-brush belt. He saw and heard a few from the bottom of Saline Valley up to the piñons in the Inyo Mountains, found it as high as 2,650 meters (8,700 feet) in the White Mountains, and also on the plateau at the head of Owens Valley. In Owens Valley a specimen was taken at the mouth of the cañon at Lone Pine, June 12; Mr. Stephens saw two at Olancha May 16–23, and others at Independence Creek June 18–23, and at the Queen mill and mine, Nevada, July 11–16. The same observer saw one at Borax Flat, near the southern end of the Argus Range, the last of April. Mr. F. W. Koch collected two fresh eggs May 6 above Maturango Spring, where it was common. At Coso it was heard or seen every evening during the latter half of May. It was common at Hot Springs in Panamint Valley, April 10–25; and at Wild Rose Spring, in the Panamint Mountains, June 25.

Record of specimens collected of Phalænoptilus nuttalli.

Collector's No.	Sex.	Locality.	Date.	Collector.	Remarks.
	♀	Death Valley, Calif	Jan. 28, 1891	E. W. Nelson	Bennett Wells.
	♂	......do............	Feb. 14, 1891	...do........	Saratoga Springs.
246	♂	Coso Mountains, Calif	May 22, 1891	A. K. Fisher	
337	♀	Owens Valley, Calif	June 12, 1891	...do.........	Lone Pine.
41	♂	Grapevine Mountains, Calif	Apr. 1, 1891	F. Stephens	Grapevine Spring.
	♀	Mount Magruder, Nev	June 4, 1891	C. Hart Merriam	

Phalænoptilus nuttalli californicus. California Poor-will.

This race of the poor-will was common in Kern Valley, where Mr. Bailey secured a specimen July 8. One was seen on the road from Kaweah to the Sequoia National Park July 31. It would await until the horse nearly stepped on it, then fly ahead some distance and alight on the road again, which manœuver it repeated several times. Mr. Bailey saw a poor-will at Trout Meadows in the High Sierra, which probably belonged to this race. Dr. Merriam shot one at Twin Oaks, at the foot of the Granite range, in San Diego County, July 10, where several were observed to alight in the same place every evening in a dusty road under the spreading branches of a live-oak tree.

Record of specimens collected of Phalœnoptilus nuttalli californicus.

Collector's No.	Sex.	Locality.	Date.	Collector.	Remarks.
	♂	Kern River, Calif. Twin Oaks, San Diego County, Calif.	July 8, 1891 July 10, 1891	V. Bailey C. Hart Merriam	South Fork.

Chordeiles virginianus henryi. Western Nighthawk.

It is a source of great regret that specimens of nighthawks were not secured at the various places where they were found by the members of the expedition. This neglect makes it impossible to properly separate the range of the present from that of the following species in the region under consideration.

The only specimen of the western nighthawk secured was one collected by the writer in Death Valley, at Furnace Creek, June 19. At this place the nighthawks began to fly just after sunset and were very common over the alfalfa fields at the ranch. Nighthawks supposed to belong to this species were seen in Pahranagat Valley, Nevada, May 22–26, on Mount Magruder, Nevada, June 4–8, and in the High Sierra, at Trout, Whitney, and Big Cottonwood meadows, during the summer and autumn.

Chordeiles texensis. Texas Nighthawk.

Fortunately, a larger number of specimens of this night-hawk was taken than of the preceding species, though not enough to enable the satisfactory mapping of its distribution in California and Nevada.

The Texas nighthawk was a very common breeder in most parts of Owens Valley, where it occurred as far north at least as Bishop. Around Owens Lake and Lone Pine large numbers were observed every night, and at the former place many were seen skimming close to the water in pursuit of a small fly (*Ephydra hians*), which was swarming on and near the shore.

The species was not uncommon along the South Fork of the Kern River, where Mr. Bailey secured a specimen July 8, and at Bakersfield, in the San Joaquin Valley, where several were seen and one secured about the middle of the month.

Dr. Merriam saw it during the breeding season in Oasis Valley and Ash Meadows, Nev., and at other points in the Amargosa Desert, and also in the Mohave Desert, in California. He saw one at Saratoga Springs at the south end of Death Valley, April 26, and two at Resting Springs in the Amargosa Desert, April 27. He found it common at the mouth of Beaverdam Creek, Arizona, May 9, and secured two fresh eggs at St. George, in the Lower Santa Clara Valley, Utah, May 13. Another was shot in the Virgin Valley, near the eastern boundary of Nevada, May 8. Nighthawks which probably belonged to this species were seen in Pahrump and Vegas valleys, Nevada, and Saline Valley, California. This nighthawk had the habit of alighting on the dusty roads, just at dusk, where it sat motionless for a time, though in a few instances it was observed to make a series of hopping flights, alighting at short intervals for a moment only.

Record of specimens collected of Chordeiles texensis.

Collector's No.	Sex.	Locality.	Date.	Collector.	Remarks.
125	♂	Beaverdam Creek, Ariz.	May 10, 1891	V. Bailey	
319	♀	Owens Valley, Calif.	June 29, 1891	F. Stephens	Bishop.
327	♂	......do........	June 8, 1891	A. K. Fisher	Lone Pine.
335	♀	......do........	June 10, 1891	....do	Do.
336	♀	......do........	June 12, 1891	....do	Do.
	♂	......do........	....do	....do	Do.
285	♀	......do........	June 13, 1891	C. Hart Merriam	Do.
69	♂	......do........	June 2, 1891	A. K. Fisher	Keeler.
		......do........	May 31, 1891	F. Stephens	Ash Creek.
398	♀	Kern River, Calif.	July 8, 1891	V. Bailey	South Fork.
		Bakersfield, Calif.	July 19, 1891	A. K. Fisher	

Cypseloides niger. Black Swift.

The black swift was first observed at Owens Lake near Keeler, Calif., where a number were seen flying back and forth over the salt meadows on May 31. On June 2, twenty or more were seen feeding over the same meadow and five specimens were collected. From the condition of the ovaries of the female secured, it was evident that the eggs had been laid. When the flock left the marsh, it rose high in the air and went in the direction of the cliffs in the Inyo Mountains, near Cerro Gordo, where a colony evidently was breeding. Near the upper end of the lake, and about 6 miles north of Keeler, several were seen on June 4 and again on June 15. At Lone Pine, five passed over camp early on the morning of June 7, and a number were seen at the mouth of the cañon above the town June 12. Dr. Merriam saw a number and secured one at the north end of Owens Lake, June 12, and saw half a dozen at Olancha, at the south end of the lake, June 20. Mr. Stephens saw a dozen or more at the latter place May 23 and secured two June 4. On the former date they were flying high out of range, in company with white-throated swifts and white-bellied swallows. The same observer saw this species at Independence Creek, June 20, and at Bishop Creek, August 6.

On the South Fork of Kern River three swifts were seen which undoubtedly belonged to this species, and on several occasions black swifts were seen in Kings River Cañon, August 13–16.

Record of specimens collected of Cypseloides niger.

Collector's No.	Sex.	Locality.	Date.	Collector.	Remarks.
279	♂	Keeler, Inyo County, Calif.	June 2, 1891	A. K. Fisher	
280	♂	......do........	....do	....do	
281	♂	......do........	....do	....do	
282	♀	......do........	....do	....do	
	♂	......do........	....do	T. S. Palmer	
	♂	Owens Lake, Calif.	June 12, 1891	C. Hart Merriam	
73	♂	......do........	June 4, 1891	F. Stephens	Olancha.
74	♂	......do........	....do	....do	Do.

Chætura vauxii. Vaux's Swift.

Vaux's swift was seen a few times only in the valleys on each side of the Sierra Nevada. Mr. Stephens saw it nearly every day and secured a specimen at Olancha, near the south end of Owens Lake, where it was migrating, May 16-23.

Mr. Belding saw large flocks in the Yosemite Valley. The writer saw a few at Three Rivers, in the western foothills of the Sierra, September 13-14, and at Visalia on September 18.

Aëronautes melanoleucus. White-throated Swift.

White-throated swifts were common at a number of places in the desert valleys and ranges during the spring and summer. In Johnson Cañon, in the Panamint Mountains, Calif., Mr. Palmer saw one March 26, and Mr. Nelson secured one near the same place, April 12. The latter observer found the species to be a common summer resident in portions of the Panamint and Grapevine mountains visited. The last of May he saw them going in and out of crevices in the steep walls above Willow Creek, and in June found them frequenting the cliffs in Cottonwood Cañon, 750 meters (2,500 feet) above Salt Wells, and observed them about the cliffs in Boundary Cañon in the Grapevine Range. They were frequently seen in the morning and evening hunting over Saline Valley. In the Panimint Mountains north of Telescope Peak, Mr. Bailey and the writer saw several hundred of these swifts flying back and forth over a hillside, and a few above the summit of the peak, June 23. The males uttered at short intervals a series of notes which, when a number joined in the performance, produced a not unpleasant impression. In Death Valley Dr. Merriam saw a flock at Mesquite Wells, April 8; Mr. Burnett saw individuals flying over the reservoir at Furnace Creek, April 15; and the writer killed a number of specimens at the latter place, June 20. In the Argus Range swifts were seen in Shepherd Cañon the last of April, and along the divide above Maturango Spring during the first half of May.

In Nevada Dr. Merriam saw several at Pahroc Spring, May 22; at Ash Meadows, May 30; and in Oasis Valley and the upper part of Amargosa Desert, June 1, when they were observed in aërial coition. In Utah Dr. Merriam saw several small flocks in the Lower Santa Clara Valley, May 11-15. Mr. Nelson found it breeding in the Inyo Mountains, Calif., June 24-July 4, and sparingly in the White Mountains in July. White-throated swifts were common in many places in Owens Valley, especially about the meadows at Owens Lake and at the mouth of the cañons. Along the South Fork of the Kern River they were tolerably common the first week in July, and a few were seen flying over the Sequoia National Park the first week in August. Mr. Nelson found them at the head of Owens River; also along all the streams visited on the western slope of the Sierra, and in the Yosemite Valley up to timber line. They bred everywhere in crevices in the cañon walls. He saw several flocks in the Ojai Valley in December.

Record of specimens collected of Aëronautes melanoleucus.

Collector's No.	Sex.	Locality.	Date.	Collector.	Remarks.
43	♀	Panamint Mountains, Calif	Apr. 11, 1891	E. W. Nelson	
345	♀	Death Valley, Calif	Apr. 9, 1891	F. Stephens	Furnace Creek.
346	♀	......do........	June 20, 1891	A. K. Fisher	Do.
347	♀	......do........	...do...	...do...	Do.
	♀	......do........	...do...	...do...	Do.
95	♂	Keeler, Calif	June 2, 1891	T. S. Palmer	
	♂	Owens Lake, Calif	June 12, 1891	F. Stephens	Olancha.

Trochilus alexandri. Black-chinned Hummingbird.

The black-chinned hummingbird is common in Owens Valley, California, where it was found at the following localities: At Lone Pine a number of specimens were secured in June; At Olancha Mr. Stephens found it common, May 16–23; at Ash Creek, May 30–June 3; a few at Independence Creek, June 18–23; Alvord, June 26–28; and young of the year were common at Fish Slough, July 2–3. At Olancha he secured a very interesting specimen which in its specific characters was intermediate between this species and Costa's hummer, and was probably a hybrid. He found a nest containing three eggs in an orchard at the same place, May 16. Mr. Nelson found it common on both slopes of the Inyo Mountains from the valleys up to the piñons, wherever there was water enough to produce a growth of willows and other deciduous trees. In Walker Basin, where it was not common, Mr. Bailey secured a specimen, July 14, and another was taken at Bakersfield in the San Joaquin Valley, July 19. At Old Fort Tejon Mr. Palmer secured an immature bird in July, which he referred to this species.

Dr. Merriam saw several and secured two at the mouth of Beaverdam Creek, Arizona, May 9, and found the species common in the Lower Santa Clara Valley, Utah, where four nests containing fresh eggs were found, May 11–14. All the nests (one of which contained three eggs) were placed on low branches of cottonwoods, generally within easy reach from the ground.

Record of specimens collected of Trochilus alexandri.

Collector's No.	Sex.	Locality.	Date.	Collector.	Remarks.
	♀	Santa Clara, Utah	May 11, 1891	C. Hart Merriam	
	♂	Beaverdam Creek, Ariz	May 9, 1891	V. Bailey	
58	♀	Owens Valley, Calif	May 16, 1891	F. Stephens	Olancha, set 3 eggs.
65	♂	......do...	May 20, 1891	...do...	Ash Creek.
80	♂	......do...	June 10, 1891	...do...	Olancha.
	♂	Walker Basin, Calif	July 14, 1891	V. Bailey	
400	♀	Bakersfield, Calif	July 19, 1891	A. K. Fisher	
311	♂	Owens Valley, Calif	June 7, 1891	...do...	Lone Pine.
312	♂	......do...	...do...	...do...	Do.
314	♂	......do...	June 8, 1891	...do...	Do.

Calypte costæ. Costa's Hummingbird.

Costa's hummingbird is the common species of the desert valleys and mountains of southern California and Nevada. One was seen at

Resting Springs in the Amargosa Desert, California, February 13; a number were seen in the Funeral Mountains March 22; at Furnace Creek, Death Valley, April 12; and in Emigrant Cañon, in the Panamint Mountains, April 14. It was common in Johnson and Surprise cañons, where it was seen near all the springs and streams during April, and in the latter cañon a half-completed nest was found April 19. Several were seen at Hot Springs in Panamint Valley, April 19-25, and at Leach Point Spring April 25. Costa's hummingbird was the only species met with by Mr. Nelson in the Panamint and Grapevine Mountains, where he found it a common breeder, during May and June.

In Nevada, Dr. Merriam found it tolerably common on Mount Magruder June 4-8; in Pahranagat Valley May 22-25; at Mountain Spring, Charleston Mountains, and at Upper Cottonwood Springs at the eastern base of these mountains, April 30. In Vegas Wash he found a nest containing two full-fledged young May 3; at the Bend of the Colorado one containing two fresh eggs May 4; and at Bitter Spring in the Muddy Mountains, another containing two fresh eggs, May 5. Mr. Nelson saw one in Vegas Wash, Nevada, March 10; and Mr. Stephens reported it from the Grapevine Mountains and Oasis Valley from the middle to the latter part of the month. Dr. Merriam found it common among the junipers on the eastern side of the Beaverdam Mountains, Utah, May 11.

In the Argus Range, California, the species was very common at Maturango Spring, and in Shepherd Cañon, where several nests were found in the low bushes along the edges of the cañon. Those containing two fresh eggs each were taken April 27, April 28, and May 7, and one containing full-fledged young, April 27. At Coso the species was very abundant and several of its nests were found. Various kinds of plants were used as nesting sites, though the branching cactus (*Opuntia echinocarpa*) was most commonly chosen. Usually the structure was placed on the top of a lower branch, a foot or so from the ground, and under an overhanging mass of thick spiny branches, which formed a protection for the parent bird from the sun and weather, as well as its enemies. At Coso one of these hummers was seen on a bright moonlight evening hovering about a bunch of flowers, and was heard again later in the same night. During our last trip to Death Valley Mr. Bailey saw one at Furnace Creek June 19, and the species was abundant all through the Panamint Mountains. Just at daylight on the morning of June 25, before the shadow had risen out of Wild Rose Cañon, a Costa's hummingbird came and hovered within a foot of our camp fire, probably mistaking it from the distance for a bunch of bright flowers. It was observed on several occasions that any bright-colored object placed in a conspicuous position attracted this bird. In Owens Valley this hummingbird was more or less common, especially along the eastern slope of the Sierra Nevada, where it was associated with the black-chinned hummer. Several were seen on the eastern slope of Walker Pass July 1, and in Reche Cañon September 22-24.

The male Costa's hummingbird has a peculiar habit, probably closely associated with the season of courtship, of flying up in the air to a considerable height and then swooping down with great velocity until near the ground, when it rises to its former position, to repeat the manœuver fifteen or twenty times before settling on some perch to rest. The course taken by the bird forms a parabolic curve, and when on the descent a booming, rushing noise is made, which can be heard at a considerable distance.

Record of specimens collected of Calypte costæ.

Collector's No.	Sex.	Locality.	Date.	Collector.	Remarks.
59	♂	Owens Valley, Calif	May 20, 1891	F. Stephens	Olancha. Hybrid between *T. costæ* and *T. alexandri*.
68	♀	......do......	May 31, 1891	......do......	Ash Creek. Parent of nest and eggs.
139	♂	Panamint Mountains, Calif	Mar. 26, 1891	A. K. Fisher	Johnson Cañon.
155	♂	......do......	Apr. 14, 1891	......do......	Surprise Cañon.
163	♂	......do......	Apr. 16, 1891	......do......	Do.
166	♂	......do......	Apr. 20, 1891	......do......	Do.
167	♂	......do......	......do......	......do......	Do.
	♂	......do......	Mar. 27, 1891	E. W. Nelson	Johnson Cañon.
	♂	......do......	Mar. 28, 1891	......do......	Do.
	♂	......do......	April 4, 1891	......do......	Do.
	♂	......do......	Apr. 11, 1891	......do......	Do.
	♂	......do......	Apr. 14, 1891	......do......	Surprise Cañon.
	♂	......do......	May 12, 1891	......do......	
	♀	......do......	May 23, 1891	......do......	Willow Creek. Parent of nest and eggs.
192	♀	Argus Range, Calif	Apr. 29, 1891	A. K. Fisher	Shepherd Cañon. Parent of No. 191.
191	♂ juv.	......do......	......do......	......do......	Shepherd Cañon.
204	♀	......do......	May 7, 1891	......do......	Shepherd Cañon. Nest and eggs.
268	♀	Coso Mountains, Calif	May 28, 1891	......do......	Nest and eggs.
	♂	Ash Meadows, Nev	May 30, 1891	V. Bailey	
	♂	Charleston Mountains, Nev	Apr. 30, 1891	......do......	
	♂	Panaca, Nev	May 19, 1891	......do......	

Calypte anna. Anna's Hummingbird.

A large hummer was seen in the Cajon Pass in the San Bernardino Mountains on January 2, which was probably this species. Mr. Stephens saw a number, mostly immature males, on the side of Reche Cañon, September 22–24; Mr. Bailey found the species common at Monterey, where he secured specimens October 3 and 6, and Mr. Nelson found it common at Morro Bay, and saw a few south of that place in November.

Record of specimens collected of Calypte anna.

Collector's No.	Sex.	Locality.	Date.	Collector.	Remarks.
	♂	Monterey, Calif	Oct. 3, 1891	V. Bailey	
	♂	......do......	Oct. 6, 1891	......do......	

Selasphorus platycercus. Broad-tailed Hummingbird.

The broad-tailed hummer was found by Dr. Merriam at Sheep Spring in the Juniper Mountains, Nevada, where an adult male was secured and many others seen May 19. Mr. Nelson reported it as common on the western slope of the Sierra Nevada, California, opposite the head of Owens River, and Mr. Palmer secured a specimen in the Sequoia National Park August 4.

Selasphorus rufus. Rufous Hummingbird.

The Rufous hummingbird was seen only in the Sierra Nevada, in California. Mr. Nelson found it common at the head of Owens River, and on the western slope from timber line down into the Yosemite Valley. While crossing the divide between the heads of the San Joaquin and Merced rivers he saw a number of these birds crossing from the latter to the former river. The species was common in the Sequoia National Park, where a specimen was taken August 4; and at Horse Corral Meadows August 9-13; one was seen in Kings River Cañon August 15, and one at Kearsarge Pass August 18.

At Mineral King it was common from above timber-line down to the lower part of the pines early in August and again in September. It was unusually common on the south side of Farewell Gap, on September 8, where large numbers were observed flying about in the attempt to dry and warm themselves, after a cold rain and hail storm.

Stellula calliope. Calliope Hummingbird.

None of our party obtained this hummingbird. Mr. Belding observed it at Crocker's, near the Yosemite Valley, in May 1891, and Dr. W. J. Hoffman reported it from Owens Valley, where it was found breeding in July. "One nest with eggs was found perched over and within a short distance of a noisy mountain stream, where it was no doubt frequently subjected to the dashing spray" (Bull. U. S. Geol. and Geog. Sur., Hayden, VI, 1881, 237).

Mr. Henshaw saw a single individual in the Tejon Mountains, August 17, 1875.

Tyrannus tyrannus. Kingbird.

At Olancha, near the southern end of Owens Lake, Mr. Bailey and the writer saw a common kingbird, June 29. It was so near that identification was positive. The Arkansas flycatchers seemed to be ill disposed towards the stranger and were chasing and diving at it whenever it took wing.

Tyrannus verticalis. Arkansas Kingbird.

The Arkansas flycatcher was common in most of the valleys traversed by the expedition. In California one was seen at Raymond Well, in Salt Wells Valley, and another in the Coso Valley, May 1, in which latter place it became common a few days later. Mr. Nelson saw a few in Panamint, Saline, and Mesquite Valleys, in May and June; near the valleys on both slopes of the Inyo Mountains, the last of June; and at the head of Owens Valley, near the White Mountains, in July. In Owens Valley, it was common at Lone Pine, where many young were seen June 4-15; at Olancha, June 29; at Big Pine, June 26-28; and more or less common at various other places in the valley throughout the summer. Dr. Merriam found it breeding commonly in the tree yuccas in Antelope Valley at the west end of the Mohave Desert, June 26-27, and saw one at Resting Springs in the Amargosa Desert, April 27. At Walker Pass a pair was seen on the east slope July 1, and the species was common on the west slope the following day. It was common also along the valley of Kern River July 3-13; at Walker Basin, July 13-16; at Bakersfield, in the San Joaquin Valley, July 17-20, and at Three Rivers and along the lower part of the Kaweah River, the last of July. Mr. Palmer found it abundant at Old Fort Tejon in July, and Mr. Nelson saw several near Nordhoff the last of December.

In Nevada, Dr. Merriam saw it on Gold Mountain, June 3; found it tolerably common in Pahranagat Valley May 22-26; in Meadow Creek Valley, May 19; in the Valley of the Virgin near Bunkerville, May 8; at the Bend of the Colorado, May 4; at Vegas Ranch, May 1; and at Yount's ranch in Pahrump Valley, April 29. In the Lower Santa Clara Valley, Utah, he found it breeding and tolerably common, May 11-15.

Record of specimens collected of Tyrannus verticalis.

Collector's No.	Sex.	Locality.	Date.	Collector.	Remarks.
205	♂	Vegas Valley, Nev.	May 1, 1891	C. Hart Merriam.	
225	♀	Argus Range, Calif.	May 7, 1891	A. K. Fisher	Maturango Spring.
304	♂	......do	May 11, 1891	....do.	Do.
91	♂	Owens Valley, Calif	June 6, 1891	....do	Lone Pine.
92	♀	......do	June 12, 1891	F. Stephens	Olancha.
		......do	...do	....do	Do.

Tyrannus vociferans. Cassin's Kingbird.

Dr. Merriam found this flycatcher breeding commonly among the live oaks at Twin Oaks, in western San Diego County, in the early part of July and secured a specimen July 10. One was seen at San Bernardino January 1.

Myiarchus cinerascens. Ash-throated Flycatcher.

The ash-throated flycatcher is a common resident of the desert regions of southern California, Nevada, Utah, and northern Arizona, and is common also west of the Sierra Nevada. In California it was first seen in Panamint Valley, at Hot Springs, where it arrived April 22 and became common almost immediately. In the Argus Range it was common in Shepherd Cañon and at Maturango Spring, where it was seen along the hillsides, hovering over the flowers in search of small moths and other insects, during the first half of May. At Coso several pairs were seen, and an individual was observed to devote considerable time to examining the open end of a 2-inch water pipe, which protruded from the side of an old building, evidently with an idea of using it for a nesting site. Mr. Nelson found it a widely distributed species, breeding from the bottom of Mesquite, Panamint, and Saline valleys, up to at least 2,130 meters (7,000 feet) in the Panamint and Grapevine mountains, where it appeared to be equally at home on the open slopes of the valleys, among the mesquite and larrea bushes, or in the mountains, in the midst of a tolerably abundant growth of piñons. He found it breeding as high as the upper border of the piñons in the Inyo Mountains the last of June.

In Nevada Dr. Merriam saw it in the tree yuccas on the east side of Pahrump Valley, April 29; at the Bend of the Colorado, May 4; near Bunkerville, in the Valley of the Virgin, May 8; on the west slope of the Juniper Mountains, May 19; in Pahranagat Valley, May 23; on the Timpahute Mountains, May 26; found it common among the yuccas in Indian Spring Valley, May 28; on the south side of Gold Mountain, June 3; and tolerably common and evidently breeding among the nut pines on Mount Magruder, June 4–8. In Utah he found it breeding commonly in the Santa Clara Valley, May 11–15, and among the tree yuccas on the west side of the Beaverdam Mountains, May 10. In northwestern Arizona he saw several at the mouth of Beaverdam Creek the same day. On the summit connecting the White and Inyo mountains, in California, several were seen on June 9.

At Furnace Creek, Death Valley, a pair of these birds was seen just above the ranch at the mouth of the cañon, June 21, and the species was not uncommon in the Panamint Mountains up to an altitude of more than 2,450 meters (8,000 feet). In Owens Valley it was not uncommon at Lone Pine, June 4–15; at Olancha, May 16–23; at Ash Creek, May 30–June 3; and at Benton, July 9–10.

It was seen among the tree yuccas in Walker Pass, June 22 and July 2–3; was common in the valley of the Kern, July 3–13; abundant in Walker Basin, June 24 and July 13–16; in Tehachapi Pass, June 25; and in the Cañada de las Uvas, June 28. A few were seen among the live oaks in the Granite Range in the western part of San Diego County, July 1–10. It was common at Bakersfield, July 17–20, and at Three Rivers, July 25–30.

Record of specimens collected of Myiarchus cinerascens.

Collector's No.	Sex.	Locality.	Date.	Collector.	Remarks.
181	♂	Panamint Valley, Calif.	Apr. 22, 1891	C. Hart Merriam	Hot Springs.
	♂	......do......	Apr. 23, 1891	A. K. Fisher	Do.
305	♂	Owens Valley, Calif.	June 6, 1891	...do...	Lone Pine.
101	♀	......do......	June 13, 1891	F. Stephens	Olancha.

Sayornis saya. Say's Phœbe.

Say's phœbe is a common species throughout the desert regions, and was also found west of the Sierra Nevada. It was common in the vicinity of Owens Lake in December, 1890; was seen near Daggett, in the Mohave Desert, January 10, 1891, and at Lone Willow Spring, January 15. In Death Valley, it was observed at Bennett Wells and Furnace Creek the latter part of January; again, April 9–12 and June 19–22.

In Nevada it was observed at Ash Meadows in March, sparingly in Pahrump and Vegas valleys, and thence down to the Bend of the Colorado, and was rather common and mating in Oasis Valley in the same month. Dr. Merriam found it in Fish Lake Valley, June 8; on the north slope of Gold Mountain, June 3; at the east end of Grapevine Cañon, June 2, where a nest was observed in an old well at an abandoned mining shaft known as Thorp's mill; in Ash Meadows, where a nest was found in an old adobe, May 30; in Pahranagat Valley, May 22-26; at Pahroc Spring, May 22; at the Bend of the Colorado, May 4; and in the Virgin Valley near Bunkerville, May 8. He saw two at the mouth of Beaverdam Creek, Arizona, May 9-10, and in Utah found it common in the lower Santa Clara Valley, breeding along the cliffs near St. George, May 10-11, and among the junipers on the eastern slope of the Beaverdam Mountains, May 10-11.

In the Panamint Mountains the species was not seen in Johnson Cañon, but was common in Surprise Cañon, where a nest and eggs was found April 19, and also at Hot Springs, in Panamint Valley, April 20-25. Mr. Nelson found it commonly distributed in the bottoms of Saline, Panamint, and Mesquite valleys, ranging up in the Panamint and Grapevine mountains. He found the species breeding in various sheltered places, such as holes in clay banks, niches in rocky ledges, sides of old walls, and in crevices in deserted mining shafts. In the Argus Range it was common in Shepherd Cañon and at Maturango Spring, and at Coso a nest containing three nearly grown young was found in one of the deserted buildings the last of May. The species was found in the Inyo Range up to and among the piñons, and was a rather common breeding species in Owens Valley.

Several were seen in Walker Pass, July 1-3. Say's phœbe was common through Kern River Valley, July 3-13, and occurred in Walker Basin in about equal numbers with the black phœbe, July 13-16. One was seen at timber line near Mineral King, September 10, and the species was observed along the route to Three Rivers, September 12-16. Mr. Bailey found it common at Monterey, September 28 to October 9, and Mr. Stephens at Reche Cañon, near San Bernardino, September 22-24.

Mr. Nelson found it common and generally distributed along the coast from San Simeon to Carpenteria and Santa Paula, in November and December, and sparingly in the San Joaquin Valley, October 5-27.

Record of specimens collected of Sayornis saya.

Collector's No.	Sex.	Locality.	Date.	Collector.	Remarks.
71	♂	Death Valley, Calif	Jan. 24, 1891	A. K. Fisher	Furnace Creek.
76	♂	....do....	Jan. 25, 1891	...do	Do.
	♀ im.	....do....	June 10, 1892	V. Bailey	Do.
12	♀	Daggett, Calif	Feb. 8, 1891	F. Stephens	
257	♂ juv.	Coso, Mountains, Calif	May 26, 1891	A. K. Fisher	
102	♂ im.	Owens Valley, Calif	June 15, 1891	F. Stephens	Olancha.

Sayornis nigricans. Black Phœbe.

The black phœbe was rare in the desert regions east of the Sierra Nevada, though more or less common west of this range. At San Bernardino one was seen among some willows, associated with other birds, December 28, 1890. It was seen in Cajon Pass, March 30; at Furnace Creek, Death Valley, April 12; at Hot Springs, in the Panamint Valley, April 22; and in the Argus Range, at Shepherd Cañon, April 27. Mr. Stephens found a pair apparently breeding at Little Owens Lake the first week in May, and an immature individual at Bishop Creek, August 4–10. On the western slope, it was common along the valley of Kern River, near the water, July 3–13; common and in about equal numbers with Say's phœbe, at Walker Basin, July 13–16; common in the Cañada de las Uvas, June 28–29; and in the Sierra Liebre, June 30. It was common at Bakersfield, in the San Joaquin Valley, in July; at Three Rivers, in the foothills, July 25–30 and September 13–16; and in Kings River Cañon, August 13–16. Mr. Bailey saw one at timber line near Mineral King, August 4, and found it common at Monterey, September 18 to October 9. Mr. Nelson observed it commonly about San Emigdio, sparingly along the southern and western sides of the San Joaquin Valley, commonly and in about equal numbers with Say's phœbe along the coast from San Simeon to Carpenteria, and not numerous between Carpenteria and Santa Paula, in November and December.

Contopus borealis. Olive-sided Flycatcher.

The olive-sided flycatcher was found nowhere common. Mr. Nelson observed it migrating in considerable numbers at the head of Willow Creek in the Panamint Range, during the third week in May. The same observer found it on the east side of the Sierra Nevada, at the head of Owens River, from an altitude of 2,500 to 2,900 meters (8,200 to 9,500 feet), and on the west slope up to 3,050 meters (10,000 feet).

In the Sierra Nevada Mr. Stephens found it at Menache Meadows, May 24–26; Mr. Dutcher secured two specimens and reported it as more or less common at Big Cottonwood Meadows; and Mr. Bailey saw several at an altitude of about 2,650 meters (8,700 feet) near Mineral King, and secured a brood of young just able to fly, August 4.

The writer secured a specimen in the Coso Mountains, California, May 23; Dr. Merriam observed one on the south side of Gold Mountain, Nevada, June 3; and Mr. Palmer saw one near the summit of Frazier Mountain, California, July 9.

Record of specimens collected of Contopus borealis.

Collector's No.	Sex.	Locality.	Date.	Collector.	Remarks.
248	♂	Panamint Mountains, Calif.	May 21, 1891	E. W. Nelson	
	♂	Coso Mountains, Calif.	May 23, 1891	A. K. Fisher	
8	♀	Sierra Nevada, Calif.	June 23, 1891	B. H. Dutcher	Big Cottonwood Meadows.
26	♂	...do...	Aug. 4, 1891	...do...	Do.
	♂	...do...	...do...	V. Bailey	Mineral King.
	im	...do...	...do...	...do...	Do.

Contopus richardsonii. Western Wood Pewee.

The western wood pewee was a common species in many of the localities visited. Mr. Nelson found it a rather common breeding bird in Cottonwood, Willow Creek, and Mill Creek cañons in the Panamint Mountains, Calif., and saw it also in the Grapevine Mountains, Nevada.

In Coso Valley, California, it first appeared May 16, and by May 25 was common in the Coso Mountains. It was common all through Owens Valley, and on the White Mountains. At Keeler, on the east side of Owens Lake, it was not uncommon the 1st of June. One day when the wind was very high, a number were seen sitting on the bare alkaline flats near the lake, where they were picking up from the ground the flies which swarmed there, as grain-eating birds do seeds. On the summit of the divide in the White Mountains, between Deep Spring Valley and Owens Valley, Dr. Merriam killed two June 9. At Old Fort Tejon it was common about the 1st of July.

It was common in Walker Pass, where a nest was observed, July 2; at Kernville, July 11; Walker Basin, July 13-16; and at Bakersfield, in the San Joaquin Valley, July 17-20. In the High Sierra it was not uncommon in the Sequoia National Park, the first week in August; at Horse Corral Meadows, August 9-13; Kings River Cañon, August 13-16; Big Cottonwood Meadows, during the summer; at Menache Meadows, May 24-26; and was common along the Kaweah River from Mineral King down to Three Rivers, in September.

In Nevada, Dr. Merriam saw it among the cottonwoods at Vegas ranch, May 1; at Pahranagat Valley, May 23 (common); at Oasis Valley, June 1; and on Mount Magruder, June 8. He also saw the species at the mouth of Beaverdam Creek, Arizona, May 10.

Record of specimens collected of Contopus richardsonii.

Collector's No.	Sex.	Locality.	Date.	Collector.	Remarks.
251	♀	Coso Mountains, Calif	May 24, 1891	A. K. Fisher	
6	♂	Sierra Nevada, Calif	June 19, 1891	B. H. Dutcher	Big Cottonwood Meadows.
89	♀	Owens Lake, Calif	June 12, 1891	F. Stephens	
	♀	White Mountains, Calif	June 9, 1891	V. Bailey	
	♂	......do......	do.	...do......	
	♂	Mount Magruder, Nev	June 4, 1891	...do......	

Empidonax difficilis. Western Flycatcher.

The western flycatcher was seen in a few localities only. Dr. Merriam secured an adult male at Ash Meadows, Nevada, May 30, and a female at Mount Magruder in the same State, June 5. Mr. Palmer reported the species as common and secured one at Old Fort Tejon, July 6. Mr. Nelson saw it along the San Joaquin River in August, but does not state how common it was.

Record of specimens collected of Empidonax difficilis.

Collector's No.	Sex.	Locality.	Date.	Collector.	Remarks.
	♂ ad. ♀	Ash Meadows, Nev Mount Magruder, Nev	May 30, 1891 June 5, 1891	V. Bailey C. Hart Merriam	

Empidonax pusillus. Little Flycatcher.

In a few localities the little flycatcher was not rare. Dr. Merriam found it tolerably common where Beaverdam Creek joins the Virgin River in northwestern Arizona, May 9, and in Pahranagat Valley, Nevada, May 22–26.

In Owens Valley, California, Mr. Stephens found it a rather common migrant at Olancha, May 16–23, and the writer secured two specimens in a willow thicket along Owens River, at Lone Pine, June 11. Mr. Palmer shot one near Old Fort Tejon July 3, and Mr. Nelson saw a few among the willows along streams from 2,940 to 2,900 meters (9,000 to 9,500 feet) altitude, in the White Mountains, in the same month.

Record of specimens collected of Empidonax pusillus.

Collector's No.	Sex.	Locality.	Date.	Collector.	Remarks.
77	♂	Pahranagat Valley, Nev	May 23, 1891	C. Hart Merriam	
90	♀	Owens Valley, Calif	June 9, 1891	F. Stephens	Olancha.
		...do...	June 12, 1891	...do...	Do.
333	♂	...do...	June 11, 1891	A. K. Fisher	Lone Pine.
334	♂	...do...	...do...	...do...	Do.

Empidonax hammondi. Hammond's Flycatcher.

Hammond's flycatcher was seen in two localities only. In the Argus Range several were seen and two secured among the piñons above Maturango Spring on May 8. Dr. Merriam secured a specimen in Pahranagat Valley, Nevada, May 23.

Record of specimens collected of Empidonax hammondi.

Collector's No.	Sex.	Locality.	Date.	Collector.	Remarks.
208	♀	Argus Range, Calif	May 8, 1891	A. K. Fisher	Maturango Spring.
209	♂	...do...	...do...	...do...	Do.
	♀	Pahranagat Valley, Nev	May 23, 1891	C. Hart Merriam	

Empidonax wrightii. Wright's Flycatcher.

Wright's flycatcher was the only one of the small flycatchers found in winter in any of the region traversed. Mr. Nelson secured a specimen at Hot Springs in Panamint Valley, January 3, and the writer obtained one in the same place April 22. A specimen was secured among the willows at the edge of the reservoir at Furnace Creek, Death Valley, February 1, and two small flycatchers, probably this species, were seen there about the middle of April.

A specimen was secured in the Argus Range, at Maturango Spring, May 5, and another was seen in Shepherd Cañon a few days before. In Owens Valley Mr. Stephens found the species at Olancha about the middle of May, and at Bishop Creek August 4–10. In the High Sierra it was seen at Big Cottonwood Meadows, August 29; at Whitney Meadows, August 20; and at Kern River Lakes or Soda Springs, September 5. Dr. Merriam secured a specimen in the Virgin Valley in eastern Nevada, May 6.

Record of specimens collected of Empidonax wrightii.

Collector's No.	Sex.	Locality.	Date.	Collector.	Remarks.
	?	Panamint Valley, Calif	Jan. 3, 1891	E. W. Nelson	
95	♀	Death Valley, Calif	Feb. 1, 1891	A. K. Fisher	Furnace Creek.
180	♂	Panamint Valley, Calif	Apr. 23, 1891	...do	Hot Spring.
50	♀	Argus Range, Calif	Apr. 26, 1891	F. Stephens	
198	♀	...do	May 5, 1891	A. K. Fisher	Maturango Spring.
	♀	...do	May 12, 1891	T. S. Palmer	Do.
		St. Thomas, Nev	May 6, 1891	V. Bailey	
	im.	Sierra Nevada, Calif	Aug. 20, 1891	...do	Whitney Meadows.

Pyrocephalus rubineus mexicanus. Vermilion Flycatcher.

Dr. Merriam shot an adult female of this species at St. George, in the Lower Santa Clara Valley, Utah, May 13. She was killed in an orchard at Dodge Spring, about a mile from the settlement, and contained large ova nearly ready for the shell. This record extends the known range of the species very materially, since it had not previously been recorded north of Fort Mohave, Arizona.

Otocoris alpestris arenicola. Desert Horned Lark.

So far as specimens go, this race of the horned lark was the only one found breeding east of the Sierra Nevada in the region traversed by the expedition. A flock of twenty or more was seen at Hesperia, in the Mohave Desert, January 4, and the subspecies also was seen in the same desert at Daggett January 8–10, and Granite Wells January 13–15. Dozens were seen by Dr. Merriam, who traveled over the same ground during the latter part of March and first week in April. In January Mr. Nelson saw about one hundred at the southern end of Panamint Valley. Horned larks were not seen at any time in Death Valley.

In Nevada they were common at Ash Meadows, in the plowed fields and sand plains, and about the middle of March had mated and were preparing to nest. In Pahrump and Vegas valleys Mr. Nelson found small parties in February and March. Dr. Merriam found it common in Meadow Creek Valley May 19; in Desert and Pahroc valleys May 20–22; in the valley between Gold Mountain and Mount Magruder June 4, where it was common and two nearly full grown young were shot; on Mount Magruder, June 4–8, where it was common on the sage plain on top of the mountain. In Utah, it was not seen in the Santa Clara Valley, but several were observed in Mountain Meadows May 17.

In the north end of Panamint Valley, Mr. Nelson saw several the last of May, and others on the high tableland between Saline and Panamint valleys, in May and June. Dr. Merriam found it common in the sage brush north of Telescope Peak, April 15. Horned larks were found during the breeding season in the sage plains on the Inyo and White mountains, and in Saline and Deep Spring valleys. Below Maturango Spring, in Coso Valley, it was quite common May 11, and others were seen along the valley as far north as Darwin. In Owens Valley, the subspecies was found as a summer resident from the lower to the upper end. Mr. Palmer found it very abundant in Antelope Valley, and a few near Gorman Station the last of June.

Record of specimens collected of Otocoris alpestris arenicola.

Collector's No.	Sex.	Locality.	Date.	Collector.	Remarks.
227	♂	Coso Valley, Calif.	May 11, 1891	A. K. Fisher	
228	♂	......do	......do	......do	
229	♀	......do	......do	......do	
8	♂	Mohave Desert, Calif.	Feb. 7, 1891	F. Stephens	Daggett.
52	♂	......do	Jan. 13, 1891	A. K. Fisher	Granite Wells.
53	♀	......do	......do	......do	Do
54	♀	......do	......do	......do	Do
55	♂	......do	......do	......do	Do
56	♂	......do	......do	......do	Do
57	♂	......do	......do	......do	Do
	♂	......do	Apr. 25, 1891	V. Bailey	Leach Point Valley.
	♂	......do	June 27, 1891	T. S. Palmer	25 miles southwest of Mojave.
51	♂	Salt Wells Valley, Calif.	Apr. 29, 1891	F. Stephens	Borax Flat.
126	♂	Ash Meadows, Nev	Mar. 14, 1891	A. K. Fisher	
136	♂	......do	Mar. 19, 1891	......do	
	♀	......do	......do	E. W. Nelson	
	♂	Pahrump Valley, Nev.	Feb. 17, 1891	......do	
	♂	......do	......do	......do	
	♂	Indian Spring Valley, Nev.	May 28, 1891	V. Bailey	
	♂	Panaca, Nev	May 19, 1891	......do	
	♂ im.	Gold Mountain Valley, Nev.	June 4, 1891	C. Hart Merriam	Valley between Gold Mountain and Mount Magruder.
	♂ im.	......do	......do	......do	
	♀	Mount Piños, Calif.	Oct. 16, 1891	E. W. Nelson	San Rafael Mountains.
70	♀	Owens Valley, Calif	June 1, 1891	F. Stephens	Ash Creek.
83	♂	......do	June 10, 1891	......do	Olancha.
270	♂	......do	May 31, 1891	A. K. Fisher	Keeler.
271	♀	......do	June 1, 1891	......do	Do.
288	♂	......do	June 2, 1891	......do	Do.
289	♀	......do	......do	......do	Do.
290	♂	......do	June 3, 1891	......do	Do.
153	♀	......do	Aug. 16, 1891	F. Stephens	Do.
154	♀ juv.	......do	......do	......do	Do.
135	im.	......do	July 20, 1891	......do	Casa Diablo Spring.
136	♀	......do	July 21, 1891	......do	Do.
	♂	White Mountains, Calif	July 12, 1891	E. W. Nelson	
107	♂	Darwin, Calif	May 5, 1891	A. K. Fisher	
	♂	Coso Valley, Calif.	May 11, 1891	T. S. Palmer	Maturango Spring.
	♂	......do	......do	......do	Do.

Otocoris alpestris chrysolæma. Mexican Horned Lark.

Mr. Nelson obtained a number of specimens of this race at Keeler, on the shore of Owens Lake, December 28, 1890, though specimens taken at the same place during the breeding season are referable to *arenicola*. Mr. Stephens took one in the Panamint Mountains in April, and Mr. Bailey secured a specimen at Kernville, where the subspecies was common, July 13. The birds seen by Mr. Nelson in the San Joaquin Valley and in the vicinity of the Cañada de las Uvas probably should be referred to this race. He found it excessively abundant on the San Joaquin Plain, where it is locally known as the 'wheat bird' in the grain districts, owing to its habit of following the farmer and eating the newly-sown wheat at seeding time.

Record of specimens collected of Otocoris alpestris chrysolæma.

Collector's No.	Sex.	Locality.	Date.	Collector.	Remarks.
44	♂	Panamint Mountains, Calif.	Apr. 15, 1891	F. Stephens	5,200 feet altitude.
	♂	Kernville, Calif.	July 13, 1891	V. Bailey	
	♂	Owens Valley, Calif.	Dec. 28, 1890	E. W. Nelson	Keeler.
	♂	...do...	...do...	...do...	Do.
	♂	...do...	...do...	...do...	Do.
	♀	...do...	...do...	...do...	Do.
	♂	...do...	...do...	...do...	Do.
	♀	...do...	...do...	...do...	Do.
	♀	...do...	...do...	...do...	Do.

Pica pica hudsonica. Black-billed Magpie.

Mr. Bailey saw three individuals of this species 10 miles east of Toquerville, Utah, December, 31, 1888. The black-billed magpie was not seen by the expedition, but is known to be a common resident in the neighborhood of Carson, in western Nevada.

Pica nuttalli. Yellow-billed Magpie.

The Yellow-billed magpie is common in a number of places west of the Sierra Nevada, in California. At Visalia, several were seen among the oaks, July 23, as well as along the route from that place to Three Rivers, July 25. Near Cottage post-office, in Tulare County, about half-way between these two places, the species was common September 17.

Mr. Nelson found it common in the foothills of the Sierra Nevada, in August; and also among the oaks from La Panza to San Luis Obispo, October 28 and November 3; and from the latter place to the Santa Ynez River, beyond which places it was not noted.

Cyanocitta stelleri. Steller's Jay.

Steller's jay was met with along the coast of California, in two localities only. Mr. Bailey found it common in the thick woods in the vicinity of Monterey, where he secured a pair, October 1; and Mr. Nelson observed a few in the mountains near San Simeon in November.

Record of specimens collected of Cyanocitta stelleri.

Collector's No.	Sex.	Locality.	Date.	Collector.	Remarks.
	♂	Monterey, Calif.	Oct. 1, 1891	V. Bailey	
	♀	...do...	...do...	...do...	

Cyanocitta stelleri frontalis. Blue-fronted Jay.

The blue-fronted jay was not found in the desert ranges, although it was common in many places along the east slope of the Sierra Nevada, in California. Mr. Nelson found it common at the head of Owens River at an altitude of from 2,500 to 2,900 meters (8,200 to 9,500 feet), and Mr. Stephens found it at Bishop Creek, August 4–10, and at Menache Meadows, May 24–26. The writer secured one among the pines above Walker Basin, July 14; found it common in Sequoia National Park the first week in August; at Horse Corral Meadows, August 9–13; in Kings River Cañon, August 13–16; and Big Cottonwood Meadows, Round Valley, and Whitney Meadows, the last of the month. It was very common among the sugar and yellow pines at Soda Springs or Kern River Lakes, the first week in September. Mr. Dutcher found it common during the breeding season at Big Cottonwood Meadows, and Mr. Bailey and the writer found it common at Mineral King and down along the Kaweah River to the lower limit of the pines, in September. Mr. Palmer reported it common on Frazier Mountain, near Old Fort Tejon, July 6.

Record of specimens collected of Cyanocitta stelleri frontalis.

Collector's No.	Sex.	Locality.	Date.	Collector.	Remarks.
75	♂	Owens Lake, Calif.	June 7, 1891	F. Stephens	Altitude, 4,000 feet.
141	♂	Sierra Nevada, Calif.	July 25, 1891	....do	
17	im.	....do	July 12, 1891	B. H. Dutcher	Big Cottonwood Meadows.
	♂ im.	....do	Aug. 3, 1891	E. W. Nelson	South Fork Merced River.
390	♀	Walker Basin, Calif.	July 14, 1891	A. K. Fisher	
409	♂ im.	Sierra Nevada; Calif.	Aug. 7, 1891	....do	Sequoia National Park.
434	♀	....do	Sept. 3, 1891	....do	Soda Springs.

Aphelocoma woodhousei. Woodhouse's Jay.

Woodhouse's jay was found on all the desert ranges which furnish a growth of piñon or junipers. In California it was observed in the White Mountains, Inyo, Argus, Coso, and Panamint ranges; in Nevada, in the Charleston, Grapevine, Juniper, and Pahroc mountains, and in Utah, in the Beaverdam Mountains. In the latter part of June, young which were able to fly were found among the willows along the streams in the Panamint Mountains, north of Telescope Peak.

Record of specimens collected of Aphelocoma woodhousei.

Collector's No.	Sex.	Locality.	Date.	Collector.	Remarks.
39	♂	Grapevine Mountains, Nev.	Mar. 24, 1891	F. Stephens	
147	♀	Panamint Mountains, Calif.	Mar. 29, 1891	A. K. Fisher	Johnson Cañon.
172	♂	....do	Apr. 20, 1891	....do	Surprise Cañon.
173		....do	....do	....do	Do.
355	♀ im.	....do	June 23, 1891	....do	Wild Rose Cañon.
356	♀ im.	....do	....do	....do	
		Inyo Mountains, Calif.	June 27, 1891	E. W. Nelson	
	im.	White Mountains, Calif.	July 8, 1891	....do	

Aphelocoma californica. California Jay.

The California jay was not found east of the Sierra Nevada, it being replaced in the desert ranges by Woodhouse's jay. Although abundant on the west slope of the main Sierra, it was common in few places on the east side. Mr. Stephens found it rather common on the latter slope at Independence Creek, June 18–23; at Menache Meadows, May 24–26; and Mr. Nelson, at the head of Owens River, in the latter part of July.

The species was common in Cajon Pass in the San Bernardino Mountains, January 2–3, where it was seen and heard among the chaparral at all times of the day. Dr. Merriam found it common in the Sierra Liebre, San Bernardino, Tejon, and Tehachapi ranges, as well as in the southern Sierra from Walker Pass southward. It was tolerably common on the west slope of Walker Pass, June 21 and July 2–3; in the valley of Kern River, June 21–22 and July 3–13; thence southward to Havilah and Caliente, June 23–24; and was abundant and noisy at Old Fort Tejon late in June and early in July.

Dr. Merriam found it common in the coast ranges south of the San Bernardino plain, and in large numbers in the Granite Range between Twin Oaks and Escondido, Calif., early in July.

In the San Joaquin Valley it was common at Visalia and up along Kaweah River to the lower edge of the pines, in August and September, and a few were seen in the Sequoia National Park during the first week of August. Mr. Bailey found it common in the brush and open woods at Monterey, Calif., September 28 to October 9.

Mr. Nelson reported this jay as abundant in the Tejon and Temploa mountains and around San Luis Obispo in October, and along the route from San Simeon to Carpenteria and Santa Paula, in November and December.

Record of specimens collected of Aphelocoma californica.

Collector's No.	Sex.	Locality.	Date.	Collector.	Remarks.
62	♀	Owens Valley, Calif.	May 23, 1891	F. Stephens	Olancha.
363	♂ im.	Walker Pass, Calif.	July 3, 1891	V. Bailey	
383	♀	do	July 2, 1891	A. K. Fisher	
		Kern River, Calif.	July 9, 1891	do	South Fork.

Corvus corax sinuatus. Raven.

Ravens were seen in more or less abundance in most, if not all, of the localities visited by members of the expedition, from above timber line on the High Sierra to the bottom of Death Valley and the other desert valleys, and undoubtedly breed in all the desert ranges of southern California and Nevada. Ravens were seen in Cajon Pass in the San Bernardino Mountains, and on the Mohave Desert during the first week in January. At Daggett fifty or more remained about the slaughter house feeding on the refuse. In Death Valley they were observed by every party that visited the place from the first week in January to the last in June. In the Coso Mountains, two adults with their five young were seen flying high in the air May 25, the old birds being readily distinguished by their worn primaries.

In Nevada they were common at Ash Meadows and Pahrump Valley, and at the latter place a pair was secured the last of February. Dr. Merriam observed one, together with a large nest, on the shelf of a high cliff in Vegas Wash, May 3. He found ravens tolerably common about the Bend of the Colorado, May 4, and saw several in the Valley of the Virgin, near Bunkerville, May 8; others in the Juniper Mountains, May 19; in Desert Valley, May 20, and in Pahranagat Valley, May 22-26. In Utah he found several pairs in the Lower Santa Clara Valley, May 11-15, and thence northward to Mountain Meadows, where several were seen May 17.

Ravens were common all through Owens Valley. At Walker Basin flocks of several hundred were observed every day flying about the fields and roads, feeding on the grasshoppers which occurred in vast numbers there. All the specimens shot had nothing in their stomachs except the remains of these insects. Dr. Merriam and Mr. Palmer observed large numbers catching grasshoppers in the western part of the Mohave Desert, known as Antelope Valley, June 27-28, and near Gorman Station no less than forty-four were seen catching grasshoppers on the grassy hillsides at one time.

In the High Sierra ravens were seen at Menache, Whitney, and Big Cottonwood meadows, and at the head of Owens River. Mr. Nelson saw a few about Mount Piños and at Buena Vista Lake in October, and found them sparingly along the route from San Simeon to Carpenteria and Santa Paula, in November and December.

Record of specimens collected of Corvus corax sinuatus.

Collector's No.	Sex.	Locality.	Date.	Collector.	Remarks.
113	♀	Lone Willow Spring, Calif.	Jan. 14, 1891	E. W. Nelson	
114	♀	Pahrump Valley, Calif.	Feb. 24, 1891	A. K. Fisher	
	♂	......do......	......do......	......do......	

Corvus americanus. Crow.

At one place only was the common crow seen by any member of the expedition east of the Sierra Nevada. In Pahrump Valley, Nevada, a flock of crows kept around the ranch during February and March.

At Bakersfield, in the San Joaquin Valley, crows were common along the river bottoms, in flocks of from five to fifty, July 17-20. Crows were observed among the oaks at Visalia, July 23, and a flock of about one hundred was seen and a specimen secured near Three Rivers, the latter part of the same month. Dr. Merriam saw a flock of half a dozen in Tehachapi Valley, California, June 25, and Mr. Palmer found them common at Tejon ranch, where they were feeding on figs, early in July. At Monterey, Mr. Bailey heard them cawing in the grounds of the Hotel Del Monte, September 28 to October 9. Mr. Nelson found crows common in the San Joaquin Valley in October, along the route from San Simeon to Carpenteria, and in the Ojai Valley in November and December.

Picicorvus columbianus. Clarke's Nutcracker.

Clarke's crow was common in the High Sierra in California, as well as in a few of the higher desert ranges to the eastward. It was numerous about the camp in the Charleston Mountains, Nevada, in February. In the Panamint Mountains, California, a solitary individual was seen near the top of the ridge south of Telescope Peak, April 2, and on the north slope of the same peak several were heard, June 23. A pair was seen later in the same day which, from their actions, appeared to be parent and young. Mr. Nelson found it rather common among the *Pinus flexilis* on the Inyo Mountains, and in the same belt of the White Mountains as well as on the plateau at the head of Owens Valley; and Mr. Stephens reported it common at Queen mine, in the White Mountains, Nevada, July 11-16. Along the eastern slope of the Sierra, it was abundant at Menache Meadows, May 24-26; at Kearsarge Pass, June 18-23; at Bishop Creek, August 4-10; and from 2,450 meters (8,000 feet) altitude to timber line at the head of Owens River the latter part of July; at Big Meadows and Horse Corral Meadows it was seen August 8-13; in Big Cottonwood Meadows it was very common all summer; at Round Valley, 12 miles south of Mount Whitney, August 28; and along the route from Soda Springs or Kern River Lakes to Mineral King, early in September. Mr. Nelson found it numerous among piñons on Mount Piños the later part of October.

Record of specimens collected of Picicorvus columbianus.

Collector's No.	Sex.	Locality.	Date.	Collector.	Remarks.
63	♂	Sierra Nevada, Calif.	May 27, 1891	F. Stephens	Summit Meadows, near Olancha Peak.
421	♂	......do.........	Aug. 28, 1891	A. K. Fisher	Big Cottonwood Meadows.
430	♀	......do.........	Aug. 28, 1891	....do........	Round Valley.
		......do.........	Sept. 4, 1891	....do........	Soda Springs, Kern River.

Cyanocephalus cyanocephalus. Piñon Jay.

The piñon jay is more or less common on all the desert ranges of southern California and Nevada which are high enough to support a growth of piñons (*Pinus monophylla*), and was found in a few places on the Sierra Nevada, though in limited numbers. Mr. Nelson found it breeding in the piñon belt in the Panamint, Inyo, White, and Grapevine mountains, and Mr. Stephens saw a flock of a hundred or more in the latter range toward the end of March.

The writer found it common in the Argus Range above Maturango Spring. The stomach and gullet of one shot at this place about the middle of May contained the kernels of the pine nut, which it evidently had picked up from the ground, as some of them had already sprouted. The species was common on the Coso Mountains the last half of May. Dr. Merriam saw it on Mount Magruder and Gold Mountain, Nevada, early in June; in the Juniper Mountains, near the boundary between Nevada and Utah, May 18-19, and in the juniper belt on the east slope of the Beaverdam Mountains, in Utah, May 11.

Mr. Palmer saw a single bird in the Charleston Mountains among the tree yuccas, February 14.

In the Sierra Nevada Mr. Nelson saw it at the head of Owens River, though it was not numerous, and Mr. Stephens observed it at Bishop Creek, August 4-10, and noted one individual at Benton, July 9-10.

Record of specimens collected of Cyanocephalus cyanocephalus.

Collector's No.	Sex.	Locality.	Date.	Collector.	Remarks.
201	♂	Argus Range, Calif............	May 6, 1891	A. K. Fisher....	Maturango Spring.
206	♂	......do	May 8, 1891	....do............	Do.
207	♂	......do	....do........	....do............	Do.
233	♀	......do	May 12, 1891	....do............	Do.
249	♂	Coso Mountains, Calif.........	May 23, 1891	....do............	

Molothrus ater. Cowbird.

Dr. Merriam saw several cowbirds in the Lower Santa Clara Valley, Utah, May 11-15, and a few in Pahranagat Valley, Nevada, May 22-26. The writer shot an adult male at Furnace Creek, Death Valley, June 20, which was the only one seen there.

Xanthocephalus xanthocephalus. Yellow-headed Blackbird.

Yellow-headed blackbirds were seen sparingly at a number of localities. Mr. Bailey secured a specimen at Bennett Wells in Death Valley, April 1, and an individual came and alighted on the wagon while the party was at Darwin, in the Coso Valley, May 5. Dr. Merriam saw a few about the spring at Yount's ranch in Pahrump Valley, Nevada, April 29, and a number in the valley of the lower Muddy, May 6. Others were seen by him in Meadow Creek Valley, Nevada, near Panaca, May 19, and the species was said to breed in Pahranagat Valley, though he did not see it there, May 22-26. In the Lower Santa Clara Valley, Utah, it was tolerably common about the junction of the Santa Clara with the Virgin, May 11-15. In Salt Wells Valley, Mr. Stephens saw a small flock at Raymond Well, and at Borax Flat the last of April and first of May. At Lone Pine, in Owens Valley, one was seen among a flock of redwings in December, 1890. A number were observed in June, and several small flocks among the tules and along the fence rows, August 22. The species was seen sparingly at Bakersfield, in the San Joaquin Valley, July 17-20.

Record of specimens collected of Xanthocephalus xanthocephalus.

Collector's No.	Sex.	Locality.	Date.	Collector.	Remarks.
325	♂ ad. ♂ ad.	Death Valley, Calif. Lone Pine, Calif.	Apr. 1, 1891 June 9, 1891	V. Bailey A. K. Fisher	Bennett Wells.

Agelaius phœniceus. Red-winged Blackbird.

The red-winged blackbird is probably resident in most if not all of the tule marshes in southern California and Nevada. A small flock of eight or ten individuals was seen at Furnace Creek, Death Valley, during the latter part of January; a single specimen was secured at Resting Springs, California, in February. In Nevada a large flock was found during March around the corral of Mr. George Watkins, at Ash Meadows, where the birds fed upon grain left by the stock. Mr. Nelson stated that several hundred of these birds came to roost each night in the tules growing near the main spring at Pahrump Ranch, February 12-28. Mr. Stephens found it common in Oasis Valley, March 15-19, and at Grapevine Spring, California, the first week in April. Dr. Merriam saw it at Yount's ranch, in Pahrump Valley, April 29, and at the Bend of the Colorado, May 4. He found it breeding abundantly in the valley of the Muddy, in eastern Nevada, May 6; in Meadow Creek Valley, near Panaca, May 19; in Pahranagat Valley, May 23 and 24; in Oasis Valley, June 1; along the Santa Clara and Virgin, near St. George, Utah, May 14, and saw a few at the west end of Antelope Valley, near Gorman Station, California, June 28.

At Hot Springs, in Panamint Valley, Calif., several were seen April 20-24. In Owens Valley, Mr. Stephens found the species not common at Little Owens Lake, May 6-11; at Olancha May 16-23; abundant at Alvord, June 26-28; common at Bishop, June 30; at Fish Slough, July 2-3; at Morans, July 4-7; at Benton, July 9-10, and a few at Haway Meadows, May 12-14; and on the meadow at Bishop Creek, August 4-10. Mr. Nelson observed it at the head of Owens River up to an altitude of 2,130 meters (7,000 feet) during the latter part of July, and found it abundant about the farms at Lone Pine, in Owens Valley, December, 1890, where the writer saw numbers which were breeding in the tule marshes, the following June. The same observer also found it common along the South Fork of the Kern River, California, July 3-11; and Bakersfield, in the San Joaquin Valley, July 17-20.

Mr. Bailey saw flocks of redwings at Monterey, September 28 to October 9. Mr. Nelson found this species common and associated with *A. gubernator* about Buena Vista Lake in the San Joaquin Valley; in the wet places near San Emigdio, and along the coast between San Simeon and Carpenteria.

Record of specimens collected of Agelaius phœniceus.

Collector's No.	Sex	Locality	Date	Collector	Remarks
138	♂	Ash Meadows, Nev	Mar. 18, 1891	A. K. Fisher	
	♀ ad.	....do....	....do....	E. W. Nelson	
111	♂ ad.	Resting Springs, Calif.	Feb. 14, 1891	A. K. Fisher	
303	♂	Owens Valley, Calif.	June 6, 1891	....do....	Lone Pine.
317	♂	....do....	June 8, 1891	....do....	Do.
118	♂	....do....	June 26, 1891	F. Stephens	Alvord.
124	♀	....do....	June 28, 1891	....do....	Do.
		Fresno, Calif.	Sept. 25, 1891	V. Bailey	

Agelaius gubernator. Bicolored Blackbird.

Although this species was common, if not abundant, in some localities west of the Sierra Nevada, one specimen only was collected during the season, and this was shot by Mr. Stephens at Olancha, at the southern end of Owens Lake, California, June 11.

Mr. Nelson found a few in the Ojai Valley in December; found it common and associated with the common redwing on the border of Buena Vista Lake in the San Joaquin Valley, near San Luis Obispo, and along the route from San Simeon to Carpenteria, in November and December.

Mr. Belding recorded it from the Yosemite Valley.

Sturnella magna neglecta. Western Meadowlark.

The meadowlark is a more or less common resident in most of the valleys in the desert region, as well as in those west of the Sierra Nevada. It was common and singing at San Bernardino, December 28-29, 1890, and was seen in Cajon Pass, January 1. In Death Valley it was not uncommon at Bennett Wells, near the old Eagle borax works, at Saratoga Springs, and at Furnace Creek, where it was common in the alfalfa fields the last of January. On the last trip to the valley Mr. Bailey and the writer found it not uncommon at Furnace Creek, June 19-21. The meadowlark was not uncommon at Resting Springs in the Amargosa Desert, the first half of February and April 27, and was common about the ranches at Ash Meadows and in Pahrump and Vegas valleys, Nevada, in March. In the same State Dr. Merriam found it common in the sage-covered plateau of Mount Magruder, June 5-8; and in Oasis Valley, where it was abundant and singing in great numbers in the early evening, June 1. He also found it abundant and musical in Pahranagat Valley, May 22-26; along the valleys of the Virgin and lower Muddy May 6-8, and at Ash Meadows, May 30. In Utah it was common in alfalfa fields along the Lower Santa Clara, near its junction with the Virgin, May 11-15; thence northerly to Mountain Meadows and the Escalante Desert, May 17; and one was seen on the western side of the Beaverdam Mountains, May 10.

In California Mr. Nelson observed a few pairs breeding on the tableland between Saline and Panamint valleys, at the base and among the piñons of the Inyo Mountains, and on the plateau at the head of Owens Valley, at the base of the White Mountains. In the Coso Valley and

Mountains it was rare, only a few individuals being seen in May. It was common all through Owens Valley and on the lower part of the eastern slope of the Sierra Nevada. It was common all along Kern River Valley, July 3-13; at Walker Basin, July 13-16; in Tehachapi Valley, June 25; at Old Fort Tejon the last of June; and at Bakersfield, in the San Joaquin Valley, July 17-20. Mr. Bailey found it in flocks consisting of several hundred individuals at Monterey, September 28 to October 9, and Mr. Nelson reported it as common in the San Joaquin Valley, October 5-27, and along the route from San Simeon to Carpenteria and Santa Paula in November and December.

Record of specimens collected of Sturnella magna neglecta.

Collector's No.	Sex	Locality	Date	Collector	Remarks
98	♂	Resting Springs, Calif	Feb. 6, 1891	A. K. Fisher	
69	♀	Death Valley, Calif	Jan. 23, 1891	...do	Furnace Creek.
84	♂	......do......	Jan. 28, 1891	...do	Do.
	♂	......do......	June 19, 1891	V. Bailey	Do.
79	♂	Owens Lake, Calif	June 9, 1891	F. Stephens	

Icterus parisorum. Scott's Oriole.

Scott's oriole is one of a number of birds whose known range has been greatly extended by the observations of the different members of the expedition. It was first observed at the summit of Shepherd Cañon in the Argus Range, Calif., May 1. All along the western slope of this range and in Coso Valley it was common, and males were in full song. On May 5 a female was secured, which contained an egg in the oviduct, and on May 7 a nest containing two eggs was found. It was placed on the lower side of a branch of a tree yucca about 8 feet from the ground, and was firmly attached to the bayonet-shaped leaves of the tree by threads of plant fiber and tough grasses. A number of old nests were seen in many places through the valley. In the Coso Mountains it was also common up to the summit among the yuccas, junipers, and piñons, where, on May 27, a nest containing an egg and three young was found in a yucca in Mill Cañon.

Mr. Nelson found it breeding in the Inyo, Panamint, and Grapevine mountains in the piñon belt. On the eastern slope of the Inyo Mountains, near Cerro Gordo, one was noted on June 15. On both slopes of the Panamint Mountains, near Cottonwood Cañon, he found it ranging from the yucca belt up to the summit of the divide, and in the Grapevine Mountains found it among the piñons. Everywhere he found it in pairs, the males singing from the tops of piñons. Above the 'charcoal kilns' in Wild Rose Cañon in the Panamint Mountains, Mr. Bailey and the writer saw the species and heard the males singing, June 24-25. Mr. Stephens heard it near the Queen mine in the White Mountains, Nevada, July 11-16. In the same State Dr. Merriam secured specimens in the Charleston Mountains April 30, and in the Juniper

Mountains, east of Panaca, May 19, when several pairs were seen mating. On Mount Magruder, Nevada, he found it tolerably common among the nut pines, where the birds seemed to be hunting for nesting sites, and were very difficult to approach. Several fine specimens were taken there June 4-11. The same observer found the species in the juniper belt of the Beaverdam Mountains, in Utah, May 10-11. In Walker Pass, on the east slope of the Sierra Nevada, several were seen and one shot among the yuccas June 21, and another on the western slope of the same pass in a *Pinus sabiniana* July 2.

Record of specimens collected of *Icterus parisorum*.

Collector's No.	Sex.	Locality.	Date.	Collector.	Remarks.
196	♀	Argus Range, Calif	May 5, 1891	A. K. Fisher	Maturango Spring.
	♂	......do......	May 9, 1891	T. S. Palmer	Do.
	♂	......do......	May 11, 1891	....do......	Do.
245	♂	Coso Mountains, Calif	May 21, 1891	A. K. Fisher	
261	♂	......do......	May 27, 1891	....do......	
	♂	Panamint Mountains, Calif.	May 8, 1891	E. W. Nelson	
	♀	......do......	May 12, 1891	....do......	
	im	Walker Pass, Calif	June 21, 1891	C. Hart Merriam	
	♀	Charleston Mountains, Nev.	Apr. 30, 1891	....do......	
	♀	Mount Magruder, Nev	June 4, 1891	....do......	
	♂	......do......	....do......	....do......	
	♂	......do......	June 8, 1891	....do......	

Icterus bullocki. Bullock's Oriole.

Bullock's oriole was tolerably common in several localities, where streams large enough to nourish a more or less extensive growth of trees were found. In Owens Valley it was common at Lone Pine, where a number of nests were observed in the willows, and several specimens secured, June 4-15. In the same valley, Mr. Stephens saw a solitary male at Little Owens Lake the first week in May; at Haway Meadows, May 12-14; found the species rather common at Olancha May 16-23; common and a nest containing young at the mouth of the cañon at Independence Creek June 19; not common at Bishop, Fish Slough, and Morans July 1-7; and Benton July 9-10. Dr. Merriam saw one among the cottonwoods at Furnace Creek in Death Valley about the middle of April; in the Amargosa Cañon, and at Resting Springs, April 27. In Nevada, he saw it at Vegas Ranch, May 1; in the Valley of the Virgin and lower Muddy, May 6-8, and in Meadow Creek Valley, near Panaca, May 19. He found it tolerably common also in the Lower Santa Clara Valley, Utah, where it was breeding, May 11-15. On the western slope of the Sierra Nevada it was seen in Walker Pass, July 2; was common along the valley of the Kern June 22-23 and July 3-10; at Walker Basin July 13-16; and at Bakersfield July 17-20. It was common at Old Fort Tejon, and was seen in other parts of the Cañada de las Uvas in June and July. Mr. Nelson saw it in the Yosemite Valley, and Mr. Bailey, along the Kaweah River, in August.

Record of specimens collected of Icterus bullocki.

Collector's No.	Sex.	Locality.	Date.	Collector.	Remarks.
297	♂	Death Valley, Calif.	April 7, 1891	V. Bailey.	
298	♂	Owens Valley, Calif.	June 5, 1891	A. K. Fisher.	Lone Pine.
309	♂	......do......	......do......	......do......	Do.
322	♂ ad	......do......	June 7, 1891	......do......	Do.
323	♂ ''	......do......	June 9, 1891	......do......	Do.
324	♀ ''	......do......	......do......	......do......	Do.
87	♀	......do......	June 12, 1891	F. Stephens	Owens Lake.
	♀	Walker Pass, Calif.	July 3, 1891	V. Bailey.	

Scolecophagus cyanocephalus. Brewer's Blackbird.

Brewer's blackbird was not a common species in many localities visited by the expedition, either in the desert region or among the mountains. At San Bernardino a number of flocks were seen, together with redwings, December 29, 1890. A few individuals were found about the ranch at Furnace Creek, in Death Valley, in the latter part of January, and at Resting Springs, in the Amargosa Desert, early in February.

In Nevada a few were seen at Ash Meadows and in Pahrump and Vegas valleys, where they kept about inclosures and out-houses, in March. Dr. Merriam found it in the same valleys April 29-30; at the Bend of the Colorado May 4; at Bunkerville in the Virgin Valley, May 8; in Meadow Creek Valley near Panaca, May 19; and in Pahranagat Valley May 22. A few were seen at Hot Springs, in Panamint Valley, April 20-25; in Saline Valley the latter part of June, and on the plateau at the foot of the White Mountains in July. In Owens Valley it was common at Olancha June 29; at Alvord June 26-28; at Morans July 4-7; at Benton July 9-10; rather common at Bishop Creek August 4-10; and a few were seen at Little Owens Lake May 6-11; at Haway Meadows May 12-14; and at Ash Creek May 30 to June 3.

In the High Sierra it was common at Menache Meadows May 24-26; at the head of Owens River the latter part of July; at Whitney Meadows, where Mr. Nelson saw a flock of twenty or more sitting on the backs of sheep, August 30. A dozen or fifteen were seen at Trout Meadows September 7, and it was found breeding at Big Cottonwood Meadows during the summer. It was common in Walker Pass July 2; along the valley of the Kern July 3-13; at Walker Basin, where it was feeding on grasshoppers, July 13-16; and at Bakersfield, in the San Joaquin Valley, July 17-20. Dr. Merriam saw many catching grasshoppers in Antelope Valley, at the west end of the Mohave Desert, June 27; found the species common in the Cañada de las Uvas June 27-28; and saw a few in the San Marcos Valley, San Diego County, July 1-10.

Mr. Bailey found it common at Monterey September 28 to October 9; and Mr. Nelson saw flocks in San Joaquin Valley, and found it generally distributed along the route from San Simeon to Carpenteria, in November and December.

Record of specimens collected of Scolecophagus cyanocephalus.

Collector's No.	Sex.	Locality.	Date.	Collector.	Remarks.
77	♀	Death Valley, Calif	Jan. 25, 1891	A. K. Fisher	Furnace Creek.
82	♀	......do......................	Jan. 27, 1891	...do..............	Do.

Coccothraustes vespertinus montanus. Western Evening Grosbeak.

The evening grosbeak was seen but once by the expedition. Mr. Bailey saw a small flock at Auburn, Calif., and secured two specimens October 22.

Record of specimens collected of Coccothraustes vespertinus montanus.

Collector's No.	Sex.	Locality.	Date.	Collector.	Remarks.
	♂	Auburn, Placer Co., Calif	Oct. 22, 1891	V. Bailey	
	♀	......do......................	...do......	...do..........	

Pinicola enucleator. Pine Grosbeak.

Mr. Nelson saw a fine adult male pine grosbeak in brilliant plumage on the head of the San Joaquin River July 30. This individual was the only one seen during the year.

Carpodacus purpureus californicus. California Purple Finch.

Not obtained by any member of the expedition. Mr. Henshaw secured a single specimen near Mount Whitney, Calif., October 10, 1875.

Carpodacus cassini. Cassin's Purple Finch.

Cassin's purple finch was seen only in the higher parts of the White and Inyo mountains, and in the Sierra Nevada. Mr. Nelson saw two pairs in the *Pinus flexilis* belt on Waucoba Peak, in the Inyo Mountains, during the latter part of June, and secured two specimens at about 2,650 meters (8,700 feet) altitude in the White Mountains July 7. The same observer found it very abundant on the eastern slope, from 2,500 to 2,900 meters (8,200 to 9,500 feet) at the head of Owens River, and also at the head of the San Joaquin River, on the western slope.

It was also observed or secured at the following places in the High Sierra: at Horse Corral Meadows, August 11; at Cottonwood Meadows during the summer and as late as September 1; at Round Valley, which is 12 miles south of Mount Whitney, August 26–28; at Menache Meadows May 24–26; at Whitney Meadows the latter part of August, and near Mineral King during the latter part of August and early September.

Record of specimens collected of Carpodacus cassini.

Collector's No.	Sex.	Locality.	Date.	Collector.	Remarks.
	♂ im.	White Mountains, Calif	July 7, 1891	E. W. Nelson	
	♂	......do	...do	...do	
137	♂	Sierra Nevada, Calif	July 22, 1891	F. Stephens	
	♂ im.	......do	Aug. 11, 1891	T. S. Palmer	Horse Corral Meadows.
1	♂	......do	June 19, 1891	B. H. Dutcher	Big Cottonwood Meadows.
7	♂	......do	June 23, 1891	...do	Do.
420	♀ im.	......do	Aug. 24, 1891	A. K. Fisher	Do.
432	♂ im.	......do	Aug. 30, 1891	...do	Whitney Meadows.
	♂ im.	......do	Aug. 1, 1891	V. Bailey	East Fork of Kawah River, Calif.

Carpodacus mexicanus frontalis. House Finch.

The house finch was found wherever water was present in all localities visited by the expedition, except in the higher mountains among the pines, and undoubtedly bred wherever found. There was no other species of bird, with the possible exception of the dove, whose presence was so indicative of the nearness of water as the one under consideration. The writer never saw it more than a few hundred yards from water, except when flying high overhead.

After leaving Daggett on the Mohave Desert, Calif., house finches were seen at all the springs or water holes on the road to Death Valley. At Granite Wells flocks were found about the water at all times of day. In Death Valley a few were seen at Bennett Wells and between that place and Furnace Creek during the latter part of January. Dr. Merriam saw it at the latter place about the middle of April, and Mr. Bailey and the writer found it at both places on their last trip to the valley, June 19-22.

In the Panamint Mountains it was abundant in Johnson, Surprise, and Emigrant cañons, in April; at Willow Creek and Cottonwood Creek, in May; and in Wild Rose and Death Valley cañons, in June. In the Argus Range, the species was very abundant in Shepherd Cañon and at Maturango Spring, where it bred commonly, as it did in the Panamint Mountains.

As many as a dozen nests were found from April 25 to May 1, in various situations. A few were placed in crevices in the rocky sides of the cañon, while the majority were in bushes on the sloping hillsides, from one to several feet above the ground. The nests among the rocks were more compact, as they contained a larger amount of lining than those in the bushes, which in many cases were very loosely put together. The full complement of eggs in the different nests was four, five, and six. The species was common in the Coso, Inyo, and White mountains. It was everywhere common in Owens Valley from the lower to the upper part. In this valley, both at Independence and Lone Pine, the species was found to be very destructive to the ripened peaches during the middle of August. Flocks of birds occurred in the orchards, and in some places hardly an example of the ripe fruit could be found which was not more or less mutilated. A number of birds shot in the peach orchards at Lone Pine had little except the pulp of this fruit in their gullets or stomachs. It was known as the 'peach bird.'

It was common all along the route from Walker Pass, through the valley of Kern River, Walker Basin and Bakersfield to Visalia, June 21-23, and July 1 to 23, and at Old Fort Tejon late in June and early in July. It was seen at Ash Meadows and Pahrump Valley, Nevada, in March. In the same State, Dr. Merriam noted it among the cottonwoods at Yount's ranch in Pahrump Valley, April 29; at Mountain Spring, in the Charleston Mountains, and at Upper Cottonwood Springs near the east base of these mountains, April 30; near the summit of the Timpahute Mountains in tree yuccas, May 26; at Quartz Spring, on the west side of the Desert Mountains, May 27; at the Bend of the Colorado, May 4, and on Gold Mountain where a young one just able to fly was caught June 3, at an altitude of about 1,980 meters (6,500 feet). It was common in Tule Cañon June 4, and thence up to the plateau on top of Mount Magruder. In Arizona, he found it common at the mouth of Beaverdam Creek, May 9-10; in Utah, in the juniper belt of the Beaverdam Mountains, May 10-11, and at St. George, in the Lower Santa Clara Valley, May 11-15, where it was called 'peach bird' by the Mormons. Two nests were found at St. George, one in a cottonwood and the other in an arborescent cactus.

Mr. Nelson found the species in small numbers in the Cañada de las Uvas, at San Emigdio Creek, and in the Temploa Mountains, and rather common about the ranches in the San Joaquin Valley in October. It was common along the route from San Simeon to Carpenteria, among the farms along the coast, and not uncommon between the latter place and Santa Paula in November and December.

Record of specimens collected of Carpodacus mexicanus frontalis.

Collector's No.	Sex.	Locality.	Date.	Collector.	Remarks.
45	♂	Daggett, Calif	Jan. 9, 1891	A. K. Fisher	
13	♂	......do......	Feb. 8, 1891	F. Stephens	
	♂	Panamint Mountains, Calif	Mch. 28, 1891	E. W. Nelson	Johnson Cañon.
158	♂	......do......	Apr. 13, 1891	A. K. Fisher	Surprise Cañon.
159	♂	......do......	......do......	......do......	Do.
187	♀	Argus Range, Calif	Apr. 27, 1891	......do......	Nest and eggs.
231	♂	......do......	May 12, 1891	......do......	Maturaugo Spring.
232	♂	......do......	......do......	......do......	Do.
	♂	......do......	......do......	T. S. Palmer	Do.
	♂	......do......	......do......	......do......	Do.
348	♀	Death Valley, Calif	June 21, 1891	A. K. Fisher	Furnace Creek.

Loxia curvirostra stricklandi. Mexican Crossbill.

Crossbills were uncommon and seen only in the Sierra Nevada. At Big Cottonwood Meadows Dr. Merriam saw them just below timber line June 18, and towards the end of the season Mr. Dutcher saw a few and shot a pair. Mr. Nelson saw some on the west slope opposite the head of Owens River in August. At Horse Corral Meadows a noisy flock passed our camp August 12. Mr. Bailey saw the species at Whitney Meadows, and it was heard at Soda Springs or Kern River Lakes, September 5.

Record of specimens collected of Loxia curvirostra stricklandi.

Collector's No.	Sex.	Locality.	Date.	Collector.	Remarks.
	♀	Sierra Nevada, Calif	Aug. 20, 1891	V. Bailey	Whitney Meadows.
	♂	......do......	Aug. 28, 1891	......do......	Do.
34		......do......	Aug. 22, 1891	B. H. Dutcher	Big Cottonwood Meadows.

Leucosticte tephrocotis. Gray-crowned Leucosticte.

A very interesting discovery made by the expedition was that the gray-crowned finch is a common summer resident in the higher portions of the White Mountains and the Sierra Nevada in eastern and southern California. The knowledge that this bird breeds as stated, makes its distribution in relation to the other species of the genus a little more clear.

In the Rocky Mountain region *Leucosticte atrata* is the northern and *L. australis* the southern representative, just as *Leucosticte t. littoralis* is the northern race of *L. tephrocotis* of the more western range.

Mr. Nelson found the gray crowned finch breeding abundantly on the White Mountains, the only range except the Sierra Nevada on which the species was seen. It was found above timber line about the bases of the main peaks at an elevation from 3,350 to 3,650 meters (11,000 to 12,000 feet). He found the birds easy of approach as they were feeding on seeds and insects about the border of the melting snowdrifts.

The warm west wind coming from over Owens Valley brought many insects which became benumbed by the cold and fell on the snowdrifts. These the birds devoured eagerly, and Mr. Nelson saw them pursue and tear to pieces several grasshoppers on the surface of the snow. The condition of the skin on the abdomen showed that they were incubating and that both sexes shared in this labor. He noticed when skinning the birds that they had a double craw. One located in the usual place and the other in the form of a double gular sac divided by a median constriction. The latter when full hangs down like a lobe of bare skin outside of the feathers.

In the Sierra Nevada the same observer saw the species about timber line at the head of Owens River on the eastern slope, and at the same altitude on Kern, Kings, and Kaweah rivers on the western slope. Mr. Stephens found it abundant about the lakes at the head of Independence Creek, where it was breeding June 18–23, and also saw three above timber line at Menache Meadows, May 24–26. Mr. Dutcher saw several flocks and secured a few specimens at and above timber line at

Big Cottonwood Meadows, during the summer. Mr. Bailey found it common all along timber line and down among the *Pinus balfouriana* at Whitney Meadows. The writer did not see the species until August 18, when a flock of forty or more was seen on the west side of the Kearsarge Pass. Later in the day, during a snow storm, a flock was seen just below timber line on the east side of the Pass, and five specimens secured. The bad weather seemed to make them restless and hard to approach. At Round Valley, 12 miles south of Mount Whitney, the species was again seen just above timber line, August 28, and on the ridge north of Mineral King large flocks were seen September 8–11.

Record of specimens collected of Leucosticte tephrocotis.

Collector's No.	Sex.	Locality.	Date.	Collector.	Remarks.
	♂	White Mountains, Calif	July 15, 1891	E. W. Nelson	
	♂	....do....	....do....	....do....	
	♂	....do....	....do....	....do....	
	♂	....do....	....do....	....do....	
	♂	....do....	....do....	....do....	
	♂	....do....	....do....	....do....	
	♂	....do....	....do....	....do....	
	♂	....do....	....do....	....do....	
	♂	....do....	....do....	....do....	
	♂	....do....	....do....	....do....	
	♂	....do....	....do....	....do....	
	♂	....do....	....do....	....do....	
	♂	....do....	....do....	....do....	
	♂	....do....	....do....	....do....	
	♂	....do....	....do....	....do....	
	♀	....do....	....do....	....do....	
	♀	....do....	....do....	....do....	
	♀	....do....	....do....	....do....	
	♀	....do....	....do....	....do....	
	♀	Sierra Nevada, Calif	July 25, 1891	E. W. Nelson	Summit of Mammoth Pass, Cal.
417	♂	....do....	Aug. 18, 1891	A. K. Fisher	Kearsarge Pass, 11,000 feet altitude.
418	♀ im	....do....	....do....	....do....	Do.
419	♀ im	....do....	....do....	....do....	Do.
112	♂	....do....	June 22, 1891	F. Stephens	Independence Creek, 10,000 feet.
113	♀	....do....	....do....	....do....	Do.
114	♀	....do....	....do....	....do....	Do.
115	♂	....do....	....do....	....do....	Do.
19	im	....do....	July 30, 1891	B. H. Dutcher	Big Cottonwood Meadows.
25	♂	....do....	Aug. 2, 1891	....do....	Do.
	♀ im	....do....	Aug. 20, 1891	V. Bailey	Do.
420	♂ im	....do....	Aug. 28, 1891	A. K. Fisher	Round Valley, above timber line.
161	♀ im	....do....	Aug. 23, 1891	F. Stephens	Olancha Peak, 12,000 feet altitude.
	♂	....do....	Aug. 7, 1891	V. Bailey	Mineral King, 9,700 feet altitude.

Leucosticte atrata. Black Leucosticte.

Mr. Bailey secured one specimen of this species at St. George, Utah, January 21, 1889. It was feeding alone on a rocky hill, among low brush.

Spinus tristis. Goldfinch.

A common species throughout southern California, though not recorded by any member of the expedition.

Spinus psaltria. Arkansas Goldfinch.

The Arkansas goldfinch was observed in a number of localities throughout the mountain and desert regions visited. At San Bernardino a flock of eight or ten was seen feeding on the seeds of a wild sunflower, December 28, 1890. Small flocks were seen in Cajon Pass, January 2, again March 29–30, and in the cottonwoods bordering the Mohave River near Victor, March 30.

In Nevada, it was not uncommon at Ash Meadows in March; at Queen station and mill in the White Mountains, July 11–16. Dr. Merriam found it at Upper Cottonwood Springs at the east base of the Charleston Mountains, April 30; at the Bend of the Colorado River, May 4; and in Pahranagat Valley, where it was breeding commonly, May 23. At the mouth of Beaverdam Creek, Arizona, and on the west side of the Beaverdam Mountains, Utah, he saw several May 9–10. As no specimens were taken for identification, the Arizona and Utah records may apply to *Spinus psaltria arizonæ*.

In the Panimint Mountains it was common in Johnson and Surprise cañons, and in the latter place Mr. Albert Koebele found a nest, just completed, April 23. In the same mountains Mr. Nelson found it a common breeding species in Cottonwood, Mill Creek, and Willow Creek cañons. In the Argus Range it was common in Shepherd Cañon, where a nest and four eggs were taken April 27, and at Maturango Spring the first half of May. At Coso Mountains a few were seen along the streams in the cañons, the last of May.

Mr. Nelson found it common in the Grapevine Mountains, and rather common in the Inyo Mountains, in willow patches along the streams up to the piñons, the latter part of June. Goldfinches were common at the head of Owens River, abundant in the Yosemite, and from the base up to the nut-pines in the White Mountains. The were more or less common in Owens Valley from the lower end, at Little Owens Lake, northward to Benton and the foot of the White Mountains. A few were seen in Walker Pass, July 2–3; the species was common along the South Fork of Kern River, July 3–10; in Walker Basin, July 13–16; and at Bakersfield, in the San Joaquin Valley, July 17–20. In the High Sierra Dr. Merriam saw the species near Big Cottonwood Meadows, June 18, and the writer observed a flock near the abandoned sawmill in Sequoia National Park, August 1.

Mr. Palmer reported it common at Old Fort Tejon during the first half of July; Mr. Stephens found it rather common at Reche Cañon September 22–24, and Mr. Bailey saw it in flocks at Monterey September 28 to October 9.

It was common at Three Rivers July 25–30, and along the route from Mineral King to that place September 12–15.

Mr. Nelson found it common and generally distributed between San Simeon and Carpenteria and Santa Paula, in November and December.

Record of specimens collected of Spinus psaltria.

Collector's No.	Sex.	Locality.	Date.	Collector.	Remarks.
7	♂	San Bernardino, Calif	Dec. 28, 1890	A. K. Fisher	
188	♀	Argus Range, Calif	April 27, 1891	...do	Shepherd Cañon, nest and 4 eggs.
193	♂	...do	April 29, 1891	...do	Shepherd Cañon.
247	♂	...do	May 13, 1891	...do	Maturango Spring.
368	♂	Walker Pass, Calif	July 3, 1891	...do	
371	♂	Kern River, Calif	July 4, 1891	...do	South Fork.
	♂	Pahranagat Valley, Nevada	May 23, 1891	C. Hart Merriam	
	♂	Santa Clara, Utah	May 11, 1891	V. Bailey	

Spinus psaltria arizonæ Arizona Goldfinch.

This subspecies was found breeding in great abundance in the Lower Santa Clara Valley, Utah, by Dr. Merriam. Five nests with fresh eggs were found, and one with eggs nearly ready to hatch, May 11-15. In California Mr. Bailey secured a specimen from a flock at Three Rivers, in the western foothills of the Sierra Nevada, September 15.

Spinus lawrencei. Lawrence's Goldfinch.

Dr. Merriam reported Lawrence's goldfinch as common in the Cañada de las Uvas, June 28-29, and in the Granite Range in western San Diego County, July 1-10. Mr. Palmer saw a male near Old Fort Tejon, June 30, and shot one in the cañon July 6. A specimen was secured in Walker Basin July 16, and an individual was seen among the oaks above it, July 14. These are all the records we have for the species.

Spinus pinus. Pine Siskin.

At two places only was this species seen by members of the expedition, both in the High Sierra in California. Mr. Nelson saw it at the head of the San Joaquin River, in August, and the writer observed a flock of a dozen or fifteen near timber line above Mineral King, September 10. The birds were feeding upon seeds on or near the ground, and when flushed alighted on a pine branch within a few feet of the observer.

Poocætes gramineus confinis. Western Vesper Sparrow.

The vesper sparrow was seen in comparatively few places on either side of the Sierra Nevada. At Ash Meadows, Nevada, it was not uncommon in migration March 10, and a few were seen by Mr. Bailey at Vegas Ranch, March 10-13.

Mr. Nelson found a few among the sage brush above the piñons in the Inyo Mountains, in June; not uncommon on the White Mountains, and on the plateau at the head of Owens Valley, in July; and common at the head of Owens River, in the same month. Dr. Merriam found the species at Mountain Meadows, Utah, May 17. A single specimen was seen near Visalia, Calif., September 17, a few near the lower end of the Cañada de las Uvas and San Emigdio Cañon, and on the Carrizo Plain, in San Joaquin Valley, in October.

Ammodramus sandwichensis alaudinus. Western Savanna Sparrow.

This little sparrow was found nowhere common, though it breeds sparingly in various localities throughout the desert regions. The writer found it not uncommon in the alfalfa fields at Furnace Creek, Death Valley, in the latter part of January, and Dr. Merriam found a few at the same place April 9-12, but Mr. Bailey and the former observer did not detect it on their last trip to the valley, June 19-22. Mr. Nelson found a few at Saratoga Springs, in the lower end of the valley, late in January. A few were seen at Resting Spring, California early in February; a number of specimens were secured in the wet meadows at Ash Meadows, Nevada, during the first three weeks of March; and Mr. Nelson found it not uncommon about wet ground in Pahrump and Vegas valleys and in Vegas Wash March 3-16. Dr. Merriam shot one at the Great Bend of the Colorado May 4; one in Meadow Creek Valley, Nevada, May 19, and a number in Pahranagat Valley, Nevada, May 22-26.

In Owens Valley the writer found it not uncommon and breeding among the salt grass at Owens Lake May 30 to June 4, and at Lone Pine June 4-15; and Mr. Stephens found it not uncommon at Olancha, May 16-23; Alvord, June 26-28; and Morans, July 4-7.

A pair was seen by Mr. Nelson at the head of Owens Valley near the White Mountains about the middle of July, and by the writer at Three Rivers, in the western foothills, September 16. It was common along the coast from San Simeon to Santa Barbara, and a few were seen near Carpenteria in December.

Record of specimens collected of Ammodramus sandwichensis alaudinus.

Collector's No.	Sex.	Locality.	Date.	Collector.	Remarks.
	♀	Great Bend of Colorado River, Nev	May 4, 1891	C. Hart Merriam	
	♂	Pahrump Valley, Nev	Feb. 17, 1891	E. W. Nelson	
	♂	Ash Meadows, Nev	Mar. 4, 1891	...do	
119	♀	......do......	...do......	...do......	
120	♀	......do......	Mar. 8, 1891	A. K. Fisher	
129	♀	......do......	Mar. 9, 1891	...do	
	♂	......do......	Mar. 15, 1891	...do	
106	♂	......do......	Mar. 19, 1891	E. W. Nelson	
		Resting Springs, Calif.	Feb. 11, 1891	A. K. Fisher	
70	♀	Death Valley, Calif.	Jan. 31, 1891	E. W. Nelson	Saratoga Spring.
91	♀	......do......	Jan. 26, 1891	A. K. Fisher	Furnace Creek.
92	♂	......do......	Jan. 31, 1891	...do	Do.
179	♀	Panamint Valley, Calif.	Apr. 23, 1891	...do	Do.
283		Owens Valley, Calif.	June 2, 1891	...do	Hot Springs.
291		......do......	June 3, 1891	...do	Keeler.
61	♂	......do......	May 22, 1891	F. Stephens	Olancha.
88		......do......	June 12, 1891	...do	Do.
103	♀	......do......	June 15, 1891	...do	Do.
292	♂	......do......	June 5, 1891	A. K. Fisher	Lone Pine.
	♀	Fresno, Calif	Sept. 25, 1891	E. W. Nelson	

Ammodramus sandwichensis bryanti. Bryant's Marsh Sparrow.

Mr. Nelson found Bryant's sparrow common along the coast from Santa Barbara to Carpenteria during the first half of December.

Record of specimen collected of Ammodramus sandwichensis bryanti.

Collectors No.	Sex.	Locality.	Date.	Collector.	Remarks.
	♂	Carpenteria, Calif	Dec. 18, 1891	E. W. Nelson	
	♂	......do............	...do...	...do...	
	♀	......do............	...do...	...do...	

Chondestes grammacus strigatus. Western Lark Sparrow.

The western lark sparrow is a characteristic inhabitant of the Upper Sonoran and Transition Zones and was not found in the Lower Sonoran Zone, except west of the Sierra Nevada, and during migration. It was a common species in Owen's Valley from the lower end northward, and was breeding wherever found. The writer found it abundant along the South Fork of Kern River, at Kernville, and in Walker Basin during the first half of July. In the San Joaquin Valley it was abundant at Bakersfield, and all along the route to Visalia, July 17–23, and at Three Rivers, July 25–30 and September 14–17.

Dr. Merriam furnished the following notes on the species: "In Nevada it was common throughout the sage brush on the rolling plateau that forms the northward continuation of the Juniper Mountains, May 18, and in Desert and Pahranagat valleys, May 20–26. In Pahranagat Valley it was particularly abundant, breeding and in full song. It was common in the north part of Oasis Valley, June 1, but was not observed at the southern end of this valley. On Mount Magruder a few were seen in the sage brush June 5. Others were found at Mountain Spring in the Charleston Mountains and at Upper Cottonwood Springs at the east base of these mountains, April 30; and in the Valley of the Muddy, May 6. Several were seen in the lower edge of the junipers on both sides of the Beaverdam Mountains in southwestern Utah, May 10 and 11. It was found also in the Santa Clara Valley, Utah, May 11–15, and was common in Mountain Meadows, Utah, May 17. In Owens Valley, California, it was common in the sage brush of the Upper Sonoran Zone, June 10–19, and in Antelope Valley at the west end of the Mohave Desert, June 27–28. On the west slope of the Sierra Nevada it was abundant in the valley of Kern River, where full-grown young were conspicuous, June 22–23. It was seen in the Tehachapi Valley, June 25, and in the Cañada de las Uvas, June 28–29, where full-grown young were common."

Mr. Nelson found it rather common in the Cañada de las Uvas and San Emigdio Cañon, at various places in San Joaquin Valley and about the borders of the foothills, in October, and in the more open country along the route from San Simeon to Carpenteria, in November and part of December.

Record of specimens collected of Chondestes grammacus strigatus.

Collector's No.	Sex.	Locality.	Date.	Collector.	Remarks.
307	♀	Owens Valley, Calif............	June 6, 1891	A. K. Fisher.......	Lone Pine.
308	♂	......do...........................	...do...	......do............	Do.
320	♀	......do...........................	June 9, 1891	......do............	Do.

Zonotrichia leucophrys. White-crowned Sparrow.

The white-crowned sparrow was a common summer resident in the Sierra Nevada and White Mountains, but was not found in any other locality, even as a migrant—at least specimens were not taken elsewhere. There is uncertainty as to the race which breeds among the piñons in the Inyo Mountains, as no specimens were collected there. Mr. Nelson found the white-crowned sparrow on the plateau at the head of Owens Valley, and thence up to near timber line in the White Mountains, and Mr. Stephens saw it at the Queen mill and mine, Nevada, in the same range, July 11–16. Along the eastern slope of the Sierra it was common at the head of Owens River, the last of July; rather common at Menache Meadows, May 24–26; Onion Lake on Independence Creek, June 18–23; and at Bishop Creek, August 4–10. Mr. Dutcher found it very common among the willows at Big Cottonwood Meadows, where nests were taken. Mr. Palmer saw a nest containing three eggs near Mount Silliman, August 7, and Mr. Belding found the species in the Yosemite. White-crowned sparrows were common in flocks at Whitney Meadows, September 1, Farewell Gap, September 8, and from timber line above Mineral King down along the Kaweah River to below the pines, September 10–12.

Record of specimens collected of Zonotrichia leucophrys.

Collector's No.	Sex.	Locality.	Date.	Collector.	Remarks.
148	im	Sierra Nevada, California.....	Aug. 8, 1891	F. Stephens........	Bishop Creek.
116	♂	......do.....	June 22, 1891	....do	Independence Creek.
	♀	......do...........................	July 31, 1891	V. Bailey	Mineral King.
	♂	White Mountains	July 10, 1891	E. W. Nelson	
162	♂	Sierra Nevada...................	Aug. 26, 1891	F. Stephens........	Mulkey Meadows.
	♀	......do...........................	July 7, 1891	B. H. Dutcher.....	Big Cottonwood Meadows.
	♀	......do...........................	July 13, 1891	....do	Do.
	♂	......do...........................	July 19, 1891	....do	Do.
422	♂ im	......do...........................	Aug. 25, 1891	A. K. Fisher.......	Do.

Zonotrichia leucophrys intermedia. Intermediate Sparrow.

The intermediate sparrow was found as a migrant or winter resident only, through the desert regions, where it was often abundant among the mesquite or other thickets. In Cajon Pass it was very common January 1–2, and again March 30. In the Mohave Desert it was common at Hesperia January 4, and about Stoddard Wells January 6. In Death Valley it was common about Furnace Creek ranch the last of

January and April 9-12, and at Resting Springs the first half of February and April 27. At the latter place the flocks became very tame and came into camp to pick up the crumbs.

It was common about the ranch and among the mesquite at Ash Meadows, Nev., during the greater part of March, and Mr. Nelson found it abundant at Pahrump and Vegas ranches and among the junipers in the Charleston Mountains during the same month. Dr. Merriam found it common at Leach Point Spring, Calif., April 25; at Mountain Spring in the Charleston Mountains, Nev., April 30; in the Valley of the Virgin near Bunkerville, May 8, and a few tardy migrants in Pahranagat Valley May 22-26. In the Santa Clara Valley, Utah, the subspecies was still tolerably common May 11-15. In the Panamint Mountains it was common in Johnson, Surprise, and Emigrant cañons in April, and Mr. Nelson found a few late migrants on Willow Creek the last of May. The sparrow was abundant among the mesquite at Hot Springs, Panamint Valley, April 20-25; a few were seen at Searl's garden, near the south end of the Argus Range, about the same time, and a few in Shepherd Cañon as late as May 1. In the latter place Mr. Nelson reported it very common in January. Mr. Stephens found it rather common in the lower end of Oasis Valley, Nev., March 15-19, and at Grapevine Spring, Calif., April 1-4.

A few were observed by Mr. Nelson about the Cañada de las Uvas and San Emigdio Cañon in October, and along the coast from San Simeon to Carpenteria in November and December.

Record of specimens collected of Zonotrichia leucophrys intermedia.

Collector's No.	Sex.	Locality.	Date.	Collector.	Remarks.
26	♀ im.	Cajon Pass, Calif	Jan. 2, 1891	A. K. Fisher	
27	♀	......do......	......do......	......do......	
38	♂	Hesperia, Calif	Jan. 4, 1891	......do......	
6	♂	Daggett, Calif	Feb. 7, 1891	F. Stephens	
68	♀	Death Valley, Calif	Jan. 23, 1891	A. K. Fisher	Furnace Creek.
67	♂	......do......	......do......	......do......	Do.
81	♂ im.	......do......	Jan. 27, 1891	......do......	Do.
105	♀	Resting Springs, Calif	Feb. 10, 1891	......do......	
123	♀	Ash Meadows, Calif	Mar. 11, 1891	......do......	
137	♀	......do......	Mar. 19, 1891	......do......	
	♂	Panamint Mountains, Calif	Mar. 29, 1891	E. W. Nelson	Johnson Cañon.
	♂	......do......	......do......	......do......	Do.
	♂	......do......	......do......	......do......	Do.
	♂	Panamint Valley, Calif	Apr. 22, 1891	......do......	Hot Spring.
	♀	......do......	Apr. 23, 1891	......do......	Do.
	♀	......do......	......do......	......do......	Do.
	♂	......do......	Apr. 14, 1891	V. Bailey	Emigrant Spring.
48	♀	Argus Range, Calif	Apr. 22, 1891	F. Stephens	Borax Flat.
	♀	Carpenteria, Calif	Dec. 18, 1891	E. W. Nelson	

Zonotrichia leucophrys gambeli. Gambel's Sparrow.

Gambel's sparrow was not met with east of the Sierra Nevada, and on the western side as a migrant only. Mr. Bailey found it abundant at Monterey the first week in October, and Mr. Nelson reported it common in the San Joaquin Valley wherever a vigorous growth of bushes or weeds afforded attractive shelter. Along the route from

San Simeon to Carpenteria and Santa Paula it was abundant during November and December.

Zonotrichia coronata. Golden-crowned Sparrow.

The golden-crowned sparrow was found by Mr. Nelson to be abundant and generally distributed along the coast from San Simeon to Carpenteria and Santa Paula during November and December. This is the only region where the species was noted.

Zonotrichia albicollis. White-throated Sparrow.

Mr. Nelson secured a male specimen of the white-throated sparrow at the mission of Santa Ynez, December 6, 1891, which makes the fourth record for California.

Spizella monticola ochracea. Western Tree Sparrow.

The only place where the tree sparrow was seen was Pahrump ranch, Nevada, where Mr. Nelson found quite a number in the willow thickets, the latter part of February. They appeared quite suddenly one morning before a storm, which filled the valley with rain and covered the mountains with snow.

Spizella socialis arizonæ. Western Chipping Sparrow.

The chipping sparrow was not found to be a common migrant in the valleys, though it was more or less common as a summer resident in the mountains, from the piñons and junipers up to and among the other conifers. A number were seen in the cultivated fields about San Bernardino, December 28–29, 1890. Mr. Nelson saw a few on the Panamint Mountains the latter part of May and found the species breeding on the Grapevine Mountains, June 10–11. A few were seen about Maturango Spring, where the males were in full song, May 13–14. The species was found up to timber line in the White Mountains, and was common at the head of Owens River, in the Sierra Nevada. Dr. Merriam found it on the north slope of Telescope Peak in the Panamint Mountains, April 17–19; among the junipers in the Juniper Mountains, Nevada, May 18; and among the piñons on Mount Magruder, Nevada, June 5. In Walker Basin it was common among the pines above the valley, July 14, and Mr. Palmer found it quite common at Old Fort Tejon about the same time. In the High Sierra it was common in the Sequoia National Park the first week in August; at Horse Corral Meadows, August 9–13; in Big Cottonwood Meadows during the summer and fall; at Whitney Meadows, the first week in September; at Mineral King, near timber line, September 9–11; and along the Kaweah River, from Mineral King to the valley, September 11–13.

Record of specimens collected of Spizella sociailis arizonæ.

Collector's No.	Sex.	Locality.	Date.	Collector.	Remarks.
1	♂	San Bernardino, Calif	Dec. 28, 1890	A. K. Fisher	
158	♀	Sierra Nevada, Calif	Aug. 22, 1891	F. Stephens	Olancha Peak.
	♂ im.	...do...	Aug. 29, 1891	V. Bailey	Whitney Meadows.

Spizella breweri. Brewer's Sparrow.

Brewer's sparrow was a common species throughout the desert regions during migration, and bred in most of the mountain ranges among the sagebrush. A number were seen in Vegas Wash, March 10–13, and the species arrived at Ash Meadows, Nevada, March 17. Mr. Nelson reported it as a common breeding species among the sage, both in the Panamint and Grapevine mountains, during the latter part of May and first of June. Many of its nests were found, usually containing four eggs, and built in a sage bush a couple of feet from the ground. On the north side of Telescope Peak Dr. Merriam found it common among the sage, April 17–19, and Mr. Bailey and the writer observed it near the same place, June 22–25. It was not uncommon at Hot Springs, in Panamint Valley, April 20–23; several were seen at Leach Point Spring, April 25; and one was shot in the northwest arm of Death Valley, April 13.

In Nevada Dr. Merriam found it tolerably common in parts of Pahrump Valley, April 29, and at Mountain Spring, in the Charleston Mountains, April 30. He reported it as common in the sage brush on the plateau of the Juniper Mountains; in Pahranagat Valley, May 22–26; on Gold Mountain, June 3; in Tule Cañon, June 4; and thence up to the summit of Mount Magruder, where it was the commonest bird on the sage plateau, June 4–11, breeding abundantly, and extending thence northerly into Fish Lake Valley.

In Utah Dr. Merriam did not see it in the low St. George Valley, but found it common in the upper part of the Santa Clara Valley, May 16, beginning with the sagebrush about 8 miles north of St. George and continuing northward to Mountain Meadows and the Escalante Desert, where several nests were found, May 17. In the Beaverdam Mountains it was tolerably common throughout the sage and junipers, May 10.

Returning to California, in the Argus Range, the species was common in Shepherd Cañon, and was breeding commonly at Maturango Spring, from the summit of the range to the bottom of Coso Valley, early in May. In the Coso Mountains it was common, and a number of nests containing eggs were found during the latter part of May. Mr. Nelson found the species rather common in the Inyo Mountains, from the sage up to the summit in the White Mountains, and at the head of Owens River in the Sierra Nevada. In Owens Valley it was common throughout the summer, especially along the eastern slope of the Sierra Nevada, where Mr. Stephens noted it in a number of places, even as high as Menache Meadows. It was common on the western slope of Walker Pass, June 21 and July 2–3, and in Kern River Valley, June 22–23 and July 11–13. Mr. Palmer reported it as tolerably common in the sagebrush among the piñons at Old Fort Tejon, July 9.

Record of specimens collected of Spizella breweri.

Collector's No.	Sex.	Locality.	Date.	Collector.	Remarks.
130	♂	Ash Meadows, Nev	Mar. 17, 1891	A. K. Fisher	
	♂	....do....	Mar. 18, 1891	E. W. Nelson	
46	♀	Panamint Valley, Calif.	Apr. 22, 1891	....do....	Hot Springs.
	♂	Panamint Mts., Calif.	Apr. 16, 1891	F. Stephens	
203	♂	Argus Range, Calif.	May 6, 1891	A. K. Fisher	Maturango Springs.
213	♂	....do....	May 8, 1891	....do....	Do.
81	♀	Owens Lake, Calif.	June 10, 1891	F. Stephens	
105	♂ im	....do....	June 15, 1891	....do....	

Spizella atrigularis. Black-chinned Sparrow.

The black-chinned sparrow is one of a number of species whose known range was much extended by the observations of the expedition. It was first observed in Johnson Cañon in the Panamint Range, where an adult male was seen among the junipers, April 6. In Surprise Cañon, of the same range, the species was first seen April 15, when two specimens were secured, and subsequently it became common.

The song, which was frequently heard, resembles closely that of the Eastern field sparrow (*Spizella pusilla*). At Maturango Spring, in the Argus Range, a male was seen among the sage (*Artemisia tridentata*) on May 12, and a female was secured among the willows near the spring, which had an egg in the oviduct, almost ready for expulsion, May 15. In the Coso Mountains the species was not uncommon, and on May 27 a female with her nest and three eggs was secured. The nest was situated in a small bush about two feet from the ground, on a gradually sloping hillside bearing a scattered growth of piñon.

On the west side of Owens Valley Mr. Stephens heard several singing on Independence Creek, near the Rex Monte mill, and secured a specimen June 20. On the western slope of Walker Pass a specimen was secured in one of the cañons, as it was washing at a pool, July 3, and at Walker Basin an immature bird was shot on the ridge above the valley, July 14.

Record of specimen collected of Spizella atrigularis.

Collector's No.	Sex.	Locality.	Date.	Collector.	Remarks.
100	♂	Panamint Mountains, Calif.	Apr. 16, 1891	E. W. Nelson	Surprise Cañon.
161	♂	....do....	Apr. 15, 1891	A. K. Fisher	Do.
	♀	....do....	....do....	....do....	Do.
241	♂	Argus Range, Calif.	May 15, 1891	....do....	Maturango Spring.
259	♀	Coso Mountains, Calif.	May 27, 1891	....do....	Nest and eggs.
260	♂	....do....	....do....	....do....	
360	♀	Walker Pass, Calif.	July 3, 1891	....do....	
392	♂	Walker Basin, Calif.	July 14, 1891	....do....	
109	♂	Independence Creek, Calif.	June 20, 1891	F. Stephens	Owens Valley.

Junco hyemalis. Slate-colored Junco.

A specimen of the common eastern junco was secured by the writer in Johnson Cañon in the Panamint Range, April 3, and another was seen a day or two later in the same locality. Mr. Bailey took one near Fort Mohave, Ariz., March 4, 1889.

Junco hyemalis shufeldti. Shufeldt's Junco.

A specimen collected in the Charleston Mountains and another in the Grapevine Mountains, Nevada, in March, belong to this race. Whether the species remains in these ranges to breed, or passes further east for that purpose, it is impossible to say, as no specimens were collected there later in the season.

Record of specimens collected of Junco hyemalis shufeldti.

Collectors No.	Sex.	Locality.	Date.	Collector.	Remarks.
35	♀ ♀	Charleston Mountains, Nev. Grapevine Mountains, Nev.	Mar. 7, 1891 Mar. 21, 1891	V. Bailey F. Stephens	

Junco hyemalis thurberi. Thurber's Junco.

Thurber's junco was a common species in many places throughout the desert region of southeastern California, and bred commonly in most of the desert ranges, as well as in the Sierra Nevada. It was very common in Cajon Pass in the San Bernardino Mountains, January 2, and several were seen there March 30. Mr. Nelson found juncos common at Lone Pine, in the cañons at the foot of the Sierra Nevada, also in Surprise Cañon of the Panamint, and Shepherd Cañon of the Argus range, in December and early January. The individuals which he found in considerable numbers at Pahrump ranch, and in the Charleston Mountains, in February and March, may or may not have been wholly or in part referable to this form, as a single specimen collected in the Charleston Mountains belongs to the more eastern race, *shufeldti*. The same may be said of the few pairs of birds he found breeding near the summit of the Grapevine Mountains, in June, as no specimens were collected at that time. It was common in Johnson and Surprise cañons, in the Panamint range, during the first half of April; Dr. Merriam saw many on the north base of Telescope Peak, April 16–19, and Mr. Bailey and the writer saw it from the summit of that peak down to below the 'charcoal kilns', in Wild Rose Cañon, June 23. It was tolerably common among the piñons in the Argus range, where specimens were secured during the first half of May, and Mr. Palmer saw one in the Coso Mountains May 27, and others at Cerro Gordo, in the Inyo range, May 31. Mr. Nelson found it sparingly among the *Pinus flexilis* in the latter range the last of June, and not common in the White Mountains in July. Mr. Stephens found it not common from the Rex Monte mine to timber line in Independence Cañon, June 18–23; at Queen mine, White Mountains, Nevada, July 11–16; common at Bishop Creek, August 4–10, and Menache Meadows, May 24–26. Juncos were common on the ridge above Walker Basin, July 14, and Mr. Palmer saw three back of

Old Fort Tejon July 6, which had probably descended from the mountains where they were common among the pines July 9. Mr. Nelson reported this species as abundant at the head of Owens River, where he found a nest containing four eggs nearly ready to hatch, July 25. On the western slope it was also common. On the upper Merced he found two nests on August 3, one containing a young bird and three eggs nearly ready to hatch, and the other three fresh eggs. The first mentioned nest was nicely hidden under a projecting spruce root on the side of a small gully, and the latter was placed in a clump of aspens at the base of a small sapling, was strongly made, and was lined with the long hairs of the porcupine.

Juncos were very common in the Sequoia National Park during the first week of August. One nest with three eggs was found, and young as large as their parents were seen. They were common at Horse Corral Meadows August 9-13, Big Cottonwood Meadows and Round Valley the last of August, and at Whitney Meadows and Mineral King early in September. Mr. Dutcher found them abundant at Big Cottonwood Meadows where he discovered several nests, and Mr. Bailey observed them on the Kaweah River from the lowest conifers to above timberline. A nest with young was found among the giant redwoods July 29.

Mr. Nelson reported the species as common on high ground along the route from San Simeon to Carpenteria in November and December; it was also common on the route from La Panza to San Luis Obispo October 28 to November 3; and a few were seen at Santa Paula the last of December.

Record of specimens collected of Junco hyemalis thurberi.

Collector's No.	Sex.	Locality.	Date.	Collector.	Remarks.
	♀	Panamint Mountains, Calif.	Mar. 28, 1891	E. W. Nelson	Johnson Cañon.
	♂	......do......	...do......	...do......	Do.
149	♂	......do......	Apr. 2, 1891	A. K. Fisher	Do.
170	♀	......do......	Apr. 19, 1891	...do......	Surprise Cañon.
	♂	......do......	...do......	E. W. Nelson	Do.
353	♂	......do......	June 23, 1891	A. K. Fisher	Coal kilns.
202	♂	Argus Range, Calif.	May 6, 1891	...do......	Maturango Spring.
	♂	......do......	May 9, 1891	T. S. Palmer	Do.
	♀	......do......	...do......	...do......	Do.
111	♀	Owens Valley, Calif.	June 21, 1891	F. Stephens	Independence Creek. Sitting.
133	♂	White Mountains, Calif.	July 13, 1891	...do......	10,000 feet altitude.
	♂	......do......	July 14, 1891	E. W. Nelson	
22	♂	Cajon Pass, Calif.	Jan. 2, 1891	A. K. Fisher	
	♀	Sierra Nevada, Calif.	Aug. 7, 1891	V. Bailey	Mineral King.
5	♂	......do......	June 19, 1891	B. H. Dutcher	Big Cottonwood Meadows.
	♀	......do......	July 7, 1891	...do......	Do.
37	♂	......do......	Sept. 14, 1891	...do......	Do.
38	?	......do......	...do......	...do......	Do.
414	♀ ad.	......do......	Aug. 12, 1891	A. K. Fisher	Horse Corral Meadows.
144	♂ im.	......do......	July 27, 1891	F. Stephens	
	♂	......do......	July 22, 1891	E. W. Nelson	
	♂	......do......	July 25, 1891	...do......	Nest and eggs.
	♂	San Emigdio Cañon, Calif.	Oct. 18, 1891	...do......	

Junco pinosus. Point Pinos Junco.

This species has been described by Mr. Leverett M. Loomis since the return of the expedition. Juncos which were seen at Monterey by Dr. Merriam and Mr. Bailey undoubtedly belong to this species.

Amphispiza bilineata. Black-throated Sparrow.

The black-throated desert sparrow is one of the most abundant and characteristic birds of the Lower Sonoran zone, in which it breeds abundantly. The writer first observed the species in the Funeral Mountains, at the summit of Furnace Creek Cañon, on March 22, while on the return trip to Death Valley from Ash Meadows, Nevada. The four or five males which were seen evidently had just arrived, as Mr. Bailey and Mr. Nelson, who had passed over the same route a few days before, saw none. The bird was common on both slopes of the Panamint Mountains, in Johnson and Surprise cañons, during the first three weeks of April, where it was in full song most of the time. It was common in the Argus range from the valley to the summit. In Coso Valley, below Maturango Spring, Mr. Palmer and the writer found several nests. On May 12 two were discovered, one containing three young and the other four eggs, and on May 13 a nest was found just completed. In the Coso Mountains this sparrow was common, and its nest was found in various kinds of bushes, though the branching cactus (*Opuntia echinocarpa*) seemed to be the most common site. A nest containing eggs was found near the road between Darwin and Keeler as late as May 30.

When Mr. Bailey and the writer returned to Death Valley in the latter part of June, they did not find this bird in the valley proper, but found it a few hundred feet above, in Death Valley Cañon, and all through the Panamint Mountains. The same observers found it common both on the east and west slope of Walker Pass, in the Sierra Nevada, on July 1-3, and the former saw several on the South Fork of the Kern River July 3-10.

Dr. Merriam furnishes the following notes on the species as observed by him on the trip to and from St. George, Utah: "In California it was common on the Mohave Desert, between the mouth of Cajon Pass and Pilot Knob, in the early part of April; and at the west end of the desert (Antelope Valley) June 27, and was found also near Lone Willow Spring, in Windy Gap, in Death Valley, in Emigrant Cañon, and in Leach Point Valley. In Owens Valley, California, it was common in the Lower Sonoran zone where it ranges north on the east side of the valley as far as Alvord, and was found in Deep Spring Valley, Nevada (June 9). In Nevada it was common also in Pahrump Valley (the commonest sparrow April 29), in Vegas Valley, at the Great Bend of the Colorado (where a nest containing two fresh eggs was collected May 4), along the Virgin River Valley (nests containing fresh eggs found at Bunkerville early in May), in Desert Valley just east of the Pahroc Mountains (May 20), on the plain below Pahroc Spring (May 22), in Pahranagat

Valley (May 22-26), in Indian Spring Valley, where a nest containing three eggs was found in a bush of *Atriplex canescens* May 28, and at the extreme west end of this valley, where it slopes down toward the Amargosa Desert, young just able to fly were secured May 29. It was tolerably common on the Amargosa Desert, but rare in Oasis Valley (one seen June 1). On Sarcobatus Flat, at the mouth of Grapevine Cañon, a few were seen June 2, and a few were seen on both sides of Gold Mountain (where young nearly full-grown were secured June 3). It was common in Tule Cañon, at the extreme north end of the northwest arm of Death Valley, June 4, though it does not reach the sage plain of the Mount Magruder plateau. It reappears, however, a short distance below Pigeon Spring on the northwestern slope of Mount Magruder, and ranges thence across Fish Lake Valley (June 8). In southwestern Utah it was found on both slopes of the Beaverdam Mountains, ranging up into the junipers slightly above the upper limit of the lower division of the Lower Sonoran zone. In the Lower Santa Clara Valley, Utah, it is abundant, breeding in the greasewood bushes (*Atriplex*) and in the branching cactuses (*Opuntia echinocarpa*), where several nests were found containing two or three fresh eggs each (May 11-15)."

Mr. Nelson found it breeding from the middle of the sage brush belt on the slopes of the Panamint, Grapevine, Inyo, and White mountains, down into Panamint, Mesquite, Saline, and Owens valleys. Mr. Stephens found it common near the lower end of the Argus Range, at Borax Flat, April 28-30; and in Owens Valley, at Little Owens Lake, May 6-11; at Haway Meadows, May 12-14; at Olancha, May 16-23; at Morans, July 4-7, and at Benton July 9-10.

Record of specimens collected of Amphispiza bilineata.

Collectors' No.	Sex.	Locality.	Date.	Collector.	Remark.
162	♂	Panamint Mountains, Calif	Apr. 15, 1891	A. K. Fisher	Surprise Cañon.
171	♀	......do......	Apr. 20, 1891	....do............	Do.
189	♀	Argus Range, Calif	Apr. 27, 1891	....do............	
352	♂	Owens Valley, Calif	June 11, 1891	....do............	Lone Pine.
	♀	Coso Valley, Calif	May 11, 1891	T. S. Palmer	Nest and 4 eggs.
	♂ im.	Owens Valley, Calif	June 9, 1891	....do............	Lone Pine.
127	♀ juv.	......do......	July 6, 1891	F. Stephens	Morans.
	♀ juv.	Amargosa Desert, Nev	May 29, 1891	V. Bailey	
	juv.	Gold Mountain, Nev	June 3, 1891	C. Hart Merriam	
	♂ juv.	Mount Magruder, Nev	June 4, 1891	....do............	

Amphispiza belli. Bell's Sparrow.

Mr. Nelson found Bell's sparrow abundant in the bushes of the arid district bordering the southern and western sides of Buena Vista Lake, in San Joaquin Valley, during October.

Amphispiza belli nevadensis. Sage Sparrow.

The sage sparrow is one of the few birds characteristic of the sage plains of the Upper Sonoran and Transition zones, but does not breed in the Lower Sonoran zone, though it winters in this zone and passes through it in great numbers during migration.

In winter it was common along the entire route of the expedition. It was seen at Cajon Pass in the San Bernardino Mountains, January 2, and on the Mohave Desert, at Hesperia, in flocks of from ten to twenty, January 4-5; at Victor, Stoddard Wells, and Daggett, January 6-10; at Granite Wells, January 13-15; at Lone Willow Spring, January 15-19. It was found in Death Valley from the lower end to Furnace Creek, January 21 to February 4; at Resting Springs, February 6-17, and at Ash Meadows, Nevada, the first three weeks in March.

Mr. Stephens found it common in Oasis Valley, Nevada, March 15-19; not common at Grapevine Spring, California, April 1-4; and Mr. Nelson found it everywhere common in Pahrump Valley about the ranch, and along the route down through Vegas Valley and Wash, to the Bend of the Colorado, March 3-16. Dr. Merriam saw a few in tree yuccas on the Mohave Desert near the mouth of Cajon Pass, March 30, and a number near Daggett, April 4-6. He noted the species at Windy Gap, April 7; in Death Valley, near Bennett Wells, April 9-12; in Mesquite Valley, April 13; Emigrant Cañon, in the Panamint Mountains, April 14 and 15, and found it common in Perognathus Flat, April 15. Perognathus Flat is a high basin in the Panamint Mountains, at the lower edge of the Upper Sonoran zone, and the species may remain there to breed. At the mouth of Johnson Cañon, in the Panamint Mountains, the writer saw this species March 25, and Mr. Bailey saw one in Wild Rose Cañon, near the 'charcoal kilns,' in the same mountains, June 25. At Hot Springs, in Panamint Valley, a few were seen in *Atriplex* bushes by Dr. Merriam, April 19-24, and one was seen at Leach Point Spring, April 25. He did not find it in the Lower Santa Clara Valley near St. George, Utah, but met with it in great abundance in passing north from this valley towards the Escalante Desert. It was one of the most characteristic birds at the upper Santa Clara Crossing, Utah, May 17, thence northward through Mountain Meadows to the Escalante Desert and Shoal Creek, and westerly across the low rolling plateau of the Juniper Mountains to Meadow Creek Valley, Nevada. It was common also in Desert Valley, Nevada, and in the neighboring Pahroc Mountains, May 20-21. A few were seen in the sage plain on Mount Magruder plateau, Nevada, June 5, and in the sage brush in Owens Valley, June 10-19. In this valley Mr. Stephens found it not common at Ash Creek, May 30-June 3; at Morans, July 4-7; and common at Olancha toward the mountains and breeding; at Independence Creek, June 18-23; at Benton, July 9-10; and was seen at Bishop Creek, August 4-10. Mr. Nelson found it common at the head of Owens River the latter part of July; on both slopes of the Inyo Mountains, from the valleys up to the middle or upper part of the piñon belt, June 24-July 4; and common in the White Mountains, up to the middle of the same belt. He did not find it in the north end of the Panamint Mountains nor in Saline Valley, but noted it on the eastern slope of the Panamint Mountains, in Cottonwood Creek, and thence down to Mesquite Valley, and also in the Grapevine Mountains, May 4 to June 15. Mr. Nelson reported the sage sparrow as very common along the route from Lone Pine to Keeler, and through the Coso and Panamint valleys to Lone Willow Spring, and thence to Death Valley, during December 1890, and January 1891.

The specimens collected along the east slope of the Sierra Nevada in Owens Valley are almost intermediate, both in size and color, between *Amphispiza belli* and *Amphispiza belli nevadensis*.

Record of specimens collected of Amphispiza belli nevadensis.

Collector's No.	Sex.	Locality.	Date.	Collector.	Remarks.
35	♂	Hesperia, Calif	Jan. 4, 1891	A. K. Fisher	Mohave Desert.
36	♂	do	do	do	Do.
42	♀	Victor, Calif	Jan. 6, 1891	do	Do.
43	♂	Stoddard Wells, Calif	Jan. 7, 1891	do	Do.
46	♀	Daggett, Calif	Jan. 9, 1891	do	Do.
47		do	do	do	Do.
2	♂	do	Feb. 6, 1891	F. Stephens	Do.
3	♂	do	do	do	Do.
4	♂	do	Feb. 7, 1891	do	Do.
5	♂	do	do	do	Do.
10	♂	do	Feb. 8, 1891	do	Do.
11	♀	do	do	do	Do.
58	♂	Granite Wells, Calif	Jan. 13, 1891	A. K. Fisher	Do.
63	♀	Lone Willow Spring, Calif	Jan. 16, 1891	do	
66		Death Valley, Calif	Jan. 21, 1891	do	Furnace Creek.
80		do	Jan. 27, 1891	do	Do.
112	♂ ad.	Resting Springs, Calif	Feb. 17, 1891	do	
27	♀	12-mile Spring Calif	Feb. 21, 1891	F. Stephens	North of Resting Springs.
	♂	Mountain Meadows, Utah	May 17, 1891	V. Bailey	
331	♂ ad.	Owens Valley, Calif	June 11, 1891	A. K. Fisher	Lone Pine.
52	♂	Salt Wells Valley, Calif	May 1, 1891	F. Stephens	
84	♂	Owens Valley, Calif	June 10, 1891	do	Olancha.
96	♂	do	June 13, 1891	do	Do.
97	♀	do	do	do	Do.
98	♀	do	do	do	Do.
99	♀	do	do	do	Do.
	im.	Sierra Nevada, Calif	Aug. 20, 1891	V. Bailey	Whitney Meadows.

Peucæa cassini. Cassin's Sparrow.

The only specimen of this species noted during the entire expedition was shot by Dr. Merriam in Timpahute Valley, Nevada, May 26. It was an old male in worn breeding plumage, and attracted his attention by flying up from the desert brush and singing in the air.

Peucæa ruficeps. Rufous-crowned Sparrow.

An immature specimen of this sparrow was secured on a rocky hillside on the South Fork of Kern River, California, July 8. Mr. Palmer saw one on the west fork of Castac Cañon June 30, and Mr. Stephens saw several migrants in Reche Cañon, near San Bernardino, Calif., September 22-24. These are all the records we have of the species.

Melospiza fasciata fallax. Desert Song Sparrow.

The writer did not meet with this race, and quotes the following from Dr. Merriam's notes:

"The desert song sparrow was not found anywhere in California, but was common in suitable valleys in southeastern Nevada, southwestern Utah, and northwestern Arizona. It was found in the valley of the Muddy near St. Joe, Nev., May 7, and was a common breeder in Pahranagat Valley, Nevada, May 23. A specimen was shot and others seen at the mouth of Beaverdam Creek, Arizona, May 9, and it was common in the Lower Santa Clara Valley near the junction of the Santa Clara and Virgin, May 11-15, where a nest was found near a marshy meadow."

Record of specimens collected of Melospiza fasciata fallax.

Collector's No.	Sex.	Locality.	Date.	Collector.	Remarks.
	♂	Pahranagat Valley, Nev	May 23, 1891	C. Hart Merriam.	
	♂	Beaverdam, Ariz	May 9, 1891	....do	

Melospiza fasciata montana. Mountain Song Sparrow.

This song sparrow was tolerably common about the ranch at Furnace Creek, and among the reeds at Saratoga Springs, in Death Valley, in January, but was not seen at the former place in June. It was quite common at Resting Springs in the Amargosa Desert, February 6-17, and at Ash Meadows, Nevada, in March. Mr. Nelson found it common along the willow-grown banks of the ditches in Pahrump and Vegas valleys, and Mr. Stephens found it rather common in the lower end of Oasis valleys, March 15-19. Mr. Bailey reported it abundant at St. George, Utah, in January, 1889.

Record of specimens collected of Melospiza fasciata montana.

Collector's No.	Sex.	Locality.	Date.	Collector.	Remarks.
	♂	Death Valley, Calif	Feb. 3, 1891	E. W. Nelson	Saratoga Springs.
78	♂	......do	Jan. 25, 1891	A. K. Fisher	Furnace Creek.
117	♂	Ash Meadows, Nev	Mar. 4, 1891	....do	
118	♀	......do	Mar. 9, 1891	....do	
128	♀	......do	Mar. 15, 1891	....do	
33	♀	Oasis Valley, Nev	Mar. 16, 1891	F. Stephens	
34	♀	......do	....do	....do	
	♂	Pahrump Valley, Nev	Mar. 4, 1891	E. W. Nelson	
	♂	......do	....do	....do	
	♀	Vegas Valley, Nev	Mar. 12, 1891	....do	

Melospiza fasciata heermanni. Heermann's Song Sparrow.

This Californian subspecies was quite common at San Bernardino, where it was singing in the brush along streams, December 28-29, 1890. It was tolerably common in suitable localities in Owens Valley, along the South Fork of Kern River, July 3-10, and was heard singing at Kernville July 11-13. At Walker Basin it was seen along the sloughs, July 13-16, and at Bakersfield it was common along the river bottom, July 17-20. Mr. Palmer found it common near Old Fort Tejon early in July; Mr. Nelson observed it commonly in the Cañada de las Uvas and in San Emigdio Cañon the last of October; and along the route from La Panza to San Luis Obispo, October 28 to November 3.

Record of specimens collected of Melospiza fasciata heermanni.

Collector's No.	Sex.	Locality.	Date.	Collector.	Remarks.
5	♂	San Bernardino, Calif	Dec. 28, 1890	A. K. Fisher	
	♀	San Emigdio Cañon, Calif	Oct. 22, 1891	E. W. Nelson	
396	♀ ad	Bakersfield, Calif	July 19, 1891	A. K. Fisher	
378	♀ im	Kern River, Calif	July 5, 1891	....do	25 miles above Kernville.
	♂ Im	......do	July 4, 1891	V. Bailey	Do.
119	♂	Owens Valley, Calif	July 26, 1891	F. Stephens	Alvord.
67	♂	......do	May 30, 1891	....do	Ash Creek.
295	♂	......do	June 5, 1891	A. K. Fisher	Lone Pine.
302	♂	......do	June 6, 1891	....do	Do.
321	♂	......do	June 9, 1891	....do	Do.

Melospiza fasciata guttata. Rusty Song Sparrow.

Mr. Bailey secured a specimen of this song sparrow at Santa Clara, Utah, January 13, 1889. It was undoubtedly an accidental straggler from the northwest coast.

Melospiza fasciata rufina Sooty Song Sparrow.

Mr. Bailey took a specimen of this subspecies at Boulder Creek, California, on October 13, 1891, and stated that it was common there.

Melospiza fasciata graminea. Santa Barbara Song Sparrow.

Specimens of this new race, indistinguishable from Mr. Townsend's type, were taken by Mr. Nelson at Morro and Carpenteria, Calif. He found them common near the streams and wet places along the coast, and a few as far inland as Santa Paula. Whether it is a resident or a migrant from the Santa Barbara Islands, can not be decided at present.

Record of specimens collected of Melospiza fasciata graminea.

Collector's No.	Sex.	Locality.	Date.	Collector.	Remarks.
	♂	Carpenteria, Calif	Dec. 18, 1891	E. W. Nelson	
	♀	......do	....do	....do	
	♀	Morro, Calif	Nov. 8, 1891	....do	

Melospiza lincolni. Lincoln's Sparrow.

A few Lincoln's sparrows were seen at Ash Meadows, Nevada, and Mr. Nelson found it common in wet places among bushes at Vegas ranch and in Vegas Wash in March, where Dr. Merriam again saw it May 1. It was not uncommon in Johnson and Suprise cañons in the Panamint Range, April 1–20. The species was common at Hot Springs in Panamint Valley, April 20–23, and a few were seen in Shepherd Cañon, in the Argus Range, the last of April. Mr. Stephens found it breeding, but not commonly, at Independence Creek, June 18-23, and the writer saw several in the high grass at Horse Corral Meadows, August 9-13. Mr. Belding found a pair breeding in the meadow at Crockers, near the Yosemite Valley, in May, and Mr. Bailey saw a few at Monterey, September 28 to October 9.

Record of specimens collected of Melospiza lincolni.

Collector's No.	Sex.	Locality.	Date.	Collector.	Remarks.
154	♀	Panamint Mountains, Calif.	Mar. 27, 1891	E. W. Nelson	Johnson Cañon.
	♀	......do......	Apr. 11, 1891	A. K. Fisher	Do.
175	♀	Panamint Valley, Calif.	Apr. 21, 1891	....do......	Hot Springs.
177	♂	......do......	Apr. 22, 1891	....do......	Do.
117	♀	Sierra Nevada, Calif.	June 22, 1891	F. Stephens	

Passerella iliaca unalaschcensis. Townsend's Sparrow.

Townsend's sparrow was not uncommon in Cajon Pass in the San Bernardino Mountains January 2. It was not reported again until Mr. Bailey found it common at Monterey, September 28 to October 9. Mr. Nelson found it common and generally distributed wherever thickets occurred along the coast from San Simeon to Carpenteria, November 4 to December 18.

Record of specimens collected of Passerella iliaca unalaschcensis.

Collector's No.	Sex.	Locality.	Date.	Collector.	Remarks.
21	♂	Cajon Pass, Calif.	Jan. 2, 1891	A. K. Fisher	
		Morro, Calif.	Nov. 8, 1891	E. W. Nelson	

Passerella iliaca megarhyncha. Thick-billed Sparrow.

The thick-billed sparrow was found commonly in a number of places in the High Sierra. Mr. Nelson reported it as rather common at the head of Owens River, and on the western slope, in July and August. Mr. Stephens saw it among the thickets at Menache Meadows May 24-26; found it common at Independence Creek, where young were taken June 20; and at the lake on Bishop Creek August 4-10. In the Sequoia National Park it was common, and several broods of young just able to fly were seen the first week in August. On the East Fork of the Kaweah River Mr. Bailey found it breeding from the lower edge of the conifers up to where *Pinus monticola* grows. It was seen at Horse Corral Meadows, August 9-13; at Whitney Meadows and Soda Springs or Kern River Lakes, the last of August; at Mineral King, September 8-11, and on the brushy hillsides about the Cañada de las Uvas and San Emigdio, October 14-28.

Record of specimens collected of Passerella iliaca megarhyncha.

Collector's No.	Sex.	Locality.	Date.	Collector.	Remarks.
64	♀	Sierra Nevada, Calif..	May 27, 1891	F. Stephens....	Summit Meadow, near Olancha Peak.
108	♀	......do..............	June 20, 1891	......do.........	Independence Creek.
	♀ im.	......do..............	July 30, 1891	V. Bailey........	East Fork of Kaweah River.
407	♂	......do..............	Aug. 6, 1891	A. K. Fisher.....	Sequoia National Park.
411	♂ im.	......do..............	Aug. 11, 1891	......do.........	Horse Corral Meadows.

Passerella iliaca schistacea. Slate-colored Sparrow.

The slate-colored sparrow was not uncommon, according, to Mr. Nelson, about the heads of streams on the eastern slope of the White Mountains, where a specimen was taken, July 14. A few were seen in Johnson and Surprise cañons, in the Panamint Mountains, where a specimen was taken in the former cañon, March 28. This sparrow was not detected elsewhere by members of the expedition.

Record of specimens collected of Passerella iliaca schistacea.

Collector's No.	Sex.	Locality.	Date.	Collector.	Remarks.
	♀	Panamint Mountains, Calif....	Mar. 28, 1891	E. W. Nelson......	Johnson Cañon.
	♂	White Mountains, Calif.........	July 14, 1891	......do...........	

Pipilo maculatus megalonyx. Spurred Towhee.

The spurred towhee is common over much of the Great Basin, and also in California west of the Sierra Nevada. Mr. Nelson reported it as common among the junipers on the Charleston Mountains in the early part of March. A pair was seen in one of the cañons in the Coso Mountains, May 23, and subsequently Mr. Palmer saw others in the brush along the streams. Mr. Nelson found a few at Lone Pine in Owens Valley, in December, 1890, and the writer saw a few in the brush along the river at the same place, June 11. Dr. Merriam found it common in the northern part of the valley on the latter date. Mr. Stephens reported it as common in the lower part of the cañon at Independence Creek, where young were seen June 18–23; as not common among the piñons at Benton, July 9–10; he also saw three at Bishop Creek, August 4–10. In the Panamint Mountains, Mr. Nelson saw it in Surprise Cañon in December, 1890, and found it sparingly in the vicinity of water, where thickets of willows and rose bushes afforded it shelter, in both this range and the Grapevine Mountains during the latter part of May and the first of June. The same observer found a few in the Inyo Mountains among the piñons at Hunter's arastra, and again in willows bordering the creek near Waucoba Peak, the latter part of June; found it rather common on the west slope of the Sierra, mainly along streams; and found a few in the upper parts of the streams in the White Mountains.

In Nevada, Dr. Merriam found it in the following localities: At Mountain Spring in the Charleston Mountains, April 30; in the Juniper Mountains May 19, where it was common throughout the scrub oak and juniper down to the very edge of Meadow Creek Valley near Panaca; at Tule Cañon and on Mount Magruder, where it was abundant and a full-fledged young was shot, June 5. In Utah, he found it common among the junipers on the Beaverdam Mountains, May 11, and saw a number between the Upper Santa Clara Crossing and Mountain Meadows, in thickets of *Amelanchier* and scrub oak, May 17.

On the western slope of Walker Pass, in California, it was common July 2 and 3; along the South Fork of the Kern, July 3–10; on the hillsides in chaparral at Walker Basin, July 13–16; and at Bakersfield in the San Joaquin Valley, July 17–20.

Mr. Bailey reported it as common below the conifers on the Kaweah River the last of July, and Dr. Merriam found it common in the Granite Range in western San Diego County, July 1–10.

Record of specimens collected of Pipilo maculatus megalonyx.

Collector's No.	Sex.	Locality.	Date.	Collector.	Remarks.
	♂	Mountain Meadows, Utah	May 17, 1891	C. Hart Merriam	
	♂	Charleston Mountains, Nev	Mar. 7, 1891	V. Bailey	
	im.	Mount Magruder, Nev	June 5, 1891	...do	
36	♂	Grapevine Mountains, Nev	Mar. 21, 1891	F. Stephens	
329	♂ ad.	Lone Pine, Calif	June 11, 1891	A. K. Fisher	Owens Valley.
374	♂ im.	Kern River, Calif	July 5, 1891	...do	South Fork.

Pipilo maculatus oregonus. Oregon Towhee.

Mr. Nelson found the Oregon towhee sparingly along the coast of California from La Panza to San Luis Obispo the last of October; between San Simeon and Carpenteria November 4 to December 18, and common between the latter place and Santa Paula December 18 to January 4.

Pipilo chlorurus. Green-tailed Towhee.

The green-tailed towhee is a common summer resident in the mountain ranges visited by of the expedition. It was first observed in Johnson Cañon on the east slope of the Panamint Mountains, April 12, but was not seen in Surprise Cañon on the west slope during the following fortnight. In May and June Mr. Nelson found it common among the sage brush on the Panamint and Grapevine mountains, where it was associated with Brewer's sparrow. It was most numerous among the rank growth of vegetation along small streams and about springs, though it was not uncommon on the high benches among the *Artemisia tridentata*. On Willow Creek, May 24, he found a nest containing four eggs which was placed in a sage bush 15 inches from the ground. It was composed externally of rather coarse plant stems, and lined with fine fibrous rootlets and horsehair. On the north slope of

Telescope Peak, it was common as high as the upper limit of the sage brush, June 22-25.

In the Argus Range, it was common in Shepherd Cañon, where numbers were migrating the last week in April, and at Maturango Spring among the willows and other vegetation at the spring the first two weeks in May. Among the Coso Mountains it was very common along the streams and on the slopes among the sage and piñons, where the males often were heard singing from their perches on the tops of some dead brush or trees, the latter part of May. Dr. Merriam saw it on the northward continuation of the Kingston Range, between the Amargosa Desert, California, and Pahrump Valley, Nevada. He found it also in the following localities in Nevada: Tolerably common in the Charleston Mountains, April 30; at the Bend of the Colorado, May 4; very abundant on Mount Magruder, where it was breeding from the upper part of Tule Cañon up to 2,600 meters (8,500 feet) or higher, and where a dozen or more were often seen at one time, singing from the tops of sage brush and nut pines, and they were heard singing several times at night; a few were seen in the Juniper Mountains, May 19; in the Beaverdam Mountains, Utah, he found them tolerably common among the junipers, May 10-11, and in the Santa Clara Valley, Utah, May 11-15.

Mr. Nelson found the species from among the piñons up to the summit in the Inyo Mountains the latter part of June, and in the White Mountains and on the plateau at the head of Owens Valley, in July. Along the eastern slope of the Sierra Nevada it was common at the head of Owens River the last of July; at Independence Creek, where a nest containing two eggs just ready to hatch was found at the Rex Monte mill, June 18-23; at Bishop Creek, August 4-10; not common at Benton, July 9-10; and at Menache Meadows where it occurred nearly to timber line, May 24-26. The species was seen at Walker Pass, July 2; at Soda Springs or Kern River Lakes, September 3; and was common in the Sequoia National Park, during the first week of August; and in the vicinity of Mineral King, the last of August and 1st of September. Mr. Dutcher saw a few at Big Cottonwood Meadows during the summer, and Mr. Palmer found it common on Frazier Mountain among the pines, July 9, and in Tejon Pass, July 12.

Record of specimens collected of Pipilo chlorurus.

Collector's No.	Sex.	Locality.	Date.	Collector.	Remarks.
186	♂	Argus Range, Calif.	Apr. 27, 1891	A. K. Fisher	Shepherd Cañon.
230	♂	...do...	May 12, 1891	...do...	Maturango Spring.
258	♂	Coso Mountains, Calif.	May 27, 1891	...do...	
110	♀	Owens Valley, Calif.	June 20, 1891	F. Stephens	Independence Creek.
134	♂	White Mountains, Nev.	July 14, 1891	...do...	Queen mine.

Pipilo fuscus mesoleucus. Cañon Towhee.

Mr. Bailey found the cañon towhee abundant among the hills at Mineral Park, in western Arizona, during the middle of February, 1889, and later in the same month saw a few near Fort Mohave.

Pipilo fuscus crissalis. California Towhee.

The California towhee was common among the chaparral in a number of localities west of the Sierra Nevada. At Cajon Pass, in the San Bernardino Mountains, it was very common from the lower part of the valley, well up on the divide among the oaks, January 2–3, and Dr. Merriam found it abundant at the same place, March 29–30. It was common on the western slope of Walker Pass, July 2–3; along the valley of the Kern River, July 3–13, and abundant in Walker Basin, July 13–16. Mr. Palmer reported it as abundant at Old Fort Tejon in July; Mr. Stephens at Reche Cañon, September 22–24, and Mr. Nelson as very abundant in the western foothills of the Sierra Nevada in August. It was common at Three Rivers, July 25–30, and September 12–15, and Mr. Bailey noted it along the East Fork of the Kaweah River nearly up to the lower edge of the pines. The same observer found it common at Monterey the first week in October; Mr. Nelson reported it as abundant among the brush along the western edge of the San Joaquin Valley in October, and along the coast from San Simeon to Carpenteria and Santa Paula in November and December.

Record of specimens collected of Pipilo fuscus crissalis.

Collector's No.	Sex.	Locality.	Date.	Collector.	Remarks.
15	♀	San Bernardino, Calif.	Jan. 1, 1891	A. K. Fisher	
18	♂	......do............	...do...	...do......	
49	♂	Argus Range, Calif.	Apr. 25, 1891	F. Stephens	Searl's Garden.
364	♀ ad.	Walker Pass, Calif.	July 2, 1891	A. K. Fisher	
	Im.	......do............	July 3, 1891	V. Bailey	
	♀ im.	......do............	...do...	...do......	
372	♂ ad.	Kern River, Calif.	July 4, 1891	A. K. Fisher	South Fork.
	♂	Ventura River, Calif.	Dec. 20, 1891	E. W. Nelson	

Pipilo aberti. Abert's Towhee.

The westernmost locality at which Dr. Merriam and Mr. Bailey saw Abert's towhee is the Bend of the Colorado River, in Nevada, where it was common, and a full grown young was secured, May 4. Thence northward they found it common in the valleys of the Virgin and lower Muddy, May 6–8, where Beaverdam Creek joins the Virgin in northwestern Arizona, May 9–10, and in the Lower Santa Clara Valley, Utah, near St. George, May 11–15, where it was breeding commonly.

Habia melanocephala. Black-headed Grosbeak.

The black-headed grosbeak was first observed in Shepherd Cañon in the Argus Range, where a specimen was secured April 26. A week later it was common among the willow patches at Maturango Spring and among the tree yuccas at the western base of the range. In the Coso Mountains several were seen in the cañons during the latter part of May. Mr. Nelson found it a common breeding bird both in the Panamint and Grapevine mountains, and the writer saw a fine male in full song at the 'charcoal kilns' in Wild Rose Cañon, north of Telescope Peak, June 23. In Owens Valley Mr. Stephens found it rather common at Olancha, May 16-23; not common at Ash Creek, May 30 to June 3, and saw one male at Independence Creek, June 18-23. Mr. Nelson found it sparingly among the willows in the Inyo Mountains, June 24 to July 5, and along the western slope of the Sierra Nevada in August. Mr. Bailey reported this grosbeak as common among the pines along the East Fork of the Kaweah River, July 25 to August 10. It was observed on the western slope of Walker Pass, June 21; was common in Kern Valley, June 22-23 and July 3-10; on the ridge above Walker Basin, July 14; in the Sierra Liebre, June 30; and in Cañada de las Uvas, June 28-29.

In Nevada Dr. Merriam found a pair breeding in a thicket near Log Spring on Mount Magruder, June 8; saw it in Oasis Valley, June 1; in the valley of the Virgin near Bunkerville, May 8; and found it common in Pahranagat Valley, where it was singing in the tall cottonwoods, May 22-26. In Utah he found it breeding plentifully along the Lower Santa Clara River, May 11-15.

Record of specimens collected of Habia melanocephala.

Collector's No.	Sex.	Locality.	Date.	Collector.	Remarks.
184	♂	Argus Range, Calif	Apr. 26, 1891	A. K. Fisher	Shepherd Cañon.
240	♂	......do......	May 14, 1891	......do......	Maturango Spring.
	♀	......do......	May 15, 1891	T. S. Palmer	Do.

Guiraca cærulea eurhyncha. Western Blue Grosbeak.

The blue grosbeak is tolerably common in many of the valleys of California and Nevada. In Nevada, Dr. Merriam found it breeding commonly in Pahranagat Valley, May 22-26, and along the Lower Muddy and Virgin rivers, May 7 and 8. He saw several where Beaverdam Creek joins the Virgin River in northwestern Arizona, May 9-10, and found the species common in the Lower Santa Clara Valley, Utah, May 11-15. Several were seen in the Cañada de las Uvas, California, June 28-29. At Lone Pine, in Owens Valley, it was quite common among the fruit orchards and thick growth along streams, where two young just out of the nest were secured, June 14. Mr. Stephens found it more or less common in the same valley, at Olancha, May 16-23; Ash Creek, May 30 to June 3; Alvord, June 26-28; and at Morans, July 4-7. Mr. Bailey secured an adult male at Furnace Creek ranch, Death Valley, June 19, and Mr. Nelson saw the species in Saline Valley the latter part of the same month. Blue grosbeaks were very common along the South Fork of the Kern, where they frequented the oat fields and the thick vegetation in the river bottoms, July 3-10. They were also common at Kernville, July 11-13; at Walker Basin, July 13-16; and at Bakersfield in the San Joaquin Valley, July 17-20.

Record of specimens collected of Guiraca caerulea eurhyncha.

Collector's No.	Sex.	Locality.	Date.	Collector.	Remarks.
	♂	St. George, Utah	May 14, 1891	V. Bailey	
	♀	Beaverdam, Ariz	May 9, 1891	...do	
	♂	Bunkerville, Nev	May 8, 1891	C. Hart Merriam	
	♂	Death Valley, Calif	June 19, 1891	V. Bailey	Furnace Creek.
	♂	Owens Valley, Calif	June 5, 1891	T. S. Palmer	Lone Pine.
313	♂	......do	June 7, 1891	A. K. Fisher	Do.
316	♂	......do	June 8, 1891	...do	Do.
338	♀ juv	......do	June 14, 1891	...do	Do.
339	♀ juv	......do	...do	...do	Do.
66	♂	......do	May 30, 1891	F. Stephens	Ash Creek.
85	♀	......do	June 11, 1891	...do	Olancha.
93	♂	......do	June 12, 1891	...do	Do.
104	♀	......do	June 15, 1891	...do	Do.
121	♂	......do	June 27, 1891	...do	Alvord.
373	♂	Kern River, Calif	July 4, 1891	A. K. Fisher	South Fork.
379	♂ ad	......do	July 5, 1891	...do	Do.
384	♂ ad	......do	July 10, 1891	...do	Do.

Passerina amœna. Lazuli Bunting.

The lazuli bunting is a common breeder in many places in the Great Basin wherever there is sufficient water to produce a growth of willow or other thickets suitable for nesting sites.

In Nevada, Dr. Merriam found it breeding commonly on Mount Magruder, and in the thickets in Tule Cañon, June 4-8; in Pahranagat Valley, May 22-26, and saw a few in the Juniper Mountains, May 18, and in Oasis Valley, June 1. He found it common at the Bend of the Colorado, May 4, and at a few points in the valleys of the Muddy and Virgin rivers, May 7-8. In the Santa Clara Valley, Utah, it was an abundant breeder, May 11-15.

The writer first met with the species at Coso, Calif., where a male was secured May 25. At Furnace Creek, Death Valley, a female was secured in the brush near the ranch, June 19, and the species was common in Wild Rose Cañon in the Panamint Mountains, June 24 and 25. Mr. Nelson found it common in both the Panamint and Grapevine mountains, wherever willow thickets occurred. It was nesting in Mill Creek, Willow Creek, and Cottonwood cañons in the former, and in Wood Cañon in the latter range of mountains. The same observer found it from the bottom of the valley up to the piñons in the Inyo Mountains; at the head of Owens Valley, near the White Mountains, and along borders of streams from the foothills up to 2,450 meters (8,000 feet) altitude at the head of Owens River. In Owens Valley it was common about the orchards at Lone Pine in June; and Mr. Stephens saw several at

Olancha, May 16-23; found it common at Ash Creek, May 30-June 3; at Morans, July 4-7; abundant in the lower part of the cañon of Independence Creek, June 18-23; not common at Alvord, June 26-28; at Benton, July 9-10; at Queen station in the White Mountains, Nev., June 11-16; and saw a male at about 2,450 meters (8,000 feet) altitude, at Bishop Creek, August 4-10. Mr. Palmer secured a specimen at Horse Corral Meadows, August 11, and saw another in Kings River Cañon, August 15; and Mr. Bailey saw two at 2,450 meters (8,000 feet) altitude on the Kaweah River, about the same time. Mr. Palmer found it common at Old Fort Tejon, where a nest containing three fresh eggs was found in a willow tree 6 feet from the ground, July 4. The species was common along the valley of the Kern, July 3-13; at Walker Basin, July 13-16; and at Bakersfield in the San Joaquin Valley, July 17-20.

Record of specimens collected of Passerina amœna.

Collector's No.	Sex.	Locality.	Date.	Collector.	Remarks.
256	♂	Coso, Coso Mountains, Calif.	May 25, 1891	A. K. Fisher	
301	♂	Owens Valley, Calif	June 6, 1891	....do	Lone Pine.
241	♀	Death Valley, Calif	June 19, 1891	....do	Furnace Creek.

Calamospiza melanocorys. Lark Bunting.

A few miles north of Pilot Knob on the Mohave Desert, California, a lark bunting was killed by Mr. F. W. Koch April 6, and two others were seen by Dr. Merriam. One was shot in Pahrump Valley, Nevada, April 29, by Mr. Bailey. No others were observed by any members of the expedition.

Piranga ludoviciana. Western Tanager.

The western tanager was found commonly in many places during migration, and sparingly during the breeding season. The first individual observed was secured by Dr. Merriam in Surprise Cañon in the Panamint Mountains, California, April 23. When first seen it was in hot pursuit of a large beetle, which it failed to capture. At Maturango Spring in the Argus Range, a large flight of these tanagers occurred on May 4, where as many as a dozen males were seen at one time. From this date until the time of leaving, the middle of May, it was common among the willows in the vicinity of the spring. In the Coso Mountains a pair was seen near the top of the ridge, where they were evidently hunting for a nesting site, May 23. Mr. Nelson found it a rather common breeding species among the piñons on Willow Creek in the Panamint Mountains, and also in Mill Creek and Cottonwood cañons, though in smaller numbers, during the last of May. He saw none in the Grapevine Mountains.

Dr. Merriam saw two males of this species and one hepatic tanager in a tall cottonwood at the point where Beaverdam Creek joins the Virgin

River, in northwestern Arizona, May 9. He saw many males in the Lower Santa Clara Valley, Utah, May 11-14; six males in the Juniper Mountains, Nevada, May 18, and several in Pahranagat Valley, May 22-26.

At Keeler, early in June, an individual alighted for a few moments on the wagon during a gale. In the same valley a few were seen and two secured at Lone Pine, June 6-8; Mr. Stephens reported it a rather common migrant at Olancha May 16-23; not common at Bishop August 4-10, and rather common at Menache Meadows May 24-26. Mr. Nelson found it at the head of Owens River the latter part of July; several were seen among the hills above Walker Basin July 14, and several were observed in the Sequoia National Park during the first week of August. Mr. Palmer saw one in Tejon Pass July 12.

Record of specimens collected of Piranga ludoviciana.

Collector's No.	Sex.	Locality.	Date.	Collector.	Remarks.
	♂	Panamint Mountains, Calif.	Apr. 23, 1891	C. Hart Merriam	Surprise Cañon.
195	♂	Argus Range, Calif.	May 4, 1891	A. K Fisher	Maturango Spring.
220	♂	......do	May 10, 1891	......do	Do.
221	♂	......do	......do	......do	Do.
222	♂	......do	......do	......do	Do.
250	♂	Coso Mountains, Calif.	May 23, 1891	......do	
306	♀	Owens Valley, Calif.	June 6, 1891	......do	Lone Pine.
315	♂	......do	June 8, 1891	......do	
71	♂	......do	June 1, 1891	F. Stephens	Owens Lake.
145	♂	Sierra Nevada, Calif.	July 27, 1891	......do	

Piranga hepatica. Hepatic Tanager.

The only individual of this species observed during the entire season was seen by Dr. Merriam in a cottonwood at the point where Beaverdam Creek empties into the Virgin in northwestern Arizona, May 9. Two adult male western tanagers (*P. ludoviciana*) were in the same tree, and both species were probably migrating.

Progne subis hesperia. Western Martin.

A colony of martins was found breeding at Old Fort Tejon in the Cañada de las Uvas, California, June 28, 1891, by Dr. Merriam and Mr. Palmer. They were nesting in woodpeckers' holes in the large oaks in front of the old fort, where three were killed. Mr. Belding noted the species at Crocker's, 21 miles northwest of the Yosemite Valley, in May.

Record of specimens collected of Progne subis hesperia.

Collector's No.	Sex.	Locality.	Date.	Collector.	Remarks.
	♂ ad.	Old Fort Tejon, Calif.	June 28, 1891.	C. Hart Merriam.	
	♂ im.	......do	......do	......do	
	♂ im.	......do	......do	......do	

Petrochelidon lunifrons. Cliff Swallow.

This widely distributed species was found breeding in various localities visited by the expedition. In Nevada Dr. Merriam found a colony breeding in the cañon at the lower end of Vegas Wash, May 3, and saw several at the Bend of the Colorado, May 4; he found it common in Pahranagat Valley, May 22–26, and in Oasis Valley, June 1. In Utah he saw a colony which was breeding near St. George, in the Lower Santa Clara Valley, where many nests were found on the red sandstone cliffs a mile or two from the settlement.

The cliff swallow was common in Owens Valley, California. It was seen along the edge of the lake at Keeler, May 30–June 4; at the mouth of the cañon above Lone Pine, June 12; and Mr. Stephens found it common at Haway Meadows, May 12–14; abundant at Olancha, May 16–23; at Ash Creek, May 30 to June 3; breeding in the cañon at Benton, July 9–10; and not common at the Queen mine, Nevada, July 11–16. Mr. Nelson saw it on Willow Creek in the Panamint Mountains, the last of May, and found it at the head of Owens River, in the Sierra Nevada, up to 2,100 meters (7,000 feet) altitude. It was common in Kern Valley, July 3–13, and in Walker Basin, July 13–16. At the latter place a number of nests were found fastened against the ceiling and walls of the rooms in several of the deserted buildings. Dr. Merriam found it breeding commonly at Kernville, under the eaves and piazzas of houses, June 23, and in the Cañada de las Uvas, under the eaves of Old Fort Tejon, June 28–29.

At Twin Oaks, in western San Diego County, he was shown a large sycamore tree on the outside of which these swallows used to fasten their nests, and was told that after heavy rains the nests were frequently washed down in great numbers. The species was common at Bakersfield, in the San Joaquin Valley, July 17–20, and Mr. Stephens found it not uncommon at Roche Cañon, near San Bernardino, September 22–24.

Chelidon erythrogaster. Barn Swallow.

The barn swallow was found nowhere common except in Owens Valley, California. It was first seen at Ash Meadows, Nevada, where two were noted, March 19. In the same State, Dr. Merriam saw one at Mount Magruder, June 8; one in Oasis Valley, June 1; a number in Pahranagat Valley, May 22–26, where it was doubtless breeding, and several near Bunkerville, in the Virgin Valley, May 7–8. He saw a single bird near St. George, in the Lower Santa Clara Valley, Utah, about the middle of May.

Mr. Nelson saw it as a migrant on the divide between Panamint and Saline valleys, the last of May, and at the head of Willow Creek, in the Panamint Mountains, about the same time. He saw barn swallows at the head of Owens Valley in the White Mountains, at the head of Owens River, and also in the Yosemite Valley. Mr. Stephens found it common all through Salt Wells and Owens valleys, and the writer found it common in the latter valley at Keeler, near Owens Lake, and at Lone Pine, in June. At Keeler a male was noticed every day during our stay. He sat for hours on a wire in front of the signal station and produced a series of notes which were well worth the title of a song. The sounds were more or less disconnected, but the writer does not remember hearing so perfect a song from any swallow, and as Mr. Bicknell states (Auk, Vol. I, 1884, p. 325) the notes suggest those produced by the marsh wren.

Tachycineta bicolor. Tree Swallow.

White-bellied swallows were seen in a few places during migration. Several were seen at Ash Meadows, Nevada, March 12, and a number near the Colorado River, March 10–13. At Furnace Creek, Death Valley, it was common about the reservoir, March 23–24, and again the middle of April. A few were seen in Johnson Cañon in the Panamint Range, April 4, and Mr. Nelson observed stragglers at the head of Willow Creek in the same range, the last of May.

Tachycineta thalassina. Violet-green Swallow.

The violet-green swallow is a common summer resident among the mountains and was frequently seen in the neighboring valleys while searching for food. Two or three were seen near the upper end of Vegas Wash, Nevada, March 10, and many were observed in Death Valley, at Furnace Creek, April 10, and at Saratoga Springs, near the south end, April 26. In Nevada, Dr. Merriam found it common in Pahranagat Valley, May 22–26, saw it on Mount Magruder, June 8, and in Oasis Valley, June 1. In Utah it was common in the Lower Santa Clara Valley, May 11–15. Mr. Nelson found it a common species in the Panamint and Grapevine mountains, where it bred in the crevices of the lofty cliffs, from the summits down to the border of the surrounding valleys. In the former range violet-green swallows were common, and a specimen was secured on the summit of Telescope Peak, June 23. In the Argus Range it was common about the summit above Maturango Spring, May 12–14, and at Coso, four or five came about camp, May 28.

Mr. Nelson saw the species from the lower part of Saline Valley to the summit of the Inyo Mountains, in June; up to timber line in the White Mountains, in July, and at the heads of Owens and Merced rivers, in the Sierra Nevada, in July and August. In Owens Valley this swallow was common about the lake at Keeler and at Lone Pine during the first half of June. At the latter place it was seen flying about in company with the cliff swallows, white-throated and cloud swifts, at the mouth of the cañon, and with the barn swallows over the meadows and marshes. Mr. Stephens found it more or less common in other parts of the valley. It was common along the valley of Kern

River, July 3–13; in Walker Basin, July 13–16, and along the route to Bakersfield, July 16–20. Dr. Merriam and Mr. Palmer found it abundant at Old Fort Tejon, where it was breeding in the oaks and crevices of the adobe buildings; it was very common about the summit of Frazier Mountain, July 9, and at the summit of Tejon Pass, July 12. In the High Sierra it was common about the openings at Horse Corral Meadows, August 9–13; in Kings River Cañon, August 13–16; Big Cottonwood Meadows, August 25–26; at Soda Springs or Kern River Lakes, September 3, and above timber line at Mineral King, and along the route from that place to Three Rivers in the western foothills, September 10–13. Mr. Bailey found the species numerous at Monterey, September 28 to October 9, and Mr. Stephens saw several at Reche Cañon, September 22–24.

Record of specimens collected of Tachycineta thalassina.

Collector's No.	Sex.	Locality.	Date.	Collector.	Remarks.
269	♀	Coso, Coso Mountains, Calif.	May 28, 1891	A. K. Fisher	
272	♀	Keeler Inyo County, Calif.	June 1, 1891	....do	
263	♂	....do	....do	....do	
286	♂	....do	June 2, 1891	....do	
287	♀	....do	....do	....do	
354	♂	Panamint Mountains, Calif.	June 23, 1891	....do	Telescope Peak.

Clivicola riparia. Bank swallow.

Bank swallows were seen in two places only by members of the expedition. Mr. Nelson saw a few in company with rough-winged swallows at the Bend of the Colorado, in Nevada, about March 10. Mr. Stephens found it common at Alvord, in Owens Valley, where they were breeding in the banks along the sloughs, June 26–28.

Stelgidopteryx serripennis. Rough-winged Swallow.

The rough-winged swallow was tolerably common in a number of the desert valleys, where it was a summer resident. It was first seen at Ash Meadows, Nevada, March 10, and in Vegas Wash, near the Bend of the Colorado River, March 10–13. A specimen was secured at Hot Springs, in Panamint Valley, April 22, and Mr. Nelson observed a few migrants along Willow Creek, in the Panamint Mountains, the last of May. Dr. Merriam saw this swallow at Saratoga Springs in Death Valley, April 26; at the Bend of the Colorado River, May 4; in the Valley of the Virgin near Bunkerville, Nevada, May 8; and in Pahranagat Valley Nevada, where it was tolerably common and doubtless breeding, May 22–26. He found it common where Beaverdam Creek joins the Virgin in northwestern Arizona, May 9–10, and the commonest swallow in the Santa Clara Valley Utah, May 11–15. In Owens Valley a pair was seen about a pond at Lone Pine, June 8, and others were observed at Big Pine June 10. At Furnace Creek, Death Valley, several were secured about the reservoir June 19–21, and a number were seen in Kern River Valley June 22–23.

Record of specimens collected of *Stelgidopteryx serripennis*.

Collector's No.	Sex.	Locality.	Date.	Collector.	Remarks.
176	♂	Panamint Valley, Calif.	Apr. 22, 1891	A. K. Fisher	Hot Springs.
340	♂ im.	Death Valley, Calif	June 19, 1891	....do	Furnace Creek.
	♀ im.	....do	....do	V. Bailey	Do.

Ampelis cedrorum. Cedar Waxwing.

The only cedar birds observed during the entire trip were two seen at Lone Pine, in Owens Valley, June 14, and a flock of five, at Three Rivers, Tulare County, September 15. At the former place they were feeding on mulberries, which were cultivated along one of the irrigating ditches of a fruit ranch. This berry, when it can be obtained, seems to be their favorite food, and one which they will take in preference to any other. Among the Creoles of Louisiana the knowledge of this fact has given rise to the name of *mûrier* for the cedar bird in that locality.

At Three Rivers the specimens secured were gorged with a small wild grape (*Vitis californica*), which was ripening in abundance in the low thickets along the streams.

Phainopepla nitens. Phainopepla.

This species is a characteristic bird of the Lower Sonoran zone, where it remains throughout the year. Several were seen among the mesquite at Hot Springs in Panamint Valley, in January, and a fine male was secured at the mouth of Surprise Cañon, not far from the above place, April 23. Its stomach was filled with the berries of the mistletoe, which is a parasite on the mesquite. Several were seen at Resting Spring in the Amargosa Desert, about the middle of February, feeding on the same berries, which appear to be their principal food.

An adult male was seen at Maturango Spring in the Argus Range, May 10, and one or two were observed at Coso the latter part of May. Mr. Nelson found it rather common in the lower part of Vegas Valley and upper part of Vegas Wash and very abundant in the lower part of the Wash, near the Colorado River, in March. It was seen by Dr. Merriam at Mountain Spring in the Charleston Mountains, April 30, and was common in the Lower Santa Clara Valley, Utah, June 11-15, where several pairs were breeding in the village of St. George. An adult female was seen by Mr. Stephens at Morans, in Owens Valley, July 4-7, and Mr. Nelson found it rather common in the western foothills of the Sierra Nevada, between the San Joaquin and Merced rivers in August. One was seen in the chaparral above Kaweah, July 25, and another July 30.

At Kernville the species was abundant in cañons above the village July 11-13, where as many as a dozen were seen at once, some sitting on the tree tops, while others were busily engaged in capturing winged insects after the manner of the cedar bird.

Dr. Merriam met with unusual numbers among the live oaks and chaparral between Kernville and Havilah, June 23; saw many in Walker Basin June 24, and several in Tehachapi Pass June 25. He also noted it as common in the Sierra Liebre June 30, and in the Granite Range, in western San Diego County, July 1–10.

Mr. Palmer saw several in the San Francisquito Pass, north of Newhall, July 1, and Mr. Nelson found it common among the piñons a few miles west of the Cañada de las Uvas, the middle of October.

Mr. Bailey found a nest containing three fresh eggs in a mesquite, near Fort Mohave, Ariz., March 4, 1889, and one containing young, several days old, February 28.

Record of specimens collected of Phainopepla nitens.

Collector's No.	Sex.	Locality.	Date.	Collector.	Remarks.
109	♀	Resting Springs, Calif.	Feb. 12, 1891	A. K. Fisher	
183	♂	Panamint Mountains, Calif.	Apr. 23, 1891	....do	Surprise Cañon.

Lanius ludovicianus excubitorides: White-rumped Shrike.

The white-rumped shrike is very generally distributed over the greater part of the desert region of southern California and Nevada. From its habit of associating in pairs and not congregating in flocks, it is seldom common in the sense that other birds are, though a considerable number may be seen in the course of a day's ride through suitable localities. It is especially partial to the country covered by tree yuccas and seldom builds its nest in other growths where these abound. Many old as well as new nests were found which were so well protected by the strong, bayonet-like leaves of this plant that it was with difficulty they could be reached. The species was tolerably common at Hesperia in the Mohave Desert, January 4–5, and at Granite Wells, about the middle of January. At Furnace Creek and Saratoga Springs, in Death Valley, several were seen the last of January.

At Resting Springs, California, a number were seen each day during the first half of February, and at Ash Meadows, Nevada, in March. It was not uncommon in Vegas Valley, Nevada, where Mr. Nelson found a small *Perognathus* and lizard impaled on thorns by it. In Coso Valley, California, the writer observed a number of insects and lizards fastened on the sharp-pointed leaves of the yuccas. In the latter place several nests containing eggs were found in the tree yuccas during the first half of May, and one near Darwin, in the north end of the valley, June 17. In the Coso Mountains shrikes were in sight most of the time, and a nest containing four young was found May 27. Four other young, just able to fly, were seen on the same date.

In Nevada Dr. Merriam found a nest containing six eggs on the east slope of the Pahranagat Mountains, May 26. It was so placed in a fork of a tree yucca that although easily seen it could not be reached from any direction. He found the species at Mountain Spring in the Charleston Mountains, April 30; in Desert Valley, May 20; in the Juniper Mountains, May 18-19; and on Gold Mountain, among the yuccas on the south slope, June 3. On Mount Magruder several were seen in Tule Cañon, and thence up to an altitude of 2,450 meters (8,000 feet) in the nut pines, where it evidently was breeding, June 4-8. In Utah it was seen in the Santa Clara Valley near St. George, May 11-15; at Mountain Meadows, May 17; and among the tree yuccas on the south slope of the Beaverdam Mountains, May 10. Several were seen in the nut pines on the White and Inyo mountains, California.

In Owens Valley the species was quite common and numbers of young birds were seen about the orchards and roadsides in June. Mr. Nelson found it breeding in the Panamint, Grapevine, Inyo, and White mountains and the adjacent valleys, and Dr. Merriam saw several in the clumps of mesquite, in Death Valley and Mesquite Valley, April 8-18

It was common in Kern River Valley, Walker Pass, and Walker Basin, and in the San Joaquin Valley between Bakersfield and Visalia. It is a question whether the individuals seen by the writer at San Bernardino, December 27-30, 1890; by Dr. Merriam in the southern part of San Diego County, July 1-10, and by Mr. Nelson along the route from San Simeon to Carpenteria and Santa Paula should not be referred to the California shrike (*Lanius ludovicianus gambeli*).

Record of specimens collected of Lanius ludovicianus excubitorides.

Collector's No.	Sex.	Locality.	Date.	Collector.	Remarks.
37	♂	Hesperia, Calif.	Jan. 4, 1891	A. K. Fisher	Mohave Desert.
61	♀	Granite Wells, Calif.	Jan. 15, 1891	....do	Do.
97	♀	Death Valley, Calif.	Feb. 3, 1891	....do	Furnace Creek.
116	♂	Ash Meadows, Nev.	Mar. 4, 1891	....do	
20	♀	Twelve-mile Spring, Calif.	Feb. 21, 1891	F. Stephens	North of Resting Springs.
262	♂ juv.	Coso Mountains, Calif.	May 27, 1891	A. K. Fisher	
263	♀ juv.	....do	....do	....do	
264	♀ juv.	....do	....do	....do	
296	♂ juv.	Owens Valley, Calif.	June 5, 1891	....do	Lone Pine.
56	♀	....do	May 13, 1891	F. Stephens	Haway Meadows.
57	♂ juv.	....do	....do	....do	Do.
106	♀	....do	June 19, 1891	....do	Independence Creek

Vireo gilvus swainsoni. Western Warbling Vireo.

The warbling vireo was seen with very little regularity and was common in few localities visited by the expedition. In Owens Valley Mr. Stephens saw one among the willows at Haway Meadows, May 13; found it common and migrating at Olancha, May 16-23; common in the lower part of the cañon of Independence Creek, June 18-23; and heard several among the willows at the Queen mine in the White Mountains, Nevada, July 11-16. At Coso one was seen among the willows and rose bushes bordering a spring, May 23, and two were secured at the same place the following day. Dr. Merriam shot a specimen in worn breeding-plumage at Ash Meadows, Nevada, May 30, and saw a pair at Kernville, in Kern River Valley, June 23. It was not uncommon among the hills above Walker Basin, July 14, and Mr. Nelson noted a few at the head of Owens River the latter part of the month. Mr. Palmer found it common at Old Fort Tejon, where a nest containing four eggs, just ready to hatch, was discovered in a willow 10 or 12 feet from the ground, July 4.

Record of specimens collected of Vireo gilvus swainsoni.

Collector's No.	Sex.	Locality.	Date.	Collector.	Remarks.
252	♂	Coso, Coso Mountains, Calif	May 24, 1891	A. K. Fisher	
253	♂	......do....................	....do....	....do.......	

Vireo solitarius cassinii. Cassin's Vireo.

Cassin's vireo was observed in a number of places in the Sierra Nevada and sparingly in some of the other ranges. Dr. Merriam took a specimen in worn breeding-plumage, June 28, at Old Fort Tejon, in the Cañada de las Uvas, California, the type locality of the species. At Maturango Spring, in the Argus Range, a specimen was taken among the piñons, May 8. Mr. Nelson found it common at the head of Owens River and Dr. Merriam shot one among the junipers at Sheep Spring in the Juniper Mountains, Nevada, May 19. It was observed among the pines above Walker Basin, July 14; was common in the Sequoia National Park during the first week in August; was seen at Horse Corral Meadows, August 11; common at Kings River Cañon, August 13–16; and one was secured at Big Cottonwood Meadows, September 5.

Record of specimens collected of Vireo solitarius cassinii.

Collector's No.	Sex.	Locality.	Date.	Collector.	Remarks.
210	♂	Juniper Mountains, Nev	May 19, 1891	C. Hart Merriam	
	♀	Argus Range, Calif	May 8, 1891	A. K. Fisher	Maturango Spring.
393	♂	Old Fort Tejon, Calif	June 28, 1891	T. S. Palmer	
157	♀	Walker Basin, Calif	July 14, 1891	A. K. Fisher	
	♀ im.	Sierra Nevada, Calif	Aug. 22, 1891	F. Stephens	Olancha Peak.

Vireo solitarus plumbeus. Plumbeous Vireo.

The only specimen of this vireo taken on the expedition was a male secured by Dr. Merriam at Sheep Spring in the Juniper Mountains, Nevada, May 19, 1891. It was in full song and was shot in the same tree in which a Cassin's vireo was killed a few minutes before.

Vireo bellii pusillus. Least Vireo.

The least vireo is a tolerably common summer resident in Owens Valley, where at Lone Pine adult and young were secured in June; it was seen by Mr. Stephens at Olancha, May 16–23, and at Bishop Creek, August 4–10. A specimen was secured at Furnace Creek, Death Valley,

June 20, and the species was not uncommon in the cañon above the ranch the following day. West of the Sierra Nevada, it was common at Bakersfield, in the San Joaquin Valley, July 17-20.

Record of specimens collected of Vireo bellii pusillus.

Collector's No.	Sex.	Locality.	Date.	Collector.	Remarks.
343	♂	Ash Meadows, Nev.	May 30, 1891	V. Bailey	
351	♂	Death Valley, Calif.	June 20, 1891	A. K. Fisher	Furnace Creek.
318	♀	..... do	June 21, 1891	.... do	Do.
328	♀ juv.	Owens Valley, Calif.	June 8, 1891	.... do	Lone Pine.
397	♂	..... do	June 11, 1891	.... do	Do.
		Bakersfield, Calif.	July 19, 1891	.... do	

Vireo vicinior. Gray Vireo.

Mr. Nelson found this vireo rather common in the Grapevine Mountains, Nevada, where he secured a specimen June 8. In Wood Cañon, he saw several among the piñons, and on June 10 observed one carrying material for its nest. This is the only locality at which the bird was found.

Helminthophila luciæ. Lucy's Warbler.

This rare warbler breeds in the Lower Santa Clara Valley in southwestern Utah, where two specimens were shot by Dr. Merriam, May 11 and 13, the former in cottonwoods along the Santa Clara River and the latter at a small pond near the village of St. George.

Record of specimens collected of Helminthophila luciæ.

Collector's No.	Sex.	Locality.	Date.	Collector.	Remarks.
	♂	Santa Clara, Utah	May 11, 1891	C. Hart Merriam	
	♀	St. George, Utah	May 16, 1891	.... do	

Helminthophila ruficapilla gutturalis. Calaveras Warbler.

The Calaveras warbler, with the exception of a pair seen in Shepherd Cañon in the Argus Range, California, April 29, was seen only in the Sierra Nevada. It was common in the Sequoia National Park during the first week of August, and a few were seen at Round Valley, 12 miles south of Mount Whitney, August 28. Mr. Nelson found it common at the head of Owens River and also on the western slope in the Yosemite Valley, in July and August.

Record of specimens collected of Helminthophila ruficapilla gutturalis.

Collector's No.	Sex.	Locality.	Date.	Collector.	Remarks.
194	♀	Argus Range, Calif.	April 29, 1891	A. K. Fisher	Shepherd Cañon.
405		Sierra Nevada, Calif.	Aug. 4, 1891	.... do	Sequoia National Park.

Helminthophila celata lutescens. Lutescent Warbler.

This active little warbler was found to be abundant in a few places during migration. At San Bernardino one was seen on the border of a stream, December 29, 1890. In the Panamint Mountains it was seen in Johnson Cañon, April 12; by Mr. Nelson among the willows at the heads of Willow and Mill creeks, the last of May; and by Mr. Bailey and the writer near the 'charcoal kilns' at the head of Wild Rose Cañon, June 23. In the Argus Range, it was common both in Shepherd Cañon and at Maturango Spring the first half of May. Mr. Stephens saw a few migrating by Little Owens Lake, May 6-11; and at Haway Meadows, May 12-14.

It was common along the South Fork of the Kern, July 3-10. In the High Sierra it was abundant in the Sequoia National Park, the first week in August; common at Horse Corral Meadows, August 9-13; at Round Valley, 12 miles south of Mt. Whitney, August 28; and at Mineral King, September 10-11. Mr. Nelson found it common at the head of Owens River and in the Yosemite Valley in July and August.

Record of specimens collected of Helminthophila celata lutescens.

Collector's No.	Sex.	Locality.	Date.	Collector.	Remarks.
215	♀	Argus Range, Calif	May 8, 1891	A. K. Fisher	Maturango Spring.
216	♂	......do	May 9, 1891	....do	Do.
217	♂	......do	....do	....do	Do.
	♂ im	Panamint Mountains, Calif	June 24, 1891	V. Bailey	Coal kilns.
	♂ im	Sierra Nevada, Calif	Aug. 3, 1891	E. W. Nelson	South Fork Merced River.
159	♀ im	......do	Aug. 22, 1891	F. Stephens	Olancha Peak.

Dendroica æstiva. Yellow Warbler.

The yellow warbler was tolerably common in a number of localities visited by members of the expedition. Mr. Nelson found it a rather common breeding species among the willows along Willow Creek, Mill Creek, and Cottonwood Creek cañons in the Panamint Mountains, and noted a few in Wood Cañon in the Grapevine Mountains. The same observer found it common at the head of Owens Valley at the base of the White Mountains and up to 2,600 meters (8,500 feet) altitude at the head of Owens River, in the Sierra Nevada. The writer first observed the species at Coso, where an adult male was seen busily engaged catching insects among some willows and rose bushes on the evening of May 24 and the following morning.

At Lone Pine, in Owens Valley, yellow warblers were common among the orchards and shade trees, June 4-15. In the same valley, Mr. Stephens found it common at Independence Creek, June 18-24; not common at Benton, July 9-10, and the Queen mill, Nevada, July 11-16, and saw two or three individuals in the cottonwoods at Morans, July 4-7.

In Nevada, Dr. Merriam shot a male in Pahrump Valley, on a solitary mesquite bush at a small spring six miles south of Yount's ranch,

April 29. He saw others at Upper Cottonwood Springs, at the east base of the Charleston Mountains, April 30; at Vegas ranch, May 1; at the Bend of the Colorado River, May 4; in the valley of the Virgin and Lower Muddy, May 6 and 8, and on Mount Magruder, June 4-8. In Pahranagat Valley it was breeding commonly, May 22-26, this being the only locality in Nevada at which he observed it in any numbers. He found it common where Beaverdam Creek joins the Virgin in northwestern Arizona, May 10, and breeding plentifully in the Lower Santa Clara Valley, Utah, near St. George, May 11-15. Mr. Palmer found it very common at Old Fort Tejon the first of July. All through Kern Valley, Walker Basin, and at Bakersfield, in the San Joaquin Valley, this warbler was common in the willows along the streams during the first three weeks of July, and sparingly in the latter valley as late as October.

Record of specimens collected of Dendroica æstiva.

Collector's No.	Sex.	Locality.	Date.	Collector.	Remarks.
293	♂	Owens Valley, Calif.	June 5, 1891	A. K. Fisher	Lone Pine.
94	♀	....do....	June 12, 1891	F. Stephens	Olancha.
128	♂	....do....	July 9, 1891	....do....	Benton.
129	♂ juv	....do....	....do....	....do....	Do.

Dendroica auduboni. Audubon's Warbler.

The western yellow-rumped warbler was common as a migrant in various localities and not uncommon as a breeder in some of the mountain ranges. At San Bernardino a flock was seen in a clump of willows, and a number associated with chipping sparrows were seen gleaning insects from a field of early cabbage, December 28, 1890. A few were found among the willows bordering the reservoir at Furnace Creek, Death Valley, California, during the latter part of January, and again on April 10, and a single one was seen at Ash Meadows, Nevada, March 21. It was not uncommon at Hot Springs in Panamint Valley, April 20-23, and at Maturango Spring, in the Argus range, the first half of May.

In Nevada Audubon's warbler was seen by Mr. Nelson at Pahrump and Vegas ranches in February and March; and by Dr. Merriam in Pahrump Valley at Yount's Ranch, April 28-29; at Mountain Spring in the Charleston Mountains, and at Upper Cottonwood Springs at the east base of these mountains, April 30. In Utah a few were observed still lingering in the Santa Clara Valley, May 11-15, though the bulk of the species had gone into the mountains before this date.

In California Mr. Nelson saw a few migrants the last of May among the piñons at the head of Willow Creek in the Panamint Mountains, though none were seen later by him in these or in the Grapevine Mountains. The same observer saw a few in the Inyo Mountains from the upper edge of the piñon belt to the summit of the range, June 24 to July 4, and sparingly in the White Mountains a little later. It was common at the head of Owens River, from 2,500 to 2,900 meters (8,200 to 9,500 feet) altitude, and also on the west slope in the Yosemite Valley and on the head of the Merced River. In Owens Valley it was observed at Lone Pine in December, 1890, and at Little Owens Lake, May 6-11.

Along the east slope of the Sierra Nevada it was seen at Independence Creek, where it was probably breeding, June 18-21; at Bishop Creek August 4-10; at Menache Meadows May 24-26; and at Big Cottonwood Meadows during the summer and early fall.

It was common at Horse Corral Meadows August 10, and along the Kaweah River, where it was breeding, from 2,130 meters (7,000 feet) altitude up to timber line during the first part of August. Mr. Palmer found it rather common on the summit of Frazier Mountain, near Old Fort Tejon, on July 9. Mr. Nelson found it common at San Luis Obispo, Santa Paula, Carpenteria, and in the San Joaquin Valley in November and December, 1891.

Record of specimens collected of Dendroica auduboni.

Collector's No.	Sex.	Locality.	Date.	Collector.	Remarks.
2	♀ im.	San Bernardino, Calif.	Dec. 28, 1890	A. K. Fisher	
96	♂	Death Valley, Calif.	Feb. 1, 1891	....do	Furnace Creek.
2	♂	Sierra Nevada, Calif.	June 19, 1891	B. H. Dutcher	Big Cottonwood Meadows.
3	♂	......do	......do	....do	....do
12	♀	......do	July 7, 1891	....do	....do
142	♂	......do	July 26, 1891	F. Stephens	

Dendroica nigrescens. Black-throated Gray Warbler.

The black-throated gray warbler was first observed among the piñons above Maturango Spring, in the Argus Range, California, where a female was secured May 8, containing a large egg in the oviduct, and on the following day one was seen carrying nesting material in its beak. Mr. Nelson saw a few in the Panamint Mountains among the piñons on Willow Creek the last of May, and found them breeding among the same trees in the Grapevine Mountains. Above the 'charcoal kilns' in Wild Rose Cañon in the Panamint Mountains, males were heard singing by Mr. Bailey and the writer June 25. This warbler was found breeding in the Inyo and White Mountains and in the Sierra Nevada, at the head of Owens River. Dr. Merriam shot one at Sheep Spring in the Juniper Mountains, Nevada, May 19, and two in the nut pines on Mt. Magruder, June 5. Mr. Bailey saw a few among the pines on the Kaweah River the last of July, and the writer saw one on the Hockett trail near Little Cottonwood Creek, August 23, and secured a specimen at Three Rivers, September 14.

Mr. Nelson reported a few as seen along the coast from San Simeon to Carpenteria, Calif., November 4 to December 18.

Record of specimens collected of Dendroica nigrescens.

Collector's No.	Sex.	Locality.	Date.	Collector.	Remarks.
	♂	Argus Range, Calif	May 9, 1891	T. S. Palmer	Maturango Spring.
	♀	....do	....do	....do	Do.
211	♂	....do	May 8, 1891	A. K. Fisher	Do.
212	♂	....do	....do	....do	Do.
238	♀	....do	May 13, 1891	....do	Do.
239	♀	....do	....do	....do	Do.
435	♀	Three Rivers, Calif	Sept. 14, 1891	....do	
132	♀	Queen mine, Nev	July 11, 1891	F. Stephens	White Mountains.
	♂	Juniper Mountains, Nev	May 19, 1891	C. Hart Merriam	
	♂	Mount Magruder, Nev	June 5, 1891	V. Bailey	
	♀	....do	....do	C. Hart Merriam	

Dendroica townsendi. Townsend's Warbler.

Townsend's warbler was first noted on the ridge above Maturango Spring in the Argus Range, California, where a male in full song was secured, and others seen among the piñons May 6. From this date until the departure of the party, May 15, the species was not uncommon, though there was no evidence of its intention to remain and breed, as in the case of the black-throated gray warbler. One was seen at Coso on May 19, and Mr. Stephens saw a small flock migrating among the creosote bushes northeast of Little Owens Lake, the second week in May.

In the Sierra Nevada Mr. Nelson saw two or three on the South Fork of the Merced River August 9. They were in company with a large number of other small birds of several species, gleaning insects from among the lower branches as they passed from tree to tree. On the coast Mr. Bailey found it common at Monterey September 28 to October 9, and Mr. Nelson saw it, though very sparingly, at Morro Bay and southward.

Record of specimens collected of Dendroica townsendi.

Collector's No.	Sex.	Locality.	Date.	Collector.	Remarks.
200	♂	Argus Range, Calif	May 6, 1891	A. K. Fisher	Maturango Spring.
219	♀	....do	May 9, 1891	....do	Do.
226	♂	....do	May 11, 1891	....do	Do.
	♂	Monterey, Calif	Oct. 5, 1891	V. Bailey	
	♀	Morro	Nov. 8, 1891	E. W. Nelson	

Dendroica occidentalis. Hermit Warbler.

This rare warbler was first seen among the piñons in the Argus Range, above Maturango Spring, where a pair was observed and a female secured May 6. The following day another was seen. Mr. Nelson saw a few among a migrating flock on the South Fork of the Merced, near Wawona, August 9. Mr. Palmer saw one in a mixed flock of warblers at Halsted Meadows, in the Sequoia National Park, August 7, and the writer secured a specimen at Horse Corral Meadows August 13. Mr. Belding saw migrants at Crocker's, 21 miles northwest of Yosemite Valley, in May.

Record of specimens collected of Dendroica occidentalis.

Collector's No.	Sex.	Locality.	Date.	Collector.	Remarks.
199	♀	Argus Range, Calif	May 6, 1891	A. K. Fisher	Maturango Spring.
415	♀ im.	Sierra Nevada, Calif	Aug. 13, 1891	....do	Horse Corral Meadows.

Seiurus noveboracensis notabilis. Grinnell's Water-Thrush.

The only individual of this species obtained by the expedition was an adult male secured by Dr. Merriam and Mr. Bailey at the eastern edge of the Santa Clara settlement, in the Lower Santa Clara Valley, Utah, May 11, 1891.

Geothlypis macgillivrayi. Macgillivray's Warbler.

This warbler was first observed in Shepherd Cañon in the Argus Range, California, April 27, and afterwards at Maturango Spring, where it was common among the willow thickets. At Coso, the species was common in the shrubbery about the springs and along the cañons to the summit of the range, the latter part of May. Mr. Nelson found it a rather common migrant along the upper part of Willow and Mill Creeks in the Panamint Mountains during the last week of May. After this date comparatively few were seen, and these only within the sage belt along the willow-grown banks of springs and streams. A few were seen also in Wood Cañon in the Grapevine Mountains. In the Sierra Nevada, Mr. Nelson found it at the head of Owens River, though not common. Mr. Stephens saw a female accompanied by young at Bishop Creek, August 4–10; Mr. Dutcher secured specimens at Big Cottonwood Meadows, where the writer saw it August 26; and several were seen in the Sequoia National Park during the first week in August.

In Nevada Dr. Merriam found Macgillivray's Warbler common in Pahranagat Valley, May 22–26, immediately after a severe snowstorm, and thought it did not breed in the valley. He saw a single individual on Mount Magruder, Nevada, June 8, and Mr. Nelson found a few at the heads of streams on the east slope of the White Mountains.

Record of specimens collected of Geothlypis macgillivrayi.

Collector's No.	Sex.	Locality.	Date.	Collector.	Remarks.
218	♀	Argus Mountains, Calif	May 9, 1891	A. K. Fisher	Maturango Spring.
254	♂	Coso, Coso Mountains, Calif.	May 24, 1891	....do	
255	♂	....do	May 25, 1891	....do	
267	♀	....do	May 28, 1891	....do	

Geothlypis trichas occidentalis. Western Yellow-throat.

The western yellow-throat was common in only a few localities visited by the expedition. At San Bernardino, Calif., it was tolerably common along the streams and in the thickets, December 28-29, 1890. It was seen in Surprise Cañon in the Panamint Mountains, April 16, and was not uncommon at Hot Springs in Panamint Valley, April 20-25. Mr. Nelson found a few during the latter part of May in the willows on Mill and Willow creeks in the Panamint Mountains, but observed none in the Grapevine Mountains. He saw a few at Hunter Cañon on the east slope of the Inyo Mountains, and also among some willows in Saline Valley. In Owens Valley it was a tolerably common summer resident from Little Owens Lake up to the head of the valley at the base of the White Mountains. In Death Valley the species was not uncommon in Furnace Creek Cañon and at Bennett Wells, June 19-21.

In Nevada, Dr. Merriam found it tolerably common and breeding in Pahranagat Valley, and saw it at Vegas Ranch, May 1, and along the Lower Santa Clara in Utah, May 11-15.

It was common along the South Fork of the Kern River, California, July 3-10; at Kernville, July 11-13; in Walker Basin, July 13-16, and at Bakersfield in the San Joaquin Valley, July 17-20.

On the coast of California Mr. Nelson found it, though in limited numbers, at the head of Morro Bay, and thence southward.

Record of specimens collected of Geothlypis trichas occidentalis.

Collector's No.	Sex.	Locality.	Date.	Collector.	Remarks.
8	♀ im.	San Bernardino, Calif.	Dec. 28, 1890	A. K. Fisher	
174	♂	Panamint Valley, Calif	Apr. 21, 1891	....do	Hot Springs.
350	♂	Death Valley, Calif.	June 21, 1891	....do	Furnace Creek.
78	♂	Owens Valley, Calif	June 9, 1891	F. Stephens	Olancha.
82	♀	......do	June 10, 1891	....do	

Icteria virens longicauda. Long-tailed Chat.

Owing to the lack of suitable localities for nesting the yellow-breasted chat was found sparingly in most of the region traversed by the expedition. It was moderately common in Owens Valley, at Lone Pine, June 4-15, and Mr. Stephens found it in the same valley, though not commonly, at Olancha, May 16-23; at Ash Creek, May 30-June 3; at Independence Creek, June 18-23, and at Morans, July 4-7. Mr. Nelson saw and heard one, which sang in the evening and the greater part of the night of May 22, near his camp on Willow Creek in the Panamint Mountains, and observed others in the Inyo Mountains, from Hunter's arastra down to the bottom of Saline Valley, during the latter part of June. At Furnace Creek, Death Valley, chats were tolerably common at the ranch and in the cañon above it, June 19-21. At Kernville, Calif., and along Kern Valley, chats were common June 22-23, and

July 11-13; in Walker Basin, July 13-16, and several were seen in the Cañada de las Uvas June 28, 29. At Bakersfield, in the San Joaquin Valley, it was seen or heard every day from July 17-20.

In Nevada, Dr. Merriam found it in the lower part of Vegas Wash, May 3; at the Bend of the Colorado, May 4; in the valleys of the Virgin and Muddy, May 6-8; and in Pahranagat Valley, as a common breeder, May 22-26. In the Santa Clara Valley, Utah, it was a tolerably common breeder, May 11-15.

Record of specimens collected of Icteria virens longicauda.

Collector's No.	Sex.	Locality.	Date.	Collector.	Remarks.
294	♂	Owens Valley, Calif.	June 5, 1891	A. K. Fisher	Lone Pine.
349	♂	Death Valley, Calif.	June 21, 1891	....do	Furnace Creek.

Sylvania pusilla pileolata. Pileolated Warbler.

The black-capped warbler was first seen in Surprise Cañon in the Panamint Mountains, April 17, and Mr. Nelson found it rather common among the willows at the head of Willow, Mill, and Cottonwood creeks in the same mountains the last of May, after which time he did not see it there. A few were seen in the Argus Range in Shepherd Cañon, April 27, and the species was common about Maturango Spring, in the willows and rosebushes during the first half of May. It was seen in the Coso Mountains in the bottom of the cañons among the shrubbery, the last of May, and at the head of the streams in the White Mountains, in July. Mr. Stephens found it migrating in Salt Wells Valley, May 1-5; at Little Owens Lake, May 6-11; at Olancha, May 16-23; and in Reche Cañon, September 22-24. In the High Sierra it was seen in the Sequoia National Park the first week in August; at Horse Corral Meadows, August 9-13; at the head of Owens River and on the western slope opposite, in July and August; at Big Cottonwood Meadows, during the summer; at Round Valley, 12 miles south of Mount Whitney, the last of August; and north of Mineral King, September 10-11.

In Nevada, Dr. Merriam saw it at a large spring in Pahrump Valley, April 29; at Mountain Spring in the Charleston Mountains, April 30; at Upper Cottonwood Springs at the east base of these mountains, the same day; at Vegas ranch, May 1; at the Bend of the Colorado, May 4; and in the Valley of the Virgin and Lower Muddy, May 6.

Record of specimens collected of Sylvania pusilla pileolata.

Collector's No.	Sex.	Locality.	Date.	Collector.	Remarks.
190	♂	Argus Range, Calif.	Apr. 27, 1891	A. K. Fisher	Shepherd Cañon.
223	♀	....do	May 10, 1891	....do	Maturango Springs.
13	♂	Sierra Nevada, Calif.	July 7, 1891	B. H. Dutcher	Big Cottonwood Meadows.

Anthus pensilvanicus. Titlark.

The titlark was found as a winter resident in suitable localities in southern California and Nevada.

In California Mr. Nelson saw a few at Lone Pine, and found it very common along the shore of Owens Lake in December, 1890; he also saw a few at Hot Springs, Panamint Valley, in the early part of January, where the writer secured a specimen, April 22, 1891. At San Bernardino several flocks were seen in a wet meadow bordering a stream, on December 28, 1890. In Death Valley a flock of twenty or more was always to be found in the alfalfa fields at Furnace Creek, and a few were observed at Saratoga Springs during the latter part of January. Dr. Merriam saw two in the Mohave Desert on the sand beach bordering the Mohave River at Victor, March 30. At various places in the San Joaquin Valley Mr. Nelson found it congregated in small flocks in October, and common in fields and along the coast from San Simeon to Carpenteria, in November and December.

In Nevada the species was common at Ash Meadows in flocks on the wet marshes and plowed fields during the first three weeks of March, and Mr. Nelson found it not uncommon about wet ground in both Vegas and Pahrump valleys, and near the upper end of Vegas Wash about the same time.

Record of specimens collected of Anthus pensilvanicus.

Collector's No.	Sex.	Locality.	Date.	Collector.	Remarks.
6	♂	San Bernardino, Calif.	Dec. 28, 1890	A. K. Fisher	
89	♀	Death Valley, Calif.	Jan. 30, 1891	....do.	Furnace Creek.
90	♀	....do.	....do.	....do.	Do.
182	♀	Panamint Valley, Calif.	Apr. 23, 1891	....do.	Hot Springs.

Cinclus mexicanus. Water Ousel.

The dipper or water ousel was seen only along the streams of the Sierra Nevada, in California. In December, 1890, Mr. Nelson saw one on Owens River at the mouth of Lone Pine Creek. The writer first observed the species on the South Fork of Kern River, where a specimen was secured July 7 as it was flying from boulder to boulder in a rapid portion of the stream. It was seen at Horse Corral Meadows August 9–13, and was common in Kings River Cañon August 13–16. At the latter place an old nest was discovered in the eroded end of a drift log which hung out over a waterfall. The dipper was met with by Mr. Nelson at the head of Owens River and in the Yosemite Valley, and by Mr. Stephens at Bishop Creek. It was common in the high mountains along the streams in Big Cottonwood and Whitney Meadows, where specimens were secured. Mr. Palmer observed one at an altitude of about 3,500 meters (11,600 feet) in Langley Meadow September 10.

Record of specimens collected of Cinclus mexicanus.

Collector's No.	Sex.	Locality.	Date.	Collector.	Remarks.
381	im.	Kern River, Calif	July 7, 1891	A. K. Fisher	South Fork
433	♂	Whitney Meadows, Calif	Aug. 31, 1891	...do	
15	♂	Sierra Nevada, Calif	July 8, 1891	B. H. Dutcher	Big Cottonwood Meadows.
24	♂	......do	Aug. 2, 1891	...do	Do.
416	♂	Kings River Cañon, Calif	Aug. 11, 1891	A. K. Fisher	

Oroscoptes montanus. Sage Thrasher.

The sage thrasher is a characteristic inhabitant of the sage plains, occurring in company with the sage sparrow (*Amphispiza belli nevadensis*), Brewer's sparrow (*Spizella breweri*), and the lark sparrow (*Chondestes grammacus strigatus*). It was not found in the lower valleys except as a winter resident. A flock of six or eight was seen at Hesperia in the Mohave Desert, January 4, and about an equal number at Granite Wells, January 13–15. One was observed at Mesquite Well in Death Valley, January 20. Mr. Nelson saw about half a dozen in the sage brush on the divide between Willow and Cottonwood creeks in the Panamint Mountains, where they seemed to be breeding during the last of May. Dr. Merriam found the species common among the sage brush north of Telescope Peak April 15. A pair was observed in Coso Valley, below Maturango Spring, May 11, and Mr. Nelson reported the species common in the same place in January.

In Nevada a few were noted at Ash Meadows in March, and Mr. Nelson found them in both Pahrump and Vegas valleys. Dr. Merriam found them common in the sage brush on the rolling plateau of the Juniper Mountains, May 18; in the valley between Gold Mountain and Mount Magruder, June 4; and on Mount Magruder plateau, June 5–8, where a nest containing two fresh eggs was found in a sage bush, June 8. In the Santa Clara Valley in southwestern Utah, they were not found near St. George, but were seen first on May 15, about 8 miles northwest of that place where the sage brush begins. A few miles further north, at the upper Santa Clara Crossing, they were one of the most abundant birds, May 17; and at Mountain Meadows, Utah, where they were common, he shot an adult male sitting on a nest containing four fresh eggs, May 17. Mr. Nelson found them sparingly among the piñons in the Inyo Mountains, California, the latter part of June; saw a few on the White Mountains and found them rather common about the head of Owens Valley, in July. He reported them as common up to 2,450 meters (8,000 feet), at the head of Owens River. Mr. Stephens saw several at Morans, July 4–7; found them common at Benton, July 9–10; and at Queen mine, in the White Mountains, Nevada, where a few were heard singing, July 11–16.

Record of specimens collected of Oroscoptes montanus.

Collector's No.	Sex.	Locality.	Date.	Collector.	Remarks.
34	♂	Hesperia, Calif	Jan. 4, 1891	A. K. Fisher	
51	♂	Granite Wells, Calif	Jan. 14, 1891	....do........	
60	♂	......do......	....do......	....do........	
		Coso Valley, Calif	May 12, 1891	T. S. Palmer	
45	♂	Panamint Mountains, Calif	Apr. 15, 1891	F. Stephens	
130	♂	Owens Valley, Calif	July 9, 1891	....do........	Benton.
30	♂	Ash Meadows, Nev	Mar. 11, 1891	....do........	
	♂	St. George, Utah	May 16, 1891	V. Bailey	3,800 feet altitude.
	♂	Mountain Meadows, Utah	May 17, 1891	C. Hart Merriam	Nest and eggs.

Mimus polyglottos. Mocking Bird.

The mocking bird was found sparingly in the desert regions of California, and was more or less common in similar localities in Nevada, Utah, and Arizona. It was common about San Bernardino, Calif., and in Cajon Pass the first of January and the latter part of March. In Death Valley, one was seen at Saratoga Springs in the latter part of January, and others in various other parts of the valley proper and in the northwest arm (Mesquite Valley), April 8–13, but was not seen anywhere in the valley during the trip of June 19–21. It was found at Hot Springs in Panamint Valley, April 20–24, and was tolerably common among the yuccas in Coso Valley and Mountains, throughout May. Mr. Nelson found it through the north end of the Panamint Mountains from the divide between Cottonwood and Willow creeks down to the bottom of Mesquite and Saline valleys. In the Grapevine Mountains it ranged up to the base of the main summits, at an altitude of 2,450 meters (8,000 feet). The same observer found it common as high as the lower edge of the piñons in the Inyo Mountains, to 2,370 meters (7,800 feet) at the head of Owens River in the Sierra, and a few from the head of Owens Valley up to 2,430 meters (8,000 feet) in the White Mountains.

In Nevada, Dr. Merriam found Mocking Birds in Tule Cañon, at the extreme northern end of the northwest arm of Death Valley, June 4; on the southern slope of Gold Mountain, among the tree yuccas, June 3; in Oasis Valley, June 1; in the Timpahute Mountains, May 26 (among the tree yuccas); in Pahranagat Valley, May 22–26 (common and breeding); at Pahroc Spring, May 20–22; in Meadow Creek Valley, May 19; in the valleys of the Muddy and Virgin, May 6–8 (common); at the Bend of the Colorado May 4; in Vegas Valley and Wash, April 30–May 3; and in Pahrump Valley, April 28–29 (several in the tree yuccas on east side of valley). In Utah, he found them common in the Lower Santa Clara Valley, May 11–15, and abundant on both sides of the Beaverdam Mountains, May 10–11.

They were tolerably common in Owens Valley, Calif., where they were seen at Little Owens Lake, Keeler, and Lone Pine. A pair was seen on the eastern slope of Walker Pass, July 1, and another at Walker Basin,

July 15; they were common at Bakersfield, July 17–20; in Tehachapi Pass, June 25, and a few were observed around Visalia in July. Several were seen in Reche Cañon, by Mr Stephens, September 22–24; and a male by Mr. Nelson at Santa Paula, during the last of December.

Harporhynchus redivivus. California Thrasher.

The California thrasher is a bird of the chaparral and was not found in the desert regions east of the Sierra Nevada. At San Bernardino the writer saw one December 29, 1890, and Mr. Stephens reported the species rather common in Reche Cañon near the same place, September 22–24, 1891. A pair was seen at Cane Brake ranch on the western slope of Walker Pass, July 3, and several at Kernville, where two were secured July 12. A number were seen in Walker Basin, July 13–16, and Dr. Merriam found the species common between that place and Caliente June 24; in the Cañada de las Uvas June 28–29; and in the Sierra Liebre June 30. In the latter range it passes over the divide and occurs in the chaparral on the north slope, close to the edge of the Mohave Desert. Several were seen at Bakersfield, in the San Joaquin Valley, July 17–20. Mr. Bailey saw a pair in the oak brush just below the edge of the conifers on the Kaweah River, and others at Boulder Creek; and Mr. Nelson found them common along the coast, from Morro to Santa Paula, during November and December.

Record of specimens collected of Harporhynchus redivivus.

Collector's No.	Sex.	Locality.	Date.	Collector.	Remarks.
386	♀ im.	Kernville, Calif	July 11, 1891	A. K. Fisher	
	♀	......do......	......do......	V. Bailey	
105	♂	Hesperia, Calif.	Sept. 15, 1891	F. Stephens	

Harporhynchus lecontei. LeConte's Thrasher.

Le Conte's thrasher is a characteristic bird of the deserts of southeastern California and southern Nevada and Arizona, where it was found in all the Lower Sonoran valleys east of the Sierra visited by the expedition. It is not a migratory species and probably remains in the vicinity of its summer home the entire year. This statement is strengthened by the fact that in most places where the species was found old nests were also observed. These were placed in arborescent cactuses, mesquite, or other thorny shrubs.

This thrasher was first seen by us not far from Victor, in the Mohave Desert, California, January 7, and a number were noticed between Daggett and Granite Wells, January 8–13 and April 4–6. In Death Valley, a pair was seen at Bennett Wells January 21, others about the middle of April, and a pair with five young on June 21; at Furnace Creek one was seen the last of January. At Resting Springs the species was very common among the mesquite, where the males were frequently heard singing from their perches on the uppermost branches, February 6–17.

In Nevada it was common at Ash Meadows in March, and Mr. Nelson found it in Pahrump Valley, at the western base of the Charleston Mountains. East of Pahrump Valley Dr. Merriam saw several April 29, and a full-grown young was shot among the yuccas. He killed one in Vegas Valley May 1, and found the species tolerably common in the valley of the Virgin and Lower Muddy. A nest was found in a branching cactus (*Opuntia echinocarpa*) on the mesa between these rivers, and, although the parent bird was on the nest, no eggs had been laid. In southwestern Utah it was found on the west side of the Beaverdam Mountains almost to the summit of the range, keeping in the tree yuccas and arborescent cactuses with the cactus wren.

At Hot Springs, in Panamint Valley, California, it was seen the last of April, and in Coso Valley and Mountains through May. It is common in Owens Valley, from Little Owens Lake, where Mr. Stephens found a nest and three eggs and a brood of nearly grown young, to Benton, where both he and Mr. Nelson saw it. Mr. Stephens found it common in Salt Wells Valley, where nests and young were observed. In Walker Pass it was common among the tree yuccas on the east side, and Dr. Merriam saw several on the west slope, about 4 miles from the summit, June 22–23. He found it common throughout the western tongue of the Mohave Desert, where a nest containing two half-grown young was found in a branching cactus (*Opuntia echinocarpa*) June 27:

In the San Joaquin Valley Mr. Nelson found it common about the southern and western sides of Buena Vista Lake, and thence west and northwest for 15 to 18 miles toward the base of the Temploa Mountains. This was the actual range in which he noted the species, though it undoubtedly occupied much more territory in the vicinity, where the low growth of desert bushes and sandy arroyos near the lake formed a congenial home.

LeConte's thrasher is a sly, skulking species, quite difficult to collect, and when running about among the desert shrubbery closely resembles the road-runner in form and actions.

The song of this species like that of the other members of the genus is sweet and variable, and in many respects rivals that of the mockingbird in musical elegance. In many places throughout its range the young (just before they leave the nest) are regularly hunted by both whites and Indians for the purpose of making cage birds of them.

At Keeler, in Owens Valley, Mr. H. E. Wilkinson, meteorological observer, had one which was allowed the freedom of the house. It was very tame and would allow itself to be caught and placed in the cage for the night. One of its favorite amusements was to sit on the window sill and catch the flies which were moving on the panes.

Record of specimens collected of Harporhynchus lecontei.

Collector's No.	Sex.	Locality.	Date.	Collector.	Remarks.
19	♂	Resting Springs, Calif	Feb. 14, 1891	F. Stephens	
20	♂	.....do	.....do	....do	
23	♂	Twelve-mile Spring, Calif..	Feb. 20, 1891	....do	North of Resting Springs.
	♂	Ash Meadows, Nev	Mar. 19, 1891	E. W. Nelson	
121	♂	.....do	Mar. 19, 1891	A. K. Fisher	
133	♂	.....do	Mar. 19, 1891	....do	
	♂	Pahrump Valley, Nev	Feb. 11, 1891	E. W. Nelson	
	♀	.....do	.....do	....do	
	♂ juv.	.....do	Apr. 29, 1891	C. Hart Merriam	
	♀ im.	Vegas Valley, Nev	May 1, 1891	....do	
	♂	Beaverdam Mountains, Utah.	May 10, 1891	....do	
29	♂	Table Mountain, Nev	May 6, 1891	F. Stephens	Amargosa Desert.
	♂	Buena Vista Lake, Calif	Oct. 26, 1891	E. W. Nelson	San Joaquin Valley.
164	♀	Hesperia, Calif	Sept. 15, 1891	F. Stephens	
53	♂	Salt Wells Valley, Calif	May 4, 1891	....do	
284	♂ im.	Owens Valley, Calif	June 2, 1891	A. K. Fisher	Keeler.
	♀	.....do	Dec. 27, 1890	E. W. Nelson	Lone Pine.
126	♂ im.	.....do	July 3, 1891	F. Stephens	22 miles north of Bishop.
	♀	Coso Mountains	Dec. 31, 1890	E. W. Nelson	
	♂	.....do	.....do	V. Bailey	
	♂	Panamint Valley, Calif	Jan. 10, 1891	....do	
41	♂	Daggett, Calif	Jan. 7, 1891	A. K. Fisher	
	♂ juv.	Mohave Desert, Calif	June 27, 1891	T. S. Palmer	Willow Spring.
	♂ juv.	.....do	.....do	....do	Do.
	♀ im.	Death Valley, Calif	June 21, 1891	V. Bailey	Bennett Wells.
	♂	.....do	Jan. 30, 1891	E. W. Nelson	Saratoga Springs.
17	♀	Garlick Springs, Calif	Feb. 10, 1891	F. Stephens	
16	♀	.....do	.....do	....do	
99	♀	Resting Springs, Calif	Feb. 7, 1891	A. K. Fisher	
100	♀	.....do	.....do	....do	
101	♂	.....do	.....do	....do	
107	♀	.....do	Feb. 11, 1891	....do	

Harporhynchus crissalis. Crissal Thrasher.

The crissal thrasher was not found in the Mohave or Amargosa deserts, nor in Death, Panamint, or other valleys west of the Charleston Mountains, where LeConte's thrasher is so common. Dr. Merriam found it from Vegas Valley, Nevada, eastward. He observed it in the valley of the Virgin, near St. Joe, Nev., May 7, and near Bunkerville, May 8; and found it a common breeder in the Lower Santa Clara Valley, Utah, where a nest containing two fresh eggs was discovered in a bush of *Atriplex torreyi*, about 3 feet above the ground, May 16. Mr. Nelson also found a nest containing three eggs, at Cottonwood Spring, at the east base of the Charleston Mountains, March 8. The bird was shot from the nest, which was placed partly on one of the large branches of a desert willow (*Chilopsis saligna*) and partly on top of an *Atriplex canescens* bush growing under it. The structure was formed externally of coarse twigs, a few inches long, and lined with hemp-like strips of bark from a plant growing in the vicinity.

Heleodytes brunneicapillus. Cactus Wren.

The cactus wren is an abundant and characteristic bird of the Lower Sonoran Zone, breeding wherever there are suitable forests of tree yuccas or arborescent cactuses, and sometimes in other forms of spiny vegetation, as the desert acacia (*Acacia greggii*). It was first seen in the Mohave Desert, at Hesperia, a few miles from the summit of Cajon Pass, where the males were singing from the tops of the tree yuccas, January 4–5. Mr. Stephens found a nest containing four fresh eggs in a 'cholla' (cactus) in Salt Wells Valley, about 8 miles north of Indian Wells, the 1st of May, and saw the species sparingly in Owens Valley, a few miles north of Little Owens Lake. In the Coso Valley, and at Coso in the mountains of the same name, Mr. Palmer and the writer found this species among the tree yuccas, and the former observer found a number of old nests during the first half of May. In the early part of July, the species was very common in Walker Pass, where as many as half a dozen were seen in one yucca, and at the South Fork of the Kern River it was found to be common wherever yuccas occurred. Mr. Nelson found it rather common about the ranch in Vegas Valley, Nevada, and still more numerous among the mesquite in Vegas Wash near the Colorado River, where the birds were in full song, March 10.

Dr. Merriam furnished the following notes on this species: "In the Mohave Desert, California, many nests were found in tree yuccas between Cajon Pass and Pilot Knob, the first week in April, but none of them contained eggs. The species reaches the extreme western end of the desert (Antelope Valley), and a few were seen in yuccas and sage-brush in a wash leading south from Gorman ranch toward Peru Creek, June 30.

"From the Mohave Desert the cactus wren extends up the wash leading to Tehachapi Basin, where it was tolerably common in the yuccas and 'chollas' below Cameron. In Walker Pass, it ranges from the east or Mohave Desert side completely across the Sierra to the valley of Kern River, where it is abundant in groves of tree yuccas and in 'chollas' down to 820 meters (2,700 feet) altitude, and where dozens of their large nests were seen in the cactuses, June 22. In Nevada two nests were found in *Acacia greggii* at Bitter Springs in the Muddy Mountains, May 5; both had been used the present season, and one contained an addled egg. The species was common on the high mesa between the Muddy and Virgin rivers, May 7, where nearly every branching cactus contained the remnants of a nest, but all the young had hatched and flown away. In the Beaverdam Mountains, in southwestern Utah, they were common in yuccas and cactuses up to 1,150 meters (3,800 feet) on the west slope. In the Lower Santa Clara Valley, Utah, near St. George, they were common, breeding in the arborescent cactus, May 11–15. This valley is the extreme northeastern limit of distribution of the species. In Southern California, on the coast slope, it is abundant on the San Bernardino Plain, and thence southward. Many were seen in the Santa Clara Valley at its junction with Castac Creek, June 30, where its nests were conspicuous in the tall cactus (*Opuntia bernardina*)."

Record of specimens collected of Heleodytes brunneicapillus.

Collector's No.	Sex.	Locality.	Date.	Collector.	Remarks.
32	♂	Hesperia, Calif	Jan. 4, 1891	A. K. Fisher	
33	♂	....do	....do	....do	
389	♂	Kern River, Calif	July 6, 1891	....do	South Fork.

Salpinctes obsoletus. Rock Wren.

The rock wren was seen wherever there were bare rocks suited to its wants, from the lowest valleys to above timber line on the highest mountains. It was seen at Granite Well in the Mohave Desert, January 13; at Lone Willow Spring, January 17; at Mesquite Well, in Death Valley, January 20; and in Furnace Creek Cañon, in the Funeral Mountains, February 5. In the Panamint Mountains, it was common in Johnson, Surprise, and Emigrant cañons in April, and Mr. Nelson found it common and widely distributed along Cottonwood Cañon, where young, following their parents, were seen during the last of May. In the latter part of June several were seen in Death Valley Cañon, a few hundred feet above the valley, and thence to the summit of Telescope Peak, where a family of six or eight were seen among the loose rocks.

In Nevada this wren was not uncommon at Ash Meadows, in Oasis Valley, and in the Grapevine Mountains in March, and in the latter mountains was breeding commonly in May. Mr. Nelson found it sparingly at various places in Pahrump Valley and along the route to the Bend of the Colorado in March. Dr. Merriam found it common in Tule Cañon, and thence up to the summit of Mount Magruder, in rocky places, June 4–9; on Gold Mountain, June 3; in Pahranagat Valley, May 22–26; and in the Pahroc Mountains, near Pahroc Spring, May 21–22. In Utah, he reported it common along the cliffs of the Santa Clara Valley, May 11–15; at the Upper Santa Clara Crossing, May 16; and saw two pairs in the junipers in the Beaverdam Mountains, May 11.

In Shepherd Cañon and at Maturango Spring, in the Argus Range, California, it was common during the first half of May, and in the cañons in the Coso Mountains during the latter part of the month. Mr. Nelson found it ranging from the bottoms of the valley to the summit of Inyo and White mountains and to timber line at the head of Owens River. In the former range, at Cerro Gordo, Mr. Palmer found young just out of the nest, May 31. The species was common and well distributed in Owens Valley from the lower end of Owens Lake to the upper part, at the base of the White Mountains. It was common along the western slope of Walker Pass, along Kern River Valley and below Old Fort Tejon, in the Cañada de las Uvas. In the High Sierra it was common at Big Cottonwood Meadows during the summer, and one was seen at Round Valley, 12 miles south of Mount Whitney, above timber line, August 28, and one at Whitney Meadows about the same time.

Record of specimens collected of *Salpinctes obsoletus*.

Collector's No.	Sex.	Locality.	Date.	Collector.	Remarks.
9	♂	Daggett, Calif.	Feb. 7, 1891	F. Stephens	Mohave Desert.
64	♂	Lone Willow Spring, Calif.	Jan. 17, 1891	A. K. Fisher	
275	♂ juv.	Owens Valley, Calif.	June 1, 1891	...do...	Keeler.
330	♀	......do......	June 11, 1891	...do...	Lone Pine.
42	♂	Grapevine Spring, Calif.	April 2, 1891	F. Stephens	

Catherpes mexicanus conspersus. Cañon Wren.

The cañon wren was found in a number of the mountain ranges visited by the expedition in California and Nevada. In a few places in the Panamint Mountains it was common, but in no other of the desert ranges was it found in any numbers. We first observed it in Furnace Creek Cañon in the Funeral Mountains, on our way to the Amargosa Desert early in February, and again on the return trip in the latter part of March. Mr. Bailey saw one at Saratoga Springs in the southern end of Death Valley, in February. In Johnson and Surprise cañons, in the Panamint Range, it was common, and males were heard singing at all times of day during the first half of April. A few were seen by Mr. Nelson on the east or Saline Valley side of the Inyo Mountains in the latter part of the same month. In the Argus Range it was seen in Shepherd Cañon in January and April, and at Lookout in the latter part of June. Dr. Merriam found it among the cliffs in the juniper belt on both sides of the Beaverdam Mountains, in southwestern Utah, May 10-11. He also found it breeding along the cliffs in the Lower Santa Clara Valley, Utah, May 11-15, and at the Upper Santa Clara crossing, May 16. Two were seen in the Pahroc Mountains, near Pahroc Spring, Nevada, May 22. In the northern part of the range, and in the Grapevine Mountains, Nevada, Mr. Nelson did not find it common during May and early June.

The following notes may refer wholly or in part to the present race of the cañon wren, or to the California coast form (*punctulatus*), as no specimens were preserved for identification. Several were seen along the South Fork of Kern River, and near Kernville, Calif., in early July. Dr. Merriam saw several in the Cañada de las Uvas, and heard it in the cañon of Peru Creek below Alamo ranch, in the Sierra Liebre, June 30. A few were seen at Three Rivers, Tulare County, in the western foothills of the Sierra, July 25-29, and September 17, and in the Sequoia National Park, at Halsted Meadows, August 6. Several were seen by Mr. Palmer at Michigan Bluff, Placer County, the last week in September.

Record of specimens collected of Catherpes mexicanus conspersus.

Collector's No.	Sex.	Locality.	Date.	Collector.	Remarks.
	♀	Panamint, Calif	Jan. 10, 1891	V. Bailey	
	♂	Panamint Mountains, Calif	Mar. 30, 1891	E. W. Nelson	Johnson Cañon.
143	♂	....do	Mar. 28, 1891	....do	Do.
156	♂	....do	....do	A. K. Fisher	Do.
157	♀	....do	Apr. 13, 1891	....do	Surprise Cañon.
165	♂	....do	....do	....do	Do.
	♂	....do	Apr. 18, 1891	....do	Do.

Thryothorus bewickii spilurus. Vigors's Wren.

A specimen taken at San Bernardino, December 29, 1890, although not typical of this race, resembles it more closely than it does any other. The bird which Mr. Bailey saw commonly at Monterey was undoubtedly this subspecies. Mr. Nelson found a form of Bewick's wren which probably belongs to this race common at San Luis Obispo, the last of October, in the Tejon and Temploa mountains about the same time, and along the route from San Simon to Carpenteria and Santa Paula during November and December.

Thryothorus bewickii bairdi. Baird's Wren.

The white-throated wren was more or less common in various places visited by the expedition. One was seen among the tree yuccas at Hesperia, in the Mohave Desert, January 4. In Death Valley a specimen was secured at Furnace Creek January 31, and a few individuals were seen among the mesquite thickets at Bennett Wells, and between that place and Saratoga Springs, about the same time. A few were seen at Resting Springs in the Amargosa Desert, in February.

In the Panamint Mountains it was seen in Johnson Cañon, early in April; by Dr. Merriam in Emigrant Cañon, April 14-15; on the north side of Telescope Peak, April 17-19, and by Mr. Nelson in Surprise Cañon, in January. In the Argus Range a few were seen in Shepherd Cañon in January, and a specimen was secured at Maturango Spring May 13. In the Coso Mountains a family in which the young were full grown and able to fly was seen in one of the cañons, May 23. Dr. Merriam saw many on the summit of the White Mountains, between Deep Spring and Owens valleys, where young were following their parents about among the piñon and juniper, June 9. Mr. Nelson found it common at Lone Pine in December, 1890, and two or three were seen in Walker Pass, July 2-3. The species was common along the South Fork of Kern River to Kernville, July 3-13, and Mr. Palmer saw one in Kings River Cañon in August. Mr. Stephens saw it at the Queen mine in the White Mountains, Nevada, July 11-16.

In Nevada, several were seen at Ash Meadows, Pahrump and Vegas valleys, and in the Grapevine Mountains, in March. In the Santa Clara Valley, Utah, one was shot and several others seen, May 11-16, and an old nest was found in a hole in a cottonwood, about 3 feet above the ground.

Record of specimens collected of Thryothorus bewickii bairdi.

Collector's No.	Sex.	Locality.	Date.	Collector.	Remarks.
12	♀	San Bernardino, Calif.	Dec. 29, 1890	A. K. Fisher	Resembling closely *spilurus*.
94	♂	Death Valley, Calif.	Jan. 31, 1891	...do	Furnace Creek.
236	♂	Argus Range, Calif.	May 13, 1891	...do	Maturango Spring.
21	♂	Resting Springs, Calif.	Feb. 17, 1891	F. Stephens	
	♂	White Mountains, Calif.	June 9, 1891	V. Bailey	
	♀ juv.	...do	...do	...do	
	♂	Santa Clara, Utah	May 11, 1891	C. Hart Merriam	

Troglodytes aëdon aztecus. Western House Wren.

The western house wren was not seen in many localities, though when found it was not an uncommon species. A few were seen at Ash Meadows, Nev., about March 20. Specimens taken at San Bernardino, Calif., in the latter part of December, 1890, were intermediate between this race and Parkman's wren of the northwest coast region. In the Panamint Mountains it was first observed in Johnson Cañon, April 12, in Suprise Cañon a little later, and in Emigrant Cañon April 14–15. A few were seen in an alfalfa field at Grapevine Spring, on the western slope of the Grapevine Mountains, the first week in April, and in Shepherd Cañon, in the Argus Range, the last week of the month. Mr. Stephens found it rather common at Searl's garden, near the south end of the same range, April 23–26; at Bishop Creek, in Owens Valley, August 4–10, and among the brush on the side of Reche Cañon, September 22–24. Several were seen along the South Fork of Kern River, July 3–10, and among the oaks above Walker Basin, July 14. Mr. Palmer found the house wren abundant at Old Fort Tejon early in July, and Mr. Nelson saw several in the Cañada de las Uvas and along San Emigdio Creek about the middle of October. In the High Sierra, Mr. Nelson saw it at the head of Owens River, and on the west slope down into the Yosemite Valley. It was common in the Sequoia National Park during the first week in August; at Horse Corral Meadows, August 9–13; near timber line in Round Valley, 12 miles south of Mount Whitney, August 28; Mineral King, September 9–10; and at Three Rivers, in the western foothills of the Sierra, September 14.

Record of specimens collected of Troglodytes aëdon aztecus.

Collector's No.	Sex.	Locality.	Date.	Collector.	Remarks.
3	♂	San Bernardino, Calif.	Dec. 28, 1890	A. K. Fisher	Inclining toward *parkmanii*.
4	♀	...do	...do	...do	Do.
	♂	Panamint Mountains, Calif.	Apr. 11, 1891	E. W. Nelson	Johnson Cañon.
	♂	Kern River, Calif.	July 4, 1891	V. Bailey	South Fork.
	♂	Sierra Nevada, Calif.	July 30, 1891	E. W. Nelson	San Joaquin River.
139	♂ im	...do	July 22, 1891	F. Stephens	
155	♀ im	...do	Aug. 21, 1891	...do	Olancha Peak.
424	♀	...do	Aug. 27, 1891	A. K. Fisher	Round Valley, 12 miles south Mount Whitney.

Cistothorus palustris paludicola. Tule Wren.

The long-billed marsh wren was common in a number of places where tules and other rank vegetation occurred along the streams, lakes, or marshes. In Death Valley a few were seen at Furnace Creek and Bennett Wells, and a considerable number at Saratoga Springs during the latter part of January. Dr. Merriam found it common at the latter place among the reeds April 26. In Owens Valley Mr. Nelson found it at Keeler and Lone Pine in December, 1890, and Mr. Stephens reported it common at Little Owens Lake May 6-11. In Nevada it was common in Pahrump, Vegas, and Oasis valleys, and not uncommon at Ash Meadows in March. Dr. Merriam also found it common in the valley of the Muddy May 6, in Pahranagat Valley May 23, breeding in the tules, and Mr. Stephens saw several at Grapevine spring April 1-4.

Record of specimens collected of Cistothorus palustris paludicola.

Collector's No.	Sex.	Locality.	Date.	Collector.	Remarks.
93	♂	Death Valley, Calif.	Jan. 31, 1891	A. K. Fisher	Furnace Creek.
132	♀	Ash Meadows, Nev.	Mch. 18, 1891	....do....	

Certhia familiaris occidentalis. California Creeper.

The tree creeper was seen nowhere except in the High Sierra. Mr. Palmer and the writer saw it at the deserted Kaweah sawmill in the Sequoia National Park, and at other places in the same general region, the first week in August, and at Horse Corral Meadows a week later. Mr. Nelson found it at the head of Owens River and in the Yosemite Valley, and Mr. Dutcher at Big Cottonwood Meadows. The writer saw it at the latter place and also at Whitney Meadows and Soda Springs about the 1st of September. Mr. Nelson observed a few at Mount Piños in October.

Sitta carolinensis aculeata. Slender-billed Nuthatch.

In California the slender-billed nuthatch was seen among the pines on several of the mountain ranges and in the oaks west of the Sierra Nevada. In the Panamint Mountains it was not uncommon in Johnson and Surprise cañons among the piñons, where a pair was seen hunting for a nesting site April 20. Dr. Merriam saw several among the junipers on the north side of Telescope Peak April 17-19, and Mr. Bailey and the writer heard and saw it near the same place June 23-24. A pair was seen among the piñons above Maturango Spring May 13; Mr. Nelson found it at the head of Owens River, and on the western slope opposite, in July and August; and Mr. Stephens heard it near Queen station, Nev., July 11-16. Dr. Merriam saw one among the live oaks between Havilah and Walker Basin, June 24, one in Tehachapi Pass June 25, and Mr. Palmer reported the species as common at Old

Fort Tejon the first week in July. The writer found it rather common in the Sequoia National Park during the first week in August, at Horse Corral Meadows August 9–13, in Kings River Cañon August 13–16, and in Round Valley, 12 miles south of Mount Whitney, and Whitney Meadows the last of the month. At Three Rivers, in the western foothills of the Sierra, it was common among the oaks July 25–30; Mr. Bailey saw it along the Kaweah River up to timber line in August; Mr. Dutcher found it a common summer resident at Big Cottonwood Meadows, and Mr. Stephens reported it as rather common at Menache Meadows May 24–26. Mr. Nelson saw it from the Cañada de las Uvas to the head of San Emigdio Cañon the last of October, and in the mountains near San Simeon in November.

Record of specimens collected of Sitta carolinensis aculeata.

Collector's No.	Sex.	Locality.	Date.	Collector.	Remarks.
352	♂	Panamint Mountains, Calif..	June 23, 1891	A. K. Fisher	Telescope Peak.
427	♀	Sierra Nevada, Calif.	Aug. 27, 1891	...do	Round Valley, 12 miles south Mount Whitney.
20	♂	......do	July 30, 1891	B. H. Dutcher	Big Cottonwood Meadows.

Sitta canadensis. Red-bellied Nuthatch.

The red-bellied nuthatch was not seen in the mountain ranges east of the Sierra Nevada in California. It was common in the Sequoia National Park and Horse Corral Meadows, where it was often heard or seen during the first half of August. Mr. Nelson saw a few on the western slope of the mountains opposite the head of Owens River, and the writer found it common among the flocks of migrants in Round Valley, 12 miles south of Mount Whitney, August 27–28, and at timber line above Mineral King September 9–11. On the coast Mr. Bailey reported the red-bellied nuthatch as common at Monterey September 28 to October 9.

Record of specimens collected of Sitta canadensis.

Collector's No.	Sex.	Locality.	Date.	Collector.	Remarks.
406	♀	Sierra Nevada, Calif.	Aug. 4, 1891	A. K. Fisher	Sequoia National Park.
431	♀	......do	Aug. 28, 1891	...do	Round Valley, 12 miles south Mount Whitney.

Sitta pygmæa. Pygmy Nuthatch.

The only locality east of the Sierra Nevada where this nuthatch was met with was the Charleston Mountains, Nevada, where Mr. Palmer and Mr. Nelson found it common in February high up among the fox-tail pine (*Pinus aristata*). Mr. Stephens found it not uncommon nearly up to timber line at Menache Meadows, Calif., May 24-26, and a few at Bishop Creek August 4-10. Mr. Palmer reported it common among the pines at the summit of Frazier Mountain July 9; near the summit of Tejon Pass July 12; and Mr. Dutcher saw it frequently at Big Cottonwood Meadows during the summer. The pygmy nuthatch was not uncommon among the pines on the ridge above Walker Basin July 14, among the sequoias on the Kaweah River the first of August, at the Sequoia National Park about the same date, and at Big Cottonwood Meadows and Round Valley the last of the month.

Record of specimens collected of Sitta pygmæa.

Collector's No.	Sex.	Locality.	Date.	Collector.	Remarks.
10	♂	Sierra Nevada, Calif	July 1, 1891	B. H. Dutcher	Big Cottonwood Meadows.
32	♂	....do	Aug. 11, 1891	....do	Do.
35		....do	Aug. 24, 1891	....do	Do.
152	♀	....do	Aug. 9, 1891	F. Stephens	Bishop Creek.
391	♀ im.	Walker Basin, Calif	July 14, 1891	A. K. Fisher	
425	♂	Sierra Nevada, Calif	Aug. 27, 1891	....do	Round Valley, 12 miles south of Mount Whitney.
426	♂	....do	....do	....do	Do.

Parus inornatus. Plain Titmouse.

The plain titmouse was first met with in the Sierra Nevada in California. It was not uncommon on the western slope of Walker Pass, where a specimen was taken July 3, and the birds seen elsewhere in the Sierra Nevada may probably be correctly referred to this species. It was common along the valley of the Kern July 3-13; in Walker Basin, July 13-16; and at Three Rivers in the western foothills of the Sierra, July 25-30, and September 13-15. Dr. Merriam saw the species in the Tejon Mountains, where it was common in the Cañada de las Uvas, June 28-29, and Mr. Nelson saw it at Mount Piños the last of October, in the hills along the route from La Panza to San Luis Obispo, and sparingly from the sea to the summit of the hills between San Simeon and Carpenteria, in November and December.

A specimen taken by the writer in Cajon Pass January 2, although not typical *inornatus*, was nearer it than *griseus*.

Record of specimens collected of Parus inornatus.

Collector's No.	Sex.	Locality.	Date.	Collector.	Remarks.
25	♂	Cajon Pass, Calif	Jan. 2, 1892	A. K. Fisher	Not typical.
367	♀ im.	Walker Pass, Calif	July 3, 1891	....do	Western slope.

Parus inornatus griseus. Gray Titmouse.

The gray titmouse was seen in most of the desert ranges. In the Charleston Mountains, Nevada, it was common among the junipers in

March. In the Panamint Mountains, California, it was seen in Johnson and Surprise cañons among the piñons and junipers in April, and Dr. Merriam found it common north of Telescope Peak, where a female, containing eggs nearly ready to be deposited, was killed, April 17-19. The writer saw a few at the same place June 22. Mr. Nelson noted it sparingly among the piñons on the Panamint, Grapevine, Inyo, and White mountains during the breeding season. Along the eastern slope of the Sierra Nevada a few were seen at the head of Owens River, and at Benton, in July.

Record of specimens collected of Parus inornatus griseus.

Collector's No.	Sex.	Locality.	Date.	Collector.	Remarks.
47	♀	Panamint Mountains, Calif	Apr. 18, 1891	F. Stephens	
145	♂	...do...	Mar. 28, 1891	A. K. Fisher	Johnson Cañon.
146	♀	...do...	...do...	...do...	Do.
168	♂	...do...	Apr. 19, 1891	...do...	Surprise Cañon.
		Charleston Mountains, Nev	Mar. 7, 1891	V. Bailey	

Parus gambeli. Mountain Chickadee.

The mountain chickadee was seen on all the mountains which support a growth of pines. In Nevada Mr. Palmer reported it common about the camp in the Charleston Mountains in February, and Mr. Stephens found a few in the Grapevine Mountains in March. Dr. Merriam found it breeding on Mount Magruder, high up among the nut pines, June 5-11, and Mr. Stephens saw several at the Queen mine in the White Mountains, July 11-16.

In the Panamint Mountains, California, it was tolerably common in Johnson and Surprise cañons in April. Dr. Merriam found it common near Telescope Peak about the middle of the month, though Mr. Nelson reported it as apparently rare among the piñons in the northern end of the range as well as in the Grapevine Mountains in June. At the 'charcoal kilns' near the head of Wild Rose Cañon, the writer noted it as quite common and found a nest with young June 24.

It was not uncommon in the Argus Range, where a nest containing eight fresh eggs was found in a piñon on the ridge above Maturango Spring, May 14. The nest, which was composed of fine grass and hair, was placed in an eroded cavity behind the end of one of the lower limbs which had been partially torn and twisted from the trunk by heavy snow or violent wind. It was perfectly concealed and would never have been discovered had the bird remained quiet when the writer accidentally struck the drooping branch. Mr. Nelson reported it as breeding sparingly from the lower edge of the piñons up to the summit in the Inyo Mountains and to timber line in the White Mountains. This chickadee was common at the head of Owens River, and Mr. Stephens noted it as rather common at Independence Creek, June 18-23; at Menache Meadows, May 24-26; several at Bishop Creek, August 4-10. Mr.

Palmer found it common on Frazier Mountain July 9, sparingly at Tejon Pass, July 12; and Mr. Nelson reported it common on Mount Piños the last of October. In the High Sierra it was common in the Sequoia National Park the first week in August; at Horse Corral Meadows, August 9–13; at Round Valley, 12 miles south of Mount Whitney, August 27–28; Big Cottonwood Meadows during the summer; and at Whitney Meadows and Mineral King the last of August and first of September. Mr. Palmer saw one at an altitude of 3,900 meters (13,000 feet) near the head waters of the Kern River, September 1.

Record of specimens collected of Parus gambeli.

Collector's No.	Sex.	Locality.	Date.	Collector.	Remarks.
40	♂	Grapevine Mountains, Nev.	Mar. 24, 1891	F. Stephens	
142	♂	Panamint Mountains, Calif.	Mar. 28, 1891	A. K. Fisher	Johnson Cañon.
151		do	April 6, 1891	do	Do.
152	♂	do	April 9, 1891	do	Do.
	♂	Argus Range, Calif.	May 7, 1891	T. S. Palmer	Maturango Peak.
	♂	White Mountains, Calif.	July 12, 1891	E. W. Nelson	

Parus rufescens neglectus. California Chickadee.

Mr. Bailey found the California chickadee common at Boulder Creek, California (north of Monterey Bay), where he secured a specimen October 14, 1891.

Chamæa fasciata henshawi. Pallid Wren-Tit.

This interesting little bird was first met with by Mr. Bailey and the writer at Kernville, Calif., on July 11, where specimens were secured. It was common there, as it was the following week in Walker Basin. Mr. Nelson saw a few in the foothills between the Merced and San Joaquin rivers; Mr. Palmer heard a number among the chamisal in the San Francisquito Pass, July 1, and Mr. Stephens heard several in Reche Cañon, near San Bernardino, September 22–24. Mr. Bailey reported it common along the Kaweah River in the thick chapparal below the pines. Mr. Nelson found the ground-tit common in the thickets on the sand dunes along the coast between San Simeon and Carpenteria, and on the bushy hillsides between the latter place and Santa Paula, in November and December. Dr. Merriam reported it as a common breeder in the coast ranges of San Diego County, where he found it in March and again in July.

Record of specimens collected of Chamæa fasciata henshawi.

Collector's No.	Sex.	Locality.	Date.	Collector.	Remarks.
385	♂	Kernville, Calif	July 11, 1891	A. K. Fisher	
	♀	do	do	V. Bailey	
107	♂	San Bernardino, Calif.	Sept. 23, 1891	F. Stephens	Reche Cañon.
		Morro, Calif	Nov. 8, 1891	E. W. Nelson	

Psaltriparus minimus californicus. California Bush-Tit.

The California bush-tit is common in the coast region, on the western slope of the Sierra Nevada, and sparingly on the eastern slope of the same range. Mr. Stephens found it tolerably common in the lower part of the cañon at Independence Creek, where a nest containing young was found, June 16–23; and saw a small flock at Bishop Creek, August 4–10. Individuals were seen on the western slope of Walker Pass, July 2–3, and Dr. Merriam found it common in the chaparral from Kernville to Havilah, and thence to Walker Basin and Caliente, June 23–24. and in the Cañada de las Uvas, June 28–29. It was common at Three Rivers in the western foothills, in flocks of 25 or more, July 25–30, and Mr. Bailey reported it common along the Kaweah River up to the conifers, about the same time. The latter observer found a species of bush-tit common at Monterey, the first of October; Mr. Stephens saw two flocks at Reche Cañon, September 22–24; and Dr. Merriam noticed it near the coast in San Diego County in July. Mr. Nelson reported it common along the coast in small flocks in thickets and on bushy hillsides, from San Simeon to Carpenteria, in November and December.

Record of specimens collected of Psaltriparus minimus californicus.

Collector's No.	Sex.	Locality.	Date.	Collector.	Remarks.
76	♀	Owens Valley, Calif.	June 8, 1891	F. Stephens	Olancha.
369	♀	Walker Pass, Calif.	July 3, 1891	A. K. Fisher	Western Slope.

Psaltriparus plumbeus. Lead-colored Bush-Tit.

The lead-colored bush-tit is common in a number of the desert ranges visited. In Nevada Mr. Stephens found it rather common in the Grapevine Mountains in March, and saw one flock at the Queen mine in the White Mountains in July. Dr. Merriam found it high up on Mount Magruder in the nut pines, June 5–9, among the junipers in the Juniper Mountains May 19, and common in the Beaverdam Mountains, Utah, May 11. A few were seen by Mr. Stephens at Twelve Mile Spring, near Resting Springs, Calif., in February. In the Panamint Mountains it was observed daily in Johnson and Surprise Cañons in April, in small flocks on the north side of Telescope Peak April 17–19, and among the sage in the northern part of the range, as well as in the Grapevine Mountains May 4 to June 15. Mr. Nelson found a few among the piñons near Waucoba Peak in the Inyo Mountains the last of June, and a few on the eastern slope of the White Mountains among the same kind of trees in July.

Record of specimens collected of Psaltriparus plumbeus.

Collector's No.	Sex.	Locality.	Date.	Collector.	Remarks.
	♂	Juniper Mountains, Nev	May 19, 1891	C. Hart Merriam	
	♀	Mount Magruder, Nev	June 5, 1891	V. Bailey	
38	♀	Grapevine Mountains, Nev	Mar. 24, 1891	F. Stephens	
24	♀	Resting Springs, Calif	Feb. 21, 1891	...do	
25	♀	...do	...do	...do	
144	♀	Panamint Mountains, Calif	Mar. 28, 1891	A. K. Fisher	Johnson Cañon.
153		...do	Apr. 9, 1891	...do	Do.
169		...do	Apr. 19, 1891	...do	Surprise Cañon.
131	♀ im.	Owens Valley, Nev	July 11, 1891	F. Stephens	Queen station.

Auriparus flaviceps. Yellow-headed Tit.

The verdin is a characteristic bird of a large part of the Lower Sonoran zone. The most western locality at which it was observed by the expedition was Resting Springs, near the Amargosa River, Calif., where a male was shot by Mr. Stephens February 13, 1891. Here the yellow-headed tit was common in February, and it was seen every day among the mesquit thickets, and its nests were frequently found. As is the case with several other members of the family, the old nests, after being relined with feathers and hair, are used for winter homes. East of this point it was found wherever suitable thickets exist, all the way to Utah. Many nests were found in bushes of *Pluchea borealis* at the Great Bend of the Colorado, Nev., by Dr. Merriam. These nests were usually about five feet above the ground, and, with the exception of one containing three eggs nearly ready to hatch, were still empty. Other nests were observed along the Virgin River and the lower part of the Muddy May 7–10, and at Beaverdam Creek, Ariz., May 9–10; and a single nest was discovered near the junction of the Santa Clara with the Virgin in southwestern Utah May 14.

Regulus calendula. Ruby-crowned Kinglet.

The ruby-crowned kinglet was a common migrant or winter resident in the valleys visited, and occurred sparingly as a summer resident in the higher mountains. In Nevada a few were seen at Ash Meadows in March; in Pahrump Valley Mr. Nelson found it common among the willows at the ranch in February; Mr. Stephens observed it in full song in Oasis Valley in March; not uncommon in the Grapevine Mountains in the same month, and Dr. Merriam shot one at Mountain Spring, in the Charleston Mountains, April 30.

At San Bernardino, Calif., it was numerous in the bushes along the streams December 28–29, 1890, and on the slopes in Cajon Pass January 2. A few were seen at Furnace Creek, Death Valley, about the first of February and again April 9–12. In the Panamint Mountains this kinglet was common in Johnson and Surprise cañons, and tolerably so in Emigrant Cañon in April. It was common at Hot Springs, in Panamint Valley, April 20–25, and was observed in Shepherd Cañon, in the Argus Range, later in the month. Mr. Nelson saw a few at the heads of streams on the eastern slope of the White Mountains, and reported it common at the head of Owens River and on the western slope of the Sierra Nevada. It was common at timber line at Round Valley, 12 miles south of Mount Whitney, August 28; in the San Joaquin Valley in October; and along the route from San Simeon to Carpenteria and Santa Paula in November and December.

Regulus satrapa olivaceus. Western Golden-crowned Kinglet.

The only record of this kinglet made by the expedition was of one seen by Mr. Nelson near San Luis Obispo about the first of November. Mr. Belding reports it as rare at Crocker's, 21 miles northwest of the Yosemite Valley.

Polioptila cærulea obscura. Western Gnatcatcher.

Blue-gray gnatcatchers were common in a number of scattered localities. At San Bernardino, a small flock associated with other birds was seen December 28, and again on the following day. Several were seen at Daggett, January 8-10, and one was secured at Furnace Creek, Death Valley, January 24. The species was common in the Panamint Mountains, in both Johnson and Surprise cañons, in April, and at Hot Springs in Panamint Valley, among the mesquite, April 20-25. Mr. Nelson found it breeding in both the Panamint and Grapevine mountains. At Willow Creek, in the former range, he found a nest containing five eggs, May 19, and another containing three eggs, May 24. Both nests were placed within 3 feet of the ground, and were neat, compactly built structures, with deep cup-shaped depressions, more or less contracted at the rims. A few individuals were seen in the Argus Range, at Maturango Spring, the first half of May, and in the Coso Mountains during the latter part of the same month. Mr. Nelson saw a single bird in a mesquite clump in Saline Valley, a few in the sage near Waucoba Peak, in the Inyo Range, the last of June, and in the White Mountains in July. He saw a few in the western foothills of the Sierra Nevada in August, and on the east slope Mr. Stephens found it uncommon in the lower part of the cañon of Independence Creek, in June. One was seen on the western slope of Walker Pass, July 3; it was common in the hills above Walker Basin, July 14; along the Kaweah, below the conifers, in August and September; and Mr. Palmer saw one in Kings River Cañon, August 13. On Mount Magruder, Nevada, Dr. Merriam shot a pair June 7, and reported the species as tolerably common in the lower part of the piñons. He found it breeding commonly in the Santa Clara Valley, Utah, May 11-15, and in the junipers on the Beaverdam Mountains, May 10-11. Mr. Nelson found it common in the thickets along the coast from Morro, Calif., to Carpenteria, November 4 to December 18, and rather common from Carpenteria to Santa Paula, the last of the year.

Record of specimens collected of Polioptila cœrulea obscura.

Collector's No.	Sex.	Locality.	Date.	Collector.	Remarks.
9	♂	San Bernardino, Calif.	Dec. 28, 1890	A. K. Fisher	
10	♂	....do....	....do....	....do....	
11		....do....	Dec. 29, 1890	....do....	
50	♂	Daggett, Calif.	Jan. 10, 1891	....do....	Mohave Desert.
70		Death Valley, Calif.	Jan. 24, 1891	....do....	Furnace Creek.
164	♂	Panamint Valley, Calif.	Apr. 16, 1891	....do....	Hot Springs.
214	♂	Argus Range, Calif.	May 8, 1891	....do....	Maturango Spring.
	♂	Panamint Valley, Calif.	Apr. 22, 1891	E. W. Nelson	Hot Springs.
	♀	Mission Santa Ynez, Calif.	Dec. 6, 1891	....do....	
	♂	St. George, Utah	May 16, 1891	V. Bailey	

Polioptila plumbea. Plumbeous Gnatcatcher.

This gnatcatcher was common at Resting Springs, near the Amargosa River, California, in February, where a number of specimens were secured. In Vegas Valley, Nevada, Mr. Nelson and Mr. Bailey saw several and secured one, March 13. At Bunkerville, Nev., Mr. Bailey secured an adult male, May 9. The species may have been seen in other places, but was not distinguished from the blue-gray gnatcatcher. In March, 1889, Mr. Bailey found it common at Fort Mohave, Ariz.

Record of specimens collected of Polioptila plumbea.

Collector's No.	Sex.	Locality.	Date.	Collector.	Remarks.
103	♀	Resting Springs, Calif.	Feb. 8, 1891	A. K. Fisher	
	♀	....do....	Feb. 12, 1891	V. Bailey	
	♀	....do....	....do....	....do....	
	♀	Vegas Valley, Nev.	Mar. 13, 1891	....do....	
	♂	Bunkerville, Nev	May 9, 1891	....do....	

Polioptila californica. Black-tailed Gnatcatcher.

The only place where the Californian gnatcatcher was observed was Reche Cañon, near San Bernardino, where Mr. Stephens found it common, September 22–24.

Myadestes townsendii. Townsend's Solitaire.

Townsend's solitaire was found nowhere common by the expedition. In Cajon Pass, California, several were observed and two secured, January 2. One was shot at Lone Pine, in Owens Valley, in December, 1890, and others were seen at Hot Springs, Panamint Valley, in January.

In the Panamint Mountains, a few were seen in Johnson and Surprise cañons, in April. Mr. Nelson found a few among the piñons about the head of Willow Creek, the 1st of May, and the writer saw a family in Death Valley Cañon, June 22. In the Sierra Nevada, Mr. Nelson found it sparingly on the western slope opposite the head of Owens River; Mr. Stephens secured the young at Bishop Creek, the 1st of August; Mr. Bailey saw one among the sequoias and another among the *Pinus monticola* on the Kaweah River; a few were seen in the Giant forest, August 3; and several at Trout Meadows, September 7. Mr. Belding found a nest and four eggs, June 4, near Crocker's, on the Big Oak Flat and Yosemite Valley stage road. It was placed in a nearly perpendicular bank of a gold mine, within a short distance of the hoisting works, which were in constant use.

In Nevada Townsend's solitaire was not uncommon among the cedars on the Charleston Mountains in March, and a specimen was secured in Oasis Valley, March 15, the only one seen there.

Record of specimens collected of Myadestes townsendii.

Collector's No.	Sex.	Locality.	Date.	Collector.	Remarks.
23	♀	Cajon Pass, Calif	Jan. 2, 1891	A. K. Fisher	
24	♀	......do......	....do......	....do......	
148	♂	Panamint Mountains, Calif	Mar. 31, 1891	....do......	Johnson Cañon.
32	♂	Oasis Valley, Nev	Mar. 15, 1891	F. Stephens	
149	♂ im.	Sierra Nevada, Calif	Aug. 8, 1891	....do......	Bishop Creek; altitude, 9,000 feet.

Turdus ustulatus. Russet-backed Thrush.

A female russet-backed thrush was shot by the writer at Maturango Springs, California, in the Argus Range, May 15, 1891, the only one observed there, and Mr. Stephens saw one at Olancha, in Owens Valley, about the same time.

Turdus ustulatus swainsonii. Olive-backed Thrush.

Mr. Belding reported this thrush as common in the Yosemite Valley, California, in June, and Mr. Nelson secured a female on the northern end of the Panamint Mountains, May 18.

Turdus aonalaschkæ. Dwarf Hermit Thrush.

The dwarf thrush was seen only during migration. Several were seen in Johnson Cañon, in the Panamint Range, California, where a specimen was secured March 28. In the Argus Range, it was not uncommon in Shepherd Cañon the last week in April, and at Maturango Spring one was secured May 8. Mr. Dutcher shot another at Big Cottonwood Meadows September 11, which was probably a migrant, as the summer resident was *auduboni*, or at least what the committee on nomenclature of the American Ornithologists' Union consider Audubon's thrush.

Mr. Bailey found the dwarf thrush common at Monterey the first of October, and Mr. Nelson observed it commonly in the vicinity of San Luis Obispo the last of the month, and along the route from San Simeon to Carpenteria and Santa Paula in November and December.

Record of specimens collected of Turdus aonalaschkæ.

Collector's No.	Sex.	Locality.	Date.	Collector.	Remarks.
36	♂	Panamint Mountains, Calif.	Mar. 28, 1891	E. W. Nelson	Johnson Cañon.
	♂	Sierra Nevada, Calif.	Sept. 11, 1891	B. H. Dutcher	Big Cottonwood Meadows.
	♀ ?	Monterey, Calif	Oct. 6, 1891	V. Bailey	
	♂	Morro, Calif	Nov. 10, 1891	E. W. Nelson	
	♀	......do	......do	......do	

Turdus aonalaschkæ auduboni. Audubon's Hermit Thrush.

A race of the dwarf thrush, named *Turdus sequoiensis* by Mr. Belding, but which the committee on nomenclature of the American Ornithologists' Union decided to be not different from *auduboni* of the Rocky Mountain region, is a summer resident in the Sierra Nevada, and probably in some of the desert ranges, though this is not certain, as specimens were not taken in the latter in summer. This applies to the records of individuals seen at Willow Creek in the Panamint Mountains, during the latter part of May, and on the east side of Waucoba Peak, in the Inyo Mountains, in June. In the Sierra Nevada Mr. Dutcher found the species common during the summer at Big Cottonwood Meadows, and Mr. Nelson reported it as abundant at the head of Owens River and on the San Joaquin River. Mr. Stephens heard a thrush above the Queen mine in the White Mountains, Nevada, July 11–16; saw the species at Bishop Creek August 4–10, and about the lakes on Independence Creek June 18–23. Mr. Belding found it in the Yosemite Valley in June.

Record of specimens collected of Turdus aonalaschkæ auduboni.

Collector's No.	Sex.	Locality.	Date.	Collector.	Remarks.
9		Sierra Nevada, Calif.	June 23, 1891	B. H. Dutcher	Big Cottonwood Meadows.
16	♂	......do	July 11, 1891	......do	
	♂	White Mountains, Calif	July 10, 1891	E. W. Nelson	
	♂	Sierra Nevada, Calif.	July 23, 1891	......do	

Merula migratoria propinqua. Western Robin.

The robin is a rather rare bird in the desert regions, even during migration and in winter. In Nevada several were seen at Ash Meadows in March. Mr. Palmer found it rather common from the valley up to the piñons on the west side of the Charleston Mountains in February, and Mr. Nelson saw it about the ranches in Pahrump and Vegas valleys, and in Vegas Wash, in March. Dr. Merriam saw it on Mount Magruder June 8, and in Utah, at Mountain Meadows, May 17. In California a few were seen at Furnace Creek, Death Valley, the latter part of January, and again on April 10. Several were observed at Resting Springs, in the Amargosa Desert, the first half of February. A few robins were seen about a spring in Johnson Cañon, in the Panamint

Range, in April. Dr. Merriam saw several in the junipers in the same mountains April 16-19, and Mr. Nelson a few at the head of Willow Creek early in May, after which time none were seen. Several were seeen in the Argus Range, above Maturango Spring, the first half of May. Mr. Nelson found it in the Inyo Mountains among *Pinus flexilis* and *P. aristata*, and in the White Mountains from the piñons up to 10,000 feet. In the Sierra Nevada robins were common in many places. Mr. Nelson found them common at the head of Owens River, on the east slope, and in the Yosemite Valley, on the west slope of the Sierra, in July and August. Mr. Stephens found them common at Independence Creek, where a nest and four young was found at the edge of the creek June 18-23; at Bishop Creek, where they were feeding on a red berry locally known as buffalo berry, August 4-10, and at Menache Meadow, nearly to timber line, May 24-26. They were common also at Big Cottonwood and Whitney meadows; among the pines above Walker Basin July 14, in the Sequoia National Park, among the pines and firs, and in the meadows, the first week in August; at Horse Corral Meadows, August 9-13; in Kings River Cañon, August 13-16, and near Mineral King September 9-12. In the western foothills of the Sierra they were seen as early as July 30 at Three Rivers, and Mr. Nelson found a few in the San Joaquin Valley October 5-27; reported them as common about San Luis Obispo October 28 to November 4, and found them generally distributed along the route from San Simeon to Carpenteria and Santa Paula in November and December.

Record of specimens collected of Merula migratoria propinqua.

Collector's No.	Sex.	Locality.	Date.	Collector.	Remarks.
85	♂	Death Valley, Calif	Jan. 29, 1891	A. K. Fisher	Furnace Creek.
108	♂	Resting Springs, Calif	Feb. 11, 1891	....do	
	♂	Panamint Mountains, Calif.	Mar. 28, 1891	E. W. Nelson	Johnson Cañon.
107	♀ juv.	Owens Valley, Calif	June 19, 1891	F. Stephens	Independence Creek

Hesperocichla nævia. Varied Thrush.

Mr. Bailey saw several varied thrushes and secured a specimen at Monterey, Calif., the first week in October; he also found it common at Boulder Creek, Santa Cruz County, and at Auburn, Placer County, during the latter part of the month. Mr. Nelson observed a few in the lowlands about San Simeon, and found it common from Santa Maria south to Carpenteria and Santa Paula, where it was particularly numerous among the trees along the streams and in the cañon.

Record of specimens collected of Hesperocichla nævia.

Collector's No.	Sex.	Locality.	Date.	Collector.	Remarks.
	♀	Monterey, Calif	Oct. 5, 1891	V. Bailey	
	♂	Boulder Creek, Calif	Oct. 12, 1891	....do	

Sialia mexicana. Western Bluebird.

The western bluebird was common in a number of places. At San Bernardino a flock of twenty or more was seen December 29, 1890; in Cajon Pass, March 30; in the cottonwoods bordering the Mohave River at Victor, the same day, and at Granite Wells January 13. Mr. Nelson found the species common near Hot Springs, in Panamint Valley, California, in January, and a few at Pahrump and Vegas ranches in Nevada, in February and March. Dr. Merriam saw several small flocks on the north side of Telescope Peak, in the Panamint Mountains, April 17-19, and Mr. Nelson found it on the western slope of the Sierra Nevada in August. It was very common along the South Fork of the Kern River, July 3-10; in Walker Basin, from the valley to the summit of the ridge, July 13-16, and in the Cañada de las Uvas, June 28-29. In the High Sierra it was not uncommon at Sequoia National Park during the first week of August; was common in Horse Corral Meadows and Kings River Cañon August 9-16, and was observed at Big Cottonwood Meadows and at the head of the Kaweah River later in the season. In the western foothills of the Sierra, at Three Rivers, it was common July 25-30 and September 12-16; and at Monterey, September 28-October 9. Mr. Nelson saw a few in various parts of the San Joaquin Valley in October, and found it common along the route from San Simeon to Carpenteria and Santa Paula in November and December.

Record of specimens collected of Sialia mexicana.

Collector's No.	Sex.	Locality.	Date.	Collector.	Remarks.
13	♀	San Bernardino, Calif	Dec. 29, 1890	A. K. Fisher	
14	♂	....do	....do	....do	
15	♂	....do	....do	....do	
	♂	Charleston Mountains, Nev	Feb. 13, 1891	E. W. Nelson	
370	♀ juv.	Kern River, Calif	July 4, 1891	A. K. Fisher	South Fork.
39	♂	Sierra Nevada, Calif	Sept. 14, 1891	B. H. Butcher	Mount Whitney.

Sialia arctica. Mountain Bluebird.

The mountain bluebird is more or less common in the desert valleys during the winter, and breeds in the higher ranges among the pines.

At Granite Wells, in the Mohave Desert, a number were seen January 13-14. Unlike the western bluebird, this species was wary and difficult of approach. It is not evident what causes this shyness, unless, perhaps, contact with the Indian, that ruthless and inveterate enemy to animal life, who attacks every bird throughout the year, no matter how small or in what condition, killing the mother of a dependent brood with as much eagerness as a fattened buck in season.

In Death Valley a flock was seen at Mesquite Well, January 21. It was common at Bennett Wells and Saratoga Springs, and at Furnace Creek, associated with titlarks and savanna sparrows in the alfalfa fields, the last of January. Several were seen at Resting Springs, in the Amargosa Desert, in February. Dr. Merriam saw a pair at Mountain Meadows, Utah, May 17. In Nevada he found several in the juniper forest on the Juniper Mountains, May 18; on the Pahroc Mountains, May 21-22, and on Mount Magruder, June 4-8. In the latter locality this bluebird was breeding among the nut pines, where it was tolerably common. Several were seen at Ash Meadows, and among the cedars on the Charleston Mountains, in March, and in Pahrump Valley, near the ranch, in February. Mr. Stephens found it not common in the Grapevine Mountains in March, and Mr. Nelson saw a few pairs about the summit of the peak and among the piñons, where they were apparently breeding, June 10-11. In the Panamint Mountains, California, Dr. Merriam saw several pairs at the north base of Telescope Peak, April 17-19, and Mr. Bailey and the writer found a number among the pines (*Pinus aristata* and *P. flexilis*), near the summit of the same peak, June 23. It was not uncommon in the Argus Range above Maturango Spring during the first half of May, and a pair was seen on the summit of the Coso Mountains, May 23. Mr. Nelson found it not uncommon in the Inyo Range above the piñons in June; a few among the upper piñons in the White Mountains in July, and at the latter place Dr. Merriam saw a number of males June 9—the females evidently were sitting. In Owens Valley, according to Mr. Nelson, it was common in winter, and Mr. Stephens found it more or less common above this valley along the eastern slope of the Sierra Nevada up to timber line at Menache Meadows, May 24-26; at the lakes on Independence Creek, June 23; among the piñons at Benton, July 9-10, and at the lake on Bishop Creek, August 4-10. Mr. Nelson reported it generally distributed up to timber line at the head of Owens River the last of July, but nowhere common, and Mr. Stephens found it common at the Queen mine in the White Mountains, Nevada, July 11-16. Mr. Bailey saw a few on the western slope of Walker Pass, July 3, found it common at timber line near the head of the Kaweah River, in August, and at Whitney Meadows in September. Mr. Dutcher found it a common summer resident at Big Cottonwood Meadows and vicinity, and Mr. Nelson saw a few on the high ridge near San Luis Obispo, and in the mountains along the coast from San Simeon to Carpenteria in November and December.

Record of specimens collected of *Sialia arctica*.

Collector's No.	Sex.	Locality.	Date.	Collector.	Remarks.
59	♂	Granite Wells, Calif.	Jan. 14, 1891	A. K. Fisher	
87	♂	Death Valley, Calif.	Jan. 29, 1891	E. W. Nelson	Bennett Wells.
88	♂	......do	Jan. 30, 1891	A. K. Fisher	Furnace Creek.
14	♂	......do	......do	......do	Do.
15	♂	Garlick Spring, Calif.	Feb. 10, 1891	F. Stephens	
125	♀	......do	......do	......do	
37	♀	Ash Meadows, Nev.	Mar. 13, 1891	A. K. Fisher	
235	♂	Grapevine Mountains, Nev.	Mar. 21, 1891	F. Stephens	
		Argus Range, Calif.	May 13, 1891	A. K. Fisher	Maturango Spring.

LIST OF BIRDS OBSERVED IN DEATH VALLEY, CALIFORNIA.

1. *Colymbus nigricollis californicus.* Eared Grebe.
    A specimen was secured at Furnace Creek April 10.
2. *Anas boschas.* Mallard.
    One was secured at Furnace Creek in January.
3. *Anas americana.* Baldpate.
    The species was secured at Saratoga Springs and Furnace Creek in January.
4. *Anas carolinensis.* Green-winged Teal.
    Common at Furnace Creek and Saratoga Springs in January.
5. *Anas cyanoptera.* Cinnamon Teal.
    At Furnace Creek flocks were seen in March, and one female secured June 19.
6. *Spatula clypeata.* Shoveller.
    A small flock seen at Furnace Creek in January.
7. *Dafila acuta.* Pintail.
    Seen and secured at Saratoga Springs in February.
8. *Erismatura rubida.* Ruddy Duck.
    A small flock was seen at Furnace Creek March 22.
9. *Anser albifrons gambeli.* White-fronted Goose.
    One was seen with the following subspecies.
10. *Branta canadensis* (subspecies?)
    Four were seen at Furnace Creek in the latter part of March.
11. *Plegadis guarauna.* White-faced Glossy Ibis.
    The remains of one were seen at the ranch at Furnace Creek.
12. *Nycticorax nycticorax nævius.* Night Heron.
    An immature specimen was secured at Furnace Creek June 19.
13. *Rallus virginianus.* Virginia Rail.
    Common at Saratoga Springs in February.
14. *Fulica americana.* Coot.
    Common at Saratoga Springs in February and April.
15. *Phalaropus tricolor.* Wilson's Phalarope.
    One specimen was secured at Furnace Creek June 19.
16. *Gallinago delicata.* Wilson's Snipe.
    One seen at Furnace Creek April 11.
17. *Ægialitis vocifera.* Killdeer.
    Not uncommon; found at Furnace Creek in January, April, and June; breeds.
18. *Callipepla gambeli.* Gambel's Quail.
    Common at Furnace Creek ranch. Introduced.
19. *Zenaidura macroura.* Mourning Dove.
    Not uncommon; breeds.
20. *Cathartes aura.* Turkey Buzzard.
    Not uncommon; seen in March, April, and June.
21. *Circus hudsonius.* Marsh Hawk.
    One was secured at Furnace Creek in January.
22. *Accipiter velox.* Sharp-shinned Hawk.
    Seen at Furnace Creek and Bennett Wells in January and April.
23. *Accipiter cooperi.* Cooper's Hawk.
    Seen at Furnace Creek in January.
24. *Buteo borealis calurus.* Western Red tail.
    Seen at Furnace Creek and Bennett Wells in January, and at the latter place in June.
25. *Falco mexicanus.* Prairie Falcon.
    Seen at Furnace Creek in January and June.
26. *Falco columbarius.* Pigeon Hawk.
    Remains of one found at Furnace Creek.

27. *Falco sparverius deserticolus.* Desert Sparrow Hawk.
   Seen at Mesquite Wells, Bennett Wells, and Furnace Creek in January, March, and April.
28. *Pandion haliaëtus carolinensis.* Osprey.
   One was seen at Furnace Creek April 10.
29. *Speotyto cunicularia hypogæa.* Burrowing Owl.
   A pair was seen at Bennett Wells June 21.
30. *Geococcyx californianus.* Road-runner.
   Common resident.
31. *Coccyzus americanus occidentalis.* California Cuckoo.
   One secured at Furnace Creek June 20.
32. *Ceryle alcyon.* Kingfisher.
   One seen at Furnace Creek April 15.
33. *Colaptes cafer.* Red-shafted Flicker.
   One was seen at Furnace Creek, April 10.
34. *Phalænoptilus nuttalli.* Poor-will.
   Secured at Bennett Wells January 28, at Saratoga Springs February 4, and seen at Furnace Creek April 10.
35. *Chordeiles virginianus henryi.* Western Nighthawk.
   A specimen was secured at Furnace Creek June 19.
36. *Chordeiles texensis* Texas Nighthawk.
   Seen at Saratoga Springs April 26.
37. *Aëronautes melanoleucus.* White-throated Swift.
   Common at Furnace Creek in April and June.
38. *Calypte costæ.* Costa's Hummingbird.
   Seen at Furnace Creek April 12 and again June 19.
39. *Myiarchus cinerascens.* Ash-throated Flycatcher.
   A pair was seen in Furnace Creek Cañon June 21.
40. *Sayornis saya.* Say's Phœbe.
   Not uncommon resident.
41. *Sayornis nigricans.* Black Phœbe.
   It was seen at Furnace Creek April 12.
42. *Empidonax wrightii.* Wright's Flycatcher.
   A specimen was taken at Furnace Creek February 1.
43. *Corvus corax sinuatus.* Raven.
   Resident.
44. *Molothrus ater.* Cowbird.
   One was secured at Furnace Creek June 20.
45. *Xanthocephalus xanthocephalus.* Yellow-headed Blackbird.
   One was secured at Bennett Wells April 1.
46. *Agelaius phœniceus.* Red-winged Blackbird.
   A flock was seen at Furnace Creek the latter part of January.
47. *Sturnella magna neglecta.* Western Meadowlark.
   A not uncommon resident.
48. *Icterus bullocki.* Bullock's Oriole.
   One was observed at Furnace Creek about the middle of April.
49. *Scolecophagus cyanocephalus.* Brewer's Blackbird.
   A few were seen at Furnace Creek in January.
50. *Carpodacus mexicanus frontalis.* House Finch.
   Not uncommon resident.
51. *Ammodramus sandwichensis alaudinus.* Western Savanna Sparrow.
   Not uncommon at Furnace Creek in January and April.
52. *Zonotrichia leucophrys intermedia.* Intermediate Sparrow.
   Common at Furnace Creek in January and April.

53. *Spizella breweri.* Brewer's Sparrow.
   One was seen in Mesquite Valley April 13.
54. *Amphispiza bilineata.* Black-throated Sparrow.
   Seen on June 22 in the Panamint Mountains just above the valley.
55. *Amphispiza belli nevadensis.* Sage Sparrow.
   Common winter resident.
56. *Melospiza fasciata montana.* Mountain Song Sparrow.
   Common winter resident at Furnace Creek and Saratoga Springs.
57. *Guiraca cærulea eurhyncha.* Western Blue Grosbeak.
   One was secured at Furnace Creek, June 19.
58. *Passerina amœna.* Lazuli Bunting.
   A female was secured at Furnace Creek, June 19.
59. *Tachycineta bicolor.* Tree Swallow.
   Common at Furnace Creek in March and April.
60. *Tachycineta thalassina.* Violet Green Swallow.
   Observed at Furnace Creek and Saratoga Springs in April.
61. *Stelgidopteryx serripennis.* Rough-winged Swallow.
   A not uncommon summer resident.
62. *Lanius ludovicianus excubitorides.* White-rumped Shrike.
   Seen at Furnace Creek and Saratoga Springs in January.
63. *Vireo belli pusillus.* Least Vireo.
   A not uncommon summer resident.
64. *Dendroica auduboni.* Audubon's Warbler.
   Seen at Furnace Creek in January and April.
65. *Geothlypis trichas occidentalis.* Western Yellow-throat.
   A not uncommon summer resident.
66. *Icteria virens longicauda.* Long-tailed Chat.
   A not uncommon summer resident.
67. *Anthus pensilvanicus.* Titlark.
   Winter resident.
68. *Oroscoptes montanus.* Sage Thrasher.
   One seen at Mesquite Well in January.
69. *Mimus polyglottos.* Mockingbird.
   Observed in January and April.
70. *Harporhynchus lecontei.* Le Conte's Thrasher.
   An uncommon resident; seen at Saratoga Springs, Bennett Wells, Furnace Creek, and in the northwest arm of Mesquite Valley.
71. *Salpinctes obsoletus.* Rock Wren.
   One was seen at Mesquite Wells in January; breeds in the mountains just above the valley.
72. *Catherpes mexicanus conspersus.* Cañon Wren.
   One was seen at Saratoga Springs in February.
73. *Thryothorus bewickii bairdi.* Baird's Wren.
   Seen at Furnace Creek, Bennett Wells, and Saratoga Springs in January.
74. *Cistothorus palustris paludicola.* Tule Wren.
   Seen at Furnace Creek, Bennett Wells, and Saratoga Springs in January.
75. *Regulus calendula.* Ruby-crowned Kinglet.
   Seen at Furnace Creek in February and April.
76. *Polioptila cærulea obscura.* Western Gnatcatcher.
   One secured at Furnace Creek, January 24.
77. *Merula migratoria propinqua.* Western Robin.
   A few were seen at Furnace Creek in January.
78. *Sialia arctica.* Mountain Bluebird.
   A common winter resident.

LIST OF BIRDS FOUND IN OWENS VALLEY, CALIFORNIA.

1. *Colymbus nigricollis californicus.* Eared Grebe.
   Abundant on Owens Lake; breeds at the smaller lakes.
2. *Larus californicus.* California Gull.
   Seen in December, 1890.
3. *Larus delawarensis.* Ring-billed Gull.
   Seen at Lone Pine and Owens Lake in December, 1890.
4. *Larus philadelphia.* Bonaparte's Gull.
   One seen at Lone Pine, about the same time as the other gulls.
5. *Pelecanus erythrorhynchos.* White Pelican.
   A flock was seen at Haway Meadows in May and an individual at Lone Pine in August.
6. *Merganser serrator.* Red-breasted Merganser.
   Seen at Lone Pine and Owens Lake in winter.
7. *Anas boschas.* Mallard.
   Not uncommon; probably breeds.
8. *Anas discors.* Blue-winged Teal.
   Seen at Little Owens Lake in May.
9. *Anas cyanoptera.* Cinnamon Teal.
   Seen at Little Owens Lake; breeds.
10. *Spatula clypeata.* Shoveller.
    Common during migrations.
11. *Aythya americana.* Redhead.
    One was seen at Little Owens Lake in May.
12. *Glaucionetta clangula americana.* Golden-eye.
    Seen at Lone Pine, in December, 1890.
13. *Charitonetta albeola.* Buffle-head.
    Seen at Lone Pine in December, 1890.
14. *Branta canadensis* (subspecies?).
    A flock heard at Lone Pine in December, 1890.
15. *Dendrocygna fulva.* Fulvous Tree Duck.
    Breeds at Little Owens Lake.
16. *Plegadis guarauna.* White-faced Glossy Ibis.
    Seen at Little Owens Lake in May.
17. *Botaurus lentiginosus.* Bittern.
    Seen at Lone Pine in winter, and at Alvord and Bishop in summer.
18. *Ardea herodias.* Great Blue Heron.
    Seen at Lone Pine, and at Little Owens Lake in June.
19. *Ardea virescens.* Green Heron.
    Seen at Little Owens Lake in May.
20. *Nycticorax nycticorax nævius.* Night Heron.
    Not uncommon in the valley.
21. *Rallus virginianus.* Virginia Rail.
    Breeds at Lone Pine.
22. *Porzana carolina.* Sora.
    Seen at Little Owens Lake early in May.
23. *Fulica americana.* Coot.
    Common; breeds.
24. *Phalaropus tricolor.* Wilson's Phalarope.
    Two specimens were secured at Alvord, June 27.
25. *Recurvirostra americana.* Avocet.
    Seen at Little Owens Lake in May, 1891, at Owens Lake in June, at the north end of the valley in July, and Lone Pine in December, 1890.

26. *Gallinago delicata.* Wilson's Snipe.
   Seen at Lone Pine in winter.
27. *Tringa minutilla.* Least Sandpiper.
   Common at Owens Lake in December, 1890.
28. *Ereunetes occidentalis.* Western Sandpiper.
   Secured at Owens Lake in June.
29. *Totanus melanoleucus.* Greater Yellow-legs.
   Seen at Lone Pine in December.
30. *Numenius longirostris.* Long-billed Curlew.
   Seen at Owens Lake in December and June.
31. *Ægialitis vocifera.* Killdeer.
   Common; breeds.
32. *Ægialitis nivosa.* Snowy Plover.
   Not uncommon at Owens Lake, where it is a resident.
33. *Oreortyx pictus plumiferus.* Plumed Quail.
   Common along the eastern slope of the Sierra Nevada.
34. *Callipepla californica vallicola.* Valley Quail.
   Common resident.
35. *Zenaidura macroura.* Mourning Dove.
   Abundant breeder.
36. *Cathartes aura.* Turkey Buzzard.
   Seen all through the valley.
37. *Circus hudsonius.* Marsh Hawk.
   Not uncommon; breeds.
38. *Accipiter velox.* Sharp-shinned Hawk.
   Seen at Olancha and Bishop Creek in the latter part of May and first part of August.
39. *Accipiter cooperi.* Cooper's Hawk.
   Seen at Bishop Creek in August.
40. *Accipiter atricapillus striatulus.* Goshawk.
   A hawk thought to be this species was seen at Lone Pine in December, 1890.
41. *Buteo borealis calurus.* Western Red-tail.
   Resident; more or less common.
42. *Aquila chrysaëtos.* Golden Eagle.
   A pair was seen in June.
43. *Falco mexicanus.* Prairie Falcon.
   Not uncommon; undoubtedly breeds in the neighboring mountains.
44. *Falco columbarius.* Pigeon Hawk.
   Seen at Little Owens Lake.
45. *Falco sparverius deserticolus.* Desert Sparrow Hawk.
   A more or less common resident throughout the valley.
46. *Strix pratincola.* Barn Owl.
   The remains of one were found at Alvord.
47. *Speotyto cunicularia hypogæa.* Burrowing Owl.
   A not uncommon resident.
48. *Geococcyx californianus.* Road-runner.
   A common resident.
49. *Coccyzus americanus occidentalis.* California Cuckoo.
   One seen at Bishop, August 11.
50. *Ceryle alcyon.* Kingfisher.
   Not uncommon; breeds.
51. *Dryobates villosus hyloscopus.* Cabanis's Woodpecker.
   Seen at Bishop Creek in August.
52. *Melanerpes torquatus.* Lewis's Woodpecker.
   One seen at the head of the valley in July.

53. *Colaptes cafer.* Red-shafted Flicker.
    A not uncommon resident.
54. *Phalænoptilus nuttalli.* Poor-will.
    Not uncommon; breeding throughout the valley.
55. *Chordeiles texensis.* Texas Nighthawk.
    A common summer resident.
56. *Cypseloides niger.* Black Swift.
    Common; breeds in the mountains on each side of the valley.
57. *Chætura vauxii.* Vaux's Swift.
    Seen at Olancha about the middle of May.
58. *Aëronautes melanoleucus.* White-throated Swift.
    A common summer resident.
59. *Trochilus alexandri.* Black-chinned Humming Bird.
    A common summer resident.
60. *Calypte costæ.* Costa's Humming Bird.
    A common summer resident.
61. *Tyrannus verticalis.* Arkansas Kingbird.
    A common summer resident.
62. *Tyrannus tyrannus.* Kingbird.
    One was seen at Olancha, June 29.
63. *Myiarchus cinerascens.* Ash-throated Flycatcher.
    A not uncommon summer resident.
64. *Sayornis saya.* Say's Phœbe.
    A not uncommon breeding species.
65. *Sayornis nigricans.* Black Phœbe.
    Seen and apparently breeding at Little Owens Lake and Bishop Creek.
66. *Contopus richardsoni.* Western Wood Pewee.
    A common summer resident.
67. *Empidonax pusillus.* Little Flycatcher.
    Seen at Olancha in May, and at Lone Pine June 11.
68. *Empidonax wrightii.* Wright's Flycatcher.
    Found at Olancha in May, and at Bishop Creek in August.
69. *Otocoris alpestris arenicola.* Desert Horned Lark.
    A common summer resident.
70. *Otocoris alpestris chrysolæma.* Mexican Horned Lark.
    Found at Owens Lake in December, 1890.
71. *Cyanocitta stelleri frontalis.* Blue-fronted Jay.
    Seen at Bishop Creek in August.
72. *Aphelocoma californica.* California Jay.
    Found on the east slope of the Sierra Nevada.
73. *Corvus corax sinuatus.* Raven.
    Resident.
74. *Picicorvus columbianus.* Clarke's Nutcracker.
    Observed at the head of the valley and Bishop Creek.
75. *Cyanocephalus cyanocephalus.* Piñon Jay.
    Seen at Benton and Bishop Creek.
76. *Xanthocephalus xanthocephalus.* Yellow-headed Blackbird.
    A not uncommon resident.
77. *Agelaius phœniceus.* Red-winged Blackbird.
    A common resident.
78. *Agelaius gubernator.* Bicolored Blackbird.
    A specimen was secured at Olancha, June 11.
79. *Sturnella magna neglecta.* Western Meadowlark.
    A common resident.

80. *Icterus bullocki.* Bullock's Oriole.
    A common summer resident.
81. *Scolecophagus cyanocephalus.* Brewer's Blackbird.
    A common summer resident. It may be a resident.
82. *Carpodacus mexicanus frontalis.* House Finch.
    A common resident.
83. *Spinus psaltria.* Arkansas Goldfinch.
    A common summer resident.
84. *Poocætes gramineus confinis.* Western Vesper Sparrow.
    Not uncommon at the head of the valley.
85. *Ammodramus sandwichensis alaudinus.* Western Savanna Sparrow.
    A not uncommon resident.
86. *Chondestes grammacus strigatus.* Western Lark Sparrow.
    A common summer resident.
87. *Zonotrichia leucophrys.* White-crowned Sparrow.
    Observed along the east slope of the Sierra Nevada, where it breeds higher up.
88. *Spizella breweri.* Brewer's Sparrow.
    A common summer resident.
89. *Spizella atrigularis.* Black-chinned Sparrow.
    Secured at Independence Creek on the east slope of the Sierra Nevada.
90. *Junco hyemalis thurberi.* Thurber's Junco.
    Winter visitant in the valley; breeds on the east slope of the Sierra Nevada.
91. *Amphispiza bilineata.* Black-throated Sparrow.
    A common summer resident.
92. *Amphispiza belli nevadensis.* Sage Sparrow.
    A not uncommon resident.
93. *Melospiza fasciata heermanni.* Heermann's Song Sparrow.
    Tolerably common resident.
94. *Melospiza lincolni.* Lincoln's Sparrow.
    Found breeding at Independence Creek, on the east slope of the Sierra Nevada.
95. *Passerella iliaca megarhyncha.* Thick-billed Sparrow.
    Found in the same place as the preceding species.
96. *Pipilo maculatus megalonyx.* Spurred Towhee.
    A not uncommon resident.
97. *Pipilo chlorurus.* Green-tailed Towhee.
    A common summer resident in the upper end of the valley.
98. *Habia melanocephala.* Black-headed Grosbeak.
    Seen at Olancha and Ash Creek in May, and Independence Creek in June.
99. *Guiraca cærulea eurhyncha.* Western Blue Grosbeak.
    A common summer resident.
100. *Passerina amœna.* Lazuli Bunting.
    A common summer resident.
101. *Piranga ludoviciana.* Western Tanager.
    A not uncommon summer resident.
102. *Petrochelidon lunifrons.* Cliff Swallow.
    A common summer resident.
103. *Chelidon erythrogaster.* Barn Swallow.
    A common summer resident.
104. *Tachycineta thalassina.* Violet Green Swallow.
    A common summer resident.
105. *Clivicola riparia.* Bank Swallow.
    Common at Alvord the last of June, where it was breeding.
106. *Stelgidopteryx serripennis.* Rough-winged Swallow.
    A not uncommon summer resident.

107. *Ampelis cedrorum.* Cedar Bird.
    A pair was seen at Lone Pine June 14.
108. *Phainopepla nitens.* Phainopepla.
    One was seen at Morans in July.
109. *Lanius ludovicianus excubitorides.* White-rumped Shrike.
    A common resident.
110. *Vireo gilvus swainsoni.* Western Warbling Vireo.
    A not uncommon summer resident.
111. *Vireo belli pusillus.* Least Vireo.
    A not uncommon summer resident.
112. *Helminthophila celata lutescens.* Lutescent Warbler.
    A few migrants were seen at Little Owens Lake in May.
113. *Dendroica æstiva.* Yellow Warbler.
    A common summer resident.
114. *Dendroica auduboni.* Audubon's Warbler.
    Occurs in winter, and probably breeds on Independence and Bishop creeks.
115. *Dendroica townsendi.* Townsend's Warbler.
    Migrants were seen at Little Owens Lake.
116. *Geothlypis macgillivrayi.* Macgillivray's Warbler.
    Found with young at Bishop Creek in August.
117. *Geothlypis trichas occidentalis.* Western Yellow-throat.
    A common summer resident.
118. *Icteria virens longicauda.* Long-tailed Chat.
    A common summer resident.
119. *Sylvania pusilla pileolata.* Pileolated Warbler.
    A not uncommon migrant.
120. *Anthus pensilvanicus.* Titlark.
    A common winter resident.
121. *Cinclus mexicanus.* Water Ousel.
    Follows down the streams into the valley in winter.
122. *Oroscoptes montanus.* Sage Thrasher.
    Breeds commonly in the upper part of the valley.
123. *Mimus polyglottos.* Mockingbird.
    A not uncommon resident.
124. *Harporhynchus lecontei.* LeConte's Thrasher.
    A common resident.
125. *Heleodytes brunneicapillus.* Cactus Wren.
    Breeds in the southern end of the valley.
126. *Salpinctes obsoletus.* Rock Wren.
    A common resident.
127. *Thryothorus bewickii bairdi.* Baird's Wren.
    Common at Lone Pine in December, 1890.
128. *Troglodytes aëdon aztecus.* Western House Wren.
    Seen in migrations and probably breeds on the eastern slope of the Sierra Nevada.
129. *Cistothorus palustris paludicola.* Tule Wren.
    A not uncommon resident.
130. *Parus gambeli.* Mountain Chickadee.
    Rather common along the eastern slope of the Sierra Nevada.
131. *Psaltriparus minimus californicus.* California Bush-Tit.
    Seen on Independence and Bishop creeks.
132. *Polioptila cærula obscura.* Western Gnatcatcher.
    Seen at Independence Creek in June.
133. *Myadestes townsendii.* Townsend's Solitaire.
    Seen at Lone Pine in December, 1890.

134. *Turdus ustulatus.* Russet-backed Thrush.
   One seen at Olancha about the middle of May.
135. *Turdus aonalaschkæ auduboni.* Audubon's Hermit Thrush.
   Breeds on Independence and Bishop creeks.
136. *Merula migratoria propinqua.* Western Robin.
   Common summer resident along the eastern slope of the Sierra Nevada.
137. *Sialia arctica.* Mountain Bluebird.
   Common along the eastern slope of the Sierra Nevada.

ANNOTATED LIST OF THE REPTILES AND BATRACHIANS COLLECTED BY THE DEATH VALLEY EXPEDITION IN 1891, WITH DESCRIPTIONS OF NEW SPECIES.

By LEONHARD STEJNEGER,

Curator of the Department of Reptiles and Batrachians, U. S. National Museum.

With field notes by Dr. C. HART MERRIAM.

Since the days of the great western surveying expeditions, the United States Exploring Expedition (Wilkes'), the United States and Mexican Boundary Survey, the various Pacific Railroad surveys, and Wheeler's Survey West of the one-hundredth Meridian, no collection of North American reptiles and batrachians has been made equaling or even approaching that brought home by the Death Valley Expedition. In the extent of the series of many species it stands unrivaled, and in the accuracy and detail of its labeling it surpasses them all. To this point particularly it is desired to call attention. Many of the specimens of the older collection have the localities very vaguely indicated, as 'California;' 'From San Diego to El Paso;' in others, detailed localities are given, but in such a way that in many cases it is impossible to identify them; in others, the labels have been changed, and errors resulted; others again were never labeled, or the labels were lost. In the collection of the Death Valley Expedition all the nine hundred specimens are individually and fully labeled; altitudes are frequently given, and there is not the slightest doubt as to the correctness of the statement attached to each and every specimen.

Furthermore, the collection is particularly noteworthy as it is the first attempt in this country on a similar scale to gather the herpetological material together according to a rational plan and with a definite purpose in view. The result is a fine series of specimens, unique in its completeness with respect to geographic localities within the area explored by the expedition, a tract of almost 100,000 square miles, comprising a number of nearly parallel desert valleys separated by intervening barren mountain ranges. The effort of the expedition to collect every species in all the characteristic localities from California to Utah and Arizona resulted in a material by which it has been possible in many instances to follow the geographic variation in its various directions. The present report does not pretend to exhaust this material, which will yield more definite results when the adjoining territory shall have been searched as thoroughly and as intelligently as that covered by the present expedition.

With a material so well calculated to show the amount of individual variation within many species, and to determine the geographical distribution of others, the author was enabled to settle many a vexed question and to point out many a nice distinction where some of his colleagues had failed, chiefly from lack of suitable material. If, therefore, he has succeeded in somewhat advancing our knowledge of North American herpetology, thanks are principally due to Dr. C. Hart Merriam, the untiring organizer and leader of the expedition, and to the zeal and intelligence of his assistants who evidently spared no effort to make the expedition a success. Personally I have to thank Dr. Merriam for the privilege of working up such a valuable and interesting material.

Dr. Merriam has contributed field notes on many of the species, with special reference to geographic distribution and food habits. These notes are given in brackets over his initials at the end of the text relating to each species.

LIST OF SPECIES.

A. REPTILIA.

I.—TESTUDINES.

TESTUDINIDÆ.

1. Gopherus agassizii (Cooper).   2. Clemmys marmorata (B. & G.).

II.—SQUAMATA.

1. Sauri.

EUBLEPHARIDÆ.

3. Coleonyx variegatus (Baird).

IGUANIDÆ.

4. Dipsosaurus dorsalis (B. & G).
5. Crotaphytus baileyi Stejn.
6. Crotaphytus wislizenii B. & G.
7. Crotaphytus silus Stejn.
8. Callisaurus ventralis (Hallow.).
9. Sauromalus ater Dum.
10. Uta stansburiana B. & G.
11. Uta graciosa (Hallow.).
12. Sceloporus magister Hallow.
13. Sceloporus graciosus B. & G.
14. Sceloporus bi-seriatus Hallow.
15. Sceloporus occidentalis B. & G.
16. Phrynosoma blainvillii Gray.
17. Phrynosoma platyrhinos Girard.

HELODERMATIDÆ.

18. Heloderma suspectum Cope.

ANGUIDÆ.

19. Gerrhonotus scincicauda (Skilton).
20. Gerrhonotus scincicauda palmeri Stejn.
21. Gerrhonotus burnettii Gray.

XANTUSIIDÆ.

22. Xantusia vigilis Baird.

TEJIDÆ.

23. Cnemidophorus tigris B. & G.
24. Cnemidophorus tigris undulatus (Hallow.).

SCINCIDÆ.

25. Eumeces skiltonianus B. & G.

2. Serpentes.

LEPTOTYPHLOPIDÆ.

26. Rena humilis B. & G.

BOIDÆ.

27. Charina plumbea B. & G.

NATRICIDÆ.

28. Diadophis pulchellus B. & G.
29. Lampropeltis boylii (B. & G.).
30. Hypsiglena ochrorhynchus Cope.
31. Salvadora grahamiæ hexalepis Cope.
32. Pituophis catenifer (Blainv.).
33. Pituophis catenifer deserticola Stejn.
34. Bascanion flagellum frenatum Stejn.
35. Bascanion laterale (Hallow.).
36. Bascanion tæniatum (Hallow.).
37. Thamnophis infernalis (Blainv.).
38. Thamnophis elegans (B. & G).
39. Thamnophis hammondii (Kenn.).
40. Thamnophis vagrans (B. & G).
41. Thamnophis parietalis (Say).

CROTALIDÆ.

42. Crotalus tigris Kenn.
43. Crotalus cerastes Hallow.
44. Crotalus lucifer B. & G.

B.—BATRACHIA.

Anura.

BUFONIDÆ.

45. Bufo punctatus B. & G.
46. Bufo halophilus B. & G.
47. Bufo boreas nelsoni Stejn.
48. Bufo lentiginosus woodhousii (Gir.).

SCAPHIOPODIDÆ.

49. Scaphiopus hammondii Baird.

HYLIDÆ.

50. Hyla regilla B. & G.

RANIDÆ.

51. Rana draytonii B. & G.
52. Rana aurora B. & G.
53. Rana pretiosa B. & G.
54. Rana boylii Baird.
55. Rana fisheri Stejn.
56. Rana pipiens brachycephala (Cope).

A.—REPTILIA.

Order I. TESTUDINES.

Family TESTUDINIDÆ.

Gopherus agassizii (Cooper).

The characters pointed out for this species by Mr. F. W. True (Proc. U. S. Nat. Mus. IV, p. 440) I have found to hold in the additional specimens before me, and there is no difficulty in distinguishing it from *Gopherus polyphemus*, much less from *G. berlandieri*. The fact that a specimen named *Xerobates berlandieri* (No. 10412) is recorded in Yarrow's Catalogue of Reptiles and Batrachians in the U. S. National Museum (Bull. U. S. Nat. Mus., No. 24, p. 38), as from Fort Yuma, Cal., need not disturb anybody, as it is in reality a *G. agassizii*, and is recorded as such by True (*tom. cit.*, p. 447).

This species was originally described "from the mountains of California, near Fort Mohave" (Cooper, Proc. Calif. Ac. Nat. Sc., II, p. 121), and the National Museum has since received specimens from Fort Yuma (exact locality?). Dr. Cooper (*l. c.*) adds that "broken shells are frequent on the higher parts of the mountains west of the Colorado, where the Pah-Utes eat them."

12731—No. 7——11

The present expedition, therefore, not only extends the known range of this species considerably within California, but shows for the first time that it occurs in Nevada as well. The young one from Pahrump Valley has the carapace only 47^{mm} long, and the plastron is quite soft, while the length of the carapace collected at the Bend of the Colorado is no less than 290^{mm}.

[This tortoise is remarkable among American species for its power of living in the arid deserts of the Lower Sonoran zone, far away from water. It is tolerably common in the Mohave Desert, California, where one was caught between Daggett and Pilot Knob, April 24, and another at Leach Point Valley April 25. Two were found in Pahrump Valley, Nevada, where it is so much sought after by Pah-Ute Indians and coyotes that it is rather scarce. At the Great Bend of the Colorado many unusually large shells were found about an old Indian encampment, where they had been left after the bodies had been eaten.—C. H. M.]

List of specimens of Gopherus agassizii.

U. S. Nat. Mus. No.	Sex and age.	Locality.	Altitude.	Date.	Collector.	Remarks.
			Feet.			
18642	juv.	Pahrump Valley, Nev		Apr. 29	Bailey	Alcohol.
18643	ad.	....do....		Mar. —	Fisher	Shell.
18644	ad.	Bend of Colorado River, Nev		May —	Merriam	Carapace.
18645	ad.	Daggett, Calif.		Jan. 9	Fisher	Do.
19254	ad.	Leach Point Valley, Mohave Desert, Calif.		Apr. —	Bailey	Alcohol.

Clemmys marmorata (B. & G.).

The only specimen brought home by the expedition is a young one (No. 18641) collected by Dr. Fisher, July 5, in the South Fork of Kern River, 25 miles above Kernville, Calif. It is slightly smaller, but otherwise closely resembles Figs. 8 and 9, Pl. XXXII, in the atlas of the herpetology of the United States Exploring Expedition.

[Dr. A. K. Fisher obtained this turtle and saw many on the South Fork of Kern River, about 25 miles above Kernville, early in July, and Mr. Palmer and I saw half a dozen in a small pond 2 or 3 miles above the forks of the Kern June 25.—C. H. M.]

Order II. SQUAMATA.

Suborder I. *SAURI.*

Family EUBLEPHARIDÆ.

Coleonyx variegatus (Baird).

I am not prepared to unite most of the American species formerly referred to the genus *Coleonyx*, with the East Indian *Eublepharis* as recently proposed by Mr. Boulenger (Cat. Liz. Br. Mus., I, 1885, p. 230). The relative size of the claw sheaths is hardly of such importance as to justify a generic arrangement which would place the American forms in two genera, one of which would include the species found only in the East Indies. The presence or absence of enlarged chin shields seems to me a much more important character, and is far more satisfactory, since it effectually separates the American from the Indian species.

The three genera, by Boulenger referred to the family *Eublepharidæ*, would then stand thus:

Digits granular inferiorly { *Hemitheconyx* * (West Africa). *Eublepharis* (Southern Asia). } Enlarged chin shields.

Digits lamellar inferiorly { *Coleonyx* (America). } No chin shields.

The genus *Coleonyx* would then contain four species, as follows:

a^1 Claw sheaths very large .... *Coleonyx elegans*
a^2 Claw sheaths small
    b^1 Back with enlarged tubercles .... *Coleonyx dovii*
    b^2 Back uniformly granular
        c^1 Snout elongate.. *Coleonyx variegatus*
        c^2 Snout short.. *Coleonyx brevis*

Boulenger (*l. c.*) recognizes two species of the *C. variegatus* type, one with the snout elongate, while in the other it is shortened. The former he gives a new name, *E. fasciatus*, and retains the name given by Baird for a specimen from Texas. It should be remarked that all his material consisted of two specimens, one from Texas, the other from Ventanas, Mexico.

I have examined twelve specimens with the result that there is an appreciable difference, as indicated by Boulenger, between five Texan specimens, on the one hand, and seven specimens from Arizona and California, on the other, and the latter agree so well with Boulenger's description of his *Eublepharis fasciatus* that I have no doubt about the identity of the Mexican specimen and those from Arizona and California. But it will be observed that Prof. Baird's type of *C. variegatus* came from the Colorado Desert, in southern California, and that consequently Boulenger's *E. fasciatus* is a synonym only, while it is the Texan form, with its short snout, less developed anterior nasals, and more numerous labials, which will have to be named. This form I would propose to call *Coleonyx brevis*.†

The synonymy of the two forms would then stand as follows:

Coleonyx variegatus.

1859. *Stenodactylus variegatus* Baird, Proc. Phila. Acad., 1858, p. 254 (type No. 3217, Colorado Desert). *Id.*, Mex. Bound. Surv. Rept., II, pp. 12, 34 (part), pl. XXIII, figs. 9–18 (type from Colorado Desert) and figs. 19–27 (male from Ft. Yuma, 1859).

---

* *Hemitheconyx*, nom. nov., for *Psilodactylus* Gray, 1864, nec *Psilodactylus* Oken, 1816. Type *Hemitheconyx caudicinctus* (Dum.).

† Type, U. S. Nat. Mus., No. 13627; Helotes, Bexar Co., Texas; Marnock coll.

1866. *Coleonyx variegatus* Cope, Proc. Phila. Acad., 1866, p. 310. *Id., ibid.,* 1867 (p. 85) (Owens Valley, Calif.).
1885. *Eublepharis fasciatus* Boulenger, Cat. Liz. Br. Mus., I, p. 234 (Ventanas, Mexico).
Coleonyx brevis.
1859. *Stenodactylus variegatus* Baird, Mex. Bound. Surv. Rept. II, pp. 12–34 (part) pl. XXIV, figs. 11–19 (Jun. from Live Oak Creek, Texas).
1880. *Coleonyx variegatus* Cope, Bull. U. S. Nat. Mus., No. 17, p. 13 (Texas) (*nec* Baird).
1885. *Eublepharis variegatus* Boulenger, Cat. Liz. Br. Mus. I, p. 233 (Texas) (*nec* Baird).

The only specimen brought home by the expedition is a young one (No. 18620) collected by Mr. Bailey, January 23, on the east side of Death Valley, opposite Bennett Wells, about 50 feet above the salt flat. This is within the known range of this species, which extends east to Tucson, Ariz., north to Owens Valley, California, and west across the Colorado and Mohave Deserts to Mohave Station.

Family IGUANIDÆ.

Dipsosaurus dorsalis (B. & G.).

The sixteen specimens brought home by the expedition extend our knowledge of the geographical distribution of this species materially. We knew in a general way that it inhabits southern California and Lower California, but very few records of exact localities have ever been given. We now find that it occurs in the whole Death Valley region, extending north into Owens Valley, as high as 4,100 feet above the sea, and east to Callville, on the Great Bend of the Colorado, Nevada, making with the specimen from the Amargosa Desert, Nevada, the first record of the species in that State, so far as I know.

This species then ranges from Cape St. Lucas along the gulf coast of Lower California to the Colorado and Mohave deserts. To the east it extends at least as far as the Colorado River, but how far beyond is not known. Its northern range is indicated above.*

It is interesting to note that this species is a vegetable eater, as Dr. Merriam's subjoined notes show.

[This remarkable lizard, which in general form suggests the ancient Saurians, is more strictly limited to the torrid Lower Sonoran Zone than any other species, not excepting the gridiron-tail (*Callisaurus ventralis*). It ranges across the Lower Sonoran deserts of the Great Basin from the Mohave Desert and Death Valley to the Great Bend of the Colorado River, and thence northerly in eastern Nevada through the lower part of the valleys of the Virgin and Muddy, always keeping

---

*There is a record which would seem to indicate the occurrence of *Dipsosaurus dorsalis* on the west slope of the Sierra Nevada in California, inasmuch as the smaller specimen brought home by Dr. Heermann is said to have been collected between "Kern River and the Tejon Pass" (Pac. R. R. Rep., X, 1853, Williamson's route, p.8), but it must not be forgotten that Lieut. Williamson's parties on that expedition were repeatedly on the slope toward the desert, and there is not the slightest probability that the specimen in question was collected on the valley slope.

within the *Larrea* belt. In western Nevada it reaches its northern limit in the Amargosa Desert, and was not found in Oasis Valley or Indian Spring Valley. In the northwest arm of Death Valley it does not range northward beyond Grapevine Cañon, and in Owens Valley was not found much north of the lake. It is a strict vegetarian, feeding on buds and flowers, which it devours in large quantities. No insects were found in any of the stomachs examined; some contained beautiful boquets of the yellow blossoms of acacia, the orange malvastrum, the rich purple Dalea, and the mesquite (*Prosopis juliflora*); others contained leaves only.—C. H. M.]

List of specimens of Dipsosaurus dorsalis

U.S. Nat. Mus. No.	Sex and age.	Locality.	Altitude.	Date.	Collector.	Remarks.
			Feet.			
18345	♂ ad.	Callville, Great Bend of Colorado, Nev.	....	May 4	Merriam	
18346	juv.	......do......	....	...do...	Bailey	
18347	juv.	......do......	....	...do...	...do...	
18348	ad.	Amargosa Desert, Nev.	....	May 31	Merriam	
18349	juv.	Amargosa River, Calif.	....	Apr. 27	Bailey	
18350	juv.	......do......	....	...do...	Merriam	
18351	ad.	3 miles east of Owens Lake, Calif.	4,100	June 26	Bailey	
18352	ad.	Panamint Valley, Calif.	3,300	May 15	Nelson	
18353	ad.	......do......	....	Apr. 24	Bailey	
18354	ad.	Mohave Desert, Leach Point, Valley, Calif.	....	Apr. 25	Merriam	
18355	ad.	Borax Flat Water Station, Calif.	2,100	Apr. 22	Stephens	
18356	ad.	Mesquite Valley, Calif.	....	Apr. 13	Bailey	
18357	ad.	Bennett Wells, Calif.	....	Apr. 1	...do...	
18358	ad.	......do......	....	Apr. 4	...do...	
18359	juv.	Furnace Creek, Death Valley, Calif.	....	June 21	Fisher	
18360	ad.	Owl Holes, Death Valley, Calif.	....	Apr. 26	Merriam	

Crotaphytus baileyi Stejn.

The great number of specimens brought home by the expedition fully bear out the characters assigned by me in originally establishing this species (N. Am. Fauna, No. 3, 1890, p. 103).

When publishing the map (*op. cit.* Pl. XIII) showing localities from which specimens of *C. baileyi* and *collaris* had been examined, I was unable to point out any single definite locality in California, the only certain Californian specimen seen by me hailing from the 'Mohave Desert.' The specimens hereafter enumerated would fill quite a gap if plotted on that map.

In spite of the fact that this species, in certain localities at least, ascends the mountains as high as 5,600 feet, it does not occur anywhere within the interior valley of California, nor does it pass beyond the San Bernardino Range; in fact it does not seem to reach the coast anywhere; it is evidently an inland desert form.

[Bailey's ring-necked lizard does not inhabit the *Larrea* belt of the Lower Sonoran zone, but is common in suitable places in the Upper Sonoran, whence it descends a short distance into the *Grayia* belt. It lives among rocks, frequently in cañons, and is commonest in the desert ranges. In the Panamint Mountains, California, it was found in Surprise Cañon, in Emigrant Cañon just above the *Larrea* (altitude 1,400 meters, or 4,600 feet), and in the basin above Wild Rose Spring (at an altitude of 1,580 meters, or 5,200 feet). In the White Mountains it was secured in the cañon leading from Deep Spring Valley up over the pass (altitude 1,700 meters, or 5,600 feet), and also high up on the west slope, always among rocks; and Mr. Nelson collected it in the Inyo Mountains. Dr. Fisher and Mr. Palmer obtained specimens in the Argus Mountains and in Coso Valley. In Nevada it was rather common on the west slope of the Charleston Mountains below Mountain Spring, and was found also in Oasis Valley, at Quartz Spring at the west foot of the Desert Mountains (altitude 1,520 meters or 5,000 feet); in the Juniper Mountains along the boundary between Nevada and Utah (altitude 1,830–2,040 meters, 6,000–6,700 feet), and in the upper part of Pahranagat Valley.

In Utah, a very dark form was found in company with a black form of *Sceloporus biseriatus* on the black lava rock in Diamond Valley between St. George and the Upper Santa Clara crossing.—C. H. M.]

List of specimens of Crotaphytus baileyi.

U. S. Nat. Mus. No.	Sex and age.	Locality.	Altitude.	Date.	Collector.	Remarks.
			Feet.			
18319	♂	Diamond Valley, Utah, 10 miles northwest of St. George.	4,800	May 16	Merriam	On lava rock.
18320	♀	......do............	4,800	...do...	...do......	Do.
18321	♀	......do............	4,800	...do...	...do......	Do.
18322	♀ adol.	Oasis Valley, Nev		June 1	...do......	
18323	♂	Desert Mountains, Quartz Spring, Nev.	5,000	May 28	...do......	
18324	♂	Juniper Mountains (25 miles east of Panaca), Nev.	6,200	May 28	Bailey	In junipers.
18325	♂ adol.	North Kingston Mountains, Nev		April 28	...do......	
18326	♂ adol.	......do............		...do...	...do......	
18327	♂	White Mountains, Deep Spring Valley Slope, Calif.	5,600	June 9	Merriam	
18328	♀	......do............	5,600	...do...	...do......	
18329	♂	Emigrant Cañon, Calif., Panamint Mountains.	4,600	...do...	Stephens Nelson	
18330	♂	Inyo Mountains, Calif.	5,000	May 17		
18331	♀					
18332	♂	Death Valley, 5 miles from Bennett Wells, Calif.		Mar. 25	Fisher	
		Coso Valley, near Maturango Spring, Calif.		May 11	Palmer	
18333	♂	Argus Range, Shepherd Cañon, Calif.		April 27	Fisher	
18334	♀	......do............		...do...	...do......	
18335	♀	......do............		...do...	...do......	
18336	♂	Argus Range, Maturango Spring, Calif.		May 3	...do......	
18337	♂	Argus Range, Searl's Garden, Calif.	2,000	April 28	Stephens	
18338	♂	Panamint Mountains, Willow Creek, Calif.	4,500	May 19	Nelson	
18339	♂ adol.	......do............	4,500	...do...	...do......	
18340	♀ adol.	......do............	4,500	...do...	...do......	
18341	♀ adol.	Panamint Mountains, Mill Creek, Calif.	4,000	May 15	...do......	
18342	♂ adol.	Panamint Mountains, Surprise Cañon, Calif.		April 23	Fisher	
18343	♂	Panamint Mountains, 3 miles above Wild Rose Spring, Calif.	5,000	April 16	Stephens	
18344	♂	......do............	5,000	...do...	...do......	

Crotaphytus wislizenii B. & G.

Evidently one of the commonest lizards in all the desert localities visited by members of the expedition, as the subjoined list of specimens will show. The relative distribution of this species, as compared with *C. silus*, will be discussed under the latter.

Some of the females when received showed strong traces on the under side, particularly on the tail, of a vivid scarlet color, which had a very curious superficial appearance, as if caused by loosely adherent particles of dry color. It has faded entirely out of all the specimens in alcohol. Dr. Merriam has recorded detailed observations on this point in the accompanying note.

The ferocity and greed of this species is well illustrated by several of the specimens caught. Thus the stomach of a young male (No. 18291) was found to contain two full-grown lizards, *Uta stansburiana*, while an adult female (No. 18276) when opened gave up one full-grown horned-toad, *Phrynosoma platyrhinos*, besides remnants of a grown specimen of her own species!

[The leopard lizard is abundant in most, if not all, of the Lower Sonoran deserts of the Great Basin from southern California eastward across southern Nevada to Arizona and southwestern Utah. While properly belonging to the Lower Sonoran zone, it ranges up a certain distance into the Upper Sonoran, occurring further north and higher on the mountain sides than either *Callisaurus* or *Dipsosaurus*, and usually a little higher even than *Cnemidophorus*.

It was found in abundance in all of the Lower Sonoran deserts traversed, from the Mohave Desert, Panamint and Death Valleys, Ash Meadows, the Amargosa Desert, Indian Spring, Pahrump, and Vegas valleys to the Great Bend of the Colorado, and thence northerly through the valleys of the Virgin and Muddy across the northwest corner of Arizona to the Santa Clara Valley in Utah, and Pahranagat and Meadow Creek Valleys in Nevada. The upper limit of its range was not reached except in a few places, as indicated by the following localities: It was abundant throughout Antelope Valley, at the extreme west end of the Mohave Desert, ranging thence northerly through the wash or open cañon leading to Tehachapi Valley. (It was not seen in Tehachapi Valley, which is not strange, as a sharp, cold wind blew the only day we were there.) It ranges completely over Walker Pass (altitude of divide 1,550 meters, or 5,100 feet) and is common in Owens Valley, ranging as far north at least as Bishop Creek, and as high as 1,980 meters (6,500 feet) along the west slope of the White and Inyo Mountains (opposite Big Pine). On the east side of the White Mountains it is common in Deep Spring and Fish Lake valleys, and was found on the northwest slope of Mount Magruder (below Pigeon Spring) as high as 1,980 meters (6,500 feet). It was seen at the same elevation in Tule Cañon, but does not reach the Mount Magruder plateau (altitude about 2,450 meters, or 8,000 feet). Coming up through Grapevine Cañon from the northwest arm of Death Valley it spreads over Sarcobatus Flat, and ascends the south slope of Gold Mountain a little higher than the creosote.bush (*Larrea*), which stops at about 1,640 meters (or 5,400 feet) on the most favorable southwest exposures. It is common in Oasis Valley (coming in from both Sarcobatus Flat and the Amargosa Desert), and doubtless ranges over most of the Ralston Desert. It was found on the Desert, Timpahute and Pahranagat Mountains, as well as the intervening deserts, and on Pahroc Plain, and thence easterly across Meadow Creek Valley and the Juniper Mountain plateau (along the boundary between Nevada and Utah) to the Escalante Desert in Utah, and thence southerly through the sage brush to Mountain Meadows and the Santa Clara Valley. It was common on the Argus and Panamint mountains, and on the latter was taken as high as 1,610 meters (5,300 feet) near Wild Rose Spring, and may range higher.

Crotaphytus wislizenii, in company with two other Great Basin lizards (*Cnemidophorus tigris* and *Uta stansburiana*), two desert birds (*Harporhynchus lecontei* and *Campylorhynchus brunneicapillus*), the antelope or white-tailed squirrel (*Spermophilus leucurus*), and a number of desert plants (among which may be mentioned the tree yucca, *Yucca arborescens*, *Tetradymia spinosa*, *T. comosa*, *Lycium andersoni*, *L. cooperi*, *Hymenoclea salsola*, *Eriogonum fasciculatum*, and *Ephedra nevadensis*) passes over the low summit of Walker Pass (altitude 1,550 meters, or 5,100 feet), and descends westerly to Kern Valley on the west slope of the Sierra. From Kern Valley *Crotaphytus wislizenii* ranges southward to Havilah, if not to Walker Basin.

The leopard lizard is chiefly a vegetarian, feeding on the blossoms and leaves of plants; but is also carnivorous, devouring the smaller lizards, horned toads, and even its own kind, besides large numbers of insects, as determined by the examination of many stomachs. In the Argus Range Dr. Fisher surprised one in the act of swallowing a scaly lizard (*Sceloporus*) two-thirds its own size.

In many lizards, as well known, the male assumes a special coloration during the breeding season. The present species is a notable exception, the male remaining the same, while the female undergoes a remarkable change. The whole under surface and sides of the tail become deep salmon or even salmon red, and the sides of the body assume the same color, either uniformly or in blotches. The red markings on the sides usually begin as spots, which soon unite to form transverse stripes. The central part of the back is not affected by the change, and the dark markings on the sides remain distinct. None were seen in this condition until May 20, when the first red one was found on Pahroc Plain, Nev., but dozens were seen afterward in Pahranagat Valley, Indian Spring Valley, the Armagosa Desert, Tule Cañon, and numerous other localities. The change does not take place till late in the development of the egg. Many pairs were observed in copulation in Diamond and the Upper Santa Clara Valleys, Utah, and thence northward to Mountain Meadows and the Escalante Desert, and westerly across the Juniper Mountains to Meadow Creek Valley from May 17 to 19, but no trace of the red coloration had appeared. The red individuals were always found to contain large eggs, generally measuring from 12 to 15^{mm} in length, with the coriaceous shell already formed.—C. H. M.]

List of specimens of Crotaphytus wislizenii.

U.S. Nat. Mus. No.	Sex and age.	Locality.	Altitude.	Date.	Collector.	Remarks.
			Feet.			
18258	♂	St. George, Utah		May 13	Bailey	
18259	♂	10 miles northwest of St. George, Utah.	4,850	May 16	....do	
18260	♂	Mountain Meadows, Utah		May 17	Merriam	
18261	♀	......do		....do	....do	
18262	♂	......do		....do	....do	
18263	♂	......do		....do	....do	
18264	♂	Panaca, Nev		May 19	Bailey	
18265	♂	Vegas Valley, Nev.		May 2	....do	
18266	♀	Tule Cañon, Mount Magrader, Nev		June 5	Merriam	
18267	♂	Quartz Spring, Nev.		May 28	....do	
18268	♂	Amargosa Desert, Nev.		May 31	....do	
18269	♂	Sarcobatus Flat, Nev	4,600	June 2	Bailey	
18270	♀	East foot of Charleston Mountains (Cottonwood Springs), Nev.	4,800	Apr. 30	....do	
18271	♀	Grapevine Mountains, Nev	4,800	June 10	Nelson	
18272	♂	Timpahute Mountains, Nev		May 26	Bailey	
18273	♂	......do		....do	....do	
18274	♂	Indian Spring Valley, Nev		May 28	Merriam	
18275	♂	......do		May 29	....do	
18276	♂	Pahrump Valley, Nev		Apr. 29	Bailey	
18277	♂	......do		....do	....do	
18278	♂	......do		Apr. 28	Merriam	
18279	♂	Pahranagat Valley, Nev		May 23	Bailey	
18280	♂	......do		May 25	....do	
18281	♂	Pahranagat Mountains, Nev		May 26	Merriam	
18282	♀	Oasis Valley, Nev		June 1	....do	
18283	♂	Darwin, Calif.		May 29	Palmer	
18284	♂	Panamint Valley, Calif		Apr. 24	Merriam	
18285	♂	Panamint Mountains, Wild Rose Spring, Calif.	5,300	Apr. 16	Bailey	
18286	♂ jun.	......do	5,300	....do	....do	
18287	♂	Panamint Mountains, Cottonwood Cañon, Calif.	4,900	May 26	Nelson	
18288	♀ jun.	......do	6,200	....do	....do	
18289	♀	......do		June 14	....do	3,900 feet above Salt Wells.
18290	♂ jun.	Garlick Spring, Calif		Mar. 14	Palmer	
18291	♂ jun.	Death Valley (Saratoga Spring) Calif.		Mar. 8	....do	
18292	♂	Argus Range, Shepherd Cañon, Calif		Apr. 28	Fisher	
18293	♀	Owens Valley, Independence, Calif.		June 14	Palmer	
18294	♂	Mohave Desert, Southern Pacific Railroad, Calif., 2 miles below Cameron.		June 20	Merriam	
18295	♂	Mohave Desert, 15 miles east of Mohave, Calif.		Sept. 11	Stephens	
18296	♂	Mohave Desert, north base of Granite Mountain, Calif.		Apr. 5	Merriam	
18297	♂	Havilah, Calif.		June 24	....do	
18298	♂	Kernville, Calif.		June 23	Palmer	
18299	♀	Colorado Desert, Palm Spring, Calif		Sept. 27	Stephens	
18300	♀	Coso, Calif.		May 28	Fisher	
18301	♂ jun.	......do		May 19	Palmer	
18302	♂	Panamint Mountains (Emigrant Spring), Calif.	4,400	Apr. 14	Bailey	
18303	♀	Saline Valley, Calif	4,000	June 30	Nelson	
18304	♀ jun.	......do	2,300	May 22	....do	
18305	♀	Owens Valley, 20 miles west of Bishop, Calif.	4,500	July 3	Stephens	
18306	♂	Lone Pine, Calif.		June 8	Fisher	
18307	♀	......do		June 5	....do	
18308	♀	......do		....do	Palmer	
18309	♀	......do		June 6	....do	

Crotraphytus silus Stejn.

Nine additional specimens from the San Joaquin Valley confirm the distinctness of this species.

In addition to the very strongly marked proportional differences in the head pointed out in the original description (N. Am. Fauna, No. 3, p. 105,) it is now found that the coloration is also essentially different. In *C. silus* the rounded dorsal spots are larger, especially the two median rows, so that of the latter there is only one longitudinal series between the light cross-bands. The latter are very broad and distinct and do not seem to disappear as the animal grows larger. In some specimens the interspaces between the light bands are solidly dark, the spots indicated only by somewhat ill-defined patches of saturated ferrugineous.

This species seems to be closely restricted to the San Joaquin Valley, while the typical *C. wislizenii* reaches the west slope of the Sierra Nevada through Walker Pass, the summit of which is only 5,100 feet in altitude and, therefore, not above the vertical range of the species. This fact is demonstrated by two specimens brought home by the expedition, viz, No. 18298 which was collected by Mr. Palmer at Kernville, June 23, and No. 18297 collected by Dr. Merriam at Havilah, June 24. Kernville and Havilah are on the west slope of the Sierra, and the specimens from both are undoubted *C. wislizenii* both as to proportions and coloration. If we were ever to find intermediate forms between the two species, specimens from these localities would be expected to furnish them, but it is a significant fact that they are as typical as any of the specimens collected outside of the great interior valley of California.

List of specimens of Crotaphytus silus.

U.S. Nat. Mus. No.	Sex and age.	Locality.	Altitude.	Date.	Collector.	Remarks.
			Feet.			
18310	♂	Tejon Ranch, Calif.		July 13	Palmer	
18311	♂	5 miles north of Rose Station, Calif.		Oct. 13	Nelson	
18312	♂	....do		..do..	....do	
18313	♀ juv.	Poso, Calif.		Oct. 10	....do	
18314	♂ juv.	Bakersfield, Calif.		July 17	Bailey	
18315	♀ juv.	....do		Oct. 11	Nelson	
18316	♂ juv.	....do		..do..	....do	
18317	♀ juv.	....do		..do..	....do	
18318	♀	Pampa, Calif.		July 16	Bailey	

Callisaurus ventralis (Hallow.).

The large series of this interesting species brought home by the expedition has not only filled up gaps in our knowledge of its distribution, but has also afforded enough material to decide beyond a doubt the question as to the specific difference between the present form and typical *Callisaurus draconoides* Blainv. The differences are numerous and are found both in structure and coloration. Moreover, after an examination of about 200 specimens I can affirm that the characters are constant and that the two forms do not intergrade. That Boulenger (Cat. Liz. Br. Mus., II, 1885, p. 206) failed to appreciate the difference is probably due to the fact that he had only two specimens of one species, probably *C. ventralis*, before him.

As to the geographical distribution of the two species it may be stated that *C. draconoides* is restricted to the very southern extremity of the Lower California peninsula—that is, to the zoo-geographical district which has been termed the Cape Region, or Cape St. Lucas Region.

While this species, therefore, is of a very limited range, *C. ventralis* ranges over a comparatively large area, comprising, so far as known, the northern portion of Lower California; the coast of Sonora, Mexico, at least as far south as Guaymas; the desert regions of southern California; southern Arizona as far east as Camp Apache and Fort Buchanan, at least; southern and western Nevada as far north as Pyramid Lake; southern Utah, where it is restricted to the Lower Santa Clara Valley.*

It can be asserted with confidence that *Callisaurus ventralis* does not occur anywhere within the interior valley of California, not even in Walker Basin. Nor is there any evidence to show that it occurs anywhere southwest of the San Bernardino range, within the boundary of the State of California.

[The gridiron-tailed lizard is the most characteristic reptile of the Lower Sonoran deserts of southern California, southern Nevada, southwestern Utah, and Arizona, where it is almost universally distributed and very much more abundant than any other species. It inhabits the open deserts and runs with great swiftness over the sand and gravel beds, carrying its tail curled up over its back as if afraid to let it touch the hot surface of the earth. It starts off at full speed, as if fired from a cannon, and stops with equal suddenness, thus escaping or eluding its enemies, the coyotes, hawks, and larger lizards. When running it moves so swiftly that the eye has difficulty in following, and when at rest its colors harmonize so well with those of the desert that it can hardly be seen. The basal half of its tail is transversely barred underneath, and the bars are broad and distant, suggesting the name here applied to the species in lieu of a better one. During the breeding season the males develop a conspicuous patch of metallic greenish-blue on the sides of the body and have the power of inflating a pinkish sac under the chin.

The attitude of this lizard when at rest differs from that of most others in that the knees and elbows stand out at right angles from the body and are elevated to such a degree that they nearly reach the plane of the back. Like many other species, it has an odd habit of per-

---

* Some authors even include Texas in the geographical distribution of this species (and genus), but with no foundation in facts. I am not aware of an authentic record of its having been collected in New Mexico. The type came from what was then 'New Mexico,' but in those days that included Arizona as well.

forming a singular gymnastic exercise, consisting in rapidly dropping and elevating the body with the knees held stiff at right angles to the trunk.

This species feeds on insects and the blossoms and leaves of plants in about equal proportion; at least such was the case in the large number whose stomachs were examined.

The gridiron-tailed lizard is common throughout the Mohave Desert proper, but does not reach the extreme western end of the desert in Antelope Valley, which, owing to its greater altitude, passes out of the Lower Sonoran zone. It was last seen in this direction about 10 miles east of Liebre ranch. In the wash leading from the Mohave Desert to Tehachapi Valley it was seen up to 1,030 meters (3,400 feet) and may range higher. It is common in the Lower Sonoran zone at the south end of Owens Valley, and ranges up on the warm east side of the valley as far as Big Pine. It is common throughout Panamint and Death valleys and in the Amargosa Desert. In Nevada it inhabits the deserts of the southern part of the State, from Ash Meadows easterly across Pahrump and Vegas valleys to the Great Bend of the Colorado, where it is very common, and ranges north through the valleys of the Virgin and Lower Muddy (where it is abundant) to Pahranagat and Meadow Creek valleys. In western Nevada it comes through Grapevine Cañon (from the northwest arm of Death Valley), ranges easterly over Sarcobatus Flat, and ascends the warm south slope of Gold Mountain, with *Larrea*, to about 1,640 meters (5,400 feet). In Utah it is common in the Lower Santa Clara Valley, but does not range up into the sagebrush or Upper Sonoran Zone of the upper part of the valley.

In Desert Valley, just east of the Pahroc Mountains, a form of this species was found which seems to be subspecifically distinct from the ordinary type. It is much shorter and broader, with a shorter tail, and is bluish-gray in color. It may be the same as the animal inhabiting the desert at Pyramid Lake, Nevada, which point is about two degrees further north than Desert Valley, though in the same zoölogical subzone, for the low altitude of a series of narrow and irregular deserts in western Nevada carries this zone much further north than elsewhere. These specimens suggest the existence of a form peculiar to the upper division (or *Grayia* belt) of the Lower Sonoran Zone, *Callisaurus ventralis* proper being closely restricted to the lower division (or *Larrea* belt) of the same zone.—C. H. M.]

List of specimens of *Callisaurus ventralis*.

U.S. Nat. Mus. No.	Sex and age.	Locality.	Altitude.	Date.	Collector.	Remarks.
			Feet.			
18207	♂	Death Valley (Bennett Wells) Calif...		Apr. 4	Bailey	
18208	♀	......do		Apr. 1	....do	
18209	♀	......do		Apr. 4	....do	
18210	♀	......do		Jan. 22	....do	
18211	♂	......do		Apr. —	....do	
18212	♂	......do		Mar. 22	Nelson.....	
18213	♀	......do		Jan. 20	....do	
18214	♀	Death Valley, Furnace Creek, Calif...		June 20	Fisher	
18215	♂	Argus Range, Shepherd Cañon, Calif		Apr. 27	....do	
18216	♂	Panamint Valley, Calif		Apr. 24	Merriam....	
18217	♀	......do		...do ...	....do	
18218	♂	......do		...do ...	Fisher	
18219	♂	......do		...do ...	Bailey	
18220	♀	......do		...do ...	....do	
18221	♂ juv.	......do		...do ...	....do	
18222	♂	Death Valley (Saratoga Springs), Calif.		Mar. 8	Palmer	
18223	♂	......do		...do ...	....do	
18224	♂ juv.	......do		Feb. 2	Bailey	
18225	♂ juv.	......do		...do ...	....do	
18226	♀	Owens Lake, Olancha, Calif	3,700	May 10?	Stephens ...	
18227	♀	Water Station, Borax Flat, Calif.....	2,200	Apr. 23	....do	
18228	♂	Garlick Springs, Calif................		Mar. 14	Palmer	
18229	♂	Panamint Mountains (Emigrant Spring), Calif.		Apr. 14	Bailey	
18230	♂ juv.	......do		...do ...	....do	
18231	♂ juv.	Funeral Mountains, Calif............		Feb. 6	Nelson.....	
18232	♀ juv.	......do		...do ...	....do	
18233	♀	Owens Valley (Lone Pine), Calif		June 6	Palmer	
18234	♂	Cameron, 8 miles northwest Mohave, Calif.		June 26	....do	
18235	♀	Saline Valley, Calif.................	2,500?	Jan. 30	Nelson.....	
18236	♂	Sarcobatus Flat, Nev................	4,400	June 2	Merriam....	
18237	♂	......do	4,000	...do ...	Bailey	
18238	♂	Amargosa River, Nev................		Mar. 21	Fisher	
18239	♀	......do		...do ...	....do	
18240	♂ juv.	Amargosa River, Calif...............		Apr. 27	Bailey	
18241	♀	Ash Meadows, Nev..................		Mar. 20	Fisher	
18242	♂ juv.	......do		Mar. 18	....do	
18243	♂ juv.	......do		Mar. 4	Nelson	
18244	♀ juv.	......do		...do ...	....do	
18245	♂	Great Bend of Colorado (Callville), Nev		May 4	....do	
18246	♀	......do		...do ...	....do	
18247	♂	......do		...do ...	....do	
18248	♀ ad.	......do		...do ...	....do	
18249	♂	Pahranagat Valley, Nev		May 23	Bailey	
18250	♂	......do		...do ...	....do	
18251	♂	......do		...do ...	Merriam....	
18252	♀ ad.	......do		...do ...	....do	
18253	♂ juv.	......do		...do ...	....do	
18254	♀	Pahrump Valley, Nev		Apr. 29	Bailey	
18255	♀	......do		...do ...	Merriam....	
18256	♀	Desert Valley, Nev..................	5,300	May 21	....do	
18257	♀	Gold Mountain, Nev.................	6,000	June 3	Bailey	
18361	♀	Mohave Desert, Calif., Leach Point Valley.		Apr. 25	....do	
18362	♀ juv.	......do		...do ...	....do	

Sauromalus ater Dum. (Pl. IV).

It is quite gratifying to find in the large series of this species collected by the expedition all the diagnostic characters verified, which I indicated at the time I separated the large *Sauromalus hispidus* from the present species (Proc. U. S. Nat. Mus., XIV, 1891, pp. 409-411). This series also fully confirms my assumption that the largest of the specimens then at my command were fully adult. Some of the specimens of the Death Valley Expedition are somewhat larger than the largest specimens heretofore recorded, measuring in total length 415 mm and over (exact length not ascertainable as the tip of the tail of the largest specimen had evidently been lost by the animal when alive), and yet there is no approach whatever towards the distinctive characters of *S. hispidus.*

There is great individual variation in the coloration of this species, especially in the amount of black on the lower parts and in the dark cross bars on the upper surface, and although the latter are particularly well developed and defined in the young specimens, several of the older ones are by no means deficient in this respect. It is a curious fact, however, that the distinctness—or even the presence or absence—of these cross bars, especially on the tail, is changeable in the same individual and apparently dependent upon the intensity of the light to which the animal is exposed, an observation which I was able to make on a specimen which was sent to Washington alive.

I am informed that observations in the field show this species to be a vegetable eater as has already been demonstrated for the *S. hispidus.*

Beyond rather vague statements as to the general distribution of the present species very little exact information in regard to its range has been published. It is evident that the localities from which the expedition brought home its specimens—almost four times as many as in any museum before—form the center of the geographical range of the 'chuck-walla.' From here it extends southward along the Colorado River for an unknown distance, ranging westward into the Colorado Desert, and eastward along the Gila into Arizona. Dr. Merriam has now for the first time definitely demonstrated its occurrence in southern Nevada and southwestern Utah.

[The 'chuck-walla,' by which name this remarkable lizard is universally known to both Indians and whites (except the Mormons), inhabits many of the Lower Sonoran Desert ranges in the southern part of the Great Basin from the Mohave and Colorado Deserts easterly across southern Nevada to Arizona, and north to the southwestern corner of Utah. It is the largest lizard of the desert region except the Gila monster (*Heloderma*), which only slightly exceeds it in size. The broad body is black or blackish, and the large blunt tail is usually marbled with white or entirely white. It was generally found on lava or other dark rocks with which its coloration harmonizes. It is a vegetarian, feeding entirely, so far as our observations go, on the buds and flowers of plants, with the addition sometimes of a few leaves. It is much prized by the Panamint Indians as an article of food. A number were eaten by members or our expedition, and their flesh was reported to be tender and palatable.

Specimens were secured in the Panamint Range, the Amargosa Cañon, on a lava knoll on the west side of Pahrump Valley, Calif., and in the Lower Santa Clara Valley in Utah. In the latter locality, they are common both along the cañon of the Lower Santa Clara and among the red sandstone cliffs near the village of St. George, and are called 'alligators' by the Mormons. Dr. Fisher found them in considerable numbers in the

Argus Range, west of Panamint Valley, and examined a number of stomachs, in which he found the following plants (either flowers or foliage or both): *Dalea fremontii, Leptosyne bigelovii, Amsinckia tessellata, Lotus, Sphæralcea munroana,* and *Ephedra viridis.*—C. H. M.]

List of specimens of Sauromalus ater.

U.S. Nat. Mus. No.	Sex and age.	Locality.	Altitude.	Date.	Collector.	Remarks.
			Feet.			
18621	♂	Santa Clara Cañon, Utah............		May 11	Bailey......	
18622	♂	St. George, Utah.....................	3,000	May 13	Merriam....	
18623	♀ ad.	......do............................		May 14	....do	
18624	ad.	Pahrump Valley, Nev..................		Apr. 28	....do	
18625	ad.	Amargosa River, Calif................		Apr. 27	....do	
18626	ad.	Lookout, Inyo County, Calif...........		Mar. 27	Bailey......	
18627	juv.	Death Valley, Furnace Creek, Calif..		Mar. 22	Fisher......	
18629	♂	Panamint Mountains, Willow Creek, Calif.	4,500	May 19	Nelson......	
18630	ad.	......do............................		Apr. 21	Coville	
18631	♂	Argus Range, Shepherd Cañon, Calif.		Apr. 29	Fisher......	
18632	♂	......do............................		..do....	....do	
18633	♂	......do............................		..do....	....do	
18634	♂	......do............................		Apr. 26	....do	
18635	♀	......do............................		Apr. 23	....do	
18636	ad.	......do............................			....do	Skin.
18637	ad.	......do............................		Apr. —	....do	
18638	ad.	......do............................		Apr. —	....do	
18639	ad.	......do............................		Apr. —	....do	

Uta stansburiana B. & G.

The regions visited by the expedition falling within the known range of this species one can hardly wonder at the magnificent series sent home.

With the material already at hand it should now be possible to settle all questions as to individual and geographical variation within the species. The task of handling this material, however, is too great to be attempted in the present connection and must be reserved for some future occasion.

[This tiny brown-shouldered lizard is common over nearly the whole of the desert region traversed by the expedition, from California to Utah and Arizona and occurs also on the west slope of the Sierra Nevada, as the subjoined list of localities shows. Whether the form inhabiting the upper San Joaquin Valley is identical with that from the deserts of the Great Basin remains to be seen.

Uta stansburiana is common throughout the Mohave Desert, ranging westward to the extreme west end of Antelope Valley and down through the Cañada de las Uvas to Old Fort Tejon. It ranges also over Walker Pass and down into Kern Valley. It is common in Owens Valley, and thence easterly in the Coso Mountains, Panamint Valley and Mountains, Death Valley, the Amargosa Desert, Ash Meadows, Pahrump and Vegas Valleys, and at the Great Bend of the Colorado, whence it ranges northerly in the valleys of the Virgin and Muddy to the Santa Clara Valley in southwestern Utah, and Pahranagat Valley, Nevada. In western Nevada it was not found north of Sarcobatus Flat.—C. H. M.]

List of specimens of Uta stansburiana.

U.S. Nat. Mus. No.	Sex and age.	Locality.	Altitude.	Date.	Collector.	Remarks.
			Feet.			
18508	♂	St. George, Utah	3,000	May 13	Bailey	
18509	♂	....do		...do	....do	
18510	♂	....do		...do	Merriam	
18511	♀	....do		May 14	....do	
18512	♀	....do		...do	....do	
18513	♀	....do		May 13	....do	
18514	♀	....do		...do	Bailey	
18515	♀	....do		...do	....do	
18516	♀	....do		...do	....do	
18517	♂	Virgin River, Nev		May 6	....do	
18518	♂	Charleston Mountains, Mountain Spring, Nev.	5,000	Apr. 30	Merriam	
18519	♀	....do	5,000	...do	....do	
18520	♂	Pahrump Valley, Nev		Feb. 19	Nelson	
18521	♂	....do		Feb. 26	Palmer	
18522	♂	....do		Apr. 28	Merriam	
18523	♂	....do		Apr. 29	Bailey	
18524	♂	Pahranagat Valley, Nov		May 23	Merriam	
18525	♂	Vegas Valley, Nev	1,800	Mar. 12	Bailey	
18526		....do	1,830	...do	....do	
18527	♂	Ash Meadows, Nev		Mar. 2	Nelson	
18528	♂	....do		Mar. 4	....do	
18529	♂	....do		Mar. 17	....do	
18530	♂	....do		Mar. 13	Fisher	
18531	♂ im.	....do		Mar. 14	....do	
18532	♀	....do		Mar. 10	....do	
18533	♀	....do		Mar. 11	....do	
18534	♀	....do		Mar. 13	....do	
18535	♀	....do		Mar. 2	Stephens	
18536	♀ juv.	....do		...do	....do	
18537	♂	Death Valley, Calif		Jan. 23	Bailey	
18538	♀	....do		...do	....do	
18539	♂	....do		Mar. 22	Nelson	
18540	♂	....do		...do	....do	
18541		Death Valley, near Salt Wells, Calif		Jan. 20	Bailey	
18542	♂	Death Valley, Bennett Wells, Calif		Jan. 21	Palmer	
18543	♂	....do		...do	....do	
18544	♂	....do		...do	Fisher	
18545	♂	....do		...do	....do	
18546	♂	....do		...do	....do	
18547	♂	....do		Jan. 22	Nelson	
18548	♂	....do		Jan. 24	....do	
18549	♂	....do		Jan. 26	....do	
18550	♂	....do		...do	....do	
18551	♀	....do		...do	....do	
18552	♀	....do		Jan. 28	Bailey	
18553	♀	....do		Apr. 28	....do	
18554	♂	Death Valley, Mesquite Well, Calif		Jan. 20	Fisher	
18555		....do		...do	....do	
18556	♂	Death Valley, Furnace Creek, Calif		Feb. 1	Palmer	
18557	♂	....do		Jan. 26	....do	
18558	♂	....do		Jan. 24	....do	
18559	♂	....do		Jan. 23	Fisher	
18560	♂	....do		Jan. 30	....do	
18561	♀	....do		Apr. 10	Stephens	
18562	♀	Funeral Mountains, Calif		Feb. 6	Nelson	
18563	♀	....do		...do	....do	
18564	♂	Death Valley, Saratoga Springs, Calif		Feb. 3	Bailey	
18565	♀	....do		Jan. 30	....do	
18566	♀	....do		...do	....do	
18567	♀	....do		...do	....do	
18568	♀	....do		Feb. 2	Nelson	
18569	♂	....do		...do	....do	
18570	♂	Resting Springs, Calif		Feb. 13	Fisher	
18571	ad.	Borax Flat, Water Station, Calif	2,100	Apr. 22	Stephens	
18572	♂	Panamint Mountains, Johnson Cañon, Calif.		Mar. 30	Fisher	
18573	♂	....do		...do	....do	
18574	♀	....do	5,000	Mar. 28	....do	
18575	♀	....do	5,560	Apr. 3	Nelson	
18576	♂	....do	6,000	Mar. 31	....do	

List of specimens of *Uta stansburiana*—Continued.

U.S. Nat. Mus. No.	Sex and age.	Locality.	Altitude.	Date.	Collector.	Remarks.
			Feet.			
18577	♂	Panamint Valley, Calif.		Jan. 5	Bailey	
18578	♂	......do	1,575	Jan. 12	....do	
18579	♂	......do	1,575	...do	....do	
18580	♀	......do		Jan. 5	...do	
18581	♀	......do		Apr. 20	....do	
18582	♂	Coso Mountains, Coso, Calif.		May 22	Fisher	
18583	♀	Panamint Mountains, Emigrant Spring, Calif.		Apr. 14	Bailey	
18584	♂	Mohave Desert, Leach Point Spring, Calif.		Apr. 25	....do	
18585	♀	Keeler, Calif.		June 3	Fisher	
18586	♂	Fort Tejon, Calif.		June 28	Merriam	
18587	♂	......do		...do	...do	
18588	♀	Antelope Valley, Liebre Ranch, Calif.		...do	...do	
18589	♂	Walker Pass (west slope), Calif.	4,600	July 3	Bailey	
18590	♂	Roses Station, Calif		Oct. 13	Nelson	
18591	♂	Kernville, Calif.		June 23	Palmer	
18592	♂	......do		...do	...do	
18593	♂	Kern River, South Fork, Calif	2,700	July 9	Bailey	
18594	♂	Fresno, Calif		Sep. 23	...do	
18595	♂	......do		...do	...do	
18596	♂	Lone Pine, Calif	7,000	Dec. 19	....do	Lone Pine Cañon.
18597	♂	Caliente, Calif.		June 24	Palmer	

Uta graciosa (Hallow.).

The known range of this well-named species has been considerably extended by the few specimens brought home by Dr. Merriam, inasmuch as it carries it into Nevada, the first record for that State.

Uta graciosa has a very peculiar and considerably restricted distribution, for the only definite localities so far recorded show it to be an inhabitant of a narrow strip of country on both sides of the Colorado River, probably from its mouth up to the beginning of the Great Cañon, and, as now shown, some distance up the Virgin River.

[This slender and agile lizard was not seen in any of the deserts of southern California or Nevada, except in extreme eastern Nevada, where it was common at the Great Bend of the Colorado; thence northward it was found in a few places in the valley of the Virgin as far north as the Mormon town of Bunkerville, a' few miles from the northwestern corner of Arizona. It was never seen on the open desert but usually on mesquite trees and the faces of cliffs, over which it moves with grace and agility.—C. H. M.]

List of specimens of *Uta graciosa*.

U.S. Nat. Mus. No.	Sex and age.	Locality.	Altitude.	Date.	Collector.	Remarks.
			Feet.			
18505	♂	Bunkerville, Nev.		May 8	Bailey	
18506	♂	Callville, Nev. (Great Bend of Colorado).		May 4	Merriam	
18507	♂	......do		...do	...do	

Sceloporus magister (Hallow.). (Pl. I, fig. 2.).

The curious fate of *Sceloporus marmoratus*, or *variabilis*, in herpetological literature, as recently pointed out by me (Proc. U. S. Nat. Mus., XIV, 1891, p. 485, seq.), is equaled, if not surpassed, by that of the present species and *Sceloporus clarkii*.

The latter species was established in 1852 by Baird and Girard upon specimens from 'Sonora' (*i. e.*, Arizona). Two years later, Mr. Hallowell described another large specimen of *Sceloporus* from the vicinity of Fort Yuma as *S. magister*. With the material at hand then, and considering the insufficiency of the descriptions, it is hardly to be wondered at that Baird and Girard subsequently adduced Hallowell's name *S. magister* as a synonym to *S. clarkii*, or that they have been followed in this course by all subsequent herpetologists, with the possible exception, perhaps, of Hallowell himself, who, in 1859 still retains the name *S. magister*. They are, however, undoubtedly good species, as will be shown further on.

One of the more recent authors to monograph the genus, Mr. Bocourt, in 1874, seems to have recognized the difference between the two, as he thinks *S. clarkii* related to *S. formosus*, and *S. magister* to *spinosus* or *acanthinus*, but beyond these vague suggestions, there is nothing to indicate that he ever had the opportunity to examine specimens of either.

In 1875 *S. clarkii* is recognized by Cope, Coues, and Yarrow, in their various publications, and *zosteromus* is made a subspecies of *S. clarkii*, but not even that much recognition is given *S. magister*. In Yarrow's Catalogue and Check list of 1883 there is no change.

In Cope's 'Synopsis of the Mexican Species of the Genus *Sceloporus*,' published in 1885, there is a decided inclination towards lumping several of the North American forms (see for instance the synonymy of *S. undulatus*), but one is hardly prepared to find *S. zosteromus* raised to a distinct species again and to the total abandonment of *S. clarkii*. True, the paper by its title refers only to Mexican species, but as it includes several species confined to the United States it seems evident that the species occurring in North America were also intended to be included.

But in the same year we meet a decided novelty, as Mr. Boulenger, in the second volume of his Catalogue of the Lizards in the British Museum, makes *S. clarkii* a subspecies of *S. spinosus*, with the following synonymy: *S. magister* Hall.; *S. floridanus* Baird, and *S. thayerii* Bocourt (*nec.* B.& G.)! And in addition he remarks: "This form appears to be completely linked with *S. undulatus*." Before proceeding further I will note here that at least his specimen *a*, from the 'Colorado Bottom,' is true *S. magister*, and that possibly he has not seen *S. clarkii*, under which name this specimen was probably sent to the British Museum by the Smithsonian Institution.

The last monographer of the genus, Dr. Günther, in the reptile volume of Biologia Centrali-Americana (February, 1890), finally includes both *clarkii* and *magister* as unconditional synonyms of *S. spinosus*, evidently because he found a "want of agreement between the number of pores and the distribution of the species." However, had he first separated *clarkii* and *magister* by their proper characters which are not to be found in the number of femoral pores, he could not have missed the agreement looked for.

I must myself plead guilty of having confounded *S. clarkii* and *S. magister*, misled, as I was, by the almost unanimous verdict of herpetologists. If there was a settled question in regard to the *Sceloporī*, I thought surely to have it in the identity of these two names. I regarded no identification more secure than that of the specimens collected by Dr. Merriam in the Grand Cañon of the Colorado as *S. clarkii*.* As a matter of fact, however, they are *S. magister*.

That I was finally undeceived is principally due to Mr. P. L. Jouy, who, while collecting for the National Museum near Tucson, southern Arizona, in 1891, had the good fortune to observe both species alive. In sending the specimens, he wrote me that he had undoubtedly two species which he could distinguish not only by their color when alive, but also by their habits and the different localities which they frequented, one being shy and agile, the other fearless and sluggish; one found only on the mesa and on the ground, the other near the river, and chiefly on trees and bushes. Not being able, upon a cursory examination, to find any tangible character, I wrote back that there was only one big *Sceloporus* and *S. clarkii* was its name. Upon his return, Mr. Jouy again brought up the question, and as he was so very persistent, I promised him to examine all the material carefully, a promise made more to please him than because I expected a different result. I went to work and it just so happened that the first two specimens which I picked up belonged each to a different species. My eye at the very first glance hit upon the most distinctive character which separates the two, viz, the difference in the spiny scales which protect the anterior border of the ear opening, a difference which is quite apparent upon an examination of the accompanying figures (Pl. I, figs. 1 and 2). The constancy of the character was soon verified in a large series of specimens, as well as the concomitancy of the presence or absence of dusky cross markings on the dorsal aspect of the forearm and hand.

It would have been difficult to ascertain the correct names of the two species from the published descriptions, but the types of both *S. clarkii* and *S. magister* are still in the collection, and fortunately they belong respectively to the two species.

Upon plotting on a map the various localities from which I have examined specimens (about forty), it was shown that the two species inhabit different areas, and that the habitats come together and partly overlap in southeastern Arizona, notably around Tucson. But here

---

*North American Fauna, No. 3, p. 110.

it is useful to remember Mr. Jouy's observation that the two species live apart in separate localities.

Sceloporus magister, according to this, inhabits the desert region of southern California, as verified by numerous examples brought home by the Death Valley Expedition and enumerated hereafter. Material from the same source shows that it penetrates into southern Nevada, and easterly into southwestern Utah, while Dr. Merriam, during his San Francisco Mountain Expedition in 1889, demonstrated its occurrence in the Grand Cañon of the Colorado. The most northern locality from which the species has been brought, and which has never before been recorded, I believe, is the Big Bend of the Truckee River in Nevada, at 'Camp 12' of King's expedition, where numerous specimens were collected by Mr. Robert Ridgway. Eastward it has been found in the deserts of southern Arizona as far as Fort Verde and Tucson.

Sceloporus clarkii, on the other hand, within the United States, seems confined to southeastern Arizona, whence it is found southward into Mexico for an unknown distance, probably confined to the western slope of the Sierra Madre, for it is pretty certain that *S. clarkii* and all its allied forms, or species, are confined to the western slope of the continent.

The map used for plotting the distribution of the two species was the summer 'Rain-chart of the United States' by Charles A. Schott (published by the Smithsonian Institution in 1868) and the coincidence of the dividing line between the two species with the isohyetal line of 6 inches seems to be more than accidental.

Farther south in Mexico we find the typical *S. clarkii* replaced by a nearly related form, which, as it has received no name before, we may call *S. boulengeri*;* Boulenger's *S. spinosus* being in part this form.

Still farther south we have another modification of the same type in *Sceloporus acanthinus* Boc., with its excessively long points to the dorsal scales. The locality whence came the type is St. Augustine, on the west slope of the volcano of Atitlan, Guatemala.

Sceloporus magister has also representative forms toward the south. A very distinct species, but apparently of rather restricted distribu-

---

* **Sceloporus boulengeri**, sp. nov., Plate I, figs. 5a.–c.

Diagnosis.—Similar to *S. clarkii* but with fewer femoral pores; ear spines comparatively short and broad; interparietal very broad.

Habitat.—Mexico, west coast from Mazatlan to Guaymas.

Type.—U. S. Nat. Mus., No. 14079; Presidio, about 50 miles from Mazatlan, Sinaloa, Mexico; A. Forrer, coll.

In the width of the interparietal the present form agrees with *S. zosteromus*, but the latter has nearly twice as many femoral pores, and its ear spines are long, narrow, and numerous.

tion, of which specimens have come to hand only quite recently, is *Sceloporus orcutti*.* The only specimens seen have come from San Diego County, Southern California, and the only exact locality known is the Milquatay Valley, which Mr. C. R. Orcutt, who collected the specimens, and in whose honor the species is named, informs me "is just bordering the Mexican boundary, 50 miles east of San Diego by wagon road." It probably penetrates some distance south into the northern part of Lower California, in the southern portion of which its place is taken by *S. zosteromus*.† This species is closely allied to *S. magister*. *S. clarkii*, on the other hand, is more different from the latter than the latter is from *S. zosteromus*.

I have above alluded to Mr. Boulenger having made *S. floridanus* a synonym of his *S. spinosus* var. *clarkii*. Cope, on the other hand, makes it a synonym of *S. undulatus* (Proc. Am. Philos. Soc., XXII, 1885, p. 398), but both are wrong, as an examination of the type specimen clearly proves. The fig. 6 on Plate I from this specimen shows that it has nothing to do with *S. clarkii*, or any species of the group to which the latter belongs. On the other hand, the size of the dorsal scales easily distinguishes it from *S. undulatus*. It is in fact the same form which occurs all through southern Texas and which has commonly been called *S. spinosus*. It is fairly separable from the true Mexican *S. spinosus* by the greater number of femoral pores. The form occurring within the United States will therefore stand as *Sceloporus floridanus*, or *S. spinosus floridanus* (notwithstanding the fact that it does not occur in the peninsula of Florida) if the number of femoral pores should be found to intergrade. The most eastern point where this form has been found is Pensacola, Fla.; hence the name. It is needless to add that *S. thayeri* B. & G. does not belong here; on the other hand, the specimens so described and figured by Bocourt certainly do.

---

* Sceloporus orcutti sp. nov., plate I, figs. 4a–c.

Diagnosis.—Similar to *Sceloporus magister*, but dorsal scales smaller, seven in a head length, very obtusely keeled and the spiny point scarcely protruding beyond the rounded outline; no nuchal collar; back with cross-bands of dark and paler brown, the dark bands being broader than the pale ones; whole underside pale grayish blue, without definite patches, the large males with the blue somewhat darker on throat, flanks, and thighs.

Locality.—Milquatay Valley, San Diego County, Calif.

Type.—U. S. Nat. Mus., No. 16330; Charles R. Orcutt, coll.; January 5, 1890.

Although manifestly related to *S. magister*, this is perhaps the most distinct-looking species of the whole group, the comparative smoothness of the back and the very peculiar coloration being quite notable. The under surface is particularly remarkable when compared with the allied species, it being in fact unique among all the *Sceloporis* which I have examined. It is quite probable, however, that the blue in the old males may deepen and darken as the season advances.

The constancy of the species can be vouched for, as I have examined ten specimens, eight of which are now before me, and they are all alike.

† Plate I, fig. 3, shows some of the more essential characters of this species for comparison with the allied forms.

It will thus be seen that—even looking apart from *S. horridus*—we find ourselves compelled to recognize at least six distinct forms, or species, where so high an authority as Prof. Günther as late as 1890 has admitted only one. This different result is chiefly due, however, to the much more abundant material at my command, for while the herpetologists of the British Museum had scarcely more than 30 specimens to draw conclusions from, I am fortunate enough to have before me nearly 200 specimens, mostly from well authenticated localities, upon which to base the above results.

* [The large scaly lizard known as *Sceloporus magister* is a Lower Sonoran species ranging across the southern deserts and desert ranges of the Great Basin from California to Arizona and southwestern Utah. Unlike most of the lizards inhabiting the same region, it does not run about on the open desert, but lives on the tree yuccas, the ruins of stone or adobe dwellings, the nests of wood rats, and other objects that afford it shelter and protection. At the mouth of Beaverdam Creek in northwestern Arizona it was common among cottonwood logs and dead leaves; in Pahranagat Valley it was abundant about the ruins of stone houses and along the faces of cliffs; in the Mohave Desert and other localities it is common on the tree yuccas, where it was often found on the very summits of the highest branches, and where it was rather wary and difficult of capture without a gun.

In California it occurs throughout the Mohave Desert, ranging as far west as the tree yuccas in Antelope Valley and Walker Pass, and thence easterly in Owens Valley, Borax Flat, and the Argus and Panamint mountains.

In Nevada it was found on the Grapevine Mountains, in Ash Meadows, in Pahrump Valley at the foot of the Charleston Mountains, in Vegas and Indian Springs valleys, in Pahranagat Mountains and Valley, at the Great Bend of the Colorado River, and in the valley of the Virgin.

In Arizona it was abundant at the point where Beaverdam Creek joins the Virgin.

In Utah it was common in the Lower Santa Clara or St. George Valley.

Sceloporus magister is a mixed feeder, both insects and flowers being found in the stomachs examined. At the Great Bend of the Colorado, Nevada, and St. George, Utah, stomachs were opened that contained insects only. One from the latter locality contained a large goldsmith beetle.—C. H. M.]

List of specimens of *Sceloporus magister*.

U.S. Nat. Mus. No.	Sex and age	Locality	Altitude	Date	Collector	Remarks
18096	♀	Pahranagat Valley, Nev	Feet.	May 23	Merriam	
18097	♂	...do...		...do...	...do...	
18098	♀	...do...	4,100	...do...	...do...	
18099	♀	...do...		...do...	Bailey	
18100	♀ juv.	...do...		...do...	Merriam	
18101	♂ juv.	...do...		May 25	Bailey	
18102	♂	Pahranagat Mountains, Nev		May 26	Merriam	
18103	♂	Pahrump Valley, Nev	5,000	Apr. 29	...do...	Yucca belt.
18104	♂	Callville, Nev		May 4	Bailey	
18105	♂	Ash Meadows, Nev		Mar. 16	Nelson	
18106	♂ juv.	...do...		Mar. 20	Palmer	
18107	♂	Vegas Valley, Nev		May 1	Bailey	
18108	♂	Indian Spring Valley, Nev		May 29	Merriam	
18109	♂	...do...		...do...	Bailey	
18110	♂ juv.	Grapevine Mountains, Nev		June 8	Nelson	4,000 feet above Salt Wells, Mesquite Valley.
18111	♂ juv.	Bunkerville, Nev		May 8	Merriam	
18112	♂	St. George, Utah		May 12	Bailey	
18113	♂	...do...		May 13	...do...	
18114	♂	Diamond Valley, 10 miles north of St. George, Utah.	4,800	May 16	Merriam	Lava rock.
18115	♂	...do...	4,800	May 16	...do...	Do.
18116	♂	Panamint Mountains, Cottonwood Cañon, Calif.		June 14	Nelson	4,400 feet above Salt Wells.
18117	♂	...do...	3,900	May 29	...do...	
18118	♂	Panamint Mountains, Willow Creek, Calif.	3,800	May 22	...do...	
18119	♀ juv.	...do...	4,000	May 17	...do...	
18120	♀	Walker Pass, Calif	4,000	July 2	Bailey	
18121	♀	...do...	4,000	July 1	...do...	
18122	♀	...do...	4,000	...do...	...do...	
18123	♂	Mohave, Mohave Desert, Calif		June 26	Palmer	
18124	♂	Near Mohave, Mohave Desert, Calif.		...do...	Merriam	
18125	♂	...do...		...do...	...do...	
18126	♂	...do...		Apr. 6	...do...	
18127	♂	Mohave Desert, near base of Granite Mountains, Calif.		Apr. 25	Bailey	On rocks.
18128	♀	Argus Range, Shepherd Cañon, Calif.		Apr. 29	Fisher	
18129	♀	...do...		Apr. 27	...do...	
18130	♀	Argus Range, Searl's Garden, Calif.	3,000	Apr. 24	Stephens	
18131	♂	Owens Valley (Lone Pine), Calif		June 11	Fisher	
18132	♀ juv.	...do...		June 12	...do...	
18133	♂	Columbus, Nev		Dec. '90	Bailey	

Sceloporus graciosus B. & G.

The size of the dorsal scales in this species is very variable, the number of scales in a head length varying from eleven to sixteen. Both extremes are represented in the present collection. In the two smallest specimens the numbers are fifteen and sixteen; in a slightly larger one from Mount Magruder, Nevada, there are fourteen; in two full-grown specimens from the same locality, thirteen and twelve; one from the east slope of the High Sierra west of Lone Pine, Calif. (altitude 8,000 feet), has also twelve; and in a couple from the Juniper Mountains, Nevada altitude 6,700 feet), the number of scales in a head length is only eleven. From this it might be supposed that the difference in the ratio between the head and the dorsal scales depended upon age, but in the types of the species (U. S. Nat. Mus. 2877, Great Salt Lake, Utah, Capt. Stansbury coll.), which are fully as small as the smallest specimens mentioned above with fifteen and sixteen scales to the head length, the number is only twelve, while in two full-grown males from Fort Klamath, Oregon (U. S. Nat. Mus. Nos. 15437-15438, Dr. Merrill, coll.), there are fifteen and fourteen, respectively.

[This species, which is a characteristic inhabitant of the Upper Sonoran and Transition zones in northern Nevada, eastern Oregon, and Idaho, was very abundant on the sage-covered plateau of Mount Magruder at an altitude of about 2,450 meters (8,000 feet); in the sage plains on top of the White and Inyo mountains near the boundary between California and Nevada; and on the east slope of the Sierra Nevada west of Owens Valley (at 2,450 meters, or 8,000 feet). It was common also among the sage and juniper on the Juniper Mountains along the boundary between Nevada and Utah.

Sceloporus graciosus is generally found in company with such Transition Zone species as the sage thrasher (*Oroscoptes montanus*), Brewer's sparrow (*Spizella breweri*), the Nevada sage sparrow (*Amphispiza belli nevadensis*), the sage plains chipmunk (*Tamias minimus pictus*), the sage brush pocket mouse (*Perognathus olivaceus*), and the sage plains spermophile (*Spermophilus mollis*).—C. H. M.]

List of specimens of *Sceloporus graciosus*.

U.S. Nat. Mus. No.	Sex and Age.	Locality.	Altitude.	Date.	Collector.	Remarks.
18134	♀	Mount Magruder, Nev.	Feet. 8,000	June 6	Merriam	Sage Plain.
18135	♀	....do	8,000	..do	..do	Do.
18136	♀	....do	8,000	..do	Bailey	Do.
18137	♂	Juniper Mountains, Nev.	6,700	May 19	Merriam	In junipers.
18138	♀	Juniper Mountains (Sheep Spring, 15 miles east of Panaca), Nev.	6,700	..do	Bailey	
18139	♂	High Sierra, west of Lone Pine, Calif.	8,000	June 18	Merriam	
18140	♀	Panamint Mountains, Willow Creek, Calif.	6,400	May 12	Nelson	
18141	♂	(?)		(?)	(?)	(*)

*Without label, but with the following note by Mr. Charles W. Richmond: "Rec'd July 2, 1891, with specimens from Grapevine Mountains, Lone Pine, etc."

Sceloporus bi-seriatus Hallow.

The great majority of *Sclopori* brought home by the expedition belong to this form, which in the region visited seems to occur everywhere above the desert belt at least up to 8,000 feet altitude.

I can discover no difference between the examples from the mountains inclosing the Valley of California and those from the isolated desert ranges to the east, except that male specimens with the white of the under surface replaced by black are more common from the latter localities.

Among the localities from which specimens were brought are the type localities of Hallowell's *bi-seriatus*, with its several color varieties, of Baird's *longipes*, of Cope's *smaragdinus*, and of Boulenger's *bocourtii*;

and with the actual types of Baird and of Cope, and with specimens before me out of the same bottles upon which Boulenger founded his variety, I have no hesitation in pronouncing all these names synonymous, and in asserting that Bocourt's *S. biseriatus* is the same as Hallowell's. Boulenger's *bocourtii*, however, is somewhat composite, as I do not believe that the Monterey specimens, at least, belong to it. I have no doubt that they are referable to *S. occidentalis*, with which the present form is easily confounded, on account of the fact that both differ from typical *S. undulatus* in the females having the blue patches almost as well developed as the males.*

[*Sceloporus biseriatus* is one of the few lizards inhabiting both the desert ranges of the Great Basin and the interior valley of California. Specimens were obtained at frequent intervals all the way from the Upper San Joaquin Valley, in California, to the Upper Santa Clara Valley, in Utah, about 10 miles northwest of St. George. On the east side of the Great Divide, in California, it was obtained on the Panamint, Argus, Coso, White, and Inyo mountains, and at the east foot of the Sierra in Owens Valley (on Independence Creek). On the west side of the Great Divide it was common on the west slope of Walker Pass and thence down into Kern Valley to the neighborhood of Kernville, and southerly along the west slope of the Sierra to Havilah and Walker Basin, and northerly to Three Rivers. It was common also in the Cañada de las Uvas, and in the Upper San Joaquin Valley, where specimens were collected at Kern Lakes, Tulare, and Fresno. In Nevada it was collected on the Charleston Mountains (near Mountain Spring), on Mount Magruder, in the Juniper Mountains, and in the Grapevine Mountains.

A black form (having the belly intensely blue-black) was found on black lava rock in Diamond Valley, Utah; on the Charleston Mountains (near Mountain Spring), Nevada, where it was found both on rocks and on juniper trees, and on the White Mountains, near the eastern boundary of California. In the latter locality it was common on the summit of the divide near the road between Deep Spring and Owens valleys, where it was frequently seen on and among light colored rocks, which made it unusually conspicuous. It is entirely possible, however, that this very striking contrast is a protection, causing the lizard to resemble the dark cracks in the rocks when viewed from above by passing hawks.—C. H. M.]

---

*Yarrow's *S. undulatus thayeri* (Bull. U. S. Nat. Mus., 24, p. 60) consists mainly of *S. bi-seriatus*, but also to some extent of *S. occidentalis*. To the latter are also referable Cope's specimens similarly named in Proc. Phil. Ac., 1883, p. 28, and probably *tom. cit.*, pp. 23 and 27.

List of specimens of Sceloporus biseriatus.

U.S. Nat. Mus. No.	Sex and age.	Locality.	Altitude.	Date.	Collector.	Remarks.
			Feet.			
18147	♂	Panamint Mountains, Calif	8,000	Apr. 19	Nelson	
18148	♂	...do	6,000	Apr. 4	...do	
18149	♂	...do	6,000	...do	...do	
18150	♂	...do	6,000	Apr. 3	...do	
18151	♂	...do	6,000	...do	...do	
18152	♀ juv.	...do	6,000	...do	...do	
18153	♀ juv.	...do		Mar. —	...do	
18154	♂	...do	*6,000	Mar. —	...do	
18155	♂	Panamint Mountains, Willow Creek, Calif.	4,500	May 19	...do	
18156	♂	Panamint Mountains, Johnson Cañon, Calif.		Mar. 31	Fisher	
18157	♂	...do		...do	...do	
18158	♂	...do		Apr. [1	...do	
18159	♂	...do		Apr. 2	...do	
18160	♂	...do		Apr. 4	...do	
18161	♂	...do		Apr. 10	...do	
18162	♀	...do		Apr. 4	...do	
18163	♂	Coso Mountains, Coso, Calif		May 18	...do	
18164	♂	...do		May 23	...do	
18165	♂	...do		May 21	...do	
18166	♂	...do		May 20	...do	
18167	♀	...do		...do	...do	
18168	♀ ad.	...do		...do	...do	
18169	♂	Old Fort Tejon, Calif		June 28	Palmer	
18170	♂	...do		...do	Merriam	
18171	♂	...do		June 29	Palmer	
18172	♀	...do		July 3	...do	
18173	♀	...do		July 5	...do	
18174	♀	...do		July 8	...do	
18175	♂	South Fork Kern River, 25 miles above Kernville, Calif.		July 7	Fisher	
18176	♂	Kernville, Calif		June 23	Palmer	
18177	♂	...do		...do	...do	
18178	♂	South Fork Kern River, Calif	2,750	July 7	Bailey	
18179	♂	Walker Basin, Calif		July 14	Fisher	
18180	♀	...do		...do	...do	
18181	♂	Havilah, Calif		June 24	Palmer	
18182	♀ ad.	...do		...do	...do	
18183	♀	...do		...do	Merriam	
18184	♀	Fresno County, Horse Corral Meadow, Calif.		Aug. 11	Palmer	
18185	♀ ad.	...do		...do	...do	
18186	♀	...do		...do	Fisher	
18187	♂	Walker Pass (West Slope), Calif		July 7	...do	
18188	♂	Cañada de las Uvas, Calif		Oct. 14	Nelson	
18189	juv.	...do		...do	...do	
18190	♂	White Mountains, Calif	8,000	June 9	Merriam	
18191	♀	Soda Springs, Kern River, Calif		Aug. 15	Bailey	
18192	♂	Three Rivers, Calif		July 28	Fisher	
18193	♀	Tulare, Calif		July 21	Bailey	
18194	♂	Kaweah River, East Fork, Calif	5,600	July 29	...do	
18195	♂	San Joaquin River, Calif	7,600	...do	Nelson	
18196	♂	Argus Range, Shepherd Cañon, Calif		May 7	Fisher	
18197	♀	East Slope High Sierra, Independence Creek, Calif.	6,000	June 21	Stephens	
18198	♂	Charleston Mountains, Mountain Spring, Nev.	5,600	Apr. 30	Bailey	
18199	♂	...do	5,600	...do	...do	
18200	♀	...do	5,600	...do	Merriam	
18201	♀	...do	5,600	...do	...do	
18202	♂	Mount Magruder, Nev		June 5	...do	
18203	♀	...do		...do	...do	
18204	♂	Juniper Mountains, 12 miles east of Panaca, Nev.	6,700	May 19	Bailey	
18105	♀	Grapevine Mountains, Nev	6,400	June 10	Nelson	
18206	♂	Ten miles west of St. George, Utah	4,800	May 16	Bailey	On lava rock.

*About.

Sceloporus occidentalis B. & G.

The Monterey specimens enumerated below belong to the present form of *S. undulatus*. The status of these two forms relative to each other has not been settled yet, nor has the material necessary for such a settlement been accumulated so far in any museum. Under these circumstances nothing is gained by using a trinominal.

List of specimens of Sceloporus occidentalis.

U.S. Nat. Mus. No.	Sex and Age.	Locality.	Altitude.	Date.	Collector.	Remarks.
			Feet.			
18143	♂	Monterey, Calif.		Oct. 6	Bailey	
18144	♂	......do		Oct. 3	....do	
18145	♂ juv.	......do		Sept. 29	....do	
18146	♂ juv.	......do		Sept. 30	....do	

Phrynosoma blainvillii Gray.

That authors with only specimens of either *Ph. blainvillii* or *Ph. coronatum* before them should consider both species synonymous is perhaps not to be wondered at, but a confusion of them, with both at hand, is not so easily explained. The differences are marked, numerous, and constant, and moreover, are easily expressed. The two species inhabit two well-separated zoölogical faunas, for while *Ph. coronatum* appears to be restricted to the Cape region of Lower California—that is to say, to the comparatively small mountainous area at the extreme southern end of the peninsula, on which are located Cape St. Lucas, La Paz, and San José del Cabo—*Ph. blainvillii* is restricted, so far as we know, to Upper California. How far down the peninsula the latter species descends we do not know, and whether there is any other gap between the two species than the low, sandy plains to the north of the Cape region remains to be seen; but it is somewhat significant that Cerros Island, about halfway down the peninsula, is inhabited by a third species,* more nearly related to *Ph. blainvillii* than to *Ph. coronatum*.

The title of the Californian species to the name *Phrynosoma blainvillii* Gray is at present not entirely beyond a suspicion. The facts in the case are as follows:

In the 'Zoölogy of Capt. Beechey's Voyage' (published in 1839), J. E. Gray (p. 96), shortly and insufficiently characterized a new species of *Phrynosoma* from 'California' as *Ph. blainvillii* without stating the source of the specimen or whether more than one specimen served as a basis for his description. The text is accompanied by a wretched figure (Pl. XXIX, fig. 1). The description gives no clew to the identity of the species, but were I to go by the figure alone, I should unhesi-

---
*Phrynosoma cerroense, sp. nov.

Diagnosis.—Nostrils excessively large, pierced in the line of canthus rostralis; gular scales enlarged, in several longitudinal rows; ventral scales smooth; a long and slender spine between the sublabial rictal spine and the lower end of the ear; medium occipital spine reduced to a tubercle; no row of spines between eye and temporal spines; lower peripheral spine row obsolete and only indicated by a few scattered small spines.

Habitat.—Cerros Island, Pacific coast of Lower California.

Type.—U. S. National Museum, No. 11,977; L. Belding coll.

tatingly refer it to the Upper Californian species, had as the figure is, and not to *Ph. coronatum* from Cape St. Lucas. However, in his 'Catalogue of the Specimens of Lizards in the British Museum' (1845), Gray himself identifies his species with *Ph. coronatum* and states in so many words that his *Ph. blainvillii* was based upon a specimen presented by Prof. De Blainville (see also his statement in the introduction, p. v., that "the specimens presented by M. De Blainville may be regarded as the types of the species described by that professor in the *Nouveaux Memoires du Museum*)." In addition he enumerates three more specimens from 'California.' This would seem to settle the case in favor of making *Ph. coronatum* and *Ph. blainvillii* synonymous, but there are yet two possibilities. First, it must be remembered that Botta, whose collection was the basis of De Blainville's description, evidently collected both at the Cape St. Lucas (where he obtained *Callisaurus draconoides, Cyclura acanthura, Coluber vertebralis*), and also further north in Upper California, probably near San Diego (where he secured *Coluber catenifer; C. infernalis; C. californiae*). It is, therefore, quite possible that he collected horned-toads at both places, and that the young specimen presented to the British Museum in reality was different from *Ph. coronatum*. Whether this be the case could easily be settled in the British Museum, where the specimen is still preserved. In the second place, it is possible that Gray had figured one of the other specimens then in the British Museum, and that the specimen figured belongs to the Upper Californian species. If that be the case the name *Ph. blainvillii* would stick to the latter no matter which specimens Gray *subsequently* might designate as the type.

There is some additional inferential evidence which tends to corroborate this opinion, viz, that Boulenger with the above specimens before him and additional specimens from Monterey refers them all to one species (Cat. Liz. Brit. Mus., II, 1885, pp. 243, 244), as it seems but little probable that he should have failed to appreciate the great difference, had both species been represented in his series.

The geographical distribution of *Ph. blainvillii* includes the interior valley of California as well as the entire western slope of the various coast ranges, but it is not found, so far as I know, anywhere in the true desert region. It is true that Yarrow's Catalogue (Bull. U. S. Nat. Mus., No. 24, 1883, p. 70) enumerates two specimens as having been collected by Dr. Loew in the Mohave Desert, but I have good reasons for asserting that the locality is in all probability erroneous. In the original entry of No. 8647 only one specimen is registered, while the bottle now contains three specimens so numbered, a fact which throws discredit upon the whole entry; and as Dr. Loew collected near Santa Barbara and at Santa Cruz Island in June, 1875, as shown by the records, the probability is that the specimens in question came from one or both of those localities.

It is to *Ph. blainvillii* that the published accounts about ejecting blood from the eyes should be credited, and one of the specimens in the collection brought home (No. 18452) is the offender who gave rise to Dr. O. P. Hay's entertaining article (Proc. U. S. Nat. Mus., XV, 1892, pp. 375–378) on this subject. It transpired afterwards that this specimen had been sent me alive for the very reason that it had been ejecting blood repeatedly when caught. The letter from Mr. Bailey accompanying the specimen turned up long after Dr. Hay's experience with the animal, and it is to the following effect:

KERNVILLE, CAL., *July 11, 1891.*

DEAR SIR: I caught a horned toad to-day that very much surprised Dr. Fisher and myself by squirting blood from its eyes. It was on smooth ground and not in brush or weeds. I caught it with my hand and just got my fingers on its tail as it ran. On taking it in my hand a little jet of blood spurted from one eye a distance of 15 inches and spattered on my shoulder. Turning it over to examine the eye another stream spurted from the other eye. This he did four or five times from both eyes until my hands, clothes, and gun were sprinkled over with fine drops of bright red blood. I put it in a bag and carried it to camp, where, about four hours later, I showed it to Dr. Fisher, when it spurted three more streams from its eyes. One of the same species that I caught July 2 evidently did the same, as I found its head covered with blood when I caught it, but supposed it was injured in the weeds. It seems so strange that I send the horned toad to you alive.

VERNON BAILEY.

The specimen upon its arrival was handled a great deal, but gave no evidence of its blood-squirting tendencies until the beginning of August, when it resented Dr. Hay's handling it somewhat roughly in the manner related. In order to give the entire history of this animal, I reprint Dr. Hay's account as follows:

"About the 1st of August it was shedding its outer skin, and the process appeared to be a difficult one, since the skin was dried and adhered closely. One day it occurred to me that it might facilitate matters if I should give the animal a wetting; so, taking it up, I carried it to a wash-basin of water near by and suddenly tossed the lizard into the water. The first surprise was probably experienced by the *Phrynosoma*, but the next surprise was my own, for on one side of the basin there suddenly appeared a number of spots of red fluid, which resembled blood. . . . . . A microscope was soon procured and an examination was made, which immediately showed that the matter ejected was really blood.

"The affair now became very interesting. Just where the blood came from I could not determine with certainty, the whole thing having happened so suddenly and unexpectedly; yet the appearance seemed to indicate that the blood came from the region about one of the eyes. There appeared to be a considerable quantity of the blood, since on the sides of the vessel and on the wall near it I counted ninety of the little splotches. A consultation was had with Mr. Stejneger the next day with regard to the propriety of dashing the animal into the water again to discover, if possible, where the blood came from.

It was thought, however, that such blood-lettings must be somewhat exhausting, and that it would be better to allow the animal a day to recuperate. While talking I picked up the lizard and was holding it between my thumb and middle finger, and stroking its horns with my fore-finger. All at once a quantity of blood was thrown out against my fingers, and a portion of it ran down on the animal's neck; and this blood came directly out of the right eye. It was shot backward and appeared to issue from the outer canthus. It was impossible to determine just how much there was of the blood, but it seemed that there must have been a quarter of a teaspoonful. I went so far as to taste a small quantity of it, but all that I could detect was a slight musky flavor."

[The fact that horned toads at times eject blood from their eyes is well known in the West, and is by no means confined to the present species. I have been aware of the habit for many years.

Phrynosoma blainvillii is the horned toad of the interior valley and coastal slopes of California. Specimens were obtained by our expedition on the west slope of the Sierra Nevada in Walker Pass, in Kern Valley, Walker Basin, and at old Fort Tejon in the Cañada de las Uvas; and others were collected at Bakersfield and Fresno in the San Joaquin Valley, and on Carrizo Plain.—C. H. M.]

List of specimens of Phrynosoma blainvillii.

U.S. Nat. Mus. No.	Sex and age	Locality	Altitude	Date	Collector	Remarks
			Feet.			
18446	♂	Walker Pass, Calif		July 2	Bailey	
18447	♀	do		do	do	
18448	♂	do		do	Fisher	Western slope.
18449	♂	Walker Basin, Calif		July 14	Bailey	
18450	♀	South Fork, Kern River, Calif	2,750	July 7	do	
18451	♀	Kernville, Calif		June 23	Palmer	
18452	♂	do		July 11	Bailey	Ejected blood from eye.
18453	♂ jun.	Fresno, Calif		Sept. 23	do	
18454	♂ juv.	do		do	do	
18455	♀ jun.	do		do	do	
18456	♀	Bakersfield, Calif		Oct. 11	Nelson	
18457	♂	Carrizo Plains, Calif		do	do	
18458	♀	do		do	do	
18459	♀	Old Fort Tejon, Calif		July 4	Palmer	Pl. II, fig. 2.
18460	♂ jun.	Cañada de las Uvas, Calif		July 9	do	

Phrynosoma platyrhinos Girard.

Boulenger asserts that this species is "very closely allied" to *Ph. m'callii*, (Cat. Liz. Br. Mus., II, 1885, p. 247), but as a matter of fact these species are as distinct as any two in the genus. Boulenger's error, undoubtedly, arose from the fact that the specimen he described as *Ph. m'callii* is not this species at all, but only another specimen of *Ph. platyrhinos*. No wonder his specimens are "very closely allied!" Had he compared his specimens with the descriptions and figures quoted by him he would not have made the mistake; as it is, he has taken the identification of his specimen (U. S. Nat. Mus. No. 10785) by Dr. Yarrow as conclusive, without knowing that not a single specimen of all the horned-toads enumerated by Yarrow in his Catalogue of Reptiles in the U. S. National Museum really belongs to *Ph. m'callii*.

The fact, however, that Boulenger had given characters apparently separating northern and southern specimens, led me to examine the material at hand with a view to ascertain whether it might be possible to recognize two or more races, but an inspection of about one hundred and seventy-five specimens fails to disclose any character or combination of characters by which to separate them. The shape of the head, length, shape, and direction of head spines, length of limbs, number of femoral pores, and coloration are so variable that no separation can be built upon any of these characters. To illustrate this, let me discuss the contents of the two jars out of each of which Mr. Boulenger had one specimen, viz: U. S. Nat. Mus., No. 10785 and 11770. The former is Boulenger's so-called *Ph. m'callii*, with the occipital spines as long as the horizontal diameter of the orbit, and seven femoral pores on each side.

In No. 10785 (locality and collector now unknown), out of which came Boulenger's so-called *Ph. m'callii*, there are now left seven specimens, six males and one female. The number of femoral pores on each side in the males are respectively 9, 8, 7, 7, 9, 8, and in the female 7; in the latter the occipital horns are comparatively best developed, and in at least one of the large specimens this horn is considerably shorter than the horizontal diameter of the orbit.

In No. 11770 (Camp 12, King's Exped., Nevada, R. Ridgway, coll.) there are now six specimens, three adult males and one young, and one adult and one young female. The number of femoral pores in the adult males are respectively 9, 10, 8, and in the adult female 9; in the first-mentioned male the occipital spine is longer than the horizontal diameter of the orbit; in the second, the two dimensions are equal; in the third male and in the female the spines are shorter. As there seems to be a slight average difference between the specimens in the two jars, I was led to examine my series with a view to determine whether the southern specimens average a smaller number of femoral pores than northern ones, but without success.

The reëxamination of my material, however, led to the unexpected discovery of a new species from the sandy coast desert of the Mexican state of Sonora, which I have called *Ph. goodei*,* and dedicated to Dr.

---

*Phrynosoma goodei sp. nov. (plate ii, figs. 3, *a-c*).

Diagnosis.—Nostrils pierced within the canthi rostrales; one series of enlarged spines around the periphery of the body; tail more than twice the length of the head; tympanum entirely concealed by scales; 7-10 femoral pores; 3 temporal horns only on each side, the posterior one nearly on a line with and of the same size as the occipital horns; only three posterior inframaxillary plates spinous.

Habitat.—Coast deserts of the state of Sonora, Mexico.

Type.—U. S. Nat. Mus. No. 8567*a*; Dr. T. H. Streets coll.

G. Brown Goode, the Assistant Secretary of the Smithsonian Institution. It belongs to the same group which embraces *Ph. cornutum*, *m'callii*, and *platyrhinos*, but is hardly more closely allied to one than to the others. It may easily be distinguished by the diagnosis given in the footnote, and for comparison with *Ph. platyrhinos* I add figures of both on plate II.

Ph. platyrhinos appears to be distinctively a desert species, as it was collected nearly everywhere, outside of the interior valley of California and the Pacific slope, where members of the expedition went, and judging from the great number of specimens brought back it must be very common. The range of the species covers that of *Callisaurus ventralis* within the territory of the United States, but extends considerably further east and north.

As with the other species of this genus the ground color of the living animal is subject to great variation, more or less dependent upon the coloration of the surroundings. The specimens collected by the expedition vary from a very pale, in some nearly whitish, drab gray to a vivid brick-red.

[Horned toads abound throughout the desert regions of the West. *Phrynosoma platyrhinos* inhabits the Lower Sonoran deserts of the Great Basin from California to Utah and ranges up a short distance into the Upper Sonoran. In California it was found in greater or less abundance in the Mohave Desert, in Owens, Coso, Panamint, Death, Mesquite, and Deep Spring valleys, and in the Argus, Funeral, and Panamint mountains (up to 1,740 meters or 5,700 feet on west slope northwest of Wild Rose Spring). In Nevada it was abundant in Sarcobatus Flat, the Amargosa Desert, Ash Meadows, Indian Spring, Pahrump, Vegas, Pahranagat, and Meadow Creek valleys, and the Valley of the Virgin and Muddy. In the northwestern corner of Arizona it was very abundant about the mouth of Beaverdam Creek and thence up on the west slope of the Beaverdam Mountains. In Utah it was common in the Santa Clara Valley ranging up through the sage brush to Diamond Valley and Mountain Meadows.

At Ash Meadows in the Amargosa Desert a very white form was found living on the white alkali soil.

The horned toads of the San Joaquin Valley and west slope of the Sierra Nevada in California belong to another species, *Phrynosoma blainvillii*—C. H. M.]

List of specimens of Phrynosoma platyrhinos.

U.S. Nat. Mus. No.	Sex and age.	Locality.	Altitude.	Date.	Collector.	Remarks.
			Feet.			
18363	♂	Virgin Valley, Ariz		May 10	Merriam	
18364	♂	......do		..do..	..do..	
18365	♂	......do		..do..	..do..	
18366	♂	......do		..do..	..do..	
18367	♂	......do		..do..	..do..	
18368	♂	......do		..do..	..do..	
18369	♂	......do		..do..	..do..	
18370	♂	......do		..do..	..do..	
18371	♀	......do		..do..	..do..	
18372	♀	......do		..do..	..do..	
18373	♀	......do		May 9	..do..	
18374	♂	St. George, Utah		May 13	..do..	
18375	♀	......do		..do..	..do..	
18376	♀ jun.	......do		..do..	..do..	
18377	♀	Mountain Meadows, Utah		May 17	..do..	
18378	♂	Panaca, Nev		May 19	..do..	
18379	♂ juv.	......do		..do..	..do..	
18380	♀	......do		..do..	..do..	
18381	♂	Grapevine Mountains, Nev		June 6	Nelson	4,200 feet above Salt Wells. Colorado River.
18382	♂	Lincoln County, Nev		Mar. 12	..do..	
18383	♀	......do		..do..	..do..	
18384	♂	Indian Spring Valley, Nev.		May 29	Bailey	
18385	♀ jun.	......do		..do..	..do..	
18386	♂	Pahrump Valley, Nev		April 29	..do..	
18387	♂	......do		..do..	..do..	
18388	♂	Pahranagat Valley, Nev		May 25	..do..	
18389	♀	......do		..do..	..do..	
18390		......do		..do..	Merriam	
18391	♂	Vegas Valley, Nev		Mar. 9	Bailey	
18392	♂	......do		..do..	Nelson	
18393	♂	Amargosa Desert, Nev		May 31	Merriam	
18394	♂	......do		..do..	..do..	
18395	♀	......do		..do..	..do..	
18396	♀ juv.	Ash Meadows, Nev		Mar. 4	Bailey	
18397	♂	......do		Mar. 3	Stephens	
18398	♂	......do		Mar. 4	Palmer	
18399	♂	......do		Mar. 20	..do..	
18400	♂	......do		..do..	..do..	
18401	♂	......do		Mar. 4	Nelson	
18402	♂	......do		May 30	Merriam	
18403	♂ juv.	......do		Mar. 21	Fisher	
18404	♂	......do		..do..	..do..	
18405	♂ jun.	......do		..do..	..do..	
18406	♂	......do		May 30	Merriam	
18407	♂	Amargosa, Nev		Mar. 8	Palmer	
18408	♀	Funeral Mountains, Calif.		Mar. 16	..do..	1,000 feet above Borax works.
18409	♀	Argus Range, head of Borax Flat, Calif.	3,000	Apr. 21	Stephens	
18410	♀	Water Station, head of Borax Flat, Calif.		Apr. 22	..do..	
18411	♂	Death Valley, Calif	5,000	Apr. 3	Bailey	Panamint Mts.
18412	♀ jun.	Death Valley, Bennett Wells, Calif.		Jan. 21	Palmer	
18413	♀	Death Valley, Furnace Creek, Calif.		Jan. 30	Fisher	
18414	♂	......do		Apr. 10	Stephens	
18415	♀ jun.	10 miles from Resting Springs, Calif		Mar. 17	Palmer	
18416	♂	Saline Valley, Calif	1,500	June 30	Nelson	
18417	♂	Panamint Mountains, Wild Rose Spring, Calif.	5,300	Apr. 16	Bailey	
18418	♂	......do	..do..	..do..	..do..	
18419	♂	......do	..do..	..do..	..do..	
18420	♀	......do	..do..	..do..	..do..	
18421	♀	Panamint Mountains, Willow Creek, Calif.	5,000	May 16	Nelson	
18422	♂	Panamint Valley, Wild Rose Spring, Calif.	4,500	Mar. 20	Bailey	
18423	♀	Panamint Valley, Calif.		Mar. 27	..do..	
18424	♀	......do		Apr. 20	..do..	
18425	♂	......do		..do..	..do..	
18426	♂	......do		..do..	..do..	
18427	♀ jun.	......do		Apr. 24	..do..	
18428	♀ jun.	......do		..do..	..do..	
18429	♂	Owens Lake, Ash Creek, Calif.	3,700	May 29	Stephens	
18430	♀	Owens Valley, 10 miles north of Bishop, Calif.	4,200	July 1	..do..	
18431	♂	Argus Range, Maturango Spring, Calif.		May 6	Fisher	
18432	♀	......do		..do..	..do..	

List of specimens of *Phrynosoma platyrhinos*—Continued.

U.S. Nat. Mus. No.	Sex and age	Locality.	Altitude.	Date.	Collector.	Remarks.
			Feet.			
18433	♀ jun.	Argus Range, Maturango Spring, Calif.	....	May 6	Fisher	
18434	♂	Argus Range, Coso Valley, Calif.	....	May 11	...do...	
18435	♀ jun.	Coso, Calif.	....	May 19	Palmer	
18436	♂	Deep Spring Valley, Calif.	5,400	June 9	Merriam	
18437	♀	Lone Pine, Calif.	....	June 5	Palmer	
18438	♂ jun.	...do...	....	June 7	...do...	
18439	♂	Independence, Calif.	....	June 11	Bailey	
18440	♂	...do...	....	...do...	...do...	
18441	♂	...do...	....	June 18	Stephens	
18442	♀	Coyote Holes, 20 miles northeast of Daggett, Calif.	....	Mar. 13	Palmer	
18443	♂ juv.	Colorado Desert, Palm Spring, Calif.	....	Sept. 27	Stephens	
18444	♀	(?)	....	(?)	(?)	Received from Death Valley Expedition, April 28, 1891.
18445	....	(?)	....	(?)	(?)	
18401	♂	Ash Meadows, Nev.	....	Mar. 4	Nelson	Pl. ii, fig. 4.

Family HELODERMATIDÆ.

Heloderma suspectum Cope.

It is curious that the exact range of so conspicuous and so far-famed a species as the Gila monster is still greatly in doubt. Southern Arizona seems to be the center of its distribution, and from there we have a number of well authenticated records based upon specimens, but as soon as we get outside of that Territory the records become uncertain, and the localities given are vague. Thus we have 'Mohave River' given by Baird upon the authority of Kennerly and Möllhausen (Pac. R. R. Rep., X, Whipple's R., Zoöl., p. 38) which would introduce the species into the Californian fauna, but no specimen seems to have been brought home, and the record remains dubious. Yarrow (Wheeler's Exp., W. 100 Mer., V, p. 562) states that it is "not uncommon in Utah, New Mexico, and Arizona" and that "several specimens were secured in 1871, 1873, and 1874, but with one exception (specimen from Arizona collected in 1873) all were lost in transit to Washington." The New Mexico record refers probably to the observation near San Ildefonso of "a large lizard, presumably of this species" by one of the packers. Whether specimens were actually secured in Utah, I don't know, nor has any other Utah record come to my certain knowledge.

It is therefore very interesting to note that Dr. Merriam found the dead carcass of a *Heloderma* near the Virgin River, in eastern Nevada, the first authentic record from that state.

The specimen was in too bad shape to be preserved, but two of the feet were cut off and brought home as evidence (No. 18640). As the fourth finger, without claw, measures 22^{mm}, it is plain that the specimen was one of large dimensions.

[One of the most unexpected discoveries made by the expedition was the finding of a Gila monster by Mr. Bailey and myself in the Valley of the Virgin, about 8 miles below Bunkerville, near the eastern boundary of Nevada, May 8, 1891. It was dead when found, and measured 475ᵐᵐ (a little more than 18½ inches) in total length. We were told by the Mormons that the species occurs in the Lower Santa Clara Valley, in southwestern Utah, but is rare.—C. H. M.]

Family ANGUIDÆ.

Gerrhonotus scincicauda (Skilton).

The question of the status of the various *Gerrhonoti* credited to California is one of the most difficult and most intricate in North American saurology, partly on account of the great amount of individual variation, partly because of the comparatively scanty, and in many respects unsatisfactory material. Yet, with about one hundred specimens before me, I am able to distinguish a number of separable forms. Nothing would be easier than to bring them all together under one name, and with only a limited number of specimens I might be tempted to do so, but the result would be very far from the truth, and by so doing we would only delay the true solution of the question instead of promoting it.

Let me first remark that I regard the Cape St. Lucas form separable, and that from Bocourt's rather detailed description of the type (Miss. Sc. Mex., Rept., livr. 5, 1878, pp. 357–359) I believe that it is entitled to the name *Gerrhonotus multicarinatus*. This form does not occur in Upper California, nor do I believe that it will be found in Lower California outside of the Cape region proper.

The next question relates to the name of the present form which inhabits, so far as the localities embraced in the present report are concerned, the chaparral belt of the San Joaquin Valley and of the San Jacinto and San Bernardino Mountains. I have so far been unable to make a distinction between the so-called *G. multicarinatus* of authors, from the State of California, *G. scincicauda*, and *G. grandis*, and as *G. scincicauda* is the oldest of these, I retain it for the present form, *i. e.*, the one with all the upper scales strongly carinated, the azygos prefrontal large, the body very elongated, and the coloration characterized by about nine continuous dark bands across the back. It is possible that Wiegmann's *G. cæruleus* (1828) may belong here, but without the exact locality of the type being known, and without an opportunity to examine the specimen, which moreover seems to be very abnormally colored, it would be very unwise to adopt that name.

The nomenclature of the other separable forms will be discussed further on under their respective heads.

According to Mr. T. S. Palmer, the present form is confined to the chaparral belt. Only two specimens were secured by the expedition.

List of specimens of Gerrhonotus scincicauda.

U.S. Nat. Mus. No.	Sex and age.	Locality.	Altitude.	Date.	Collector.	Remarks.
			Feet.			
18616	♀	Three Rivers, Calif.		July 28	Fisher	
18617	♀	Kaweah River, East Fork, Calif.	3,600	July 27	Bailey	

Gerrhonotus scincicauda palmeri, subsp. nov.

Diagnosis —Similar to *G. scincicauda*, but body much less elongated and coloration above essentially different, being, according to age and sex, either uniform dark olive brown with numerous black and white dots on the sides, or pale bluish drab clouded with numerous ill-defined and irregular blotches of brownish drab, blotches not arranged in cross bands.

Habitat.—High elevations of western slope of southern [only?] Sierra Nevada.

Type.—U. S. Nat. Mus., No. 18606 ♂ ad. South Fork Kings River, Calif., T. S. Palmer coll.

Most of the *Gerrhonoti* brought home by the expedition belong to this form, of which there is no specimen in the Museum collection from any definite and undoubted locality before, and all the specimens of the expedition were collected in a comparatively small area near the headwaters of the Kern, Kings, and Kaweah rivers, at an altitude of from about 7,000 to 9,000 feet above the sea.

It might seem strange that there should be no name available among the many defunct synonyms of Californian *Gerrhonoti* by which to distinguish this form, but the fact seems to be that most of the specimens so far brought to the notice of herpetologists have been collected in the lower altitudes, while the present form seems to be restricted to the higher altitudes of the Sierra.

The general aspect of this form is strikingly different from all the other Californian *Gerrhonoti*, and this difference is equally well marked in the youngest specimen and in the oldest. I have before me a nearly unbroken series of ten specimens, from a very young one, with a body only 40^{mm} long, up to the dark old males, and none of them can for an instant be mistaken for the typical *G. scincicauda* from the lower valleys. The whole figure is shorter and more thick set, and the broad and rather distant cross-bands on the back are conspicuously abrupt, the coloration being either uniform dark or else an ill-defined, often obscure, 'pepper-and-salt' mixture. Only in one specimen (No. 18612) there is a more definite arrangement of the light and dark spots, but these ill-defined cross-bands are much more numerous than in *G. scincicauda*, being about fifteen on the back (between anterior and posterior limbs) as against nine to ten in the latter. A similar pattern may also be traced in the youngest specimen referred to (No. 18613) with a similar result.

I take great pleasure in dedicating this interesting form to Mr. T. S. Palmer, who not only collected the type, but also assisted me materially in clearly pointing out the difference in distribution of the present form and its typical representative in the chaparral belt.

List of specimens of Gerrhonotus scincicauda palmeri.

U.S. Nat. Mus. No.	Sex and age.	Locality.	Altitude.	Date.	Collector.	Remarks.
			Feet.			
18606	♂	South Fork King's River, Calif.			Palmer	Type.
18607	♀	East Fork Kaweah River, Calif.	*8,800	Aug. 8	Bailey	
18608	♀ jun.	....do....	*8,890	..do...	...do...	
18609	♂ jun.	....do....	*8,500	Aug. 1	...do...	
18610	♂	Soda Springs, North Fork Kern River, Calif.	7,200	Sept. 6	Nelson	
18611	♀	....do....	7,200	..do...	...do...	
18612	♀	North Fork Kern River, Calif.		Sept. 15	...do...	
18613	♂ juv.	Soda Springs, North Fork Kern River, Calif.		Aug. 15	Bailey	
18614	♀	Sequoia National Park, Calif.	*7,000	Aug. 2	Fisher	Near Kaweah saw-mill.
18615	♀	Mineral King, Calif.	*8,800	Aug. 6	Bailey	

* About.

Gerrhonotus burnettii Gray.

I have no hesitation in declaring this form to be exactly the same as Baird and Girard's *G. formosus*, and a comparison of the excellent figure of the type of *G. burnettii* by Bocourt (Miss. Sc. Mex., Rept., livr. 5, 1878, Pl. XXI C. fig. 4–4 *a*) with that of the type of *G. formosus* in the atlas of the herpetology of the United States Exploring Expedition (Pl. XXIII, figs. 10 and 12) will at once substantiate this assertion. The essential characters consist in the comparatively short snout with its very arched profile, the great development of the paired prefrontals at the expense of the azygos prefrontal, which therefor is of small size, and the peculiar coloration, the dorsal cross-bands being broken up into three portions, one median and two lateral by two longitudinal lines which in some specimens are emphasized by being lighter than the ground color.

This form is only distantly related to *G. scincicauda*, but very closely to *Gerrhonotus principis*, so close, in fact, that I believe that the name of the latter will become reduced to a trinominal when the geographical distribution of the two forms shall have been ascertained in all its details. *G. burnettii* is now known to occur along the coast at least from Monterey to Humboldt Bay. How far inland it extends its range and how and where it meets or grades into *G. principis* is as yet undeterminable. One thing is certain, however, and that is, that the range of *G. burnetti* and *G. scincicauda* overlap considerably, and in this fact alone I see sufficient proof of their specific distinctness. The differences between them are certainly due neither to sexual, nor to seasonal, nor to individual variation, great as the latter is in the Gerrhonoti.

List of specimens of *Gerrhonotus burnettii*.

U.S. Nat. Mus. No.	Sex and age.	Locality.	Altitude.	Date.	Collector.	Remarks.
18605	♂ juv.	Monterey, Calif.	Feet.	Sept. 29	Bailey	

Family XANTUSIIDÆ.

Xantusia vigilis Baird. (Pl. III, fig. 1).

The present species was described in 1858 by Prof. Baird from specimens sent home by Xantus from 'Fort Tejon,' Calif. Nothing has been published concerning it since then, and this, perhaps our most interesting lizard, has also been one of the rarest and supposed to possess a very restricted range.

Two additional specimens are now before us, one collected by Dr. Fisher at Hesperia, on the south side of the Mohave Desert, on January 4, 1891, while Mr. Palmer secured the other on February 24, in Pahrump Valley, Nevada, thus extending the range of the species nearly 200 miles eastward. The type locality, Fort Tejon, is in an open cañon—the celebrated Cañada de las Uvas of the early exploring expeditions—connecting the west end of the Mohave Desert with the San Joaquin Valley. The fauna and flora of this cañon present a mixture of Mohave Desert and interior valley forms.

In all probability this species is more or less nocturnal in habits, which may account for the scarcity of specimens collected.

Both specimens are somewhat larger than the largest of the types, and, judging from the condition of the femoral pores, I take them to be adults.

There appears to be some slight variation in the shape of the individual head shields and in the shape of the head, the Death Valley expedition specimens having it somewhat more elongate; but the differences are not greater than between the type specimens themselves.

List of specimens of *Xantusia vigilis*.

U.S. Nat. Mus. No.	Sex and age.	Locality.	Altitude.	Date.	Collector.	Remarks.
18618	....	Pahrump Valley, Nev	Feet.	Feb. 24	Palmer	....
18619	....	Hesperia, Mohave Desert, Calif	3,200	Jan. 4	Fisher	Pl. III, fig. 1.

Family TEJIDÆ.

Cnemidophorus tigris B. & G.

All the *Cnemidophori* brought home by the expedition belong to one species, those from the deserts of the Great Basin in California, Nevada, and Utah being typical of the above name, while those from the great interior valley of California are referable to a subspecies, *C. tigris undulatus*.

Owing to the fact that nearly the entire collection of North American *Cnemidophori* are inaccessible to me at the present writing, I have been unable to settle the question as to the proper name of the present species to my own satisfaction. It may be that *C. tigris* is only a synonym pure and simple of *C. tesselatus* (Say) or they may be trinominally separable. I have therefore retained the name *C. tigris*, as the specimens before me agree perfectly with the type of the latter.

There is a great deal of individual variation in the amount of black markings and in their intensity, the dorsal pattern being quite distinct in some, while in others it looks as if it had faded out. On the other hand, the black suffusion on throat and breast is equally variable, but neither sex, age, season, nor locality seem to account for the variation, except that it is usually absent in the very youngest. In all the specimens the longitudinal striping is very evident, and, in fact, the difference between the general pattern in the only very young specimen collected (No. 18481) and the full-grown ones, apart from individual variation, is but very slight.

[The whip-tail lizard (*Cnemidophorus tigris*) is nearly as common as the gridiron-tail in much of the area traversed, but is not so strictly confined to the Lower Sonoran Zone, ranging up a short distance into the Upper Sonoran and consequently reaching some valleys in which the former species is absent. In this respect it resembles the leopard lizard (*Crotaphytus wislizenii*), with which it is usually found. It lives on the open desert and runs with great rapidity when alarmed.

In California it is abundant in the Mohave Desert, where it ranges westward through Antelope Valley to the Cañada de las Uvas (changing to subspecies *undulatus*), and southward in the wash leading from near Gorman station toward Peru Creek in the Sierra Liebré. In the open cañon leading up to Tehachapi Valley from the Mohave Desert it ranges all the way to the summit of the pass (at Cameron) and probably throughout Tehachapi Valley also, but was not seen there because of a severe cold wind, which lasted all day at the time we passed through. It ranges up from the Mohave Desert over Walker Pass and down on the west slope to the valley of Kern River, where it changes to subspecies *undulatus*. It is common in Owens Valley, and ranges thence up on the warm, west slope of the Inyo and White Mountains to 2,130 meters (7,000 feet) or higher, opposite Big Pine; and is tolerably common also in Deep Spring Valley. It is common in Panamint, Death, and Mesquite Valleys, ranging from the latter through Grapevine Cañon to Sarcobatus Flat. In Nevada it is common in the Amargosa, Pahrump, and Vegas Valleys, at the Bend of the Colorado, in the valleys of the Virgin and Muddy, and reaches Oasis, Pahranagat, Desert, and Meadow Creek Valleys, and from the latter ranges up among the junipers on the west slope of the Juniper Mountains, to an altitude of 1,980 meters (6,500 feet). In Utah it is common in the Lower Santa Clara Valley, and thence ranges northward to the Upper Santa Clara Crossing, but disappears before reaching Mountain Meadows.

The food of *Cnemidophorus tigris* consists of grasshoppers and other insects—no leaves or flowers were found in the numerous stomachs examined.—C. H. M.]

List of specimens of Cnemidophorus tigris.

U.S. Nat. Mus. No.	Sex and age.	Locality.	Altitude.	Date.	Collector.	Remarks.
			Feet.			
18462	ad.	Santa Clara Valley, Utah		May 11	Merriam	
18463	♂	Pahrump Valley, Nev		Apr. 28	...do	
18464	♂	......do		Apr. 29	Bailey	
18465	ad.	Pahranagat Valley, Nev		May 25	Merriam	
18466	ad.	......do		May 25	Bailey	
18467	ad.	Oasis Valley, Nev	4,600	June 2	...do	
18468	adol.	Callville, Nev		May 4	...do	
18469	♂	Coso Mountains, Coso, Calif		May 18	Fisher	
18470	♀	......do		May 20	...do	
18471	♂	Argus Range, Shepherd Cañon, Calif.		Apr. 27	...do	
18472	♂	......do		Apr. 28	...do	
18473	♀	......do		Apr. 28	...do	
18474	♂ juv.	......do		Apr. 28	...do	
18475	♂	Argus Range, Coso Valley, Calif.		May 11	...do	
18476	♂	Argus Range, Searl's Garden, Calif.		Apr. 24	Stephens	
18477	ad.	Panamint Mountains, Willow Creek, Calif.	4,600	May 18	Nelson	
18478	♂	Panamint Valley, Hot Springs, Calif.		Apr. 22	Merriam	
18479	ad.	Lone Pine, Calif		June 11	Fisher	
18480	ad.	......do		June 6	Palmer	
18481	juv.	Death Valley, Calif.		Mch. 22	Nelson	
18482	ad.	Death Valley, Furnace Creek, Calif.		June 20	Fisher	
18483	jun.	......do		Jan. 29	...do	
18484	ad.	......do		Apr. 10	Merriam	
18485	ad.	Death Valley Bennett Wells, Calif.		Apr. 1	Bailey	
18486	ad.	......do		...do	...do	
18487	ad.	......do		Apr. 4	...do	
18488	ad.	......do		...do	...do	
18489	jun.	......do		Jan. 22	...do	
18490	♂	Mohave Desert, Leach Pt. Valley, Calif.		Apr. 25	Merriam	
18491	♀	......do		...do	...do	
18492	♀	Owens Lake, mouth of cañon 5 miles southwest of Olancha, Calif.	4,000	June 8	Stephens	
18493	♀	Owens Lake, Olancha, Calif.	3,700	May 19	...do	
18494	ad.	Deep Spring Valley, Calif	5,300	June 9	Merriam	

Cnemidophorus tigris undulatus (Hallow).

Ten specimens from the west slope of the Sierra Nevada differ so much from the desert specimens that I must regard them as entitled to a separate trinominal appellation. So far as I can see there is no structural difference, nor is there a very radical difference in the color or the pattern. The latter is considerably coarser, better defined, and deeper in color. The difference between the two forms in this respect is particularly well marked on the sides of the head, the dark marks being nearly obsolete in the desert form, while in the latter the slate-colored suffusion on the under side seems to be the rule. I have yet to see a specimen from the great interior valley of California in which it is present.

As to the name of this form, I have to remark that the specimens have been carefully compared and found identical with Hallowell's type specimen. It will be observed that in the original description (Pr. Phil. Ac., 1854, p. 94) the locality of the type is stated to be "near Fort Yuma, in San Joaquin Valley," but the self-contradiction of this statement is explained by the fact that Fort Miller, Fresno County, is meant, and not Fort Yuma, on the Colorado River (cf. Heermann's list in Pac. R. R. Rep., X, Williamson's Route, Zoöl., Rept., p. 24).

Two very young specimens of this form (No. 18503 and 18504), which are quite alike, differ considerably from the typical Death Valley specimen (No. 18481) of precisely the same size. In the latter the three median dark dorsal bands are more or less broken up by light spots adjacent to the light stripes, while in the young *C. undulatus* these bands are well defined and uniform blackish. It would therefore seem that, while there is but little difference between adult and young in the former, the young of the latter are considerably different from the adults.

[This subspecies replaces the typical *C. tigris* on the west or coast slope of the Sierra Nevada in California, where it was found from Kernville south to Havilah and Walker Basin, and north to Three Rivers and the East Fork of Kaweah River. It was collected also in the Cañada de las Uvas, near Old Fort Tejon. The range of *C. tigris* seems to be continuous with that of *C. tigris undulatus* through the three low passes by which communication is established between the Mohave Desert and the upper San Joaquin Valley—namely Walker and Tehachapi Passes and the Cañada de las Uvas.—C. H. M.]

List of specimens of Cnemidophorus tigris undulatus.

U. S. Nat Mus. No.	Sex and age.	Locality.	Altitude.	Date.	Collector.	Remarks.
			Feet.			
18495	ad.	East Fork, Kaweah River, Calif	5,600	July 29	Bailey	
18496	ad.	Walker Basin, Calif		July 14	Fisher	
18497	ad.	......do		....do	...do	
18498	ad.	Old Fort Tejon, Calif		July 7	Palmer	
18499	ad.	Kernville, Calif		June 23	...do	
18500	ad.	......do		...do	...do	
18501	adol.	South Fork, Kern River, Calif	2,750	July 7	Bailey	
18502	ad.	Three Rivers, Calif		July 28	Palmer	
18503	juv.	......do		Sep. 10	Bailey	
18504	juv.	......do		Sep. 14	...do	

Family SCINCIDÆ.

Eumeces skiltonianus (B. & G.).

The extent of variation in color, scale formula, and proportions is well illustrated by the material brought home by the expedition. Thus in the two examples from Maturango Spring in the Argus Range, both quite adult and nearly of the same size, one (No. 18598) is nearly uniformly brownish-gray above, with hardly a trace of dark stripes, while in the other (No. 18599) the longitudinal stripes are quite visible, though the ground color is nearly the same; the former has the head greatly swollen at the temples and has 24 rows of scales round the middle of the body, while the latter has the head narrow and 26 scale rows; moreover, in the former the limbs are overlapping when pressed against the body, a character relied upon by Boulenger for separating *E. skiltonianus*, etc., from *E. leptogrammus*, while in the last mentioned specimen the limbs do not meet by the length of several scales, in the latter character agreeing with No. 18600 from the Panamint Mountains. Both specimens from Old Fort Tejon are uniformly brownish-gray, one (No. 18603) considerably paler than the other, both with swollen temples. No. 18601 is colored like the latter, but has a very long tail, and has, moreover, the frontal in contact with the azygos prefrontal.

All the specimens have two azygos postmentals, but in the collection of the National Museum there is plenty of material to show that Bocourt's *Eumeces hallowelli*, the distinguishing character of which is the single postmental, is nothing but an individual variation of *E. skiltonianus*.

It is interesting to note that *E. skiltonianus*, as it grows old, is subject to the same swelling of the head at the temples and the concomitant disappearance of the striped pattern as well as the loss of the blue color of the tail, as *Eumeces fasciatus*.

A glance at the subjoined list of specimens shows that the expedition has materially extended our knowledge of the geographical distribution of this species, all the specimens previously recorded having been obtained within the Pacific slope, while now we have specimens both from the Argus Range and the Panamint Mountains. It is evident, however, that it is not a species of the desert plains or valleys.

[Specimens of this small lizard were obtained in the Panamint and Argus ranges in the Great Basin, and in Kern River Valley and the Cañada de las Uvas (near Old Fort Tejon) on the coastal slope of the Great Divide in California.—C. H. M.]

List of specimens of Eumeces skiltonianus.

U.S. Nat. Mus. No.	Sex and age.	Locality.	Altitude.	Date.	Collector.	Remarks.
			Feet.			
18598	ad.	Argus Range, Maturango Spring, Calif.		May 8	Fisher	
18599	ad.	......do......		May 3	...do...	
18600	adol.	Panamint Mountains, head of Willow Creek, Calif.	*7,000	May 10	Nelson	
18601	ad.	Kern River, 25 miles above Kernville, Calif.		July 4	Fisher	
18602	juv.	Soda Springs, North Fork Kern River, Calif.		Aug. 15	Bailey	
18603	ad.	Old Fort Tejon, Calif		July 5	Palmer	
18604	ad.	......do......		July 8	...do...	

*About.

Suborder II. OPHIDIA.

Family LEPTOTYPHLOPIDÆ.

Rena humilis B. & G.

A single specimen (No. 18686) was collected in Death Valley, 6 miles from Bennett Wells, by Mr. Palmer, March 25. This is the most northern record of the species as well as of the family *Leptotyphlopidæ* in North America. The type of this species came from the Colorado Desert.

Family BOIDÆ.

Charina plumbea (B. & G.).

The specimen (No. 18685) which Dr. Fisher collected in Redwood Cañon, on the East Fork of the Kaweah River, September 12, 1891, is entirely within the limits of the extraordinary variation of this species demonstrated by me some time ago (Proc. U. S. Nat. Mus., XIII, 1890, p. 177 seqv.), and does not in any way approach either *Ch. bottæ* or *Ch. brachyops*. It has forty-five scale rows, posterior nasal not in contact with anteorbital; prefrontals not entering orbits; one loreal, four prefrontals, no internasals, one anteorbital, one supraorbital, three to four postorbitals, no suborbitals, two to three labials in contact with eye.

Prof. Cope has recently (Proc. U. S. Nat. Mus., XIV, 1891, p. 593) discussed the status of *Ch. plumbea* and *bottæ*, without the slightest reference however to my paper quoted above, and comes to the conclusion that both are identical, chiefly, it seems, on the ground that when he, himself, in 1864, examined the alleged type of de Blainville's *Ch. bottæ* he counted forty-three scale rows. It will be remembered that I retained the two species for the reason that both Jan and Bocourt count thirty-nine scale rows as against a minimum of forty-three in twenty specimens of *Ch. plumbea*.* There seems to be good ground for doubting that the specimen which Cope examined really was the type and the same specimen which Jan and Bocourt have described and figured in detail. Moreover, some of Prof. Cope's notes concerning this matter (*l. c.*) are not calculated to inspire confidence in the exactness of all the statements.

Consequently I can see no reason for changing my views of three years ago, viz, that there is as yet no good reason for uniting the two species.

Family NATRICIDÆ.

Diadophis pulchellus B. & G.

I have seen no intergradation between this form and *D. amabilis* which would justify a trinominal appellation for the present.

---

*Cope (*l. c.*) calls attention to Bocourt's lapsus of giving twenty-nine scale rows. That it is a lapsus is evident from Bocourt's comparison of the two species, in which he distinctly credits *Ch. bottæ* with thirty-nine.

The only specimen (No. 18684) collected is typical in coloration and within the known range of this form. It was obtained by Mr. E. W. Nelson in Yosemite Valley, California, August 7, 1891.

Lampropeltis boylii (B. & G.)

The six specimens brought home by the expedition give no occasion for any extended remarks, as they are quite typical in every respect, with no leaning toward var. *conjuncta* Cope, from Cape St. Lucas and Yuma; *californæ* Blainville, from San Diego, or *eisenii* Yarrow, from Fresno.

The two Nevada specimens differ from those from California in having the frontal longer than the interparietal suture, but in a lot of true *L. boylii* from Fresno (U. S. Nat. Mus. No. 11787) I find a specimen exactly like the above from Nevada.

[This large and conspicuous snake, whose cream colored body is sharply marked by rings of black, was first found in the Valley of the Lower Muddy near an abandoned mill at Overton, Nevada, where several were secured in dense thickets of *Atriplex torreyi*. About dark they began to emerge from these retreats, making a great noise in crawling over the dry leaves, and were soon found in the open. The species was obtained also in Pahranagat Valley, Nevada, a little north of the middle of the valley. On the west slope of the Sierra Nevada, in California, specimens were collected in Kern Valley, at Three Rivers, and on the east fork of Kaweah River.—C. H. M.]

List of specimens of Lampropeltis boylii.

U. S. Nat. Mus. No.	Sex and age.	Locality.	Altitude.	Date.	Collector.	Remarks.
			Feet.			
18090	....	Three Rivers, Calif........	....	July 27	Palmer......	
18091	....	......do......	....	...do...	Fisher......	
18092	....	South fork, Kern River, 25 miles above Kernville, Calif.	....	July 9	...do......	
18093	juv.	East fork, Kaweah River, Calif....	1,700	July 27	Bailey......	•
18094	....	Overton, Muddy Valley, Nevada..	....	May 6	Merriam....	
18095	....	......do......	....	...do...	Bailey......	

Hypsiglena ochrorhynchus Cope.

The only specimen obtained by the expedition was collected by Dr. A. K. Fisher in Shepherd Cañon, in the Argus Range, California, April 24, 1891. It (No. 18071) is somewhat peculiar on account of the small size of the dorsal spots, though otherwise it agrees well with the types from Cape St. Lucas, Lower California, as well as with a number of specimens from Arizona. The characters pointed out by Cope as distinguishing *H. chlorophæa*, types from Fort Buchanan, southern Arizona, are so variable in the specimens before me that they will not serve the purpose. I am not quite prepared to give up the latter species as yet, inasmuch as the type specimen (U. S. Nat. Mus., No.

4676; only one specimen is now in the collection) has no pseudopreocular, a character only shared by a specimen from the city of Chihuahua, Mexico (U. S. Nat. Mus. No., 14287), while it is present in all the other specimens. These two specimens, therefore, I shall continue to call *H. chlorophæa* until it be shown that the absence of the pseudopreocular is only an individual variation.

The specimen collected by the expedition adds a new species to the fauna of the State of California, if I am not mistaken.

Assuming, for the present at least, the distinctness of *H. chlorophæa*, we would have three species or forms within the United States, including an undescribed species from southwestern Texas,* which may be distinguished as follows:

a^1. Upper surface of head flat.
   b^1. No pseudopreocular .... *H. chlorophæa*.
   b^2. Pseudopreocular present .... *H. ochrorhynchus*.
a^2. Upper surface of head convex .... *H. texana*.

Salvadora grahamiæ hexalepis Cope. (Pl. III, fig. 2).

The four specimens collected by the expedition belong to this form, as I now understand it, that is to say, to the form which possesses at least one true subocular (by this term excluding the subpreocular, or pseudopreocular). One of the specimens (No. 18062 Virgin River, Nevada) possesses only one subocular (anterior), and agrees in this respect perfectly with specimens from Fort Whipple, Arizona (type locality); Mohave Villages, Arizona; Cottonwood Cañon, Utah, and Valle de la Viejas, San Diego County, California. The three other specimens, however, differ from all the other specimens I have seen in also having a posterior subocular, thus isolating the eye entirely from the labials.

The individual variation in this species is too great, however, to allow a subdivision on these lines without a much greater material to support it. There is evidently a tendency towards dividing up the labials transversely in the region indicated by the localities mentioned above, and as this subdivision seems to be proportionate to the greater width of the rostral, it would be natural to conclude that the two characters may have a common origin. The fact that these localities are the most arid of all those from which I have specimens of *Salvadora* is very suggestive, since these snakes to a great extent live in holes in the ground.

---

* **Hypsiglena texana**, sp. n.
Diagnosis.—Similar to *H. ochrorhynchus*, but with the upper surface of the head convex, the lateral outline of the frontal curved outward, and the dark eye stripe covering more than upper half of the sixth supralabial.

Scale rows, 21; gastrosteges, 175; urosteges, 43; supralabials, 8; preoculars, 1; pseudopreoculars, 1; postoculars, 2; temporals, 1.

Type.—U. S. Nat. Mus., No. 1782; between Laredo and Camargo, Tex.; U. S. Mex. Bound. Surv., Arthur Schott, coll.

Habitat.—Southwestern Texas

In addition to the type specimen the museum possesses two other specimens, one collected by Mr. W. Taylor at San Diego, Texas (U. S. Nat. Mus., No. 15672), and one by Mr. Butcher at Laredo (No. 7124). Both agree in every respect with the type.

The gradation of this form into *S. grahamiæ*, without suboculars, is shown by a specimen collected by Dr. Edward Palmer at St. Thomas, Nev. (U. S. Nat. Mus. No. 15616), which has one on one side but none on the other.

[St. Thomas is less than 30 miles from the point where my specimen (No. 18062) was collected, and is in the same valley.—C. H. M.]

List of specimens of Salvadora grahamiæ hexalepis.

U.S. Nat. Mus. No.	Sex and age.	Locality.	Altitude.	Date.	Collector.	Remarks.
18059	....	Argus Range, Shepherd Cañon, Calif.	*Feet.*	Apr. 26	Fisher	....
18060	....	Argus Range, Maturango Spring, Calif.	....	May 2	....do	Pl. III, fig. 2.
18061	....	Amargosa Borax Works, Calif.	....	Mar. 16	Palmer	1,000 feet above the Amargosa river.
18062	....	Virgin River, near Bunkerville, Nev.	....	May 8	Merriam ...	....

Pituophis catenifer (Blainv.).

The only two specimens which I can refer to the typical form of this species are from the coastal or west slope of the Sierra Nevada, and from Old Fort Tejon, in the Cañada de las Uvas, California, and are better recognized as such by their coloration and general aspect than by any exclusive structural character. True, the carination of the scales is weak and the eight outer scales are smooth in both, but the character derived from the carination is a very elusive one, as will be demonstrated under the heading of the next form, and can not alone be relied upon to define these very difficult and variable snakes.

List of specimens of Pituophis catenifer.

U.S. Nat. Mus. No.	Sex and age.	Locality.	Altitude.	Date.	Collector.	Remarks.
18063	....	South Fork Kings River, Calif	*Feet.* 8,000	Aug. 17	Palmer	Bubb's Creek.
18064	....	Old Fort Tejon, Calif	....	July 8	....do	

Pituophis catenifer deserticola, subsp. nov.

By this name I propose to designate the form usually called *P. bellona*, or *P. sayi bellona*, as there can be no doubt that Baird's and Girard's, original *Churchillia bellona*, which came from Presidio del Norte, Chihuahua, Mexico, was a typical *P. sayi*. The type appears now to be lost, but I have before me a specimen from the identical locality (U. S. Nat. Mus. No. 1542) with a most pronouncedly narrow rostral and agreeing with *P. sayi* in all other respects also. Of all the later names applied to various forms or individuals of the present species none seem to have been based upon the richly-colored form from the Great Basin and the southwestern deserts, which agrees with true *P. catenifer* in having a broad and low rostral. That Baird and Girard later referred specimens of this form to *P. bellona* can not, of course, justify the shifting of this name to another type.

As a general rule this form has a more pronounced carination of the scales and a less number of smooth scales on the sides, but this character can not be relied upon at all, and whether a specimen shall be referred to either typical *P. catenifer* or to this desert form must be decided upon the totality of the characters, as a reliance upon the carination leads to very erroneous results. This will be plain at once to any one who will take the trouble to examine and compare the descriptions of the various species described by Baird and Girard in their Catalogue of North American Serpents, and as I have examined a number of their specimens I am able to state that the descriptions are generally correct. It will then be found that these Pacific coast specimens have only three to five outer rows perfectly smooth, while as synonyms of *P. catenifer*, the types of *P. wilkesii*, etc., 'ought' to have nine rows of smooth lateral scales. Again, both types of *P. mcclellanii* which 'ought' to have only five smooth rows, because being true *P. sayi*, have at least seven smooth rows. Furthermore, it has been asserted that the typical *P. catenifer* occurs as far east as Pyrmont,* Nev., upon the strength of U. S. National Museum No. 8139. This number contains two specimens so alike otherwise as to preclude the possibility of their belonging to two different species. Why they should be referred to *P. catenifer* I can not discover, for one has only three perfectly smooth scale rows, while in the other the number is four or five. On the other hand, of two specimens in the present collection, both from the Panamint Mountains, Calif. (Nos. 18065 and 18066), one has only four rows of smooth scales on each side, while the other has ten. In every other respect the two are practically alike and no one could reasonably refer them to two different species. Yet that would have to be done were we to use the number of smooth scale rows as a character.

[This subspecies, according to Mr. Stejneger, is the form inhabiting the Great Basin, while, as pointed out above, typical *P. catenifer* is restricted to the coastal slope of California.

On the east side of Pahrump Valley, Nevada, one of these snakes measuring 5 feet in length was killed April 29, among the tree yuccas along the upper edge of the *Larrea* belt, at an altitude of 1,340 meters

---

*The name 'Pyrmont' appears in the Rept. Wheeler Survey, v, 1875, Zoölogy, p. 541. the specimens referred to having been taken there by the Wheeler Expedition of 1872. This is probably the same place as *Piermont*, which is given on map sheet No. 49 of the Wheeler Survey, and on the 'Map of California and Nevada with Parts of Utah and Arizona,' published by the Chief of Engineers, U. S. Army, 1879. Piermont is on the west side of Spring Valley and on the east slope of the Shell Creek Range. It is in White Pine County, Nev., about 75 miles due east of the town of Eureka.

(4,400 feet). Another was obtained on the east slope of the Beaverdam mountains, in southwestern Utah, May 11.

In California, specimens were obtained at Lone Pine and Haway Meadows in Owens Valley, and in the Panamint and Argus mountains.—C. H. M.]

List of specimens of *Pituophis catenifer deserticola*.

U.S. Nat. Mus. No.	Sex and age.	Locality.	Altitude.	Date.	Collector.	Remarks.
			Feet.			
18065	....	Panamint Mountains, Jackass Spring, Calif.	....	May 7	Nelson....	
18066	....	Surprise Cañon, Calif.	....	April 23	Fisher....	
18067	....	Argus Range, Shepherd Cañon, Calif	....	April 26	...do.....	
18068	....	Ten miles south of Owens Lake, Calif	3,750	May 12	Stephens.	Haway Meadows.
18069	....	Owens Valley (Lone Pine), Calif....	....	June 4	Fisher....	
18070	....	Beaverdam Mountain, Utah...........	....	May 11	Merriam..	

Bascanion flagellum frenatum, subsp. nov.

Diagnosis.—Adults with permanent brownish or blackish bars across the nape; young with a distinct whitish line from nostrils through eye and across temporals, this stripe often persistent in adults; chin and throat speckled with blackish.

Habitat.—Southern Arizona, Utah, Nevada, California, and Lower California.

Type.—U. S. National Museum, No. 16340. Mountain Spring, Colorado Desert, San Diego County, Calif.; C. R. Orcutt coll.

There is no good reason why the various geographical forms of *Bascanion flagellum* should not be recognized by name, inasmuch as they are well marked, fairly constant, and characteristic of circumscribed geographical areas.

It is somewhat doubtful whether the form from the Cape St. Lucas region should not be recognized by a separate name also, but the material at hand is too scant to warrant any separation for the present.

Say's *Coluber testaceus*, the adults of which are uniform above, is apparently confined to the country east of the Rocky Mountains, and the name inapplicable to the form so strongly marked, as indicated in the diagnosis above. In the search for a possible name among the various synonyms I was led to examine the type of Baird and Girard's *Masticophis mormon* (U. S. Nat. Mus., No. 2012), from the Great Salt Lake, in the hope that it might be available for the present form, since it is sometimes found quoted in the synonymies of '*Bascanium testaceum*,' but it proved to be a young *B. flaviventre*, and a new name had consequently to be adopted.

This species was not collected by the expedition in the interior valley of California, but specimens in the U. S. National Museum from various localities show that it occurs there.

The present form has undoubtedly as much right to a separate name as *Bascanion piceum* Cope, the chief character of which, in addition to the uniform dusky coloration above, seems to be the nineteen scale-rows of the type and only specimen hitherto recorded, against the normal seventeen rows in *B. flagellum* and its allies. I have, however, before me a specimen (U. S. Nat. Mus., No. 17950) collected by Mr. P. L. Jouy, near Tucson, Ariz., which, though evidently by color a *B. piceum*, has only seventeen scale rows.

Of the specimens collected, No. 18088 is particularly interesting, as having an undivided anal. The fact that an undivided anal has been observed several times in *B. flagellum* and allies is quite an argument in their favor who would not attribute 'generic value' *per se* to the division or nondivision of the anal plate.

List of specimens of Bascanion flagellum frenatum.

U. S. Nat. Mus. No.	Sex and age.	Locality.	Altitude.	Date.	Collector.	Remarks.
			Feet.			
18081	....	Overton (Muddy Valley), Nev	....	May 6	Merriam	
18082	....	Vegas Valley, Nev	....	May 1	....do	
18083	jun.	Death Valley, Bennett Wells, Calif. ...	....	Jan. 21	Nelson	
18084	....	Death Valley, Furnace Creek, Calif. ..	....	June 20	Fisher	
18085	jun.	Panamint Valley, Calif	4,100	May 15	Nelson	
18086	....	Panamint Valley, Hot Springs, Calif.	....	Apr. 22	Merriam	*Sitomys* in stomach.
18087	....	Colorado Desert, Palm Springs, Calif.	....	Sept. 27	Stephens ...	
18088	....	Keeler, Owens Lake, Calif	....	June 12	Palmer	Killed in a cellar.
18089	....	Deep Spring Valley, Calif	....	June 9	Merriam	Head only.

Bascanion laterale (Hallow.).

Three typical specimens were collected on the west or coastal slope of the Sierra Nevada and Tejon Range, California, and one from the western slope of the Coast Range, in San Diego County, Calif.

This species seems to be comparatively rare, and considerable additional material is necessary to enable us to satisfactorily map out its geographical distribution.

List of specimens of Bascanion laterale.

U. S. Nat. Mus. No.	Sex and age.	Locality.	Altitude.	Date.	Collector.	Remarks.
			Feet.			
18077	....	Old Fort Tejon, Calif	....	July 2	Palmer	
18078	....	Three Rivers, Calif	850	Sept. 14	Bailey	
18079	....	Walker Pass, west slope, Calif	....	July 3	Fisher	
18080	....	Santa Ysabel, Calif	....	Oct. 6	Stephens ...	

Bascanion tæniatum (Hallow.).

The range of the present species is somewhat better understood than that of *B. laterale*. It is much more widely distributed, as specimens have been taken in Idaho, Utah, Nevada, California, Arizona, New Mexico, and Mexico, but it does not seem to reach the coast, nor does it appear to occur in the Valley of California, except at two points. These are Walker Basin (U. S. Nat. Mus., No. 9498) and Shasta County, northern California, where it probably enters by way of the Pit River Valley, as one specimen is from Baird, on the McCloud River (U. S. Nat. Mus., No. 13618), the other from Canoe Creek (No. 1983), both tributaries of Pit River.

List of specimens of Bascanion tæniatum.

U. S. Nat. Mus. No.	Sex and age.	Locality.	Altitude.	Date.	Collector.	Remarks.
			Feet.			
18072	....	Argus Range, Maturango Spring, Calif.		May 4	Fisher	
18073	....	Coso Valley, Calif.		May 5	Do.	
18074	....	Coso Valley, near Maturango Spring, Calif.		May 11	Palmer	
18075	....	Coso Mountains, Coso, Calif.		May 18	Fisher	
18076	....	Panamint Mountains, Willow Creek, Calif.	5,400	May 19	Nelson	

Thamnophis* infernalis (Blainv.).

The status of the various forms of garter snakes in North America is one of the most difficult problems, and as yet an unsolved one. Much more material than is at present available will be necessary in order to establish the limits of the species and subspecies, to define their characters, to ascertain the range of individual variation within each form, and to settle the many knotty points of nomenclature. For the present, the reference of many specimens must necessarily be a provisional one, and individuals which one herpetologist might identify as belonging to one form are very likely to be named quite differently by another, and our knowledge of the geographical distribution of a number of these forms must consequently also be defective. It would therefore hardly be wise to make any generalizations in this direction. Under such circumstances, when the limits and true characters of the various forms are yet unsettled, it seems unnecessary to make an attempt at recognizing a distinction between specific and subspecific terms. With

---

* According to the A. O. U. Code of Zoölogical Nomenclature (canon XLII), *Thamnophis* Fitzinger, 1843 (type *Th. saurita*), takes the precedence over *Eutainia* Baird & Girard. Apropos of my introduction of *Leptotyphlops* of Fitzinger for *Stenostoma*, preoccupied, it has been asserted that Fitzinger's names are *nomina nuda*. The simple fact that Fitzinger expressly indicated the type of the genus at once removes them from that category, and moreover, the code referred to states in so many words that the indication of the type species is sufficient for the establishment of the generic term.

this proviso I shall designate the forms which I have recognized among the material of the Death Valley Expedition by binominals.

Whether the form called *Eutainia infernalis* by Baird and Girard, and later by Prof. Cope, really is the same as Blainville's *Coluber infernalis* is to me a question which even Bocourt's recent paper (Bull. Soc. Zool. France, XVII, Jan. 26, 1892, p. 40) fails to settle, because he evidently includes several forms which we on this side of the Atlantic would not think of uniting. As the four specimens before me (Nos. 18711-18714) agree with the specimens which are usually called *E. infernalis*, I have adopted this term for the present.

Two of these specimens have nineteen scale-rows and eight supralabials (Nos. 18711, 18712), and all are uniform dark above with three well-defined buff-colored bands. No. 18711, the larger specimen, has the supralabials well bordered with blackish, while in No. 18712 these marks are obsolete. The latter is somewhat abnormal in having the second row of temporals fused together. The two specimens from Morro (Nos. 18713-18714), on the other hand, have twenty-one scale-rows and the labials (eight) well bordered with black.

List of specimens of *Thamnophis infernalis*.

U.S. Nat. Mus. No.	Sex and age.	Locality.	Altitude.	Date.	Collector.	Remarks.
18711	ad.	San Joaquin River, High Sierra, Calif.	Feet. 8,100	July 29	Nelson	Near Mammoth Pass.
18712	......	Monterey, Calif	......	Oct. 5	Bailey	
18713	......	Morro, San Luis Obispo County, Calif	......	Nov. 10	Nelson	
18714	......	...do	......	...do	...do	

Thamnophis elegans (B. & G.).

Of the three specimens which I refer to this species, the large one (No. 18708) is strikingly like the type of Baird and Girard. The number of scale-rows, however, is only nineteen, as in Baird and Girard's second specimen. The eye is somewhat larger, and the posterior supralabials lower, but in both respects it agrees closely with No. 878, from Fort Reading, Calif., which has always been referred to *T. elegans* without hesitation. In the two younger specimens, from Mount Whitney (Nos. 18709 and 18710), the general color is slightly more olive, not quite so bluish, and the labials are margined with blackish, in this respect resembling No. 878, referred to above. I do not believe that too much stress should be laid upon the absence or presence of these marks in this and allied forms. But instead of having the space between the dorsal and lateral stripes uniform dark, as in the larger specimen, these younger ones are distinctly spotted on a rather dark ground, quite resembling the subspecies recently described by Cope as *T. elegans lineolata*. An examination of No. 878, however, establishes the fact that the dorsal spots are present and that consequently the absence or presence of spots is only due to the darker or lighter shade of the ground color.

A great amount of collecting and observing will have to be done before we can know anything definite about the individual variation of these snakes. Each species and form will have to be investigated by itself, for it is plain that conclusions based upon analogies from allied forms are not to be relied upon, and it seems as if the only safe way would be to commence an examination on as large a scale as possible of the unborn young, cut out of the mother snake. A careful and detailed record of such examinations would settle many a mooted point, and is recommended to the attention of California naturalists.

List of specimens of Thamnophis elegans.

U. S. Nat. Mus. No.	Sex and age.	Locality.	Altitude.	Date.	Collector.	Remarks.
			Feet.			
18708	ad.	Yosemite Valley, Calif.	4,000	Aug. 6	Nelson	
18709		10 miles south of Mount Whitney, Calif.		Aug. 31	Dutcher	
18710		...do		...do	...do	

Thamnophis hammondii (Kenn.).

Fortunately there attaches no doubt to specimens belonging to this well-defined species, and all here referred to it are typical in every way, scutellation as well as coloration. Its range overlaps to a great extent that of *Th. vagrans* without affecting the purity of the type, and as both are found in the identical localities, as well proved by the present collection, there seems no valid reason for regarding them as subspecies of the same species. The distinctive characters of this form are well pointed out and emphasized by Kennicott in the original description.

Neither does there seem to be any good reason for substituting the name *Th. couchii* for that of *Th. hammondii*. The two forms have been considered distinct up to the present time, and there has been collected no additional material of recent years which could tend to show that they are identical.

The twelve specimens of *Th. hammondii* contained in the present collection show a great constancy of some of the structural characters. All have twenty-one scale rows, eight supralabials, and one preocular.

In nearly all of them there are distinct indications of a dorsal band which in No. 18691, a young specimen, is quite well marked the whole length of the animal, while in most others it is chiefly developed on the portion nearest to the head.

List of specimens of Thamnophis hammondii.

U. S. Nat. Mus. No.	Sex and age.	Locality.	Altitude.	Date.	Collector.	Remarks.
			Feet.			
18687	♀ ad.	Owens Valley, Alvord, Calif.	4,000	June 27	Stephens	
18688	ad.	Owens Valley, Fish Slough, 10 miles north of Bishop, Calif.		July 2	....do	
18689	♀ ad.	Owens Lake, Cartago, Calif.	3,700	June 10	....do	
18690		Old Fort Tejon, Calif.		July 3	Palmer	
18691	juv.	Lone Pine, Calif.		Aug. 21	Fisher	
18692	jun.	Kern River, 25 miles above Kernville, Calif.		July 9	....do	South Fork.
18693	jun.	....do		July 5	....do	
18694	jun.	Kern River, South Fork, Calif.		July 7	....do	
18695	ad.	Kern River, Calif.	7,200	Sept. 8	Nelson	
18696		Kern River, South Fork, Calif.	2,700	June 22	Palmer	
18697	ad.	Soda Springs, Kern River, Calif.		Sept. 4	Fisher	
18698	jun.	....do		Aug. 14	Bailey	

Thamnophis vagrans (B. & G.).

The material brought home by the Death Valley Expedition seems clearly to demonstrate the impracticability of recognizing a subspecies *lineolata*. Among the specimens from southern California there are specimens which are typical and unquestionable *Th. vagrans* (for instance, No. 18706), which combine all the characters of this species, both as to scutellation and coloration. Practically from the same locality we have another specimen (No. 18707), which might properly be referred to *Th. lineolata*. Those from Soda Springs on the North Fork of Kern River, and Whitney Creek are more like the former than the latter, while the light-colored specimen from Ash Meadows, Nevada (No. 18700), is a true *vagrans*, so far as its dorsal spots are concerned, but a *lineolata* if we pay attention to the dorsal stripe only.

The other specimen from this latter locality (No. 18701) is abnormal in several respects, it being quite melanistic in coloration with a well-defined dorsal band. The dorsal scale rows are very irregular, so that it is difficult to make out the exact scale formula, but the prevailing number seems to be nineteen.

The amount of black on the belly is very variable; in fact, not two specimens are alike in this respect. No. 18707, from Lone Pine, has no trace of it, while No. 18706, from practically the same locality, Owens Lake, has the anterior half of each gastrostege black, and No. 18704, from Soda Springs, has the middle of the under side almost solid bluish black.

List of specimens of Thamnophis vagrans.

U.S. Nat. Mus. No.	Sex and age.	Locality.	Altitude.	Date.	Collector.	Remarks.
			Feet.			
18699	......	Silver Creek, Nev	......	Nov. 8, 1890	Bailey	......
18700	......	Ash Meadows, Nev	......	Mar. 3, 1891	Palmer	......
18701	......	......do	......	Mar. 4, 1891	....do	......
18702	......	North Fork, Kern River, Calif	......	Sept. 12, 1891	....do	......
18703	juv.	......do	7,000	Sept. 10, 1891	Nelson	......
18704	juv.	Soda Springs, North Fork, Kern River, Calif.	......	Aug. 15, 1891	Bailey	......
18705	......	Whitney Creek, Calif	8,500	Sept. 5, 1891	....do	......
18706	......	Owens River, Calif	6,000	July 20, 1891	Nelson	......
18707	......	Lone Pine, Calif	......	June 11, 1891	Palmer	......

Thamnophis parietalis (Say).

A single specimen (No. 18715) from Horse Corral Meadows, Fresno County, Calif., collected by Dr. A. K. Fisher, August 10, 1891, having nineteen scale rows, seven supralabials, and one preocular, has been referred to the present form in spite of the fact that the superior spots along the dorsal stripe are not fused into a solid black band. I have, however, before me a specimen from San Francisco (No. 893), referred to *Th. parietalis* by Cope, which in this respect agrees with the present specimen, but the dorsal is broader. On the other hand our specimen presents many points of resemblance to so-called *Th. leptocephala*, but I am unable to distinguish specimens of the latter with the above scale formula from specimens of the *Th. sirtalis* group. I have failed so far to distinguish any specific difference between *Th. sirtalis* and *leptocephala*, and am inclined to think that the latter is made up of similarly degenerate specimens belonging to different species or forms.

Family CROTALIDÆ.

Crotalus tigris Kenn.

The 'tiger-rattler,' of which the expedition has brought home quite a series, is one of the rarest species in collections. Discovered during the survey of the boundary between the United States and Mexico, and described by Kennicott, the habitat of the species was given in general terms as "Deserts of Gila and Colorado," but I can find no evidence of specimens recorded from anywhere except from the Sierra del Pozo Verde,* in Arizona. A specimen was afterwards collected by Dr. Irwin at Fort Buchanan, Ariz., and recorded by Dr. Yarrow in his

---

* The name is written both Sierra del Pozo Verde and Sierra Verde in the Rept. U. S. and Mex. Bound. Surv. (cf. vol. I, pt. I, p. 121 and pt. II, p. 70). This range is situated on the boundary between Arizona and Sonora, nearly due south of Baboquivari Peak, and about 50 miles northwest of Nogales. A spring known as 'Agua del Pozo Verde (Green Well)' is situated at the foot of the western slope near the southern end of the range.

Catalogue of the Reptiles and Batrachians in the U.S. National Museum (No. 5271). Dr. J. G. Cooper has since enumerated *C. tigris* from the California side of the 'Colorado Valley,'* but whether he based his record upon specimens actually collected (in which case, probably near Fort Mohave), or only upon the general statement in the report of the Mexican Boundary Survey, I do not know.

It does not appear to have been collected by any of the many parties of the Pacific Railroad Surveys, nor was it brought home by the herpetologists of the Wheeler Expedition west of the one hundredth meridian.

The extension of its known range by the present expedition is therefore very material, and is the more interesting since it was found almost over the entire desert area visited. So far from being restricted to the Colorado Valley proper, as surmised by Dr. Cooper, it seems to be chiefly confined to the desert mountain ranges, in which it ascends to a considerable altitude, as shown by the table below, while horizontally its range has been extended over quite a considerable area of southern Nevada.

A study of the present series convinces me that the nearest affinity of the 'tiger rattler' is with the true *Crotalus confluentus* of the plains, in spite of the rather striking and in many respects peculiar aspect of the former.

[The known range of this exceedingly rare rattlesnake has been greatly extended by the expedition, specimens having been secured at frequent intervals from Owens Valley in California to the Great Bend of the Colorado on the boundary between Nevada and Arizona. It was usually found in rocky places in the desert ranges—rarely in the intervening valleys.

When passing through Emigrant Cañon in the Panamint Mountains, in California, April 15, two large rattlesnakes of this species were killed at one shot by Mr. Stephens, at an altitude of 1,400 meters (4,600 feet). They were on a ledge of rock, and were standing erect with their heads near together, apparently playing. In Indian Spring Valley, north of the Charleston Mountains, in Nevada, one was found in a wood-rat's nest that was dug open to secure a large scaly lizard (*Sceloporus magister*) which had taken refuge there. Its stomach contained a kangaroo rat (*Dipodomys*) and a pocket mouse (*Perognathus*), indicating nocturnal habits. Others were killed in the upper part of Vegas Valley (near Cottonwood Springs) and Vegas Wash, Nevada, and in Owens Valley (on Independence Creek), Coso Valley, the Argus Range, Slate Range, Panamint Range, and Grapevine Mountains, California. In the Argus Range nineteen were killed in or near Shepherd Cañon, during the latter part of April and first week of May, by Dr. Fisher's party.—C. H. M.]

---

*Proc. Calif. Acad. Nat. Sci., IV, p. 66 (1870).

List of specimens of Crotalus tigris.

U.S. Nat. Mus. No.	Sex and age.	Locality.	Altitude.	Date.	Collector.	Remarks.
			Feet.			
18661	ad.	Vegas Valley, Nev		May 1	Merriam	
18662	ad.	Vegas Wash, Nev		May 2	Bailey	
18663	juv.	Indian Spring Valley, Nev		May 29	Merriam	
18664	juv.	Grapevine Mountains, Nev		June 6	Nelson	3,000 feet above Salt Wells.
18665	ad.	Slate Range, Calif	3,100	Apr. 21	Stephens	
18666	ad.	Panamint Mountains, Willow Creek, Calif.	5,500	May 17	Nelson	
18667	juv.	Panamint Mountains, Johnson Cañon, Calif.	5,000	Mar. 30	Fisher	
18668	ad.	Panamint Mountains, Emigrant Cañon, Calif.	4,600	Apr. 16	Stephens	
18669	ad.	......do	4,600	....do	....do	
18670	ad.	Argus Range, Shepherd Cañon, Calif.		Apr. 29	Fisher	
18671	ad.	......do		Apr. 27	....do	
18672	ad.	Coso Valley, Maturango Springs, Calif.		May 11	Palmer	
18673	ad.	......do		....do	....do	
18674	♀ ad.	Owens Valley, Independence Creek, Calif.	6,500	June 20	Stephens	

Crotalus cerastes Hallow.

The horned rattlesnake has a record somewhat different from that of the foregoing species (*C. tigris*), although inhabiting, in a general way, the same country. It was described much earlier, is less rare in collections, and the geographical range was better known. This difference is probably due to the fact that it is more confined to the desert plains and valleys, while *C. tigris* seems to take its place in the mountains.

The material brought home by the Death Valley Expedition adds considerable detail to our knowledge of the geographical range of the present species, and is, therefore, very valuable and interesting, for the previous material although better than that of *C. tigris*, as intimated above, was scanty and indefinite enough. Thus, if we take the Catalogue of the specimens in the U. S. National Museum (Bull. U. S. Nat. Mus., No. 24, p. 73), we note at once that there is no specimen from the type locality, which is the Mohave Desert and borders of the Mohave River. Dr. Merriam has now supplied this desideratum by the specimen collected April 6, 1891 (No. 18656). We next note that a specimen (No. 8923) was collected by Dr. Yarrow in 'Southern Utah.' The locality is indefinite enough and more than dubious, if for no other reason than the complete absence of any reference to such a specimen in Dr. Yarrow's report upon the reptiles in the fifth volume of Wheeler's Survey West of the One Hundredth Meridian. Another specimen (No. 9116) is said to have been collected by John Kohler in 'Cottonwood Cañon, Nevada.' Turning to the record book we find 'Cottonwood Cañon, Arizona,' and on p. 98 of the catalogue referred to we find that John Kohler collected a *Salvadora grahamiæ* in 'Cottonwood Cañon, Utah.'

The locality is certainly indefinite, to say the least, and a more favorable expression can hardly be used about 'Colorado River, Colorado,' for specimen No. 482, which was probably collected near Fort Yuma, California, and certainly not in the State of Colorado, as the catalogue referred to would seem to indicate.

It is refreshing to turn from these unreliable and confusing statements to the list of exact localities furnished below for each individual specimen taken, and nothing will better illustrate the value of the work done by the Death Valley Expedition than the parallel just drawn.

[The horned rattlesnake or 'sidewinder,' as it is locally known throughout the region it inhabits, is the characteristic snake of the Lower Sonoran deserts of the Great Basin, from southern California easterly across southern Nevada to Arizona and southwestern Utah. It inhabits the open deserts, while its congener of the same region (*C. tigris*) lives in the desert ranges. Its local name is derived from its peculiar mode of progression: when disturbed it moves away sideways, keeping its broadside toward the observer instead of proceeding in the usual serpentine manner. Its bite is said to be fatal, which is probably not the case under ordinary circumstances. A large number were secured by the expedition and many others were killed, but no one was bitten by it. It was found on both sides of Pilot Knob in the Mohave Desert (April 5 and 6) in Pahrump Valley, where four were caught in a space of a mile and half (April 28 and 29); in Vegas Valley (May 1); in Vegas Wash (May 3); in Indian Spring Valley (May 29), where one was shot containing a kangaroo rat (*Dipodomys*) and two pocket mice (*Perognathus*); in the Amargosa Desert (May 31), and in Sarcobatus Flat (June 2). It was common in the valley of the Virgin and Lower Muddy (May 6 and 7), and was said to inhabit Pahranagat Valley, though we did not find it there.

During the latter part of April and the early part of May these rattlesnakes were often found in pairs and were doubtless mating. At such times they remained out in plain sight over night instead of retreating to holes or shelter under desert brush, and on two occasions they were found by us on cold mornings so early that they were too chilled to move until considerably disturbed. I stepped on one of these by accident as it lay in a compact coil with its head in the center, but it was held so firmly by my weight that it was unable to strike. A moment before, I had killed its mate. I killed three on the mesa east of St. Joe, in the valley of the Muddy, in eastern Nevada, May 7.— C. H. M.]

List of specimens of Crotalus cerastes.

U.S. Nat. Mus. No.	Sex and age.	Locality.	Altitude.	Date.	Collector.	Remarks.
			Feet.			
18646	ad.	Pahrump Valley, Nev		Apr. 29	Merriam	
18647	ad.	......do......		...do...	...do...	
18648	ad.	......do......		...do...	...do...	
18649	ad.	......do......		Apr. 28	...do...	
18650	ad.	Indian Spring Valley, Nev		May 29	Bailey	
18651	ad.	......do......		...do...	Merriam	
18652	jun.	Ash Meadows (14 miles north of), Nev		Mar. 11	Stephens	
18653	jun.	Sarcobatus Flat, Nev	4,500	June 2	Bailey	
18654	jun.	Amargosa Desert, Nev		May 31	Merriam	
18655	jun.	Death Valley (Bennett Wells), Calif		Apr. 3	Bailey	
18656	jun.	Mohave Desert, Calif		Apr. 6	Merriam	Type locality.
18657	jun.	Borax Flat (water station), Calif	2,20)	Apr. 22	Stephens	
18658	ad.	Panamint Valley, Calif		Apr. 24	Nelson	
18659	ad.	......do......		Apr. 23	Bailey	
18660	ad.	Lone Pine, Calif		June 7	Palmer	

Crotalus lucifer B. & G.

The questions whether there is more than one separable form of this species within the Pacific region and, in case of an affirmative answer, what names are to be employed for the various forms, are yet open, awaiting the accumulation of much additional material. It may even be found that the name adopted above for the species is not the oldest tenable; but, not being able to settle that point at present, I retain *C. lucifer* as undoubted in its application. On the other hand, that it is a good and distinct species, well separated from *C. confluentus*, and not a subspecies of the latter, I feel perfectly confident.

The present species is characteristic of the interior valley and slopes of California as contrasted with the Great Basin, and the boundary between the two forms seems to be quite sharply drawn, at least in the regions visited by the expedition. There is probably no stronger contrast among the reptiles of the same genus met with by the Death Valley explorers than that between the pale and clay colored rattlesnakes in the desert plains and mountains and the dark colored *C. lucifer* which they obtained only in the San Joaquin Valley and in the mountain slopes encircling it.

[This species does not inhabit the Great Basin, but was found in a number of localities on the west or coastal slope of the Sierra, and in the San Joaquin Valley. Specimens were obtained at Old Fort Tejon, in the Cañada de las Uvas, and thence northward on the west slope of the mountains to Tehachapi Pass, Kern Valley, Kaweah River, Kings River Cañon, the San Joaquin River, and the Merced River (on the latter as high as 2,620 meters or 8,600 feet).—C. H. M.]

List of specimens of Crotalus lucifer.

U.S. Nat. Mus. No.	Sex and age.	Locality.	Altitude.	Date.	Collector.	Remarks.
			Feet.			
18675	ad.	Old Fort Tejon, Calif.		July 7	Palmer	
18676	adol.	Bakersfield, Calif.		July 17	Bailey	
18677	ad.	Kernville, Calif.	2,400	July 10	....do	
18678	jun.	Soda Springs, North Fork Kern River, Calif.		Aug. 12	....do	
18679	♂	East Fork Kaweah River, Calif.	4,500	July 28	....do	Skin.
18680	ad.	Klug's River Cañon, Calif.		Aug. 14	Palmer	
18681	ad.	North Fork San Joaquin River, Calif.	6,600	July 29	Nelson	
18682	ad.	Merced River, Calif.	8,000	Aug. 4	....do	
18683	ad.	....do	8,600	...do	....do	

B.—BATRACHIA.

Order ANURA.

Family BUFONIDÆ.

Bufo punctatus B. & G.

This species of rather wide distribution belongs to the Lower Sonoran fauna, and is not known from the interior valley of California. It probably finds its northern limit not far from where the numerous specimens of the expedition were collected.

List of specimens of Bufo punctatus.

U.S. Nat. Mus. No.	Sex and age.	Locality.	Altitude.	Date.	Collector.	Remarks.
			Feet.			
18748	ad.	Death Valley, Calif.		Mar. 22	Nelson	
18749	ad.	....do		...do	....do	
18750	ad.	....do		...do	....do	
18751	ad.	....do		...do	....do	
18752	ad.	....do		...do	....do	
18753	ad.	....do		...do	....do	
18754	ad.	....do		...do	....do	
18755	ad.	....do		...do	....do	
18756	ad.	Death Valley, Furnace Creek, Calif.		Mar. 21	....do	
18757	ad.	....do		...do	....do	
18758	ad.	....do		...do	....do	
18759	ad.	....do		...do	....do	
18760	ad.	....do		...do	....do	
18761	ad.	....do		...do	....do	
18762	ad.	....do		...do	....do	
18763	ad.	....do		...do	....do	
18764	ad.	....do		...do	....do	
18765	ad.	....do		...do	....do	
18766	ad.	....do		...do	....do	
18767	ad.	....do		...do	....do	
18768	ad.	....do		...do	....do	
18769	ad.	....do		...do	....do	
18770	ad.	....do		...do	....do	
18771	ad.	....do		...do	....do	
18772	ad.	....do		...do	....do	
18773	ad.	....do		...do	....do	
18774	ad.	....do		...do	....do	
18775	ad.	....do		...do	....do	
18776	ad.	....do		...do	....do	
18777	ad.	....do		...do	....do	
18778	ad.	....do		...do	....do	
18779	ad.	....do		...do	....do	
18780	ad.	....do		...do	....do	
18781	ad.	....do		...do	....do	
18782	ad.	....do		Apr. 10	Stephens	
18783	larvæ.	....do		Feb. 4	Fisher	
18784	ad.	Panamint Mountains, Cottonwood Cañon, Calif.	2,700	May 29	Nelson	
18785	adol.	....do		...do	....do	

Bufo halophilus B. & G. (Plate III, figs. 3 a-b).

Of rather general distribution, as specimens were collected by the expedition inside the great interior valley of California, on the Pacific coast near Monterey, and in various localities in Owens Valley, east of the Sierra Nevada. Its vertical range is hardly less extended, having been found from the level of the sea to more than 10,000 feet above.

List of specimens of Bufo halophilus.

U.S. Nat. Mus. No.	Sex and Age.	Locality.	Altitude.	Date.	Collector.	Remarks.
			Feet.			
18719	adol.	Owens Valley, Alvord, Calif.	4,000	June 26	Stephens.	
18720	juv.	Owens Valley, Bishop Creek, Calif.	4,000	June 29	....do......	
18721	juv.	......do......	4,000	June 29	....do......	
18722	juv.	......do......	4,000	June 29	....do......	
18723	ad.	Owens Valley, Independence Creek, Calif.	6,000	June 19	....do......	
18724	jun.	......do......	6,000	June 19	....do......	
18725	ad.	Owens Valley, Lone Pine, Calif.		June 18	Nelson.	
18726	ad.	......do......		June 7	Palmer.	Pl. III. fig. 3 a-b.
18727	adol.	......do......		June 6	....do......	
18728	jun.	......do......		June 6	....do......	
18729	adol.	Round Valley, Tulare County, Calif.	10,000	Aug. 22	....do......	
18730	adol.	Whitney Meadows, Calif.		Aug. 20	Bailey.	
18731	adol.	Kings River, Calif.	5,200	Aug. 19	Nelson.	
18732	adol.	Elizabeth Lake, Calif.		July 2	Palmer.	
18733	jun.	Monterey, Calif.	About sea level.	Sept. 30	Bailey.	
18734	jun.	......do......	...do...	Oct. 1	....do......	
18735	tadpoles	East Fork, Kaweah River, Calif.	10,200	Aug. 7	....do......	
18736	do	......do......	10,200	Aug. 7	....do......	
18737	do	......do......	10,200	Aug. 7	....do......	

Bufo boreas nelsoni, subsp. nov. (Pl. III, figs. 4 a-b).

Diagnosis.—Similar to *B. boreas:* Skin between warts smooth; snout protracted, pointed in profile; webs of hind legs very large; soles rather smooth; limbs shorter, elbows and knees not meeting when adpressed to the sides of the body; inner metacarpal tubercle usually very large.

Habitat.—Southeastern California and western Nevada.

Type.—U. S. Nat. Mus., No. 18742; Oasis Valley, Nevada, March 16, 1891; F. Stephens, coll.

This seems to be the southern form of *Bufo boreas*, distinguished from the latter as above. Extreme examples of both forms are very different and would readily pass for distinct species, but specimens occur in which one or the other of the characters are less developed, making it expedient to use a trinominal appellation.

On the other hand, both *B. boreas* and the new form here described are quite well separated from *B. halophilus* and its northern race, *B. halophilus columbiensis*, the difference in profile of the snout being quite sufficient (comp. pl. III, figs. 3a and 4a), not to mention the other characters indicated in the diagnosis above. Their geographical distribution, as examplified by the material brought home by the Death Valley Expedition, furnishes sufficient proof of the specific value of their differences, for while we find *B. halophilus* alone in the valley of California, both species were collected in the same localities east of the Sierra Nevada.

The name of this form is selected in honor of Mr. E. W. Nelson for his valuable zoögeographical work both in the extreme south and in the extreme north of our country.

List of specimens of Bufo boreas nelsoni.

U.S. Nat. Mus. No.	Sex and age.	Locality.	Altitude.	Date.	Collector.	Remarks.
			Feet.			
18738	ad.	Oasis Valley, Nev		Mar. 16	Stephens	
18739	ad.	......do		...do...	....do	
18740	ad.	......do		...do...	....do	
18741	ad.	......do		...do...	....do	
18742	ad.	......do		...do...	....do	Type.
18743	ad.	......do		...do...	Nelson	
18744	adol.	Resting Springs, Calif		Feb. 7	Fisher	
18745	jun.	......do		...do...	....do	
18746	ad.	Owens Valley, Morans, Calif	5,000	July 4	Stephens	
18747	ad.	Owens Valley, Lone Pine, Calif		June 18	Nelson	

Bufo lentiginosus woodhousii (Gir.).

The three specimens mentioned below are rather young, and are referred to under the above name more because they occur in the region commonly assigned to this form than because they conform to the characters ascribed to it. As a matter of fact, I have yet to discover a character, or a combination of characters of *sufficient* stability to enable me to distinguish *B. woodhousii* from *B. americanus*. Proportions, parallelism or divergence of cranial ridges, and single or double subarticular tubercles on the toes, seem all entirely valueless as characters.

[Specimens of this toad were collected in Pahranagat and Vegas valleys, Nevada; and toads, probably the same species, were common in the Lower Muddy and Virgin valleys, Nevada, and at the mouth of Beverdam Creek, Arizona.—C. H. M.]

List of specimens of Bufo lentiginosus woodhousii.

U.S. Nat. Mus. No.	Sex and age.	Locality.	Altitude.	Date.	Collector.	Remarks.
			Feet.			
18716	jun.	Pahranagat Valley, Nev		May 25	Bailey	
18717	jun.	Vegas Valley, Nev		Mar. 13	Nelson	
18718	jun.	......do		Mar. 14	Bailey	

Family SCAPHIOPODIDÆ.

Scaphiopus hammondii Baird.

The four specimens representing various sizes and ages from the same locality will ultimately be of great help in better understanding the status of this species. The few specimens now in the collections from a number of localities scattered over a very wide area, and often in a bad state of preservation, form a very unsatisfactory material upon which to base a rational discussion of the question.

List of specimens of Scaphiopus hammondii

U.S. Nat. Mus. No.	Sex and age	Locality	Altitude	Date	Collector	Remarks
			Feet.			
18746	ad.	Owens Lake, Olancha, Calif	3,700	May 21	Stephens	
18787	adol.	......do......		May 18	....do......	
18788	adol.	......do......	3,700	May 15	....do......	
18789	jun.	......do......		May 18	....do......	

Family HYLIDÆ.

Hyla regilla B. & G.

We have been so accustomed to regard this species as chiefly 'Pacific' in its distribution that it was rather a surprise to receive such an enormous number of specimens from so many localities in the desert regions visited by the expedition. Our knowledge as to the geographical distribution of this species has consequently been considerably extended, and there can be no doubt that the material gathered will be of extreme importance whenever it shall be possible to work up in detail the unequaled series in the National Museum. As my assistant, Mr. Frederick C. Test, has been engaged for some time upon this work, I shall refrain from further remarks in order not to forestall any of his conclusions.

[On the west or coastal slope of the Great Divide in California, tree toads of this species were found in Kern Valley, Walker Basin, and at Old Fort Tejon in the Cañada de las Uvas. On the east or Great Basin side of the divide they were tolerably common about the spring in Surprise Cañon in the Panamint Mountains, at Hot Springs in Panamint Valley, at Saratoga Spring at the south end of Death Valley, and at Resting Springs. In Nevada they were found in Ash Meadows, Oasis, Pahrump, and Vegas valleys.—C. H. M.]

List of specimens of *Hyla regilla*.

U.S. Nat. Mus. No.	Sex and age.	Locality.	Altitude.	Date.	Collector.	Remarks.
			Feet.			
18790	ad.	Panamint Mountains, Johnson Cañon, Calif.	6,000	Mar. 31	Fisher	
18791	ad.	......do	6,000	...do...	...do	
18792	ad.	......do	6,000	...do...	...do	
18793	ad.	......do	6,000	...do...	...do	
18794	ad.	......do	6,000	...do...	...do	
18795	ad.	......do	6,000	...do...	...do	
18796	ad.	......do	6,000	...do...	...do	
18797	ad.	......do	6,000	...do...	...do	
18798	ad.	......do	6,000	...do...	...do	
18799	ad.	......do	6,000	...do...	...do	
18800	ad.	......do	6,000	...do...	...do	
18801	ad.	......do	6,000	...do...	...do	
18802	ad.	......do	6,000	...do...	...do	
18803	ad.	......do	6,000	...do...	...do	
18804	ad.	......do	6,000	...do...	...do	
18805	ad.	......do	6,000	...do...	...do	
18806	ad.	......do	6,000	...do...	...do	
18807	ad.	......do	6,000	...do...	...do	
18808	ad.	......do	6,000	...do...	...do	
18809	ad.	......do	6,000	...do...	...do	
18810	ad.	......do	6,000	...do...	...do	
18811	ad.	......do	6,000	...do...	...do	
18812	ad.	......do	6,000	...do...	...do	
18813	ad.	......do	6,000	...do...	...do	
18814	ad.	......do	6,000	...do...	...do	
18815	ad.	......do	6,000	...do...	...do	
18816	ad.	......do	6,000	...do...	...do	
18817	ad.	......do	6,000	...do...	...do	
18818	ad.	......do	6,000	...do...	...do	
18819	ad.	......do	6,000	...do...	...do	
18820	ad.	......do	6,000	...do...	...do	
18821	ad.	......do	6,000	...do...	...do	
18822	ad.	......do	6,000	...do...	...do	
18823	ad.	......do	6,000	...do...	...do	
18824	ad.	Panamint Mountains, Surprise Cañon, Calif.		Apr. 23	...do	
18825	ad.	......do		...do...	...do	
18826	ad.	......do		...do...	...do	
18827	ad.	......do		...do...	...do	
18828	ad.	......do	2,600	Apr. 21	Bailey	
18829	ad.	......do	2,600	...do...	...do	
18830	juv.	Whitney Creek, Calif		Aug. 18	...do	
18831	ad.	Whitney Meadows, Calif		Sept. 1	Fisher	
18832	adol.	......do		Aug. 20	Bailey	
18833	juv.	......do		Aug. 20	...do	
18834	juv.	......do		...do...	...do	
18835	juv.	......do		...do...	...do	
18836	juv.	......do		...do...	...do	
18837	ad.	Near Whitney Meadows, Calif.		Aug. 23	...do	Among granite rocks.
18838	ad.	Panamint Mountains, Calif		Apr. 22	Nelson	
18839	ad.	......do		...do...	...do	
18840	ad.	Panamint Valley, Hot Springs, Calif.		...do...	Fisher	
18841	ad.	......do		...do...	...do	
18842	juv.	......do		...do...	...do	
18843	juv.	......do		...do...	...do	
18844	juv.	......do		...do...	...do	
18845	juv.	......do		...do...	...do	
18846	ad.	Resting Springs, Calif.		Feb. 8	Palmer	
18847	ad.	......do		Feb. 7	Fisher	
18848	ad.	......do		...do...	...do	
18849	ad.	......do		Feb. 17	...do	
18850	ad.	......do		...do...	...do	
18851	ad.	......do		...do...	...do	
18852	ad.	......do		...do...	...do	
18853	adol.	Saratoga Springs, Calif.		Jan. 30	Bailey	In pond at spring.
18854	adol.	......do		...do...	...do	
18855	adol.	......do		...do...	...do	
18856	ad.	Hot Springs, Calif		Jan. 9	...do	
18857	♂ ad.	South Fork Kern River, 25 miles above Kernville, Calif.		July 4	Fisher	
18858	juv.	Kern River, Calif.		...do...	...do	

*About.

List of specimens of *Hyla regilla*—Continued.

U.S. Nat. Mus. No.	Sex and age.	Locality.	Altitude.	Date.	Collector.	Remarks.
			Feet.			
18859	ad.	Walker Basin, Calif		July 15	Fisher	
18860	juv.	Antelope Valley, near La Liebre Rancho, Calif.		June 27	Palmer	
18861	ad.	Old Fort Tejon, Calif		July 3	....do	
18862	ad.	......do		July 6	....do	
18863	ad.	......do		....do	....do	
18864	ad.	......do		July 11	....do	
18865	ad.	South Fork Merced River, Calif	8,900	July 31	Nelson	
18866	ad.	Horse Corral Meadows, Calif	8,000	Aug. 12	Palmer	
18867	ad.	Kings River, Calif	7,500	Aug. 19	Nelson	
18868	juv.	Cottonwood Meadows, Calif		Aug. 24	Dutcher	
18869	juv.	......do		....do	....do	
18870	juv.	......do		....do	....do	
18871	ad.	Monterey, Calif		Oct. 2	Bailey	In vine on an arbor.
18872	juv.	......do		Sept. 29	....do	
18873	juv.	......do		Sept. 30	....do	
18874	juv.	......do		....do	....do	
18875	ad.	Charleston Mountains, in Mountain Spring, Nev.	5,600	Apr. 30	....do	
18876	ad.	......do	5,000	....do	....do	
18877	ad.	......do	5,000	....do	....do	
18878	ad.	......do	5,000	....do	....do	
18879	ad.	......do	5,000	....do	....do	
18880	ad.	Pahrump Valley, Nev		Feb. 21	Nelson	
18881	ad.	Pahrump Valley, Yount's Ranch, Nev.		Apr. 28	Bailey	
18882	ad.	......do		....do	....do	
18883	juv.	......do		....do	....do	
18884	juv.	......do		....do	....do	
18885	ad.	Mountain Spring, Charleston Mountains, Nev.		Mar. 6	....do	
18886	ad.	......do		....do	....do	
18887	ad.	Corn Creek, Vegas Valley, Nev		Mar. 15	....do	
18888	ad.	......do		....do	....do	
18889	ad.	Vegas Valley, Nev		Mar. 13	....do	
18890	ad.	......do	1,800	Mar. 14	....do	In spring.
18891	ad.	......do		Mar. 13	Nelson	
18892	ad.	......do		....do	....do	
18893	ad.	......do		....do	....do	
18894	ad.	......do		....do	....do	
18895	ad.	......do		....do	....do	
18896	ad.	......do		....do	....do	
18897	juv.	......do		....do	....do	
18898	juv.	......do		....do	....do	
18899	juv.	......do		....do	....do	
18900	adol.	Vegas Valley, Cottonwood Spring, Nev.		Apr. 30	Bailey	
18901	adol.	......do		....do	....do	
18902	ad.	Oasis Valley, Nev		Mar. 16	Stephens	
18903	ad.	......do		....do	....do	
18904	ad.	......do		....do	....do	
18905	ad.	......do		....do	....do	
18906	ad.	......do		....do	....do	
18907	ad.	......do		....do	....do	
18908	ad.	......do		....do	....do	
18909	ad.	......do		....do	....do	
18910	ad.	......do		....do	....do	
18911	ad.	......do		....do	....do	
18912	ad.	......do		....do	....do	
18913	ad.	Ash Meadows, Nev		Mar. 20	Fisher	
18914	ad.	......do		....do	....do	
18915	ad.	......do		....do	....do	
18916	ad.	......do		....do	....do	
18917	ad.	......do		....do	....do	
18918	ad.	......do		Mar. 13	....do	
18919	ad.	......do		....do	....do	
18920	ad.	......do		....do	....do	
18921	ad.	......do		Mar. 18	Palmer	
18922	juv.	......do		Mar. 4	....do	
18923	juv.	......do		Mar. 2	Bailey	
18924	ad.	......do		Mar. 4	Stephens	
18925	ad.	......do		Mar. 17	Nelson	
18926	ad.	......do		Feb. 28	....do	

Family RANIDÆ.

Rana draytonii B. & G.

Of this well-marked species, Mr. Bailey collected two adults and two young ones at Monterey, the latter in a spring near the beach. The specimens are in fine condition, and display the distinctive characters very well. The vicissitudes of this species demonstrate beautifully the disastrous results of prejudiced desires of 'lumping' species.

List of specimens of Rana draytonii.

U.S. Nat. Mus. No.	Sex and age.	Locality.	Altitude.	Date.	Collector.	Remarks.
			Feet.			
18953	ad.	Monterey, Calif	Near sea level.	Oct. 3	Bailey	In spring, near beach.
18954	ad.	....do..............	..do...	..do......	....do........	Do.
18955	juv.	....do..............	..do...	Sept. 30	....do........	
18956	juv.	....do..............	..do...	..do......	....do........	

Rana aurora B. & G.

The specimens referred to this species agree in such essential points with the types of *R. aurora*, that I have been obliged to so name them, the only other alternative being to describe them as new. It is my conviction that the result of a careful study of a large number of specimens from the Pacific province will result in the establishment of several more species or subspecies than at present recognized, but I also feel that the final settlement must be deferred until a more propitious time for a monographic essay on the various forms which cluster around *R. aurora*, *pretiosa*, and *draytonii*. Under these circumstances I deem it inadvisable to establish any new names, the more so since I hope it will not be long before I shall be able to devote the necessary time to this question.

It is hardly necessary to add that it is out of the question to base any generalizations upon the supposed geographical distribution of these forms as they are defined for the present.

The character which associates the present specimens so strongly with *R. aurora* is the smoothness of the skin, although very minutely pitted, and the very strong pitting of the line which takes the place of the dorso-lateral fold in the other species. The differences consist chiefly in shorter snout, fuller webbing of the toes, broader tongue, and darker color.

List of specimens of Rana aurora.

U.S. Nat. Mus. No.	Sex and age.	Locality.	Altitude.	Date.	Collector.	Remarks.
			Feet.			
18947	ad.	Sequoia National Park, Calif	7,000	Aug. 2	Palmer	
18948	ad.	....do..............	7,000	Aug. 6	....do........	Halsted Meadows.
18949	ad.	....do..............	7,000	..do...	Fisher	Do.

Rana pretiosa B. & G.

The remarks under *R. aurora* refer as well to the present species. The southern specimens which have come under my notice have the white (or yellow) supralabial stripe ill-defined and more or less interrupted, especially behind the angle of the mouth; while in the northern specimens this stripe usually is well-defined and uninterrupted.

List of specimens of Rana pretiosa.

U. S. Nat. Mus. No.	Sex and age.	Locality.	Altitude.	Date.	Collector.	Remarks.
			Feet.			
18028	ad.	Sierra Nevada, Calif	8,400	July 24	Stephens	
18029	ad.	Mulkey Meadows, Sierra Nevada, Calif.	9,000	....do	....do	
18030	ad.	......do	9,000	....do	....do	
18031	ad.	Chiquito, San Joaquin River, Calif.	9,800	July 31	Nelson	Head of river east of Mt. Raymond.
18032	ad.	......do	9,800	....do	....do	Do.
18033	adol.	Head of Big Cottonwood Creek, Calif	11,000	Sept. 11	Dutcher	Near Mount Whitney.
18034	adol.	......do	11,000	Sept. 13	....do	
18035	adol.	......do	11,000	....do	....do	
18036	adol.	......do	11,000	....do	....do	
18037	adol.	......do	11,000	....do	....do	
18038	juv.	......do	11,000	....do	....do	
18039	ad.	Whitney Creek, Calif		Aug. 18	Bailey	
18040	ad.	East Fork Kaweah River, Calif	10,200	Aug. 7	....do	In little lake.
18041	ad.	......do	10,200	....do	....do	Do.
18042	adol.	......do	10,200	....do	....do	Do.
18043	juv.	......do	10,200	....do	....do	Do.
18044	adol.	Mineral King, Calif.	7,500	July 31	....do	
18045	adol.	Lone Pine, Calif		Aug. 21	Fisher	
18046	ad.	South Fork Merced River, Calif	8,800	July 31	Nelson	

Rana boylii Baird.

In a recent paper* (December, 1891) Boulenger expresses the opinion that *R. boylii* is only a synonym of *R. draytonii*. It is evident that he has arrived at this conclusion without having had opportunity to compare authentic specimens of both species, for otherwise it would be impossible to make such a mistake. The two species differ in all essential points, and among the many puzzling Western forms of this genus none are more easily separated. Dentition, tympanum, and dorsolateral glands are so different that once seen the two species can not well be confounded. *R. boylii* has the tympanum almost concealed and covered with tubercles, the vomerine teeth in an oblique longitudinal series on each side, and the dorso-lateral fold flattened out so as to be nearly, or entirely, imperceptible, while *R. draytonii* has a smooth, distinct tympanum, vomerine teeth in clusters, and very prominent dorso-lateral folds.

The specimens which I have referred to *R. boylii* differ from the type of the latter in a few minor points, chief of which is the narrowness of the tongue; but as the specimens are rather small, much stress ought not to be attached to this point. Moreover, I would again refer to my

---
*Ann. Mag. Nat. Hist. (6), VIII, p. 453.

remarks under *R. aurora* as to the inadvisability of meddling with the status of the Californian frogs in the present connection.

List of specimens of Rana boylii.

U.S. Nat. Mus. No.	Sex and age.	Locality.	Altitude.	Date.	Collector.	Remarks.
			Feet.			
18950	ad.	South Fork Kern River, Calif.		July 4	Fisher	25 miles above Kernville.
18951	ad.	Kernville, Calif.		June 23	Palmer	
18952	ad.	....do....		...do...	...do...	

Rana fisheri, sp. nov. (Plate III, figs. 5a–c.)

Diagnosis.—Heel of extended hind limb reaching anterior eye canthus, falling considerably short of tip of snout; vomerine teeth between and projecting posteriorly beyond choanae; no black ear patch; vertical diameter of tympanic disc greater than distance between nostrils and eye; hind feet webbed for about two-thirds; one small metatarsal tubercle; one weak dorso-lateral dermal fold, no dorsal folds between; posterior lower aspect of femur granular; back and sides with numerous small, distinct, dark spots, surrounded by lighter; no external vocal sacs.

Habitat.—Vegas Valley, Nevada.

Type.—U. S. Nat. Mus., No. 18957; Vegas Valley, Nevada, March 13, 1891; V. Bailey coll.

Not closely allied to any of the known species. The coloration is very distinct, resembling somewhat that of *R. aesopus;* the great size of the tympanic disc is also quite characteristic, being larger than in any of our species, except *R. catesbiana, clamitans,* and *septentrionalis.*

I should have considered it rather risky to describe a new species of *Rana* from the West had it not been for the fact that the great number of the specimens collected established beyond a doubt the constancy of the characters mentioned.

This species is dedicated to Dr. A. K. Fisher in recognition of his share in the herpetological success of the Death Valley Expedition.

[Frogs were tolerably common in Beaverdam Creek near its junction with the Virgin in northwestern Arizona, May 8, but whether *Rana fisheri* or *R. pipiens brachycephala* is not certain. The former was collected in Vegas Valley (type locality); the latter in Pahranagat Valley.—C. H. M.]

List of specimens of Rana fisheri.

U.S. Nat. Mus. No.	Sex and age.	Locality.	Altitude.	Date.	Collector.	Remarks.
			Feet.			
18057	ad.	Vegas Valley, Nev.		Mar. 13	Bailey	Type.
18958	ad.	......do		Mar. 9	....do	
18959	ad.	......do		Mar. 13	....do	
18960	ad.	Las Vegas Ranch, Vegas Valley, Nev.		Mar. 9	Nelson	
18961	ad.	......do		...do	...do	
18962	ad.	......do		...do	...do	
18963	ad.	......do		...do	...do	
18964	ad.	......do		...do	...do	
18965	ad.	......do		...do	...do	
18966	ad.	......do		...do	...do	

Rana pipiens brachycephala (Cope).

The western form of the green frog evidently reaches its western limit in Nevada, and from the fact that the expedition only brought home one specimen it may probably be concluded that it is rare in that region. This specimen was collected in Pahranagat Valley, Nevada, May 25, 1891, by Vernon Bailey (No. 18927).

As to the name *Rana pipiens* Schreber, adopted in preference to *R. virescens* 'Kalm,'1 may remark that as the latter was never used by Kalm in a binominal sense, it being only the first word of his diagnosis of the species, the former is beyond doubt the oldest tenable name for the species. From some of the recent synonymies it might be inferred that *Rana virginiana* of Laurenti (1768) would be the name, but I need only quote his diagnosis, viz, "corpore cinereo, dorso quinqueangulato quinquestriato; maculis rubris; abdomine, pedibusque flavescentibus," to show that it can never be identified as our shad-frog.

This question has already been settled by Prof. S. Garman in 1888 (Bull. Ess. Inst., xx, pp. 90, 100), and I am only induced to repeat and corroborate it here, as one might be led to believe, from Cope's treatment of the matter (Man. N. Am. Batr., 1889, p. 399), that Garman is responsible for the adoption of *Rana virescens*.

REPORT ON THE FISHES OF THE DEATH VALLEY EXPEDITION COLLECTED IN SOUTHERN CALIFORNIA AND NEVADA IN 1891, WITH DESCRIPTIONS OF NEW SPECIES.

By CHARLES H. GILBERT, Ph. D.

LIST OF SPECIES.

Ameiurus nebulosus Le Sueur.
Catostomus araeopus Jordan.
Rhinichthys (Apocope) velifer, sp. nov.
Rhinichthys (Apocope) nevadensis, sp. nov.
Rutilus symmetricus (B. & G.).
Lepidomeda vittata Cope.
Cyprinus carpio Linn.
Salmo irideus Gibbons.
Salmo mykiss agua-bonita Jordan.
Cyprinodon macularius Girard.
Cyprinodon macularius baileyi, subsp. nov.
Empetrichthys merriami, gen. et sp. nov.
Gastrosteus williamsoni Girard.

Ameiurus nebulosus Le Sueur.

Two specimens of this introduced species were procured at Lone Pine, on Owens River, where the species was reported as abundant.

Catostomus aræopus Jordan.

Type locality.—South Fork of Kern River, California.

One specimen from Reese River, Nevada. Collected by Vernon Bailey.

Rhinichthys (Apocope) velifer, sp. nov. (Plate VI, Fig. 2.)

Type locality.—Pahranagat Valley, Nevada.

This species is closely related to *Rhinichthys yarrowi*, from which it differs in the much larger scales, the lateral line traversing 55 instead of 74 to 83 scales. Both species mark such perfect transition between *Apocope* and *Rhinichthys* that it seems best to reduce the former to the rank of a subgenus. About half the specimens of *yarrowi* have a narrow frenum, and this is present in each of the three type specimens of *velifer*. In both *yarrowi* and *velifer* the teeth are 2-4-4-2, as in typical *Rhinichthys*. The only character left to distinguish *Apocope* is the narrowness of the frenum when present, it being very wide in typical *Rhinichthys*.

Head 4 in length; depth, 4¾. Snout narrow, but bluntly rounded, not projecting beyond the front of premaxillaries. Frenum joining premaxillaries to skin of forehead very narrow, varying in width in the three type specimens. It will probably be found that some specimens of this species, as of *yarrowi*, have protractile premaxillaries. Mouth small, horizontal, the maxillary reaching vertical from front of orbit, equaling diameter of eye, 3½ in length of head. Interorbital width, 3 in head.

Teeth 2, 4–4, 2, hooked, with sharp edges.

Pectorals nearly reaching base of ventrals, the latter long, overlapping front of anal fin. Origin of dorsal fin midway between base of caudal and middle of eye.

D., 8; A., 7. Lat. l. 56 (pores). 10 scales in a series obliquely forward to lateral line from base of first dorsal ray.

Color in spirits, brown along back, a black band from snout across cheeks and along middle of sides, with a narrow silvery streak above it. Lower half of sides and belly silvery; an ill-defined dark streak from base of pectorals back along sides to the end of the anal fin. A small black spot on base of caudal.

Three specimens were taken in a hot spring in Pahranagat Valley, Nevada, May 25, 1891, by C. Hart Merriam and Vernon Bailey. Temperature of spring 36.11° C. (97° F.).

Rhinichthys (Apocope) nevadensis, sp. nov. (Plate VI, Fig. 1.)

Type locality.—Ash Meadows, Amargosa Desert, on boundary between California and Nevada.

Differing from other known species in the large head, the short deep body, very small eye, and in the reduction of the outer ventral ray to a mere rudiment.

Head, $3\frac{2}{3}$ in length (varying from $3\frac{1}{2}$ to 4); depth, $3\frac{2}{3}$ (varying from $3\frac{1}{2}$ to 4). D., 8; A., 7. Lat. l. 65. Ventrals apparently with seven rays, the outer one rudimentary, and often to be detected with difficulty.

Body robust, with broad heavy head, the least depth of caudal peduncle less than half the greatest height of body. Greatest depth of head at occiput 5 in length of body ($6\frac{1}{4}$ in nubila of equal size). Eye very small, half interorbital width, which equals distance from tip of snout to middle of eye, and is contained $2\frac{2}{3}$ times in head.

Mouth terminal, very oblique, the lower jaw included, the premaxillaries not at all overlapped by the snout. The maxillary reaches the vertical from front of eye, and is one-third length of head. Maxillary barble well developed.

Scales very irregularly placed, and difficult to enumerate. The lateral line is incomplete in adults, and usually does not reach to opposite dorsal fin. In the young it is variously developed, often extending, though with many interruptions, to end of dorsal or base of caudal. Pores in lateral line (when complete) 58, about 66 oblique series, counted above lateral line.

Fins small, the pectorals not reaching ventrals, the latter not to vent. Front of dorsal midway between base of caudal and middle of occiput.

In spirits, the upper half of sides is speckled and marbled with brown; the belly and lower half of sides immaculate or sparsely spotted. A broad dark lateral stripe usually present, becoming more conspicuous posteriorly, and ending in an obscure black spot on base of tail. A dark stripe sometimes present along middle of lower half of sides.

Numerous specimens were procured in the warm springs at Ash Meadows, Indian Creek, and Vegas Creek, Nevada.

Rutilus symmetricus (Baird and Girard).

Type locality.—Old Fort Miller, Fresno Co., San Joaquin Valley, California.

Specimens from Owens Lake, California, seem to agree with those reported on by Jordan and Henshaw (*Leucos formosus*, Rep. Chief Engineer, Wheeler Surv. W. 100th Mer., App. NN, 1878, 193) from Washoe Lake, Nevada, and Kern Lake, California. There are 11 scales between lateral line and front of dorsal, and 52 scales in lateral line. Teeth 4-5. There are seven or eight rays in the anal fin, and the head is $3\frac{2}{3}$ in the length. The lateral line is imperfect in the young.

The American species of this genus are poorly defined, and may be reducible to one or two species. If the specific forms prove to be numerous there is no assurance that these specimens are identical with the types of *Pogonichthys symmetricus* and *Algansea formosus* from the San Joaquin and Mohave rivers.

Lepidomeda vittata Cope.

Type locality.—Little Colorado River, Arizona.

Three small specimens from Pahranagat Valley, Nevada, agree well with the original description of this species, and are probably referable to it. It has been recorded hitherto only from the original locality, the Colorado Chiquito River, Arizona, and its occurrence in the present locality is full of interest. Not only *Lepidomeda* but the whole subfamily (the *Plagopterinæ*) to which it belongs, is peculiar to the basin of the Colorado River, to which the Pahranagat waters must belong.

Cyprinus carpio Linn.

A specimen of this introduced species was found dead on the shores of Owens Lake. Carp and catfish are both common in the lower Owens River, and when they enter the lake are soon killed by the alkalinity of the water.

Mr. Palmer and Dr. Fisher reported carp as the staple food fish at Three Rivers on the Kaweah River, where numerous large individuals were taken.

Salmo irideus Gibbons.

Type locality.—San Leandro Creek, Alameda Co., California.

A single specimen of the 'Rainbow Trout' was preserved by Dr. A. K. Fisher from the Cañon of Kings River. Compared with specimens from the Santa Cruz Mountains in the vicinity of Palo Alto, this is found to agree in all respects. The coloration is very bright as is usual in the colder mountain streams. The scales above the lateral line are arranged in 135 oblique series.

Salmo mykiss agua-bonita Jordan.

Type locality.—Whitney Creek south of Mt. Whitney, High Sierra, California. (Jordan, Report State Fish Commissioners of California, 1892, p. 62.)

Several specimens of this, the 'Golden Trout' of Kern River, were collected in Whitney Creek, whence came the original types, and from Cottonwood Creek, a tributary of Owens Lake, to which they have been transplanted. Two specimens were also preserved, taken from the South Fork of Kern River. They agree perfectly with the original description cited. The scale formula should read 180 to 200, not 130 to 200, as in the original description.

Cyprinodon macularius Girard.

Type locality.—Rio San Pedro, Arizona.

(*Cyprinodon nevadensis* Eigenmann, Proc. Cal'a Acad. Nat. Sci., 1889, 270.)

This small Cyprinodont inhabits the springs and wells throughout the desert region of southern California, Arizona and Nevada, and is the characteristic denizen of the more or less alkaline waters of this district. The original types are from the Rio San Pedro, a tributary of the Rio Gila, and I have found it abundant at a pond at Lerdo, Mexico, on the lower Colorado River. Specimens obtained at Lerdo have been compared with those from Death Valley and found identical.

The species varies in form and color, and apparently in the size which it reaches in different localities. The males have the back and sides uniform dusky, the lower parts lighter, all the fins in the most brightly colored individuals being broadly margined with black. The females have the lower half of sides as well as belly lighter, often silvery white, the sides crossed by black bars, which are wide along middle of body, but become much narrower than the interspaces on the lower half of sides. The bars vary in number and size and often alternate with narrower, fainter, and shorter ones. The fins are light, and the dorsal either with or without a black blotch on its posterior rays. Although usually uniform in coloration, the males occasionally show lateral bars, which, however, contrast little with the general dusky color of the sides.

The dorsal varies from 9 to 11, and the anal from 10 to 11. There are 24 or 25 transverse series of scales, and the humeral scale is but little enlarged. The head is contained 3 to $3\frac{1}{4}$ times in the length. Adults are very short and deep, the depth being nearly or quite half the length; in half-grown specimens 1 inch long, the depth is contained $2\frac{2}{5}$ in the length. The eye is very small, about equaling the snout, contained $1\frac{1}{2}$ to $1\frac{2}{3}$ times in the interorbital width, and $3\frac{3}{4}$ times in the head. The front of dorsal is usually midway between occiput and base of caudal.

The normal number of ventral rays in this species seems to be six. No specimen examined has shown more than this number, and in several but five are present. In one specimen from Ash Meadows, Nevada, the ventral of one side only is present, and contains but three or four rays. Four young specimens from the same locality and two from Medbury Springs, Amargosa Desert, California, have the ventrals wholly aborted, and show on dissection no trace of the basals. These occur in the same lots with other specimens having normal ventrals, and are otherwise indistinguishable from them. No full-grown adults were found without ventrals, the largest being a half-grown specimen about one inch long with the characteristic coloration of the males already developed. Ten young specimens from the 'Devil's Hole,' Ash Meadows, are all without ventrals, and further collections from this locality would be of interest.

In the intestines were found fragments of insects, and in one series of specimens from Saratoga Springs at the south end of Death Valley, California, very numerous shells of a small Gasteropod mollusk.

Specimens are in the collection from the following localities: Medbury Spring (6 miles north of the Borax Works), Amargosa Desert, California; Ash Meadows, Amargosa Desert, Nevada; Saratoga Springs, Death Valley, California; Amargosa Creek, California.

Cyprinodon macularius baileyi, subsp. nov.

Type locality.—Pahranagat Valley, Nevada, collected by C. Hart Merriam and Vernon Bailey, May 25, 1891.

Eleven immature specimens from Pahranagat Valley, Nevada, show no trace of ventral fins. They are olivaceous above, bright silvery on the lower half of sides and below, and have two lengthwise series of coarse black spots, one along middle line of body, the other on a level with the lower edge of caudal peduncle. The anal fin is larger than in typical *macularius*, the eleven specimens having each 13 rays instead of 10 or 11, as constantly in the latter. The material is insufficient to fully decide the status of this form. Except in the characters noted it agrees in proportions and formulæ with *macularius*.

EMPETRICHTHYS gen. nov. (Plate V.)

(Cyprinodontidæ).

Intestines short, 1½ times length of body. Teeth conic, fixed, in each jaw arranged in a band consisting of two or three rows, the outer series somewhat enlarged. Ventrals absent. Branchiostegals five. Both upper and lower pharyngeals greatly enlarged and bearing molar teeth, tubercular in shape. The lower pharyngeals are firmly attached to the ceratobranchials of the fourth arch, while the massive epibranchials of the same arch serve to connect them firmly at the sides with the pharyngobranchials above. The fourth branchial arch bears normal gills. Its median portion is produced anteriorly, forming a triangular extension of the lower pharyngeals in the middle line. On the oral surface this is indistinguishable from the pharyngeals proper, and like them bears molar teeth.

Scales normal, large, regularly imbricated, nowhere tubercular or ridged.

This genus seems most nearly allied to *Orestias*, of which numerous species have been described from lakes in the high Andes of South America.

Empetrichthys merriami, sp. nov. (Plate v.)

Type locality.—Ash Meadows, Amargosa Desert, on boundary between California and Nevada.

In form and general appearance much resembling the mud minnow (*Umbra limi*), though somewhat deeper and more compressed.

Head compressed, its upper surface slightly convex. Mouth very oblique, with a distinct lateral cleft, the maxillary free at tip only, reaching slightly behind front of eye. Length of gape (measured from tip of snout to end of maxillary), $3\frac{1}{2}$ in head; interorbital width, $2\frac{1}{4}$; length of snout (from front of orbit to middle of upper jaw), $3\frac{3}{4}$. Eye small, its greatest oblique diameter 5 to $5\frac{1}{2}$ in head.

Distance from front of dorsal to middle of base of tail equals one-half its distance from tip of snout. The dorsal begins slightly in advance of anal, and ends above its posterior third. Its greatest height equals length of snout and eye.

Caudal truncate when spread. Pectorals broadly rounded, reaching half way to vent. D., 11 or 12 (13 in one specimen); A., 14 (from 13 to 15). Lat. l., 30 or 31, counted to base of caudal rays; 33 or 34 in all.

In spirits the color is dark brown above, sides and below lighter, often irregularly blotched with brown and white. The belly often appears checkered, having centers of scales brown and margins white, or the reverse. Fins all dusky, the basal portions of dorsal and caudal with elongated brown spots on the interradial membranes.

Several specimens were secured at Ash Meadows and in Pahrump Valley, Nevada.

Gasterosteus williamsoni Girard.

Type locality.—Williamson Pass, California.

Four specimens of this species collected by Dr. A. K. Fisher at San Bernardino, California, seem to differ from *G. microcephalus* only in the entire absence of plates on the sides. In *microcephalus* the plates vary from 3 to 7 in number, but no specimens wholly without plates have been reported from the more northern parts of its range. It is probable that *williamsoni* will prove a southern subspecies of this widely distributed form, in which case the plated specimens must bear the name *Gasterosteus williamsoni microcephalus*. The naked form has been reported heretofore from San Bernardino (by Miss Rosa Smith), and from Williamson's Pass by the original describer. The locality of the pass I have not been able to make out.

REPORT ON A SMALL COLLECTION OF INSECTS MADE DURING THE DEATH VALLEY EXPEDITION.

By C. V. RILEY,

With supplementary reports and descriptions of new species by
S. W. WILLISTON, P. R. UHLER, and LAWRENCE BRUNER.

INTRODUCTION.

In connection with the Death Valley Expedition organized by Dr. Merriam arrangements were made to have Mr. Albert Koebele, one of the agents of the Division of Entomology, stationed at Alameda, in California, join the party with a view of making a collection of the insects of the region. He collected assiduously during the brief period of his connection with the expedition, which was suddenly interrupted by a decision to have him proceed to Australia to study and introduce into California certain beneficial insects. He separated from the rest of the party to return to Alameda the latter part of May and the collecting was done during the months of April and May. The material was forwarded without report prior to his leaving for Australia, so that the specimens are, as a rule, without notes, whether of food-plant, or habit. The collection is also necessarily very incomplete in not representing the fauna of the region in the same degree as it would have done had Mr. Koebele been allowed to continue throughout the expedition.

It may be premised in making a report on any such collection as this, that there are few parts of the country, however well explored, that will not yield to the entomologist, in a few days' collecting, a good percentage of species that are new or undescribed, if all orders are taken into consideration, and this being true of the older settled portions of the country, it is true to a far greater extent of such exceptional regions as those included in the Death Valley Expedition. Insects are, also, so numerous in species and specimens, and the undescribed material so vast, that the orders may be compared with the classes in the other groups of animals so far as reporting on them is concerned, and no entomologist would consider himself competent at the present day to intelligently report on any general collection, which must be dealt with by the several specialists who have made particular study of specific families and orders. The part which I have prepared is simply a list of the species easily determinable either by comparison with the national collection or by reference to authorities in the several families, and until the undescribed species and genera are all worked up deductions from the list as to the bearings of the fauna on geographical distribution, must be more or less imperfect and unsatisfactory. Nevertheless, a few suggestions as they occur may not be out of place.

Taking first the Coleoptera, which represent by far the larger part of the collectings, they have for the most part been carefully compared with the national collection, and I have had the assistance, in the verifications, of Mr. M. L. Linell and Mr. E. A. Schwarz, both well acquainted with our North American Coleoptera. Mr. Schwarz has also materially aided in the analysis of the collection. As the chief localities from which the beetles were obtained do not exceed seven, the list has been arranged in tabular series to prevent repetition of localities. This arrangement at once shows that the collection comprises some 258 species, representing 170 genera in 39 families. Of the total number of species arranged according to localities, twenty-eight (*a*) are of general distribution in North America, *i. e.*, they cross the whole continent, and among these are six cosmopolitan species (*a b*), while only a single species (*Bradycellus cognatus*), found in the Argus Mountains, belongs to the circumpolar fauna. About fifty of the species (*c*) are widely distributed throughout the more arid regions of the West, and about twenty species (*d*) belong more properly to the fauna of maritime or upper California. The bulk of these species, as will be noted, were collected in San Bernardino County. Deducting the three sets of species and a few others, *e. g.*, the genera Homalota, Scopæus, Scymnus, and Cryptophagus, of the distribution of which very little can be definitely said, there remain about 140 species (those unlettered) which are more or less characteristic of the lower Sonoran fauna.

Some nineteen species are undoubtedly new, but only a small number of these belong to families that have been worked up and that can be satisfactorily described. They have not been sent away to specialists, as probably no one would care to describe them at once. They will, I hope, be worked up by Mr. Schwarz or Mr. Linell, but not in time for this report. I may mention that the Coleopterous fauna of this general region has been collected and studied by several competent observers. Dr. J. L. LeConte early visited the Colorado Desert and adjacent parts of Arizona; Dr. George H. Horn has also explored the fauna of Owens Valley; Mr. G. R. Crotch collected in a trip across the Mohave Desert; Dr. Edward Palmer collected in southern Utah, while Mr. W. G. Wright has recently made collections in San Bernardino County, and Mr. H. F. Wickham along the line of the Atlantic and Pacific Railroad in northwestern Arizona. Thus Mr. Koebele's small collection adds very little to our knowledge of the species already worked up.

Among the more interesting species Mr. Schwarz has indicated, may be mentioned *Pseudopsis* n. sp., *Mecomycter* n. sp., *Elasmocerus* n. sp., *Cremastochilus westwoodii*, *Alaudes singularis*, *Tanarthrus* n. sp., *Calo-*

spasta n. sp., and a remarkable new genus of Scolytidæ. Perhaps the chief interest attaching to the collection is that it permits us to make some comparison between the beetles of the valleys and intervening mountain chains within the region explored. If we omit those collected in San Bernardino County, which have no exact localities, and also the very few from Coso and Owens Valleys, the following deduction may be made: In Death Valley and Panamint Valley 140 species were found (including 23 species common to both valleys), while in Panamint Mountains and Argus Mountains 160 species were found (including 16 species common to both ranges). Comparing the faunas of the valleys and mountains, it will be noted that they have only 36 species in common. This difference is due principally to the marked preponderance of the Staphylinidæ in the mountain fauna, the complete absence of the family Meloidæ and the marked prevalence of Elateridæ and Chrysomelidæ in the mountain regions. Continued collecting later in the season might have largely changed this condition of things, however, and hence too much importance should not be attached to the deduction. The Carabidæ are the best represented in the collection, 22 genera with 44 species having been collected. The genera are all of wide distribution, and only a few species, *e. g.*, *Omophron dentatum*, *Calosoma prominens*, *Tetragonoderus pallidus*, and *Pinacodera punctigera*, are peculiar to the lower Sonoran region and have all been found in the valleys. The single representative (*Bradycellus cognatus*) of the circumpolar fauna belongs to this family. In most other families the material collected is too small or not characteristic enough to warrant any generalization.

In the Lepidoptera, the Rhopalocera have been determined by comparison with the national collection or by reference to W. H. Edwards, of Coalburgh, W. Va. The majority of the species are characteristic of the southwestern United States, but I have not had time to fully analyze the distribution of the species. The representatives in most of the other families of the Lepidoptera, outside of the Noctuidæ and Geometridæ, are so very few as not to justify consideration. In the Noctuidæ, which are better represented, most of the species have been reported before, but there are a certain number of new species, and Prof. J. B. Smith, of New Brunswick, N. J., to whom these have been referred, finds that they represent even three new genera. In the Geometridæ there are six species which can not be determined either generically or specifically, and which are not included in the list. These undescribed forms have been referred to Dr. George D. Hulst, of Brooklyn, N. Y., who will, I hope, in due time characterize them.

Among the Hymenoptera the Aculeate species comprise genera not restricted to California and include several species which are evidently new. In the parasitic Hymenoptera very little can be said about the collection. The species are most of them new, but this same statement would have to be made of almost any collection of the parasitic forms in this order from any part of the Pacific coast, and would be largely true of almost any part of the country. It is a singular fact, however, that no new genera occur, as will be noticed, in the parasitic families, the most interesting fact worthy of mention being the discovery of what is probably a representative of the genus Scolobates, found heretofore only in northern Europe. The parasitic Hymenoptera were referred to my assistants, Mr. L. O. Howard for the Chalcididæ, and Mr. William H. Ashmead for the other families, and the generic references of the undescribed forms are upon their intimate knowledge of the subject. They will not be able to characterize the many new forms in time for this report.

The Diptera were few in number and were referred to Dr. S. W. Williston, who has characterized the new forms, and whose report shows that, small as was the collection, it added three genera to the American fauna.

In the Heteroptera the list represents merely the species that were readily determinable, while the balance, including the more interesting forms, have been referred to Mr. P. R. Uhler, of Baltimore, Md., who has kindly reported on them, with definitions of the new genera and species.

In the Homoptera, as will be noticed, there are some interesting new species, especially in the family Psyllidæ, but until they are carefully compared, I do not feel justified in making any remarks upon them. Nor have I time just now to characterize the undetermined forms which I prefer to do in connection with the very many new species in the National Collection to which I have already given much study.

The Orthoptera are of considerable interest, although the collection is small. In the Acridiidæ, which probably have been most thoroughly studied in this country, three new species occur and one new genus. The undescribed material has been referred to Mr. Lawrence Bruner, of Lincoln, Nebr., who has reported on the new forms. Probably the most interesting find in this order is the rediscovery of *Scyllina delicatula* Scudder. The type of the species, and the only one hitherto found was taken in the Garden of the Gods. Most of the other species are of rather wide distribution.

The Arachnida were referred to Dr. Geo. Marx and are determined by him.

ORDER COLEOPTERA.

	San Bernardino County.	Death Valley.	Panamint Valley.	Panamint Mountains.	Argus Mountains.	Coso Valley.	Owens Valley.
Family CICINDELIDÆ.							
Cicindela senilis Horn............................							38
Family CARABIDÆ.							
Omophron dentatum Lec............................	4						19
Calosoma prominens Lec............................		1	13				
Clivina punctulata Lec............................	1						
Dyschirius tridentatus Lec........................	1						
Dyschirius basalis Lec............................	1						
Dyschirius sphæricollis Say (a)...................	1						
Schizogenius depressus Lec........................				1			
Bembidium erosum Mots.............................		9					
Bembidium lugubre Lec. (c)........................		21	2				
Bembidium sculpturatum Mots.......................							1
Bembidium aratum Lec..............................		8		14			
Bembidium n. sp...................................							1
Bembidium iridescens Lec. (c).....................			9	7			
Bembidium n. sp...................................							6
Bembidium ephippiger Lec..........................							2
Bembidium flavopictum Mots.(c)....................		1					
Tachys rapax Lec..................................	1		30	5			
Tachys anthrax Lec................................			1		2		
Tachys corax Lec..................................			1	2			3
Tachys edax Lec...................................				1			
Tachys n. sp......................................			26	1			
Amara californica Dej. (d)........................			1				
Platynus brunneomarginatus Mannh. (d).............	1		1	1	2		
Platynus funebris Lec. (d)........................	3						
Lachnophorus elegantulus Mannh....................	1						
Galerita lecontei Dej. (a)........................			1	1			
Tetragonoderus pallidus Horn......................			1				
Lebia pleuritica Lec. (a).........................					8		
Lebia guttula Lec. (c)............................					1		
Apristus laticollis Lec. (c)......................		1					
Tecnophilus croceicollis Men......................		3					
Pinacodera punctigera Lec.........................		1					
Brachynus tschernikhii Mannh. (d).................	5						
Brachynus costipennis Mots. (d)...................	10						
Chlænius obsoletus Lec............................			13	2			
Chlænius nemoralis Say (a)........................	2						
Chlænius variabilipes Eschsch. (d)................	2						
Stenolophus limballs Lec. (c).....................		18					
Stenolophus flavipes Lec. (c).....................		10			1		
Bradycellus rupestris Say (a).....................		12		4	11		
Bradycellus cognatus Gyllh. (a)...................				1	1		
Tachycellus nitidus Dej. (c)......................	2		1				
Anisodactylus californicus Dej. (d)...............	1		1	1			
Anisodactylus consobrinus Lec.(d).................			1	1			
Family DYTISCIDÆ.							
Cœlambus lutescens Lec. (c).......................			1				
Hydroporus vilis Lec. (c).........................					5		
Hydroporus n. sp..................................			20				
Agabinus glabrellus Mots..........................			1				
Agabus n. sp. ?...................................			3				
Ababus lecontei Crotch (c)........................			1				
Agabus griseipennis Lec. (c)......................					1		
Agabus lugens Lec.................................					2		
Cybister ellipticus Lec...........................			2				
Family HYDROPHILIDÆ.							
Hydrophilus triangularis Say (a)..................			2				
Hydrophilus californicus Lec......................			4				
Ochthebius rectus Lec.............................			3				
Helochares normatus Lec...........................			16				
Cymbiodyta imbellis Lec...........................						11	
Family SILPHIDÆ.							
Necrophorus nigrita Mannh. (d)....................			1				
Necrophorus guttula Mots. (d).....................			1				

ORDER COLEOPTERA—Continued.

	San Bernardino County.	Death Valley.	Panamint Valley.	Panamint Mountains.	Argus Mountains.	Coso Valley.	Owens Valley.
Family PSELAPHIDÆ.							
Bryaxis deformata Lec				22			
Bryaxis foveata Lec				47			
Family STAPHYLINIDÆ.							
Falagria sp			2	26			
Falagria sp				2			
Falagria sp				2			
Myrmedonia sallei Sharp (a)				14			
Homalota sp					10		
Homalota sp			1				
Homalota sp				8			
Homalota sp		6	1				
Aleochara bimaculata Grav. (ab)					2		
Gyrophæna sp. (c)			2				
Quedius limbifer Horn (c)			1	15	12		
Philonthus filicornis Horn					8		
Philonthus decipiens Horn					1		
Philonthus parvus Horn				20	17		
Actobius puncticeps Horn				10	32		
Xantholinus pusillus Sachse. (a)			3				
Leptacinus brunnescens Lec. (c)					1		
Cryptobium californicum Lec. (d)					20		
Scopœus sp					1		
Scopœus sp				10	1		
Scopœus sp					1		
Scopœus sp					3		
Tachinus debilis Horn					9		
Tachyporus californicus Horn (c)					10		
Bledius ferratus Lec			9	20			
Bledius nitidiceps Lec							
Bledius armatus Er	1						1
Trogophlœus sp							
Pseudopsis n. sp				1	1		
Homalium n. sp					4		
Anthobium n. sp. (princeps Fauv. i. litt.) (c)					19		
Orobanus densus Casey				1			
Family PHALACRIDÆ.							
Phalacrus ovalis Lec. (c)			1				
Family CORYLOPHIDÆ.							
Sericoderus subtilis Lec. (c)				21			
Family COCCINELLIDÆ.							
Hippodamia convergens Guér. (a)		3	3	2	1		
Hippodamia 5-signata Kirb. (a)		3	1	20	1		
Coccinella abdominalis Say (a)		1					
Mysia hornii Crotch (c)					1		
Psyllobora tædata Lec. (a)		2	3		15		
Pentilia n. sp					11		
Scymnus coniferarum Crotch					18		
Scymnus sp			1				
Scymnus sp				1			
Scymnus sp					1		
Family COLYDIIDÆ.							
Anchomma costatum Lec					1		
Family CRYPTOPHAGIDÆ.							
Cryptophagus sp				12			
Family DERMESTIDÆ.							
Attagenus piceus Oliv. (ab)					3		
Perimegatoma cylindricum Kirb. (c)					3		
Perimegatoma variegatum Horn				1	1		
Trogoderma ornatum Say (ab)		2	6				
Anthrenus scrophulariæ Linn. (ab)		3					

ORDER COLEOPTERA—Continued.

	San Bernardino County.	Death Valley.	Panamint Valley.	Panamint Mountains.	Argus Mountains.	Coso Valley.	Owens Valley.
Family HISTERIDÆ.							
Saprinus ciliatus Lec. (c)					1		
Saprinus lubricus Lec. (c)					9		
Saprinus laridus Lec							3
Family NITIDULIDÆ.							
Carpophilus yuccæ Crotch					5		
Carpophilus pallipenuis Say (a)				29			
Family LATHRIDIIDÆ.							
Stephostethus liratus Lec. (a)				1	3		
Lathridius filiformis Gyllh. (ab)				3			
Corticaria cavicollis Mannh. (a)				9	9	5	
Family BYRRHIDÆ.							
Limnichus californicus Lec				1			
Family DASCYLLIDÆ.							
Cyphon concinnus Lec. (c)					1		
Family ELATERIDÆ.							
Cardiophorus seniculus Blanch					1		
Cardiophorus obscurus Lec					1		
Anchastus sericeus Horn					1		
Melanotus longulus Lec					1		
Dolopius lateralis Eschsch. (a)	2			1	3		
Melanactes densus Lec					1		
Family BUPRESTIDÆ.							
Buprestis lauta Lec. (c)				1	1		
Anthaxia æneogaster Lap. (a)			2	2			
Chrysobothris octocola Lec			9	15			
Chrysobothris debilis Lec							
Acmæodera tuta Horn			2		1		
Acmæodera connexa Lec					1		
Family LAMPYRIDÆ.							
Podabrus tomentosus Say (a)					1		
Silis n. sp					2		
Silis filigera Lec			1				
Malthodes n. sp					1		
Family MALACHIIDÆ.							
Malachius macer Horn					2		
Malachius mirandus Lec					1		
Malachius n. sp					5		
Attalus trimaculatus Mots		2	4				
Pristoscelis conformis Lec			3				
Pristoscelis sp			28	14			
Pristoscelis sp							2
Pristoscelis sp			14		2		
Listrus luteipes Lec					11		
Listrus difficilis Lec					9		
Listrus sp		2	4				
Dolichosoma n. sp			9	6			
Dolichosoma n. sp					2		
Allonyx sculptilis Lec					12		
Eschatocrepis constrictus Lec					12		
Mecomycter n. sp			90				
Family CLERIDÆ.							
Elasmocerus n. sp			1				
Trichodes ornatus Say (c)			29		2		
Hydnocera discoidea Lec		12	7				
Lebasiella n. sp			1	1			

ORDER COLEOPTERA—Continued.

	San Bernardino County.	Death Valley.	Panamint Valley.	Panamint Mountains.	Argus Mountains.	Coso Valley.	Owens Valley.
Family PTINIDÆ.							
Ernobius sp.					8		
Sinoxylon declive Lec.					1		
Amphicerus fortis Lec.				3			
Family SCARABÆIDÆ.							
Aphodius granarius Linn. (ab)					2		
Aphodius rubidus Lec.	1						
Atœnius abditus Hald. (a)	4						
Oncerus floralis Lec.				2			
Diplotaxis corvina Lec.		3					
Cotalpa granicollis Hald.					1		
Cremastochilus westwoodii Horn.						1	
Family CERAMBYCIDÆ.							
Haplidus testaceus Lec.					2		
Family CHRYSOMELIDÆ.							
Coscinoptera vittigera Lec. (c)					1		
Lema nigrovittata Guér.			4	2			
Exema conspersa Mannh. (a)	1						
Cryptocephalus sanguinicollis Suffr (c)					2		
Pachybrachys n. sp.	1						
Pachybrachys sp.		27		1	1		
Pachybrachys lustrans Lec.			1				
Glyptoscelis illustris Crotch					10		
Metachroma californicum Lec.				1			
Pingidera n. sp.					1		
Monoxia consputa Lec. (c)				1			
Haltica carinata Germ. (a)					11		1
Epitrix suberinita Lec. (c)					11		
Phyllotreta albionica Lec. (c)					7		
Psylliodes convexior Lec. (c)					2		
Family BRUCHIDÆ.							
Bruchus prosopis Lec.		8	6				
Bruchus protractus Horn		7	1				
Bruchus n. sp.		18	1				
Family TENEBRIONIDÆ.							
Triorophus lævis Lec.	2		1				
Triorophus subpubescens Horn					1		
Eurymetopon rufipes Eschsch. (d)	4	12	2				
Anepsius delicatulus Lec.	1						
Centrioptera muricata Lec.	1						
Schizillus laticeps Horn						3	
Cryptoglossa verrucosa Lec.	1	15	1			1	
Coniontis viatica Eschsch. (d)	2						
Eusattus productus Lec.				1			
Eleodes granosa Lec.				1		2	
Eleodes grandicollis Mannh. (d)					2		
Eleodes armata Lec.					2	3	
Eleodes carbonaria Say (c)	2	7		1		1	
Eleodes gracilis Lec.						1	
Eulabis rufipes Eschsch.					2		
Cerenopus concolor Lec.	1						
Cœlocnemis magna Lec.				8		8	8
Blapstinus dilatatus Lec.	1						
Blapstinus brevicollis Lec.			2				
Blapstinus rufipes Casey			5				
Conibiosoma elongatum Horn	1		5		2		
Notibius puberulus Lec.	1		3				
Alaudes singularis Horn					1		
Family OTHNIIDÆ.							
Othnius umbrosus Lec. (c)					1		
Family PYTHIDÆ.							
Cononotus macer Horn					1		

INSECTS OF THE DEATH VALLEY EXPEDITION. 243

ORDER COLEOPTERA—Continued.

	San Bernardino County.	Death Valley.	Panamint Valley.	Panamint Mountains.	Argus Mountains.	Coso Valley.	Owens Valley.
Family MORDELLIDÆ.							
Anaspis pusio Lec				6			
Family ANTHICIDÆ.							
Notoxus cavicornis Lec					4		
Anthicus confinis Lec			1				
Anthicus difficilis Lec (a)	2						
Anthicus nitidulus Lec (c)					10		
Anthicus californicus Laf (a)							7
Tanarthrus n. sp			3				
Family MELOIDÆ.							
Megetra opaca Horn			1				
Cysteodemus armatus Lec			23				
Nemognatha lutea Lec			2				
Nemognatha apicalis Lec	1						
Epicauta n. sp	1		1				
Cantharis magister Horn			28				
Calospasta n. sp			26				
Calospasta mirabilis Horn			1				
Phodaga alticeps Lec	1		5				
Family OTIORHYNCHIDÆ.							
Eupagoderus varius Lec		1	1		1		
Eupagoderus geminatus Lec		11	1				
Eupagoderus n. sp		15					
Nov. gen. and n. sp			2				
Nov. gen. and n. sp	1						
Family CURCULIONIDÆ.							
Sitones vittatus Lec (d)				3			
Apion ventricosum Lec		39	3	2			
Apion vicinum Smith				20			
Apion antennatum Smith			22		13		
Lixus 4-lineatus Chevr (c)					1		
Cleonus vittatus Kirb (c)			1				
Smicronyx n. sp				1			
Smicronyx cinereus (a)		10	5	1	53		
Anthonomus peninsularis Dietz				4			
Anthonomus ebeninus Dietz				14			
Macrorhoptus estriatus Lec (c)				10			
Tychius semisquamosus Lec				1			
Tychius setosus Lec		13	29	1			
Copturus longulus Lec (a)				1			
Centorhynchus rapæ Gyllh (ab)				3			
Centorhynchus n. sp			1				
Family CALANDRIDÆ.							
Scyphophorus yuccæ Horn				14			
Sphenophorus pictus Lec			1				
Sphenophorus simplex Lec (c)			4				
Family SCOLYTIDÆ.							
Pityophthorus sp				28			
Pityophthorus sp				22			
Nov. gen. (near Cryphalus), n. sp				2			
Family ANTHRIBIDÆ.							
Brachytarsus tomentosus Say (a)				1			

Order LEPIDOPTERA.

Family NYMPHALIDÆ.

Melitæa acastus Edw ....13 ex., Argus Mountains.
Melitæa alma Streck.......................15 ex., Coso Valley; 1 ex., Panamint Valley; 1 ex., Argus Mountains.
Pyrameis cardui L..........................1 ex., San Bernardino County, and abundant everywhere on trip, and migrating towards northwest.
Pyrameis caryæ Hb ....2 ex., Argus Mountains.

Family LYCÆNIDÆ.

Lemonias mormo Feld ....1 ex., Argus Mountains; 1 ex., Panamint Mountains; 1 ex., Panamint Valley.
Thecla dumetorum Bd......................1 ex., San Bernardino County; 5, Coso Valley; 2, Argus Mountains.
Thecla spinetorum Bd......................3 ex., Argus Mountains; 1, Panamint Mountains.
Lycæna acmon Doubl......................1 ex., Panamint Valley; 1, Argus Mountains.
Lycæna amyntula Bd ....8 ex., Coso Valley; 1, Panamint Valley; 2 Argus Mountains.
Lycæna exilis Bd ....1 ex., Argus Mountains; 1, Death Valley; 2, Panamint Valley.
Lycæna daedalus Behr ....1 ex., Death Valley.
Lycæna neglecta Edw ....1 ex., Coso Valley; 1, Death Valley.
Lycæna lygdamas Dd ....2 ex., Argus Mountains.
Lycæna oro Scudd ....4 ex., Argus Mountains.
Lycæna pheres, var. *orius* Bd.............1 ex., Argus Mountains; 2, Coso Valley.
Lycæna battoides Behr ....2 ex., Argus Mountains.

Family PAPILIONIDÆ.

Pieris beckerii Edw..........................2 ex., Argus Mountains.
Pieris sisymbrii Bd..........................26 ex., Argus Mountains.
Anthocharis cethura Feld..................19 ex., Argus Mountains.
Anthocharis ansonides Bd.................15 ex., Argus Mountains; 2, Panamint Mountains; 5, Coso Valley; 6, Paradise Valley.
Colias ariadne Edw.........................1 ex., Coso Valley.
Papilio zolicaon Bd.........................5 ex., Argus Mountains; 1, San Bernardino County.

Family HESPERIDÆ.

Copæodes procris Edw ....1 ex., Argus Mountains.
Pamphila nevada Scud.....................1 ex., Argus Mountains.
Pamphila phylæus Dru ....1 ex., Death Valley.
Pyrgus tesselata Scud......................1 ex., Argus Mountains.
Pyrgus ericetorum Bd......................9 ex., Coso Valley; 3, Argus Mountains.
Nisoniades alpheus Edw ....2 ex., Argus Mountains; 1, Coso Valley.
Eudamus nevada Scud ....1 ex., Argus Mountains.

Family SPHINGIDÆ.

Lepisesia phaëton G. and R....................1 ex., San Bernardino County.

Family SESIIDÆ.

Sesia sp..2 ex., Argus Mountains.

Family AGARISTIDÆ.

Alypia ridingsii Gr..........................3 ex., Argus Mountains; 1, Panamint Mountains; 1, San Bernardino County.

Family PYROMORPHIDÆ.

Triprocris smithsonianus Clem..............,5 ex., Argus Mountains.

Family ARCTIIDAE.

Leptarctia decia Bd........................2 ex., Argus Mountains.

Family NOTODONTIDÆ.

Cerura n. sp..................................3 ex., Owens Valley.

Family COSSIDÆ.

Hypopta bertholdi Grt......................1 ex., Argus Mountains.

Family NOCTUIDÆ.

Melipotis jucunda Hb ....1 ex., Panamint Mountains.
Syneda howlandii Gr ....1 ex., Argus Mountains.
Cirrhobolina deducta Morr..................1 ex., Death Valley
Hypena polligera Smith....................1 ex., Panamint Valley.
Grotella dis Gr ....24 ex., Argus Mountains.
Thalpochares arizonæ H. Edw ....10 ex., Argus Mountains.
Mamestra curialis Grt......................18 ex., Argus Mountains.
Mamestra crotchii Grt......................2 ex., Argus Mountains
Acontia cretata Grt. and Robs..............8 ex., Argus Mountains.
Acontia lanceoluta Grt ....6 ex., Argus Mountains.
Triocnemis saporis Grt ....1 ex., Argus Mountains.
 (Much paler than typical form.)
Melicleptria n. sp..........................1 ex., Argus Mountains.
Oncocnemis ? n. sp.........................5 ex., Argus Mountains.
Schinia sp..................................3 ex., Argus Mountains.
Schinia n. sp..............................20 ex., Argus Mountains.
Antaplaga n. sp............................5 ex., Argus Mountains.
Heliophana n. sp...........................1 ex., Argus Mountains.
Nov. gen. et n. sp...........................7 ex., Argus Mountains.
Nov. gen. et n. sp...........................3 ex., Argus Mountains.
Nov. gen. et n. sp. (congeneric with above.)..6 ex., Argus Mountains.
Scotogramma n. sp. (?).....................8 ex., Argus Mountains.
Nov. gen. et n. sp...........................1 ex., Argus Mountains.
Noctua havilae Grt.........................2 ex., Argus Mountains.
Plusia sp. (badly rubbed.).................2 ex., Argus Mountains.
Agrotis (sens. lat.) n. sp.................3 ex., San Bernardino County.
Homoptera mima var.........................4 ex., Death Valley.
Pleonectyptera n. sp.......................2 ex., Argus Mountains.

Family GEOMETRIDÆ.

Azelina hübnerata Gn........................4 ex., Argus Mountains.
Azelina meskearia Pack....................8 ex., Argus Mountains.
Hetœra ephelidaria Hulst................1 ex., Panamint Valley; 1 ex., Argus Mountains.
Anaplodes festaria Hulst.................2 ex., Argus Mountains.
Nemoria phyllinaria Zell..................2 ex., Panamint Valley.
Semiothisa metanemaria Hulst.........2 ex., Argus Mountains.
Semiothisa californiata Pack...........12 ex., Argus Mountains; 3 ex., Death Valley; 2 ex., San Bernardino County; 1 ex., Coso Valley.
Phasiane sp....................................1 ex., Argus Mountains.
Phasiane meadiata Pack..................8 ex., Panamint Valley.
Phasiane neptata Gn.......................1 ex., Panamint Mountains.
Marmopteryx tesselata Pack............1 ex., Coso Valley; 1, Argus Mountains.
Lepiodes escaria Gr........................1 ex., Panamint Valley.
Lepiodes behrensata Pack...............1 ex., San Bernardino County.
Gorytodes n. sp..............................3 ex., Argus Mountains.
Boarmia furfuraria Hulst..................2 ex., Argus Mountains.
Eupithæcia rotundopennata Pack....1 ex., Death Valley.
Eupithæcia zygadæniata Pack.........1 ex., Argus Mountains.
Eupithæcia taeniata Hulst...............2 ex., Argus Mountains.
"*Coremia defensaria*" according to label by Packard in collection, Hulst.........9 ex., Argus Mountains; 1 ex., Death Valley.

Family PHYCITIDÆ.

Ortholepis near *jugosella* Rag........12 ex., Argus Mountains.
Ephestia nigrella Hulst....................1 ex., Death Valley.
Lipographis fenestrella Pack. var....1 ex., Death Valley.
Homeosoma mucidellum Rag..........2 ex., Death Valley.

Order HYMENOPTERA.

Family APIDÆ.

Xylocopa sp....................................2 ex., Panamint Valley.
Xylocopa sp....................................2 ex., Panamint Mountains.
Anthophora sp................................2 ex., Panamint Mountains.
Diadasia sp....................................10 ex., Coso Valley.
Diadasia sp....................................1 ex., Panamint Valley.
Melissodes sp.................................1 ex., Panamint Valley.
Anthidium sp..................................1 ex., Panamint Valley.
Osmia sp..1 ex., Death Valley.
Nomada sp.....................................1 ex., Death Valley.
Perdita (Macrotera) cephalotes Cr..2 ex., Panamint Mountains.
Panurgus sp...................................1 ex., Panamint Valley.
Panurgus sp...................................5 ex., Panamint Mountains.

Family ANDRENIDÆ.

Macropis sp....................................5 ex., Panamint Valley.
Cilissa albihirta Ashm....................1 ex., Panamint Valley.
Cilissa sp.......................................2 ex., Panamint Valley.
Halictus sp.....................................1 ex., Panamint Valley.

Family SPHECIDÆ.

Prionouyx thomæ Fabr .... 1 ex., Panamint Valley.

Family MASARIDÆ.

Masaris sp .... 1 ex., Death Valley.

Family EUMENIDÆ.

Odynerus sp .... 1 ex., Panamint Valley.
Odynerus sp .... 1 ex., Death Valley.
Ancistrocerus sp .... 2 ex., Argus Mountains.
Ancistrocerus sp .... 1 ex., Death Valley.
Ancistrocerus sp .... 1 ex., Argus Mountains.

Family MUTILLIDÆ.

Sphærophthalma sp .... 2 ex., Death Valley.
Sphærophthalma sp .... 1 ex., Panamint Valley.
Sphærophthalma sp .... 1 ex., Argus Mountains.

Family FORMICIDÆ.

Camponotus castaneus Latr .... 1 ex., Argus Mountains.
Formica integra Nyl .... 1 ex., Argus Mountains.
——— ——— male .... 1 ex., Panamint Mountains.

Family MYRMECIDÆ.

Aphænogaster pergandei Mayr .... Lone Pine.

Family BRACONIDÆ.

Bracon sp .... 1 ex., Argus Mountains.
Bracon sp .... 2 ex., Argus Mountains.
Bracon sp .... 1 ex., San Bernardino County.
Microbracon sp .... 1 ex., Argus Mountains.
Microbracon sp .... 1 ex., Monterey County.
Microbracon sp .... 2 ex., Argus Mountains.
Microbracon sp .... 1 ex., Santa Clara County.
Microbracon sp .... 1 ex., Argus Mountains.
Heterospilus sp .... 1 ex., Argus Mountains.
Bathystomus sp .... 1 ex., Argus Mountains.
Chelonus sp .... 1 ex., Argus Mountains.
Acælius sp .... 1 ex., Death Valley.
Apanteles sp .... 8 ex., Argus Mountains.
Apanteles sp .... 1 ex., Death Valley.
Microplitis sp .... 1 ex., Panamint Valley.
Agathis vulgaris Cr .... 2 ex.: 1, Argus Mountains; 1, Panamint Valley.
Agathis nigripes Cr .... 1 ex., Argus Mountains.
Euphorus mellipes Cr .... 1 ex., Argus Mountains.
Lysiphlebus cucurbitaphis Ashm .... 2 ex., Monterey County.

Family ICHNEUMONIDÆ.

Cryptus sonorius Cr., female .... 2 ex., Death Valley.
Ophion bilineatum Say .... 1 ex., Sonoma County.
Limneria cupressi Ashm .... 1 ex., Argus Mountains.

Limneria fugitiva Say........................1 ex., Monterey County.
Scolobates sp. (or a new genus closely allied)..1 ex., Argus Mountains. (Collected on *Pinus monophylla*.)
Anomalon sp ....1 ex., Argus Mountains.
Plectiscus sp...............................1 ex., Death Valley.
Exetastes sp................................1 ex., Argus Mountains.
Banchus spinosus Cr ....1 ex., Panamint Valley.
Orthocentrus sp.............................2 ex., Argus Mountains.
Pimpla novita Cr............................9 ex., Argus Mountains. (Collected on *Pinus monophylla*.)

Family PROCTOTRYPIDÆ.

Ceraphron sp ....1 ex., Argus Mountains.
Ceraphron sp ....2 ex., Panamint Mountains.

Family CHALCIDIDÆ.

Leucaspis affinis Say........................1 ex., San Bernardino County.
Chalcis sp..................................2 ex., Death Valley.
Chalcis sp..................................1 ex., San Bernardino County.
Chalcis sp..................................1 ex., San Bernardino County.
Acanthochalcis sp...........................1 ex., Panamint Valley.
Decatoma sp.................................1 ex., San Bernardino County.
Isosoma sp ....15 ex., Argus Mountains.
Ashmeadia sp................................2 ex. (Collected on *Pinus monophylla*.)
Systole sp ....1 ex., Argus Mountains.
Perilampus sp ....2 ex., San Bernardino County.
Perilampus sp ....1 ex., San Bernardino County.
Holaspis sp.................................1 ex., Death Valley.
Torymus sp..................................3 ex., Argus Mountains; 1 on *Pinus monophylla.*
Torymus sp..................................29 ex., Argus Mountains; 13 on *Pinus monophylla.*
Syntomaspis sp ....1 ex., San Bernardino County.
Metapelma sp................................1 ex., Panamint Mountains.
Ratzeburgia sp..............................1 ex., Argus Mountains.
Eupelmus sp.................................1 ex., Argus Mountains. (Collected on *Pinus monophylla*.)
Eupelmus sp.................................1 ex., Argus Mountains. (Collected on *Pinus monophylla*.)
Antigaster sp., male........................1 ex., San Bernardino County. Reared from eggs of a *Phaneroptera.*
Polychroma sp...............................1 ex., Death Valley; 1, Panamint Valley; 1, Argus Mountains.
Encyrtus sp ....2 ex., Argus Mountains.
Dibrachys sp................................32 ex., Argus Mountains.
Eutelus sp..................................1 ex., Argus Mountains.
Isocyrtus sp................................2 ex., Owens Valley.
Arthrolytus sp..............................1 ex., Panamint Mountains.
Meraporus sp................................2 ex., Argus Mountains.
Platyterma sp...............................2 ex., Argus Mountains.
Anogmus sp ....1 ex., Argus Mountains.
Euplectrus sp...............................1 ex., Argus Mountains.
Teleogmus sp................................1 ex., Monterey County.
Olinx sp....................................2 ex., Argus Mountains.

Sympiesus sp ....1 ex., Argus Mountains.
Omphale sp. ....1 ex., Argus Mountains.
Entedon sp ....1 ex., Argus Mountains.
Chrysocharis sp..........................1 ex., Argus Mountains.
Euderus sp ....4 ex., Argus Mountains.
Tetrastichus sp. (3 species)..........................8 ex., Argus Mountains, Panamint Valley, and Death Valley.

Order HETEROPTERA.

Family CORIMELÆNIDÆ.

Corimelœna extensa Uhler..........................11 ex., Panamint Mountains; 2 Panamint Valley; 1 Argus Mountains.

Family PENTATOMIDÆ.

Brochymena obscura H. Sch..........................1 ex., Panamint Valley.
Lioderma sayi Stål..........................1 ex., Panamint Valley.
Peribalus limbolarius Stål..........................1 ex., Panamint Valley.
Thyanta rugulosa Say..........................1 ex., Argus Mountains.
                                                                     14 ex., Nev. 671.
Carpocoris lynx Fabr..........................1 ex., Panamint Valley.
Dendrocoris pini Mont..........................9 ex., Argus Mountains, on *Pinus monophylla*.

Family COREIDÆ.

Ficana apicalis Dall..........................3 ex., Argus Mountains, on *Pinus monophylla*.
                                                                     4 ex., Panamint Valley.
Harmostes reflexulus Stål..........................1 ex., Death Valley.
Corizus lateralis Say..........................1 ex., Argus Mountains, on *Pinus monophylla*.

Family BERYTRIDÆ.

Neides muticus Say..........................1 ex., Argus Mountains.

Family LYGÆIDÆ.

Nysius angustatus Uhler..........................15 ex., Argus Mountains.
Ischnorhynchus didymus Zett..........................1 ex., Argus Mountains.
Cymodema tabida Spin..........................1 ex., Owens Valley; 1 Panamint Mountains.
Eremocoris-tropicus Dist..........................4 ex., Argus Mountains.
Melanocoryphus bicrucis Say..........................1 ex., Argus Mountains, on *Pinus monophylla*.
Lygœus reclivatus Say..........................1 ex., Panamint Valley.

Family PYRRHOCORIDÆ.

Largus cinctus H. Sch..........................1 ex., Argus Mountains; 1 ex., Coso Valley; 1 ex., Panamint Valley.

Family CAPSIDÆ.

Campsocerocoris annulicornis Rent..........................2 ex., Argus Mountains, on *Pinus monophylla*.
Hadronema robusta Uhler..........................1 ex., Owens Valley.

Lygus pratensis Linn........................1 ex., Death Valley.
Lygus inritus Say............................2 ex., Death Valley.
Dicyphus secundus Uhler....................5 ex., Argus Mountains.

Family ANTHOCORIDÆ.

Triphleps insidiosus Say....................1 ex., Panamint Valley.

Family TINGITIDÆ.

Tingis arcuata Say..........................5 ex., Argus Mountains.
Corythuca ciliata Say. var.................25 ex., Argus Mountains.

Family NABIDÆ.

Coriscus ferus Linn........................1 ex., Death Valley.

Family REDUVIIDÆ.

Diplodus socius Uhler......................2 ex., Panamint Valley; 1, Panamint Mountains.
Apiomerus ventralis Say....................1 ex., Panamint Valley.
Ginea rileyi Mont..........................5 ex., Death Valley; 4 ex., Panamint Valley.

Family VELIIDÆ.

Hebrus pucellus Burm.......................2 ex., Panamint Mountains.
Macrovelia hornii Uhler....................2 ex., Argus Mountains.

Family SALDIDÆ.

Species of Salda undetermined.

Family GALGULIDÆ.

Mononyx stygicus Say.......................3 ex., Panamint Valley.

Family NOTONECTIDÆ.

Anisops platycnemis Fieb...................1 ex., Death Valley.

Order HOMOPTERA.

Family FULGORIDÆ.

Delphax tricarinatus Say...................1 ex., Argus Mountains, on *Pinus monophylla*.
Cixius stigmatus Say.......................1 ex., Argus Mountains, on *Pinus monophylla*.

Family MEMBRACIDÆ.

Platycentrus acuticornis Stål..............20 ex., San Bernardino County.
Centrodus atlas Goding.....................48 ex., Death Valley.
Multareis cornutus Goding..................2 ex., Panamint Valley.

Family BYTHOSCOPIDÆ.

Agallia siccifolia Uhler...................12 ex., Argus Mountains, on *Pinus monophylla*.

Family CERCOPIDÆ.

Proconia hieroglyphica Say .... 1 ex., Argus Mountains.
Proconia costalis Fabr .... 1 ex., Argus Mountains, on *Pinus monophylla*.

Family JASSIDÆ.

Several species not determined.

Family PSYLLIDÆ.

Aphalara n. sp .... 23 ex., Argus Mountains, May, 1891.
Aphalara n. sp .... 5 ex., Argus Mountains, May, 1891.
Aphalara n. sp .... 5 ex., Argus Mountains, May, 1891.
Aphalara n. sp .... 23 ex., Death Valley, April, 1891.
N. g. et. n. sp .... 34 ex., Panamint Mountains and Argus Mountains.
Psylla n. sp .... 47 ex., Argus Mountains, April and May, 1891.
Psylla n. sp .... 40 ex., Argus Mountains, April and May, 1891.
(?) *Psylla* n. sp .... 1 ex., Argus Mountains, May, 1891.
Trioza n. sp .... 136 ex., Death Valley and Argus Mountains.

Order ORTHOPTERA.

Family FORFICULIDÆ.

Tridactylus n. sp .... 3 ex., San Bernardino County; 1 ex., Lone Pine. (A. K. Fisher.)

Family BLATTIDÆ.

Heterogamia sp. (probably new) .... 1 ex.

Family GRYLLIDÆ.

Nemobius sp. (probably new) .... 1 ex.
Gryllus abbreviatus Serv. (?) .... 4 ex., Panamint Valley; 2, Argus Mountains.

Family LOCUSTIDÆ.

Stenopelmatus talpa Burm .... 1 ex., Panamint Valley.

Family ACRIDIIDÆ.

Paratettix mexicanus Sauss .... 8 ex., Panamint Valley.
Paratettix tollecus Sauss. (not quite typical).. 17 ex., Panamint Valley.
Dracotettex n. sp .... 6 ex., Panamint Valley.
Haldemanella robusta Brun .... 1 ex., Argus Mountains.
Hippiscus latertius Sauss (var) .... 8 ex., Argus Mountains; 4, Panamint Valley.
Hippiscus aurilegulus Scudd .... 1 ex.
Auconia integra Scudd. (modified in color)... 8 ex., Death Valley.

Eucoptolophus n. sp............................19 ex., Panamint Valley; 5 ex., Death Valley.
Scirtettica n. sp.............................1 ex.
Scyllina delicatula Scudd....................1 ex.
N. gen. et n. sp.; between *Œdipoda* and *Erimobia* ....1 ex.
Leptysma mexicana Sauss.....................18 ex., Panamint Valley.
Psoloessa texana Scudd ....3 ex., Coso Valley
Trimerotropis vinculata Scudd ....3 ex., Panamint Valley.
Thrincus aridus Brun ....2 ex., Panamint Valley.
Camnula pellucida ....Several ex., Walker Basin. (Dr. A. K. Fisher.)

ARACHNIDA.

Family IXODIDÆ.

Argas occidentalis Marx ....From dog's ear, Ash Meadows, Nov., March 9, 1891. (A. K. Fisher.)
Rhipistoma leporis Marx ....From rabbit's ear, Kern River, Calif., July 4, 1891. (A. K. Fisher.)
Ixodes ricinus L ....From Thomomys, Walker Pass, Calif., July 1. 1891. (A. K. Fisher.)
Rhipicephalus angustipalpis Marx ....From jack rabbit, Daggett, Calif., Jan. 7, 1891. (A. K. Fisher.)
Dermacentor americanus L....................From child's ear, Lone Pine, Calif., June 9, 1891. (A. K. Fisher.)

Family SCORPIONIDÆ.

Vejovis punctipalpis Wood....................1 ex. (A. K. Fisher), Panamint Mountains, April.

LIST OF DIPTERA OF THE DEATH VALLEY EXPEDITION.

By S. W. WILLISTON.

The following pages include a list of the species contained in a small collection of Diptera from Death Valley and the adjoining regions, sent me recently for determination by Prof. Riley. That the larger part of them should be new to science is not at all strange, inasmuch as they are, for the greater part, members of families which have been but little studied in America. The collection is of considerable interest as adding three European or African genera hitherto unrecorded from America, among which the wingless *Apterina* is the most remarkable. After careful search I have found it necessary to describe two new genera—one among the Dexiidæ, the other an Ephydrinid.

Culex inornatus n. sp.

Female.—Palpi yellowish brown. Proboscis yellowish, black at the tip. Antennæ black, the basal joints yellowish. Occiput black, clothed mostly with whitish pubescence. Thorax red, the dorsum reddish brown, thinly clothed with light yellow and white tomentum, and blackish bristly hairs. Pleuræ with white tomentum. Abdomen black, somewhat yellowish in ground-color on the second and third segments, covered with white scale-like tomentum on the front and sides of the segments, on the posterior part of the segments with blackish tomentum. Legs brownish; on the inner side thickly, on the outer side thinly, covered with white tomentum. Wings nearly hyaline, the tomentum of the veins blackish. Length, 5-6^{mm}.

One specimen, Argus Mountains, April, 1891 (Koebele). Both this and the following species belong to the genus *Culex* in the restricted sense of Lynch.

Culex n. sp.

Female.—Dark brown or black, the occiput covered with white and brown tomentum. Palpi black, at the tip silvery. Proboscis black, with a white ring beyond the middle. Antennæ black. Dorsum of thorax covered with brown and white tomentum, the white toward either side posteriorly, and forming two slender lines, abbreviated anteriorly. Pleuræ with white tomentum. Abdomen deep brown, with six conspicuous rings of white tomentum on the anterior part of the segments, the ground-color under them yellow; on the second segment a white tomentose spot in front. Legs nearly black, the base of all the femora yellowish. On the outer side of the femora, in large part, and along the whole inner side of the legs, as also moderately broad rings at the articulations of all the tarsal joints, white. Wings nearly hyaline; tomentum blackish, distributed nearly evenly on the veins. Length, 6^{mm}.

One specimen, Argus Mountains, Calif., April. This species is closely allied to *C. annulatus* Meigen, which occurs in the western regions and in Mexico, but seems to differ in the uniformly distributed tomentum of the wings.

Simulium argus n. sp.

Female.—Black, the legs in part light yellow. Front black, opaque. Face cinereous, with whitish pubescence. Antennæ brownish black, the basal joint yellowish. Thorax black, the dorsum thinly pollinose, not shining; pleuræ densely white pollinose, with a black spot. Abdomen opaque velvety black, the first three segments with a narrow silvery white spot on either side at the hind margin; the next three segments similarly marked, but the interval between the spots successively wider, and each with two other, successively larger, white spots, leaving a black space in the middle and a narrower one at the outer sides. Venter white. Legs brownish black, the distal part of the femora, base of tibiæ, and the greater part of the metatarsi light yellow. Wings pure hyaline, the veins light colored, those posteriorly very delicate. Length, 2¼ᵐᵐ.

One specimen, Argus Mountains, Calif., May, 1891.

Psilocephala n. sp.?

A single male specimen. Panamint Valley, April.

Thereva vialis Osten Sacken, Western Dipt., 274.

A single male specimen, Death Valley, Calif., April, 1891.

Erax aridus sp. [var.] n.

A single female specimen, considerably larger than the type of *E. latrunculus* Will. differs from that species in the legs being wholly black, the hair of the face being wholly white, and in the furcation of the third vein taking place opposite, instead of distinctly beyond the base of the second posterior cell. I am not sure till the male is examined, that these differences are specific. The very marked difference in the color of the legs will, however, justify the varietal name.

Anthrax n. sp.

This species, represented by a single specimen from Panamint Valley, I can not identify with any described species. In Coquillett's most recent synopsis, it is brought straight to *A. scitula*, from which it differs, however, in important particulars, aside from the markings of the wings, the figure of which, herewith given, will permit the recognition of the species.

Anthrax fenestratoides Coquillett, Trans. Amer. Ent. Soc. xix, 185, 1892.

A single specimen, agreeing well with the description, from Panamint Valley, Calif.

Anthrax (Stonyx) sodom, n. sp.

Female.—Black, the legs chiefly yellowish. Face produced conically; clothed, like the front, with black pile slightly intermixed with white tomentum. Proboscis not projecting beyond the epistoma. Style of antennæ about twice the length of the bulbous portion. Occiput with yellowish tomentum. Mesonotum clothed with white tomentum and sparse, erect, black hairs. Abdomen white tomentose, with a moderate amount of black tomentum, and with sparse, erect, long black hairs; the margins of the abdomen with black and white pile. Base of femora somewhat blackish: front tibiæ without spinules; front ungues small, the pulvilli apparently wanting. Wings with brown markings, as in the figure. Length 7ᵐᵐ.

One specimen, Death Valley, Calif., April, 1891 (Koebele).

Anthrax n. sp.

A single specimen, from Panamint Valley, Calif., seems to belong to a new species. It is taken to be *A.* (*Dipalta*) *serpentina* in Coquillett's table, from which it differs decidedly. The figure herewith given will enable it to be recognized.

Aphœbantus vittatus Coquillett, Can. Entom. May, 1886.

A single specimen from Panamint Valley, Calif., April 21 (Koebele), seems to be this, though the thorax and abdomen do not have a very "vittate" appearance.

Argyramœba daphne Osten Sacken, Biol. Centr. Amer. Diptera, i, 104, pl. 11, f. 6, 1886.—Mexico.

One male, from Panamint Valley, Calif. It agrees so closely with the description and figure of this species that I believe the determination very probable. It has, however, *three* submarginal cells in each wing, a fact which sustains Coquillett's objections to the acceptation of *Stonyx* and *Dipalta*.

Triplasius novus n. sp.

Male.—Head narrower than the thorax. Eyes broadly contiguous, the facets markedly larger above, but without a dividing line, the posterior orbits with a distinct incision. Antennæ inserted close together, slender, second joint short, about as long as broad, and about one-third the length of first joint; third joint longer than the first two together, a little thickened at the base, slender on the distal half, terminating in a minute bristle. Frontal triangle with a median impression; triangle and face clothed with abundant pile. Oral opening large, its upper margin nearly opposite the middle of the eyes. Proboscis long, palpi slender. Thorax and abdomen clothed with thick, bushy pile. Abdomen a little longer than the thorax and abdomen together. Legs not strong; ungues gently curved; pulvilli about half of the length of the claws, distinct. Three marginal cells present, the neuration otherwise as in *Bombylius*. Front light-grayish pollinose, clothed with black hairs in the middle. First two joints of the antennæ with abundant black hair. Face with abundant light-yellowish hair, intermixed with black; the uppermost part of the face in ground-color is black; along the oral margin, reaching the eyes, broadly yellow. Cheeks black, grayish pollinose. Antennæ, palpi, and proboscis black. Pile of the occiput light yellowish or white. Thorax and scutellum opaque black, but almost wholly obscured by the long and abundant light yellow or white pile. Abdomen with long and abundant light yellowish or white pile; the sides of the second segment and the terminal segment with bushy, black hair. Legs black. Wings dark brown, more yellowish along the costa, and lighter colored distally. Length, 11^{mm}.

One specimen, Panamint Valley, Calif., April, 1891. The species is in all respects a *Bombylius* with three submarginal cells.

Comastes sackeni n. sp.

Female.—Differs from *C. robustus* in the smaller size, the presence of black hairs on the face and thorax, the wholly black scutellum, which is without bristles on its margin, in the abdomen being rather uniformly clothed with shorter white pile, intermixed with numerous long black hairs, and in the greater infuscation of the basal portion of the wings. The femora and tibiæ are black. Length, 9^{mm}.

One specimen, Argus Mountains, Calif., May, 1892.

Geron, n. sp.

A single, injured specimen, agreeing somewhat with specimens of *G. albidipennis*, but apparently different. Death Valley, Calif., May.

Lordotus sororculus n. sp.

Deep black, shining. Face, first two joints of the antennæ and the front clothed wholly with deep black pile. First antennal joint about half of the length of the slender third joint, the second joint but little longer than wide. Pile of the occiput, yellowish gray; that of the mesonotum and scutellum of the same color, abundant; some black pile on the pectus. Scutellum convex, without impression or groove. Knob of the halteres, yellow. Abdomen, both above and below, with long, nearly white pile. Legs black, with light-yellowish tomentum and black pile. Wings, pure hyaline. Length, 8^{mm}.

Two specimens, Coso Valley, May 21, and Kern County, Calif.

Melanostoma n. sp.

A single male specimen from Argus Mountains, Calif., May, 1891, evidently belongs to an undescribed species. It is nearest related to *M. cærulescens* Will., but has the abdomen oval and elongate.

Oncunyia abbreviata Loew. Williston, etc.

A single specimen of this widely distributed insect from Panamint Valley, Calif., April, 1891.

Pipunculus aridus n. sp.

Male.—Front and face black, with silvery pubescence. Antennæ black; third joint silvery on the lower part, produced below into a spinous point. Thorax black, dorsum a little shining, faintly brownish dusted on the disk. Abdomen greenish black, shining. Legs black, the immediate tip of the femora, the base of the tibiæ, and all the tarsi, save their tip yellow. Hind femora without bristles below. Wings hyaline; last section of the fourth vein sinuous, the three outer sections of the same vein of nearly equal length. Small cross vein much beyond the tip of the auxiliary vein. Length 3^{mm}.

One specimen, Argus Mountain, California, April, 1891. Is most nearly allied to *P. flavitarsis* Will., but differs in the color of the abdomen, and the more produced third joint of the antennæ.

Blepharopeza adusta Loew. Centur. x, 67.

A single specimen from Sonoma County, Calif. (Riley), agreeing well with the description, save that all the tibiæ are reddish.

Prospherysa similis n. sp.

Male.—Front somewhat narrowed behind; frontal stripe dark brown, on each side a single row of bristles descending below the base of the third antennal joint. Sides of the face and the cheeks wholly without bristles. Antennæ black; third joint four or five times the length of the second joint, not reaching the vibrissæ; arista thickened to about the middle. Face and sides of the front yellowish gray, a darker spot on the lower part of the cheeks. Palpi yellow, thorax black, lightly dusted, with three linear, darker stripes, scarcely visible behind. Tip of scutellum red, with four marginal bristles on each side, a small, medium, decussate pair and two small, subdiscal ones. Abdomen somewhat elongate; first segment only a little shorter than the second; all the segments marmorate with white; first and second segments each with a pair of marginal bristles, the third segment with six before the hind margin, the fourth segment with a subdiscal pair and numerous ones near the margin; hypopygium, red. Thorax, abdomen, and legs clothed with long and abundant black hair. Legs, deep black; pulvilli and claws elongate, the former light yellow, the latter yellowish; front tibiæ with a row of short bristles on the outer side; middle tibiæ with two or three median stout bristles; hind tibiæ with numerous bristles, of which two are longer than the rest. Tegulæ, white. Wings, grayish hyaline; the small cross vein situated a little before the middle of the discal cell. Length 13^{mm}.

Female.—Front broader, about one-third of the width of the head; a pair of orbital bristles present; hair of thorax and abdomen less abundant, and that of the abdomen more recumbent and bristly; claws and pulvilli not elongate. Length, 10^{mm}.

Two specimens, Sonoma County, Calif. The female bears the label "Clisiocampa," sp. The species is nearest allied to *P. apicalis* v. d. Wulp, where it is clearly brought by Wulp's table. It will be distinguished from *P. promiscua* Towns., as also *P. websteri* Towns., by the bare eyes, as well as other characters.

Prospherysa sp.

A single male specimen from Alameda County, Calif. (Riley), seems to agree well with *P. plagiodes* v. d. Wulp in its neurational characters, but has the third vein bristly for a short distance only.

Melanodexia gen. nov.

Eyes of male separated above by the ocellar prominence; front in the female very broad. Bristles of the front numerous and hair-like in the male; in the female shorter, fewer, and stouter; not descending below the base of the antennæ. Eyes bare. Second joint of the antennæ somewhat swollen, the third joint not three times the length of the second; arista short plumose. Sides of face and the cheeks hairy. Vibrissal ridges nearly parallel; vibrissæ slender, situated a considerable distance above the oral margin, the epistoma not projecting. Bottom of the facial groove only gently convex. Width of the cheeks less than one-half of the greater diameter of the eyes. Proboscis short, palpi slender. Thorax and scutellum with well developed bristles. Abdomen short-conical, without distinct macrochætæ, save on the distal part; in the male, with abundant erect hair on the anterior segments, and thin bristles posteriorly; in the female, with short recumbent bristles anteriorly, and longer bristles posteriorly. Third longitudinal vein strongly convex in front, terminating very near the tip of the wing; antepenultimate section of the fourth vein fully twice the length of the penultimate section, the latter joining the ultimate section in an angle, which may be slightly rounded in the female. Legs not elongate, the bristles of ordinary size; hind tibiae not ciliate; pulvilli and ungues small in both sexes.

This genus is nearest allied to *Morinia* and *Pseudomorinia*, but differs in the small claws of the male, the higher position of the vibrissae, the situation of the posterior cross-vein, the closed first posterior cell, and the absence of discal and marginal bristles on the anterior abdominal segment.

Melanodexia tristis n. sp.

Male.—Wholly black, shining, with black bristles and hair. Tegulae blackish; pulvilli yellow. Frontal stripe opaque, very narrow above, separating the eyes; three or four times as wide below; the narrow lunula shining. Hair of the lower part of the cheeks long. Thorax and scutellum with long bristles and moderately abundant erect hair. First two segments of the abdomen with abundant erect hair, posteriorly the abdomen is, for the greater part, clothed with numerous, erect, slender bristles. Wings tinged with blackish, especially along the veins. Length, 6^{mm}.

Female.—Frontal stripe very broad, on each side with a row of short bristles; orbital and ocellar bristles present. Thorax and abdomen not hairy, but nearly bare, with short, recumbent bristles instead. Length, 7^{mm}.

One male, Southern California (Baron), and one female, Monterey County, Calif. (Riley).

Lispa tentaculata Degeer, Ins. vi, 42, 15, 1776 (Musca) Latreille, Gen. Crust. et Ins. iv, 347, 1809; Fallen, Dipt. Succ. Musc. 93, i, 1820; Meigen, Syst. Beschr. v, 226, 1826; Macquart, Hist. Nat. Dipt. ii, 314, 1835; Zetterstedt, Dipt. Scand. v, 1796, 1846; Walker, Ins. Dipt. Brit. ii, 147, 1853; Schiner, Fauna Austr. i, 660, 1862; Rondani, Dipt. Ital. Prodr. vi, 289, 1877; v. d. Wulp, Tijdschr. v. Ent. xi, 1868, pl. ii, f. 6; Kowarz, Wien. Ent. Zeit. xi, 000, 1892.

Habitat.—All Europe (Kowarz), New England, Michigan, South Dakota, California.

Two specimens, Panamint Valley, April, 1892. The species is especially characterized by the slender spur-like projection of the front metatarsi in the male.

Euxesta spoliata n. sp.

Female.—Shining, somewhat metallic green. Front, red or reddish yellow, with moderately coarse hairs. Antennae, reddish or brownish yellow, third joint rounded. Face, reddish yellow, of a little lighter color than the front, not pollinose. Thorax, bright green, somewhat shining, thinly pruinose. Abdomen, black or pitchy black, the first two segments red or yellowish. Legs, yellowish or brownish red, the distal joints of all the tarsi blackish. Halteres, light yellow. Wings, whitish hyaline, with light-colored veins, except in the dark spots, where they are blackish; the costal and subcostal cells are blackish throughout, encroaching somewhat on the marginal cell. The large blackish spot at the tip begins on the costa a little beyond the middle of the antepenultimate section and reaches nearly to the fourth vein; the last section of the fourth vein converges markedly toward the third. Length, 4^{mm}.

Three specimens, Death Valley and Panamint Mountains, Calif.

Ephydra tarsata n. sp.

Front shining greenish black, with two pairs of proclinate ocellar bristles; about three pairs of reclinate bristles below, a row along the orbit, directed inward, and a vertical bristle to the inner side of the row, directed inward. Antennae black; a small bristle on the upper side of the second joint; arista very short, pubescent on the much thickened basal portion. Face showing somewhat greenish beneath the grayish pruinosity; hair long and black. Thorax black, with a thin gray pruinosity; the dorsum faintly striate. Abdomen black, olivaceous grayish pollinose, not shining; hypopygium small, mostly concealed. Legs black, grayish or greenish pruinose; front metatarsi in the male thickened and longer than the following three joints together; in the female, simple but elongate. Wings grayish, hyaline; small cross vein opposite the tip of the first longitudinal vein; posterior cross vein oblique. Length, 5–6^{mm}.

Two specimens, Owens Valley, May 21, 1891.

This species will be readily recognized by the small hypopygium of the male, and the thickened front metatarsus in the same sex, together with the nearly bare arista.

Notiphila decoris n. sp.

Female.—Front gray or brownish gray, with two black stripes, separated by the triangular, brownish ocellar triangle; the median, anteriorly directed pair of bristles well developed. Antennæ and palpi black. Face opaque, light golden yellow. Dorsum of thorax and scutellum opaque yellowish brown, somewhat grayish anteriorly; the stripes only feebly indicated. Pleuræ more grayish-yellow below, with two shining black spots. Abdomen chiefly dark coffee-brown, with the posterior part and a median stripe on each segment gray. Legs black, the base of the front metatarsi and the first three joints of the four posterior tarsi reddish yellow. Wings cinereous. Length, 3½^{mm}.

One specimen, Panamint Valley, Calif., April.

Pelomyia gen. nov. *Ephydridarum.*

Third joint of antennæ rounded, second joint not unguiculated; arista long, very finely pubescent, nearly bare. Eyes wholly bare. Face of only moderate breadth, moderately convex. Cheeks moderately broad. Front moderately broad with well-developed bristles. Clypeus not projecting. Thorax with four rows of bristles, extending to the anterior part. Middle tibiæ without bristles on the outer side.

The genus seems nearest related to *Pelina*, from which it differs in the retracted clypeus, the bristles of the anterior part of the thorax, etc. The eyes are bare under the highest magnification. The neuration does not differ from *Notiphila,* etc.

Pelomyia occidentalis n. sp.

Male, female.—Vertical triangle large, yellowish gray; front, below the triangle, opaque yellow, the orbital margins narrowly white, pollinose; vertical triangle, with two proclinate bristles; a row of three bristles on the orbital margin. Antennæ brownish black, the under side of the third joint yellowish; second joint with a weak bristle at its extremity. Face yellow, not broad, somewhat whitish, pollinose; on either side with a few short, weak bristles. Dorsum of thorax brownish gray, with three slender brown stripes. Scutellum large, bare, with two pairs of bristles, the intermediate pair near the apex and large, the outer pair small. Abdomen black, with a brownish pubescence, opaque, the small hypopygium shining black; in shape elongate oval; sixth and seventh segments of the female very short. Legs black, or somewhat luteous, rather slender; femora with some short bristles. Wings nearly hyaline. Length, 2½^{mm}. Two specimens, Monterey, Calif.

Scarcely any attention has hitherto been given to the Borboridæ of America, a group of considerable interest, as including several of the few wingless forms of Diptera. I have examined about twenty species of the family from the United States and West Indies, nearly all of which are yet undescribed. I give here a table of genera based upon these species, and will shortly publish descriptions of them:

North American genera of Borboridæ:

1. Wingless species... APTERINA
    Wings fully developed... 2

2. Fourth and fifth veins of the wings incomplete beyond the discal cell, not reaching the border...LIMOSINA
   Fourth vein, at least, fully developed and reaching the border.................. 3
3. Scutellum with well-developed bristles; the fifth vein incomplete beyond the discal cell..BORBORUS
   Scutellum without bristles; fifth vein complete ....SPHÆROCERA

Borborus, sp.:
Two specimens, Argus Mountains, which seem to belong to a new species.

Limosina aldrichi n. sp.

Male.—Black, but little shining, nearly bare. Face somewhat whitish. Front, but little shining in the middle. Antennæ black, arista long, distinctly pubescent. Thorax shining. Scutellum flattened, bare, with six bristles, the pair near the apex much larger than the ones toward the base. Abdomen opaque, somewhat pruinose. Legs black, the tibiæ and tarsi more or less dark luteous; hind metatarsi only a little dilated, and but little shorter than the following joint. Wings nearly hyaline; the third vein ends beyond the small cross-vein, gradually and nearly uniformly curved forwards; the tip of the second is nearly midway between the terminations of the first and third veins, the latter ending near the tip of the wing; fourth vein beyond the discal cell faintly indicated. Hind cross-vein rectangular to the fourth vein. Length, 3^{mm}.

One specimen, Argus Mountains, April, 1891.

Apterina polita sp. nov.

Female.—Very small, shining black, without wings and apparently without halteres. Scutellum large, flattened, trapezoidal, with four well-developed bristles. Face excavated in profile; oral margin on either side with a conspicuous bristle. Cheeks moderately broad. Clypeus retracted into the oral cavity. Antennæ short, third joint rounded, hairy, with a long, pubescent arista. Eyes bare. Front broad, with a row of orbital, proclinate bristles. Thorax with bristles. Abdomen broadly oval, depressed, with six visible segments, the second, third, and fourth of nearly equal length. Legs slender, with bristles, the middle tibiæ, at least, with a preapical bristle; first joint of the hind metatarsi short, and dilated. Front opaque, with a shining median stripe or elongated triangle; face and cheeks whitish dusted. Dorsum of thorax, scutellum and abdomen shining, the hair very short and sparse. Tip of femora, base of tibiæ, and the tarsi, save the tip, yellowish. Length $1\frac{1}{4}^{mm}$.

Three specimens, Panamint Valley, April, 1891.

Apterina is subordinated to *Borborus* by Schiner, and he may be right in doing so. The present species is in all respects a wingless *Limosina*, but that genus has no tangible differences from *Borborus* save such as are found in the neuration. A mere excresence, of a yellowish color, is all there is to be seen of the wings. I therefore locate the species, provisionally, at least, in Macquart's genus.

NOTE.—In addition to the Diptera reported upon above by Dr. Williston, the collection contains 7 species easily named which were not sent to him, nor was it thought worth while to introduce these few names into the tabulated list which precedes. They are added here, however, for the purpose of completing the report.—C. V. R.

Tabanus punctifer O. S :.......................4 ex., Panamint Valley and Death Valley.
Pantarbes capito O. S.........................1 ex., Argus Mountains.
Triodites mus O. S............................1 ex., Coso Valley.
Lordotus diversus Coq ....5 ex., Panamint Valley and Death Valley.
Ploas fenestrata O. S ....3 ex., Death Valley.
Platychirus peltatus Meig ....,.............1 ex., Argus Mountains.
Bibio hirtus Loew............................1 ex., Santa Cruz Mountains.

HEMIPTERA, HETEROPTERA OF THE DEATH VALLEY EXPEDITION.

By P. R. Uhler.

COREIDÆ.

Harmostes propinquus Dist., Biol. Cent. Amer. Hemipt., p. 168, No. 7; pl. xv, fig. 19.

A damaged specimen, of somewhat larger size than usual, was secured on the Argus Mountains in May, 1891.

BERYTINÆ.

Pronotacantha n. gen.

Form of *Parajalysus* Distant, but with long, erect, remote spines on all sides of the pronotum, those of the front border directed obliquely forwards, those of the sides pointing outwards, the posterior pair pointing backwards, and the single one on each humerus curved at tip, posterior portion of the pronotum convex, very much elevated behind, emarginated for the base of the corium. Scutellum small, flat, armed with a long slender spine. Epipleura with a short tooth beneath the base of the wing-cover. Antennæ and legs with the usual knobs at end of joints. Wing-covers flat, very much wider and longer than the abdomen, nearly spindle-shaped in outline, almost membranous and translucent throughout, the costal areole wide, crossed by a coarse diagonal vein, followed by a longer areole which is also bounded at tip by a diagonal vein which sends off a thinner vein to curve outward and bound a narrow, cuneus-like areole running to the tip of the wing-cover, behind this, extending inwardly, are four long areoles which constitute the end of the wing-cover. Abdomen a little swollen at base, narrow behind. Middle coxæ placed far back from the anterior pair, but not remote from the posterior coxæ.

P. annulata n. sp.

Pale fulvous, with the head, front, and back of the pronotum polished black. Head short, subglobose, with the tylus forming a prominent vertical ridge, bounded by swollen cheeks; eyes prominent, brown; rostrum reaching to behind the middle coxæ, dark piceous, paler on the middle and beneath. Antennæ long and slender, annulated with black, the basal joint longer than the head and pronotum united, a little thickened at tip, second joint about one-half as long as the basal, the third a little longer, the fourth joint black, pale at tip, very short and thick, fusiform but acute at both ends. Pronotum stout, broad and tumid behind, black, polished, with a broad yellow band which narrows below and extends upon the sternum, spines chiefly yellow, those of the base longer. Scutellum narrow, testaceous, armed with a long, erect, yellow spine. Legs slender, testaceous, banded with black, the femora clavate and wax-yellow at tip. Wing-covers testaceo-hyaline, almost membranous throughout, the veins delicate and a little deeper colored than the integument, those of the corium thick, brown, especially the costal one, the corium unevenly punctate, very short, triangular at tip, with the costal rib carried far beyond its tip; the membrane is much longer than the corium and extending well along its inner border, and has a series of four long and wide areoles. The cubital area is long, narrow, oblique at tip, and from it is continued a much narrower apical areolar extension, and these areas are all punctate and minutely bristly along the veins. Abdomen polished, somewhat piceous at base and tip, tinged with rufo-ferrugineous on the sides superiorly, acutely narrowing towards the tip in the male.

Length to end of abdomen, 4 ^{mm}; width of pronotum, $\frac{3}{4}$ ^{mm}. One specimen, a male, was taken on the Argus Mountains in April. This specimen has the greater portion of the veins of hemelytra pale brown. Several other specimens from different parts of Arizona have been submitted to me for examination.

This genus comes near to *Metacanthus*, but it differs widely therefrom in the venation of the wing covers. It has also close affinities with *Parajalysus* Dist., from which it differs also in venation, armature, etc.

Acanthophysa n. gen.

Apparently related to *Hoplinus* Stål., but quite abnormal by reason of the broad fusiform figure, emphasized by the upwardly inflated hemelytra, which appears semicoriaceous throughout, terminate in an acute point behind, and have the veins arranged longitudinally like ridges, and which carry series of remote, long, erect spines. Head acutely produced, conforming to the front of the pronotum, and armed each side with a series of long, anteriorly directed, almost procumbent, sharp spines. Rostrum reaching the posterior coxæ, the basal joint thick and long; antennæ long and slender, the basal joint as long as the two following united, clavate at tip, the apical joint short, fusiform, acute at tip. Pronotum subcampanuliform, flattened above, encircled and set with long, oblique spines pointing outward, the middle with a strong transverse section. Scutellum triangular, acute. Hemelytra with rows of long, remote spines on the veins, and fringed with a series on the costal and cubital border all the way to the tip; the discoidal vein closely forked, and the central areole narrow and long, acutely narrowed at tip and crossed by about three veinlets before the tip, veins minutely, remotely punctate. Legs long and slender, the femora clavate at tip, and the posterior ones shorter than the abdomen. Venter almost flat, slightly convex.

A. echinata n. sp.

Grayish white, with the legs and antennæ wax yellow, and the hemelytra marked with short, fuscous streaks on the coarse veins and a few irregular spots on the disk, bases of the spines mostly fuscous, and the head and pronotum a little fuscous in spaces; the apical joint of antennæ blackish. Head long and acute, yellowish, with a sharp spine above, and others each side, all projecting forward; rostrum yellowish; antennæ darker on the swollen tip of first joint. Pronotum moderately flat, having a dark band in front, the posterior lobe pale yellow, the basal margin almost truncated, with a short spine in the middle pointing backward, all the margins and the humeral angles armed with long, slanting spines, those of the anterior lobe longest and projecting over the head. Scutellum with the central carina and lateral raised margins ivory yellow. Legs banded with fuscous with the apex of the femora greatly swollen, piceous. Hemelytra with the spines chiefly white and directed obliquely outward and backward, the veins, especially on the disk and next the claws, interrupted with pale brown or fuscous membrane, forming an almost acuminate tip, having two approximate veinlets running throughout its length. Venter yellowish, spread with white, marked with interrupted raised longitudinal lines, a little sprinkled with fuscous, and the entire surface hispid with short bristly spines, the apex infuscated.

Length to tip of venter, $3\frac{1}{4}^{mm}$.; width of pronotum, $\frac{3}{4}^{mm}$.; width of hemelytra across the middle, $1\frac{1}{4}^{mm}$.

One specimen, a male, was secured at the Argus Mountains in April, and I have examined two other specimens which were collected near Los Angeles, Calif., by Mr. Coquillett. The costal rib is sharply raised, and is protracted to the very tip of the subcoriaceous corium; and the apexes of this corium are widely separated by a triangular interval.

This most remarkable insect might perhaps be confounded with the prickly seed vessel of some of the sand ticks or beggars' lice which grow in sandy places.

Although unquestionably a member of the family *Berytidæ*, it is the most aberrant genus of this group as yet discovered, and it helps to set forth the principle that there is a wide divergence of composition in the adjustment of the parts of the wing-covers in this remarkable group.

Lygæosoma Feib.

L. solida n. sp.

Narrow and deep, gradually narrowing from the middle of corium to the front of pronotum; the surface dull, minutely grayish, pubescent all over, black, with the corium and humeral angles and a spot on the middle of the basal margin of pronotum dull red. Head broad, convex, appearing longer from the acutely projecting tylus, each side of which the cheeks are sunken toward the antennal lobes; antennæ stout, coated with minute gray pubescence; rostrum black, piceous, reaching to behind the middle coxæ. Pronotum longer than wide, almost flat, crossed next the middle by an indistinct ridge, humeral angles tubercular. Prosternum in front and margins of the pleural segments dull yellowish. Legs polished, black, hoary pubescent. Scutellum minutely pubescent, the carinate cross acute and pale at tip. Corium and clavus a little rough, closely pubescent, with the edge next the membrane a little dusky, the costal margin curved, and the membrane dusky black; tergum polished black, venter dull black, rendered a little gray by the hoary pubescence.

Length to tip of venter, $4\frac{1}{2}^{mm}$; width of base of pronotum, $1\frac{1}{2}^{mm}$.

Two specimens, a male and a female, of the brachypterous form were secured in Mariposa County, Calif.

The membrane has an obscure pale lunule on the middle, and a very narrow whitish outer border.

Lygæus Fab.

L. melanopleurus n. sp.

Form of *histriangularis* Say, but having the pronotum a little shorter, more depressed behind the middle, and with the lateral margins a little sinuated. Color mainly dull black, rendered grayish by the close, whitish pubescence which invests both the upper and lower surface. Head stout, moderately wide, convex above, marked with a red dot next the middle of base, the front narrow, with the cheeks compressed from the antenniferous lobes downward; the rostrum piceous, black, reaching upon the posterior coxæ, antennæ black, thick, grayish, pubescent; pronotum a little wider than long, depressed, and with a few coarse, dragged punctures behind the anterior margin; callosities transverse, distinct, the surface behind them depressed, a little rough, and with a few coarse punctures; lateral margins moderately oblique, feebly sinuated before the middle, with the humeri a little raised into a longitudinal ridge, the posterior margin nearly straight and slenderly edged with yellow; scutellum a little rough, depressed behind the middle, with the tip carinate and acute. Hemelytra paler and more lead-colored than the thorax, with the costal border broadly yellowish red, the posterior border more slenderly yellow, the surface pubescent and remotely minutely punctate; membrane long, black, broadly bordered with white. Pectus black, hoary, pubescent, marked each side of line of legs with a row of pale spots. Legs black, pubescent. Venter reddish, black at tip, and with a broad blackish stripe on the side following the line of the stigmata.

Length to end of venter, $4\frac{1}{2}$ to 5^{mm}.; to tip of membrane, 6^{mm}.; width of base of pronotum, 2^{mm}.

Two specimens were obtained on the Panamint Mountains in April. It inhabits also Colorado.

Lygæosoma sp.

A specimen with robust figure and of the brachypterous form was collected in Mariposa County, Calif., but it is too greasy for description.

Pamera Say.

P. nitidula n. sp.

Dull blackish, with the head and thorax polished, chestnut brown, and the hemelytra pale testaceous, with a broad black band across the posterior part of the corium, an irregular spot near its base, and a spot at tip of cuneus, which runs back slenderly on the outer margin. Head long, subacute at tip, set with erect bristly hairs, transversely wrinkled; rostrum yellowish, slender, reaching behind the middle coxæ; antennæ pale yellow, slender, a little brown at points of articulation, the second joint as long as from the front of the eye to the pronotal stricture, the apical joint scarcely darker than the others, equally as long as the second, first and third much shorter, subequal in length. Pronotum highly polished, a little darker across the base, the anterior lobe globosely convex, much narrower than the basal lobe, having a constriction and collum in front, the latter being punctate and a little produced behind, bounded by a deeply incised line, the surface spread with some bristly hairs; posterior lobe depressed, about as wide as the length of the anterior lobe, coarsely remotely punctate, with the humeral angles callous and elevated. Legs pale yellow, the anterior femora very stout, pale chestnut brown, with the knees and teeth darker, the anterior tibiæ strongly bent, pectoral and pleural areas polished roughly and coarsely punctate and clothed with stiff pale hairs. Scutellum piceous, remotely punctate, sparingly pubescent, ridged from the middle to the tip, and with the tip pale and acute. Corium pale yellowish testaceous, darker at base, whitish at tip and on the cuneus, remotely punctate with brown in longitudinal lines, the embolium a little dusky and punctate in the crease, membrane dusky excepting the outer border, with pale veins. Venter pale reddish chestnut, dusky at base, the female with a sickle-shaped callosity running backward from the base.

Length to tip of venter 6^{mm}, to end of membrane $6\frac{1}{2}^{mm}$, width of base of pronotum $1\frac{3}{4}^{mm}$.

A single specimen (♀) was obtained in the Argus Mountains, Calif., April. I have also examined two others from Texas and New Mexico. Only females have thus far been sent to me for examination.

Crophius Stål.

C. disconotus Say. Heteropt. New Harm., p. 14, No. 6.

One specimen was collected on the Argus Mountains in May. This is *Lygæus diconotus* Say, the specific name of which is a misprint for *disconotus*, and would have been more correctly *disconotatus*.

TINGITIDÆ.

Gargaphia Stål.

G. opacula n. sp.

Oblong, ovate, with the head, breast, abdomen, basal and last joint of antennæ and base of second joint black. Head produced in front, pale beneath, the rostrum extending to the middle coxæ, having the bucculæ white and continuous, with the white raised border which bounds the whole length of the mesosternum on its sides. Pronotum tri-carinate, convex, woolly over most of the surface and sides. The short anteriorly blunt and twice-tufted bulla stands next behind the head, the surface yellowish white, with a narrow reflexed border along the curved lateral margin, the scutellum narrow and less depressed than usual; also whitish, pubescent. Legs pale rufo-testaceous, slender. Wing-covers white, with the veins a little tinged with fuscous near the tip, the exterior margin bluntly curved, regularly curved at tip, the areoles small, unusually regular in size, a double series of them occupying the costal area, but tapering off to a single series at tip, the clavus opaque, coriaceous, coarsely punctate, minutely pubescent in common with the disk of corium. Beneath dull black, minutely pubescent.

Length to end of abdomen, $2\frac{1}{2}^{mm}$.; to tip of hemelytra, 3^{mm}.; width of pronotum, 1^{mm}.

Only a single specimen of this peculiar species was secured. It was taken on the Argus Mountains in April. The prominent convexity of the pronotum with its fur-like covering of hair and narrow pronotum will serve to quickly distinguish this species from the others thus far described.

Monanthia Fab.

M. labeculata n. sp.

Form similar to that of *M. nassata* Puton, but with a shorter pronotum and smaller meshes to the hemelytra, color fuscogriseus. Head short, convex, bronze-black, closely punctate, convex, the tylus vertical, buccule large, lamelliform, whitish, coarsely pitted in common with the gula; antennæ rufous, the basal and apical joints and the base of the second joint black; rostrum piceous, reaching to between the middle coxæ. Pronotum a little darker than the hemelytra, convex, prominently lobate each side, the lobes long-oval, occupying the whole length, and divaricating posteriorly, the sunken longitudinal between them occupied by a piceous carina which is continued back to the tip of the scutellum, the surface covered with coarse sunken punctures, with short, yellowish hairs in the spaces, collum whitish, prominent in the middle, granulated and blackish piceous behind; humeri strongly convex, blackish and granulated at the faintly carinated lateral margin; beneath black, the propleuræ piceous, coarsely punctate, but the tumid pieces of the meso— and metasternum smooth. Scutellum grayish testaceous, with the baso-lateral divaricating carinæ short, piceous, granulate, confined to the outer angles, the medial carina pale testaceous except at base, the surface granulate in lines, a little punctate and minutely, remotely pubescent. Corium pale-grayish testaceous, a little tinged with bronze, remotely punctate and pubescent, studded with piceous granules, and with the discoidal vein especially prominent; blackish, bullate and uneven, the cells of the membrane usually with dusky veins, and the cross veinlets of the costal border, including those of the membrane, black, the coarse vein bordering the corium often piceous black. Venter dull black, obsoletely rostrate.

Length to tip of wing-covers, 3^{mm}; width of pronotum, 1^{mm}. Nine specimens were taken from *Pinus monophylla*, on the Argus mountains in May, 1891.

The species bears some resemblance to others of this genus common in Brazil and Central America.

Leptoypha Stål.

L. mutica Say. *Tingis mutica* Leconte Ed. Say's Writings, vol. i, p. 319.

A dozen or more specimens of this common insect were collected on the Argus mountains in April and May. I find no difference to separate these specimens from those of Texas and other parts of the United States.

CAPSIDÆ.

Hoplomachus Fieb.

H. consors n. sp.

Robust, tapering anteriorly, cinereous tinged with olive, clothed with long pile on the head and fore part of pronotum, and with shorter pubescence on the remainder of the body. Head long, conical, acute as seen from above, indented each side near the eyes, with a pale yellow or orange line on the carinate middle, running back over the pronotum and continuing to the tip of the scutellum, tylus almost vertical, bounded by deeply cut sutures, covered with pale gray pile, the middle cheeks small, prominent, black, sharply defined; rostrum pale piceous, darker and acute at tip, reaching behind the posterior coxæ, the basal joint stout, inflated at tip, longer than the throat; eyes brown, with a bullate black space beneath them, and with one or two black raised dots near the base of tylus; antennæ rather slender, reaching behind the tip of the scutellum, the basal joint and lobe piceous black, the second joint as long as from the front of eye to the base of pronotum, pale olive, darker on the ends, the two following darker, short, more slender, pronotum trapeziform, convex behind a little scabrous over most of the surface, the lateral margins oblique, sharp edged, a line of obsolete dark spots occurs across the base, in front of this each side is an oblique mark, and farther forward is a larger transverse spot each side; scutellum darker each side of basal portion; pectus dark in the depressions, the plural pieces coarsely punctate, the prosternum, including the xyphus, pale, but blackish at base; legs dusky testaceous, with the nails, tips of tarsi and spines piceous; hemelytra wide, almost translucent, closely hoary pubescent, the costal margin broadly curved, the disk and claws dusky olive, membrane pale dusky olive, venter dark olive with a fuscous tinge, finely pale pubescent, with the genital pieces paler.

Length to end of abdomen, 4^{mm}; to tip of membrane, 4½^{mm}; width of base of pronotum, 1½^{mm}.

One specimen was taken on the Argus Mountains in May. The species occurs in the vicinity of Los Angeles and in other parts of southern California.

Some five or six other new species of genera related to *Lygus*, *Macrotylus*, and *Psallus*, belong to this collection, but they are not in condition for description.

ANTHOCORIDÆ.

Anthocoris Fall.

A. musculus Say. Heteropt. New Harmony, p. 3J; No. 6.

One specimen was secured on the Argus Mountains in April.

SALDIDÆ.

Salda Fab.

1. S. interstitialis Say. Journ. Philada. Acad., vol, iv; p. 324; No. 1.

Two specimens were secured in the Panamint and Argus mountains in April. They belong to two varieties with the white spots not widely distributed.

2. S. explanata, new sp.

In form similar to *S. brachynota* Fieb,, of Europe. Deep black, dull, covered with minute golden pubescence. The head but little wider than the front of the pronotum, and the eyes moderately prominent, the clypeus margined each side and the tylus entirely testaceous; antennæ stout, black, white on the outside of the basal joint. Pronotum short, transversely wrinkled behind, the base deeply sinuated, the lateral margins oblique and a little curved, the submargin broadly, deeply depressed, remotely punctate, with the edge a little recurved, the humeral angles with the button-like callosity near the border; callosities transversely prominent, with a sunken dot in the middle between them; pleural depression coarsely and remotely punctate. Tip of femora, the tibiæ excepting the base and tip, and the tarsi excepting the tip, pale testaceous. Hemelytra obsoletely and minutely punctate, remotely pubescent, marked with whitish oblong flecks, an obsolete pair being placed near the tip of the clavus, a few minute ones from near the base to behind the middle, an angular spot next the middle of the posterior margin and a more distinct white dot exterior to this; the membrane has four long, narrow, pale areoles marked with the ordinary smoky oblong spots, and the posterior border is also smoke-brown with a white dot at the inner angle. Venter dull black, minutely pubescent, with the sixth segment of the female broadly and unevenly bordered behind with white.

Length to tip of membrane, 4½ to 5^{mm}; width of base of pronotum, 1⅞ to 3^{mm}.

This species occurs in various regions west of the Rocky Mountains. I have examined specimens taken in Nevada, Olympia, in Washington State, various parts of Utah, and California. A pair of specimens in the present collection were secured in the Panamint and Argus mountains in the month of April.

DESCRIPTIONS OF NEW SPECIES OF ORTHOPTERA FROM THE DEATH VALLEY EXPEDITION.

By LAWRENCE BRUNER.

Ameles sp.

Possibly new, but the specimen is in too bad a condition to be described, it having been broken while en route in the mail, besides being immature. This same insect has been examined by me on several former occasions. It appears to be quite widely distributed in the arid and semiarid regions of the Southwest, as I have it from various points in New Mexico, Arizona, and California. I have also seen specimens from southern Idaho and middle Nevada.

Heterogamia sp.

Like the preceding, this insect is also probably undescribed. It is a female specimen, and can not well be characterized now. This form seems to be not at all rare in some portions of Arizona and southwestern United States, and also occurs in portions of old Mexico.

Tridactylus sp.

The collection contains a specimen of an apparently undescribed species of this genus, but until I have had a little more time to study these peculiar little crickets, I would prefer not to name it. Other specimens of the genus have been taken along the Colorado River during the past summer, and have just lately come to my notice.

Nemobius sp.

This insect may also be new. I have seen specimens very similar to this from the vicinity of Los Angeles, Calif., and if represented in the collection, I can not at present find it. I will not try to describe the species from the single male before me.

Encoptolophus pallidus n. sp.

General color dull yellowish brown, varied with faint dusky markings common to the representatives of the genus. Head moderately large, a little wider than front edge of pronotum. Vertex about as wide as the eyes, depressed in front where the lateral carinæ meet in less than a right angle, these carinæ bowed and approaching slightly behind, but fading away into the sides of the occiput along the hind margin of the eyes; the sulcus quite deep and provided with a well-defined central carina posteriorly; frontal costa quite prominent above, of nearly equal width throughout, but slightly sulcate at the ocellus and below (♀), or more deeply grooved throughout (♂); antennæ not quite as long (♀) as head and pronotum combined, or slightly surpassing the latter (♂), a little enlarged and slightly flattened toward their tips in the male; pronotum small, with the sides nearly parallel when seen from above, the lateral carinæ well defined, but interrupted a little in advance of the middle carina, not prominent, equal throughout, cut a little in advance of the middle by last transverse sulcus, the hind border a little obtuse-angled. Tegmina and wings of about equal length, surpassing the tip of the abdomen in both sexes. Posterior femora not much inflated basally, but passing the tip of abdomen slightly in both sexes.

Color.—Male and female dull dry-grass color, marked faintly back of the eyes, along sides of pronotum, on front edge of tegmina and on posterior femora with the characteristic fuscous blotches and bands. Posterior wings hyaline, with the tips apparently but little darker than the disk and base. Hind tibiæ pale glaucous with basal third pale.

Length of body, ♂, 18 mm., ♀, 21 mm.; of antennæ, ♂, 7 mm., ♀, 6.5 mm.; of pronotum, ♂, 3.75 mm., ♀, 4.7 mm.; of tegmina, ♂, 15.5 mm., ♀, 19 mm.: of hind femora, ♂, 10.5 mm., ♀, 13 mm.

Habitat.—Panamint Valley, Cal., April 6, 1891.

Scirtettica occidentalis n. sp.

The collection also contains a single female specimen of locust which has the general appearance at first glance of a *Trachyrrhachys*, but upon closer examination proves to be more nearly related to *Scirtettica marmorata* Uhl. of the New England coast.

Head, with the occiput rugulose, rather small and deeply set into the front edge of the pronotum, which latter is also quite rough; vertex between the eyes a little narrower than their shortest diameter, deeply grooved and provided with a deep triangular pit in front, the lateral walls prominent and farthest apart at front edge of eyes, approaching posteriorly but not quite meeting; frontal costa deeply sulcate with the walls prominent, diverging below. Antennae not quite reaching the posterior edge of the pronotum, filiform, but gently compressed. Pronotum short, about as broad as long, strongly compressed near the front above, the median carina prominent but not arched, once severed a little in advance of the middle by the last transverse impressed line; lateral carinae obliterated in front, but prominent behind; posterior angle a right angle. Tegmina and wings extending slightly beyond the tips of the abdomen, the former rather narrow. Hind femora with the base a little inflated; hind tibiae with the apical spines strong and longer than usual. Entire insect more or less thickly clothed with short whitish hairs.

General color, grayish brown mottled and specked with plain brown and dull black. Middle of sides of pronotum with a short oblique whitish blotch. Tegmina with a median and postbasal brown spot on costal edge, apical third and posterior half irregularly flecked with quadrate flecks of varying sizes. Wings with disklike waxy yellow, crossed just beyond the middle by a dull, rather narrow fuscous band that sends a dark ray nearly to the base along the costal edge, apex hyaline with two or three small fuscous spots along the principal veins. Posterior femora crossed above by three blackish bands, the middle one showing on the outer face as a very oblique band, anteriorly with the basal half black, beyond this with a yellow and then a black band, the knees dusky; hind tibiae yellowish, infuscated apically and provided with an obscure dusky annulus near the basal third.

Length of body, ♀, 20^{mm}.; of antennae, 6^{mm}.; of pronotum, 4^{mm}.; of tegmina, 19^{mm}.; of hind femora, 12.25^{mm}.

Habitat.—A single specimen from Argus Mountains, Calif., May, 1891.

This insect does not properly fall in this genus, but appears to approach the members belonging here more closely than it does any of the other forms known to me, and for that reason is placed here, for the present at least.

Dracotettix plutonius n. sp.

A smaller species than the *D. monstrosus*, with a much lower median pronotal carina and the vertex shorter and more depressed.

Vertex between the eyes about as wide (♂), or a little wider than the shortest diameter of the eyes, shallowly sulcate throughout and divided into longitudinal halves by a rather prominent median carina, most marked behind, the lateral edges raised so as to form low walls; frontal costa of nearly equal width throughout, quite prominent to just below the ocellus; below this point the face is perpendicular; antennae short, heavy, slightly broadened and flattened near the base, bluntly pointed. Pronotum in front a little wider than the head, the dorsum somewhat flattened, with the lateral carinae evenly divergent posteriorly, nearly as prominent as the median, which has its lobes rounded, anterior margin obtuse-angled, the posterior acute-angled. Tegmina and wings abbreviated, acute, the inner margins not quite touching in the female, and but very slightly overlapping in the male, reaching past the back edge of the third abdominal segment in the former and nearly to the base of the supra-anal plate in the latter. Prosternal spine quite large, rounded behind, straight or slightly concave in front and very bluntly pointed.

The general color of this insect is dull grayish brown, the lighter color inclining to testaceous in the female and whitish in the male. Face, pronotum and tegmina, with the hind femora streaked with white (♂) or dirty yellowish white (♀). Hind femora crossed above with three fuscous and three lighter bands, the inner face for the most part black. Hind tibiæ and tarsi reddish on inner edges, gray outside. Antennæ infuscated on apical half.

Length of body, ♂, 19^{mm}., ♀, 39^{mm}.; of antennæ, ♂, 6.5^{mm}.; ♀ 8^{mm}.; of vertex, ♂, 1.3^{mm}., ♀, 2.1^{mm}.; of pronotum, ♂. 8^{mm}., ♀, 12.30^{mm}.; of tegmina, ♂, 8.5^{mm}., ♀, 13^{mm}.; of hind femora, ♂, 10.75^{mm}., ♀, 15.2^{mm}.

Habitat.—Panamint Valley, April, and Argus Mountains, May, 1891.

Other representatives of the genus Dracotettix have been taken in Arizona, at Los Angeles, in Napa County, and at Gilroy, Calif. Among the material thus gathered at least three well-defined species are represented.

REPORT ON THE LAND AND FRESH-WATER SHELLS COLLECTED IN CALIFORNIA AND NEVADA BY THE DEATH VALLEY EXPEDITION, INCLUDING A FEW ADDITIONAL SPECIES OBTAINED BY DR. C. HART MERRIAM AND ASSISTANTS IN PARTS OF THE SOUTHWESTERN UNITED STATES.

By ROBT. E. C. STEARNS, Ph. D.,
Adjunct Curator of the Department of Mollusks, U. S. National Museum.

The present report treats of the land and fresh-water shells collected in 1891 by the several subdivisions of the Death Valley Expedition, in southern California and Nevada, between latitude 34° and latitude 38° N. The routes followed by several of these parties led them into regions previously unexplored by naturalists, and specimens were secured from numerous thermal and mineral springs in the arid deserts of the southern part of the Great Basin, within the Colorado drainage area. The most interesting forms obtained were the two species heretofore referred to *Tryonia*, until recently regarded as obsolescent or absolutely extinct, but which were found to be living, as elsewhere remarked. *Helix magdalenensis*, another interesting species described from examples collected in the Mexican State of Sonora in 1889–'90 by Mr. Bailey, of Dr. Merriam's Division of Biological Exploration, was detected by Fisher and Nelson several degrees of latitude farther to the north than the habitat of Bailey's original examples and at a very much higher altitude. This latter, by its presence at this northerly station, contributes to our previous knowledge and data bearing upon the relations between the geographical distribution of species and environmental conditions or influences; and two fresh-water forms, not before known, were added to the molluscan fauna of the region traversed by the expedition.

In addition to the desert material, small collections were made in the High Sierra and other parts of California, and a few species are included from Arizona, New Mexico, and Texas, collected by Dr. C. Hart Merriam and assistants, while engaged in biological surveys of these regions under the Department of Agriculture. This latter material is important, as illustrating the geographical distribution of the species concerned.

LIST OF SHELLS.

Glandina decussata.
 singleyana.
 texasiana.
Streptostyla sololensis.
Limax campestris.
Patula striatella.
Helix (Arionta) magdalenensis.
 coloradoënsis.
 mormonum.
 indicntata.
 cypreophila.
 arrosa.
 (*Praticola*) *griseola.*
  berlandieriana.
 (*Mesodon*) *thyroides.*
 (*Polygyra*) *texasiana.*
  bicruris.
Pupa (*Vertigo*) *pentodon.*
Bulimulus dealbatus.
 alternatus.
 serperastrus.
Succinea luteola.
 oregonensis.
Limnæa caperata.

Limnæa nuttalliana.
 humilis.
 bulimoides.
Planorbis lentus.
 liebmanni.
 parrus
 trivolvis.
Physa gyrina.
 heterostropha.
Carinifex newberryi.
Amnicola micrococcus, sp. nov.
 porata.
Tryonia clathrata.
Fluminicola fusca.
 merriami.
 fusca minor.
 nuttalliana.
Helicina chrysocheila.
 tropica.
Anodonta nuttalliana.
Unio anodontoides.
 berlandieri.
Pisidium occidentale.

Class GASTROPODA.

Order PULMONATA.

Suborder GEOPHILA.

Glandina decussata Pfr.

Hidalgo, Tamaulipas, Mexico (Mus. No. 123571), William Lloyd, March, 1891.

 These examples, three in number, are not decussated, but are sculptured *only* by the longitudinal incremental lines; they have the usual glossy or semipolished surface characteristic of the group. These specimens are rather between the variety *singleyana* and the typical *decussata*, and indicate what is exhibited in other related forms, conspicuously in the shells of *G. truncata* of Florida, a considerable range of variation.

Glandina singleyana W. G. B.
 ? = *G. decussata* Pfr., variety.

Hidalgo, Tamaulipas, Mexico (Mus. No. 123572); also Monterey, Mexico (Mus. No. 123906), Feb., 1891, William Lloyd.

 Two examples very close to *G. texasiana*, the principal difference being the curve and form of the termination of the columella. This seems to be the form that Mr. Binney refers to as collected by Prof. Wetherby in Bexar County, Tex., which he figures and calls *decussata* var. *singleyana* in Bull. Mus. Comp. Zoöl., Vol. XXII, No. 4, Pl. 1, Fig. 4, pp. 163–203.

Glandina texasiana Pfr.
Brownsville, Tex. (Mus. No. 123573), William Lloyd.

Two specimens. An ample series of the above, and the west Mexican *G. albersi* of the same author, might result in the reduction of the first to a synonymous position.

Streptostyla sololensis C. & F.
Victoria, Tamaulipas, Mexico (Mus. No. 123574), William Lloyd, March 30, 1891.

"In the Sierra." Though both examples are dead, and one broken, they are sufficient to validate the above determination. The species was described by Crosse and Fisher from Sololo (Guatemala) specimens.

Limax campestris Binney.
South Fork of Kern River, California (Mus. No. 123575), Vernon Bailey, July 8, 1891.

At an elevation of 2,700 feet; a single example. This may be Ingersoll's *L. montanus* or a variety thereof, which he obtained in Colorado. Ingersoll's *montanus* and *montanus* var. *castaneus*, Binney's *ingersolli* and Heynemann's *wienlandi* may be regarded, or at least strongly suspected, of close relationship to Binney's *campestris*, which latter may perhaps include Cooper's *L.* var. *occidentalis*.

Patula striatella Anth.
Kern River region, California (Mus. No. 123577), Vernon Bailey.

Numerous living examples at an altitude of 2,700 feet.

Helix (Arionta) magdalenensis Stearns.
Johnson Cañon, Panamint Mountains, California (Mus. No. 123578), April 11, 1891, Dr. A. K. Fisher; also additional specimens in the same region (Mus. No. 123579), April 18, 1891, Dr. Fisher and E. W. Nelson.

The foregoing species was described by me in the Proc. U. S. National Museum, Vol. XIII, pp. 207–208, from a few examples collected at or near the town of Magdalena, State of Sonora, Mexico, November 6, 1889, by Mr. Vernon Bailey. He detected it on a hill or mountain at an elevation of about 1,000 feet above the town. The latitude of Magdalena is about 31° N. The investigations of the Death Valley Expedition have carried it far to the north of the above, to the Panamint region of California, where both Dr. Fisher and Mr. Nelson obtained numerous living individuals. This discovery extends the area of the distribution of *H. magdalenensis* northerly between six and seven degrees of latitude. The place where these specimens were found in Johnson Cañon has an elevation of about 6,000 feet above the sea; the first lot (No. 123578) were mostly bleached shells. The Fisher-Nelson series (No. 123579) subsequently collected, is from a still higher elevation, viz, 8,000 feet: here twenty-five living examples were obtained, most of them mature. The Mexican locality may ultimately prove to be about the southerly limit of its distribution.

Helix (Arionta) coloradoensis Stearns.
Resting Springs, California (Mus. No. 123907), Vernon Bailey, February 12, 1891.

A single example, either alive when collected or quite fresh, was detected by Mr. Bailey, who found it among rocks on a dry hill 900 feet above the springs. It is nearly white, with the single band quite pale. This gives another locality to the above species, first found in the Grand Cañon of the Colorado, opposite the Kaibab plateau at an elevation of 3,500 feet, by Dr. C. Hart Merriam in 1890. The Resting Springs locality is in the southeastern part of Inyo County.

Helix (Arionta) mormonum Pfr.

Mineral King, Tulare County, Calif. (Mus. No. 123580), September 10, 1891, Vernon Bailey.

The single fresh specimen, hardly mature, was found among rocks about 1,000 feet below the timber line, above the Empire mine.

Helix (Arionta) tudiculata W. G. B.

Three Rivers, Tulare County, Calif. (Mus. No. 123581), T. S. Palmer, July 27, 1891.

Three specimens, one a fine living example, found at a point 850 feet above the sea. These illustrate the trifling value that should be given to the umbilical character in many of the land shells. The specimens from which the author wrote his description were *imperforate*, while the best example of Palmer's has an entirely open umbilicus, the same as many other individuals that I have observed before. A large series will be seen to run from one extreme to the other, the variability of this feature being the constant factor, paradoxical as it may appear.

Helix (Arionta) cypreophila Newc.

?=*H. tudiculata* W. G. B., variety.

Three Rivers, Tulare County, Calif. (Mus. No. 123582), July 27, 1891. T. S. Palmer.

Two examples, probably whole and fresh if not living at the time they were collected, were detected by Mr. Palmer in the above region, at an elevation of 850 feet. Dr. Newcomb's specimens were found at or near Copperopolis, in Calaveras County, Calif. Binney regards it as a variety of *tudiculata*; it may be so. It is, however, so rare that I have never seen specimens enough to enable me to come to a conclusion. Mr. Palmer's examples, though imperfect, conspicuously exhibit the characters that separate it from *tudiculata*. Perhaps a large series of specimens might satisfactorily connect the two. The dentition and genitalia have been investigated and were found by Mr. Binney to be the same as in *tudiculata*. Judging by the Palmer shell it is, to say the least, a decidedly well-marked variety.

Helix (Arionta) arrosa Gould.

Boulder Creek, Santa Cruz County, Calif. (Mus. No. 123583), Vernon Bailey, October, 1891.

A single example, which may be regarded either as a dwarfed *arrosa* or an elevated form of *exarata*; the latter is probably a geographical aspect of *arrosa*; Hemphill catalogues *exarata* as a variety of *arrosa*.

Helix (Praticola) griseola Pfr.

Hidalgo, Tamaulipas (Mus. No. 123584), and Monterey, Mexico (Mus. No. 123908), February, 1891; also Brownsville, Tex. (Mus. No. 123585), William Lloyd, July, 1891.

The three Texas shells are fine, broadly banded examples and dark colored; the others of the general or usual aspect.

Helix (Praticola) berlandieriana Mor.
Nueces Bay, San Patricio County (Mus. No. 123586), December, 1891, and Matagorda Peninsula, Texas (Mus. No. 123587). January 30, 1892, William Lloyd.

Numerous examples from the former and two from the latter locality.

Helix (Mesodon) thyroides Say.
Natividad River, Texas (Mus. No. 123588), William Lloyd, January 1, 1892.

Four fine specimens, one immature; two with a small parietal tooth, all of a dark amber horn color, and lustrous glazing. These beautiful examples, while fully as elevated as the larger of the three figures (337) in Binney's Manual of American Land Shells, Bull. U. S. National Museum, No. 28, p. 315 (*M. bucculentus*), are somewhat larger and slightly angulated at the periphery. The umbilicus is covered, peristome moderately thick, size of shell considered. These are links in the chain of connection of the typical *thyroides* with the *bucculentus* aspect.

Helix (Polygyra) texasiana Mor.
Natividad River, Texas (Mus. No. 123589), William Lloyd, Janunary 4, 1892.

Two examples of this somewhat puzzling group. A comparison of Bland's *triodontoides* and Pfeiffer's *bicruris* creates the suspicion that a large geographical series might result in placing two of the three species in the waste basket of synonymy.

Helix (Polygyra) bicruris Pfr.
Brownsville, Tex. (Mus. No. 123594); Mouth of Rio Grande, Texas. (Mus. No. 123168). William Lloyd.

Two examples, mature and perfect, from the first and one from the last named locality. Heretofore credited to Mexico.

Pupa (Vertigo) pentodon Say.
Vegas Valley, Lincoln County, Nev. (Mus. No. 123590), Vernon Bailey, March 7, 1891.

The dozen or more examples of this tiny shell were detected by Mr. Bailey at Cottonwood Springs at the east base of the Charleston Mountains, otherwise known as the Spring Mountain range, of which the principal elevation is called Charleston Peak. The region is in the most southern part of Nevada. This species has not before been detected so far to the west or anywhere within the vast area of the Great Basin or the Pacific States.

Bulimulus dealbatus Say.
Monterey, Mexico (Mus. No. 123909), William Lloyd, February, 1891.

Four characteristic examples, mature and immature; dead shells.

Bulimulus alternatus Say.
Hidalgo, Tamaulipas, Mexico (Mus. No. 123592); Brownsville (Mus. No. 123691); and Nueces Bay, San Patricio County, Tex. (Mus. No. 123593), William Lloyd, December, 1891.

The four Mexican specimens are very fine examples of this species and well illustrate the propriety of Say's specific name. The alternation of the irregular, somewhat diaphanous, longitudinal bands with others of a more opaque aspect is quite striking. The examples from the Texan localities are of the ordinary aspect.

Bulimulus serperastrus Say.

Hidalgo, Tamaulipas, Mexico (Mus. No. 123595), William Lloyd.

Three good examples of this pretty species, the largest 25^{mm} long. Like other species of the group, it varies considerably. Some individuals are much slenderer than others; hence, quite likely, the following synonyms from Binney's Land and Fresh Water Shells of North America (Part I, fig. 335, p. 192):

> *Bulimus liebmanni* Pfr.
> *Bulimus ziebmanni* Rve.
> *Bulimus nitelinus* Rve.

I agree with Binney; he is no doubt correct in the above inclusion. Perhaps the *californicus* of Reeve, Conch. Icon., 378, is a geographical aspect of *serperastrus*.

Succinea luteola Gould.

Hidalgo, Mexico (Mus. No. 123596), William Lloyd.

Three examples of fresh specimens.

Succinea oregonensis Lea.

Kern River, California (Mus. No. 123597), Vernon Bailey.

The four living examples were detected by Mr. Bailey at an elevation of 2,700 feet.

Suborder *HYGROPHILA*.

Limnæa caperata Say.

Ash Meadows, Nevada (Mus. No. 123598), Dr. A. K. Fisher.

Numerous specimens, all dead and bleached. Some of these are moderately angulated on the upper part of the basal whorl following the suture; others strongly malleated; all of them are rather solid, and the surface in many instances nearly smooth; in some examples the incremental lines are sharply defined; in one the basal whorl is quite shouldered above and malleated below, with hints of interrupted threadlike keels (liræ), on the same whorl near the columella. Cooper (Geog. Cat. No. 348) credits this species to 'S. F. to Oregon,' 'Eastern States.' Hemphill includes it (No. 91) in his little catalogue of the land and fresh water shells of Utah. Call credits it living to 'Warm Springs Lake' in the Bonneville Basin, Bull. U. S. Geol. Survey, No. 11, 1884. My remarks relating to *Limnæa palustris* in Proc. U. S. National Museum, Vol. XIV, 1891, are also applicable to the foregoing species.

Limnæa nuttalliana Lea.

=*L. palustris* Mull., var.

Panamint Valley, California (Mus. No. 123599), Dr. C. Hart Merriam.

Several examples with an unusually acute drawn-out spire; the largest a nearly typical *nuttalliana*; nevertheless, this, like many other so-called species of *Limnæa*, is but a local expression or variety of the world-wide *palustris*.

Attention is called to my remarks under *Limnæa lepida* of the previous year's collection (1890), in Proc. U. S. National Museum, Vol. XIV, 1891.

Limnæa humilis Say.
Kelton, Utah Territory (Mus. No. 123600), Vernon Bailey, November 7, 1891.

One specimen in the "dry clay wash, about 100 feet above the level of the lake."

Limnæa bulimoides Lea.
Mohave River, near Daggett, Mohave Desert, San Bernardino County, Calif. (Mus. No. 123910), Dr. C. Hart Merriam, March 31, 1891.

Six examples of this rather rare form, all dead and bleached. Described by the late Dr. Lea, in 1841, from examples collected by Nuttall in Oregon. Since found at many places in the Pacific States and in the Yellowstone region by Hayden's Survey.

Planorbis lentus Say.
Ash Meadows, Nevada (Mus. No. 123601), F. Stephens, March 2, 1891. Same region (Mus. No. 123602), Dr. A. K. Fisher, March 15, 1891. Panamint Valley, California (Mus. No. 123603), Dr. C. Hart Merriam. Brownsville, Tex. (Mus. No. 123604), William Lloyd.

Only a few examples of the above are mature or full grown; these, though of rather rude growth compared with specimens from more southerly and less arid regions, are much closer to what Say describes as *lentus* than to his *trivolvis*.

Planorbis liebmanni Dkr.
Hidalgo, Tamaulipas, Mexico (Mus. No. 123606), William Lloyd, March, 1891.

Numerous examples of this easily recognizable species.

Planorbis parvus Say.
Mohave River near Daggett, Mohave Desert, San Bernardino County, Calif. (Mus. No. 123911), Dr. C. Hart Merriam, March 31, 1891.

Three examples, bleached.

Planorbis trivolvis Say.
Fresno, Calif. (Mus. No. 123605), Vernon Bailey, September 22, 1891. Keeler, Calif. (Mus. No. 123615), T. S. Palmer, June 1, 1891. Daggett, Calif. (Mus. No. 123912), Dr. C. Hart Merriam, March 31, 1891.

Mr. Bailey's Fresno shells were collected by him in an irrigation ditch. The specimens, of which there are several, were found living. None of them are adult, being most of them but half grown; at this stage they might be labeled *P. tumens* Cpr. Palmer's Inyo County examples are dead shells, none adult, being about the same age as Bailey's. All of the above are simply young *trivolvis*. Dr. Merriam's locality is in the Mohave Desert, near the river of the same name, in San Bernardino County. Some of the examples are nearly typical *trivolvis*, others exhibit the *corpulentus* aspect. In both the growth lines are quite conspicuous. The latter are listed herein as *P. trivolvis* var. (Mus. No. 123913.)

Physa gyrina Say.

Hot Springs, Panamint Valley, California (Mus. No. 123607), April 22, 1891; also Pahranagat Valley, Nevada (Mus. No. 123608), May 25, 1891; Daggett, Mohave Desert, California, March 31, 1891 (Mus. No. 123914), Dr. C. Hart Merriam. Garlick Springs, San Bernardino County, Cal. (Mus. No. 123609), March 14, 1891; Resting Springs, Inyo County, February 9, 1891 (Mus. No. 123916); Keeler, Inyo County, Calif. (Mus. No. 123610), June 1, 1891; Gorman Station, 8 miles south of Fort Tejon, Cal., July 2, 1891 (Mus. No. 123611), T. S. Palmer. Kern River, California (Mus. No. 123612), and Fairfield, Utah (Mus. No. 123613), June 25, 1890, Vernon Bailey. Hidalgo, Tamaulipas, Mexico (Mus. No. 123614); Monterey, Mexico (Mus. No. 123915), William Lloyd.

Dr. Merriam's Hot Springs examples of the above are fine large dark-colored shells; they vary considerably in elevation of spire. In the shorter spired individuals there is a tendency to tabulation or flattening of the upper part of the body whorl, following the suture, suggesting the shouldered aspect of *Physa humerosa*, a common form on the surface of the Colorado Desert. His Pahranagat Valley lot are paler and more elongated, with a higher and more acute spire, suggestive of *P. hypnorum*.

Palmer's Garlick Springs shells are nearer the typical form; taken as a whole, in size, color, and general facies; some of them hint of Tryon's species *diaphana*, a local varietal aspect of *gyrina*, found in the neighborhood of San Francisco Bay. His Keeler examples, from the shores of Owens Lake, are few in number; two of these are over rather than of the usual size, and two are hardly adult; all are characteristic, form considered. The Gorman Station lot, of which there is a large number, also collected by Palmer, at a point 8 miles south of Fort Tejon, are exceedingly uniform in size, color, and proportions; they are all adults, of medium size, rather slenderer on the whole than the typical form, but not as slender as Merriam's Pahranagat examples. Bailey's five specimens from the South Fork of Kern River, at an elevation of 2,700 feet, are apparently adults of a dwarfed form, less than half the size of average typical adults; his Fairfield specimens were found in a spring. At the first Mexican locality Mr. Lloyd found a single individual; at Monterey, seven specimens; these latter exhibit the modifications in texture, solidity, etc., which so frequently characterize northerly forms of this and allied groups, where the distribution extends into southerly or warmer regions.

Physa heterostropha Say.

Bennett Spring, Meadow Valley, Nevada (Mus. No. 123616), Dr. C. Hart Merriam, May 20, 1891. Owens Valley, Inyo County, Calif. (Mus. No. 123617), F. Stephens, July 7, 1891. Hot Springs, Panamint Valley, California (Mus. No. 123618), Vernon Bailey, January 9, 1891. Brownsville, Tex. (Mus. No. 123619), William Lloyd.

Dr. Merriam's Bennett Spring shells were found by him at a point 7 miles west of Meadow Creek, at an elevation of 6,000 feet; they range from adolescent to mature, the largest being rather under than up to the usual adult mean. Stephens' specimens are all of one size, under rather than up to the average mean of adults, and of that perplexing aspect so frequently exhibited in the fresh-water snails, that make the use of one specific name instead of another simply an arbitrary matter. They would pass as subspecies of the above, or *gyrina*. The numerous examples were detected at Moran's, near Benton, Calif., at an altitude of 5,000 feet. Bailey's Panamint Hot Springs specimens are hardly more characteristic; they point suggestively to the *humerosa* form, of the Colorado desert. Lloyd's two Texas examples are dark amber colored and rather solid shells.

Carinifex newberryi Lea.
Keeler, Inyo County, Calif. (Mus. No. 123620), T. S. Palmer.

Numerous examples, in a bleached and semi-fossilized condition. These exhibit, as is not unusual with this form, considerable variation. As additional information comes to us from time to time, the great range of this species, first detected by Dr. J. S. Newberry, in the Klamath Lake region of northern California, near the Oregon line, and described by Dr. Lea in 1858, becomes exceedingly instructive and interesting. Hemphill collected it living in the neighborhood of Keeler, which is near the margin of Owens Lake, several years ago. Dr. Edward Palmer obtained it in Utah Territory, near Utah Lake, in the Wahsatch Mountains, and it has been found in the Tertiaries of Nevada (King's Survey). "In the Lahontan Basin it ranges from the shores of Walker's Lake, north to Button's Ranch, Christmas Lakes, Oregon, where it is found semi-fossil" [Call]. Utah Lake is the easternmost locality as yet known.

Order PROSOBRANCHIATA.

Suborder *PECTINIBRANCHIATA*.

Section TAENIOGLOSSA.

Amnicola micrococcus Pilsbry, sp. nov.

Shell minute, globose, with short conic spire and narrow umbilicus. Whorls $3\frac{2}{3}$, convex, especially below the sutures, the apex very obtuse. Surface smooth, light olive colored. Aperture ovate, about half the length of the entire shell, bluntly angled above; the inner lip is either free from the preceding whorl, or in contact only at the upper part. Alt. 1.5, diam. 1.3^{mm}.

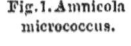
Fig. 1. Amnicola micrococcus.

A smaller species than *A. granum* Say, with oval instead of round aperture and shorter spire.

Type from small spring in Oasis Valley, Nevada (Mus. No. 123622), Dr. C. Hart Merriam, June, 1891. Collected also in Death Valley by Nelson and Bailey, February 4, 1891 (Mus. No. 123901).

Several examples of this quite minute shell were detected in a small spring. This is a form not heretofore observed and an exceedingly interesting little species. It was referred to Mr. Pilsbry for determination and description.

Amnicola porata Say.
Kelton, Utah (Mus. No. 123625), Vernon Bailey, November 7, 1891.

Two examples in the dry clay wash about 100 feet above the lake.

Bythinella protea Gould (Stearns).
  = *Amnicola protea* Gould, 1855.*
  = *Melania exigua* Conrad, 1855.
  = *Tryonia protea* Binney et auct.
  + *Bythinella seemani* Frau. (Pilsbry).
  = *Hydrobia seemani* Frau. 1863.†

Saratoga Springs, Death Valley (Mus. No. 123905); January 30, 1891, E. W. Nelson; February 4, 1891, Vernon Bailey.

Several hundred living specimens were obtained at the springs by Mr. Nelson and a large number in a marsh near the springs by Mr. Bailey. Associated with them were a few examples of *Amnicola micrococcus* Pilsbry before mentioned.

In explanation of the foregoing synonymy it should be stated that *Bythinella protea* is an exceedingly variable form, including examples that have a perfectly smooth surface, and others that are variously sculptured. In all, whether sculptured or otherwise, *the apex whorls are smooth.* The smooth form, like those referred to below, has the appearance in every respect of an attenuated, slender drawn out *Bythinella*, like *nickliniana*, described by the late Dr. Lea in 1839, and it, *protea*, may ultimately be regarded as belonging to Lea's species.

B. seemani as identified by Mr. Pilsbry appears to be the smooth variety or aspect of Gould's *Tryonia protea* (=*Melania exigua* Conrad).

Frauenfeld's description is based upon examples from Durango, Mexico. The National Museum contains a number of specimens from Andocutira in the State of Michoacan, Mexico, from the bed of an ancient lake. These latter are no doubt the same as the Durango shells; they are perfectly smooth, of a porcellaneous whiteness and texture, and in no way different from the smooth form of *B. protea*, with which they have been repeatedly and carefully compared. The Michoacan region is nearly 1,800 miles south of the Colorado desert.

The granulose form or variety agreeing with figs. 141 and 142 of Binney,‡ was detected near the line of the Southern Pacific Railroad in June, 1888, by Mr. C. R. Orcutt, of San Diego. He found them living in pools at Indian or Fish Springs, some 15 miles northwest of the station on said road, known as Salton. The pools, of which there are several, varying from 10 to 20 feet across, are situated at the base of the San Jacinto range of mountains. They are only a few feet deep and are

---
* Pacific Railroad Reports, v, 1855, p. 332.
† Verhandlungen der k. k. zoologisch-botanischen Gesellschaft in Wien, Jahrgang 1863, p. 1025.
‡ See Land and Fresh Water Shells of North America, Smithsonian Misc. Collections 144, Sept. 1865, p. 72.

surrounded and shaded by tules. The water is warm; in Mr. Orcutt's judgment not under 100° F., and tastes like the water of the Dos Palmas Spring, 6 miles north of Salton on the opposite side of the desert, at the base of the Chuckawalla or Lizard Mountains. "An analysis of the Dos Palmas Spring water gives slight traces of alum, soda and sulphur and shows that considerable salt is held in solution, but it is not too salt for use. These springs are all below the present sea level about 100 feet, judging from the fact that Salton lying in the depression between Dos Palmas and Indian Springs, is reported to be 250 feet below sea level from actual measurements." Specimens from this place kindly presented by Mr. Orcutt* are contained in the National Museum (No. 104886).

Mr. Pilsbry remarks as to *B. seemani*, "it is indeed much like a smooth *Tryonia*. I wonder whether the *Tryonias* are not simply examples of this, isolated in a gradually evaporating basin, becoming more and more saline! However this may be, the shells you submitted to me for my determination are the real *seemani*."

Gould's name *protea* is eminently appropriate; besides the smooth form herein discussed and inclusively regarded as the same as Frauenfeld's, and Orcutt's Indian Springs granulose examples, we find other varietal aspects and the sculpture varying between faint or barely discernible, to moderately defined or conspicuous. Sometimes the shells are shouldered or angulated on the upper side of the whorls, often traversed spirally by slender liræ or threads, and these again modified by longitudinal ribs or costæ. And the proportions of the shells in shape also vary exceedingly; sometimes drawn out, elongated, attenuated, and slender, again short and robust. The mouth smaller or larger; the whorls varying in convexity and all of these aspects of sculpture and form, are seen, when hundreds of specimens are examined, to intergrade or blend together in a greater or less degree. Occasionally there is an example that hints of Stimpson's *elathrata*, but I have not thus far been able to connect the two forms. Again referring to Mr. Pilsbry's note, writing of *seemani* he says "it is no doubt a *Bythinella*† related quite closely to our *niekliniana*."

Without here considering the niceties of generic distinction between *Hydrobia*‡ (in which Frauenfeld placed his species *seemani*), and *Bythinella*, it will readily occur to the reader, that a form so variable, would be likely in some phase of its variation to closely approach if not absolutely and inseparably resemble individuals of other species belonging to more or less intimately related, though geographically widely separated groups.

*See Orcutt's notes in West American Scientist, September, 1888, and May, 1889.

†Agreeing with Mr. Pilsbry on this point, it will be seen that I have adopted the generic name, *Bythinella*, for Dr. Gould's species.

‡*Vide* Stimpson's Researches upon the Hydrobiinæ, etc., Smithsonian Misc. Coll., 201, August, 1865.

The suggestion that arises from the study of the forms above reviewed, and the regions and conditions to which they are related, point to the causes that induce variation, and to the permanency of species and genera, or to the mutability of the same, as dependent on environmental factors, forces, or conditions. If we are warranted in assuming or to indulge in the speculation, that with volume of water ample or *maximum* and *chemical proportions as related to volume minimum* our *Tryonias* would be smooth; and that the smooth form that so largely prevails or dominates in the various species of the *Bythinellas* and related groups is in a conventional sense of the word, normal, then we may reasonably assume that upon the reversal of these conditions which are environmental and apparently fundamental, with volume of *water mimimum* and with *chemical proportions as related to volume of water maximum*, these phenomena of variation may be attributed, because they are so generally coincident with the latter or alternative character of the environment, though temperature conditions probably have more or less influence.*

At times, no doubt, the flow of water from the springs where these forms occur is comparatively excessive, and there follows a limited local extension of distribution or occupancy in the immediate region, equal to the area covered by the overflow. With the decline of the waters and the evaporation or drying up that follows, the larger areas are inhabitable for awhile, as the mollusks of this general group possess remarkable vitality, and can live for a long time away from, or without water, in damp mud, by burying themselves below the surface.

The soil or mud in the immediate region of alkaline or saline springs, through repeated overflow and evaporation, becomes supersaturated with the bitter chemicals, and it would seem that in course of time these conditions might play some part in inducing variation in the progeny of those individuals that possessed sufficient vitality to survive or to adapt themselves to these conditions. In many places, it is not unreasonable to suppose that such or similar conditions are an ever-present and operative influence within the environment.

I have heretofore† called attention to the remarkable variation exhibited by the pond snails, *Physa*, of the Colorado Desert, so abundant in and around Indio. In these the sculptural feature has no part, but the forms present not only the normal aspect of several well-known species, but the varietal phases, furnish connecting links between them, as well as extraordinary extremes to the extent of distortion.

Now these alternations of conditions are exactly what have occurred within the vast area, in various places of which, these forms occur.

No doubt there are many other springs still living (flowing) within the general region that await examination. The territory inhabited by Gould's species includes not only the localities from whence Merriam,

---

*In this connection see Call's interesting and able paper "On the Quaternary and Recent Mollusca of the Great Basin," etc., Bull. 11, U. S. Geol. Survey, 1884.

†Am. Naturalist, October, 1883, pp. 1011–1020.

Nelson, Bailey, and Orcutt collected living examples, but places still farther north, in the Great Basin so-called; for certain forms collected by Dr. Yarrow* in 1872 on the shores of Sevier Lake, middle Utah, though unfortunately few in number and somewhat weathered, were regarded by the late Mr. Tryon, to whom the specimens were submitted, as "a representative of the genus *Tryonia*," and are referable to no other form. (Mus. No. 73960.)

In course of time living specimens from new localities may come to our knowledge, as they have within the past five years, since Orcutt led the way with his Indian Springs collection, and it may be found, that in springs where the water is comparatively permanent in volume and sweet, the smooth form prevails, and *vice versa*, so far as quantity and quality of water and the matter of shell characters. Information on these points is now what is wanted.

Tryonia clathrata Stimpson.
Pahranagat Valley, Nevada (Mus. No. 123,621), Dr. C. Hart Merriam, May 25, 1891.

This is the veritable form described by the late Dr. William Stimpson in February, 1865, from the dead bleached specimens collected by Prof. William P. Blake on the surface of the Colorado Desert, while connected with one of the Pacific Railroad surveys, nearly forty years ago. Prof. Blake found it together with other small fresh-water gastropod shells, including Gould's *Amnicola protea*. Subsequently Gen. Carlton collected several examples of *T. clathrata* while on his way east with his command in 1861–'62, but in neither case is the exact locality of Blake's or Carlton's specimens stated. In neither of the lots collected by them were there any living examples; all were of a porcelaneous whiteness, the same as the innumerable bleached specimens of the more common *protea-exigua* form, that are spread over the surface of the desert. Of the thousands of these latter that I have received and collected along the line of the Southern Pacific Railroad, not a single example of *clathrata* has rewarded me for the time expended in the effort to find a specimen by the subsequent examination of the material from this part of the desert. Dr. Merriam's find indicates a more easterly and less southerly distribution for *clathrata*, and quite likely it may prove to be less abundant than its ally. Dr. Merriam's examples were found in a hot spring; the temperature of the water as noted being 97° F.

Fluminicola fusca Hald.
Kelton, Utah Territory (Mus. No. 123623), Vernon Bailey, November 7, 1891.

Five semifossilized examples were detected in the dry wash of a clay bank at an elevation of about 100 feet above the lake.

Fluminicola merriami Pilsbry and Beecher. †

"Shell small, globose-turbinate, narrowly but distinctly and deeply umbilicated. Spire low-conic, acute; whorls four, slightly shouldered

---
*U. S. Geol. Survey, W. of the 100th Meridian, vol. v, p. 948.
†The Nautilus, vol. v, April 1892, p. 143.

below the sutures, the upper-lateral portion rather flattened, periphery and base convex. Surface smooth, horn-colored. Aperture oblique, ovate, angled above, broadly rounded below; upper portion of the inner lip adherent to the body-whorl, lower portion arcuate, without a callous thickening.

"Alt. 3, diam. 2½mm.

"Collected from a warm spring (temperature 97° F.) in Pahranagat Valley, Nevada, by Dr. C. Hart Merriam, and submitted to the writer by Dr. R. E. C. Stearns.

"This species differs from *F. fusca* Hald., in the much more distinct umbilicus, thin texture, and the *non-thickened* inner lip.

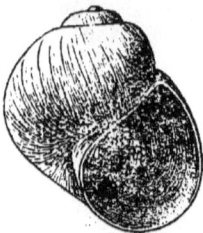

Fig. 2. Fluminicola merriami.

"Specimens may be seen in the National Museum (No. 123626) collected at Warm Springs, Pahranagat Valley, Nevada, by Dr. C. Hart Merriam, May 25, 1891."

This form, not previously described, is regarded by Mr. Pilsbry, who is an authority on the shells of this and allied groups, as a new species. It was found associated with *Tryonia clathrata*, elsewhere noted, the temperature of the water being 97° F.

Fluminicola fusca Hald. var. minor.
Ash Meadows, Nye County, Nevada (Mus. No. 123624), F. Stephens, March 4, 1891.

Numerous (200) living specimens of nearly uniform size in spring.

Fluminicola nuttalliana * Lea.
Shoshone Falls, Idaho (Mus. No. 58596).

A large number of specimens, probably as many as two hundred and fifty, were collected at this locality by Dr. Merriam (October 10, 1890), who found them clinging to the rocks in the stream. They vary considerably in elevation of the spire, etc., but the form of the mouth is quite persistent.

A dwarfed but characteristic aspect of this species occurs among the surface shells in the Colorado Desert.

Suborder *SCUTIBRANCHIATA*.

Section RHIPODOGLOSSA.

Helicina chrysocheila Binney.
Hidalgo, Tamaulipas, Mexico (Mus. No. 123627); also Texas near the mouth of the Rio Grande (Mus. No. 123167), William Lloyd.

Four characteristic illustrations of this well marked and handsome species described in Binney's Terr. Air-breathing Moll., U. S., Vol. II, p. 354, 1851. In addition to the above number, two were obtained at the Texan locality.

---

* Inadvertently omitted in my previous list, but included in list published in *N. Am. Fauna*, No. 5, 1891, p. 27.

Helicina tropica Jan.
Brownsville, Tex. (Mus. No. 123628), William Lloyd.

A single example.

Class PELECYPODA.

Order TETRABRANCHIATA.

Suborder *SUBMYTILACEA*.

Anodonta nuttalliana Lea.
Keeler, Calif. (Mus. No. 123629), T. S. Palmer.

One semifossil example.

Unio anodontoides Lea.
Brownsville, Tex. (Mus. No. 123630); Mier, Tamaulipas, Mexico, May 4, 1891 (Mus. No. 123632), William Lloyd.

The Brownsville examples are less elongated than usual in this species. The Mexican specimens are full grown and of the usual proportions.

These localities are believed to be much farther south than heretofore reported.

Unio berlandieri Lea.
Mier, Tamaulipas, Mexico (Mus. No. 123631), William Lloyd, May 4, 1891.

The examples of this species are nearly full grown adults and of the characteristic aspect.

Suborder *CONCHACEA*.

Pisidium occidentale Newc.
Oasis Valley, Nevada (Mus. No. 123633), Dr. C. Hart Merriam, June 2, 1891.

Several examples. The above place is on the western edge of the Ralston Desert, in Nye County, Nevada.

NOTES ON THE DISTRIBUTION OF TREES AND SHRUBS IN THE DESERTS AND DESERT RANGES OF SOUTHERN CALIFORNIA, SOUTHERN NEVADA, NORTHWESTERN ARIZONA, AND SOUTHWESTERN UTAH.

By C. HART MERRIAM, M. D.

The present chapter is made up of a multitude of disconnected notes, jotted down on horseback while traversing the deserts and desert ranges of the southern part of the Great Basin. These notes relate to the vertical and geographical distribution of the trees and shrubs observed by me in April, May, and June, 1891, along the route traveled from the north end of Cajon Pass, in the San Bernardino Mountains, California, to the St. George Valley, at the foot of the Hurricane Cliffs, in southwestern Utah, and thence westerly across Nevada to Owens Valley, California, and southward and southwestward to the extreme end of the western tongue of the Mohave Desert (Antelope Valley), including the several passes (Walker, Tehachapi, and the Cañada de las Uvas) by means of which communication is established between the Mohave Desert on the southeast, and the Bakersfield Plain, or upper San Joaquin Valley, on the northwest. A detailed itinerary of this trip may be found in Part I of the report. In a few instances, notes made by other members of the expedition are added and duly accredited; a small number of non-woody plants are admitted to render the list more useful, and in addition to the desert species a few from the Sierra Nevada, mainly conifers, are included.

Most of the desert shrubs are social plants and are distributed in well-marked belts or zones, the vertical limits of which are fixed by the temperature during the period of growth and reproduction. Since the temperature at this season in places of the same latitude depends mainly on altitude, base level, and slope exposure, it follows that the boundaries of the several belts conform largely to the contours of altitude, with such flexures as variations in base level and slope exposure impose.

The principal plant zones conform also to the animal zones, as defined by the limits of distribution of terrestrial mammals, birds, and reptiles. But since these *Life Zones* are discussed in the first part of the report they will not be considered here. It should be mentioned, however, that each of the life zones is subdivisible both latitudinally and longitudinally, and that while the former divisions are clearly dependent on temperature, the causes controlling the latter are not always well understood. Such local factors as soil and slope are not here referred to. The most marked longitudinal divisions, so far as the Great Basin is concerned, are those of the Lower Sonoran Zone, which may be designated the *Larrea* belt and the *Grayia* belt. The creosote bush (*Larrea tridentata*) is the most conspicuous, most widely distributed, and best-known bush of the torrid deserts of the southwest, where it covers the gravel soils up to a certain line, which probably marks the southern limit of killing frost. The *Larrea* belt is the most important of all from the horticultural standpoint, because it is suited to the requirements of the citrus fruits, the olive, almond, fig, and raisin grape. Associated with the *Larrea*, and coinciding with it in distribution, is the inconspicuous *Franseria dumosa*. Another species occupying the same gravel soils, but less generally distributed, is the beautiful and fragrant *Krameria parvifolia*. The alkali soils of the same belt are covered with greasewoods of the genus *Atriplex*, of which *A. polycarpa* is the most characteristic. The *Grayia* belt, named from its most distinctive and widespread bush (*Grayia spinosa*), occupies the strip between the upper limit of *Larrea* and the lower border of the true sage brush (*Artemisia tridentata*), which latter indicates the beginning of the Upper Sonoran Zone. Other shrubs of the *Grayia* belt are the dark *Coleogyne ramosissima*, which resembles *Krameria parvifolia* in general appearance, but belongs to a different order and has yellow flowers; the handsome *Tetradymia spinosa* and *T. glabrata*; the fetid *Thamnosma montana*; the stunted *Menodora spinosa*, whose conspicuous green berries always grow in pairs; and the singular *Salazaria mexicana*, whose inflated capsules are borne away by the wind and lodge in great numbers upon the spiny cactuses. Certain shrubs range over the whole breadth of the Lower Sonoran Zone, occurring alike in the *Larrea* and *Grayia* belts. The most noticeable members of this category are the olive-colored *Ephedra nevadensis*, which has no apparent foliage and is used as a medicine by the Indians and miners; the handsome *Daleas*, with their blue and purple flowers, and *Lycium andersoni*, which bears a small edible fruit.

The true sage brush (*Artemisia tridentata*) begins with a solid front along the southern border of the Upper Sonoran Zone and spreads northward over the Great Basin like a monstrous sheet, covering almost without a break hundreds of thousands of square miles. It is not only the most striking and widely diffused plant of the Upper Sonoran and Transition zones, but as a social plant has few equals, often occupying immense areas to the exclusion of all but the humblest and least conspicuous forms. Wherever one travels in this vast region, the aromatic odor of the sage brush is always present, and sometimes, particularly after rains, is so powerful as to cause pain in the nostrils.

In addition to the sage, many of the desert ranges support a growth of shrubs and small trees rarely if ever found on the intervening deserts and plains, whatever the altitude. This seems to be due in part to increased moisture and in part to the physical character of the slopes. The so-called cedar (*Juniperus californica utahensis*) and the piñon or nut pine (*Pinus monophylla*) clothe the summits and higher slopes of many of the ranges, forming stunted open forests of much beauty. Mixed with these are scattered clumps of bushes representing a number of genera, most of which bear green foliage and handsome flowers. Conspicuous among them are *Berberis fremonti*, *Ceanothus fremonti*, *Rhus trilobata*, *Robinia neomexicana*, *Cercis occidentalis*, *Prunus fasciculata*, *Kunzia tridentata* [until recently known as *Purshia*], *Cowania mexicana*, *Fallugia paradoxa*, *Amelanchier alnifolia*, *Peraphyllum ramosissimum*, *Garrya veatchii flavescens*, and *Symphoricarpos longifolius*. Scrub oaks of two species (*Quercus gambelii* and *Q. undulata*) are common in places; the green *Ephedra viridis* is almost universally present, and the mescal (*Agave utahensis*) occurs on a few of the slopes.

Some of the desert ranges, as the Funeral Mountains, are too excessively hot and arid to support even these forms of vegetation; others, as the Charleston Mountains, push their lofty summits into so cold an atmosphere that they obtain a covering of the boreal pines and firs. These higher mountains, when rising from the Lower Sonoran deserts, present in succession all the extra tropical zones of North America, which, from their close juxtaposition, may be here studied to unusual advantage.

In ascending or descending such slopes the change from one zone to another is quickly recognized and the altitude of first appearance of the various new species encountered may be recorded with considerable confidence. Not so, however, with the species lost, for, except in the case of trees and such strikingly conspicuous forms as the yuccas, some of the cactuses, the creosote bush (*Larrea*), and a few others, it is exceedingly difficult to detect the disappearance of species when passing out of their ranges. A close parallel occurs in the study of bird migration. Every observer reports the first appearance of the newcomers in spring, while but few have any record of disappearance in autumn.

In order to make sure of the upper and lower limits of species on a mountain side the same line should be traversed both up and down the slope, which it was impossible to do in the limited time at our disposal. In cases where this is done the resulting altitudes relate to a particular slope only and too often to a cañon or wash on that slope, so that they can not always be accepted as fair averages for the base level and slope exposure to which they properly pertain.

Most of the altitudes were determined by aneroid barometer and are only approximate, because of the scarcity of base stations of known elevation. All altitudes are recorded in meters, and equivalents in English feet are given in parentheses. These equivalents are stated in round numbers to avoid the appearance of a degree of precision unwarranted by the altitudes themselves. While in some instances the absolute altitudes are doubtless considerably in error, their relative values are not impaired, for they still serve to show the vertical extent of the belts occupied by the various species and the elevation in respect to fixed points.

For aid in the determination of species I am indebted to my assistant, Mr. Vernon Bailey, who was with me in the field, and to Mr. F. V. Coville, botanist of the expedition, who unfortunately was with me only ten days at the end of the trip. Mr. Coville is responsible for the nomenclature and sequence of genera here adopted.

LIST OF TREES AND SHRUBS.

Berberis fremonti.
Arctomecon californicum.
  merriami.
Stanleya pinnata.
Isomeris arborea.
  arborea globosa.
Krameria parvifolia.
  canescens.
Malvastrum rotundifolium.
Sphæralcea monroana.
Fremontodendron californicum.
Larrea tridentata.
Thamnosma montana.
Mortonia scabrella.
Glossapetalon nevadense.
  spinescens.
Rhamnus crocea.
Ceanothus fendleri.
  divaricatus.
  cuneatus.
Æsculus californica.
Acer negundo.
Rhus trilobata.
  diversiloba.
Dalea polyadenia.
  fremonti.
  johnsoni.
Robinia neomexicana.
Cassia armata.
Cercis occidentalis.
Prosopis juliflora.
  pubescens.
Acacia greggii.
Prunus fasciculata.
  virginiana (or *demissa*).
  andersoni.

Basilima millefolium.
Holodiscus discolor.
Adenostoma fasciculatum.
Kunzia glandulosa.
  tridentata.
Coleogyne ramosissima.
Cercocarpus ledifolius.
  parvifolius.
Cowania mexicana.
Fallugia paradoxa.
Rosa sp. —?
Heteromeles arbutifolia.
Amelanchier alnifolia.
Peraphyllum ramosissimum.
Ribes leptanthum brachyanthum.
  menziesii.
Petalonyx parryi.
Eucnide urens.
Garrya veatchii flavescens.
Symphoricarpos longiflorus.
Amphiachyris fremontii.
Acamptopappus sphærocephalus.
Aplopappus monactis.
Bigelovia douglassi.
  graveolens.
  teretifolia.
Baccharis glutinosa.
Pluchea sericea.
Hymenoclea salsola.
Franseria dumosa.
  eriocentra.
Encelia frutescens.
Artemisia tridentata.
  spinescens.
  arbuscula.
  filifolia.

LIST OF TREES AND SHRUBS—continued.

Peucephyllum schottii.
Tetradymia canescens.
    glabrata.
    spinosa.
    comosa (or stenolepis).
Arctostaphylos glauca.
    pungens.
Menodora spinescens.
Fraxinus coriacea.
    anomala.
Eriodictyon tomentosum.
Lycium andersoni.
    cooperi.
    pallidum.
    torreyi.
Chilopsis linearis.
Salvia carnosa.
    pilosa.
Salazaria mexicana.
Atriplex canescens.
    confertifolia.
    hymenelytra.
    lentiformis.
    parryi.
    polycarpa.
    torreyi.
Grayia spinosa.
Eurotia lanata.
Allenrolfea occidentalis.
Suæda suffrutescens.
Sarcobatus baileyi.
    vermiculatus.
Eriogonum polifolium.
    inflatum.
Chorizanthe rigida.
Platanus occidentalis.
Betula occidentalis.

Alnus rhombifolia.
Quercus undulata.
    gambelii.
    lobata.
    douglasii.
    wislizeni.
    kelloggii.
    dumosa.
Castanopsis chrysophylla.
Salix longifolia.
    lævigata.
    nigra.
Populus fremontii.
Ephedra nevadensis.
    viridis.
Pinus monophylla.
    ponderosa.
    ponderosa scopulorum.
    jeffreyi.
    murrayana.
    balfouriana.
    aristata.
    sabiniana.
    monticola.
    lambertiana.
    flexilis.
Abies magnifica.
    concolor.
Pseudotsuga macrocarpa.
Sequoia gigantea.
Libocedrus decurrens.
Juniperus californica.
    californica utahensis.
    occidentalis.
    occidentalis monosperma.
Tumion californicum.

Berberis fremonti.

This large shrub, bearing handsome yellow flowers, is common on the less arid of the desert ranges, where it was observed in the following localities:

NEVADA.

Charleston Mountains.—Found on west slope, near Mountain Spring, at an altitude of 1,680 to 1,770 meters (5,500–5,800 feet).

Pahranagat Mountains.—Common, and ranges down on the east slope to 1,580 meters (5,200 feet).

Hungry Hill Summit.—Common, beginning just north of the summit and passing down the south side toward the North Arm of Indian Spring Valley to 1,525 meters (5,000 feet).

12731—No. 7——19

UTAH.

Beaverdam Mountains.—Abundant, ranging down to 1,350 meters (4,400 feet) on the west slope, and to 1,100 meters (3,600 feet) on the east slope. In full bloom May 11; flowers deep rich yellow.

Upper Santa Clara Valley.—Begins about 13 kilometers (8 miles) northwest of St. George, at an altitude of about 1,280 meters (4,200 feet), and ranges thence northerly, scattering over the rocky hillsides.

Arctomecon californicum.

One of the most interesting incidents in the botanical line connected with the present expedition is the rediscovery of this elegant poppy, the type of which was collected by Fremont in Vegas Desert, southern Nevada, May 3, 1844.* On the very same spot, and within forty-eight hours of the same day of the month (May 1, 1891), Mr. Bailey and I found the species in full bloom, growing in large patches, and secured a fine series of specimens. With it was a second species equally large and handsome, but having white instead of yellow flowers, which proved to be undescribed, and which has been since named *A. merriami*. *A. californicum* was afterward found near Bitter Springs in the Muddy Mountains (May 5), and in the Amargosa Desert between Ash Meadows and Oasis Valley (May 31).

Arctomecon merriami.

As stated above, this new and handsome poppy, with white flowers measuring 50^{mm} (about 2 inches) in diameter, was discovered by Mr. Vernon Bailey and myself in Vegas Desert, southern Nevada, between Lower Cottonwood Springs and Vegas Spring, May 1, 1891. It was found in company with the yellow-flowered species (*A. californicum*), from which it differs in the leaves and fruit as well as in the flower. The botanist of the expedition, Mr. F. V. Coville, has paid me the compliment of attaching my name to the species and has figured it in his forthcoming report.†

Stanleya pinnata.

This miserable crucifer, which attains a height of 4 or 5 feet, has a woody base, while the top is herbaceous. It was not seen in Utah nor eastern Nevada, but was common in some of the deserts of western Nevada and eastern California. It or a closely allied species was noted at the following localities:

CALIFORNIA.

Owens Valley.—Common in places, and ranging up the west slope of the White Mountains to 1,970 meters (6,500 feet).

Deep Spring Valley.—Common in the higher parts of the valley.

---

*Rept. of Exploring Expedition to Rocky Mountains in 1842 and to Oregon and North California in 1843-'44, by Capt. J. C. Fremont, Washington, 1845 (Senate Doc. 174, Twenty-eighth Congress, second session), p. 312, Botany, Pl. II.

†Proc. Biol. Soc., Washington, vol. VII, May 18, 1892, p. 66.

NEVADA.

Fish Lake Valley.—Not found in the bottom of the valley, but tolerably common on the southeast side up to an altitude of 1,950 meters (6,400 feet) in a wash leading up towards Pigeon Spring, on the northwest slope of Mount Magruder.

Grapevine Cañon.—Occurs in the upper part of the cañon.

Sarcobatus Flat.—Tolerably common in places in the northern part of the flat.

Oasis Valley.—Occurs sparingly.

Pahranagat Valley.—Common in places, ranging up to about 1,525 meters (5,000 feet) on the west side of the valley.

Isomeris arborea.

The hills at the head of Antelope Valley, at the extreme west end of the Mohave Desert (altitude 1,160 meters, or 3,800 feet) were dotted with clumps of *Isomeris*, bearing yellow flowers and large inflated pods, the last week in June. It was abundant in a wash leading south from this point toward Peru Creek, and was found also in the lower part of the open cañon leading from Mohave up to Tehachapi.

Isomeris arborea globosa.*

This new subspecies of *Isomeris* was described by Mr. Coville from specimens collected near Caliente, at the head of the San Joaquin Valley, California, where we found it common along Caliente Creek, a few miles east of the station, June 24, 1891.

Krameria parvifolia.

This small and scrubby bush is very characteristic of the lower Sonoran deserts, but is not so generally distributed as some other species—notably *Larrea* and *Franseria*. It flowers profusely throughout the month of May, when it is literally buried in a mass of fragrant violet-purple blossoms. During the latter part of the month its spiny berries begin to show before it is wholly out of flower. During the remainder of the year it is easily mistaken for *Coleogyne*, though growing at a lower altitude. The following notes on its distribution were recorded:

NEVADA.

Pahrump Valley.—Common on the east side of the valley, ranging up to 1,340 meters (4,400 feet) on the west slope of the Charleston Mountains.

Indian Spring Valley.—Common throughout the valley, reaching up in the North Arm among most of the *Larrea* areas. It was still in flower in Indian Spring Valley May 29, and in fruit the same date in the Amargosa country.

Pahranagat Valley.—Common on gravel soil, where it is mixed with *Grayia*, *Lycium*, *Larrea*, and *Dalea*. In a wash leading from Pahroc Plain to Pahranagat Valley it occurs as high as 1,310 meters (4,300 feet) in company with *Franseria dumosa* (still in bloom May 22–26).

---

* Proc. Biol. Soc. Wash., vol. VII, May 18, 1892, p. 73.

Valley of the Virgin and Lower Muddy.—Common in the dry parts of the valley.

UTAH.

Santa Clara Valley.—Abundant in the lower part of the valley, disappearing at an altitude of 1,220 to 1,275 meters (4,000–4,200 feet).

Beaverdam Mountains.—On the west slope of the Beaverdam Mountains *Krameria* ranges up from the Virgin Valley to 1,150 meters (3,800 feet).

Krameria canescens.

This species was common in dry parts of the valleys of the Muddy and Virgin, Nevada. It is larger than *Krameria parvifolia*, from which its flowers differ in color and fragrance.

Malvastrum rotundifolium.

This exquisite species, whose large cup-shaped orange-pink flowers seemed disproportionately heavy for its slender stems, is common in the hottest deserts of eastern California and southwestern Nevada. It was found in the Mohave Desert, and in Panamint and Death valleys and the Amargosa Desert, but not in the deserts of eastern Nevada. It was common on the west side of the cañon leading from the Amargosa to the west end of Indian Spring Valley, but was not observed in the latter valley. It blossoms early and was in fruit about the end of May.

Sphæralcea monroana.

This common and widely distributed species (if only one species is covered by the notes), grows in enormous patches in some of the deserts of the Great Basin, where it becomes a truly social plant, the individuals standing so near together that their large salmon-colored flowers give color to areas miles in extent. Among the many places where it was seen are the following:

CALIFORNIA.

Mohave Desert.—Common in places.

Leach Point Valley.—Common.

Owens Valley.—Common, ranging up to 1,980 meters (6,500 feet) on the west slope of the White Mountains opposite Big Pine.

NEVADA.

Fish Lake Valley.—Common, ranging up on the northwest slope of Mount Magruder to 1,980 or 2,040 meters (6,500 or 6,700 feet).

Grapevine Cañon.—Common.

Sarcobatus Flat.—Common in places.

Amargosa Desert.—Occurs.

North Arm of Indian Spring Valley.—Abundant everywhere.

Emigrant Valley.—Abundant, and reaches up on the Desert Range nearly to the divide near Summit or Mud Spring.

Timpahute Valley.—One of the principal plants.

Pahranagat Valley.—Common, ranging up to 1,580 meters (5,200 feet) on the Pahranagat Mountains.

Pahrump Valley.—Common.

Vegas Valley.—Enormously abundant, giving color to more than half the area of the valley between Lower Cottonwood and Vegas springs.

Fremontodendron californicum.

This handsome small tree (6 to 7 meters or 20 to 25 feet in height), which bears large and showy yellow flowers, grows in great abundance and perfection on the lower slopes of the Sierra Nevada, west of the divide, and on the Coast Ranges, but does not occur anywhere within the limits of the Great Basin.

CALIFORNIA.

Walker Pass.—Reaches the summit of the pass from the west and is abundant thence down into the valley of Kern River, and from Kernville north to Havilah and Walker Basin (in full flower June 20-24).

Cañada de las Uvas.—Common, and still in flower on the higher mountains, June 28.

Larrea tridentata.

The creosote bush (*Larrea tridentata*) is the most characteristic, conspicuous, and widely distributed of the desert brush of the Lower Sonoran Zone, covering the gravel soils, wherever of suitable altitude, everywhere from the east foot of the Sierra Nevada in California to the valley of the Lower Santa Clara in Utah. Its dark green leaves and blackish stems render it conspicuous among all the other species with which it happens to be associated, so that it is easily distinguished at a distance, and hence is the most important zone plant in tracing the boundary between the upper and lower divisions of the Lower Sonoran Zone. It is true that several other species—notably *Franseria dumosa*—agree with it essentially in distribution, but they are so inconspicuous that it would be difficult to trace the zones by their aid alone. The following notes respecting the details of its distribution were recorded:

CALIFORNIA.

Mohave Desert.—Universally distributed over suitable soils, reaching as far west as the extreme upper limit of the lower division of the Lower Sonoran Zone in Antelope Valley, which is about 6½ kilometers (4 miles) east of the Liebre ranch along the middle and north part of the valley, but not quite so far west on the south side. On the north side of the Mohave Desert, opposite the town of Mohave, it finds its upper limit at 940 meters (3,100 feet), just reaching the mouth of the open cañon leading to Tehachapi Valley. On the south side of the Mohave Desert near Cajon Pass it reaches its northern limit at 1,020 meters (3,350 feet). It does not cover the desert ranges in the Mohave Desert, and falls short of the divide at Pilot Knob or Granite Mountain (altitude 1,400 meters or 4,600 feet).

Walker Pass.—At the east end of Walker Pass it ascends to 1,050 meters (3,400 feet), and on the south slope of the hills on the north side of the entrance to this pass reaches 60 meters (200 feet) higher, or to 1,100 meters (3,600 feet).

Salt Wells Valley.—This valley is a true *Larrea* plain, and the *Larrea* is continuous with that of the Mohave Desert.

Panamint Valley.—Common on the gravel soils, reaching up on the west slope of the Panamint Mountains as high as 1,500 meters (5,000 feet), and on favorable slopes to a still greater altitude. In Emigrant Cañon (which slopes to the northeast) it stops at about 1,200 meters (4,000 feet).

Death Valley.—Common throughout the gravel slopes on both sides of the salt bottom, where it was just beginning to flower April 7. (It was seen in flower in southern Arizona two weeks earlier.) It reaches north through the lower part of the Northwest Arm of Death Valley (Mesquite Valley) as far as Grapevine Cañon, keeping on the gravel slopes, but does not occur much further north, the altitude being too great.

Owens Valley.—In Owens Valley, *Larrea* is restricted to the extreme southern end of the valley, except along the east side where it ranges for some miles north of Owens Lake, along the warm west slope at the foot of the Inyo Mountains, this being the hottest slope exposure of the valley. South of Owens Lake it occurs in scattering patches for several miles, and completely covers the broad valley between Haway Meadows and Little Owens Lake, this valley being a true *Larrea* plain.

NEVADA.

Amargosa Desert.—At the point where the clay soil of Ash Meadows changes to the gravel of the Amargosa Desert proper, *Larrea* begins with a solid front and ranges northward without interruption over the whole of the north arm of the Amargosa Desert, forming one of the purest *Larrea* plains met with. Throughout the greater part of this desert the *Larrea* is hardly invaded by any other plant except the small and inconspicuous *Chorizanthe rigida*. The *Larrea* on this desert is stunted, hardly averaging more than ⅔ of a meter (about 2 feet) in height, and along the northern edge of the desert is mostly dead; perhaps winter killed. It was heavy with its woolly fruit May 30, though a few blossoms were seen here and there. At the same date it was still in flower in Indian Spring Valley.

Oasis Valley.—Most parts of Oasis Valley are a little too high for *Larrea*, which forms a belt on favorable slopes hardly more than three miles wide. On good south and southwest slopes a scattering growth reaches as high as 1,370 meters (4,500 feet). To the east of the north end of Oasis Valley is a small valley draining into the east fork of Amargosa Creek in which a little *Larrea* occurs. It does not grow east of the main part of Bare Mountains, or anywhere to the east or northeast, the whole country being too high and the Lower Sonoran zone here reaching its northern limit for this part of Nevada.

Grapevine Cañon.—*Larrea* comes up solid through Grapevine Cañon from Death Valley, almost, but not quite, reaching Sarcobatus Flat, where it does not grow. On a southwest slope on the south side of Gold Mountain it attains an altitude of 1,620 or 1,650 meters (5,300 to 5,400 feet).

Indian Spring Valley.—*Larrea* completely covers Indian Spring Valley, here reaching its northern limit at the base of the low range of mountains which forms the northern boundary of the valley. In the north arm of Indian Spring Valley it reaches northward a little beyond Quartz Spring to an altitude of 1,525 meters (5,000 feet), or even a little higher on favorable slopes. It was still in flower in Indian Spring Valley May 29, and in fruit in the Amargosa country at the same date. It does not occur in Timpahute Valley.

Pahranagat Valley.—Common on the gravel benches and slopes of the southern half of the valley, but not evenly distributed. It reaches Pahranagat Valley from the south, coming up from the Muddy Valley through the broad cañon south of Pahranagat Lake and passing over the low divide (1,160 meters or 3,800 feet), whence it spreads northward over the low gravel slopes, becoming less abundant and more scattering until at an altitude of 1,250 to 1,280 meters (4,100 to 4,200 feet) it is found on south slopes only. It occurs in isolated patches in the broad wash leading into the valley from Pahroc Plain, where it has a southwest slope exposure, as high as 1,340 meters (4,400 feet). On the west side of the valley (east slope of Pahranagat Mountains) it is common about as far north as the middle of the valley, stopping, except in struggling patches, about 16 kilometers (10 miles) south of the latitude of Eisemann's ranch. It was still in full flower May 22-26.

Pahrump Valley.—Scarce on the west side of the valley and absent from the extensive clay flat in the bottom, but abundant everywhere on the long gravel slope on the east side, ranging up the west slope of the Charleston Mountains to 1,340 meters (4,400 feet), where it overlaps the tree yuccas.

Vegas Valley.—Abundant, covering the gravel soil of the whole valley and ranging up on the west side to 1,130 meters (3,700 feet), at the east foot of the Charleston Mountains.

Bend of Colorado and Muddy Mountains.—Common on suitable soils throughout the region bordering the Great Bend of the Colorado, and passing abundantly over the low summits of the Muddy Mountains west of the Virgin Valley.

Valley of the Virgin and Lower Muddy.—Abundant on suitable soil throughout these valleys and over the high gravel mesa between them, where it is the dominant bush along the boundary between Nevada and Arizona.

It does not reach northward as far as Meadow Creek Valley.

ARIZONA.

Beaverdam Mountains.—*Larrea* is abundant in the Virgin Valley near the mouth of Beaverdam Creek in northwestern Arizona, and reaches up on the west slope of the Beaverdam Mountains to 1,160 meters (3,800 feet).

UTAH.

Santa Clara Valley.—*Larrea* finds the extreme northeastern limit of its range in the Lower Santa Clara or St. George Valley in southwestern Utah, where it forms a sparse growth on gravel soils and disappears on southerly exposures on the north side of the valley at an altitude of 1,200 to 1,280 meters (4,000 to 4,200 feet).

Thamnosma montana.

This stinking bush, of a yellowish-green color and generally sprinkled with berry-like fruit about the size of peas, was common in many of the southern deserts traversed. It was noted in the following localities:

CALIFORNIA.

Mohave Desert.—Common in places.
Leach Point Valley.—Found sparingly.

NEVADA.

Charleston Mountains.—Common on the Charleston Mountains, where it ranges on the west slope from about 1,340 to 1,825 meters (4,400 to 6,000 feet). On the east slope it descends to 1,219 meters (4,000 feet) with *Coleogyne*.
Indian Spring Valley.—A few plants seen.
Valley of the Virgin and Lower Muddy.—Occurs sparingly.

ARIZONA.

Virgin Valley.—Found on the east side of the Virgin Valley near the mouth of Beaverdam Creek, whence it ranges up to 1,340 meters (4,400 feet) on the west slope of the Beaverdam Mountains.

UTAH.

Santa Clara Valley.—Occurs along the foot of the Beaverdam Mountains, ranging from 1,090 to 2,130 meters (3,600 to 4,300 feet).

Mortonia scabrella.

This bush was found by Mr. Bailey and myself on a limestone knoll in the valley of the Muddy, near Overton, Nev., May 6. It is remarkable for the peculiarity of its leaves, which are oval, conspicuously granular, and have thick margins that at first sight seem to be everted.

Glossapetalon nevadense.

This small bush was collected on the Pahroc Mountains near Pahroc Spring, Nevada, and a species supposed to be the same was found on the Beaverdam Mountains in southwestern Utah.

Glossapetalon spinescens.

This species was found on the Charleston Mountains, Nevada, near Mountain Spring.

Rhamnus crocea.

Common in California in the Cañada de las Uvas, and also on the Sierra Liebre; not recorded elsewhere.

Ceanothus fendleri.

Common on some of the desert ranges in the Great Basin, where it was observed in the following localities:

NEVADA.

Mount Magruder.—Common on the main peak with *Symphoricarpos.*

Charleston Mountains.—Common on the west slope, in the neighborhood of Mountain Spring, from 1,550 to 1,770 meters (5,100 to 5,800 feet), and perhaps higher.

Highland Range.—Found on the west slope.

UTAH.

Beaverdam Mountains.—Common on the east slope, at an altitude of 1,340 to 1,370 meters (4,400 to 4,500 feet).

Ceanothus divaricatus and C. cuneatus.

These species are common in the chaparral of the west slope of the Sierra and Coast Ranges in California. In Walker Pass they are common on the west slope from 1,430 meters (4,700 feet) downward, and range thence southerly along the west slope of the Sierra nearly to Caliente.

They are common also on the south slope of the Sierra Liebre.

Æsculus californica.

The handsome California buckeye, which grows to be a small tree, was in full bloom when we first saw it, the last week in June, on the west slope of the Sierra Nevada between Kernville and Walker Basin, and in the Cañada de las Uvas in the Tejon Mountains, a few days later. It usually grows on the sidehills, towering above the chaparral.

Acer negundo.

The box elder requires too much water to be common anywhere in the desert region proper. We found it along a running stream below Old Fort Tejon in the Cañada de las Uvas, in California, and along the Santa Clara River, in Utah, but not elsewhere.

Rhus trilobata.

In California this species was common on the west slope of the Sierra between Walker Basin and Caliente, and on the Sierra Liebre. In Nevada it was found in scattered clumps on the Charleston Mountains, where it reaches its lower limit on the west slope at 1,550 meters (5,100 feet), and on the Pahranagat Mountains, where it ranges down on the east slope to 1,580 meters (5,200 feet). On the Beaverdam Mountains in southwestern Utah it descends to 1,150 meters (3,800 feet) on the west slope, and to 970 meters (3,200 feet) on the east slope, thus reaching the Santa Clara Valley.

Rhus diversiloba.

Common on the west slope of the Sierra Nevada and in the Coast Ranges. It was observed along the road between Walker Basin and Caliente, and also in the Cañada de las Uvas.

Dalea polyadenia.

This small, glandular, strongly scented, purple-flowered species of *Dalea* is common over many of the desert valleys of the southern part of the Great Basin, where it was noted in the following localities:

CALIFORNIA.

Mohave Desert.—Common in places; seen in Leach Point Valley.

Owens Valley.—Common in places in the lower parts of the valley, particularly between Owens Lake and Haway Meadows.

Deep Spring Valley.—Occurs in company with *D. fremonti*, *Grayia*, *Menodora*, and a few other shrubs.

NEVADA.

Fish Lake Valley.—Tolerably common on the southeast side of the valley and ranging up to an altitude of 1,765 meters (5,800 feet).

Grapevine Cañon.—Tolerably common in the bottom of the cañon near Sarcobatus Flat.

Sarcobatus Flat.—Rather common in places in the northern part of the flat.

Oasis Valley.—A single bush seen.

Pahranagat Valley.—Common at the extreme south end of the valley in company with the large blue-flowered species (*D. fremonti*), and extends thence northerly over the gravel soil and lower gravel slopes up to 1,340 or 1,370 meters (4,400–4,500 feet). In full flower May 22–26.

Great Bend of Colorado River.—Common; in flower May 4.

Muddy Mountains.—Rather common; in full flower May 5.

Dalea fremonti.

The *Daleas* rank among the most characteristic and, when in flower, among the most beautiful and showy of the desert brush. Some doubt attaches to the determination of the species observed by Mr. Bailey and myself. The large blue-flowered species believed to be *Dalea fremonti* was noted at the following localities:

CALIFORNIA.

Mohave Desert.—Common in places; noted in Leach Point Valley.

Owens Valley.—Common along the west side of the valley from Lone Pine to Olancha, and less common south to Haway Meadows. From the east side of Owens Valley it ranges up on the west slope of the White Mountains to 1,980 meters (6,500 feet).

Deep Spring Valley.—Found in company with *D. polyadenia*, *Grayia*, and other bushes of the upper division of the Lower Sonoran Zone.

NEVADA.

Fish Lake Valley.—Common in the southeast corner of the valley, whence it ranges up to an altitude of 1,765 meters (5,800 feet).

Gold Mountain.—Common on the north slope of Gold Mountain a little below 2,135 meters (7,000 feet) in altitude.

Indian Spring Valley.—Common in the *Larrea* in the north arm of Indian Spring Valley.

Pahranagat Valley.—This large blue-flowered species was found in company with the small purple-flowered *Dalea polyadenia*, and with *Coleogyne ramosissima*, on the gravel divide at the extreme south end of the valley, south of Pahranagat Lake, at an altitude of 1,155 meters (3,800 feet). Like *Coleogyne*, it stops about half a mile north of this divide and does not occur in Pahranagat Valley proper. It does occur, however, also in company with *Coleogyne*, on the west side of the valley on the gavel slope at the east foot of the Pahranagat Mountains, between 1,280 and 1,370 meters (4,200 and 4,500 feet), but is rather scarce there. It was in full flower May 22–26.

Dalea johnsoni.

Specimens of the large and showy *Dalea johnsoni* were collected near St. George, in the Lower Santa Clara Valley, Utah; and the species was common from the Santa Clara Valley (altitude 970 meters, or 3,200 feet) up to 1,090 meters (3,600 feet) on the east slope of the Beaverdam Mountains.

Robinia neomexicana.

This dwarf locust was found in the Santa Clara Valley, in Utah, and thence up along the east slope of the Beaverdam Mountains to 1,040 meters (3,400 feet), but was not observed elsewhere.

Cassia armata.

This handsome *Cassia* was found flowering abundantly at the Great Bend of the Colorado River (May 4), in Leach Point Valley (April 25), and near the south end of Death Valley (April 26).

Cercis occidentalis.

The Judas bush was found in but one spot in the Great Basin, namely, the Charleston Mountains, Nevada, where Mr. Bailey and I found it flowering in profusion in a rocky cañon a little east of Mountain Spring, April 30. The seed pods of the previous year were still clinging to the branches, together with the handsome red flowers. On the west slope of the Sierra Nevada, in California, it was found in Kern Valley as low down as 820 meters (2,700 feet) on northerly exposures.

Prosopis juliflora.

The two species of mesquite are commonly ranked as trees and are the only trees besides cottonwoods that inhabit the arid Sonoran deserts of the Great Basin. The cottonwoods are never found except near water; the mesquite, on the other hand, occur at long distances from visible water and often occupy the tops of sand dunes. They usually grow in clumps from 3 to 9 meters (10 to 30 feet) in height. Their roots are very long and are said to travel 30 meters (100 feet) or more in search of moisture. The two species occur either together or singly, and their fruit, called 'mesquite beans,' is much sought after by the native animals and birds of the region, and also by the Indians. The pods are sweet and nutritious, and are sometimes gathered and fed to horses and mules instead of grain. The present species (*Prosopis juliflora*) was observed at the following localities:

CALIFORNIA.

Hot Springs, Panamint Valley.—Tolerably common.

Death Valley.—Occurs in clumps and irregular patches on the west side of the valley, beginning several miles south of Mesquite Well and ranging thence northward. It is abundant also on sand dunes in the northwest arm of Death Valley, from which circumstance the place is commonly known as 'Mesquite Valley.' In Death Valley it was just coming into leaf on clayey soil April 10, while adjoining clumps on sand soil were in full leaf at the same date.

Amargosa Cañon.—Common in places.

Resting Spring.—Tolerably common.

NEVADA.

Ash Meadows.—Common.

Indian Spring Valley.—Common in a few places.

Virgin and Lower Muddy Valleys.—Common in many places. (In full flower May 6.)

Great Bend of the Colorado.—Abundant on the sand hills on the south side of Vegas Wash.

UTAH.

Santa Clara Valley.—Occurs sparingly on sandy soil in the lower valley.

Prosopis pubescens.

This mesquite, commonly known as 'screw bean,' is widely distributed over the deserts of the southwest, usually in company with the preceding. It was noted in the following localities:

CALIFORNIA.

Panamint Valley.—Common about Hot Springs.

Death Valley.—Common along the west side of the valley.

Amargosa Cañon.—Occurs with *P. juliflora* and is enormously abundant in the upper part of the cañon, where Tecopa Cañon comes in.

NEVADA.

Ash Meadows.—Abundant.

Virgin and Lower Muddy Valleys.—Common in places.

Indian Spring Valley.—Occurs in places.

UTAH.

Santa Clara Valley.—Occurs sparingly on sandy soil in the lower valley.

Acacia greggii.

This Lower Sonoran shrub, which grows to be 2½ to 3 meters (8 to 10 feet) in height, perhaps higher, was not found in California, or in Nevada west of the Charleston Mountains. It is tolerably common along the upper and lower Cottonwood Springs at the east foot of the Charleston Mountains, and thence easterly was found at Bitter Springs in the Muddy Mountains, and in the valley of the Virgin and Lower Muddy, and thence northerly to the mouth of Beaverdam Creek, in northwestern Arizona, where it was abundant on the flat at the junction of Beaverdam Creek with the Virgin.

Prunus fasciculata.

This species is so characteristic of the desert ranges in the southern part of the Great Basin that it might properly be called the 'Desert Range Almond.' It is known to the Mormons as the wild almond and grows in dense clumps of bushes about as high as a man's head or lower, with irregular and very tough branches. It was noted in the following localities:

CALIFORNIA.

White Mountains.—Found in places along the summit and in cañons.

Walker Pass and Kern Valley.—Occurs sparingly, descending as low as 820 meters (2,700 feet) on northerly exposures in Kern Valley.

NEVADA.

Mount Magruder.—Not common, but found in the upper part of Tule Cañon and in a few other places.

Gold Mountain.—Tolerably common on the north slope in scattered clumps a little below 2,135 meters (7,000 feet).

Highland Range.—Occurs sparingly, mixed with *Artemisia tridentata.*

Pahroc Mountains.—Tolerably common, mixed with sagebrush and Kunzia.

Juniper Mountains.—Rather common, mixed with sagebrush and juniper, beginning at an altitude of about 1,830 meters (6,000 feet) on the Meadow Valley side and ranging up to the divide.

Charleston Mountains.—Common, reaching its lower limit on the west slope (Pahrump Valley side) at about 1,435 meters (4,700 feet).

UTAH.

Beaverdam Mountains.—Common, ranging down on the west slope to about 1,160 meters (3,800 feet) and on the east slope to about 1,100 meters (3,600 feet).

Santa Clara Valley.—Occurs in scattering patches on the rocky hillsides in the Upper Santa Clara Valley, beginning about 13 kilometers (8 miles) northwest of St. George at an altitude of 1,280 meters (4,200 feet) and ranging thence northerly to the Upper Santa Clara Crossing.

Prunus virginiana (or demissa).

The chokecherry grows sparingly about Sheep Spring in the Juniper Mountains between Panaca, Nevada, and Hebron, Utah, but was not observed elsewhere.

Prunus andersoni.

This species was found on the west slope of Walker Pass in the southern Sierra Nevada, California, at an altitude of about 1,370 meters (4,500 feet).

Basilima millefolium.

This beautiful shrub was observed on the Beaverdam Mountains in southwestern Utah, and on the east slope of the High Sierra in California, where it was abundant at and a little below 2,900 meters (9,500 feet).

Holodiscus discolor.

Found on the east slope of the Sierra Nevada in California at an altitude of about 2,130 meters (7,000 feet).

Adenostoma fasciculatum.

The California chemisal or chemise does not enter the desert region of the Great Basin, though it occurs on the north or Mohave Desert slope of the Sierra Liebre and throughout Cajon Pass in the San Bernardino Mountains. It is the prevailing chaparral of the coast ranges of southern California and is generally mixed with scrub oaks and *Ceanothus*, forming impenetrable thickets. It is abundant on the west slope of the Sierra Nevada on the east side of the upper San Joaquin Valley. On the north slope of the Sierra Liebre it begins a little north of Alamo ranch at an altitude of 730 meters (2,400 feet), whence southward it is the prevailing chaparral. It was in flower in the Sierra Liebre the last week in June.

Kunzia glandulosa [= *Purshia glandulosa*].

Mr. Coville tells me that this is the species found by us on the summit of Walker Pass in the southern Sierra Nevada, and thence down on the west slope to 940 meters (4,100 feet).

On the east slope of the Beaverdam Mountains (which cross the boundary between Utah and Arizona) Mr. Bailey and I collected a form very close to *K. glandulosa*, and also the typical *K. tridentata*, apparently at different altitudes. Some of the records under the latter species may belong to the former.

Kunzia tridentata [= *Purshia tridentata*].

Kunzia tridentata is common on many of the desert ranges, where it usually grows in company with *Cowania mexicana* and *Fallugia paradoxa*. When not in flower these three genera resemble one another so closely that they are sometimes confounded. *Kunzia* has yellow flowers on very short peduncles; *Fallugia* has pure white flowers on very long peduncles; *Cowania* has handsome cream-colored flowers on moderate peduncles. It is possible that the two species of *Kunzia* (*K. tridentata* and *K. glandulosa*) have been confounded in some of the following localities:

CALIFORNIA.

White Mountains.—Common on the east slope, ranging down to 1,700 meters (5,600 feet) on the Fish Lake Valley side.

NEVADA.

Mount Magruder.—Common in places, ranging down into Tule Cañon.

Gold Mountain.—Common, ranging down on the south side nearly as low as sagebrush (a little above 1,860 meters or 6,100 feet).

Hungry Hill Summit.—Common just north of the summit, whence it ranges over the divide (1,760 meters or 5,800 feet) and passes south toward the north arm of Indian Spring Valley to about 1,520 meters meters (5,000 feet).

Timpahute and Desert mountains.—A little was seen near Mud or Summit Spring.

Pahranagat Mountains.—Common, ranging down to 1,580 meters (5,200 feet) on the east slope.

Hyko Mountains.—Common in places, descending into the broad wash that leads from Pahroc Plain into the middle of Pahranagat Valley.

Pahroc Mountains.—Common, mixed with *Cowania mexicana*, *Artemisia tridentata*, and *Prunus fasciculata*.

Juniper Mountains.—Common in the juniper forest between Meadow Creek Valley, Nevada, and Shoal Creek, Utah, where it was just coming into flower May 18. A week earlier (May 10-11) it was past flowering in the Beaverdam Mountains.

UTAH.

Upper Santa Clara Valley.—Common from an altitude of 1,640 meters (5,400 feet) upwards to 1,830 meters (6,000 feet), and ranging thence northward to the Upper Santa Clara Crossing and Shoal Creek. Mostly past flowering in the Upper Santa Clara Valley May 17.

Beaverdam Mountains.—Common, descending to 1,280 meters (4,200 feet) on the east or northeast slope, and ranging down on the west slope to 1,340 meters (4,400 feet). Past flowering and petals all off May 11.

Coleogyne ramosissima.

This important zone plant grows in the *Grayia* belt just above the upper limit of the *Larrea*; it belongs therefore to the upper division of the Lower Sonoran Zone. The altitude which it requires takes it out of most of the desert valleys and places it on the sides of the desert ranges, where it commonly grows in a narrow belt between the creosote bush (*Larrea tridentata*) and the sage (*Artemisia tridentata*).

It is a low, dark-colored bush bearing small yellow flowers. The following notes respecting the details of its distribution were recorded:

CALIFORNIA.

Owens Valley.—Common along the west side of the valley on the lower slope of the Sierra Nevada, between the altitudes of 1,375 and 1,900 meters (4,500 and 6,200 feet).

Panamint Mountains.—On the west slope of the Panamint Mountains, in a broad basin above Wild Rose Spring, a well-defined zone of *Coleogyne* crosses the basin obliquely between the upper edge of the *Larrea* and the southern edge of the juniper at an altitude of about 1,525 meters (5,000 feet). On the east slope of the Panamint range Mr. Bailey found it in a zone between about 1,340 and 1,710 meters (4,400 to 5,600 feet).

NEVADA.

Charleston Mountains.—Common on the west slope, beginning at the upper edge of the *Larrea* at 1,340 meters (4,400 feet) and ranging up to about 1,825 meters (6,000 feet) in the neighborhood of Mountain Spring, where it passes over the divide and descends on the east slope to about 1,200 meters (4,000 feet) with *Yucca baccata* and *Thamnosma montana*. In full bloom April 30 on the east slope of Charleston Mountains.

Hungry Hill Summit.—Begins just north of the summit, passes over it and descends the south slope toward the North Arm of Indian Spring Valley to about 1,525 meters (5,000 feet) altitude.

Timpahute and Desert mountains.—Common in the saddle between the Timpahute and Desert mountains.

Pahranagat Mountains.—Common at 1,825 meters (6,000 feet) on the west or Timpahute side and ranging thence down to 1,525 meters (5,000 feet). On the east (Pahranagat Valley) side it grows in a zone between 1,275 and 1,500 meters (4,200 and 4,900 feet).

Pahranagat Valley.—Not found anywhere on the east side of the valley proper, but common on the gravel slope on the west side, beginning 1 mile from the bottom at 1,275 meters (4,200 feet) and ranging up to 1,500 meters (4,900 feet) at the east foot of the Pahranagat Mountains. At the south end of Pahranagat Valley it comes up over the divide below the lake at 1,150 meters (3,800 feet) and stops about half a mile north of the divide. (It was not found anywhere in Meadow Creek Valley.)

UTAH.

Beaverdam Mountains.—Common on the west slope from 1,040 meters (3,400 feet) up to the summit of the pass at 1,525 meters (5,000 feet), and on the northeast slope between 975 and 1,340 meters (3,200 and 4,400 feet), and straggling still higher.

Santa Clara Valley.—Occurs on cold slopes in the Lower Santa Clara Valley, near St. George, whence it ranges up on the north side of the valley (south exposure) to 1,525 meters (5,000 feet), but is not evenly distributed.

Cercocarpus ledifolius.

The mountain mahogany is common on the higher summits of some of the desert ranges, and was recorded from the following localities:

CALIFORNIA.

Panamint Mountains.—A grove of large and handsome mountain mahogany trees occupies the bottom of a cañon above the abandoned charcoal kilns at the north base of Telescope Peak, whence straggling trees pass over the summit of the Panamint Range north of the Peak at an altitude of 2,560 meters (8,400 feet). Others were found on the north slope as high as 3,060 meters (9,300 feet).

High Sierra.—On the east (Owens Valley) slope of the High Sierra the mountain mahogany is found in abundance, and of unusually large size. West of Lone Pine it grows in a zone from 2,285 to 2,900 meters (7,500 to 9,500 feet) altitude, and many of the individual trees attain a diameter of a foot.

NEVADA.

Mount Magruder.—Common and of large size on the main peak, above 2,590 meters (8,500 feet), but not reaching summit.

UTAH.

Upper Santa Clara Valley.—Common in places on the west slope of Pine Valley Mountain.

Cercocarpus parvifolius.

Common in the chaparral on the west slope of the Sierra Nevada and on the coast ranges. It was found in abundance also in the Cañada de las Uvas and on the south slope of the Sierra Liebre, along the upper part of the valley of Peru Creek.

Cowania mexicana.

This beautiful shrub, which attains a height of 2 or 3 meters (6 to 9 feet), is common on many of the desert ranges, where it flowers in such profusion that its large cream-colored blossoms often hide the deep green of its foliage.

CALIFORNIA.

Panamint Mountains.—Found on the summit of the range, northwest of Telescope Peak, at an altitude of about 2,560 meters (8,400 feet).

NEVADA.

Mount Magruder.—Found sparingly in the upper part of the Tule Cañon on the south slope of Mount Magruder.

Gold Mountain.—Common, and ranging down on the south side to about 1,990 meters (6,200 feet).

Hungry Hill Summit.—Begins just north of the summit, passes over the divide and down on the south side, toward Indian Spring Valley, to about 1,525 meters (5,000 feet).

Pahranagat Mountains.—Common, descending to about 1,580 meters (5,200 feet) on the east slope.

Pahroc Mountains.—Common in the sage brush near Pahroc Spring; just coming into flower May 20.

Highland Range.—Found on the west slope.

Charleston Mountains.—Found on the west slope from 1,550 to 1,830 meters (5,100 to 6,000 feet) in the neighborhood of Mountain Spring.

Juniper Mountains (between Panaca, Nevada, and Shoal Creek, Utah).—Abundant in places on south exposures, where it was hardly in bud May 17, while a week earlier (May 10) it was flowering in the height of perfection on the Beaverdam Mountains. *Kunzia tridentata* was common with *Cowania* in the Juniper Mountains and was just coming into flower May 17, while it had past flowering in the Beaverdam Mountains May 10.

UTAH.

Beaverdam Mountains.—Abundant, ranging from 1,100 to 1,430 meters (3,600 to 4,700 feet) in altitude on the northeast slope; flowering profusely May 10–11.

Santa Clara Valley.—In ascending the Santa Clara Valley, *Cowania* begins in the sage brush about 13 kilometers (8 miles) northwest of St. George (altitude 1,280 meters, or 4,200 feet), and extends thence northerly to and beyond the Upper Santa Clara Crossing, reaching an altitude of about 1,645 meters (5,400 feet) where it stops and *Kunzia* begins. In other localities it is mixed with *Kunzia*, though the latter generally ranges higher.

Fallugia paradoxa.

This species occurs on many of the desert ranges of the Great Basin, often associated with *Cowania mexicana* and *Kunzia tridentata*, from which it has not always been discriminated by travelers. *Fallugia* averages hardly more than a meter in height, being a much smaller bush than *Cowania*. Its pure white flowers are larger than the cream-colored blossoms of *Cowania*, and are borne on longer peduncles. The flowers of *Kunzia* are yellow. *Fallugia* was found in the following localities:

NEVADA.

Charleston Mountains.—Common on the west slope above 1,430 meters (4,700 feet), in the neighborhood of Mountain Spring, ranging up to at least 1,700 meters (5,600 feet). On the east slope it was not seen above 1,525 meters (5,000 feet).

Pahranagat Mountains.—Common on the east slope a little above 1,580 meters (5,200 feet), and on the west slope reaches the summit.

Hungry Hill Summit.—Begins just north of summit and passes over the divide (1,770 meters, or 5,800 feet) and down on the south side toward the North Arm of Indian Spring Valley to 1,525 meters (5,000 feet).

UTAH.

Beaverdam Mountains.—Common on the east and northeast slopes of the Beaverdam Mountains, between 1,160 and 1,370 meters (3,800 to 4,500 feet), where it was just coming into flower May 11.

Rosa sp.—?

A wild rose was found in large patches in Pahranagat Valley, Nevada, where it was in full bloom May 22-25.

Heteromeles arbutifolia.

This is one of the characteristic shrubs of the Coast Ranges of California. It is common on the south slope of the Sierra Liebre, but hardly enters the region covered by the expedition.

Amelanchier alnifolia.

The service berry does not grow in the deserts, but occurs sparingly on some of the desert ranges.

In Nevada it was found on the west slope of the Charleston Mountains, between 1,675 and 1,765 meters (5,500 to 5,800 feet) altitude; on the Juniper Mountains, on the Pahroc Mountains, and on Mount Magruder, where it descends into the upper part of Tule Cañon.

In Utah it was found sparingly between the Upper Santa Clara Crossing and Mountain Meadows, and in some places formed dense thickets; and on the east slope of the Beaverdam Mountains it was common between an altitude of 1,100 meters (3,600 feet) and the summit of the pass at 1,525 meters (5,000 feet).

Peraphyllum ramosissimum.

This dwarf cherry, whose handsome flowers are disproportionately large for so small a bush, was found in the following localities on the mountain sides of the Transition Zone.

NEVADA.

Mount Magruder.—Very abundant in large patches from an altitude of about 2,130 meters (7,000 feet) up to about 2,590 meters (8,500 feet) and descending into Tule Cañon. Flowering profusely June 6.

Charleston Mountains.—Found near Mountain Spring.

Hungry Hill Summit.—Begins a little north of the summit, passes over the divide (1,760 meters, or 5,800 feet) and down on the south side toward the North Arm of Indian Spring Valley to about 1,525 meters (5,000 feet).

Highland Range.—Found on the west slope.

Juniper Mountains.—Found in scattered clumps at an altitude of about 1,825 meters, (6,000 feet) and upwards from the Upper Santa Clara Crossing to Shoal Creek and thence northwesterly across the Juniper Plateau.

Ribes leptanthum brachyanthum.

This species was collected on Gold Mountain, Nevada, at an altitude of about 2,130 meters (7,000 feet).

Others, probably the same species, were found at Sheep Spring in the Juniper Mountains, Nevada; in the cañon at the south end of Pahranagat Valley, and on Mount Magruder.

Ribes menziesii.

Common in places in the Cañada de las Uvas, California, especially in the vicinity of Old Fort Tejon.

Petalonyx parryi.

This bush was found in but one locality, namely, the mesa on the south side of Vegas Wash, Nevada, where it was abundant on gypsum soil and in full bloom May 2. It is a small bush averaging 450 to 600^{mm} (about 1½ or 2 feet) in height, and having pale, yellowish flowers.

Eucnide urens.

This singular plant, which grows in crevices in rocky cañons, was found in suitable places along the bases of many of the desert ranges in southern California and western Nevada, and also along the Lower Santa Clara River in southwestern Utah.

Garrya veatchii flavescens.

This willow-like bush, about 1½ meters (5 feet) in height, is common on the west slope of the Charleston Mountains, Nevada, near Mountain Spring, between 1,670 and 1,760 meters (5,500 and 5,800 feet), and on the Beaverdam Mountains in southwestern Utah.

Symphoricarpos longiflorus.

Symphoricarpos bushes were found on many of the desert ranges of Nevada, in the Upper Sonoran and Transition zones. *S. longiflorus* was common at Pahroc Spring, where it was in full flower May 21 (specimens collected). Others, supposed to belong to the same species, but not collected and not positively identified, were recorded from the following localities:

NEVADA.

Highland Range.—Common in places, particularly in cañons.

Timpahute and Desert mountains.—Common in places on the higher parts of the range.

Hyko Range.—Found sparingly in a cañon leading from Pahroc Plain to Pahranagat Valley.

Pahranagat Mountains.—Common, descending on the east slope to 1,580 meters (5,200 feet).

Gold Mountain.—Common on the north side.

Mount Magruder.—Common high up on the main peak and on side hills lower down, and also in several of the cañons, particularly in the upper part of Tule Cañon.

UTAH.

Beaverdam Mountains.—Found on the east slope.

Amphiachyris fremontii.

This handsome little bush, which is common on parts of the Mohave Desert, was collected in the Valley of the Virgin near Bunkerville, Nevada.

Acamptopappus sphærocephalus.

This composite desert shrub is abundant on many of the deserts and was common in the narrow valley between Owens Lake and Haway Meadows, California.

Aplopappus monactis.

Collected on Sarcobatus Flat, on the southwestern edge of the Ralston Desert, Nevada.

Bigelovia douglassi.

This species is not found in the desert bottoms, but is common among the sage brush and junipers on many of the mountain sides.

CALIFORNIA.

Walker Pass.—Becomes abundant at an altitude of 1,430 meters (4,700 feet) on the east side and ranges up over the summit of the pass. On the west side it descends plentifully to 1,250 meters (4,100 feet).

Kern Valley.—Occurs on the north exposures as low down as 820 meters (2,700 feet).

Tehachapi Basin.—Occurs.

Cañada de las Uvas.—Common.

Bigelovia graveolens.

This Upper Sonoran desert species was common in the extreme western end of the Mohave Desert (Antelope Valley) and was found in a wash leading thence southerly toward Peru Creek, along with tree yuccas, sage brush, and *Isomeris*. Specimens provisionally referred to the same species by Mr. Coville were collected at Beaverdam, Arizona.

Bigelovia teretifolia.

Collected on Gold Mountain, Nevada, at an altitude of 1,830 meters (6,000 feet) June 3.

A large and rank species, supposed to be the same, was found in abundance in many of the dry washes of the desert ranges from Emigrant Cañon in the Panamint Mountains, California, eastward to the Pahranagat and Hyko ranges, Nevada, and the Beaverdam Mountains, Utah. On the west slope of the latter range it was found up to 1,340 meters (4,400 feet).

Baccharis glutinosa.

No species of *Baccharis* was observed on the western side of the Great Basin, but one or more species were found in great abundance at the Bend of the Colorado River, in Nevada, and in the Valley of the Virgin and Lower Muddy, and also on the flat at the mouth of Beaverdam Creek, in northwestern Arizona.

Pluchea sericea.

This slender, willow-like plant, sometimes called 'arrow-wood,' forms low thickets in the neighborhood of water in some parts of the desert region, but was not found west of Death Valley. It is common at Furnace Creek on the east side of Death Valley, the only locality in California where it was seen by the expedition. In Nevada it is common about some of the warm springs in Ash Meadows, and very abundant in Vegas Wash and about the Great Bend of the Colorado River, and also in parts of the Muddy and Virgin valleys. In the Lower Santa Clara Valley, Utah, near the junction of the Santa Clara with the Virgin, it forms dense thickets along the river.

Hymenoclea salsola.

This small shrub, which suggests a *Bigeloria* in general appearance, but is profusely beset with small glomerate heads, is common in many parts of the desert region, particularly along the courses of washes on the mountain sides, in which it frequently attains a considerable altitude. The following notes on its distribution were recorded:

CALIFORNIA.

Mohave Desert.—Common in places and found as far west as Antelope Valley, between the town of Mohave and Willow Spring; also extends up the open cañon leading from Mohave to Tehachapi Basin, where it reaches an altitude of 1,050 meters (3,450 feet).

Walker Pass.—On the east side of the pass it ranges up to 1,430 meters (4,700 feet) in the tree yuccas. On the west side of the pass it runs down into Kern Valley as low as 820 meters (2,700 feet), perhaps lower.

Owens Valley.—Abundant in the southern part of the valley and one of the commonest shrubs on the west side between Lone Pine and Haway Meadows. It ranges up along the foot of the Sierra slope to 1,525 or 1,550 meters (5,000 or 5,100 feet).

Deep Spring Valley.—Found in the wash leading up to the pass across the White Mountains.

NEVADA.

Graperine Cañon.—Common in the bottom of the cañon.

Oasis Valley.—Common along the bottom of the valley.

Indian Spring Valley.—Common in the wash at the extreme west end of Indian Spring Valley.

Emigrant Valley.—Common and reaching thence up on the west side of the Desert Mountains to about 1,680 meters (5,500 feet) near Mud or Summit Spring.

Timpahute Valley.—One of the principal plants in the bottom.

Pahranagat Valley.—Common throughout the dryer parts of the valley up to about 1,340 meters (4,400 feet). On the west side (Pahranagat Mountain slope) it runs up a gravel wash to nearly 1,525 meters

(5,000 feet). On the east side it is common in a wash leading down from Pahroc Plain through the Hyko Mountains.

Virgin Valley.—Common in places.

UTAH.

Beaverdam Mountains.—Reaches up the west slope of the Beaverdam Mountains to 1,340 meters (4,400 feet).

Santa Clara Valley.—Common over most of the valley, reaching upon the east slope of the Beaverdam Mountains to 1,100 meters (3,600 feet).

Franseria dumosa.

This small and inconspicuous shrub is one of the most important zone plants of the Lower Sonoran Zone, because of its wide distribution and strict adherence to the lower division of this zone. It occurs almost invariably in company with *Larrea tridentata*. The following notes on its distribution were recorded:

CALIFORNIA.

Mohave Desert.—Abundant, finding its upper limit on the north side of the desert at about 1,000 meters (3,250 feet), where it enters the mouth of the open cañon leading from Mohave to Tehachapi, and ranges about 45 meters (150 feet) higher than *Larrea*. It reaches its western limit in Antelope Valley.

Walker Pass.—Common at the east mouth of Walker Pass, ranging up to about 1,100 meters (3,600 feet) thus exceeding the *Larrea* by about 30 meters (100 feet).

Owens Valley.—Common in the extreme south end of the valley on the east side, and found in scattered patches from Lone Pine south, and all along the west side of Owens Lake and thence south to Haway Meadows.

NEVADA.

Pahrump Valley.—Common in the *Larrea* on the east side of the valley, where it finds its upper limit with that of *Larrea* on the southwest slope of the Charleston Mountains at 1,310 meters (4,400 feet).

Vegas Valley.—Covers the valley with *Larrea* and ranges up on the west side to about 1,130 meters (3,700 feet).

Muddy Mountains.—Common in *Larrea* at the Great Bend of the Colorado whence it extends northward over the low summits of the Muddy Mountains between Callville and the Virgin.

Valley of the Virgin and Lower Muddy.—Abundant in dry places with *Larrea*, particularly on gravel slopes. Common also on the high mesa between these two rivers, where it is abundant along the boundary between Arizona and Nevada.

Pahranagat Valley.—Common on the gravel benches with *Larrea* in the southern and southwestern parts of the valley, but not evenly distributed and not reaching the northern part of the valley at all. It runs up an open cañon leading from Pahroc Plain into Pahranagat Valley, reaching an altitude of 1,310 meters (4,300 feet) on the southwesterly slope exposures, but falling a little short of the extreme limit of the scattered patches of *Larrea* in the same cañon.

Indian Spring Valley.—Common throughout the valley in *Larrea*.

Oasis Valley.—Occurs sparsely in the lower part of the valley along with *Larrea*, both species here finding their northern limit in this part of Nevada.

Grapevine Cañon.—*Franseria* comes up in Grapevine Cañon from Death Valley and reaches up on the southern slope of Gold Mountain as high as 1,610 meters (5,300 feet) in company with *Larrea*. (It was not found in Sarcobatus Flat or in Meadow Creek Valley.)

ARIZONA.

Common with *Larrea* in the Valley of the Virgin near the mouth of Beaverdam Creek, and ranging thence easterly up the west slope of the Beaverdam Mountains to 1,160 meters (3,800 feet).

UTAH.

Santa Clara Valley.—Occurs sparingly in the lower part of the valley, disappearing a little above 1,220 meters (4,000 feet).

Franseria eriocentra.

This species was first found at the mouth of Beaverdam Creek in northwestern Arizona. On the opposite side of the mountains it is common in parts of the Santa Clara Valley in Utah. In Nevada it is abundant in the higher parts of Pahranagat Valley, whence it ranges up through a cañon in the Hyko Mountains; it reaches the summit of the pass over the Pahranagat Mountains (1,825 meters or 6,000 feet) from the west (Timpahute) slope; and occurs also at Hungry Hill Summit, whence it extends southerly to about 1,675 meters (5,500 feet).

Encelia frutescens.

This species is common in places on the Mohave Desert, whence it ranges up completely through the open cañon leading from Mohave to Tehachapi Valley (altitude of divide 1,100 meters or 3,600 feet), and up the east slope of Walker Pass to 1,430 meters (4,700 feet).

Artemisia tridentata.

This species, the true aromatic sagebrush of the Great Basin, does not grow anywhere in the deserts of the Lower Sonoran zone, but begins with the Upper Sonoran and ranges thence northward over the plains of the Transition zone, and on many mountain sides covers the gravel slopes well up into the Boreal. In the southern part of the Great Basin, therefore, it was found only on the mountains. Coming down from the plains of Oregon, Washington, and Idaho, it covers the whole of the northern part of the State of Nevada, and California east of the Sierra Nevada, and reaches southward uninterruptedly along the bottom of Owens Valley nearly to Owens Lake, and still further south along the Sierra, White, and Inyo mountains. On the treeless plains it is much prized as firewood. The following detailed notes on its distribution were recorded:

CALIFORNIA.

Cañada de las Uvas.—Common at an altitude of 1,070 meters (3,500 feet), ranging from Castac Lake eastward to the extreme west foot of Antelope Valley and also occurring in a wash leading thence southward toward Peru Creek, where it is mixed with stunted tree yuccas (altitude 760 to 910 meters or 2,500 to 3,000 feet).

Walker Pass.—Common on the east side of the pass from 1,430 meters (4,700 feet) to summit (1,550 meters or 5,100 feet), and much higher on mountains on both sides. On the west slope it covers the whole pass down to 1,240 meters (4,100 feet).

Kern Valley.—Found on a steep north slope in the Kern River Valley as low as 820 meters (2,700 feet).

East slope of Sierra Nevada.—Abundant all along the west side of Owens Valley and ranging thence up on the Sierra as high as 2,740 meters (9,000 feet).

Owens Valley.—Covers the whole valley from its northern end down to within a few miles of Lone Pine, descending to about 1,160 meters (3,800 feet). South of Lone Pine it is confined to the west side of the valley, where it follows the cold streams that come down from the High Sierra and is common on the slope above 1,550 meters (5,100 feet). In a few places it reaches the narrow valley between Owens Lake and Haway Meadows. It is absent from the warm slope at the foot of the White and Inyo mountains on the east side of Owens Valley, but begins as low as 1,980 meters (6,500 feet) on northerly exposures in the latitude of Big Pine, and ranges up over the White Mountains.

White and Inyo mountains.—Abundant over most parts of the summit of the range, often forming pure sage plains of considerable extent and ranging down to about 2,280 meters (7,500 feet) on the west slope (Owens Valley side) and to 1,920 meters (6,300 feet) on the east slope (Deep Spring Valley side), but does not descend into Deep Spring Valley.

Panamint Mountains.—Common along the summit of the range, descending as low in places as 1,980 meters (6,500 feet) or even 1,920 meters (6,300 feet). On the west slope of Telescope Peak it grows as high as 3,050 meters (10,000 feet).

Mohave Desert.—Found on the summit of Cajon Pass and thence along the upper part of the Mohave Desert at the foot of the San Bernardino Mountains, occurring sparsely among the junipers down to an altitude of 1,160 meters (3,800 feet), where it is replaced by *Atriplex* and other genera. The altitude of the Mohave Desert as a whole is too low for sagebrush.

NEVADA.

Fish Lake Valley.—Not found in the bottom of the valley, but descends from the White Mountains to about 1,680 meters (5,500 feet) along the west side of the valley; and from Mount Magruder to about 2,040 meters (6,700 feet) on the southeast side of the valley (northwest exposure), and still lower on northerly exposures.

Mount Magruder.—Covers the whole Mount Magruder plateau and the hills and peaks that rise from it even to the extreme summit of Mount Magruder itself. On the latter peak it grows in a peculiar way, forming distinct lines that are conspicuous at a distance. These lines are horizontal on the peaks and vertical on the saddles. On the south side of Mount Magruder it descends into Tule Cañon (in the upper part of which it is the prevailing brush) and into the valley between Mount Magruder and Gold Mountain, where it is mixed with *Grayia spinosa*, *Tetradymia glabrata*, *Atriplex confertifolia*, and other species. On the northwest slope of Mount Magruder it descends to Pigeon Spring (altitude 2,040 meters, or 6,700 feet) and reaches several hundred feet lower on the south side of the cañon (north exposure).

Gold Mountain.—Sagebrush is the prevailing brush on Gold Mountain, on the south slope of which it descends to 1,830 meters (6,000 feet).

Timpahute and Desert ranges.—Common along the summit, descending to the divide at Hungry Hill summit, 1,780 meters (5,850 feet), and extending thence southward toward the North Arm of Indian Spring Valley to 1,740 meters (5,700 feet), and northward toward Emigrant Valley to 1,700 meters (5,600 feet).

Pahranagat Mountains.—Abundant, descending as low as 1,525 meters (5,000 feet) on the east slope (Pahranagat Valley side) at the latitude of the middle of the valley, and still lower in the northern part of the valley.

Pahroc Mountains.—Common, reaching down to 1,740 meters (5,700 feet) or a little lower on the upper levels of Desert Valley.

Highland range.—Abundant, descending to 1,830 meters (6,000 feet) on the west side (Desert Valley side), and down into the valley of Meadow Creek on the east side, covering the valley excepting the flat bordering the creek.

Juniper Mountains.—The whole of the high plateau here spoken of as the Juniper Plateau or Mountains, extending from Meadow Creek Valley, Nevada, easterly to and across the western boundary of Utah, is continuously covered with sagebrush mixed with junipers.

Charleston Mountains.—Abundant throughout the higher parts of the Charleston Mountains, descending on the west slope (Pahrump Valley side) to 1,550 meters (5,100 feet).

UTAH.

In western Utah the true sage spreads southward continuously, covering the Escalante Desert and Shoal Creek country and Mountain Meadows (which is a true sage plain), and extending south continuously far enough to include the Upper Santa Clara Valley above 1,280 meters

(4,200 feet) altitude, where its southern edge reaches within 13 kilometers (8 miles) of the town of St. George. To the west it ranges continuously over the Juniper Plateau to Meadow Creek Valley as already mentioned, and reaches southward, along the Beaverdam Mountains, descending to 1,340 meters (4,400 feet) on the west (Arizona) slope and to 1,100 meters (3,600 feet) on the east (Utah) slope.

Artemisia spinescens.

This compact little species is abundant on many of the higher valleys and slopes of the desert region in the southern part of the Great Basin, in California and Nevada. The following notes on its distribution were recorded:

CALIFORNIA.

Walker Pass.—Found on the summit at an altitude of 1,830 meters (5,100 feet).

Deep Spring Valley.—Common, in company with *Menodora spinosa*, *Grayia spinosa*, *Eurotia lanata*, *Dalea fremonti*, *D. polyadenia*, *Lycium andersoni*, and *Tetradymia spinosa*.

Panamint Mountains.—Common in many parts of the range. The little basin between Wild Rose Spring and Emigrant Cañon, named 'Perognathus Flat' by our expedition, is covered with this species, very pure and little mixed with other plants.

NEVADA.

Fish Lake Valley.—Abundant, covering the flat on the east side of the valley in company with *Eurotia lanata*, and ranging thence up on the northwest slope of Mount Magruder nearly to Pigeon Spring (altitude 2,040 meters or 6,700 feet).

Valley between Mount Magruder and Gold Mountain.—Not abundant, but found in company with *Artemisia tridentata*, *Grayia spinosa*, *Atriplex confertifolia*, and *Tetradymia glabrata*.

Grapevine Cañon.—Tolerably common in the upper part of the cañon.

Sarcobatus Flat.—Common in northern part.

Oasis Valley.—Common in the upper part of the valley above 1,220 meters (4,000 feet) and ranging thence westerly.

Emigrant Valley.—One of the commonest plants of the bottom (altitude a little above 1,525 meters or 5,000 feet), and ranging thence easterly up on the Timpahute Mountains to 1,680 meters (5,500 feet).

Timpahute Valley.—One of the principal plants.

Pahranagat Valley.—Common on the higher levels above 1,220 meters (4,000 feet). In places on the west side of the valley it reaches 2,440 meters or 5,300 feet (on the east slope of the Pahranagat Mountains).

Desert Valley.—The dominant plant in the gravelly soil surrounding the dry lake.

Meadow Creek Valley.—Common below 1,770 meters (5,800 feet), on the west slope of the Juniper Plateau.

Artemisia arbuscula.

This sage, which grows at greater elevations than most species, was found in Nevada on the summit of the Pahranagat Mountains and on Mount Magruder.

Artemisia filifolia.

This species was rare in the region traversed, but was found covering a large flat near St. George in the Lower Santa Clara Valley, Utah. It differs widely from the other species of the genus, its long linear or filiform whitish leaves giving it a peculiarly soft and beautiful appearance.

Peucephyllum schottii.

This large shrub, resembling a *Bigelovia* in general aspect, was found in many of the dry washes on the lower parts of the desert ranges and in some of the higher valleys. It is common in Owens Valley, California, where it ranges up on the east slope of the Sierra to 1,550 meters (about 5,100 feet). On the opposite side of the valley it reaches up on the west slope of the White Mountains to about 1,980 meters (6,500 feet). It is common also on the Panamint Mountains, California, in the Muddy Mountains, Nevada, and in many other localities.

Tetradymia canescens.

This species is common on many of the higher levels, particularly on the desert ranges. In Nevada it was common on Mount Magruder; in the upper part of Pahranagat Valley; in the Juniper Mountains (between Meadow Creek, Nevada, and the Escalante Desert, Utah); and in Utah in the upper part of the Santa Clara Valley (mixed with the true sage brush, *Artemisia tridentata*).

Tetradymia glabrata.

This fine species was not seen in the southern deserts traversed in going from Panamint and Death valleys across southern Nevada to Utah, but was found in a number of places on the return trip, which was a little further north and covered higher ground. Before going to seed it may be easily recognized by its deep-green cylindrical branches, which are nearly vertical. It was found between the east slope of the Sierra in Owens Valley, California, and Meadow Creek Valley, Nevada, in the following localities:

CALIFORNIA.

Owens Valley.—Common, ranging up to 1,550 meters (5,100 feet) on the west slope.

NEVADA.

Valley between Gold Mountain and Mount Magruder.—Occurs sparingly in this valley with *Artemisia tridentata*, *Grayia spinosa* and other brush.

Grapevine Cañon.—Found in the upper part of the cañon.

Sarcobatus Flat.—Tolerably common in places in the northern part of the flat.

Oasis Valley.—Scarce. Found sparingly above 1,200 meters (4,000 feet).

Emigrant Valley.—Common on the higher slopes and ranging thence easterly over the west slope of the Desert Mountains.

Timpahute Valley.—One of the principal plants ranging easterly to the summit of the pass over the Pahranagat Mountains (1,830 meters or 6,000 feet.)

Pahranagat Valley.—Tolerably common in dry places, running up to 1,650 meters (5,400 feet) on the west side of the valley (Pahranagat Mountain side) with *T. spinosa* and *Grayia spinosa*. Some of it was in full flower May 22–26, though it was mostly in bud at that date.

Desert Valley.—Ranges throughout the low pass across the Highland Range between Meadow Creek and Desert valleys.

Meadow Creek Valley.—Common, ranging easterly for about 13 kilometers (8 miles) east of Panaca, where it was first seen. This point constitutes the easternmost limit of the range of the species so far as observed by us.

Tetradymia spinosa.

This elegant bush, with conspicuous long straw-yellow spines, is common on many of the higher levels in the southern part of the Great Basin. In early spring when the foliage is freshest it is very handsome, and later in the season when in fruit and covered with its white woolly tufts of soft feathery plumes it is still more beautiful. It was found in the following localities:

CALIFORNIA.

Walker Pass.—Tolerably common among the tree yuccas on the east side of the pass as high up as 1,430 meters (4,700 feet); found also on the west slope between 1,250 and 1,400 meters (4,100 and 4,600 feet).

Kern Valley.—Common on northerly exposures as low as 820 meters (2,700 feet).

Owens Valley.—Common along the west side of the valley, where it ranges up the east slope of the Sierra opposite Lone Pine to 1,830 or 1,890 meters (6,000 to 6,200 feet). On the opposite side of the valley it ranges up the White Mountain slope to 1,980 meters (6,500 feet) or higher.

Deep Spring Valley.—Occurs in the bottom of the valley with *Grayia spinosa, Menodora spinosa, Eurotia lanata, Daleas,* and a few others (altitude about 1,675 meters or 5,500 feet).

NEVADA.

Gold Mountain.—Common on the south slope above 1,675 meters (5,500), and on the north slope below 2,135 meters (7,000 feet).

Oasis Valley.—Common on gravel soil at the head of the valley at an altitude of about 1,340 meters (4,400 feet).

Emigrant Valley.—Found on the east side of the valley, ranging thence over the lower parts of the Desert and Timpahute mountains.

Timpahute Valley.—Common on the higher levels, and ranges up on the Pahranagat Mountain slope to the summit of the divide at 1,830 meters (6,000 feet). On the west side of the valley it begins at 1,460 meters (4,800 feet) and ranges up on the Timpahute Mountains.

Pahranagat Valley.—Common in places, generally on gravel soil, ascending on the west side of the valley (east slope of Pahranagat Mountains) to 1,645 meters (5,400 feet).

Highland Range.—Found sparingly on the west slope.

Charleston Mountains.—On the west slope of the Charleston Mountains *Tetradymia spinosa* was found in a zone between 1,340 and 1,765 meters (4,400–5,800 feet).

UTAH.

Beaverdam Mountains.—Occurs sparingly.

Tetradymia comosa (or stenolepis).

This beautiful shrub, which may be recognized at a distance by its whiteness, is common in part of the region traversed. It was found in the following localities:

CALIFORNIA.

Owens Valley.—Common in the higher parts of the valley, ranging up on the west side opposite Lone Pine to 1,520 or 1,550 meters (5,000 or 5,100 feet.)

Walker Pass.—Occurs on the east side of the pass where it was seen at 1,250 meters (4,100 feet).

Kern Valley.—Found on northerly exposures as low as 820 meters (2,700 feet).

Mohave Desert.—Found in places, ranging westward nearly to Willow Spring in Antelope Valley, and extending northward through the open cañon leading from Mohave to Tehachapi.

Arctostaphylos glauca.

In Cajon Pass this manzanita begins at about 670 meters (2,200 feet) and ranges up to the summit of the pass.

Arctostaphylos pungens.

This species of manzanita was found on the Charleston Mountains, Nevada, near Mountain Spring, and on the east slope of the Beaverdam Mountains in Utah, from 1,100 to 1,300 meters (3,600 to 4,300 feet) altitude. It was not found on any of the other desert ranges.

NOTE.—Other species of manzanita are common on both slopes of the Sierra Nevada in California, and on the coast ranges.

Menodora spinescens.

The beautiful little bush provisionally referred to this species, but which may have been *Menodora scoparia*, grows in dense tufts over many of the higher desert levels, where it is easily recognized by the peculiar green of its foliage and by the circumstance that it fruits early and its large green berries are distributed in pairs along the branches, growing sessile, one on each side of the stem. It was found in the following localities:

CALIFORNIA.

Deep Spring Valley.—Occurs in company with *Grayia, Eurotia, Dalea, Lycium,* and *Tetradymia spinosa;* altitude about 1,680 meters (5,500 feet).

NEVADA.

Fish Lake Valley.—Common on the upper levels, ranging up on the northwest side of Mount Magruder to 1,950 meters (6,400 feet).

Gold Mountain.—Common on the south slope, ranging upward from 1,550 meters (5,100 feet).

Oasis Valley.—Occurs sparingly above 1,220 meters (4,000 feet).

Indian Spring Valley.—Tolerably common throughout the valley.

Timpahute Valley.—One of the principal plants.

Pahranagat Valley.—Rather common on gravelly soil above an altitude of 1,190 meters (3,900 feet); on the west side of the valley (Pahranagat Mountain slope) it ranges up to 1,525 meters (5,000 feet). It was heavily laden with fruit May 22-26.

Charleston Mountains.—On the west slope of the Charleston Mountains *Menodora spinosa* ranges from about 1,525 meters (5,000 feet) down to the upper levels of Pahrump Valley.

NOTE.—Another species of *Menodora*, considerably larger than the one above mentioned (perhaps true *spinescens*), was found on the divide south of Pahranagat Lake, Nevada, at an altitude of about 1,150 meters (3,800 feet).

Fraxinus coriacea.

This ash was observed in the following localities:

CALIFORNIA.

Owens Valley.—Common in open groves along Cottonwood and Ash creeks on the west side of Owens Lake, where it was heavily laden with fruit June 19. Another and very distinct species occurs in company with *F. coriacea* and was in fruit on the same date.

NEVADA.

Ash Meadows.—Ash Meadows takes its name from the circumstance that this small ash is common about many of the warm springs. Ash Meadows is the type locality of the species.

Upper Cottonwood Springs.—Small ash trees, supposed to be this species, are common with the desert willows (*Chilopsis linearis*) along the Upper Cottonwood Springs at the east base of the Charleston Mountains.

UTAH.

Santa Clara Valley.—A small ash, supposed to be this species, is common along the banks of the Lower Santa Clara River, where it occurs in company with *F. anomala*, the latter reaching the Santa Clara from the neighboring slope of the Beaverdam Mountains.

Fraxinus anomala.

This single-leaved dwarf ash was found near Mountain Springs on the west slope of the Charleston Mountains, Nevada, from 1,600 to 1,760 meters (5,300 to 5,800 feet); and on the east slope of the Beaverdam Mountains, Utah, from an altitude of 1,275 meters (4,200 feet) down to the Lower Santa Clara Valley, where it occurs along the river with another species believed to be *F. coriacea*.

Eriodictyon tomentosum.

This species was common in the Cañada de las Uvas, California, particularly on north and east exposures, and was found also on the south slope of the Sierra Liebre along the Valley of Peru Creek.

Lycium andersoni.

The members of the genus *Lycium* rank among the characteristic bushes of the Great Basin in California, Nevada, Utah, and Arizona. They rarely inhabit the lower deserts, but are found plentifully on the upper levels and on many of the desert ranges. They are not social plants, but occur here and there among the other kinds of desert brush. Their flowers are usually greenish yellow and inconspicuous. The berries of *L. andersoni* are brownish in color, acid, and rather pleasant, suggesting currants. This species, which is the smallest of the genus, was found in the following localities:

CALIFORNIA.

Antelope Valley (west end of Mohave Desert).—A little was seen between Mohave and Willow Spring. It occurs also along the northwest edge of the Mohave Desert, and ascends the open cañon leading up to Tehachapi Valley as high as 1,030 meters (3,400 feet).

Walker Pass and Kern Valley.—Runs up to 1,430 meters (4,700 feet) on the east slope. On the west slope it was observed from 1,220 meters (a little over 4,000 feet) down to 820 meters (2,700 feet) in the valley of Kern River.

Owens Valley.—Occurs sparingly on the west side of the valley, ranging up to 1,525 or 1,550 meters (5,000 or 5,100 feet) on the Sierra slope opposite Lone Pine.

Deep Spring Valley.—Occurs in company with *Grayia*, *Eurotia*, *Dalea fremonti*, *D. polyadenia*, *Menodora spinosa*, *Tetradymia spinosa*, *Artemisia spinescens*, and *Atriplex canescens*.

NEVADA.

Fish Lake Valley.—Found on the east side of the valley, whence it ranges up on the northwest slope of Mount Magruder as high as 1,860 meters (6,100 feet).

Meadow Creek Valley.—Common in places, and ranging up to 1,765 meters (5,800 feet) on the west slope of the Juniper Range.

Grapevine Cañon.—Occurs at the upper end of the cañon near Sarcobatus Flat.

Oasis Valley.—Rather common, beginning at the foot of the valley at 1,140 meters (3,750 feet), and following the bottom to the head of the valley.

Amargosa Desert.—Occurs sparingly, mixed with the upper edge of the *Larrea*.

Indian Spring Valley.—Common; berries ripe May 29.

Emigrant Valley.—Common, and runs up on the west slope of the Desert Mountains to the divide near Summit or Mud Spring.

Timpahute Valley.—One of the principal plants.

Pahranagat Valley.—Common on dry gravelly levels, mixed with other shrubs. Extends up from the valley to 1,580 meters (5,200 feet) or higher on the Pahranagat Mountains. Fruit ripening May 22–26.

Pakroc Plain.—Rather common, mixed with *Grayia spinosa*, *Eurotia lanata*, and *Atriplex canescens*.

UTAH.

Beaverdam Mountains.—Tolerably common on the east slope, ranging up to 1,100 meters (3,600 feet), and down to the Santa Clara Valley.

Lycium cooperi.

This large species was found in the following localities:

CALIFORNIA.

Mohave Desert.—Common in the upper levels, reaching west in Antelope Valley nearly to Willow Spring, and extending northward throughout the open cañon leading up to Tehachapi.

Tehachapi Valley.—Occurs in places, coming from the Mohave Desert and extending northward sparingly into Tehachapi Pass.

Kern Valley.—Occurs on northerly exposures down to 820 meters (2,700 feet).

Owens Valley.—Common in large clumps on the west side of the valley, ranging up on the Sierra slope as high as 1,830 or 1,890 meters (6,000 or 6,200 feet) opposite Lone Pine, and common in places all the way south to Haway Meadows and the Mohave Desert.

Panamint Mountains.—Common in places.

NEVADA.

Gold Mountain.—Occurs sparingly on the north slope (collected).

Amargosa Desert.—Found mixed with the *Larrea* in the upper part of the *Larrea* zone.

Oasis Valley.—Occurs.

Mount Magruder.—Found near Pigeon Spring, on the northwest slope of Mount Magruder.

Lycium torreyi.

This large species was collected in fruit in the Muddy Valley near St. Thomas, Nevada, where it was common in dry parts of the valley, and also in the Valley of the Virgin (nearly out of flower May 6). In Utah it was found in the Santa Clara Valley.

Lycium pallidum.

This large species, which has large trumpet shaped flowers and large leaves, is common in the Upper Santa Clara Valley, Utah, about 8 miles northwest of St. George, at an altitude of 1,275 meters (4,200 feet), ranging thence up to or above the Upper Santa Clara crossing. It was collected on the east slope of the Beaverdam Mountains, where it runs up to 1,090 meters (3,600 feet). A large species, probably the same, was found on the west slope of the Beaverdam Mountains, from 730 up to 1,340 meters (2,400 to 4,400 feet).

NOTE.—*Lyciums* were found in a number of localities not mentioned under the four species above enumerated for the reason that doubt attaches to the identification of the species. In many places two kinds were found growing together. One or more species were found in the following localities:

Leach Point Valley, and Perognathus Flat (in the Panamint Mountains), California; Pahrump Valley, Indian Spring Valley, and Highland Range, Nevada; Beaverdam Mountains and Lower Santa Clara Valley, Utah.

Chilopsis linearis.

Mr. Bailey and I did not find the desert willow in California or western Nevada, but encountered it for the first time at Upper Cottonwood Springs, at the east foot of the Charleston Mountains, Nevada, where it was common. It was common also at Bitter Springs in the Muddy Mountains, Nevada; at the point where Beaverdam Creek joins the Virgin in northwestern Arizona; on the east slope of the Beaverdam Mountains in Utah, where it reaches an altitude of 1,280 meters (4,200 feet), and in the Lower Santa Clara Valley.

Mr. F. V. Coville informs me that he found it in California, on the Mohave River, near Daggett.

Salvia carnosa.

This species was noted in the following localities in California:

Walker Pass.—Common up to 1,430 meters (4,700 feet) on the east side of the pass.

Kern Valley.—Common down to 820 meters (2,700 feet), or lower on northerly exposures.

Antelope Valley.—Abundant in places in a wash leading south from near Gorman Station toward Pern Creek; still lower down it is mixed with *Audibertia alba.*

Salvia pilosa [=*Audibertia pilosa*].

This small-leaved species (until recently known as *Audibertia incana pilosa*) was found at the following localities:

NEVADA.

Charleston Mountains.—Common in the neighborhood of Mountain Spring, from about 1,525 to 1,770 meters (5,000 to 5,800 feet).

Pahroc Mountains.—Found near Pahroc Spring.
Highland Range.—Common on the west slope.
Juniper Mountains.—Collected at an elevation of 1,680 meters (5,500 feet).

UTAH.

Beaverdam Mountains.—Abundant and in full flower May 10-11; ranges down to 1,100 meters (3,600 feet) on the east slope, and to 1,160 meters (3,800 feet) on the west slope.

NOTE.—A large-leaved species of *Audibertia* was found on several of the desert ranges. On the north slope of Gold Mountain a species was found as high as 2,100 meters (7,000 feet).

Salazaria mexicana.

This small shrub, which presents a very odd appearance when covered with its large inflated gibbous pods, is common in many parts of the desert region. It was noted in the following localities:

CALIFORNIA.

Mohave Desert.—Common in many places, reaching westward to Antelope Valley, and entering the mouth of Walker Pass, and also of the pass leading from Mohave to Tehachapi, where it attains an altitude of 1,035 meters (3,400 feet).

NEVADA.

Gold Mountain.—Found on the south slope of Gold Mountain, beginning at an altitude of 1,550 meters (5,100 feet) and ranging upward.

Oasis Valley.—A little is found in Oasis Valley above 1,220 meters (4,000 feet).

Indian Spring Valley.—Common throughout the valley. (Covered with inflated gibbous fruit globes May 29).

Pahranagat Valley.—Not found in the valley proper, but tolerably common on the divide south of Pahranagat Lake (altitude 1,150 meters, or 3,800 feet), and on the west side of the valley at the east foot of the Pahranagat Mountains above an altitude of 1,340 meters (4,400 feet).

Charleston Mountains.—Common on the west slope, ranging up from Pahrump Valley to 1,580 meters (5,200 feet), and on the east slope up to 1,525 meters (5,000 feet).

Muddy Mountains.—Common on east slope at an altitude of 600 to 760 meters (2,000 to 2,500 feet).

UTAH.

Santa Clara Valley.—Occurs sparingly in the valley, disappearing on the north side between 1,220 and 1,280 meters (4,000 and 4,200 feet).

Beaverdam Mountains.—Common on the lower slopes, ranging up to 1,100 meters (3,600 feet) on the east slope, and up to 1,340 meters (4,400 feet) on the west slope.

Atriplex confertifolia.

Atriplex confertifolia is the most characteristic species of desert brush on the clayey alkaline soils of the Upper Sonoran zone, from the Snake

Plains of Idaho southward, and reaches downward into the Lower Sonoran also.

CALIFORNIA.

Mohave Desert.—Common in suitable parts of the desert, and found as far west as a point a little north of Willow Spring, in Antelope Valley.

Owens Valley.—The commonest plant throughout a large part of Owens Valley, predominating over all other species; particularly abundant on suitable soil from Big Pine southward to a point 9 miles south of Owens Lake. On the east side of the valley it reaches up on the White and Inyo mountains to about 1,980 meters (6,500 feet) in the latitude of Big Pine.

NEVADA.

Fish Lake Valley.—Very abundant, and ranging thence up on the northwest slope of Mount Magruder in the wash leading to Pigeon Spring as high as 1,950 meters (6,400 feet), where it grows in company with *Sarcobatus vermiculatus* and *Stanleya pinnata*.

Valley between Mount Magruder and Gold Mountain.—Common, and mixed with *Artemisia tridentata*, *Grayia spinosa*, *Tetradymia glabrata*, and other species.

Grapevine Cañon.—Abundant.

Sarcobatus Flat.—The southern half of Sarcobatus Flat is covered with this species, very pure and free from admixture with other plants. To the north it becomes invaded by *Atriplex parryi*, *A. canescens*, *Artemisia spinescens*, *Tetradymia glabrata*, *Grayia spinosa*, and several other shrubs.

Oasis Valley.—Common throughout the valley, but disappearing abruptly at the south end, and not seen on the Amargosa Desert.

Ash Meadows.—The commonest plant on the dry, alkali soil, stopping with the alkali flat at the south end of the Amargosa Desert proper.

Indian Spring Valley.—Common about the large dry lake at the junction of the north arm with the main valley.

Emigrant Valley.—One of the commonest plants in the bottom at an altitude of a little more than 1,525 meters (5,000 feet) and extending thence easterly up the west slope of the Desert Range to 1,675 meters (5,500 feet) or higher.

Timpahute Desert.—One of the principal plants.

Pahranagat Valley.—Abundant in large patches on the bottoms and lower gravel slopes, and in the lower part of the wash coming into Pahranagat Valley from Pahroc Plain; ranges up on the west side of the valley to 1,430 meters (4,700 feet).

Desert Valley.—Common in the flat bordering the dry lake.

Meadow Creek Valley.—Abundant in the flat along the creek.

Pahrump Valley.—Very abundant on the flats in the bottom of the valley.

Virgin and Lower Muddy Valleys.—Common on the dry bottoms.

UTAH.

Santa Clara Valley.—Common in places in the lower valley.

Atriplex parryi.

This species apparently has the most restricted range of any of the shrubby forms of the genus. In California it was found in parts of Owens Valley between Big Pine and Lone Pine, and also along the west side of Owens Lake. In Ash Meadows, on the boundary between California and Nevada, it is one of the commonest bushes, covering the alkali flats and reaching north to the gravel *Larrea* plain that marks the beginning of the Amargosa Desert proper, where it ends abruptly because the soil is unsuitable. It reappears in Oasis Valley (beginning in the cañon at the foot of the valley at an altitude of 1,140 meters or 3,750 feet) where it extends all the way along the bottom, associated with *Atriplex confertifolia, A. canescens,* and *Sarcobatus vermiculatus.* A little was found at the bottom of Grapevine Cañon about a mile and a half from its east mouth, whence it extends easterly over the north part of Sarcobatus Flat, where, however, it is not abundant.

Atriplex hymenelytra.

This striking species, which grows on salty and alkaline soil in the Lower Sonoran zone, is not widely distributed over the deserts of southern California and Nevada. It is common in Death Valley, Panamint Valley, and Ash Meadows, and also in places in the Muddy and Virgin valleys in eastern Nevada, but was not found in Oasis Valley or in any of the other valleys of southern Nevada.

Atriplex polycarpa.

Of all the greasewoods, *Atriplex polycarpa* is the most distinctive of the lower division of the Lower Sonoran Zone, occupying the bottoms of the lowest deserts, and never occurring above, if as high as, the upper edge of the *Larrea.*

CALIFORNIA.

Mohave Desert.—Common in suitable bottoms; the principal brush on the clay flat a few miles west of Willow Spring, in Antelope Valley.

Owens Valley.—One of the commonest shrubs in the lower part of the valley from Lone Pine south to Haway Meadows (about 16 kilometers, or 10 miles, south of Owens Lake).

NEVADA.

Grapevine Cañon.—Grows in the bottom of the cañon about a mile and a half from Sarcobatus Flat.

Oasis Valley.—Common in the lower part of the valley.

Pahranagat Valley.—Not found in Pahranagat Valley proper, but common on the flat south of Pahranagat Lake at an altitude of about 1,070 meters (3,500 feet).

Virgin and Lower Muddy valleys.—Common on dry bottoms.

Pahrump Valley.—Common on the east side of the valley in the *Larrea* belt.

Atriplex canescens.

Atriplex canescens is one of the commonest and most generally distributed greasewoods of the Lower Sonoran Zone. It is abundant from the western arm of the Mohave Desert (Antelope Valley) in California to the foot of the Hurricane Cliffs in western Utah and Arizona. The following notes on its distribution were recorded.

CALIFORNIA.

Mohave Desert.—Abundant over most parts of the desert where the soil is alkaline and clayey. It reaches the extreme western end of Antelope Valley near Gorman Station, and occurs in the wash leading thence southerly toward Peru Creek, at an altitude of about 760 meters (2,500 feet).

Tehachapi Valley.—Tolerably common, coming in from the Mohave Desert through the open cañon at Cameron; seen also in Tehachapi Pass.

Walker Pass.—Runs up the east side of Walker Pass from the Mohave Desert to an altitude of about 1,425 meters (4,700 feet).

Owens Valley.—Common along the bottom and east side of Owens Valley up to about 1,980 meters (6,500 feet) along the west foot of the White and Inyo mountains; abundant in the narrow valley for about 9 miles south of Owens Lake.

Deep Spring Valley.—Grows in the bottom of the valley with *Grayia spinosa*, *Tetradymia spinosa*, *Menodora spinosa*, *Dalea polyadenia*, *D. fremonti*, *Lycium andersoni*, *Eurotia lanata*, and *Artemisia spinescens*.

NEVADA.

Fish Lake Valley.—Common in the bottom of Fish Lake Valley on the boundary between California and Nevada, and ranges thence up on the northwest slope of Mount Magruder nearly to Pigeon Spring, reaching an altitude of 1,980 or 2,010 meters (6,500 or 6,600 feet).

Sarcobatus Flat.—Common in the northern part of the flat.

Grapevine Cañon.—Found in the bottom of this broad and open cañon about a mile or a mile and a half west of Sarcobatus Flat.

Oasis Valley.—Common, beginning in the cañon at the foot of the valley at an altitude of about 1,150 meters (3,750 feet), and growing in company with *Atriplex confertifolia*, *A. parryi*, and *Sarcobatus vermiculatus*.

Indian Spring Valley.—Common about the dry lake a little north of the point where the north arm of Indian Spring Valley joins the main valley.

Emigrant Valley.—Common, and ranges thence easterly to the summit of the Desert Mountains near Mud Spring.

Timpahute Valley.—One of the principal plants; ranges easterly up the west slope of the Pahranagat Mountains to the divide.

Pahranagat Valley.—Abundant on most of the dry parts of the bottom and on gravel slopes, and ranging up a little above 1,500 meters (5,000 feet) on the west or Pahranagat Mountain side (much of it in flower May 22-26).

Desert Valley.—Common in places with *Artemisia spinescens* and *Eurotia lanata*.

Pahroc Plain.—Common, mixed with *Grayia*, *Eurotia*, and *Lycium andersoni*, and ranging as high as 1,980 meters (6,500 feet) on the Pahroc Mountains.

Meadow Creek Valley.—Common, and ranging up to 1,980 meters (6,500 feet) on west slope of Juniper Plateau.

Virgin and Lower Muddy valleys.—Common in the dryer parts of the valleys.

Pahrump Valley.—The most abundant brush on the alkaline bottoms, whence it ranges up the west slope of the Charleston Mountains to about 1,700 meters (5,600 feet).

UTAH.

Santa Clara Valley.—Common in places in the lower part of the valley.

Atriplex lentiformis.

This large species is not so generally distributed as most of the other members of the genus, and in places it may have been confounded with *A. torreyi*, from which it is not always easily distinguishable.

CALIFORNIA.

Mohave Desert.—Found growing north of Willow Spring, in Antelope Valley.

Amargosa Cañon.—Rather common with *A. torreyi*.

NEVADA.

Oasis Valley.—A few clumps seen.

Pahranagat Valley.—Common in patches on suitable soil, usually sand or fine gravel; generally rank and large.

Virgin and Lower Muddy valleys.—Common in dry parts of the valleys; sometimes in company with *A. torreyi*.

Great Bend of the Colorado River.—Occurs on the sand banks on the south side of Vegas Wash.

UTAH.

Santa Clara Valley.—Grows in the lower part of the valley.

Atriplex torreyi.

Atriplex torreyi is the largest species of the genus and grows in isolated localities throughout the Lower Sonoran zone. Small bushes are sometimes difficult to distinguish from *A. lentiformis*.

CALIFORNIA.

Owens Valley.—A little was seen on the west side of Owens Lake, and a few patches in the narrow valley between Owens Lake and Haway Meadows.

Amargosa Cañon.—Abundant, forming dense thickets.

NEVADA.

Valley of the Virgin and Lower Muddy.—Common in places in the dryer parts of the valley. Near an abandoned mill at St. Joe, on the Muddy, it forms dense and impenetrable thickets and grows to immense size, single bushes attaining a height of $4\frac{1}{2}$ to $5\frac{1}{2}$ meters (15 to 18 feet), with trunks 150 millimeters (about 6 inches) in diameter.

Pahranagat Valley.—A few scattering patches of rather small size were found.

UTAH.

Santa Clara Valley.—Grows in the lower valley.

Grayia spinosa [=*Grayia polygaloides*].

Grayia spinosa is one of the most characteristic bushes of the upper division of the Lower Sonoran Zone in the deserts of the southern part of the Great Basin. Owing to the peculiar green of its leaves and their tendency to assume a pinkish tint, it is easily distinguishable from the other brush with which it is associated. It was recorded from the following localities:

CALIFORNIA.

Mohave Desert.—*Grayia* is common in many of the higher levels of the Mohave Desert. It was found as far west as Antelope Valley a short distance east of Willow Spring, and a little was seen in the open cañon leading from Mohave to Tehachapi.

Walker Pass.—In Walker Pass it extends up the east slope from the Mohave Desert to an altitude of 1,330 meters (4,400 feet) or higher.

Owens Valley.—Common and ranges up on the west side (Sierra Nevada slope) to 1,525 or 1,550 meters (5,000 or 5,100 feet). On the opposite or White Mountain slope it ranges up to 1,980 meters (6,500 feet).

Deep Spring Valley.—Found in the bottom of the valley with *Tetradymia spinosa, Menodora spinosa, Atriplex canescens, Dalea polyadenia, D. fremonti, Artemisia spinescens, Lycium andersoni,* and *Eurotia lanata.*

NEVADA.

Fish Lake Valley.—Abundant, ranging up nearly to Pigeon Spring on the northwest slope of Mount Magruder, at an altitude of 1,980 to 2,040 meters (6,500 to 6,700 feet).

Valley between Gold Mountain and Mount Magruder.—Common, mixed with *Artemisia tridentata, Tetradymia glabrata, Atriplex confertifolia,* and a little *Artemisia spinescens.*

Gold Mountain.—Common below 2,135 meters (7,000 feet) altitude on the north slope, and down to 1,675 meters (5,500 feet) on the south slope.

Sarcobatus Flat.—Tolerably common in places in the northern part of the flat.

Oasis Valley.—Not common. Found from 1,220 meters (4,000 feet) upwards.

Timpahute Valley.—Scarce.

Pahranagat Valley.—Abundant on the gravel slopes and on dry gravel soil in the bottom of the valley and thence up to 1,645 meters (5,400 feet) on the west side (east slope Pahranagat Mountains). In fruit May 22-26.

Pahroc Plain.—Abundant on the gravel slopes, where it is the prevailing bush all the way from Pahroc Spring to Pahranagat Valley.

Desert Valley.—Abundant, in places forming large patches by itself unmixed with other species, and continuous with that of Pahroc Plain.

Meadow Creek Valley.—Common, mixed with the sage brush, and ranging up to 1,920 meters (6,300 feet) on the west slope of the Juniper Plateau, but this is above its usual limit.

Charleston Mountains.—Found on the east slope below 1,200 meters (4,000 feet).

UTAH.

Beaverdam Mountains.—Found on the east slope of the mountains from 1,095 meters (3,600 feet) down into the valley.

Santa Clara Valley.—Occurs in the lower valley, but disappears at about 1,220 to 1,280 meters (4,000 to 4,200 feet) on the north side of the valley (south exposure).

Eurotia lanata.

This well-known species, which is a valuable food plant for sheep, and is also eaten by horses, is common throughout the sage plains of Idaho and Nevada, and was found on many of the higher levels of the deserts traversed by the expedition. In the north it is commonly known as 'white sage,' but is a widely different plant from the so-called 'white sage' of the coastal slope and coast ranges of southern California, the latter being *Audibertia alba.*

CALIFORNIA.

Mohave Desert.—Common on the upper levels and extending up to 1,035 meters (3,400 feet), in the open cañon leading from Mohave to Tehachapi Valley.

Owens Valley.—Common among the sagebrush, and ranging up to a little above 1,550 meters (5,100 feet) on the Sierra slope.

Deep Spring Valley.—Tolerably common, with *Grayia spinosa, Menodora spinosa, Tetradymia spinosa, Dalea fremonti, D. polyadenia, Artemisia spinescens, Lycium andersoni,* and *Atriplex canescens* (altitude about 1,680 meters or 5,500 feet).

NEVADA.

Fish Lake Valley.—Abundant on the east side of the valley, ranging up to Pigeon Spring on the northwest slope of Mount Magruder (altitude 2,040 meters or 6,700 feet).

Sarcobatus Flat.—Tolerably common in places in the northern part of the flat.

Oasis Valley.—Common on the gravel slopes at the head of the valley at an altitude of about 1,340 meters (4,400 feet).

Emigrant Valley.—One of the commonest plants in the bottom of the valley at an altitude of 1,525 meters (a little above 5,000 feet).

Timpahute Valley.—One of the principal plants.

Pahroc Plain.—Common, mixed with *Grayia spinosa*, *Lycium andersoni*, and *Atriplex canescens*.

Desert Valley.—This valley is a remarkably typical *Eurotia* plain, thousands of acres between Pahroc Mountains and the Highland Range showing no other plant.

Meadow Creek Valley.—Extensive tracts (comprising many acres) are covered with this species alone.

Juniper Mountains (between Panaca, Nevada, and Shoal Creek, Utah).—Common in places among the sage and juniper.

UTAH.

Santa Clara Valley.—Rather common in places.

Allenrolfea occidentalis [= *Spyrostachys occidentalis*].

This small, scrubby plant (commonly known as *Spyrostachys occidentalis*) can endure more alkali and salt in the soil than any other species, and consequently is abundant on many of the salt flats where no other species grows. In Death Valley it forms a distinct border around the salt flat; and it occurs in similar soils easterly as far as the valley of the Virgin and Lower Muddy.

Suæda suffrutescens.

Suæda suffrutescens is a saline plant, requiring both salt and alkali in the soil in which it thrives. It can not stand so much salt as *Allenrolfea*, and consequently is found outside of the *Allenrolfea* belt around the true salt flats. It was recorded from the following localities:

NEVADA.

Grapevine Cañon.—Common in places.

Sarcobatus Flat.—Common in places in the northern part of the flat.

Oasis Valley.—Common throughout the bottom of the valley.

Pahranagat Valley.—Common in the lower part of the valley.

Valley of the Virgin and Lower Muddy.—Abundant on the salt flats.

Indian Spring Valley.—Common about the dry lake at the base of the north arm of Indian Spring Valley.

Sarcobatus baileyi.[*]

This new species of *Sarcobatus*, the second known in the genus, was first discovered by Mr. Vernon Bailey in the Candelaria salt marshes near Columbus, Nev., in winter. It was afterward found by Mr. Bailey and myself in Sarcobatus Flat, on the west side of the Ralston Desert, where it was common and in full fruit June 2, and on the east side of Fish Lake Valley, where it forms a narrow zone at an altitude

---

[*]Coville, Proc. Biol. Soc. Wash., vol. VII, May 18, 1892, pp. 77–78.

of about 2,010 meters (6,600 feet). It grows on gravel soil, while *S. vermiculatus*, as well known, grows on alkaline clayey soils.

Sarcobatus vermiculatus.

This characteristic desert shrub grows on clayey alkaline soils throughout the Upper Sonoran Zone, descending in places into the Lower Sonoran. It was observed in the following localities:

CALIFORNIA.

Owens Valley.—Common on the alkaline flats in the narrow valley between Owens Lake and Haway Meadows, and in places on the west side of the valley between Owens Lake and Lone Pine.

NEVADA.

Fish Lake Valley.—The most conspicuous plant on the mud flat in the bottom of the valley, whence it extends easterly on suitable soils to an altitude of 2,040 meters (6,700 feet) in the wash leading up to Pigeon Spring on the northwest slope of Mount Magruder.

Sarcobatus Flat.—Abundant on the clayey soil, growing on clay dunes as high as a man's head or higher. These *Sarcobatus* dunes were not found elsewhere and were such a peculiar feature of this desert that the name Sarcobatus Flat was given it on this account.

Oasis Valley.—Common throughout the bottom of the valley along with *Atriplex confertifolia* and *A. parryi*.

Pahranagat Valley.—Abounds throughout the clayey mud flats of the valley up to an altitude of about 1,280 meters (4,200 feet), and is distinguishable at a distance from the other shrubs by its peculiar green color.

Meadow Creek Valley.—Common along the bottom.

Desert Valley.—Common in large patches on the flat bordering the dry lake.

UTAH.

Shoal Creek.—Occurs in places on the mud flats bordering the creek.

Eriogonum polifolium.

This woody *Eriogonum*, the lower part of which is a true bush, is common on the upper levels of many of the deserts and along the bases of many of the desert ranges, where it was recorded from the following localities:

CALIFORNIA.

Mohave Desert.—Common on the higher levels.

Antelope Valley.—Common at the extreme west end of Antelope Valley in a wash leading south toward Peru Creek.

Tehachapi Basin.—Occurs, coming up from the Mohave Desert.

Walker Pass.—In Walker Pass it was common up to 1,430 meters (4,700 feet) on the east side; on the west or Kern River side it was found as low as 820 meters (2,700 feet) on northerly exposures.

Owens Valley.—West of Lone Pine this species is common and ranges up on the east slope of the Sierra to about 1,890 meters (6,205 feet).

Eriogonum inflatum.

This singular species, which was discovered by Fremont in his notable journey across the Mohave Desert in 1844, is common on most of the deserts in the southern part of the Great Basin, from California to Utah, usually occurring on gravelly soil. It is of slight value as a food plant for stock, being devoured by some mules and horses. On the east slope of Walker Pass it ranges up from the Mohave Desert to an altitude of 1,430 meters (4,700 feet).

Chorizanthe rigida.

This singular little plant flourishes on the hottest gravel beds of the hottest deserts of California, Nevada, Arizona, and southwestern Utah, where it flowers in the early spring. It is the only species besides the creosote bush (*Larrea tridentata*) that grows on many of the black pebble beds which become so hot in the sun that all ordinary plants would be baked in a few moments. It was recorded in the following localities:

CALIFORNIA.

Panamint Valley.—Common in places.
Death Valley.—Common on the gravel slopes.

NEVADA.

Amargosa Desert.—Common, and over large areas the only plant growing with the *Larrea* on the hot pebble beds.
Grapevine Cañon.—Common, coming up from the northwest arm of Death Valley and ranging upward on the southwest slope of Mount Magruder as high as 1,830 meters (6,000 feet).
Oasis Valley.—Rather common.
Indian Spring Valley.—Common on the black pebble beds.

UTAH.

Santa Clara Valley.—Common on the warm gravel slopes.

Platanus occidentalis.

The sycamore was not found by us in the Great Basin, but is common in southern California. It grows in considerable abundance in the valley and gorge that the road follows in leading up from Caliente toward Walker Basin (on the west slope of the divide), where it ranges up from the valley to an altitude of 820 meters (2,700 feet). It was common also in the upper part of Cajon Pass in the San Bernardino Mountains, where it was coming into leaf March 30.

Betula occidentalis.

The western birch is common along some of the mountain streams on the west side of Owens Valley at the foot of the Sierra.

Alnus rhombifolia.

This alder, which grows to be a large tree, 9 meters (30 feet) or more in height, with a tall compact trunk, is common in the valley of the Kern River, on the west side of the Sierra in California.

Quercus undulata.

This evergreen scrub oak was found in the following localities:

NEVADA.

Charleston Mountains.—Common in scattered patches near Mountain Spring, and down on the west slope to 1,520 meters (5,000 feet).

Juniper Mountains.—Common in places in the juniper between Panaca, Nevada, and Shoal Creek, Utah.

UTAH.

Upper Santa Clara Valley.—Found in patches in the Upper Santa Clara Valley, beginning about 13 kilometers (8 miles) northwest of St. George, at an altitude of about 1,275 meters (4,200 feet) and ranging northward through Diamond Valley to the Upper Santa Clara Crossing and Mountain Meadows.

Beaverdam Mountains.—Occurs in places on the east slope between 1,100 and 1,300 meters (3,600 to 4,600 feet).

Quercus gambelii.

The Desert Range scrub oak was found in the following localities:

NEVADA.

Juniper Mountains.—Found sparingly from Shoal Creek, Utah, across the Juniper Mountain Plateau in eastern Nevada.

UTAH.

Mountain Meadows.—Common in scattered patches from the Upper Santa Clara Crossing northward to and beyond Mountain Meadows.

Quercus lobata.

The white oak is common in the Cañada de las Uvas, California, particularly on the grounds immediately about Old Fort Tejon, where it grows to a great and unusual size. Many trees near the old fort measure 6 meters (20 feet) or more in circumference a meter or more (3 or 4 feet) above the ground, and one measures 8 meters (26 feet 4 inches). A colony of purple martens (*Progne subis hesperia*) was found breeding in holes high up in these oaks at the time of our visit, the last week in June, 1891. *Quercus lobata* is common also about the borders of Tehachapi Valley. One we measured near summit, in the west end of the valley, was about 2 meters (6 feet) in diameter 2 meters (6 feet) above ground (circumference 5.8 meters or 19 feet 1 inch).

Quercus douglasii.

The blue oak is common in Kern Valley and thence southerly along the west slope of the Sierra Nevada to Walker Basin and Caliente. Between the two last-mentioned localities it forms open groves on the grassy hilltops, particularly along the main divide. It is common also at Liebre ranch, on the south side of Antelope Valley, which it reaches from the adjoining Sierra Liebre.

Quercus wislizeni.

This live oak is common along the western foothills of the Sierra Nevada, in California, and thence southward.

Quercus kelloggii.

Common on the west slope of the Sierra Nevada, where Mr. Bailey found it occupying a zone between the altitudes of 1,470 and 2,160 meters (4,900—7,200 feet) along the East Fork of Kaweah River.

Quercus dumosa.

Quercus dumosa is the scrub oak of the Sierra Liebre and Coast Ranges generally. It is common on the side hills about Antelope Valley, at the extreme west end of the Mohave desert, and thence down through the Cañada de las Uvas. It is common also in Cajon Pass.

Castanopsis chrysophylla.

The California chinquapin grows abundantly on the east slope of the High Sierra, in a narrow zone between 2,750 and 2,895 meters (9,000 and 9,500 feet) altitude, opposite Lone Pine.

Salix longifolia.

This small and slender willow forms open thickets about water courses and warm springs in some of the Lower Sonoran deserts. It was found in the following localities:

CALIFORNIA.

Death Valley.—Common along Furnace Creek, on the east side of Death Valley, mixed with *Pluchea sericea*.

Amargosa Cañon.—Found sparingly along the creek in the upper part of the cañon.

NEVADA.

Great Bend of the Colorado.—A slender willow forms extensive thickets along the river on both sides of the Great Bend.

Ash Meadows.—Abundant about the hot springs.

ARIZONA.

Beaverdam Creek.—Small willows are abundant on the flats bordering Beaverdam Creek, near its junction with the Virgin, in northwestern Arizona.

UTAH.

Santa Clara Valley.—Common along the Virgin, near the mouth of the Santa Clara.

Salix lævigata.

A single tree of this species marks the position of Lone Willow Spring, at the east foot of the Slate Range, near the extreme south end of Panamint Valley, California.

Salix nigra.

This large and handsome willow tree is common about the large springs at the two ranches in Pahrump Valley, Nevada.

Other tree willows (species not determined) were found about the ranches in Pahranagat Valley, Nevada; along streams on the west side of Owens Valley, California, in Kern River Valley, and in the lower part of the Cañada de las Uvas, below Old Fort Tejon.

Populus fremontii.

Cottonwood trees grow along some of the permanent water courses of the desert region and are often planted along irrigation ditches in the settlements. They were found at the following localities:

CALIFORNIA.

Kern Valley.—Common along the river.

Mohave Desert.—Common along the Mohave River near Victor, and in a few other places.

NEVADA.

Pahranagat Valley.—Common.

Pahrump Valley.—Common about the large springs.

Vegas Valley.—Common at Vegas Spring and ranch.

Valley of the Virgin and Muddy.—Very abundant along the streams in the Mormon settlements of St. Thomas, Bunkerville, and St. Joe.

ARIZONA.

Beaverdam Creek.—Abundant, forming a large forest on the flats bordering Beaverdam Creek, near its junction with the Virgin.

UTAH.

Santa Clara Valley.—Common along the Santa Clara and Virgin rivers.

Ephedra nevadensis.

This Lower Sonoran species differs conspicuously from the green species of the mountains (*Ephedra viridis*) by its olive color. It is common in many of the desert valleys and was noted in the following localities:

CALIFORNIA.

Mohave Desert.—Common, reaching west as far as Willow Spring, in Antelope Valley.

Tehachapi Valley.—Tolerably common, coming up from the Mohave Desert through the open cañon leading up from near Mohave. Found also in Tehachapi Pass.

Walker Pass.—On the east slope of Walker Pass the olive *Ephedra* runs up to 1,430 meters (4,700 feet), where it disappears and the green species (*E. viridis*) begins.

Kern Valley.—Observed at about 820 meters (2,700 feet).

NEVADA.

Pahrump Valley.—Common, reaching its upper limit on the east side (west slope of Charleston Mountains) at 1,370 meters (4,500 feet).

Pahranagat Valley.—Common everywhere on the gravel slopes.

Indian Spring Valley.—Common in the north arm.

Sarcobatus Flat.—Tolerably common in places.

Grapevine Cañon.—Found in the bottom of the cañon.

Emigrant Valley.—Common and ranging well up on the west slope of the Desert Mountains.

UTAH.

Beaverdam Mountains.—Found on the west slope of the Beaverdam Mountains up to 1,340 meters (4,400 feet), and on the east slope up to 1,100 meters (3,600 feet).

Santa Clara Valley.—Occurs sparingly in the lower part of the valley.

Ephreda viridis Coville.

This green *Ephedra* does not occur in any of the Lower Sonoran deserts, but grows on the mountain sides and plateaus of the Upper Sonoran and Transition zones with sagebrush (*Artemisia tridentata*) and juniper (*Juniperus californica utahensis*). The following notes on its distribution were recorded:

CALIFORNIA.

Mohave Desert.—Tolerably common at the summit of Cajon Pass and thence along the north base of the San Bernardino Mountains, in the juniper belt.

Walker Pass.—On the east slope of Walker Pass this species begins at 1,430 meters (4,700 feet) with *Artemisia tridentata* and ranges up; on the west slope it is common between 1,250 and 1,400 meters (4,100 and 4,600 feet).

Sierra Nevada.—Common on the east (Owens Valley) slope from 2,750 meters (9,000 feet) or higher, down to 1,830 meters (6,000 feet); and still lower in places on the Alabama Range.

White Mountains.—Rather common along the summit.

Panamint Mountains.—Common on the higher parts of the range.

In the basin above Wild Rose Spring it begins above *Coleogyne* at 2,740–2,980 meters (6,300–6,500 feet) and runs up to the summit at the west base of Telescope Peak, altitude 2,560 meters (8,400 feet).

NEVADA.

Mount Magruder.—Common over the higher parts of the mountain, ranging all the way up to the summit of the main peak with *Artemisia tridentata*; occurs also in the upper part of Tule Cañon.

Gold Mountain.—Common on the summit and ranges down on the south slope to 1,830 meters (6,000 feet) with *Artemisia tridentata*.

Pahranagat Mountains.—Tolerably common.

Highland Range.—Occurs.

Charleston Mountains.—Common, ranging down on the west slope to 1,430 meters (4,700 feet).

UTAH.

Beaverdam Mountains.—Common, descending to 1,340 meters (4,400 feet) on the west slope, and to 1,100 meters (3,600 feet) on the east slope.

Pinus monophylla.

Pinus monophylla is the only pine belonging properly to the Great Basin region, where it occupies the summits of the desert ranges in company with *Juniperus californica utahensis*. It belongs to the Upper Sonoran and Transition zones, and consequently is absent from the highest peaks of the White and Charleston mountains, whose summits are truly Boreal. It usually begins a few hundred feet above the lower border of the juniper belt and ranges up a little higher than the juniper, though the two are mixed over the greater part of their ranges. In some areas the juniper predominates, as in the Juniper Plateau between Meadow Creek Valley, Nevada, and the Escalante Desert in Utah, while in other areas the nut pine predominates, as on Mount Magruder.

Pinus monophylla is easily distinguished from the piñon of Arizona (*Pinus edulis*) by its greater size, larger nuts, and single leaf. *P. edulis* has two leaves. Both species have short and open cones from which the nuts are easily dislodged by shaking. The nuts are eagerly devoured by wild turkeys, piñon jays, and many other species.

The nut pine furnishes the most important food of the Indians inhabiting the southern part of the Great Basin, namely, the Paiutes, Shoshones, and Panamints, who gather its cones in large quantities and roast them in heaps, after which the nuts are extracted and placed in large caches for winter use. They are eaten in a raw state as well as roasted, and are pounded into flour and baked into a sort of bread.

Mount Magruder is notable for the luxuriance of the nut pine forests which clothe its higher hills and peaks, and has long been a favorite resort of the Paiute Indians, who speak of it as 'Nut Pine Mountain,' and spend a considerable part of each year there for the sole purpose of collecting the nuts. The trees often attain a height of 12 or even 15 meters (40 to 50 feet) and a diameter of half a meter (nearly 20 inches). The following notes were recorded on the distribution of the nut pine in the region traversed:

CALIFORNIA.

Sierra Nevada.—On the east slope of the Sierra opposite Lone Pine the nut pine belt ranges from 1,830 to 2,440 meters (6,000 to 8,000 feet) in width.

Walker Pass.—On the east side of Walker Pass it begins a little above 1,430 meters (4,700 feet) on northerly exposures and ranges up over the summit of the pass at 1,525 meters (5,000 feet) and down on the west slope as low as 1,310 meters (4,300 feet) in places.

Tehachapi Mountains.—Common, and ranging down to about 1,130 meters (3,700 feet) on the side of the open cañon leading from Tehachapi Valley to the Mohave Desert.

Panamint Mountains.—Common with the juniper along the summit of the Panamint Range. In the basin above Wild Rose Spring on the northwest slope of Telescope Peak it descends to 1,980 or 1,920 meters (6,500 or 6,300 feet), and ranges up on this peak to 2,740 meters (9,000 feet), or higher. Heaps of cones were found in many places in the Panamint Mountains, where they had been left by the Indians after the nuts had been extracted.

White Mountains.—Common, descending to 2,040 meters (6,700 feet) on the east slope above Deep Spring Valley.

NEVADA.

Charleston Mountains.—Common with the juniper, descending on the west slope to about 1,550 meters (5,100 feet).

Pahroc Mountains.—Common on the higher parts of the range, and lower down in the cañons.

Gold Mountain.—Common along the summit, descending on the south side as low at least as 2,070 meters (6,800 feet).

Mount Magruder.—As already stated, the nut pine grows in greater abundance on Mount Magruder than in any other locality visited by the expedition, forming handsome forests on many of the knobs and peaks that rise from the mountain plateau, where it is very little mixed with juniper.

Juniper Mountains.—Scarce in the dense juniper forest extending from Meadow Creek Valley, Nevada, to the Escalante Desert in Utah.

UTAH.

Upper Santa Clara Valley.—Begins about 13 kilometers (8 miles) northwest of St. George on south exposures at an altitude of about 1,270 meters (4,200 feet) and grows scattering on the side hills in the Upper Santa Clara Valley, ranging thence westerly to the Shoal Creek country.

Beaverdam Mountains.—Tolerably common on the Beaverdam Mountains, ranging down on the east side to about 1,160 meters (3,800 feet), and on the west slope to about 1,340 meters (4,400 feet).

ARIZONA.

Virgin Mountains.—On the west side of the Virgin Mountains the nut pine forms a broad zone, mixed with juniper, coming fully halfway down to the foot of the range.

Pinus ponderosa.

Mr. Bailey tells me that *Pinus ponderosa* is common on the west slope of the Sierra Nevada along the East Fork of Kaweah River, growing with *Sequoia gigantea* in a belt between the altitude of 1,830 and 2,100 meters (6,000 to 7,000 feet). Its range is below that of *Pinus jeffreyi.*

Pinus ponderosa scopulorum.

The yellow pine grows in a broad zone on Charleston Peak, Nevada, and on Pine Valley Mountain, Utah, in both of which localities it is cut for lumber. It is said to be common in the higher parts of the Virgin and Highland ranges. A few scattering trees were found on the higher hills of the Juniper Mountains near Sheep Spring (between Panaca, Nevada, and Shoal Creek, Utah), at an altitude of about 2,040 meters (6,700 feet).

Pinus jeffreyi.

This large pine is common in the High Sierra in California, ranging upward on the east slope from about 2,750 meters (9,000 feet) to 2,900 meters (9,500 feet).

Pinus murrayana.

On the High Sierra in California *Pinus murrayana* reaches timberline with *P. balfouriana*, and ranges down on the east side to an altitude of about 2,900 meters (9,500 feet) or lower, growing to be a large tree.

Pinus balfouriana.

In the High Sierra in California, *Pinus balfouriana* and *P. murrayana* reach timber-line, whence they descend on the east slope to an altitude of about 2,900 meters (9,500 feet) or a little lower, where they grow to be large trees 15 to 20 meters (50 to 65 feet) in height and a meter or more (3 or 4 feet) in diameter.

Pinus aristata.

P. aristata was found on the summit of the Panamint Mountains, in California, by Mr. Bailey and Dr. Fisher, and on Charleston Peak, Nevada, by Mr. Coville and Mr. Palmer.

A pine of this type was found by Mr. Nelson on the higher parts of the White and Inyo mountains, California, but whether *P. aristata* or *P. balfouriana* is not certain.

Pinus sabiniana.

This remarkable tree, with very open foliage and huge cones, is characteristic of the west slope of the Sierra and the Coast Ranges of California, and does not occur anywhere within the Great Basin. It was common along the route traversed from a mile west of the summit of Walker Pass to Kernville, and thence southward to Walker Basin, and was found also on the Sierra Liebre, growing with and below *Pinus monophylla*, and descending on the north slope nearly to Antelope Valley in the neighborhood of Liebre ranch.

Pinus monticola.

Pinus monticola is one of the timber-line trees. On the rocky west slope of the Sierra Nevada, above Mineral King, Mr. Bailey found it at an altitude of 2,930 meters (9,600 feet), and thence upward to 3,120 meters (10,400 feet). In that locality but one pine (*Pinus balfouriana*) extended higher.

Pinus lambertiana.

Common on the west slope of the Sierra Nevada in a well-marked belt, the vertical breadth of which along the East Fork of Kaweah River was determined by Mr. Bailey to be about 360 meters (1,200 feet), or from 1,830 to 2,160 meters (6,000 to 7,200 feet) in altitude. Mr. Bailey found it common at Trout Meadows, and thence along the upper Kern River to above Soda Springs.

Pinus flexilis.

In California this species was found on the Panamint Mountains above an altitude of about 3,050 meters (10,000 feet), and on the High Sierra, where it ranges from 2,830 to 3,050 meters (9,300 to 10,000 feet). In Nevada it was found on Charleston Peak by Mr. Coville and Mr. Palmer.

Abies magnifica.

Common on the High Sierra. Mr. Bailey informs me that he observed it on the west slope near Mineral King at an altitude of 2,230 meters (7,450 feet), and thence up to about 3,090 meters (10,300 feet), where it nearly reaches timber-line.

Abies concolor.

Common on the High Sierra. On the west slope Mr. Bailey found it between the altitudes of 1,830 and 2,160 meters (6,000 to 7,200 feet) on the East Fork of Kaweah River, and up to 2,300 meters (7,700 feet) on Kern River.

Pseudotsuga macrocarpa.

This species of spruce occurs in gulches on the west side of Cajon Pass at an altitude of 670 meters (2,200 feet) and upwards, and was found also on the south side of the Sierra Liebre along the upper valley of Peru Creek, just below Alamo ranch. Cajon Pass is the type locality of this species.

Sequoia gigantea.

Sequoia gigantea forms a conspicuous but narrow and interrupted belt on the west slope of the Sierra Nevada. Mr. Bailey informs me that along the East Fork of Kaweah River he found it between the altitudes of 1,830 to 2,000 meters (6,000 to 6,600 feet), on a very gradual slope, so that the actual breadth of the forest was about 5 miles.

Libocedrus decurrens.

Mr. Bailey found *Libocedrus decurrens* common on the west slope of the Sierra Nevada, along the East Fork of Kaweah River, from 1,830 to 2,160 meters (6,000 to 7,200 feet) altitude, and along the North Fork of Kern River up to the cliffs above Soda Springs.

Juniperus californica.

The typical form occurs on the coastal slope of the Great Divide in California, sometimes ranging over a short distance on the Great Basin side, as along the north base of the San Bernardino Mountains.

It was observed in the following localities:

CALIFORNIA.

West slope of the Sierra.—Common on the sidehills about Kernville, where it descends as low as 790 meters (2,600 feet) on the north slopes, and ranges southward along the road from Kernville to Havilah. It reaches the summit of Walker Pass (1,550 meters, or 5,100 feet).

Sierra Liebre.—Common on the north slope opposite the western part of Antelope Valley.

Tehachapi Mountains.—Common, ranging down into the tree yuccas on the side of the open cañon leading from Tehachapi Valley down to Mohave (altitude, about 1,090 meters, or 3,600 feet).

Mohave Desert and San Bernardino Mountains.—Along the north foot of San Bernardino Mountains, at the extreme southern edge of the Mohave Desert, is a well-defined belt of juniper about 8 miles in width, ranging from the summit of Cajon Pass at an altitude of 1,215 meters (4,000 feet) down through the upper part of the tree yucca zone to an altitude of 1,060 meters (3,500).

Juniperus californica utahensis.

Juniperus californicus utahensis, either alone or in company with the nut pine (*Pinus monophylla*), clothes the summits of most of the desert ranges, where it reaches as high as the upper limit of the Transition zone. It is the only juniper inhabiting the southern part of the Great Basin, and does not grow below the Upper Sonoran zone; consequently it is absent from the lower ranges and also from the excessively barren Funeral and Amargosa ranges between Death Valley and the Amargosa Desert. The following notes on its distribution were recorded:

CALIFORNIA.

White and Inyo mountains.—Abundant along the summit of the range (except on the higher peaks of the White Mountains, which are too high for it and are clothed with pines and spruces). On the east slope of the White Mountains, opposite Deep Spring Valley, junipers descend with nut pines to 2,040 meters (6,700 feet).

Panamint Mountains.—Common throughout the higher parts of the range. In the basin above Wild Rose Spring on the northwest slope of Telescope Peak, junipers begin at 1,900 meters (about 6,300 feet), and run up to 2,550 meters (8,400 feet) or higher.

NEVADA.

Mount Magruder.—The juniper is scarce on Mount Magruder, where its place is taken by the nut pine (*Pinus monophylla*).

Gold Mountain—Common in sheltered cañons, and in places on the summit.

Hungry Hill Summit.—Common on the divide and neighboring hills, reaching down on the south side to about 1,525 meters (5,000 feet).

Pahranagat Mountains.—Common on the summit of the range, reaching down to 1,585 meters (5,200 feet) on the east slope.

Pahroc Mountains.—Common on the higher parts of the range and in cañons.

Hyko Range.—Common on the higher parts.

Highland Range.—Abundant, descending to about 1,830 meters (6,000 feet) on the west side. On the east side of the Highland Range it descends to 1,700 meters (5,600 feet), thus reaching within a few hundred feet of the bottom of Meadow Creek Valley.

Juniper Mountains (between Meadow Creek Valley, Nevada, and Shoal Creek, Utah).—The most extensive and purest juniper forest I have ever seen covers the rolling plateau along the boundary between Nevada and Utah, reaching from an altitude of 1,765 meters (about 5,800 feet) on the east side of Meadow Creek Valley, Nevada, all the way across to Shoal Creek on the borders of the Escalante Desert in Utah. This continuous juniper forest is more than 20 miles in breadth without a break and is mixed with very little nut pine. On the Shoal Creek side it descends to 1,830 meters (6,000 feet). The altitude of the plateau which it occupies, and which is here called the Juniper Mountains for lack of a better name, varies from a little over 1,830 meters (6,000 feet) up to about 2,100 meters (7,000 feet).

Charleston Mountains.—Common throughout the Charleston Mountains, except on the summit of the main peak, which is too high for it. On the west slope (Pahrump Valley side) it descends to 1,550 meters (5,100 feet).

ARIZONA AND UTAH.

Virgin and Beaverdam mountains.—Common in a broad zone on the Virgin Mountains, reaching down more than halfway to the valley; and on the west slope of the Beaverdam Mountains down to 1,340 meters (4,400 feet).

UTAH.

Beaverdam Mountains.—On the east slope junipers descend to 1,095 meters (3,600 feet) spreading out to the northward over the upper part of the Upper Santa Clara Valley, where they cover all the sidehills.

Pine Valley Mountain.—Abundant in a broad zone around the base of the mountain, and stretching thence northwesterly over the Upper Santa Clara Valley, forming a sparse forest on the hillsides until it reaches the Shoal Creek country, where it joins the continuous forest already described. In the Upper Santa Clara Valley it descends to 1,280 meters (about 4,200 feet) at a distance of only 13 kilometers (8 miles) northwest of St. George, thence forming a scattered forest over the sidehills in a belt at least 10 miles wide south of the Upper Santa Clara crossing, and reaching thence northerly to the borders of the Escalante Desert, south of which it is continuous with the **great** forest covering the Juniper Plateau.

Juniperus occidentalis.

This species grows on the higher summits of the Panamint Mountains, California, above the upper limit of *Juniperus californica utahensis*. On the north slope of Telescope Peak Mr. Bailey found it as high as 2,830 meters (9,300 feet).

Juniperus occidentalis monosperma.

This subspecies was identified by Mr. Coville as the form growing high up in the Charleston Mountains, Nevada.

Tumion californicum.

This singular tree grows along the west slope of the Sierra Nevada. Mr. Bailey found it on the East Fork of Kaweah River between the altitudes of 1,170 and 1,830 meters (3,950 to 6,000 feet).

NOTES ON THE GEOGRAPHIC AND VERTICAL DISTRIBUTION OF CACTUSES, YUCCAS, AND AGAVE, IN THE DESERTS AND DESERT RANGES OF SOUTHERN CALIFORNIA, SOUTHERN NEVADA, NORTHWESTERN ARIZONA, AND SOUTHWESTERN UTAH.

By C. HART MERRIAM, M. D.

The following notes on the vertical and geographic distribution of the desert cactuses, yuccas, and agave were made by me in April, May, and June, 1891, along the route traversed from the north end of Cajon Pass, in the San Bernardino Mountains, to the St. George Valley at the foot of the Hurricane Cliffs, in southwestern Utah, and thence westerly across Nevada to Owens Valley, California, and southward and southwestward to the extreme end of the western tongue of the Mohave Desert (Antelope Valley), including the several passes (Walker, Tehachapi, and the Cañada de las Uvas), by means of which communication is established between the Mohave Desert on the east and the Bakersfield Plain or upper San Joaquin Valley on the west. A detailed itinerary of this trip may be found in Part I of the present report.

Nearly all of the species were photographed by me in the field, and in most instances parts of the individual plant photographed were brought back for positive identification. As in the case of the desert shrubs, Mr. F. V. Coville is responsible for the nomenclature employed.

LIST OF CACTUSES, YUCCAS, AND AGAVE.

Cereus engelmanni.
    mohavensis.
Opuntia acanthocarpa.
    bernardina.
    echinocarpa.
    whipplei.
    parryi.
    ramosissima.
    pulchella.
    basilaris.
    engelmanni occidentalis.
    rutila.

Echinocactus johnsoni.
    polycephalus.
    polyancistrus.
    wislizeni lecontei.
Mamillaria sp.
Yucca baccata.
    arborescens.
    elata?
    macrocarpa.
    whipplei.
Agave utahensis.

Cereus engelmanni.

This is the commonest and most widely diffused cactus of the genus *Cereus* over the deserts of southern Nevada and southeastern California, where it was found in the following localities:

CALIFORNIA.

Deep Spring Valley.—Tolerably common in the wash leading up from Deep Spring Valley to the pass over the White Mountains; in full flower June 10. Found also on the Inyo Mountains.

Panamint Mountains.—Common in places.

NEVADA.

Gold Mountain.—Tolerably common on the south slope above 1,550 meters (5,100 feet); in flower June 3.

Timpahute and Desert Mountains.—Tolerably common on both slopes.

Pahranagat Valley.—Common on rocky slopes; in full flower May 22–26.

Pahranagat Mountains.—Common in places.

Juniper Mountains.—Common; in flower May 5.

Muddy Mountains.—Rather common; in full flower May 5.

UTAH.

Beaverdam Mountains.—Common, ranging from 730 to 1,350 meters (2,400 to 4,400 feet) on the west slope, and from 1,100 to 1,300 meters (3,600 to 4,300 feet) on the east slope; in flower May 10–11.

Santa Clara Valley.—Occurs in places; in flower May 11–15.

Cereus mohavensis.

This cactus grows in dense clumps in rocky places on the sides of the Desert Ranges, usually in cañons, and bears dark, purple-red flowers. It was observed in the following localities:

CALIFORNIA.

White Mountains.—Common in places on the east slope above Deep Spring Valley, beginning at an altitude of 1,900 meters (6,300 feet) and ranging up to the summit of the divide; in flower June 10.

Panamint Mountains.—Common in places along the summit, particularly north of Telescope Peak; not yet in flower, April 17–19.

NEVADA.

Charleston Mountains.—Found in a few places on the west slope of the Charleston Mountains above 1,550 meters (5,100 feet); beginning to flower April 29.

Pahranagat Mountains.—Found along the summit of the range; in flower May 26.

Highland Range.—Found on the west slope of the range; in flower May 20.

Juniper Mountains.—Tolerably common in places among the junipers from 1,820 to 2,050 meters (6,000 to 6,700 feet) in altitude; in flower May 18–19.

UTAH.

Santa Clara Valley.—Found in the Upper Santa Clara Valley at an altitude of 1,500 or 1,525 meters (4,900 or 5,000 feet). Its deep red flowers were fully open May 16.

Opuntia acanthocarpa. (Plates VII and VIII.)

This cylindrical-stemmed cactus, which is considerably larger than *O. echinocarpa*, from which it differs also in having more distant branches and fewer spines, was not observed in California or western Nevada, but was found in eastern Nevada, on the east side of the valley of the Virgin, a few miles from the Mormon town of Bunkerville, and thence easterly to an altitude of 1,340 meters (4,400 feet) on the west slope of the Beaverdam Mountains, in Utah. On the east slope of the Beaverdam Mountains it was found between 1,090 and 1,300 meters (3,600–4,300 feet). It was found also in the Lower Santa Clara Valley, Utah.

Opuntia bernardina.

This tall, arborescent, cylindrical cactus barely enters the region explored by the expedition. In southern California it is common on the San Bernardino Plain, and ranges northward through Cajon Pass, becoming scarce toward the summit. A little further west it is common in the Santa Clara Valley near the mouth of Castac Creek (about 4 miles north of the railroad switch 'Castac') at an altitude of 335 meters (1,100 feet) and thence southerly. In the region in which it grows it forms the favorite nesting sites for the cactus wren (*Campylorhynchus brunneicapillus*).

Opuntia echinocarpa.

This is the common arborescent cactus of the Mohave Desert region and the deserts of southern Nevada, over which it is widely distributed. It has inconspicuous green flowers, and was in blossom at the south end of Death Valley April 26, and at Bitter Springs, Nevada, May 5.

Two characteristic desert birds build their nests in this cactus almost exclusively, namely, Leconte's thrasher (*Harporhynchus lecontei*) and the cactus wren (*Campylorhynchus brunneicapillus*), and another species, the black-throated desert sparrow (*Amphispiza bilineata*), nests in it and in other situations also.

CALIFORNIA.

Mohave Desert.—Common and widely distributed, reaching westerly throughout Antelope Valley. It runs up the open cañon leading from Mohave to Tehachapi as high as 1,050 meters (3,450 feet).

Walker Pass.—Common among the tree yuccas on both sides of the pass, descending in Kern Valley as low as 820 meters (2,700 feet) or perhaps still lower.

Owens Valley.—Common, and ranging up on the west side (east slope of Sierra) to 1,830 or 1,900 meters (6,000 or 6,200 feet).

Panamint Valley.—Common.

Death Valley.—Common, beginning to flower at Saratoga Springs April 26 (flowers green).

Deep Spring Valley.—Occurs on the west side in the wash leading up to the pass over the White Mountains.

NEVADA.

Pahrump Valley.—Common, reaching up to the divide near Mountain Spring on the Charleston Mountains, at an altitude of 1,700 meters (5,600 feet).

Vegas Valley.—Common.

Bitter Springs.—Common in the Muddy Mountains and in flower May 5.

Valley of the Virgin and Lower Muddy.—Common on the gravel mesa between the Muddy and Virgin rivers.

Fish Lake Valley.—Occurs and ranges up on northwest slope of Mount Magruder to 1,950 meters (6,400 feet).

Grapevine Cañon.—Occurs.

Timpahute and Desert mountains.—Occurs.

Pahranagat Valley.—Common.

Pahranagat Mountains.—Occurs.

UTAH.

Beaverdam Mountains.—Comes up on the northwest slope of the Beaverdam Mountains to 1,150 meters (3,800 feet) from the Upper Virgin Valley.

Santa Clara Valley.—Common in the Lower Santa Clara Valley in the neighborhood of St. George, but not observed on the east slope of the Beaverdam Mountains. In the Upper Santa Clara Valley it is replaced by the larger and much handsomer densely-spined species *O. whipplei.*

Opuntia whipplei. (Plate IX.)

This remarkable species, noteworthy on account of the closeness of its branches, the shortness of its joints, and the multitude of its spines, is abundant in patches among the juniper and sagebrush along the Upper Santa Clara River, near the upper crossing in Utah, at an altitude of about 1,525 meters (5,000 feet); and was found also on the west slopes of the Highland and Juniper ranges in Nevada, but was not seen elsewhere. On the west slope of the Juniper Plateau it was found between the altitude of 1,830 and 1,980 meters (6,000 and 6,500 feet). The fruit differs from that of *O. echinocarpa* in bearing few or no spines.

Opuntia parryi. (Plate X.)

This species was found only in Indian Spring Valley, Nevada, and on the west slope of the Charleston Mountains, below Mountain Spring. In Indian Spring Valley it is confined to a limited area about 17 miles west of Indian Spring on and near the low divide between this valley and Ash Meadows. It is a remarkably prostrate form of the cylindrical-stemmed section of the genus, and its characters are well shown in the accompanying photograph.

Opuntia ramosissima.

This very characteristic species, easily recognized by the small diameter of its stems and branches, was not found in California or in Nevada west of the North Kingston Mountains, where it was first seen, and where it seems to reach its western limit. It was found also throughout Indian Spring Valley and on both slopes of the Timpahute and Desert mountains, ranging down on the east side (west side of Timpahute Desert) to 1,500 meters (4,900 feet), and was seen on the east side of the Valley of the Virgin, near Bunkerville, Nev., and near the mouth of Beaverdam Creek, Arizona.

Opuntia pulchella.

This singular little species, having a remarkably large root, was observed in but a single locality, namely, the south end of Fish Lake Valley, on the boundary between California and Nevada, where it was in full flower June 8. The blossoms are pink.

Opuntia basilaris.

Opuntia basiláris is one of the commonest cactuses of the Sonoran deserts, and may be recognized by the obcordate shape of its pads and the scantiness of its spines. Its purple-red flowers grow in great numbers on the upper edges of the pads, as many as eight open blossoms and several buds having been seen on a single pad at one time. The species was observed in the following localities:

CALIFORNIA.

Mohave Desert.—Common in places.

Tehachapi Valley and Pass.—Tolerably common, and still in flower as late as June 25.

Walker Pass and Kern Valley.—Common on the east slope up to 1,430 meters (4,700 feet). On the west slope it descends into the valley of Kern River, where it is tolerably common on northerly exposures as low as 820 meters (2,700 feet).

Owens Valley.—Tolerably common in places.

Deep Spring Valley.—Found in the wash leading up from Deep Spring Valley to the pass over the White Mountains.

Panamint Valley.—Common in places, running over the greater part of the Panamint Mountains, where it was tolerably common in Perognathus Flat.

Death Valley.—Common in places, particularly at Saratoga Springs at the south end of the valley, where it was in full flower as early as April 26.

NEVADA.

Fish Lake Valley.—Tolerably common, ranging up on the northwest slope of Mount Magruder to about 1,850 meters (6,100 feet).

Grapevine Cañon.—Common on the north side of the cañon and ranging up on the Gold Mountain slope between 1,525 and 1,830 meters (5,000 and 6,000 feet).

Timpahute Mountains.—Abundant and flowering profusely. Ranges up to 1,275 or 1,300 meters (4,200 or 4,300 feet) on the road to Pahroc Plain. Occurs also on Pahranagat Mountains.

Muddy Mountains.—Common near Bitter Spring (in full flower May 5).

Valley of the Virgin and Lower Muddy.—Common on dry gravel soils.

ARIZONA AND UTAH.

Beaverdam Mountains.—Common on the east side of the Virgin Valley, ranging thence up on the west slope of the Beaverdam Mountains to 1,150 meters (3,800 feet).

Opuntia engelmanni occidentalis.

Abundant throughout the San Bernardino Plain, ranging up to the base of the San Bernardino Mountains and entering the lower part of Cajon Pass, where it reaches an altitude of about 730 meters (2,400 feet). It occurs in patches in the Santa Clara Valley near the mouth of Castac Creek. In Castac Valley the highest plant was seen on the north side at an altitude of 600 meters (2,000 feet), but it was rare above 330 meters (1,100 feet), where, both it and *Opuntia bernardina* became common together about 4 miles north of the railway switch known as 'Castac.'

A related cactus, which Mr. Coville informs me is probably *Opuntia chlorotica*, was found along the Colorado River, in the western part of Vegas Desert near Lower Cottonwood Springs, and on the west slope of the Charleston Mountains between 1,675 and 1,730 meters (5,500 and 5,700 feet) altitude.

Sheep Spring, Juniper Mountains.—A cactus resembling *Opuntia engelmanni*, but with smaller and more spiny pads, which differ further from those of *O. engelmanni* in not growing on top of one another several tiers high, was common in the sage and juniper in the Juniper Mountains between Meadow Creek Valley, Nevada, and Shoal Creek, Utah, from 1,920 to 2,070 meters (6,300 to 6,800 feet) altitude.

Opuntia rutila. (Plate XI.)

This species, which has enormously long and slender spines, was not found in California except on the Panamint Mountains, where it was common along the summit, ranging down on the west slope above Wild Rose Spring to an altitude of 1,900 meters (6,300 feet). In Nevada it was found on the Charleston, Pahranagat, Desert, and Timpahute mountains, and in the Virgin Valley. In Utah it was found on the west slope of the Beaverdam Mountains, up to 1,150 meters (3,800 feet), and occurred in places in the Santa Clara Valley.

Along the west base of the Desert Mountains near Quartz Spring it was common and in flower May 27, and the flowers were yellow. All of the other flowers seen were red. It is possible that two species are here confounded.

Echinocactus johnsoni.

This species is about one-third the size of *E. wislizeni*, which it greatly resembles. Its flowers are deep red. It was found on the west slope of the Beaverdam Mountains in southwestern Utah, at an altitude of 1,030 meters (3,400 feet), and ranged thence up over the divide to 1,525 meters (5,000 feet). A small form referred to the same species was common on steep gravel slopes in Vegas Wash, Nevada, where it was in full flower May 3. It was eaten by the Paiute Indians, who peel it as we would a cucumber.

Echinocactus polycephalus.

This striking species, commonly called 'nigger-head' in the desert region, and resembling loose clusters of cocoanuts, is common on many of the desert valleys in the southern part of the Great Basin. It was observed in the following localities:

CALIFORNIA.

Inyo Mountains.—Found along the west side of the range in Owens Valley.

Panamint Mountains.—Found in the upper part of the *Larrea* on the west side of the divide between Perognathus Flat and Wild Rose Spring.

NEVADA.

Indian Spring Valley.—Common on the rocky walls of the cañon leading from the extreme west end of Indian Spring Valley down toward Ash Meadows.

Desert Mountains.—Grows sparingly along the west base of the Desert Mountains, near Quartz Spring.

North Kingston Range.—Common in places.

Ash Meadows.—Common on the low rocky mountains on the east side of Ash Meadows.

Pahranagat Valley.—A few clusters of heads were seen in rocky places on the east side of the valley.

Muddy Mountains.—A few seen in the Muddy Mountains above Bitter Springs.

Valley of the Virgin and Lower Muddy.—Found in a few places among rocks, particularly on the gravel mesa near the boundary line between Arizona and Nevada. Common on the high mesa between the Virgin and Muddy.

[The species was not seen on the east slope of the Beaverdam Mountains, in Utah.]

Echinocactus polyancistrus.

This species, which resembles a pineapple in general size and appearance, was found in flower on the east slope of the White Mountains,

California, a little above the south end of Fish Lake Valley, June 9. The flowers are red.

Echinocactus wislizeni lecontei.

This large barrel-cactus is not common in the region traversed. In California it was found in the Panamint Mountains (common in Surprise Cañon).

NEVADA.

Virgin Mesa.—Common on the high gravel mesa between the Virgin and Muddy valleys.

UTAH.

Beaverdam Mountains.—Found on the west slope of the Beaverdam Mountains between 730 and 1,340 meters (2,400-4,400 feet), but not seen on the east slope.

Mamillaria.

Owing to the uncertainty respecting the species of *Mamillaria* observed, our notes are of very little value. Representatives of the genus were found in the following localities in Nevada: Mountain Spring, Charleston Mountains; Great Bend of the Colorado River; Bitter Springs (where it was in flower May 5, flowers rich red); and on steep gravel slopes near the boundary between Arizona and Nevada on the west side of the Virgin Valley.

Yucca baccata. (Plate XII.)

This elegant yucca is by far the handsomest species growing in the desert regions of the Southwest, where it was found in the following localities:

NEVADA.

Charleston Mountains.—*Yucca baccata* was first seen on the west slope (Pahrump Valley side) of the Charleston Mountains, in the upper part of the tree yucca belt, at an altitude of about 1,430 meters (4,700 feet), whence it ranges up to the divide at Mountain Spring, a little less than 1,830 meters (or 6,000 feet), and down on the east side to 1,340 meters (4,400 feet), where it was mixed with *Yucca macrocarpa*. It was budding abundantly April 30, but only a few flowers had expanded.

Indian Spring Valley.—Tolerably common at the north end of the north arm of Indian Spring Valley at an altitude of about 1,400 meters (4,600 feet), whence it ranges up toward Hungry Hill Summit to 1,700 meters (5,600 feet), where it was flowering in great perfection May 27.

Timpahute and Desert Mountains.—Occurs sparingly in the neighborhood of Mud or Summit Spring.

Pahranagat Valley.—Occurs sparingly on the west side of the valley, beginning about a mile from the bottom at an altitude of 1,270 meters (4,200 feet) and ranging up to 1,400 meters (4,600 feet).

Hyko Mountains.—Occurs sparingly along the open cañon or wash leading from Pahroc Plain into Pahranagat Valley.

Pahroc Mountains.—Tolerably common near Pahroc Spring.

Highland Range.—Occurs sparingly on the west slope.

Juniper Mountains.—Found sparingly on the west slope of the Juniper Mountains between Panaca and Sheep Spring, at an altitude of 1,830 to 1,970 meters (6,000 to 6,500 feet). Here it was only in bud May 19, though it was in flower on the Beaverdam Mountains and on the south slope of Pine Valley Mountain, Utah, a week or ten days earlier.

UTAH.

Santa Clara Valley.—In the Upper Santa Clara Valley, north of St. George, this handsome species occurs in a belt a few miles wide, beginning at about 1,150 meters (3,800 feet) and reaching up to 1,460 meters (4,800 feet).

Beaverdam Mountains.—Common, ranging down to 1,080 meters (3,600 feet) on the east slope, and 1,030 meters (3,400 feet) on the west slope. It was beginning to flower May 10, though some plants were only in bud at that time.

Yucca arborescens [=*Yucca brevifolia*]. (Plate XIII and frontispiece.)

Among the many unusual and peculiar modifications of plant life of the desert regions of the southwestern United States, none is more remarkable or striking than the tree yucca (*Yucca arborescens*).

Tree yuccas form open forests or groves, usually of small size, but sometimes 15 or 20 miles or more in length, according to the extent of the area suitable to their requirements. The individual trees are well spaced and vary from 6 to 9 meters (20 to 30 feet) in height. They branch in a very peculiar manner and are abundantly clothed with stiff, spiny leaves set so near together that their bases are in actual contact. As the tree grows the leaves die from below upward, and the dead ones at first point outward at right angles to the trunk, and then downward, their points surrounding the branch or trunk like a belt of bayonets, effectually preventing most animals from climbing up from below. The dead leaves fall off after a year or two, so that the trunks and lower parts of the main branches finally become bare.

Tree yuccas are abundant about the borders of the Mohave Desert and on many of the included 'lost ranges,' and also in places of suitable elevation throughout the deserts of southeastern California, southern Nevada, western Arizona, and the extreme southwestern corner of Utah. They do not grow in the bottoms of the arid basins, or upon the steep declivities of the mountains, but thrive best on the higher gravel slopes that skirt the deserts and upon the basal slopes of the included desert ranges, always in a definite zone or belt the extreme vertical width of which rarely exceeds 450 meters (1,500 feet), and usually is much less. The altitude of this belt varies with the base level, but invariably marks the upper limit of the Lower Sonoran zone.

Looking northward over the Mohave Desert from the summit of Cajon

Pass a continuous forest of tree yuccas stretches away in the distance until lost in the desert haze, adding a singularly weird element to the peculiar physiognomy of the region.

Some years ago an attempt was made to make paper pulp from the trunks of tree yuccas. The attempt was successful so far as the production of good pulp was concerned, but the cost of manufacture proved greater than the projectors of the enterprise expected and it was abandoned. Mr. Charles H. Shinn, in an article in the American Agriculturist for December, 1891 (p. 689), states that a small pulp mill was built at Ravenna in Soledad Pass, just south of Mohave Desert in California (of which two figures are given), and that large quantities of paper were manufactured and shipped to England, on which a few editions of the London Daily Telegraph were printed. He states further that some of it was used in New York and in San Francisco.

The following detailed notes were recorded respecting the distribution of this species:

CALIFORNIA.

Mohave Desert.—Tree yuccas are common on the higher levels of the Mohave Desert, where they form a belt several miles in width around the west arm of the desert, covering the slope at the north foot of the San Bernardino range of mountains and stretching thence westerly nearly to the west end of Antelope Valley. On the north side of the desert they cover the slope at the foot of the Tehachapi Mountains and extend northeasterly in scattered patches nearly to Walker Pass, in which they again become abundant. This belt is not continuous throughout, but is interrupted by the absence of suitable conditions. Opposite Cajon Pass the forest is fully 20 kilometers (12 miles) in breadth, covering the slope between the altitudes of 730 and 1,180 meters (2,500 and 3,900 feet), though the trees are scarce and scattering below 920 meters (3,300 feet). Above 1,060 meters (3,500 feet) they are mixed with juniper, and between 1,150 and 1,180 meters (3,800–3,900 feet) with the true sagebrush (*Artemisia tridentata*). An isolated clump grows within the mouth of the pass on the south side of the divide at an altitude of 1,170 meters (3,850 feet). On the divide between Dagget and Pilot Knob they occur sparingly on the south side of the summit, but are more common on the long slope leading down to Paradise Valley from the south (north exposure), where a sparse growth continues for many miles. A few scattered and stunted trees were found also on and near the divide at Pilot Knob. On the north side of the Mohave Desert, just north of the town of Mohave, they begin at an altitude of 900 meters (3,000 feet) and extend up through the wash or open cañon leading to Tehachapi Valley, reaching Cameron at an altitude of 1,090 meters (3,600 feet). They range thence easterly a few miles, and westerly along the base of the Tehachapi Mountains as far as the eye can reach. They come down from the north side of the desert to within a mile of Mohave Station, and extend thence westerly and southwesterly over Antelope Valley with hardly a break between Mohave and Willow Spring, though they are absent from the dry flat extending from Willow Spring southerly and westerly. On the south side of the desert they reappear on a low ridge a few miles south of Mohave, and extend thence southerly past Lancaster to and into Soledad Pass. In the extreme western end of the Mohave Desert, known as Antelope Valley, they reach westward along the middle and north part of the valley to a point about 6 kilometers (4 miles) east of Liebre ranch, but on the south side (north slope) they do not extend quite so far west. They reappear in an open cañon or broad wash leading south from near Gorman's ranch to Peru Creek, where they occur in clumps and irregular patches for a mile or so at an altitude of 850 to 900 meters (2,800–3,000 feet).

Walker Pass.—At the east end of Walker Pass tree yuccas begin at 1,090 meters (3,600 feet) and form a fine forest in the pass, filling it all the way across up to 1,430 meters (4,700 feet), and straggling on singly and in little clumps up to and over the summit at 1,550 meters (5,100 feet) and down on the west side, with several interruptions, to the valley of Kern River. The total length of the yucca strip in the pass proper is 18 or 20 kilometers (11 or 12 miles). From Walker Pass they descend into Kern Valley, where a number of small interrupted groves are scattered irregularly along the bottom of the valley nearly all the way down to the forks of Kern River, at an altitude of 850 meters (2,800 feet).

Coso Mountains.—A yucca grove covers part of the west slope of the Coso Mountains, beginning about 5 kilometers (3 miles) south of Owens Lake and reaching thence southerly nearly to Haway Meadows. Its lower edge comes down almost to the level of the valley (probably to about 1,120 meters or 3,700 feet). A few scattering trees occur still further south, but they are not numerous enough to form a grove. [Dr. A. K. Fisher tells me that this grove spreads easterly over nearly the whole of the Coso mountains and valley.]

Panamint Mountains.—A few stunted tree yuccas occur on the west side of the divide between Perognathus Flat and Wild Rose Spring in the Panamint Mountains.

Nelson Range.—Mr. E. W. Nelson found tree yuccas in abundance on the low range (here named 'Nelson Range') separating Panamint Valley from Saline Valley, where they stretch all the way across from the Inyo Mountains to the Panamint Mountains.

Ivawatch Mountains.—Mr. T. S. Palmer found a few scattering trees on the southwest slope of the Ivawatch Mountains.

NEVADA.

Mount Magruder.—Tree yuccas occur sparingly on the northwest slope of Mount Magruder and adjacent hillsides from an altitude of 2,070 meters (6,800 feet) down almost to the upper level of Fish Lake Valley at

1,730 meters (5,700 feet). Another and better defined grove occupies the southeast base of Mount Magruder, facing the north part of Sarcobatus Flat.

Gold Mountain.—Tree yuccas occur sparingly in the valley between Mount Magruder and Gold Mountain at an altitude of 1,740 meters (5,700 feet) and range thence southerly over the south slope of Gold Mountain and adjacent hills, reaching westward almost to the edge of the northwest arm of Death Valley at 1,770 meters (5,800 feet), and occurring throughout the east and west trough or valley which occupies the north slope of Gold Mountain north of the Gold Mountain mining camp (also known as 'State Line'), reaching as high as 2,100 meters (7,000 feet) on south exposures on spurs and hills north of the main peak, though not occurring on the north slope of the main ridge proper. On the south side of Gold Mountain they descend to 1,550 meters (5,100 feet), thus reaching well down on the north side of Grapevine Cañon. Several were found in flower near the summit of Gold Mountain June 3, the only flowers of this species seen during the trip. They are sessile in dense clumps at the ends of the branches, and are coarser and less attractive than those of any of the other species.

Grapevine Mountains.—A yucca forest of considerable size occupies the east base of the Grapevine Mountains west of the southern half of Sarcobatus Flat.

Ralston Desert.—A forest of tree yuccas was seen on the north side of the east fork of Amargosa Creek northeast of the north end of Oasis Valley and is probably the northern limit of the species in this direction.

Table Mountain.—Mr. F. Stephens found a large forest of tree yuccas on the mesa known as 'Table Mountain,' about 40 kilometers (25 miles) north of Ash Meadows.

Timpahute and Desert Mountains.—Tree yuccas begin on the west side of Timpahute Desert at the very bottom of the east slope of the Timpahute Mountains (altitude 1,450 to 1,490 meters or 4,800 to 4,900 feet) and continue all the way to and over the summit of the saddle between the Timpahute and Desert Mountains (summit 1,750 meters or 5,750 feet). They do not occur immediately below Summit Spring, but soon reappear and reach down to Emigrant Valley at 1,580 meters (5,200 feet), forming a broad zone along the west slope of the Desert Range, whence they extend all the way around the south end of Emigrant Valley, and reach several miles north on the west side. Continuing southward without interruption they pass over the low divide at Hungry Hill Summit (1,760 meters or 5,800 feet) and extend down the narrow North Arm of Indian Spring Valley to 1,200 meters (4,000 feet), where they are sufficiently abundant most of the way to form a regular yucca forest. In the lower part many trees were in fruit May 27, bearing large green pods containing flat seeds.

Pahranagat Mountains.—Common on the Pahranagat Mountains from the summit of the pass between Pahranagat and Timpahute valleys (altitude 1,830 meters or 6,000 feet) down on the west side to the edge of Timpahute Desert at an altitude of 1,525 meters (5,000 feet), and down on the east side sparingly to within a mile of the bottom of Pahranagat Valley at an altitude of 1,280 meters (4,200 feet), and forming a fair forest above 1,400 meters (4,600 feet). Stunted and scattered trees stretch thence southerly all along the gravel slope on the west side of Pahranagat Valley at the foot of the Pahranagat Range. On the west slope of the Pahranagat Range (on the east side of Timpahute Valley) the trees are sufficiently near together to form a fair yucca forest between an altitude of 1,390 meters (4,600 feet) and the summit of the divide.

Highland Range.—The most northerly forest of tree yuccas found in eastern Nevada is on the west slope of the Highland Range south of the dry lake in Desert Valley, and southeast of Pahroc Spring. This forest is at least 5 miles wide and 10 miles long, and may stretch away much further to the south. Apparently it begins at an altitude of about 1,670 meters (5,500 feet) on the desert side, and ranges up to 2,000 meters or higher (probably to 6,500 or 7,000 feet) on the west slope of the mountains.

Pahroc Range.—A few scattering and stunted tree yuccas grow at Point of Rocks, the southernmost spur of the Pahroc Range near Pahroc Spring. These are the northernmost trees of which we have any knowledge. The high base level of Pahroc Plain explains the unusually high altitude at which they grow.

Charleston Mountains.—On the west slope of the Charleston Mountains (Pahrump Valley side), below Mountain Spring, tree yuccas begin at an altitude of about 1,060 meters (3,500 feet), and become more and more abundant until they form an open forest in the upper *Larrea* and *Coleogyne* belt, mixing with the junipers at 1,525 meters (5,000 feet), and pushing 60 to 90 meters (200 or 300 feet) higher on favorable slopes, finally stopping at an altitude of about 1,600 meters (5,300 feet). The individual trees are smaller than those of the Mohave Desert, rarely exceeding 4½ meters (15 feet) in height. In the lower part of this belt *Yucca arborescens* is mixed with unusually large examples of *Yucca macrocarpa*, and in the upper part with the elegant *Yucca baccata*.

ARIZONA.

Northwestern corner.—On the mesa west of the Virgin River and about 8 miles south of the mouth of Beaverdam Creek, near the boundary between Arizona and Nevada, is a scattering belt of tree yuccas a mile or a mile and a half in breadth, ranging from an altitude of about 670 meters (2,250 feet) on the Virgin Valley slope to the top of the mesa at 740 meters (2,450 feet).

Detrital Valley.—Mr. Vernon Bailey informs me that *Yucca arborescens* forms an extensive forest on the low divide between Detrital and

Sacramento Valleys, reaching northward along the sides of Detrital Valley for about 24 kilometers (15 miles) north of Mountain Spring.

UTAH.

Beaverdam Mountains.—Tree yuccas begin at the foot of the west slope of the Beaverdam Mountains in southwestern Utah at an altitude of about 700 meters (2,300 feet), and range up to 1,340 meters (4,400 feet), forming a belt 8 or 9 kilometers (5 or 6 miles) in width. The trees rarely exceed 3 meters (10 feet) in height and are more scattering than in the Mohave Desert.

Yucca elata?

A narrow-leaved yucca provisionally referred to this species was found sparingly in the Lower Santa Clara Valley, Utah, on the mesa near the town of St. George, where it was in full bloom and very handsome May 11–15. Its flower-stalks are tall and slender, and its leaves narrow and thin. A form resembling this, but with somewhat thicker and heavier leaves, was found on the west slope of the Juniper Mountains between Sheep Spring and Panaca, between the altitudes of 1,760 and 2,130 meters (5,800–6,700 feet). It was budding plentifully May 19, but was not found in flower.

Yucca macrocarpa. (Plate XIV.)

This large yucca was found in but few localities traversed by the expedition. It finds its western limit along with *Opuntia ramosissima* on the North Kingston Mountains, between Resting Springs and Pahrump Valley, Nevada. It begins again on the east side of Pahrump Valley at an altitude of about 970 meters (3,200 feet), and ranges up on the west slope of the Charleston Mountains to 1,090 meters (3,600 feet), forming a well-marked zone mixed with scattering trees of *Yucca arborescens*, which latter species becomes more and more abundant until it forms a true yucca forest in the upper *Larrea* and *Coleogyne* belt, where *Y. macrocarpa* disappears. In this zone *Yucca macrocarpa* grows larger than observed elsewhere, many plants reaching the height of $2\frac{1}{2}$ meters (8 feet), and some growing as high as 3 or even 4 meters (10 to 13 feet). It never branches like *Yucca arborescens* but has a heavy, irregular trunk, well shown in the accompanying photograph. On warm soil a few plants were in full flower April 29, though most of them were not yet in bud. On the east side of the Charleston Mountains it begins at an altitude of 1,525 meters (about 5,000 feet), and descends to the upper part of Vegas Valley, near Cottonwood Springs, at an altitude of 900 meters (3,000 feet), where dozens were found in flower April 30.

On the north side of the Charleston Mountains this species occurs sparingly throughout the higher parts of Indian Spring Valley above 1,180 meters (3,900 feet). It is common on the low divide about $27\frac{1}{2}$ kilometers (17 miles) west of Indian Spring at an altitude of 1,220 meters or 4,000 feet, and thence is continuous westerly along the south (or highest) side of the valley to the cañon separating Indian Spring Valley from the Amargosa country, and occurs scattering on the west or Amargosa side, skirting the higher slopes. In the north arm of Indian Spring Valley it is common and conspicuous, ranging from 1,370 meters (4,500 feet) northward to about 1,670 meters (5,500 feet). It was not found on the Beaverdam Mountains or in any other locality.

ARIZONA.

Detrital Valley.—Mr. Vernon Bailey informs me that he found this species abundant and of unusually large size throughout the south end of Detrital Valley and north end of Sacramento Valley, covering the divide and extending for some distance along the foothills of the bordering mountains.

Yucca whipplei.

This is the characteristic yucca of the Coast Ranges of California, whence it extends easterly along the west slope of the Sierra Nevada, where we found it flowering abundantly between Kernville and Walker Basin June 23, its creamy flowers on tall white stalks dotting the sidehills above the chaparral. It is common also in the Tehachapi Mountains, ranging down as low as 1,060 meters (3,500 feet) in the upper part of the cañon leading from Tehachapi to Mohave, and on the hills at the head of Antelope Valley, near Gorman's ranch (altitude about 1,150 meters or 3,850 feet), whence it spreads over the Sierra Liebre range.

Agave utahensis.

This species, the only true agave met with by the expedition, was found in but two localities, namely, the Charleston Mountains in Nevada and the Beaverdam Mountains in southwestern Utah. In the former locality it was common on rocky hillsides in the neighborhood of Mountain Spring, from an altitude of 1,600 meters (5,300 feet) up to 1,830 meters (6,000 feet), where many 'mescal' pits were found where the Indians had baked the edible butts of the plants. These pits average a little more than a meter (about 4 feet) in depth, and from $3\frac{1}{2}$ to 6 meters (12 to 20 feet) in diameter. On the west slope of the Beaverdam Mountains in Utah the agave begins at 1,180 meters (3,800 feet) and grows in a narrow zone upward toward the summit of the pass.

LIST OF LOCALITIES VISITED BY THE DEATH VALLEY EXPEDITION.

By T. S. PALMER.

The delay in the appearance of the first part of the report, containing descriptions of the various points visited by the expedition, makes it desirable to furnish a brief statement concerning the places referred to. In describing an area like the desert region of California great difficulty is experienced in fixing localities, and recourse must often be had to cañons, washes, and springs for names with which to indicate places. For this reason a large number of seemingly unimportant localities occur in the report, which can be found on few, if any, published maps and are more or less meaningless to one unfamiliar with the country. The following list, while making no pretense to include all the localities mentioned in the report, gives brief descriptions of the more important places, which will serve to locate them with reference to well-known points. Many of these places will be described more fully elsewhere.

The altitudes have been compiled chiefly from Gannett's Dictionary of Altitudes in the United States* and the map sheets of the Wheeler Survey West of the 100th Meridian. These have been supplemented by observations made by the expedition; but except in the case of points in Death Valley (which were determined by a topographer of the U. S. Geological Survey), such altitudes are based mainly on observations made with aneroid barometers. Since the list is intended primarily as a help in finding places on the map, distances, unless otherwise stated, indicate the number of miles measured in a straight line between two points, and not the distance by the road. In the case of railroad points, however, the distances between stations are taken from the railroad figures. This will explain the apparent discrepancy in many cases between the distances given and the actual distances as measured by an odometer. The metric equivalents for altitudes and distances are only approximate, all fractions having been discarded in converting the measurements into the metric system. Under each locality will be found the names of the members of the expedition who visited it and

---

* Bull. U. S. Geol. Survey, No. 76, 1891.

who assisted in making the collections described in this report.† A list of several names under one locality usually indicates that the place was visited by different members at different dates—particularly in the case of points in Death Valley, Owens Valley, and the Sierra Nevada.

NOTE.—Reference letters and figures follow names of places which appear on the accompanying map. Altitudes based on observations made by the expedition are marked with an asterisk.

Adobe Station, Kern County, Calif. Altitude, 231 feet (86 meters).

An abandoned stage station on the wagon road from Bakersfield to Los Angeles, situated northeast of Kern Lake in the San Joaquin Valley..................NELSON.

Alila, Tulare County, Calif. Altitude, 280 feet (85 meters).

A station on the Southern Pacific Railroad, 30 miles (48 kilometers) south of Visalia...BAILEY, FISHER, NELSON.

Alvord, Inyo County, Calif. Altitude, 3,956 feet (1,206 meters).

The station on the Carson and Colorado Railroad for Big Pine, 54 miles (86 kilometers) north of Keeler on Owens Lake..................................STEPHENS.

Amargosa Borax Works, Inyo County, Calif. F, 12.

An abandoned station and borax works of the Pacific Coast Borax Company, situated on the Amargosa River, about 20 miles (32 kilometers) north of the Great Bend and 6 miles (10 kilometers) west of Resting Springs.
PALMER, BAILEY, FISHER, NELSON.

Amargosa Range, Inyo County, Calif. D–E, 11.

The name given to the central part of the range which forms the eastern wall of Death Valley. It is usually restricted to that portion of the range between Boundary Cañon on the north (beyond which are the Grapevine Mountains), and Furnace Creek on the south, which marks the beginning of the Funeral Mountains. The highest point, Pyramid Peak, has an altitude of 6,754 feet, or 2,058 meters. (See also Funeral Mountains.)

Amargosa River. D–F, 11–12.

A 'stream' (usually nothing more than a dry wash) running from Oasis Valley, Nevada, southward through Ash Meadows to the end of the Funeral Mountains, where it turns at the 'Great Bend' to the west and northwest and sinks in Death Valley.

Antelope Valley, Los Angeles County, Calif. H, 7–8.

The name applied to the western part of the Mohave Desert immediately north of the Sierra Liebre...MERRIAM, PALMER.

Argus Mountains, Inyo County, Calif. E–F, 10.

The range situated immediately west of Panamint Valley between the Coso and Panamint mountains. Its highest point, Maturango Peak, has an altitude of 8,814 feet (2,696 meters)...PALMER, FISHER.

---

†Mr. Albert Koebele, the entomologist, joined the expedition at Daggett on April 3, and remained only about six weeks. He crossed the Mohave Desert to Death Valley with one of the parties and then proceeded to Keeler by way of Panamint Valley, Shepherd Cañon, and Darwin, making collections along the road wherever practicable. He visited Daggett, Paradise Valley, Granite Wells, and Lone Willow Spring in San Bernardino County; Furnace Creek, Bennett, and Mesquite Wells in Death Valley; Windy Gap; Hot Springs in Panamint Valley; Shepherd Cañon and Maturango Spring in the Argus Mountains; Darwin and Keeler.

Ash Creek, Inyo County, Calif. E, 8.

A small stream entering Owens Lake from the west, about 9 miles (14 kilometers) north of Olancha. Named from the ash trees that grow on its borders... STEPHENS.

Ash Meadows, Nye County, Nev. E, 11–12.

The large valley or plain east of the Amargosa Range and 50 miles (80 kilometers) north of the Great Bend of the Amargosa River, named on account of the presence of a small desert ash (*Fraxinus coriacea*) which was formerly abundant. The boundary line between California and Nevada passes through Ash Meadows. Collections were made by Merriam, Bailey, and Stephens at the 'King Spring' or 'Stone House' (altitude about 3,800* feet or 1,160 meters), on the eastern side of the valley, and by the rest of the party at Watkins' Ranch, 3 or 4 miles west of this point—all in Nevada.

Bakersfield, the county seat of Kern County, Calif. Altitude, 415 feet (126 meters). G, 6........................MERRIAM, PALMER, NELSON, FISHER, BAILEY.

Banning, San Bernardino County, Calif. Altitude, 2,317 feet (706 meters).

A station on the Southern Pacific Railroad, about 30 miles (50 kilometers) southeast of San Bernardino and near the summit of the San Gorgonio Pass........STEPHENS.

Beaverdam Mountains, Washington County, Utah. C, 17.

A north-and-south range west of the town of St. George, constituting the northward extension of the Virgin Mountains........................MERRIAM, BAILEY.

Bennett Wells, Inyo County, Calif. Altitude, 323* feet (98 meters) below sea level. E, 11.

Two shallow wells dug in the bottom of Death Valley, on the west side of the salt marsh, and nearly due east of Telescope Peak. Named in memory of one of the survivors of the ill-fated party of emigrants who entered the valley in 1850. The lowest point in the valley (480* feet or 146 meters *below sea level*, according to observations of the U. S. Geological Survey) is a little northeast of this place.
MERRIAM, PALMER, FISHER, NELSON, BAILEY.

Benton, Mono County, Calif. Altitude, 5,515 feet (1,681 meters). B, 8.

A station on the Carson and Colorado Railroad, 100 miles (160 kilometers) north of Keeler. The town is about 4 miles (6 kilometers) west of the station of the same name, and about 200 feet (60 meters) higher....................NELSON, STEPHENS.

Big Cottonwood Meadows, Inyo County, Calif. Altitude about 10,000* feet (3,050 meters).

The large meadows near the head of Big Cottonwood Creek, a stream rising near Mount Corcoran, and flowing into Owens Lake. A meteorological station was established in the meadow (about 8 miles or 13 kilometers southeast of Mount Whitney) June 15, and observations were continued by Dutcher and Koch until September 15.......................MERRIAM, PALMER, FISHER, BAILEY, NELSON.

Big Pine, Inyo County, Calif. Altitude, about 4,000 feet (1,220 meters). C, 8.

A town in Owens Valley, about 50 miles (80 kilometers) north of Owens Lake. (See also Alvord.)........................MERRIAM, BAILEY, NELSON.

Big Tree Cañon, Tulare County, Calif.

A cañon on the East Fork of the Kaweah, named on account of the presence of Big Trees (*Sequoia gigantea*)........................BAILEY.

Bishop, Inyo County, Calif. Altitude [of station], 4,104 feet (1,251 meters). C, 8.

A station on the Carson and Colorado Railroad, about 70 miles (113 kilometers) north of Keeler. The town of Bishop, or Bishop Creek, is on the creek of the same name, and is west of the station........................NELSON, STEPHENS.

Bishop Creek, Inyo County, Calif. C, 8.

A small stream rising on the east slope of the Sierra Nevada and flowing into Owens River. Collections were made by Stephens at Lewis Lake on the west fork of the creek at an altitude of about 9,000 feet (2,740 meters)..................STEPHENS.

Bitter Spring, Lincoln County, Nev. Altitude, 1,800-1,900* feet (550-580 meters). F, 15.

A spring on the east slope of the Muddy Mountains, about 16 miles (25 kilometers) northeast of the site of Callville ....MERRIAM, BAILEY.

Borax Flat or Lake, San Bernardino County, Calif. Altitude, 1,808 feet (551 meters). F, 10.

A borax marsh on the boundary line between San Bernardino and Inyo counties, just west of the Slate Range and near the southern end of the Argus Range, about 25 miles (40 kilometers) west of Browns Peak. Searles' borax works are located on the northwest side of the marsh .... STEPHENS.

Browns Peak, Calif. Altitude, 5,392 feet (1,643 meters). F, 10.

A prominent peak opposite the south end of the Panamint Range and east of Lone Willow Spring ....BAILEY.

Bubbs Creek, Fresno County, Calif.

The main branch of the South Fork of Kings River, which rises near Kearsarge Pass and unites with the South Fork at the east end of the Kings River Cañon.
PALMER, FISHER, NELSON.

Bunkerville, Lincoln County, Nev. D, 16.

A Mormon town in the Virgin Valley on the road from Callville, Nev., to St. George, Utah, 5 miles (8 kilometers) west of the eastern boundary of the State of Nevada...MERRIAM, BAILEY.

Cajon Pass, San Bernardino County, Calif. Altitude [of wagon pass], 4,195 feet (1,279 meters). I, 9-10.

A pass in the Sierra Madre, leading north from the San Bernardino Valley to the Mohave Desert ....MERRIAM, PALMER, FISHER, STEPHENS.

Caliente, Kern County, Calif. Altitude 1,290 feet (393 meters). G, 7.

A station and post-office on the Southern Pacific Railroad at the north foot of Tehachapi Pass...MERRIAM, PALMER.

Callville, Lincoln County, Nev. Altitude, 945 feet (288 meters). E, 15.

An abandoned Mormon settlement on the north bank of the Colorado River at the head of navigation and about 4 miles (6 kilometers) east of the Great Bend.
MERRIAM, BAILEY.

Cameron, Kern County, Calif. Altitude 3,786 feet (1,154 meters).

A station on the Southern Pacific Railroad, 10 miles (16 kilometers) northwest of Mohave and 6 miles (10 kilometers) southeast of Tehachapi.....MERRIAM, PALMER.

Cañada de las Uvas, Kern County, Calif. Altitude about 4,288 feet (1,307 meters). H, 7.

A wagon pass in the Tejon or Tehachapi mountains, leading from the south end of the San Joaquin Valley across to the west end of the Mohave Desert. Situated east of Mt. Piños and about 30 miles (50 kilometers) southwest of Tehachapi Pass.
MERRIAM, PALMER, NELSON.

Canebrake Ranch, Kern County, Calif. Altitude 3,904 feet (1,190 meters).

A ranch at the northwest foot of Walker Pass on the road from Kernville to Coyote Holes...........................MERRIAM, PALMER, FISHER, BAILEY.

Carpenteria, Santa Barbara County, Calif. I, 5.

A town on the Southern Pacific Railroad, 10 miles (16 kilometers) east of Santa Barbara .... NELSON.

Carrizo Plains, San Luis Obispo County, Calif. G, 4–5.

The name given to the valley or plain east of the headwaters of the San Juan River and separated from the main San Joaquin Valley by the low ridge of the Temploa Mountains.. NELSON.

Castac Lake, Kern County, Calif. H, 7.

A small lake in the Cañada de las Uvas, 2 miles (3 kilometers) south of Old Fort Tejon, but in the San Joaquin drainage†................... MERRIAM, PALMER.

Cave Wells, Calif., commonly known as the 'The Caves.' F, 12.

A spring and abandoned stage station in the Ivawatch Mountains, about 15 miles (24 kilometers) south of Saratoga Springs in Death Valley. The spring is on the main road from Daggett to Resting Springs .... PALMER, STEPHENS.

Centerville, Fresno County, Calif.

A town on Kings River in the western foothills of the Sierra, about 20 miles (32 kilometers) east of Fresno... NELSON.

Charcoal Kilns, Inyo County, Calif. Altitude about 7,500* feet (2,286 meters).

A number of abandoned charcoal kilns on the west slope of the Panamint Mountains, in the upper part of Wild Rose Cañon, about 7 miles (11 kilometers) above the spring of the same name........................... MERRIAM, FISHER, BAILEY, STEPHENS.

Charleston Mountains, Lincoln County, Nev. E–F, 13–14.

A high range of mountains, marked Spring Mountains on the Land Office and some other maps. The culminating point, Charleston Peak, has an elevation of 10,874 feet (3,314 meters), and is the highest peak in southern Nevada. Collections were made by Nelson and Palmer at a saw mill (altitude about 8,000* feet or 2,438 meters) on the west slope northwest of the main peak, and by Merriam and Bailey at Mountain Spring (altitude 5,501 feet or 1,677 meters), at the southern end of the range on the road from Pahrump Valley to Las Vegas Ranch.

Chiquito Peak, Fresno County, Calif. Altitude 8,136 feet (2,480 meters). C, 6.

A peak on the west slope of the Sierra Nevada, south of Mount Lyell.

Chiquito San Joaquin or **Chiquito Creek**, Fresno County, Calif.

A small stream in the High Sierra, which rises southeast of Mount Raymond and, flowing southward, enters the San Joaquin River a little below the mouth of the South Fork.. NELSON.

Corn Creek, Lincoln County, Nev.

A spring in the Vegas Valley, about 25 miles (40 kilometers) northwest of Las Vegas Ranch... BAILEY, NELSON.

Coso, Inyo County, Calif. Altitude about 5,800 feet (1,768 meters). E, 9.

A deserted mining camp, about 7 miles (11 kilometers) southwest of Darwin. The camp is situated at the head of a rocky cañon, about 3 miles (5 kilometers) southeast of the peak of the same name................................ PALMER, FISHER.

Coso Mountains, Inyo County, Calif. E, 9.

A range southeast of Owens Lake, between the Sierra Nevada and the Argus Range. Its highest point, Coso Peak, has an altitude of 8,425 feet (2,568 meters).

PALMER, FISHER.

---

†On some maps the name Castac Lake is given to a lake in the Mohave Desert, south of the divide in the Cañada de las Uvas.

Cottonwood Cañon, Inyo County, Calif. D. 10.

A cañon in the northern part of the Panamint Mountains, leading from the southern part of Saline Valley to the northwestern arm of Death Valley or Mesquite Valley... NELSON.

Cottonwood Springs, Lincoln County, Nev. Altitude of lower spring 3,449 feet (1,051 meters). E, 14.

(1) Upper Cottonwood Springs. A series of running springs at the east base of the Charleston Mountains, about 7 miles (11 kilometers) northeast of Mount Olcott.
MERRIAM, BAILEY, NELSON.

(2) The lower spring (the Cottonwood Spring of the Wheeler survey) is in a gap in a low range of hills between the Charleston Mountains and Vegas Valley, some distance east of the upper springs..................... MERRIAM, BAILEY, NELSON.

Coyote Holes, Calif.

A name commonly applied to small springs or 'tanks' of water on the desert whether fresh or alkaline.

(1) Kern County. Altitude 3,368 feet (1,027 meters).

A spring and ranch on the Mohave and Keeler stage road, just south of the entrance to Walker Pass; also known as Freeman Post-Office............ PALMER, STEPHENS.

(2) San Bernardino County. G, 11.

An alkaline spring on the Daggett and Resting springs road, 19 miles (30 kilometers) by the road northeast of Daggett............................... PALMER, STEPHENS.

Crane Lake, Los Angeles County, Calif.

A small lake 2 miles (3 kilometers) southeast of Gorman Station, in the extreme west end of Antelope Valley.................................. MERRIAM, PALMER.

Crocker's Ranch, California. Altitude 4,497 feet (1,371 meters).

A station on the Big Oak Flat and Yosemite Valley stage road, 23 miles (37 kilometers) northwest of the Yosemite Valley (by the road). It is near the boundary line between Tuolumne and Mariposa counties, and 2 miles (3 kilometers) west of Hodgdon, the nearest point given on the Wheeler map sheet No. 56 D.

Cuddy Peak, California. (See Frazier Mountain.)

Daggett, San Bernardino County, Calif. Altitude 2,002 feet (610 meters). H, 11.

A town on the Atlantic and Pacific Railroad, 9 miles (14 kilometers) east of Barstow. Daggett is the base of supplies for the town of Calico and the Death Valley region............................... MERRIAM, PALMER, FISHER, STEPHENS.

Darwin, Inyo County, Calif. Altitude 4,840 feet (1,475 meters). E, 9.

A small town 22 miles (35 kilometers) southeast of Keeler. Formerly an important mining camp............................ PALMER, FISHER, BAILEY, NELSON.

Death Valley, Inyo County, Calif. D–F, 10–11.

The valley lying between the Panamint Mountains on the west and the range on the east known by the names of the Funeral, Amargosa, and Grapevine mountains. There are several springs of drinkable water in the valley, of which the most important are Saratoga Springs (altitude 352* feet, or 107 meters) at the southeast end, Bennett Wells (altitude 323* feet, or 98 meters, *below sea level*) on the west side, and the springs near the mouth of Furnace Creek, in the northern part of the Funeral Mountains. Death Valley proper extends from the vicinity of Saratoga Springs to a point about 10 miles (16 kilometers) north of Furnace Creek; but with the northwest arm, or Mesquite Valley, it has an extreme length of about 135 miles (215 kilometers). It is chiefly remarkable for its depth; observations taken by the U. S. Geological

Survey show that the lowest point northeast of Bennett Wells is 480* feet (146 meters) *below sea level*, thus making the valley the deepest depression in North America.
................................MERRIAM, PALMER, FISHER, BAILEY, NELSON, STEPHENS.

Death Valley Cañon, Inyo County, Calif.

A cañon on the east slope of the Panamint Mountains, leading down into Death Valley. The head of the cañon is about 10 miles (16 kilometers) north of Telescope Peak. An Indian trail from Darwin to Furnace Creek, after crossing the Panamint Valley, ascends Wild Rose Cañon and crosses the summit of the Panamint Mountains to the head of Death Valley Cañon.............................BAILEY, FISHER.

Deep Spring Valley, Inyo County, Calif. C, 8-9.

A basin about 10 miles (16 kilometers) long, in the White Mountains near the Nevada boundary, and between Fish Lake and Owens valleys...MERRIAM, BAILEY.

Delano, Kern County, Calif. Altitude 313 feet (95 meters). F, 6.

A station on the Southern Pacific Railroad, 32 miles (51 kilometers) north of Bakersfield..BAILEY, FISHER, NELSON.

Desert Range, Lincoln County, Nev. C-D, 14.

A range north of the Charleston Mountains, inclosing the north arm of Indian Spring Valley. The Desert Range is the southern continuation of the Timpahute Mountains.

Desert Valley, Lincoln County, Nev. B, 15.

A narrow valley containing a large dry lake, between the Pahroc Range on the west and the Highland Range on the east, which latter separates it from the town of Panaca. A second Desert Valley is given on the Land Office map of Nevada just east of the Desert Range and some distance southwest of the one just described. The latter is the Timpahute Valley of the present report.........MERRIAM, BAILEY.

Diamond Valley, Utah.

A small valley in the southwestern part of the Territory, south of Pine Valley Mountain and north of St. George..................................MERRIAM, BAILEY.

Diaz Meadows, Inyo County, Calif. (See Big Cottonwood Meadows.)

Dolan Spring, Mohave County, Ariz. F, 16.

A spring on the east side of Detrital Valley, about 50 miles (80 kilometers) northeast of The Needles, Calif. Collections were made here in 1889 by.........BAILEY.

Elizabeth Lake, Los Angeles County, Calif. Altitude 3,317 feet (1,011 meters). H, 8.

A body of brackish water, a mile long and about one-half mile wide (1.6 by .8 kilometers), situated on the north side of the Sierra Liebre, 2 or 3 miles (3 to 5 kilometers) from the north end of the San Francisquito Pass..............PALMER.

Elk Bayou, Tulare County, Calif.

A small stream emptying into the Tulare River. Collections were made near the line of the Southern Pacific Railroad, about 6 miles (10 kilometers) south of the town of Tulare...BAILEY, FISHER.

Emigrant Cañon, Inyo County, Calif. D-E, 10.

A cañon in the Panamint Mountains, about 10 miles (16 kilometers) north of Wild Rose Cañon, and 15 or 20 miles (24 to 32 kilometers) north of Telescope Peak. Emigrant Cañon heads in Perognathus Flat and opens into the northwest arm of Death Valley...MERRIAM, BAILEY, STEPHENS.

Emigrant Spring, Inyo County, Calif. Altitude about 4,400* feet (1,340 meters). E, 10.

A spring, in a cañon of the same name, in the Panamint Mountains. There are two springs, about one-half mile apart, both on the west side of the cañon.
....MERRIAM, BAILEY, STEPHENS.

Emigrant Valley, Nev. C, 13.

A small valley containing a dry lake. It is on the boundary line between Nye and Lincoln counties and west of the Desert and Timpahute mountains.

MERRIAM, BAILEY.

Escalante Desert, Utah. B, 17-18.

An extensive desert in southwestern Utah, north of Pine Valley Mountain and south of Sevier Lake...MERRIAM, BAILEY.

Farewell Gap, Tulare County, Calif. Altitude about 11,000* feet (3,350 meters).

A pass from the headwaters of the East Fork of the Kaweah River above Mineral King to the head of Little Kern River...........PALMER, BAILEY, FISHER, NELSON.

Fish Lake Valley, Esmeralda County, Nev. B, 8-9.

On the boundary line between California and Nevada, lying mainly in the latter State, between the White Mountains on the west and the Silver Peak Mountains on the east ....MERRIAM, BAILEY.

Fish Slough, Owens Valley, California.

An old stage station at several large springs on the road from Bishop Creek to Benton, near the boundary line between Inyo and Mono counties; about 11 miles (18 kilometers) north of Bishop Creek ....STEPHENS.

Fort Miller, Fresno County, Calif.

An abandoned military post on the San Joaquin River, about 20 miles (32 kilometers) northeast of Fresno.

Fort Tejon, Kern County, Calif. Altitude 3,245 feet (989 meters). H, 7.

An abandoned military post situated in the Cañada de las Uvas, 4 miles (6 kilometers) from the north entrance of the cañon....................MERRIAM, PALMER.

Frazier Mountain, Ventura County, Calif. Altitude 7,750 feet, or 2,362 meters (Rothrock). H, 7.

A high peak 10 miles (16 kilometers) southeast of Mount Piños. Also known as Cuddy Peak, and this name appears on map sheets Nos. 73 and 73C of the Wheeler Survey..PALMER.

Fresno, the county seat of Fresno County, Calif. Altitude 294 feet (90 meters). D, 5 ....BAILEY.

Funeral Mountains, Inyo County, Calif. E-F, 11-12.

A barren range, forming the eastern boundary of Death Valley and separating it from the Amargosa Desert. The Grapevine, Amargosa, and Funeral mountains form a continuous range from Mount Magruder south to Saratoga Springs, the name Funeral Mountains being given to the southern end of the range south of Furnace Creek. The highest peaks in the Funeral Mountains are Le Conte, 6,580 feet (2,005 meters); Mount Smith, 6,300 feet (1,920 meters); and Mount Perry, 5,500* feet (1,676 meters). Pyramid Peak (altitude 6,754 feet or 2,058 meters) is more properly in the Amargosa Range...PALMER, FISHER, BAILEY.

Furnace Creek, Death Valley, California. E, 11.

A small stream entering the east side of Death Valley from a cañon of the same name in the northern part of the Funeral Mountains. A mile or two from the mouth of the cañon is the 'Greenland ranch' of the Pacific Coast Borax Company, which is supplied by water from Furnace Creek. The altitude of the ranch is said to be about 200* feet (61 meters) *below sea level*. Collections were made here by

MERRIAM, FISHER, PALMER, BAILEY, NELSON, STEPHENS.

Garlick Spring, San Bernardino County, Calif. G, 11.

A spring of good water in the Mohave Desert, on the Daggett and Resting Springs road, 25 or 30 miles (40 or 48 kilometers) northeast of Daggett...PALMER, STEPHENS.

Gaviota Pass, Santa Barbara County, Calif. H-I, 4.

A pass in the Santa Ynez Mountains about 30 miles (48 kilometers) northwest of Santa Barbara, running north from the coast to the Santa Ynez Valley......NELSON.

Giant Forest, Tulare County, Calif.

The most extensive grove of *Sequoia gigantea*. It is in the Sequoia National Park, on the divide between the Marble and East Forks of the Kaweah River and 5 to 10 miles (8 to 16 kilometers) south of Mount Silliman................PALMER, FISHER.

Gold Mountain, Esmeralda County, Nev. Altitude 7,400* feet (2,255 meters). C, 10.

A high east-and-west ridge at the northern end of the Grapevine Mountains, from which it is separated by a broad, open cañon (Grapevine Cañon), about 20 miles (32 kilometers) northwest of Grapevine Peak....................MERRIAM, BAILEY.

Gorman Station, Los Angeles County, Calif. Altitude 3,838 feet (1,170 meters). H, 7.

A post-office on the wagon road from Bakersfield to Los Angeles, just south of the summit of the divide in the Cañada de las Uvas.................MERRIAM, PALMER.

Granite Mountains, San Bernardino County, Calif. G, 10-11.

A low east-and-west range in the Mohave Desert lying south of the Slate and Panamint ranges. At the eastern end it runs into the Ivawatch Mountains, and on the west terminates in Pilot Knob or Granite Mountain, the altitude of which is 5,525 feet (1,683 meters)..................................PALMER, STEPHENS.

Granite Wells, San Bernardino County, Calif. Altitude, about 4,200* feet (1,280 meters).

A spring in the Mohave Desert on the northwest slope of Pilot Knob or Granite Mountain, 40 or 45 miles (64 to 72 kilometers) northwest of Daggett, on the wagon road to Death Valley ....MERRIAM, PALMER, FISHER.

Grapevine Peak, Esmeralda County, Nev. Altitude, 8,657 feet (2,638 meters). D, 10.

The highest peak of the Grapevine Mountains, which lie along the California-Nevada boundary, separating the northwestern arm of Death Valley from Sarcobatus Flat and the Ralston Desert. The peak is about 15 or 20 miles (24 or 32 kilometers) south-southeast of Gold Mountain................................NELSON.

Grapevine Spring, Inyo County, Calif. C, 10.

A spring in the northwestern arm of Death Valley, on the western slope of the Grapevine Mountains, 5 miles (8 kilometers) west of Grapevine Peak, and on the California side of the line...................................STEPHENS.

Greenland Ranch, Calif. (See Furnace Creek.)

Halsted Meadows, Tulare County, Calif. Altitude, about 7,000* feet (2,134 meters).

A small meadow in the Sequoia National Park, 6 or 8 miles (10 or 13 kilometers) southwest of Mount Silliman...........................FISHER, PALMER.

Havilah, Kern County, Calif. Altitude 3,150 feet (959 meters). F, 8.

A town and post-office about 15 miles (24 kilometers) south of Kernville, on the road to Caliente....................MERRIAM, PALMER, BAILEY, FISHER.

Haway Meadows, Inyo County, Calif. Altitude, 3,782 feet (1,152 meters). E, 9.

A ranch and stage station on the Mohave and Keeler stage road, about 9 miles (14 kilometers) south of Olancha and 10 miles (16 kilometers) south of Owens Lake.
MERRIAM, PALMER, BAILEY, STEPHENS, FISHER.

Hesperia, San Bernardino County, Calif. Altitude, 3,184 feet or 969 meters (S. C. Ry.). I, 10.

A town on the Southern California Railway, just north of Cajon Pass and 36 miles (58 kilometers) north of San Bernardino ...MERRIAM, PALMER, FISHER, STEPHENS.

Hockett Trail, California.

An old military trail from Visalia, Tulare County, to Lone Pine, Inyo County. The main trail runs up the South Fork of the Kaweah River, thence across the divide and up the North Fork to Soda Springs, where it follows Whitney Creek to Big Cottonwood Meadows; from this point it descends the steep eastern slope of the Sierra to Lone Pine. A side trail runs from Mineral King through Farewell Gap to the head of Little Kern River and strikes the old trail near Trout Meadows.

PALMER, BAILEY, FISHER, NELSON.

Horse Corral Meadows, Fresno County, Calif. Altitude, about 8,000* feet (2,438 meters).

A small meadow on the trail from Camp Badger to Kings River Cañon, situated north of Mount Silliman..................PALMER, FISHER.

Hot Springs, Inyo County, Calif. E, 10.

Warm springs on the east side of Panamint Valley, near the mouth of Surprise Cañon......................MERRIAM, BAILEY, FISHER, NELSON, STEPHENS.

Hot Springs Valley, Inyo County, Calif. E, 9.

This name is applied to the northern end of Salt Wells Valley, which lies about 10 or 15 miles (16 or 24 kilometers) southwest of Coso Peak......PALMER, STEPHENS.

Hungry Hill Summit, Lincoln County, Nev. C, 13.

A divide in the Desert Mountains between Emigrant Valley and the head of the north arm of Indian Spring Valley..................MERRIAM, BAILEY.

Independence, county seat of Inyo County, Calif. D, 8.

The station on the Carson and Colorado Railroad (26 miles or 42 kilometers north of Keeler, at an altitude of 3,718 feet or 1,133 meters), is about 2 or 3 miles (3 to 5 kilometers) east of the town. Old Camp Independence, an abandoned military post, was located about 2 miles (3 kilometers) north of the town.

MERRIAM, BAILEY, PALMER, FISHER, NELSON, STEPHENS.

Independence Creek, Inyo County, Calif.

A small stream on the east slope of the Sierra Nevada, which rises on the east slope of Kearsarge Pass and flows into Owens River near Independence.

PALMER, FISHER, NELSON, STEPHENS.

Indian Spring Valley, Lincoln County, Nev. D, 13.

A narrow east-and-west valley north of the Charleston Mountains, with a north arm west of the Desert Range ....MERRIAM, BAILEY, NELSON.

Indian Wells, Kern County, Calif. Altitude, 2,608 feet (795 meters). F, 9.

A stage station on the road from Mohave to Keeler, near the southeast entrance to Walker Pass..................MERRIAM, PALMER, FISHER, BAILEY, STEPHENS.

Inyo Mountains, Inyo County, Calif. C-D, 8-9.

The first of the desert ranges east of the Sierra Nevada, forming the eastern wall of Owens Valley. Remarkable for its height and the steepness of its slopes. The name Cerro Górdo Range is sometimes given to the southern part of these mountains; but the Cerro Gordo, Inyo, and White mountains practically form one continuous range. The highest points are Wancoba Peak (altitude, 11,267 feet, or 3,403 meters), Mount Hahn (altitude, 11,030 feet, or 3,362 meters), and New York Butte (altitude, 10,675 feet, or 3,254 meters)..................NELSON.

Jackass Spring, Inyo County, Calif. Altitude, 6,489 feet (1,977 meters).

A spring on the west slope of the Panamint Mountains, at the point where Nelson Range joins the Panamint Mountains, not far from the entrance to Cottonwood Cañon..NELSON.

Johnson Cañon, Inyo County, Calif.

A cañon on the east slope of the Panamint Mountains, opening into Death Valley. Collections were made here by Fisher and Nelson 6 or 8 miles (10 or 13 kilometers) southeast of Telescope Peak, at altitudes varying from 5,000 to 9,000 feet (1,524 to 2,743 meters).................................PALMER, BAILEY, FISHER, NELSON.

Juniper Mountains, Lincoln County, Nev. B, 16.

A north-and-south range between Meadow Valley, Nevada, and the Escalante Desert, Utah...MERRIAM, BAILEY.

Kaweah Peak, Tulare County, Calif. Altitude, about 14,000 feet (4,267 meters). D, 8.

The highest peak in the western ridge of the southern Sierra Nevada west of Mount Whitney.

Kaweah River, Tulare County, Calif. D-E, 6-7.

An important stream whose five main branches (the North, Marble, Middle, East, and South Forks) drain the west slope of the Sierra south of the basin of Kings River, and uniting near Three Rivers flow into Tulare Lake.

PALMER, BAILEY, FISHER, NELSON.

Kaweah Sawmill, Tulare County, Calif.

A sawmill about 15 or 20 miles (24 or 32 kilometers) north of Three Rivers, on the divide between the North and Marble Forks of the Kaweah River. The mill is at the lower edge of the pine forest and just within the western boundary of the Sequoia National Park. An excellent wagon road leads to it from Three Rivers.

PALMER, FISHER.

Kearsarge Pass, California. Altitude, about 12,000* feet (3,658 meters). D, 8.

One of the highest passes in the Sierra Nevada, crossing the range just south of Mount Kearsarge. The trail from Fresno to Independence runs through this pass.

PALMER, FISHER, NELSON.

Keeler, Inyo County, Calif. Altitude 3,622 feet (1,103 meters). E, 9.

A town on the east shore of Owens Lake. The present terminus of the Carson and Colorado Railroad.......MERRIAM, PALMER, BAILEY, FISHER, NELSON, STEPHENS.

Keene, Kern County, Calif. Altitude 2,705 feet (824 meters).

A station on the Southern Pacific Railroad, between Caliente and Tehachapi, about 12 miles (19 kilometers) below the summit of the pass............MERRIAM, PALMER.

Kern River, California. E-G, 6-8.

A large river draining the trough between the two ridges of the southern Sierra Nevada. The South or East Fork rises on the west slope of Olancha Peak and flows south, then turning to the west, unites near the town of Kernville with the North or West Fork, which heads near Mount Whitney. The main river flows into Kern Lake. It was named by Fremont in honor of Edward M. Kern, topographer of the third Fremont expedition.

(1). **Head of North Fork,** Tulare County, Calif.

Specimens so labeled were collected in the basin between Mount Whitney and Kaweah Peak (altitude 9,000 to 12,000 feet, or 2,743 to 3,658 meters) north of Soda Springs and the cañon of the North Fork.............PALMER, BAILEY, DUTCHER.

(2) South Fork, California.

This locality refers to a camp near the northwest base of Walker Pass and 25 miles (40 kilometers) above Kernville, on the road to Coyote Holes.
MERRIAM, PALMER, BAILEY, FISHER.

Kern River Lakes, California. (See Soda Springs.)

Kernville, Kern County, Calif. Altitude 2,551 feet (777 meters). F, 8.

A small town near the junction of the North and South forks of Kern River.
MERRIAM, PALMER, BAILEY, FISHER.

Kings River, Fresno County, Calif. C-E, 5-7.

This river drains the west slope of the Sierra between the basins of the San Joaquin and the Kaweah Rivers. Its branches rise near the crest of the range between Mounts Brewer and Goddard and flow southwest into the San Joaquin River.

Kings River Cañon, Fresno County, Calif. Altitude 4,500 to 5,000 feet (1,371 to 1,524 meters).

The main cañon on the South Fork of Kings River, about 10 miles (16 kilometers) in length..PALMER, FISHER, NELSON.

Kingston Peak, San Bernardino County, Calif. F, 13.

A peak in the northeastern part of the county near the boundary between California and Nevada, and about 45 miles (72 kilometers) southwest of Charleston Peak, Nevada.

Lake Charlotte, Fresno County, Calif. D, 8.

A small lake near timber-line in the High Sierra on the trail from Kings River Cañon to Independence, about 3 miles (5 kilometers) west of the summit of Kearsarge Pass..PALMER, FISHER, NELSON.

Lancaster, Los Angeles County, Calif. Altitude 2,350 feet (716 meters). H, 8.

A station on the Southern Pacific Railroad in the Mohave Desert, 25 miles (40 kilometers) south of Mohave..STEPHENS.

Langley Meadow, Tulare County, Calif. Altitude 11,625 feet† (3,542 meters).

A small meadow containing a lake immediately west of and under the peak of Mount Whitney. Langley Creek, which rises in this meadow, is one of the three main streams which flow into the North Fork of Kern River from the east, above Whitney Creek. Named in honor of Prof. S. P. Langley, Secretary of the Smithsonian Institution, who established his Mountain Camp in this meadow while making observations on solar heat on Mount Whitney in the summer of 1881........PALMER, DUTCHER.

La Panza, San Obispo County, Calif. G, 4.

A post-office near the San Juan River, about 25 miles (40 kilometers) northeast of San Luis Obispo..NELSON.

Las Vegas Ranch, Lincoln County, Nev. (See Vegas Valley.)

Leach Point Valley, San Bernardino County, Calif. F, 11.

A valley in the Mohave Desert north of the Granite Mountains.

Leach Point Spring on the north slope of the Granite Mountains and south side of the valley, is about 25 miles (40 kilometers) northeast of Pilot Knob, on the so-called Leach Point road from Pilot Knob to Saratoga Springs in Death Valley. Altitude about 3,500* feet (1,066 meters)..MERRIAM, BAILEY.

Lerdo, Kern County, Calif. Altitude about 414 feet (126 meters). G, 6.

A station on the Southern Pacific Railroad 12 miles (19 kilometers) northwest of Bakersfield..NELSON.

---

† Langley: Researches on Solar Heat, 1884, p. 194.

Lewis Lake, Inyo County, Calif. Altitude about 9,000* feet (2,743 meters).

A small lake on the west fork and near the head of Bishop Creek......STEPHENS.

Liebre Ranch, Los Angeles County, Calif.

A ranch at the north base of the Sierra Liebre, about 20 miles (32 kilometers) northwest of Elizabeth Lake......................................MERRIAM, PALMER.

Little Lake or **Little Owens Lake**, Inyo County, Calif. Altitude about 3,100* feet (944 meters). F, 9.

A small lake about 25 miles (40 kilometers) south of Owens Lake, on the road from Mohave to Keeler................MERRIAM, PALMER, FISHER, BAILEY, STEPHENS.

Lone Pine, Inyo County, Calif. Altitude [of station] 3,638 feet (1,115 meters). D, 8.

A town on the west side of Owens Valley, 4 miles (6 kilometers) north of Owens Lake. The railroad station is on the east side of the valley.

MERRIAM, PALMER, BAILEY, FISHER, NELSON, STEPHENS.

Lone Willow Spring, San Bernardino County, Calif. F, 10.

A spring on the east slope of the Slate Range, opposite Browns Peak. The spring is in the hills some distance above the wagon road and is almost the only good water on the road between Pilot Knob and Mesquite Wells in Death Valley.

MERRIAM, BAILEY, FISHER, NELSON, PALMER.

Lookout or **Lookout Hill**, Inyo County, Calif. Alt. about 4,000* feet (1,219 meters).

A mining camp on the east slope of the Argus Mountains near the north end of the range, about 10 miles (16 kilometers) east of Darwin...........FISHER, BAILEY.

Los Olivos, Santa Barbara County, Calif. H, 4.

A town on the road from San Luis Obispo to Santa Barbara, north of the Santa Yñez Mission...MERRIAM, NELSON.

Mammoth Pass, California. Altitude about 9,500* feet (2,900 meters).

A pass in the Sierra Nevada from the head of Owens River to the head of the San Joaquin...NELSON, STEPHENS.

Maturango Peak, Inyo County, Calif. Altitude 8,844 feet (2,695 meters). E, 10.

The highest peak of the Argus Mountains, about 13 miles (21 kilometers) southeast of the town of Darwin..PALMER.

Maturango Spring, Inyo County, Calif. Altitude about 6,000 feet (1,829 meters).

A small spring on the western slope of the Argus Mountains, 2 or 3 miles (3 or 5 kilometers) south of Maturango Peak, and about 15 miles (24 kilometers) southeast of the town of Darwin. Collections were made at the spring and also near the summit of the Argus Range, about 1,300 feet (396 meters) above.

BAILEY, FISHER, NELSON, PALMER.

McGill Peak, California. (See Mount Piños).

Meadow Creek Valley, Lincoln County, Nev. B, 15-16.

A valley east of the Highland Range, in which is situated the town of Panaca, about 10 miles (16 kilometers) south of Pioche. The name is given on some maps as Meadow Valley..MERRIAM, BAILEY.

Menache Meadows, California.

In the High Sierra north or northwest of Olancha Peak..............STEPHENS.

Merced River, California. B-C, 3-6.

Rises near Mount Lyell and Mount Dana and drains the west slope of the Sierra, between the basins of the Tuolumne and the San Joaquin rivers...........NELSON.

Mesquite Well, Death Valley, California. Altitude —351* feet (107 meters) E, 11.

A well on the west side of the valley, about 6 miles (10 kilometers) south of Bennet Wells ....MERRIAM, BAILEY, FISHER, PALMER.

Mesquite Valley, Inyo County, Calif. D, 10–11.

The name given to the northwest arm of Death Valley, 60 or 70 miles (95 or 110 kilometers) in length, which heads under Mount Magruder. The valley lies between the Grapevine Mountains on the east and the northern part of the Panamint Range on the west...................................MERRIAM, BAILEY, STEPHENS, NELSON.

Mill Creek, Inyo County, Calif.

A small stream at the extreme northwest end of Panamint Valley..........NELSON.

Mineral King, Tulare County, Calif. Altitude about 9,000° feet (2,740 meters). E, 7.

A summer resort and mining camp near the head of the East Fork of the Kaweah River, north of Farewell Gap ....PALMER, BAILEY, FISHER, NELSON.

Mohave,† Kern County, Calif. Altitude, 2,751 feet (838 meters). G, 8.

A railroad station in the west end of the Mohave Desert, at the junction of the Atlantic and Pacific with the Southern Pacific Railroad.

MERRIAM, PALMER, STEPHENS.

Mohave † River, San Bernardino County, Calif. G–I, 10–12.

The largest stream in the Mohave Desert, usually dry throughout the greater part of its course; it rises on the north slope of the San Bernardino Mountains, east of Cajon Pass, and flows north and then east into a sink known as 'Soda Lake' or the 'Sink of the Mohave.' The river was named by Fremont in 1844, who spelled the word *Mohahve*.

Monterey, Calif. D, 1.

A town on the bay of Monterey. Collections were made between Cypress Point and Pacific Grove..MERRIAM, BAILEY.

Mormon Mountains, Lincoln County, Nev. C–D, 16.

A range in the eastern part of the State near the Utah line.

Moran's, Mono County, Calif.

A ranch near the head of Owens Valley, about 6 miles (10 kilometers) east of Benton ....STEPHENS.

Morro, San Luis Obispo County, Calif. G, 3.

A town on the coast about 10 miles (16 kilometers) northwest of San Luis Obispo.

NELSON.

Mountain Meadows, Washington County, Utah. B–C, 17.

A valley in the southwestern part of the Territory northwest of Pine Valley Mountain. The scene of the Mountain Meadow massacre........MERRIAM, BAILEY.

Mountain Springs, Lincoln County, Nev. Altitude, 5,501 feet (1,677 meters). E, 14.

Springs near the summit of the pass over the Charleston Mountains on the road from Pahrump to Vegas Valley, about 6 or 8 miles (10 or 13 kilometers) north-northwest of Olcott Peak..........................MERRIAM, BAILEY, NELSON.

Mount Corcoran, California. Altitude, 14,093 feet (4,295 meters). E, 8.

The 'Old Mount Whitney;' renamed by Albert Bierstadt, the artist, in honor of W. W. Corcoran, of Washington, D. C., the first name having been transferred to a higher peak. (See Geog. Rept. Wheeler Survey, I, 1889, p. 99.)

Mount LeConte, Inyo County, Calif. Altitude, 6,580 feet (2,005 meters). E, 11.

This is the most prominent peak in the Funeral Mountains, as seen from Bennett Wells in Death Valley. It is the highest point in the range and is nearly due east of Telescope Peak. It was named in honor of Prof. Joseph LeConte, of the University of California, by James J. McGillivray,‡ of New York, who visited Death Valley in 1883–4.

---

† The spelling is that adopted by the U. S. Board on Geographic Names.

‡ See article entitled: 'In the Valley of Death.' in New York Times, May (?), 1891.

Mount Lyell, California. Altitude, 13,012 feet (3,975 meters). B, 6.

A high peak in the Sierra Nevada east of the Yosemite Valley and near the headwaters of the Merced River.

Mount Magruder, Esmeralda County, Nev. Altitude about 9,500* feet (2,900 meters). C, 9.

An important mountain standing at the extreme head of the northwestern arm of Death Valley and at the southern end of the Red or Silver Peak Mountains. The Mount Magruder plateau connects the Grapevine, Panamint and Silver Peak ranges.
MERRIAM, BAILEY.

Mount Perry, Inyo County, Calif. E, 11.

The highest peak in the northern part of the Funeral Mountains. It is named after Mr. J. W. S. Perry, Superintendent of the Pacific Coast Borax Company, at Daggett, to whom the expedition is indebted for many favors and for much valuable information. Mount Perry has an altitude of about 5,500* feet (1,676 meters), its summit being about 5,700 feet (by aneroid) above Greenland ranch in Death Valley.† ....PALMER.

Mount Piños, Ventura County, Calif. Altitude, 9,214 feet (2,808 meters). H, 6.

The culminating peak of the southern Coast Ranges standing near the northern boundary of the county and at the headwaters of the Cuyama River. Mount Piños, also known as McGill Peak, may be considered the center from which diverge the various ridges of the Coast Range in this region ....NELSON.

Mount Silliman, Tulare County, Calif. Altitude, 11,623 feet (3,543 meters). D, 7.

A high peak in the southern Sierra Nevada situated in the northeast corner of the Sequoia National Park ....PALMER.

Mount Smith, Inyo County, Calif. Altitude, 6,300 feet (1,920 meters). F, 11.

The highest peak at the southern end of the Funeral Mountains and opposite the entrance of Death Valley at Windy Gap. It is named after Mr. F. M. Smith, of San Francisco, President of the Pacific Coast Borax Company, who aided the expedition in Death Valley in every possible way.

Mount Whitney, California. Altitude, 14,522 feet (4,426 meters). D, 8.

The highest point in the United States, first called Fisherman Peak, but afterward renamed by Clarence King in honor of Prof. J. D. Whitney, Director of the Geological Survey of California. The peak was first ascended August 18, 1873, ‡ and the records of the fourth party who ascended it (July 7, 1875), were still in the monument on the summit when Mr. Dutcher and the writer climbed the peak September 10, 1891. The altitude adopted is that determined by Prof. S. P. Langley, and is based on a series of barometric observations made simultaneously on the peak and at Lone Pine. The elevation given by Whitney is 14,898 feet (4,541 meters) and that adopted by the Wheeler Survey 14,470 feet (4,410 meters).......PALMER, DUTCHER.

Mud Spring.

(1) Lincoln County, Nev. [C, 13.] Altitude about 5,600* feet (1,705 meters). A spring in the north end of the Desert Mountains, about 30 miles (48 kilometers) west of Pahranagat Lake...MERRIAM, BAILEY.

(2) Mohave County, Ariz. [G, 16.] A spring at the north end of the Sacramento Valley, about 35 miles (56 kilometers) northeast of The Needles, Calif. Collections were made in 1889 by ....BAILEY.

---

† There is a peak immediately north of Mount Perry, which is almost as prominent from Death Valley but which is 300 feet (90 meters) lower.

‡ See Geog. Rept. Wheeler Survey, I, 1889, p. 100.

Muddy Valley, Lincoln County, Nev. D-E, 15-16.

A valley northeast of the Muddy Mountains. The stream of the same name flowing through the valley empties into the Virgin River.................MERRIAM, BAILEY.

Mulkey Meadows, Inyo County, Calif.

A small meadow on the east slope of the Sierra, about 7 miles (11 kilometers) southeast of Big Cottonwood Meadows and about 12 or 15 miles (19-24 kilometers) south of Mount Whitney.................DUTCHER, KOCH.

Nelson Range, Inyo County, Calif. D, 9.

A low east-and-west range connecting the Cerro Gordo with the Panamint Mountains and separating Saline Valley from the head of Panamint Valley. Named after Mr. E. W. Nelson, who explored the range and the adjoining valleys.......NELSON.

Nordhoff, Ventura County, Calif. Altitude, 819 feet (249 meters). I, 6.

A town in the Ojai Valley, northeast of Ventura....................NELSON.

Oasis Valley, Nye County, Nev. C-D, 11.

A narrow valley in the southern part of the Ralston Desert southeast of Sarcobatus Flat. It contains the head of Amargosa Creek.......MERRIAM, BAILEY, STEPHENS.

Olancha, Inyo County, Calif. Altitude, 3,708 feet (1,130 meters). E, 9.

A ranch and post-office 1 mile (0.6 kilometers) south of Owens Lake.

MERRIAM, PALMER, BAILEY, FISHER, STEPHENS.

Olancha Peak, California. Altitude, 12,250 feet (3,734 meters). E, 8.

One of the highest peaks in the southern Sierra Nevada, about 25 miles (40 kilometers) southeast of Mount Whitney.................STEPHENS.

Onion Valley, Inyo County, Calif. Altitude, about 9,000 or 10,000 feet* (2,740 or 3,050 meters).

A meadow or small valley on the east slope of the Sierra at the junction of the three forks of Independence Creek.................STEPHENS.

Overton, Lincoln County, Nev. Altitude, 1,360 feet (414 meters). E, 16.

An abandoned Mormon town in the valley of the Muddy, northwest of St. Thomas and 4 miles (6 kilometers) southeast of St. Joe.................MERRIAM, BAILEY.

Owens Lake, California. Altitude. 3,567 feet (1,087 meters). D-E, 9.

A shallow alkaline lake 15 miles (24 kilometers) long, 9 miles (14 kilometers) wide, and about 50 feet (15 meters) deep. It is situated at the east base of the Sierra Nevada, southeast of Mount Whitney. Named by Fremont, in honor of Richard Owens, one of the members of Fremont's third expedition.

MERRIAM, PALMER, FISHER, NELSON, BAILEY, STEPHENS.

Owens River, California. B-D, 7-8.

The largest river on the east side of the southern Sierra Nevada. It rises near Mount Lyell and flows south through a valley of the same name into Owens Lake.

Owl Holes, San Bernardino County, Calif. Altitude 1,790" feet (545 meters). F, 11.

Holes containing hot water on the Leach Point road from Pilot Knob to Death Valley, situated on the south side of Owls Head Peak and about 13 miles (21 kilometers) west-southwest of Saratoga Springs.................MERRIAM, BAILEY.

Pahranagat Lake, Lincoln County, Nev. Altitude, 3,400 feet (1,036 meters). C, 14.

A small lake in the south end of the valley of the same name, lying east of the Pahranagat Mountains and about 60 miles (96 kilometers) southwest of the mining camp of Pioche.................MERRIAM, BAILEY.

Pahranagat Range, Lincoln County, Nev. C, 14.

A desert range separating Timpahute Valley on the west from Pahranagat Valley on the east .... MERRIAM, BAILEY.

Pahroc Spring, Lincoln County, Nev. Altitude 5,700* feet (1,737 meters), (approximate). B, 15.

A spring near the southern end of the Pahroc Range on the east side of the plain of the same name and about 30 miles (48 kilometers) southwest of Pioche.

MERRIAM, BAILEY.

Pahrump Valley. E-F, 12-13.

A valley lying on the boundary line between California and Nevada immediately west of the Charleston Mountains and north of Kingston Peak. Collections were made by Fisher, Nelson, and Palmer in the northwest arm near the boundary line; by Nelson and Palmer at Winters' Ranch in the north central part of the valley, and by Merriam and Bailey at Yount's Ranch, 6 or 7 miles (10 or 11 kilometers) southeast of Winters' Ranch.

Palm Springs, San Diego County, Calif.

The springs formerly known as Agua Caliente in Palm Valley on the Colorado Desert about 15 miles (24 kilometers) southeast of the San Gorgonio Pass and 6 or 7 miles (10 or 11 kilometers) south of the station of Seven Palms on the Southern Pacific Railroad .... STEPHENS.

Pampa, Kern County, Calif. Altitude, 871 feet (265 meters).

A station on the Southern Pacific railroad 15 miles (24 kilometers) southeast of Bakersfield .... BAILEY, FISHER.

Panaca, Lincoln County, Nev. Altitude, 4,770 (?) feet (1,550 meters). B, 16.

A Mormon town in Meadow Creek Valley, about 10 miles (16 kilometers) south of Pioche .... MERRIAM, BAILEY.

Panamint, Inyo County, Calif. Altitude, 6,605 feet (2,013 meters). E, 10.

A deserted mining camp on the west slope of the Panamint Mountains, about 4 or 5 miles (6 or 8 kilometers) south of Telescope Peak .... BAILEY, FISHER, NELSON.

Panamint Mountains, Inyo County, Calif. C-F, 9-10.

A high range lying immediately west of Death Valley, which it separates from Panamint Valley. The highest point, Telescope Peak, has an altitude of 10,938 feet (3,333 meters) .... MERRIAM, BAILEY, FISHER, NELSON, STEPHENS.

Panamint Valley, Inyo County, Calif. E-F, 10.

A large valley lying between the Panamint Range on the east and the Argus Mountains on the west. The bottom of the valley on the east side of the alkali flat has an altitude of about 1,300 feet (395 meters).

MERRIAM, BAILEY, FISHER, NELSON, STEPHENS.

Paradise Valley, San Bernardino County, Calif. G, 10.

A valley in the Mohave Desert southeast of Pilot Knob. The dry lake in the bottom of the valley has an altitude of about 3,000* feet (915 meters).

MERRIAM, PALMER, FISHER.

Perognathus Flat, Inyo County, Calif. Altitude, about 5,200* feet (1,585 meters).

A basin on the west slope of the Panamint Mountains at the head of Emigrant Cañon. Named on account of the unusual abundance of pocket mice of the genus *Perognathus*... MERRIAM, BAILEY, STEPHENS.

Peru Creek, California. H-I, 6-7.

A stream flowing south from Alamo Peak (near the line between Ventura and Los Angeles counties) into the Santa Clara River .... MERRIAM, PALMER.

Pigeon Spring, Esmeralda County, Nev. Altitude, about 6,700 feet (2,040 meters). C, 9.

A spring on the northwest slope of Mount Magruder near the California boundary.
MERRIAM, BAILEY.

Pilot Knob or Granite Mountain, San Bernardino County, Calif. Altitude, 5,525 feet (1,683 meters). G, 10.

A high butte or peak forming one of the most conspicuous landmarks in the Mohave Desert. It is at the west end of the Granite Mountains and about 75 miles (120 kilometers) southeast of the lower end of Owens Lake and about 35 miles (56 kilometers) northwest of Daggett and Barstow. On a clear day it can be distinctly seen from the summit of Mount Whitney and Telescope Peak. (See also Granite Mountains.)

Pine City.

(1) Mariposa County, Calif. A settlement, formerly a post-office, on the west slope of the Sierra, about 4 miles (6 kilometers) south of Wawona, near the southern boundary of the county.

(2) Mono County, Calif. A deserted mining camp near the head of Owens River and a few hundred feet below the summit of Mammoth Pass....NELSON, STEPHENS.

Pioche, county seat of Lincoln County, Nev. Altitude, 6,220 feet (1,895 meters). B, 16.

Formerly an important mining camp; in the northern part of the county.

Poso, Kern County, Calif. F, 6.

A station on the Southern Pacific Railroad in the San Joaquin Valley, 20 miles (32 kilometers) northwest of Bakersfield....................BAILEY, FISHER, NELSON.

Pozo, San Luis Obispo County, Calif. G, 4.

A post-office about 15 miles (24 kilometers) east of San Luis Obispo. To be distinguished from Poso, Kern County...NELSON.

Quartz Spring, Lincoln County, Nev. Altitude, about 5,200* feet (1,585 meters). D, 13.

A spring at the west base of the Desert Mountains in the north arm of Indian Spring Valley...MERRIAM, BAILEY.

Queen, Esmeralda County, Nev. Altitude, 6,254 feet (1,906 meters).

A station on the Carson and Colorado Railroad 10 miles (16 kilometers) northeast of Benton, Calif. The Indian Queen mine is situated in the northern end of the White Mountains, about 9 miles (14 kilometers) from the station, and at an altitude of about 9,500* feet (2,895 meters); the mill connected with it is 5 miles (8 kilometers) from the station, at an elevation of about 7,400* feet (2,250 meters)......STEPHENS.

Raymond Well, Kern County, Calif.

A spring in the south end of Salt Wells Valley in the Mohave Desert, about 16 miles (26 kilometers) southeast of Coyote Holes or Freeman Post-office...STEPHENS.

Rêche Cañon, San Bernardino County, Calif.

A narrow valley on the north side of the Box Spring Mountains, about 4 miles (6 kilometers) south of San Bernardino ....STEPHENS.

Resting Springs, Inyo County, Calif. Altitude about 1,750* feet (5,320 meters). F, 12.

The springs near the Amargosa River, about 6 miles (10 kilometers) east of the Amargosa borax works....MERRIAM, PALMER, BAILEY, FISHER, NELSON, STEPHENS.

Rose Store or Station, Kern County, Calif. Altitude, 1,334 feet (406 meters).

An old stage station on the road from Bakersfield to Los Angeles, about 6 miles (10 kilometers) north of Old Fort Tejon, near the mouth of the Cañada de las Uvas.
PALMER, NELSON.

Round Valley, Inyo County, Calif.

A small meadow in the High Sierra, 2 miles (3 kilometers) south of Big Cottonwood Meadows and about 12 miles (19 kilometers) south of Mount Whitney.
PALMER, FISHER.

Saint George, Washington County, Utah. Altitude, 2,880 feet (877 meters). C, 17.

A flourishing Mormon town near the junction of the Santa Clara and Virgin rivers in the extreme southwestern corner of Utah .... MERRIAM, BAILEY.

St. Joe, Lincoln County, Nev. Altitude, 1,650* feet or 503 meters (1,490 feet or 454 meters, Powell). D, 16.

A small Mormon settlement in the valley of the Muddy about 15 miles (24 kilometers) northwest of St. Thomas .... MERRIAM, BAILEY.

St. Thomas, Lincoln County, Nev. Altitude, 1,450* feet or 442 meters (1,180 feet or 360 meters, Powell). E, 16.

A small Mormon settlement near the Virgin River, about 30 miles (48 kilometers) northeast of the great bend of the Colorado River .... MERRIAM, BAILEY.

Saline Valley, Inyo County, Calif. D, 9.

A valley lying northeast of Owens Lake, between the Inyo Mountains and the northern extension of the Panamint Mountains........................... NELSON.

Salt Wells, Death Valley, California.

(1) A spring of strongly alkaline water unfit for use, at the south end of Death Valley near the entrance from Windy Gap and about 15 miles (24 kilometers) south of Bennett Wells. Observations made by the U. S. Geological Survey show the altitude of this spring to be 307 feet (93 meters) below sea level.
MERRIAM, PALMER, FISHER, BAILEY, NELSON.

(2) A spring in Mesquite Valley (the northwestern arm of Death Valley) opposite the mouth of Cottonwood Cañon. Altitude, about 150? feet or 45 meters (Wheeler). D, 10.. STEPHENS, NELSON.

Salt Wells Valley, California. F, 9.

The name applied to that portion of the Mohave Desert lying south of the Coso Mountains and west of the southern end of the Argus Mountains.
MERRIAM, PALMER, BAILEY, FISHER, STEPHENS.

San Bernardino Range, California (see also Sierra Madre).

A high range of mountains between the Mohave Desert and the San Bernardino Valley. The highest point, San Bernardino Peak, reaches an altitude of 11,000 feet (3,535 meters). The name is frequently restricted to that part of the range east of the Cajon Pass.. STEPHENS.

San Emigdio, Kern County, Calif. H, 6.

A sheep ranch in the cañon of the same name, about 10 or 15 miles (16 or 24 kilometers) north of Mount Piños... NELSON.

San Francisquito Pass, Los Angeles County, Calif. Altitude, 3,718 feet (1,133 meters). H–I, 7-8.

A pass in the Sierra Liebre leading north from the Santa Clara Valley to Elizabeth Lake and the Mohave Desert .... PALMER.

San Gorgonio Pass, California. Altitude, about 2,800 feet (850 meters).

A pass leading from the San Bernardino Valley to the Colorado Desert, through which runs the Southern Pacific Railroad. It is on the boundary line between San Diego and San Bernardino counties...................................... STEPHENS.

San Joaquin River, California. B—C, 6.

This river rises near the summit of the Sierra Nevada, flows southwest to the San Joaquin Valley, and turning northward empties into San Francisco Bay. The stream referred to in the report is the head of the main river............. NELSON.

San Luis Obispo, county seat of San Luis Obispo County, Calif. G, 3.
....MERRIAM, NELSON.

San Simeon, San Luis Obispo County, Calif. F, 2.

A port on bay of same name about 40 miles (65 kilometers) northwest of San Luis Obispo...NELSON.

Santa Clara Valley.

(1) Washington County, Utah. [C, 17.] The valley of the Santa Clara River (a branch of the Virgin River) in the lower part of which the town of St. George is situated ....MERRIAM, BAILEY.

(2) Ventura County, California. [H-I, 6-8.] The valley of the Santa Clara River, a stream rising in the Soledad Pass and flowing westward into the Santa Barbara Channel.

(3) Santa Clara County, California. A large valley at the southern end of San Francisco Bay in which are the towns of San Jose and Santa Clara.

Santa Margarita, San Luis Obispo County, Calif. Altitude, 996 feet (304 meters). G, 3.

A post-office and station on the coast division of the Southern Pacific Railroad about 10 miles (16 kilometers) northeast of San Luis Obispo...............NELSON.

Santa Maria, Santa Barbara County, Calif. H, 4.

A town on the road from San Luis Obispo to Santa Barbara, about 25 or 30 miles (40-50 kilometers) southeast of San Luis Obispo ....NELSON.

Santa Paula, Ventura County, Calif. Altitude 286 feet (87 meters).

A station on the Southern Pacific Railroad, 44 miles (70 kilometers) east of Santa Barbara...NELSON.

Santa Yñez Mission, Santa Barbara County, Calif. H, 4.

An old Spanish mission on the road from Santa Barbara to San Luis Obispo, 25 or 30 miles (40 or 48 kilometers) northwest of Santa Barbara.................NELSON.

Saratoga Springs, Inyo County, Calif. Altitude 352* feet (107 meters). F, 12.

Warm springs in the extreme southeast end of Death Valley, near the bend of the Amargosa River, on the road from Daggett to Resting Springs.
....MERRIAM, BAILEY, PALMER, NELSON, STEPHENS.

Sarcobatus Flat, Nevada. Altitude about 4,400* feet (1,340 meters). C, 10-11.

A flat or valley between the Grapevine Mountains and the Ralston Desert, on the boundary between Nye and Esmeralda counties. Named from the greasewood (*Sarcobatus vermiculatus*) which covers the clay dunes in the lower part of the flat.
....MERRIAM, BAILEY, STEPHENS.

Searles' Borax Works, California. (See Borax Flat).

Sheep Spring, Lincoln County, Nev. Altitude about 6,700* feet (2,041 meters). B, 16.

A spring on the east slope of the Juniper Mountains, about 20 miles (32 kilometers) southeast of Pioche...MERRIAM, BAILEY.

Shepherd Cañon, Inyo County, Calif. E, 10.

A pass in the Argus Mountains on the road between Coso and Panamint valleys, about 6 or 8 miles (10 or 13 kilometers) south of Maturango Peak.
....BAILEY, FISHER, NELSON.

Shoal Creek, Utah. B, 17.

A small stream on the east slope of the southern part of the Juniper Mountains, sinking before reaching the Escalante Desert; about 30 or 35 miles (48 or 55 kilometers) northwest of St. George..MERRIAM, BAILEY.

Sierra Liebre, Los Angeles County, Calif. H, 7-8.

The name applied to the western part of the Sierra Madre, between Frazier Mountain and the San Francisquito Pass, and lying immediately south of Antelope Valley. The portion of the range between the San Francisquito and Soledad passes is known as the Sierra Pelona .... MERRIAM, PALMER.

Sierra Madre, California. I, 8-10.

A high range of mountains, also known as the San Bernardino Range, forming the southern boundary of the Mohave Desert, and separating it from the San Gabriel and San Bernardino valleys. The name Sierra Madre is commonly restricted to that part of the range west of Cajon Pass. The highest peak is Mount San Antonio, also known as Baldy (altitude 9,931 feet, or 3,026 meters).

Slate Range, California. F, 10.

A spur of the Argus Range, separating Panamint Valley from Searles' Borax Flat. The highest peak west of Lone Willow Spring has an altitude of 5,598 feet (1,706 meters).

Soda Springs, Tulare County, Calif. Altitude about 7,000 * feet (2,134 meters).

A camping resort on the North Fork of Kern River on the 'Hockett Trail,' at the mouth of Whitney Creek. Locally known as 'Kern River Lakes.'

PALMER, BAILEY, FISHER, NELSON.

Stewart Wells, Inyo County, California.

A spring in the extreme northwestern part of Pahrump Valley (near the California and Nevada line), on the road from Resting Springs to Ash Meadows.

PALMER, FISHER, NELSON, STEPHENS.

Stoddard Wells, San Bernardino County, Calif.

A spring in the Mohave Desert, on the direct road from Victor to Daggett, about 20 miles (32 kilometers) southwest of the latter point............. PALMER, FISHER.

Surprise Cañon, Inyo County, Calif.

A cañon on the west slope of the Panamint Mountains, a little south of Telescope Peak. The abandoned mining camp of Panamint is situated in the cañon, about 6 miles (10 kilometers) above its mouth, at an altitude of 6,605 feet (2,013 meters).

BAILEY, FISHER, NELSON.

Table Mountain, Nye County, Nev. C, 12.

A high mountain or mesa in the southern part of the Ralston Desert some distance north of Ash Meadows.. STEPHENS.

Tehachapi, Kern County, Calif. Altitude 4,025 feet (1,226 meters). G, 8.

A town and station on the Southern Pacific Railroad, situated in a valley of the same name, at the summit of Tehachapi Pass................... MERRIAM, PALMER.

Tehachapi Mountains, California. (See Tejon Mountains).

Tehachapi Pass, Kern County, Calif. Altitude 3,832 feet (1,168 meters). G, 8.

A pass in the Tehachapi Mountains, through which the Southern Pacific Railroad runs, just east of the peak of the same name and about 45 miles (72 kilometers) southwest of Walker Pass.. MERRIAM, PALMER.

Tejon Mountains, Kern County, Calif. G-H, 7-8.

A range known also as the Tehachapi Mountains, running southwest and northeast, separating the San Joaquin Valley from the Mohave Desert and connecting the southern Sierra Nevada with the southern Coast Ranges. The highest points are Tehachapi Peak (altitude 8,056 feet, or 2,455 meters), Double Peak (8,263 feet, or 2,518 meters), and Mount Piños (altitude 9,214 feet, or 2,808 meters). The four principal passes are Walker, Tehachapi, Tejon, and the Cañada de las Uvas.

Tejon Pass, Kern County, Calif. H, 7.

A pass in the Tejon Mountains, southwest of Tehachapi Pass and the mountain of the same name. Formerly used as a wagon pass from the head of the San Joaquin Valley to the Mohave Desert ....PALMER.

Tejon Ranch, Kern County, Calif. Altitude about 1,450 feet (440 meters).

Three miles west of the mouth of Tejon Pass, at the extreme southeast end of the San Joaquin Valley and about 10 miles (16 kilometers) northeast of the mouth of the Cañada de las Uvas ....PALMER.

Telescope Peak, Inyo County, Calif. Altitude 10,938 feet (3,333 meters). E, 10.

The highest peak in the Panamint Mountains, west of Bennett Wells in Death Valley ....FISHER, BAILEY.

Temploa Mountains, California.

A low range of mountains between the San Joaquin Valley and the Carrizo Plains. On the boundary between San Luis Obispo and Kern counties..............NELSON.

Thorpe Mill, Esmeralda County, Nev.

An abandoned quartz mill at the east foot of the Grapevine Mountains and on the west side of Sarcobatus Flat, about 10 miles (16 kilometers) southeast of Gold Mountain .... MERRIAM, BAILEY, STEPHENS.

Timpahute Valley, Nevada. B–C, 13–14.

A desert valley lying near the boundary line between Nye and Lincoln counties, between the Timpahute Range on the west and Pahranagat Range on the east.
MERRIAM, BAILEY.

Three Rivers, Tulare County, Calif. E, 7.

A post-office about 25 miles (40 kilometers) northeast of Visalia, in the foothills of the Sierra near the junction of the North, East, and South forks of the Kaweah River...PALMER, BAILEY, FISHER, NELSON.

Trout Meadows, Tulare County, Calif. Altitude about 6,000* feet (1,829 meters).

The meadows on the trail from Mineral King to Soda Springs, just west of the divide between Little Kern River and the North Fork.
PALMER, BAILEY, FISHER, NELSON.

Tulare, Tulare County, Calif. Altitude 282 feet (85 meters). E, 6.

A town on the Southern Pacific Railroad, 11 miles (18 kilometers) southwest of Visalia ....PALMER, BAILEY, FISHER, NELSON.

Tule Spring, Esmeralda County, Nev. C, 9.

A spring in Tule Cañon, on the south slope of Mount Magruder.
MERRIAM, BAILEY.

Twelve Mile Spring, Inyo County, Calif.

A spring on the road from Resting Springs to Pahrump Valley, 12 miles (19 kilometers) north of Resting Springs..............PALMER, FISHER, NELSON, STEPHENS.

Twin Oaks, San Diego County, Calif.

A post-office in Merriam Valley, about 15 miles (24 kilometers) southeast of the old mission of San Luis Rey and 5 miles west of Escondido ....MERRIAM, KOCH.

Vegas Valley, Lincoln County, Nev. E, 14.

A large valley in the southern part of the State, directly east of the Charleston Mountains. Vegas Ranch, on the east side of the valley, has an altitude of 2,074 feet (631 meters) ....MERRIAM, BAILEY, NELSON.

Vegas Wash, Lincoln County, Nev. E, 15.

The wash running from Vegas Valley to the Colorado River near the Great Bend, and 4 miles south of the site of Callville................MERRIAM, BAILEY, NELSON.

Victor, San Bernardino County, Calif. Altitude, 2,713 feet or 827 meters (S. C. Ry.). I, 10.

A station on the Southern California Railway, on the Mohave River, a few miles north of Cajon Pass and 45 miles (72 kilometers) north of San Bernardino.

MERRIAM, PALMER, FISHER.

Virgin River, Utah, Arizona, and Nevada. C-E, 16-18.

A large stream which rises in southwestern Utah and empties into the Colorado River about 15 miles (24 kilometers) east of the Great Bend. The Virgin Valley referred to in the report is the valley along the lower part of the river, in the State of Nevada ....MERRIAM, BAILEY.

Visalia, the county seat of Tulare County, Calif. Altitude, 318 feet (105 meters). E, 6..PALMER, BAILEY, FISHER, NELSON.

Walker Basin, Kern County, Calif. G, 7-8.

A valley about 8 or 10 miles (13 or 16 kilometers) south of Havilah, on the road between that point and Caliente. Mossman's Ranch in the south end of the valley has an altitude of 3,157 feet (961 meters)......MERRIAM, PALMER, BAILEY, FISHER.

Walker Pass, Kern County, Calif. Altitude 5,100* feet or 1,555 meters (5,322 feet or 1,622 meters, Wheeler). F, 8.

A wagon pass through the south end of the Sierra Nevada from the South Fork of Kern River to the Mohave Desert. Named by Fremont in honor of Joseph Walker, guide on the third Fremont expedition.........MERRIAM, PALMER, FISHER, BAILEY.

Watkins' Ranch, Nye County, Nev.

A ranch in Ash Meadows 3 or 4 miles (4 or 6 kilometers) west of King Spring, owned by George Watkins. The base camp of the expedition was located here for several weeks in March, 1891, and collections were made by

PALMER, BAILEY, FISHER, NELSON.

Waucoba Peak, Inyo County, Calif. Altitude 11,267 feet (3,434 meters).

One of the highest peaks in the Inyo Mountains, situated at the head of Saline Valley, about 25 miles (40 kilometers) northeast of the town of Independence..NELSON.

Wawona, Mariposa County, Calif.

A stage station in the western foothills of the Sierra Nevada on the Raymond and Yosemite Valley road, 36 miles or 58 kilometers (by road) north of Raymond, Fresno County..NELSON.

White Mountains, Inyo County, Calif. B, 8.

A high range on the east side of Owens Valley, forming a northern continuation of the Inyo Mountains. The highest point, White Mountain Peak, has an altitude of 14,245 feet (4,342 meters)............................MERRIAM, BAILEY, NELSON.

Whitney Creek, Tulare County, Calif.

The largest stream entering the North Fork of Kern River from the east; it rises in Whitney Meadows 8 or 10 miles (13 or 16 kilometers) south of Mount Whitney and empties into the North Fork of Kern River near Soda Springs.

Whitney Meadows, Tulare County, Calif. Altitude 9,371 feet (2,856 meters).

Large meadows near timber-line at the head of Whitney Creek, about 10 miles (16 kilometers) south of Mount Whitney and 3 miles (5 kilometers) southwest of Big Cottonwood Meadows.........PALMER, BAILEY, FISHER, NELSON, STEPHENS, DUTCHER.

Wild Rose Spring, Inyo County, Calif. Altitude 4,060 feet (1,237 meters). E, 10.

A spring situated in a cañon of the same name on the west slope of the Panamint Mountains, about 10 miles (16 kilometers) northwest of Telescope Peak.

MERRIAM, BAILEY, FISHER, STEPHENS.

Willow Creek, Inyo County, Calif.

A small stream in the Panamint Mountains rising on the west side, near the summit of the divide in Cottonwood Cañon. It flows down a rocky cañon and sinks at the border of of Saline Valley..NELSON.

Willow Spring, Kern County, Calif. Altitude 2,573 feet (783 meters). H, 8.

A spring in the western part of the Mohave Desert about 13 miles (21 kilometers) southwest of Mohave on the road from Tehachapi to Los Angeles via the San Francisquito Pass. It should be distinguished from Lone Willow Spring, San Bernardino County, near the entrance to Panamint Valley..................MERRIAM, PALMER.

Windy Gap, Inyo County, Calif. F, 10–11.

A broad, open cañon (also known as Long Valley), connecting the south end of Panamint Valley with Death Valley. The name is sometimes restricted to the eastern end of the cañon near the entrance to Death Valley.

MERRIAM, PALMER, BAILEY, FISHER, NELSON.

Winters' Ranch, Nye County, Nev.

A ranch in the northeastern part of the Pahrump Valley, about 4 miles (6 kilometers) from the west base of the Charleston Mountains....PALMER, NELSON, BAILEY.

Wood Cañon, Calif.

A cañon on the east slope of the Grapevine Mountains southeast of Grapevine Peak and near the eastern boundary of California ....NELSON.

Yosemite Valley, Mariposa County, Calif. Altitude about 4,000 feet (1,219 meters). B, 5.

The well known valley on the Merced River celebrated for its scenery....NELSON.

Yount's Ranch, Nye County, Nev.

A ranch in Pahrump Valley, near the west base of the Charleston Monutains.

MERRIAM, BAILEY.

INDEX.

[Names of new genera and species are given in heavy type.]

Abies concolor, 340.
　　magnifica, 340.
Acacia greggii, 301.
Acamptopappus sphærocephalus, 309.
Acanthophysa, gen. nov., 262.
Acanthophysa echinata, sp. nov., 262.
Accipiter atricapillus striatulus, 37, 154.
　　cooperi, 36, 150, 154.
　　velox, 35-36, 150, 154.
Acer negundo, 297.
Acorns eaten by band-tailed pigeon, 31.
　　California woodpecker, 50.
　　valley quail, 28.
Acridiidæ, 251-252.
Actitis macularia, 23-24.
Adenostoma fasciculatum, 302.
Æchmophorus occidentalis, 12.
Ægialitis montana, 26.
　　nivosa, 25-26, 154.
　　vocifera, 24-25, 150, 154.
Aëronautes melanoleucus, 55-56, 151, 155.
Æsculus californica, 297.
Agaristidæ, 245.
Agave utahensis, 287, 359.
Agelaius gubernator, 75, 155.
　　phœniceus, 74-75, 151, 155.
Alaudes singularis, 236.
Alnus rhombifolia, 333.
Ameiurus nebulosus, 229.
Amelanchier alnifolia, 287, 307.
Ameles, 266.
Ammodramus sandwichensis alaudinus, 86, 151, 156.
　　sandwichensis bryanti, 86-87.
Amnicola microcoscus, sp. nov., 277-278.
　　porata, 278.
Ampelis cedrorum, 113, 157.
Amphiachyris fremontii, 309.
Amphispiza belli, 96.
　　belli nevadensis, 96-98, 152, 156.
　　bilineata, 95-96, 152, 156.
Anas americana, 16, 150.
　　boschas, 15, 150, 143.
　　carolinensis, 16, 150.
　　cyanoptera, 16-17, 150, 153.
　　discors, 16, 153.
　　strepera, 15-16.
Andrenidæ, 246.
Anodonta nuttalliana, 283.
Anser albifrons gambeli, 18, 150.
Anthicidæ, 243.
Anthocoridæ, 250.

Anthocoris musculus, 265.
Anthrax, 254.
　　fenestratoides, 254.
Anthrax (Stonyx) sodom, sp. nov., 254.
Anthribidæ, 243.
Anthus pensilvanicus, 125, 152, 157.
Aphelocoma californica, 70, 155.
　　woodhousei, 69.
Aphœbantus vittatus, 254.
Apidæ, 246.
Aplopappus monactis, 309.
Apterina polita, sp. nov., 259.
Aquila chrysaëtos, 38-39, 154.
Arachnida, 252.
Arbutus menziesii, eaten by band-tailed pigeons, 31.
Archibuteo ferrugineus, 38.
Arctiidæ, 245.
Arctomecon californicum, 290.
　　merriami, 290.
Arctostaphylos glauca, 318.
　　pungens, 318.
Ardea egretta, 20.
　　herodias, 19-20, 153.
　　virescens, 20, 153.
Argyromeba daphne, 254.
Artemisia arbuscula, 316.
　　filifolia, 316.
　　spinescens, 315.
　　tridentata, 312-313.
Ash, 320-321.
Asio accipitrinus, 42.
　　wilsonianus, 42.
Atriplex canescens, 326-327.
　　confertifolia, 323-325.
　　hymenelytra, 325.
　　lentiformis, 327.
　　parryi, 325.
　　polycarpa, 286, 325-326.
　　torreyi, 327-328.
Audibertia, *see* Salvia.
Auriparus flaviceps, 142.
Aythya americana, 17, 153.
　　collaris, 18.
　　vallisneria, 18.
Baccharis glutinosa, 309.
Bascanion flagellum frenatum, subsp. nov., 208-209.
　　laterale, 209.
　　tæniatum, 210.
Basilima millefolium, 302.

Batrachians, list of, 161.
    report on, 219-228.
Beechey's spermophile eaten by Cooper's hawk, 36
Berberis fremonti, 287, 289, 290.
Berytidae, 249.
Betula occidentalis, 332.
Bibio hirtus, 259.
Bigelovia douglassi, 309.
    graveolens, 309.
    teretifolia, 309.
Birch, 332.
Birds of Death Valley, Calif., 150-152.
    of Owens Valley, Calif., 153-158.
    report on, 7-158.
Bittern, 19, 153.
Blackbird, bicolored, 75, 155.
    Brewer's, 78-79, 151, 156.
    red-winged, 74-75, 151, 155.
    yellow-headed, 73-74, 151, 155.
Blattidae, 251.
Blepharopeza adusta, 256.
Bluebird, mountain, 148-149, 152-153.
    western, 148.
Botaurus lentiginosus, 19, 153.
Boxelder, 297.
Braconidae, 247.
Bradycellus cognatus, 236, 237.
Branta canadensis (subspecies?). 150, 153.
    canadensis hutchinsii, 19.
    canadensis occidentalis, 19.
Bruchidae, 242.
Bubo virginianus subarcticus, 43.
Buckeye, 297.
Bufo boreas nelsoni subsp. nov., 220-221.
    halophilus, 220.
    lentiginosus woodhousei, 221.
    punctatus, 219.
Bulimulus alternatus, 273.
    dealbatus, 273.
    serperastrus, 274.
Bunting, lark, 108.
    lazuli, 107-108, 152, 156.
Buprestidae, 241.
Bush-Tit, California, 141, 157.
    lead-colored, 141-142.
Buteo borealis calurus, 37-38, 150, 151.
    lineatus elegans, 38.
    swainsoni, 38.
Buzzard, turkey, 150, 154.
Byrrhidae, 241.
Bythinella protea, 278-281.
    seemani, 278.
Bythoscopidae, 250.
Cactuses, report on, 345-352.
Calamospiza melanocorys, 108.
Calandridae, 243.
Calidris arenaria, 23.
Callipepla californica, 27.
    californica vallicola, 28-29, 154.
    gambeli, 29-30, 150.
Callisaurus ventralis, 170-173.
Calosoma prominens, 237.
Calospasta, 236-237.
Calypte anna, 58.
    costae, 7, 8, 56-58, 151, 155.

Campylorhynchus, see Heleodytes.
Capsidae, 249-250.
Carabidae, 239.
Carinifex newberryi, 277.
Carpodacus cassini, 79-80.
    mexicanus frontalis, 80-81, 151, 156
    purpureus californicus, 79.
Cassia armata, 299.
Castanopsis chrysophylla, 334.
Cathartes aura, 31, 150, 154.
Catherpes mexicanus conspersus, 133-134, 152.
Catostomus araeopus, 229.
Ceanothus cuneatus, 297.
    divaricatus, 297.
    fendleri, 297.
Cedarbird, 157.
Centrocereus urophasianus, 31.
Ceophlœus pileatus, 49.
Cerambycidae, 242.
Cercis occidentalis, 287, 299.
Cercocarpus ledifolius, 305.
    parvifolius, 305.
Cercopidae, 251.
Cereus engelmanni, 346.
    mohavensis, 346-347.
Ceryle alcyon, 46, 151, 154.
Chaetura vauxii, 55, 155.
Chalcididae, 248-249.
Chamaea fasciata henshawi, 110.
Charadrius squatarola, 24.
Charina plumbea, 203.
Charitonetta albeola, 18, 153.
Chat, long-tailed, 123-124, 152, 157.
Chelidon erythrogaster, 110-111, 156.
Chelopus, see Clemmys.
Chemisal, 302.
Chen hyberborea, 18.
Chickadee, California, 140.
    mountain, 139-140, 157.
Chilopsis linearis, 322.
Chondestes grammacus strigatus, 87-88, 156.
Chordeiles texensis, 7, 8, 53-54, 151, 155.
    virginianus henryi, 53, 151.
Chorizanthe rigida, 332.
Chrysomelidae, 242.
Cicindelidae, 239.
Cinclus mexicanus, 125-126, 157.
Circus hudsonius, 35, 150, 154.
Cistothorus palustris paludicola, 136, 152, 157.
Clemmys marmorata, 162.
Cleridae, 241.
Clivicola riparia, 112, 156.
Cnemidophorus tigris, 198-200.
    tigris undulatus, 200-201.
Coccinellidae, 240.
Coccothraustes vespertinus montanus, 79.
Coccyzus americanus occidentalis, 45, 151, 154.
Colaptes cafer, 50-51, 151, 155.
Coleogyne ramosissima, 286, 302-305.
Coleonyx brevis (Key), 163, 164.
    dovii (Key), 163.
    elegans (Key), 163.
    variegatus, 162-163, 164.
Coleoptera, 239-243.
Columba fasciata, 31.
Colydiidae, 240.

Colymbus auritus, 13.
    nigricollis californicus, 12, 13, 150, 153.
Comastes sackeni, sp. nov., 255.
Contopus borealis, 63.
    richardsoni, 64, 153.
Coot, 21-22, 150, 153.
Corcidæ, 249.
Corimelænidæ, 249.
Cormorant, Baird's, 14.
    Brandt's, 14.
    Farallon, 14.
Corvus americanus, 71-72.
    corax sinuatus, 70-71, 151, 153.
Corylophidæ, 240.
Cossidæ, 245.
Cottonwood, 335.
Cowania mexicana, 287, 305-306.
Cowbird, 73, 157.
Crane, little brown, 20-21.
Creeper, California, 136.
Cremastochilus westwoodii, 236.
Creosote bush, 286, 293-295.
Crophius disconotus, 263.
Crossbill, Mexican, 81-82.
Crotalus cerastes, 216-218.
    lucifer, 218-219.
    tigris, 214-216.
Crotaphytus baileyi, 165-166.
    silus, 170.
    wislizenii, 167-169.
Crow, 71-72.
Cryptophagidæ, 240.
Cuckoo, California, 45, 151, 154.
Culex, 253.
Culex inornatus, sp. nov., 253.
Curculionidæ, 243.
Curlew, Hudsonian, 24.
    long-billed, 24, 154.
Cyanocephalus cyanocephalus, 72-73, 155.
Cyanocitta stelleri, 63.
    stelleri frontalis, 60, 155.
Cypseloides niger, 54, 155.
Cyprinodon macularius, 232-233.
Cyprinodon macularius baileyi, subsp. nov., 233.
Cyprinus carpio, 231.
Dafila acuta, 17, 150.
Dalea fremonti, 298-299.
    johnsoni, 299.
    polyadenia, 293.
Dascyllidæ, 241.
Dendragapus obscurus fuliginosus, 30-31.
Dendrocygna fulva, 19, 153.
Dendroica æstiva, 118-119, 157.
    auduboni, 119, 120, 152, 157.
    nigrescens, 120-121.
    occidentalis, 121-122.
    townsendi, 121-122.
Dermestidæ, 240.
Desert willow, 322.
Diadophis pulchellus, 200-201.
Dipsosaurus dorsalis, 164-165.
Dove, mourning, 32-33, 150, 154.
Dracotettix plutonius, sp. nov. 267-263.
Dryobates nuttalli, 47-48.
    pubescens gairdnerii, 47.
    scalaris bairdi, 7, 8, 47.

Dryobates villosus hyloscopus, 46-47, 151.
Duck, baldpate, 16, 150.
    blue-winged teal, 16, 153.
    bufflehead, 18, 153.
    canvasback, 18.
    cinnamon teal, 16-17, 150, 153.
    fulvous tree, 19, 153.
    gadwall, 15-16.
    golden-eye, 18, 153.
    green-winged teal, 16, 150.
    harlequin, 18.
    mallard, 15, 150, 153.
    merganser, 15.
    pintail, 17, 150.
    red-breasted merganser, 15, 153.
    redhead, 17, 153.
    ring-necked, 18.
    ruddy, 18, 150.
    scoter, 18.
    shoveller, 17, 150, 153.
    surf scoter, 18.
    widgeon, 16.
Dytiscidæ, 239.
Eagle, bald, 39.
    golden, 38-39, 154.
Echinocactus johnsoni, 351.
    polyancistrus, 351-352.
    polycephalus, 351.
    wislizeni lecontei, 352.
Egret, 20.
Elanus leucurus, 34.
Elasmocerus, 236.
Elateridæ, 241.
Empetrichthys merriami, gen. et. sp. nov. 233-234.
Empidonax difficilis, 64-65.
    hammondi, 65.
    pusillus, 65, 155.
    wrightii, 65-66, 151, 155.
Encelia frutescens, 312.
Eucoptolophus pallidus, sp. nov., 266.
Ephedra nevadensis, 286, 335-336.
    viridis, 287, 336-337.
Ephydra hians, eaten by shoveller, 17.
    snowy plover, 25-26.
    Texas nighthawk, 53.
    western wood pewee, 64.
Ephydra tarsata, sp. nov., 257-258.
Erax aridus, 254.
Ereunetes occidentalis, 23, 154.
Eriodictyon tomentosum, 320.
Eriogonum inflatum, 332.
    polifolium, 331-332.
Erismatura rubida, 18, 150.
Euchide urens, 308.
Eumeces skiltonianus, 201-202.
Eumenidæ, 247.
Eurotia lanata, 329-330.
Eutænia, see Thamnophis.
Euxesta spoliata, sp. nov., 257.
Falco columbarius, 40, 154.
    mexicanus, 39-40, 150, 154.
    peregrinus anatum, 40.
    sparverius deserticolus, 40-41, 154.
Falcon, prairie, 39-40, 150, 154.
Fallugia paradoxa, 287, 306-307.
Finch, California purple, 79.
    Cassin's purple, 79-80.

Finch, house, 80-81, 151, 156.
Fishes, list of, 229.
　　report on, 229-234.
Flicker, red-shafted, 50-51, 151, 155.
Fluminicola fusca, 281.
　　fusca minor, 282.
　　merriami, 281-282.
　　nuttalliana, 282.
Flycatcher, Arkansas, 155.
　　ash-throated, 60-61, 131, 155.
　　Baird's, 64-65.
　　Hammond's, 65.
　　little, 65, 155.
　　olive-sided, 63.
　　vermilion, 7, 8, 66.
　　Wright's, 65-66, 151, 155.
Formicidæ, 247.
Forficulidæ, 251.
Franseria dumosa, 286, 311-312.
　　eriocentra, 312.
Fraxinus anomala, 320.
　　coriacea, 319.
Fremontodendron californicum 293.
Fulica americana, 21-22, 150, 153.
Fulgoridæ, 250.
Galgulidæ, 250.
Gallinago delicata, 22-23, 150, 154.
Gargaphia opacula, sp. nov., 263.
Garrya veatchii flavescens, 287-303.
Gasterosteus williamsoni, 234.
Geococcyx californianus, 44-45, 151, 154.
Geometridæ, 246.
Geothlypis macgillivrayi, 122, 157.
　　trichas occidentalis, 123, 152, 157.
Geron, 255.
Gerrhonotus burnettii, 197-198.
　　scincicauda, 195, 196.
Gerrhonotus scincicauda palmeri, subsp. nov., 196, 197.
Glandina decussata, 270.
　　singleyana, 270.
　　texasiana, 271.
Glaucionetta clangula americana, 18, 153.
Glossapetalon nevadense, 296.
　　spinescens, 297.
Gnatcatcher, black-tailed, 144.
　　plumbeous, 144.
　　western, 143-144, 152, 157.
Godwit, marbled, 23.
Goldfinch, 83.
　　Arizona, 85.
　　Arkansas, 84-85, 156.
　　Lawrence's, 85.
Goose, Hutchin's, 19.
　　lesser snow, 18.
　　white-cheeked, 19.
　　white-fronted, 18, 150.
Gopherus agassizii, 161-162.
Goshawk, 37, 154.
Grasshoppers, eaten by Brewer's blackbird, 78.
　　burrowing owl, 44.
　　California woodpecker, 50.
　　desert sparrow hawk, 41.
　　gray-crowned leucosticte, 82.
　　Lewis's woodpecker, 50.

Grasshoppers, eaten by mallard, 15.
　　raven, 70.
　　Swainson's hawk, 38.
　　western red-tailed hawk, 37.
Grayia polygaloides (*see G. spinosa.*)
　　spinosa, 286, 328-329.
Grebe, eared, 12, 150, 153.
　　horned, 13.
　　pied-billed, 13.
　　western, 12.
Grosbeak, black-headed, 105-106, 156.
　　pine, 79.
　　western blue, 106-107, 152, 156.
　　western evening, 79.
Grouse, sage, 31.
　　sooty, 30-31.
Grus canadensis, 20-21.
Gryllidæ, 251.
Guiraca cœrulea eurhyncha, 106-107, 152, 156.
Gull, Bonaparte's, 14, 153.
　　California, 13, 14, 153.
　　glaucous-winged, 13.
　　Heermann's, 14.
　　ring-billed, 14, 153.
Habia melanocephala, 105-106, 153.
Haliæetus leucocephalus, 39.
Harmostes propinquus, 260.
Harporhynchus crissalis, 130.
　　lecontei, 7, 9, 128-130, 152, 157.
　　redivivus, 128.
Hawk, Cooper's, 36, 150, 154.
　　desert sparrow, 40-41, 151, 154.
　　duck, 40.
　　ferruginous roughleg, 38.
　　marsh, 35, 150, 154.
　　pigeon, 40, 150, 154.
　　red-bellied, 38.
　　sharp-shinned, 35-36, 150, 154.
　　Swainson's, 38.
　　western red-tail, 37-38, 150, 154.
Helcodytes brunneicapillus, 130-132, 157.
Helicina chrysicheila, 282.
　　tropica, 283.
Helix (Arionta) arrosa, 272.
　　(Arionta) coloradoensis, 271-272.
　　(Arionta) cypreophila, 272.
　　(Arionta) magdalenensis, 269, 271.
　　(Arionta) mormonum, 272.
　　(Arionta) tudiculata, 272.
　　(Mesodon) thyroides, 273.
　　(Polygyra) biernrus, 273.
　　(Polygyra) texasiana, 273.
　　(Praticola) berlandieriana, 273.
　　(Praticola) griseola, 272.
Helminthophila celata lutescens, 118.
　　luciæ, 117.
　　ruficapilla gutturalis, 117.
Heloderma suspectum, 194-195.
Heron, black-crowned night, 20, 150, 153.
　　great blue, 19-20, 153.
　　green, 20, 153.
Hesperidæ, 244.
Hesperocichla nævia, 147.
Heteractitis incanus, 23.
Heterogamea, 266.

Heteromeles arbutifolia, 307.
Heteroptera, 249-250.
Himantopus mexicanus, 22.
Histeridæ, 241.
Histrionicus histrionicus, 18.
Holodiscus discolor, 302.
Homoptera, 250-251.
Hoplomachus consors, sp. nov., 264-265.
Humming-bird, Anna's, 58.
    black-chinned, 56, 155.
    broad-tailed, 58-59.
    calliope, 59.
    Costa's, 7, 8, 56-58, 151, 155.
    rufous, 59.
Hydrophilidæ, 239.
Hyla regilla, 222-224.
Hymenoclea salsola, 310-311.
Hymenoptera, 246-249.
Hypsiglena chlorophæa (Key), 205.
    ochrorhynchus (Key), 204-205.
Hypsiglena texana, sp. nov., 205.
Ibis, white-faced glossy, 19, 150, 153.
Ichneumonidæ, 247-248.
Icteria virens longicauda, 123-124, 152, 157.
Icterus bullocki, 77-78, 151, 156.
    parisorum, 7, 8, 76-77.
Insects, reports on, 235-268.
Isomeris arborea, 291.
    arborea globosa, 291.
Ixodilæ, 252.
Jay, blue-fronted, 69, 155.
    California, 70, 155.
    piñon, 72-73, 155.
    Steller's, 68.
    Woodhouse's, 69.
Jassidæ, 251.
Joshua, *see* Tree Yucca.
Judas bush, 299.
Junco hyemalis, 92-93.
    hyemalis shufeldti, 8, 93.
    hyemalis thurberi, 7, 8, 93-94, 156.
    pinosus, 95.
Junco, Point Piños, 95.
    Shufeldt's, 8, 93.
    slate-colored, 92-93.
    Thurber's, 7, 8, 93-94, 156.
Juniperus californica, 340-341.
    californica utahensis, 287, 341-342.
    occidentalis, 343.
    occidentalis monosperma, 343.
Killdeer, 24-25, 150, 154.
Kingbird, 59, 155.
    Arkansas, 59-60.
    Cassin's, 60.
Kingfisher, belted, 46, 151, 154.
Kinglet, ruby-crowned, 142-143, 152.
    western golden-crowned, 143.
Kite, white-tailed, 34.
Krameria canescens, 292.
    parvifolia, 286, 291-292.
Kunzia glandulosa, 302.
    tridentata, 287, 302-303.
Lampropeltis boylii, 204.
Lampyridæ, 241.
Lanius ludovicianus excubitorides, 114-115, 152, 157.

Lark, desert horned, 66-67, 155.
    Mexican horned, 67-68, 155.
Larrea tridentata, 286, 293-295.
Larus californicus, 13-14, 153.
    delawarensis, 14, 153.
    glaucescens, 13.
    heermanni, 14.
    philadelphia, 14, 153.
Lathridiidæ, 241.
Lepidomeda vittata, 231.
Lepidoptera, 244-246.
Leptoypha mutica, 264.
Leucosticte atrata, 83.
    tephrocotis, 7, 8, 82-83.
Leucostiete, black, 83.
    gray-crowned, 7, 8, 82-83.
Libocedrus decurrens, 340.
Limax campestris, 271.
Limnæa bulimoides, 275.
    caperata, 274.
    humilis, 275.
    nuttalliana, 274-275.
Limosa fedoa, 23.
Limosina aldrichi, sp. nov., 259.
Lizards, eaten by western red-tailed hawk, 37.
Localities visited by the expedition, 361-384.
Locustidæ, 251.
Loon, 13.
Lordotus diversus, 259.
Lordotus sororculus, sp. nov., 255.
Loxia curvirostra stricklandi, 81-82.
Lycænidæ, 244.
Lycium andersoni, 286, 320-321.
    cooperi, 321.
    pallidum, 322.
    torreyi, 321.
Lygæidæ, 249.
Lygæosoma, 262.
Lygæosoma solida sp. nov., 262.
Lygæus melanopleurus sp. nov., 262.
Magpie, black-billed, 68.
    yellow-billed, 68.
Malachiidæ, 241.
Malvastrum rotundifolium, 292.
Mammillaria, 352.
Manzanita, 318.
Martin, western, 109.
Masaridæ, 247.
Meadowlark, western, 75-76, 151, 155.
Mecomyctor, 236.
Megascops asio bendirei, 43.
Melanerpes formicivorus bairdi, 49-50.
    torquatus, 50, 154.
    uropygialis, 50.
Melanodexia, gen. nov., 256-257.
Melanodexia tristis, sp. nov., 257.
Melanostoma, 255.
Meloidæ, 243.
Melospiza fasciata fallax, 98-99.
    fasciata graminea, 100.
    fasciata guttata, 100.
    fasciata heermanni, 89-100, 156.
    fasciata montana, 99, 152.
    fasciata rufina, 100.
    lincolni, 100-101, 156.
Membracidæ, 250.

Menodora spinosa, 286.
　　spinescens, 318-319.
Merganser americanus, 15.
　　serrator, 15, 153.
　　red-breasted, 15, 153.
Merula migratoria propinqua, 146-147, 152, 153.
Mesquite, 299-300.
Micropus, see Aëronautes.
Mimus polyglottos, 127-128, 152, 157.
Mistletoe berries, eaten by phainopepla, 113.
Mocking bird, 127-128, 152, 157.
Molothrus ater, 73-74, 151.
Mollusks, report on, 269-283.
Monanthia labeculata sp. nov., 264.
Mordellidæ, 243.
Mortania scabrella, 296.
Mountain mahogany, 305.
Mulberries, eaten by cedar-waxwing, 113.
Murre, California, 13.
Mutillidæ, 247.
Myadestes townsendii, 144-145, 157.
Myiarchus cinerascens, 60-61, 151, 153.
Myrmecidæ, 247.
Nabidæ, 250.
Nemobius, 266.
Nighthawk, Texas, 7, 8, 53-54, 151, 153.
　　western, 53, 151.
Nitidulidæ, 241.
Noctuidæ, 245.
Notiphila decoris, sp. nov., 253.
Notodontidæ, 245.
Notonectidæ, 250.
Numenius hudsonicus, 24.
　　longirostris, 24, 151.
Nutcracker, Clark's, 72, 155.
Nuthatch, pygmy, 137-138.
　　red-bellied, 137.
　　slender-billed, 136-137.
Nycticorax nycticorax nævius, 20, 150, 153.
Nymphalidæ, 244.
Oaks, 333-334.
Oidemia americana, 18.
　　perspicillata, 19.
Omophron dentatum, 237.
Oncunyia, abbreviata, 253.
Ophibolus, see Lampropeltis.
Opuntia acanthocarpa, 347.
　　basilaris, 349-350.
　　bernardina, 347.
　　echinocarpa, 347-348.
　　engelmanni occidentalis, 350.
　　parryi, 348-349.
　　pulchella, 349.
　　ramosissima, 349.
　　rutila, 350-351.
　　whipplei, 348.
Oreortyx pictus plumiferus, 7, 8, 26-27, 151.
Oriole, Bullock's, 77-78, 151, 156.
　　Scott's, 7, 8, 76-77.
Oroscoptes montanus, 126-127, 152, 157.
Orthoptera, 251-252.
Osprey, 41-42, 151.
Othniidæ, 242.
Otiorhynchidæ, 243.
Otocoris alpestris arenicola, 66-67, 153.
　　alpestris chrysolæma, 67-68, 153.

Ousel, water, 125-126, 157.
Owl, barn, 42, 151.
　　burrowing, 44, 151, 154.
　　California screech, 43.
　　long-eared, 42.
　　short-eared, 42.
　　spotted, 42.
　　western horned, 43.
Pamera nitidula, sp. nov., 262-263.
Pandion haliaëtus carolinensis, 41-42, 151.
Pautarbes capito, 259.
Papilionidæ, 244.
Partridge, plumed, 7, 8, 26-27.
Parus gambeli, 139-140, 157.
　　inornatus, 138.
　　inornatus griseus, 138-139.
　　rufescens neglectus, 140.
Passerella iliaca megarhyncha, 101-102, 156.
　　iliaca schistacea, 102.
　　iliaca unalaschcensis, 101.
Passerina amœna, 107-108, 152, 156.
Patula striatella, 271.
Peaches eaten by house finch, 80-81.
Pelecanus californicus, 14, 15.
　　erythrorhynchos, 14, 153.
Pelican, California brown, 14, 15.
　　white, 14, 153.
Pelomyia, gen. nov., 258.
Pelomyia occidentalis, sp. nov., 258.
Pentatomidæ, 249.
Peraphyllum ramosissimum, 287, 307.
Perognathus impaled by white-rumped shrike, 114.
Petalonyx parryi, 308.
Petrochelidon lunifrons, 110, 156.
Peucæa cassini, 7, 98.
　　ruficeps, 98.
Peuceaphyllum schottii, 316.
Pewee, western wood, 64, 155.
Phainopepla nitens, 113-114, 157.
Phalacridæ, 240.
Phalacrocorax dilophus albociliatus, 14.
　　pelagicus resplendens, 14.
　　penicillatus, 14.
Phalænoptilus nuttalli, 51-52, 151, 155.
　　nuttalli californicus, 52-53.
Phalarope, Wilson's, 22, 150, 153.
Phalaropus tricolor, 22, 150, 153.
Phœbe, black, 63, 151, 153.
　　Say's, 61-62, 151, 155.
Phrynosoma blainvillii, 187-190.
Phrynosoma cerrœnse, sp. nov. 187.
Phrynosoma goodei, sp. nov., 191-192.
　　platyrhinos, 190-194.
Physa gyrina, 276.
　　heterostropha, 276-277.
Phycitidæ, 246.
Pica pica hudsonica, 68.
　　nuttalli, 68.
Picicorvus columbianus, 72, 153.
Pigeon, band-tailed, 31.
Pinacodera punctigera, 237.
Pine nut eaten by piñon jay, 73.
Pine siskin, 85.
Pinicola enucleator, 79.
Piñon, 287, 337, 338.

Pinus aristata, 339.
 balfouriana, 339.
 flexilis, 340.
 jeffreyi, 339.
 lambertiana, 340.
 monophylla, 287, 337-338.
 monticola, 339.
 murrayana, 339.
 ponderosa, 338.
 ponderosa scopulorum, 339.
 sabiniana, 339.
Pipilo aberti, 105.
 chlorurus, 103-104, 156.
 fuscus mesoleucus, 105.
 fuscus crissalis, 105.
 maculatus megalonyx, 102-103, 156.
 maculatus oregonus, 103.
Pipunculus aridus, sp. nov., 255-256.
Piranga hepatica, 109.
 ludoviciana, 108-109, 156.
Pisidium occidentale, 283.
Pituophis catenifer, 206.
 catenifer deserticola, 206-208.
Planorbis liebmanni, 275.
 lentus, 275.
 parvus, 275.
 trivolvis, 275.
Platanus occidentalis, 332.
Platychirus peltatus, 257.
Plegadis guarauna, 19, 150, 153.
Ploas fenestrato, 259.
Plover, black-bellied, 24.
 killdeer, 24-25, 150, 154.
 mountain, 26.
 snowy, 25-26, 154.
Pluchea sericea, 310.
Pocket gopher eaten by western red-tailed hawk, 37.
Podilymbus podiceps, 13.
Polioptila caerulea obscura, 143-144, 152, 157.
 californica, 144.
 plumbea, 144.
Poocætes gramineus confinis, 85, 156.
Poor-will, 51-52, 151, 155.
Populus fremontii, 335.
Porzana carolina, 21, 153.
Proctotrypidæ, 248.
Progne subis hesperia, 109.
Pronotacantha annulata, gen. et sp. nov., 260-261.
Prospherysa sp., 256.
Prospherysa similis, sp. nov., 256.
Prosopis juliflora, 299-300.
 pubescens, 300-301.
Prunus andersoni, 302.
 fasciculata, 287, 301.
 virginiana (or demissa), 302.
Psaltriparus minimus californicus, 141, 157.
 plumbeus, 141-142.
Pselaphidæ, 240.
Pseudogryphus californianus, 33-34.
Pseudopis, 236.
Pseudotsuga macrocarpa, 340.
Psilocephala, 254.
Psyllidæ, 251.
Ptinidæ, 242.
Pupa (Vertigo) pentodon, 273.

Purshia, see Kunzia.
Pyrocephalus rubineus mexicanus, 7, 8, 66.
Pyromorphidæ, 215.
Pyrrhocoridæ, 249.
Pythidæ, 242.
Quail, California, 27.
 Gambel's, 29-30, 150.
 plumed, 7, 8, 26-27, 154.
 valley, 28-29, 154.
Quercus douglasii, 333-334.
 dumosa, 334.
 gambelii, 287, 333.
 kelloggii, 334.
 lobata, 333.
 undulata, 287, 333.
 wislizeni, 334.
Rail, Carolina, 21, 153.
 Virginia, 21, 150, 153.
Rallus virginianus, 21, 150, 153.
Rana aurora, 225-226.
 boylii, 226-227.
 draytonii, 225.
Rana fisheri sp. nov., 227-228.
Rana pipiens brachycephala, 223.
 pretiosa, 226.
Raven, 70-71, 151, 155.
Recurvirostra americana, 22, 153.
Reduviidæ, 250.
Regulus calendula, 142-143, 152.
 satrapa olivaceus, 143.
Rena humilis, 203.
Reptiles, list of, 160-161.
Reptiles, report on, 159-219.
Rhamnus crocea, 297.
Rhinichthys (Apocope) nevadensis, sp. nov., 230-231.
 (Apocope) velifer, sp. nov., 229-230.
Rhus diversiloba, 298.
 trilobata, 287, 297-298.
Ribes leptanthum brachyanthum, 307-308.
 menziesii, 308.
Road-runner, 44-45, 151, 154.
Robin, western, 146-147, 152, 158.
Robinia neomexicana, 287 299.
Rosa sp.?, 307.
Round-tail spermophile eaten by western red-tailed hawk, 37.
Rutilus symmetricus, 231.
Sagebrush, 312-315.
Salazaria mexicana, 286, 323.
Salda explanata, sp. nov., 265.
 interstitialis, 265.
Saldidæ, 250.
Salix lævigata, 334.
 longifolia, 334.
 nigra, 335.
Salmo iridens, 231.
 mykiss agua-bonita, 232.
Salpinctes obsoletus, 132-133, 152, 157.
Salvadora grahamiæ hexalepis, 205-206.
Salvia carnosa, 322.
 pilosa, 322.
Sand cricket, eaten by western red-tailed hawk, 37.
Sanderling, 23.
Sandpiper, least, 23, 154.

Sandpiper, spotted, 23-24.
　　　　western, 23, 154.
Sapsucker, red-breasted, 48-49.
　　　　red-naped, 48.
　　　　Williamson's 49.
Sarcobatus baileyi, 330.
　　　　vermiculatus, 331.
Sauromalus ater, 173-175.
Sayornis saya, 61-62, 151, 155.
　　　　nigricans, 63, 151, 155.
Scaphiopus hammondi, 222.
Scarabaeidae, 242.
Sceloporus bi-seriatus, 184-186.
Sceloporus boulengeri, sp. nov., 180.
　　　　graciosus, 183 184.
　　　　magister, 178-183.
　　　　occidentalis, 186-187.
Sceloporus orcutti, sp. nov., 181.
Scirtettica occidentalis, sp. nov., 267
Scolocophagus cyanocephalus, 78-79, 151, 155.
Scolytidae, 243.
Scorpion eaten by western horned owl, 43.
Screw bean, 300.
Scorpionidae, 252.
Scyllina delicatula, 238.
Seiurus noveboracensis notabilis, 122.
Selasphorus platycercus, 58 59.
　　　　rufus, 59.
Sequoia gigantea, 340.
Service berry, 307.
Sesiidae, 245.
Shells, list of, 270.
Shrike, white-rumped, 114-115, 152, 157.
Shrubs, report on, 286-332, 335-337.
Sialia arctica, 148-149, 152, 158.
　　　　mexicana, 148.
Silphidae, 239.
Simulium argus, sp. nov., 253-254.
Sitta canadensis, 137.
　　　　carolinensis aculeata, 136-137.
　　　　pygmaea, 137-138.
Snake eaten by desert sparrow hawk, 41.
Snipe, Wilson's, 22-23, 150,151.
Solitaire, Townsend's, 144-145, 157.
Sora, 21, 153.
Sparrow, Bell's, 96.
　　　　black-chinned, 7, 8, 92, 156.
　　　　black-throated, 95-96, 152, 156.
　　　　Brewer's, 91-92, 152, 156.
　　　　Bryant's marsh, 86-87.
　　　　Cassin's 7, 98.
　　　　desert song, 98-99.
　　　　Gambel's, 89-90.
　　　　golden-crowned, 90.
　　　　Heermann's song, 99-100, 156.
　　　　intermediate, 88-89, 151.
　　　　Lincoln's, 100-101, 156.
　　　　mountain song, 90, 152.
　　　　rufous-crowned, 98.
　　　　rusty song, 100.
　　　　sage, 96-98, 152, 156.
　　　　Santa Barbara song, 103.
　　　　slate-colored, 102.
　　　　sooty song, 100.
　　　　thick-billed, 101-102.
　　　　Townsend's, 101.

Sparrow, western chipping, 90.
　　　　western lark, 87-88, 156.
　　　　western savanna, 86, 151, 156.
　　　　western tree, 90.
　　　　western vesper, 85, 156.
　　　　white-crowned, 90.
　　　　white-throated, 90.
Spatula clypeata, 17, 150, 153.
Speotyto cunicularia hypogaea, 44, 151, 154.
Sphingidae, 245.
Sphaeralcea monroana, 292-293.
Sphecidae, 247.
Sphyrapicus ruber, 48-49.
　　　　thyroideus, 49.
　　　　varius nuchalis, 48.
Spinus lawrencei, 85.
　　　　pinus, 85.
　　　　psaltria, 84-85, 156.
　　　　psaltria arizonae, 85.
　　　　tristis, 83.
Spizella atrigularis, 7, 8, 92, 156.
　　　　breweri, 91-92, 152, 156.
　　　　monticola ochracea, 90.
　　　　socialis arizonae, 90.
Spyrostachys, see Allenrolfea.
Stanleya pinnata, 290-291.
Staphylinidae, 240.
Stelgidopteryx serripennis, 112-113, 152, 155.
Stellula calliope, 59.
Stenodactylus variegatus, 163, 164.
Sterna maxima, 14.
Stilt, black-necked, 22.
Sturnella magna neglecta, 75-76, 151, 155.
Streptostyla sololensis, 271.
Strix pratincola, 42, 154.
Suaeda suffrutescens, 330.
Succinea luteola, 274.
　　　　oregonensis, 274.
Swallow, bank, 112, 156.
　　　　barn, 110-111, 156.
　　　　cliff, 110, 156.
　　　　rough-winged, 112-113, 152, 156.
　　　　tree, 111, 152.
　　　　violet-green, 111-112, 152, 156.
Swift, black, 54, 155.
　　　　Vaux's, 55, 155.
　　　　white-throated, 55-56, 151, 155.
Sycamore, 332.
Sylvania pusilla pileolata, 124, 157.
Symphemia semipalmata inornata, 23.
Symphoricarpos longifolius, 287, 308.
Syrnium occidentale, 42.
Tabanus punctifer, 259.
Tachycineta bicolor, 11, 152.
　　　　thalassina, 111-112, 152, 156.
Tanager, hepatic, 109.
　　　　western, 108-109, 156.
Tanarthrus, 236.
Tattler, wandering, 23.
Tenebrionidae, 242.
Tern, royal, 14.
Tetradymia canescens, 316.
　　　　comosa, 318.
　　　　glabrata, 286, 316-317.
　　　　spinosa, 286, 317-318.
　　　　stenolepis, 318.

Tetragonoderus pallidus, 237.
Thamnophis elegans, 211-212.
    hammondii, 212-213.
    infernalis, 210-211.
    parietalis, 214.
    vagrans, 213-214.
Thamnosma montana, 286, 296.
Thereva vialis, 254.
Thrasher, California, 128.
    crissal, 130.
    LeConte's, 7, 9, 128-130, 152, 157.
    sage, 126-127, 152, 157.
Thrush, Audubon's hermit, 143, 158.
    dwarf hermit, 145-146.
    Grinnell's water, 122.
    olive-backed, 145.
    russet-backed, 145, 158.
    varied, 147.
Thryothorus bewickii bairdi, 134-135, 152, 157.
    bewickii spilurus, 134.
Tingitidæ, 250.
Titlark, 125, 152, 157.
Titmouse, gray, 138.
    plain, 138-139.
Torreya, *see* Tumion.
Totanus melanoleucus, 23, 154.
Towhee, Abert's, 105.
    California, 105.
    cañon, 105.
    green-tailed, 103-104, 156.
    Oregon, 103.
    spurred, 102-103, 156.
Trees, report on, 332-335, 337-343.
Tridactylus, 266.
Tringa minutilla, 23, 154.
Triodites mus, 259.
Triplasius novus, sp. nov., 254-255.
Trochilus alexandri, 56, 155.
Troglodytes aëdon aztecus, 135, 157.
Tyrannus tyrannus, 59, 155.
    verticalis, 59-60, 155.
    vociferans, 60.
Tryonia fusca, 281.
Tumion californicum, 343.
Turdus aonalaschkæ, 145-146.
    aonalaschkæ audoboni, 146, 158.
    ustulatus, 145, 158.
    ustulatus swainsonii, 145.
Unio anodontoides, 283.
    berlandieri, 283.
Uria troile californica, 13.
Urinator, 13.
Uta graciosa, 177.
    stansburiana, 175-177.
Veliidæ, 250.
Vireo bellii pusillus, 116-117, 152, 157.
    gilvus swainsonii, 115-116, 157.
    solitarius cassinii, 116.
    solitarius plumbeus, 116.
    vicinior, 117.
    Cassin's, 116.

Vireo, gray, 117.
    least, 116-117, 152, 157.
    plumbeous, 116.
    western warbling, 115-116, 157.
Vitis californica, eaten by cedar waxwing, 113.
Vulture, California, 33-34.
    turkey, 34.
Warbler, Audubon's, 119-120, 152, 157.
    black-throated gray, 120-121.
    Calaveras, 117.
    hermit, 121-122.
    Lucy's, 117.
    lutescent, 118, 157.
    Macgillivray's, 122, 157.
    pileolated, 124, 157.
    yellow, 118-119, 157.
    Townsend's, 121, 157.
Waxwing, cedar, 113.
Wild sunflower, eaten by Arkansas goldfinch, 84.
Willet, western, 23.
Willows, 334-335.
Woodpecker, Baird's, 7, 8, 47.
    Cabanis's, 46-47, 154.
    California, 49-50.
    Gairdner's, 47.
    Gila, 50.
    Lewis's, 50, 154.
    Nuttall's, 47-48.
    pileated, 49.
    white-headed, 48.
Wood rat, eaten by western horned owl, 43.
Wren, Baird's, 134-135, 152, 157.
    cactus, 130-132, 157.
    cañon, 133-134, 152.
    rock, 132-133, 152, 157.
    tule, 136, 152, 157.
    Vigor's, 134.
    western, 135, 157.
Wren-tit, pallid, 140.
Xanthocephalus xanthocephalus, 73-74, 151, 155.
Xantusia vigilis, 198.
Xenopicus albolarvatus, 48.
Xerobates, *see* Gopherus.
Yellow-headed tit, 152.
Yellow-throat, western, 123, 152, 157.
Yellow-legs, greater, 23, 154.
Yucca arborescens, 353.
    baccata, 352-353.
    brevifolia, 353-358.
    elata? 358-359.
    macrocarpa, 358.
    whipplei, 359.
Yuccas, report on, 352-359.
Zenaidura macroura, 32-33, 150, 154.
Zonotrichia albicollis, 90.
    coronata, 90.
    leucophrys, 88, 156.
    leucophrys gambeli, 89-90.
    leucophrys intermedia, 88-89, 151.

PLATE I.

1. *Sceloporus clarkii* B. & G.   *Type.*   (2940)
   'Sonora.'
2. *Sceloporus magister* Hallow.   (18126).
   Mohave Desert, California.
3. *Sceloporus zosteromus* Cope.   *Type.*   (5298).
   Cape St. Lucas, Lower California.
4. *Sceloporus orcutti* Stejn., sp. nov.   *Type.*   (16330).
   Milquatay Valley, San Diego County, Calif.
5. *Sceloporus boulengeri* Stejn., sp. nov.   *Type.*   (14079).
   Presidio, western Mexico.
6. *Sceloporus floridanus* Baird.   *Type.*   (2874).
   Pensacola, Fla.
   On all the figures—
       a represents top of head; all natural size except fig. 6, which is $1\frac{1}{3}$ times natural size.
       b represents the scales bordering the left ear anteriorly; all twice natural size.
       c represents one of the dorsal scales; all $2\frac{2}{3}$ times natural size.

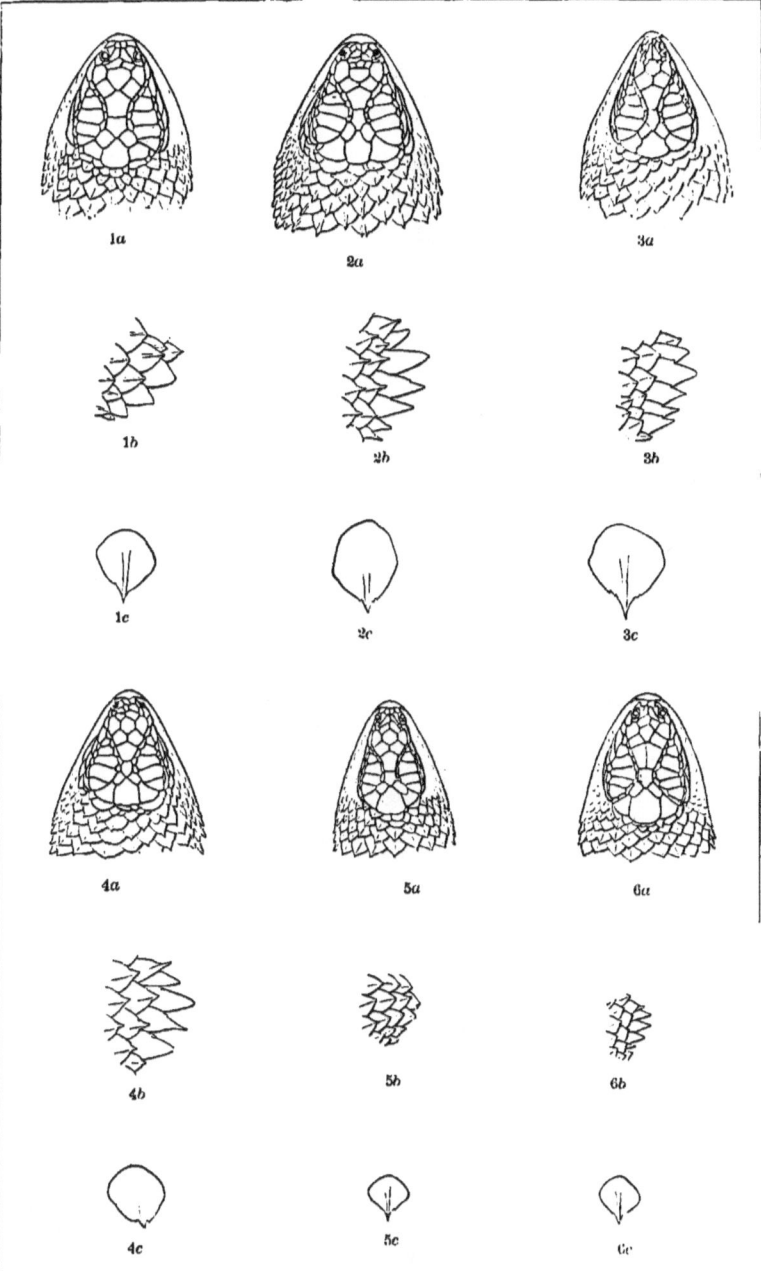

1. *Sceloporus clarkii.* 2. *S. magister.* 3. *S. zosteromus.* 4. *S. orcutti.* 5. *S. boulengeri.* 6. *S. floridanus.*

PLATE II.

[All natural size.]

1. *Phrynosoma cornutum* Blainv. (12618).
    Cape St. Lucas, Lower California.
2. *Phrynosoma blainvillii* Gray. (18459).
    Old Fort Tejon, Calif.
3. *Phrynosoma goodei* Stejn., sp. nov.   Type.   (8567a).
    Coast of Sonora, Mexico.
4. *Phrynosoma platyrhinos* Girard. (18461).
    Ash Meadows, Nevada.
     On all the figures—
        a represents head in profile.
        b represents top of head, mandibular spines excluded.
        c represents mandible from below, maxillar and other cephalic spines excluded.

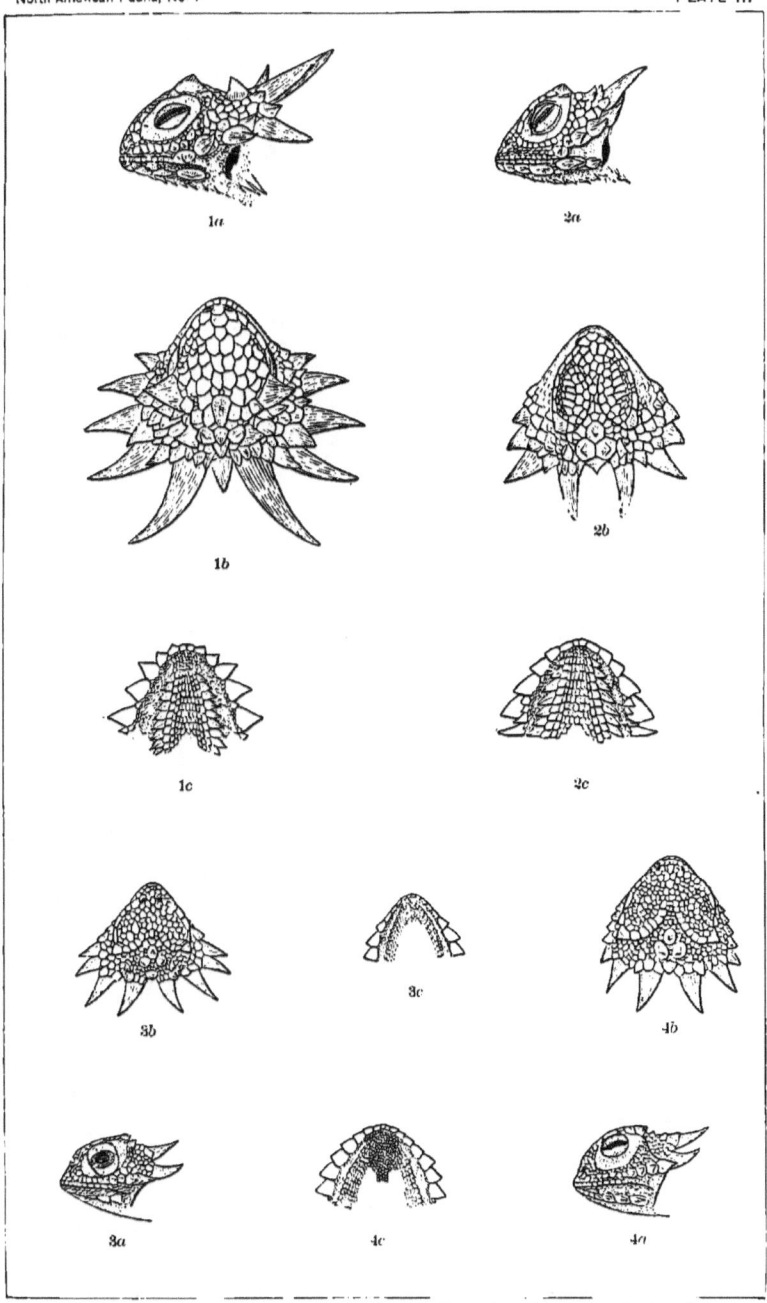

1. Phrynosoma cornutum. 2. P. blainvillii. 3. P. goodei. Type. 4. P. platyrhinos.

PLATE III.

1. *a, b, c, Xantusia vigilis* Baird. (18619.)
   Hesperia, Calif. (Twice natural size.)
2. *a, b, c, Salvadora hexalepis* (Cope). (18060.)
   Argus Range, California. (Natural size.)
3. *a, b, Bufo halophilus* B. & G. (18726.)
   Lone Pine, California. (Natural size.)
4. *a, b, Bufo boreas nelsoni* Stejn., subsp. nov. *Type.* (18742.)
   Oasis Valley, Nevada. (Natural size.)
5. *a, b, c, Rana fisheri* Stejn., sp. nov. *Type.* (18957.)
   Vegas Valley, Nevada. (Natural size.)

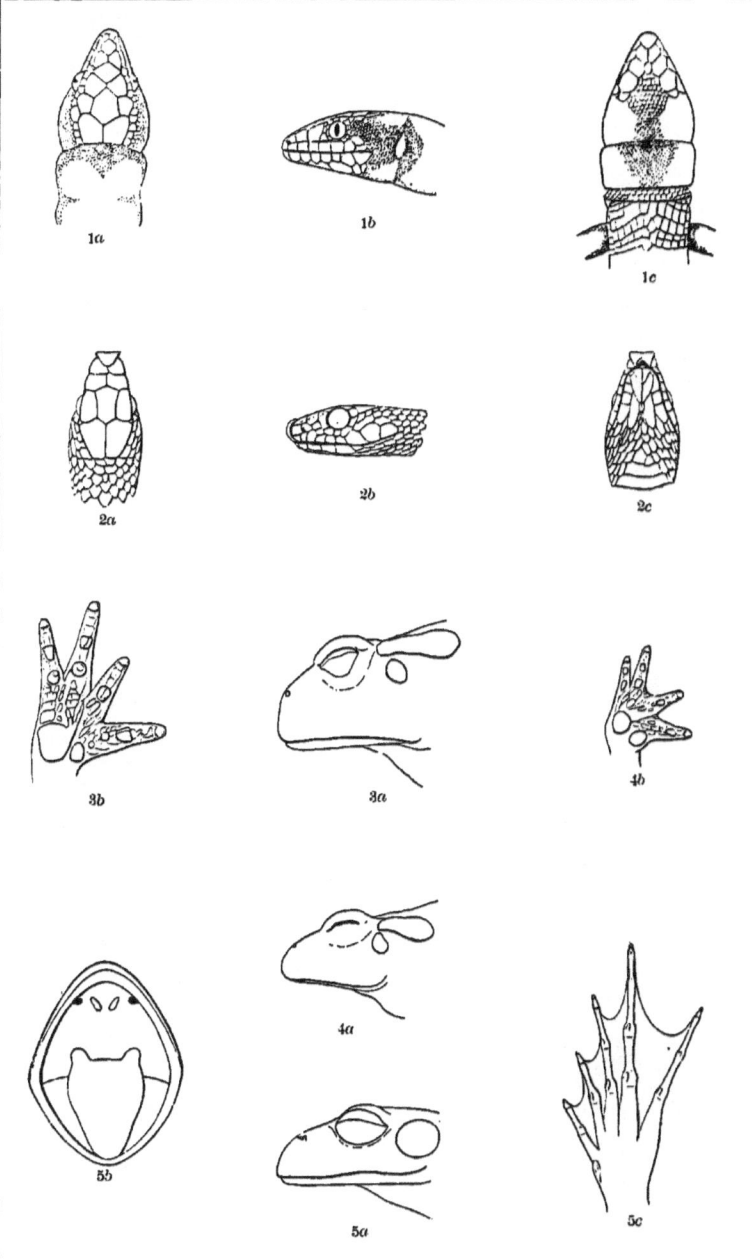

1. *Xantusia vigilis.* 2. *Salvadora hexalepis.* 3. *Bufo halophilus.*
4. *Bufo boreas nelsoni.* subsp. nov. 5. *Rana fisheri,* sp. nov.

THE CHUCK-WALLA (*Sauromalus ater*).
Argus Range, California.

PLATE V.

Fig. 1. *Empetrichthys merriami* Gilbert, sp. nov. *Type.*
  Ash Meadows, Nevada.
Fig. 2. Pharyngeals and gill arches from the side. (4½ times natural size.)
Fig. 3. Pharyngeals and gill arches from behind. (4½ times natural size.)
Fig. 4. Lower pharyngeals from above with adherent ceratobranchials of fourth gill arch. (5¼ times natural size.)
Fig. 5. Same from below. (5¼ times natural size.)
  On all the figures—
    a represents ceratobranchials of fourth gill arch.
    b represents lower pharyngeal bones.
    c represents epibranchial of fourth arch.
    d represents upper pharyngeal bones.

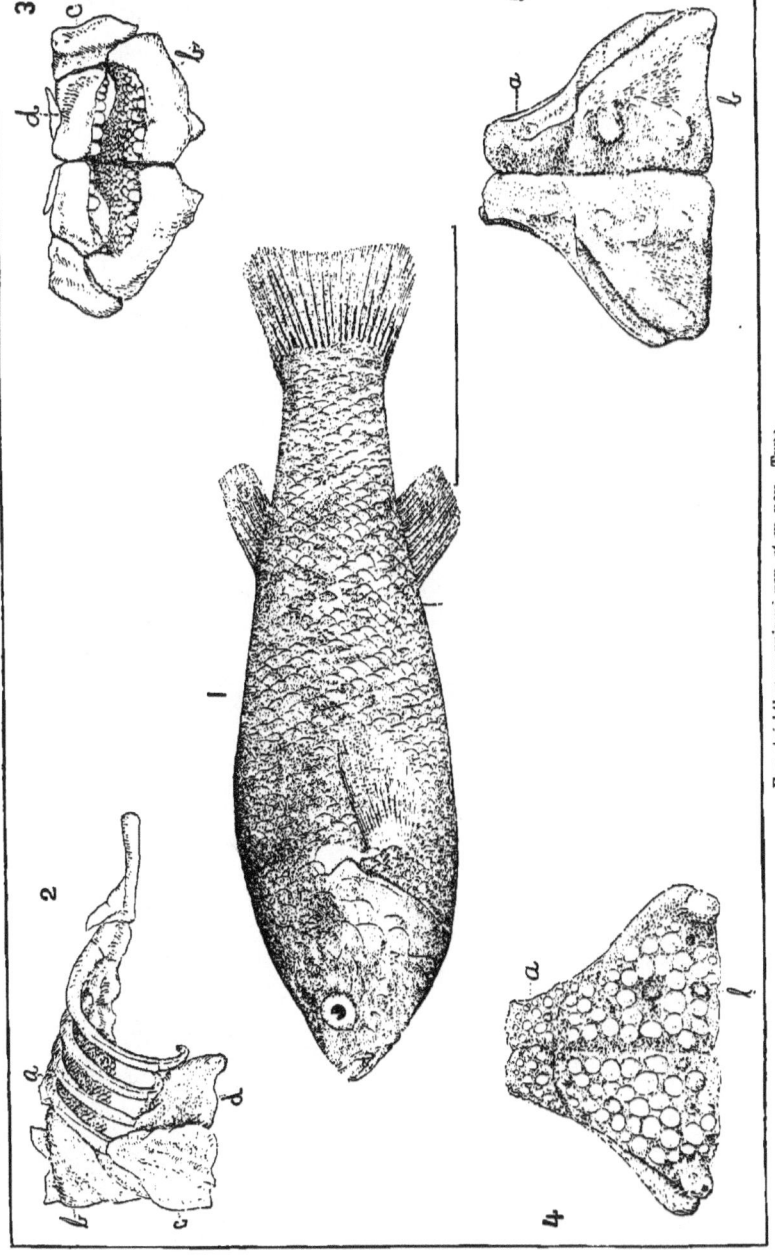

PLATE V.

Eumylodichthys merriami gen. et sp. nov. Type.

PLATE VI.

1. *Rhinichthys (Apocope) nevadensis* Gilbert, sp. nov.
    Type. Ash Meadows, Nevada.
2. *Rhinichthys (Apocope) velifer* Gilbert, sp. nov.
    Type. Pahranagat Valley, Nevada.

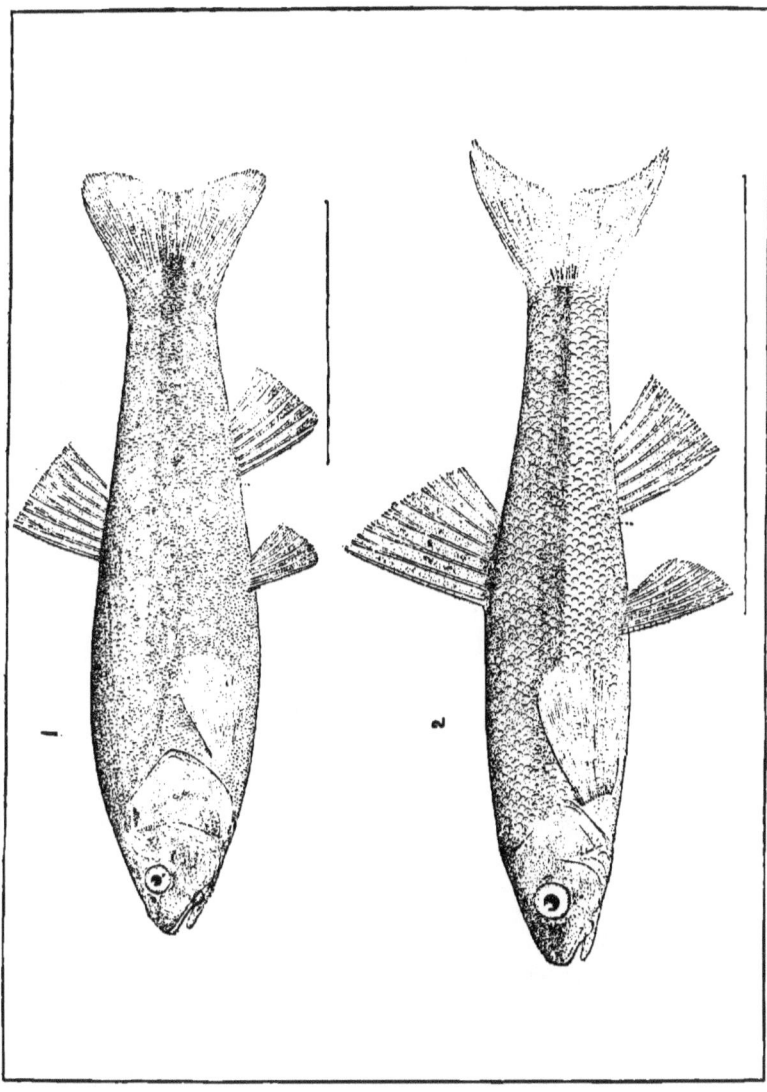

1. *Rhinichthys (Apocope) nevadensis* sp. nov. Type.
2. *Rhinichthys (Apocope) velifer* sp. nov. Type.

OPUNTIA ACANTHOCARPA. West slope Beaverdam Mountains, Utah.

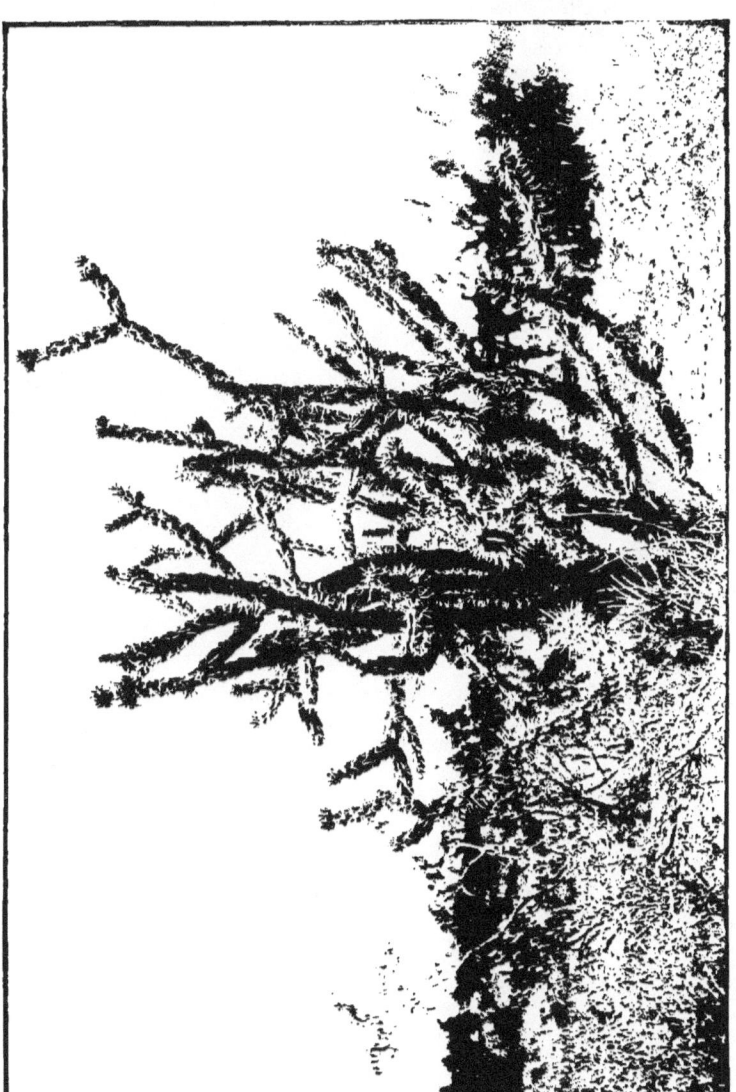

OPUNTIA ACANTHOCARPA. West slope Beaverdam Mountains, Utah.

OPUNTIA WHIPPLEI. Upper Santa Clara Crossing, Utah.

OPUNTIA PARRYI. Indian Spring Valley, Nevada.

OPUNTIA RUTILA. West slope Beaverdam Mountains, Utah.

YUCCA BACCATA. Desert Mountains, Nevada.

YUCCA ARBORESCENS. Mohave Desert, California.

YUCCA MACROCARPA. Pahrump Valley, Nevada.
(Charleston Mountains in distance.)

MAP
of part of
CALIFORNIA, NEVADA,
ARIZONA, and UTAH
traversed in 1891 by
THE DEATH VALLEY EXPEDITION

THE COLORED AREA IS THE LOWER DIVISION OF THE *LOWER SONORAN LIFE ZONE* (THE AREA IN WHICH THE RAISIN-GRAPE MAY BE SUCCESSFULLY PRODUCED).

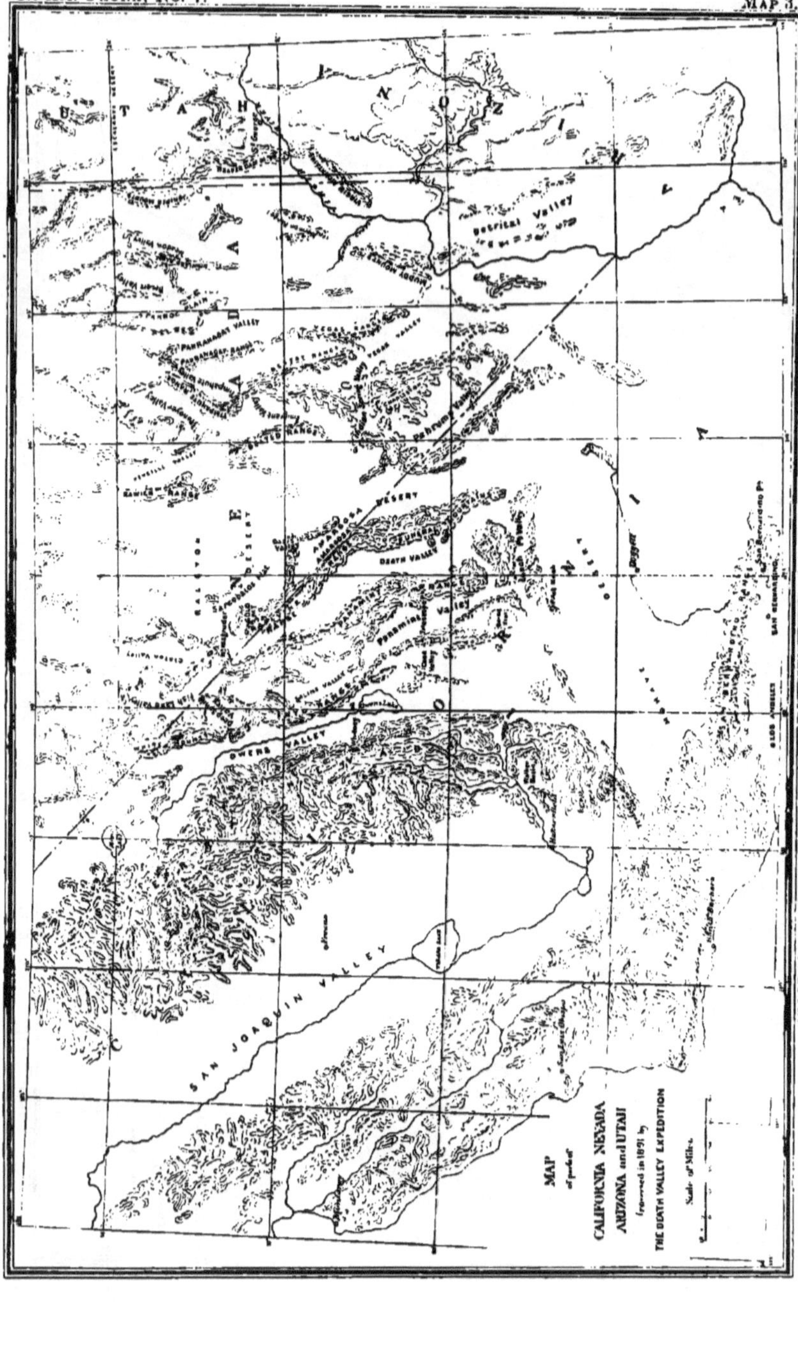

GEOGRAPHIC DISTRIBUTION OF LECONTE'S THRASHER (HARPORHYNCHUS LECONTEI).

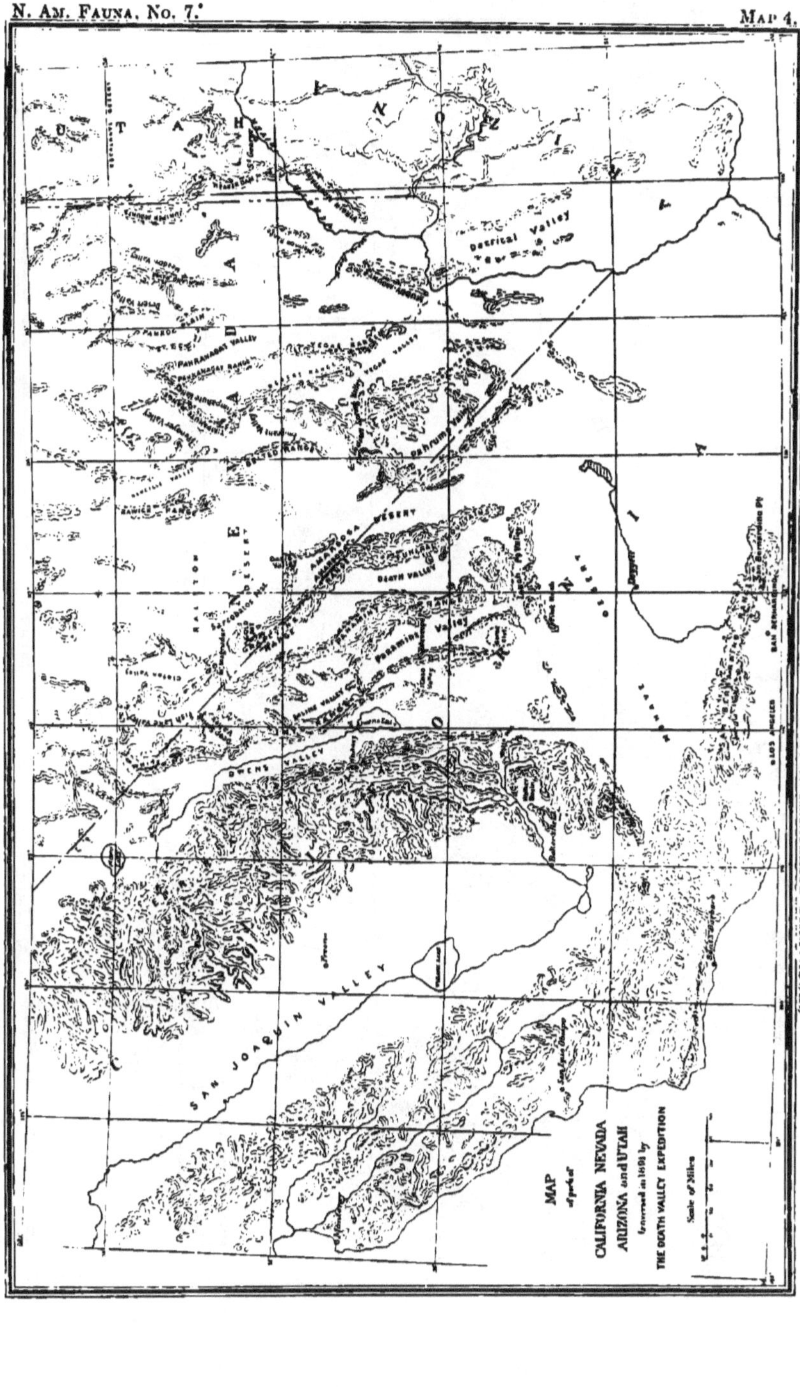

GEOGRAPHIC DISTRIBUTION OF THE CREOSOTE BUSH (*LARREA TRIDENTATA*).

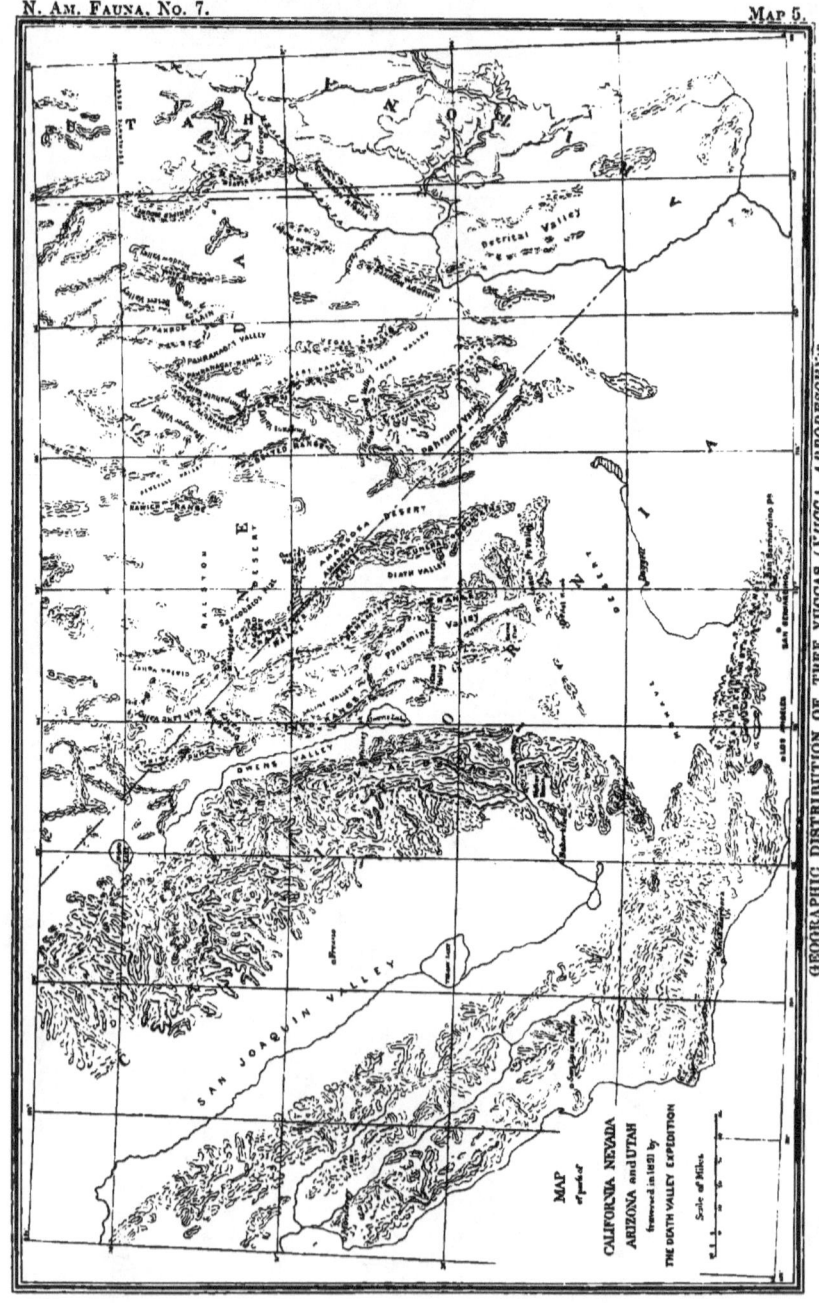

www.ingramcontent.com/pod-product-compliance
Lightning Source LLC
Chambersburg PA
CBHW051738300426
44115CB00007B/610